W9-AJU-984

# Secretarial Procedures and Administration

## SIXTH EDITION

**J MARSHALL HANNA**
Professor of Business Education
The Ohio State University, Columbus, Ohio

**ESTELLE L. POPHAM**
Professor of Business Education Emeritus
Hunter College of the City University
   of New York

**RITA SLOAN TILTON**
Associate Professor of Business Education
Wright State University, Dayton, Ohio

*Published by*

K72   SOUTH-WESTERN PUBLISHING CO.

CINCINNATI   WEST CHICAGO, ILL.   DALLAS   PELHAM MANOR, N.Y.
PALO ALTO, CALIF.   BRIGHTON, ENGLAND

# Preface

Congratulations for having decided on a secretarial career. With the requisite training, the essential personal qualities, and a dedication to your objective, you can become that poised, charming, efficient person in the business office who provides the "assist" role to top management. This book was written to help you achieve that goal.

The top-level secretary performs both operational and managerial functions. In her operational role, she demonstrates an in-depth knowledge of office and secretarial procedures; but she needs a high degree of competency in administrative skills, as well.

A basic aim of *Secretarial Procedures and Administration*, Sixth Edition, is to acquaint you with a wide range of office activities. More importantly, this book can provide you with the means to attain skill and confidence in performing secretarial-managerial operations. Stated in current business usage, the *output* (the degree of competency) depends upon your *imput* (your willingness to work and to learn).

*Secretarial Procedures and Administration* is planned for use by both the secretary-in-training and the experienced one. Basic skills in typewriting and in shorthand are assumed; other skills are presented as if they were new to you. The authors feel, however, that acquiring techniques is of little value unless this acquisition is accompanied by the development of a secretarial personality — the ability to work with people. Consequently, the activities that are provided in the text and in the related materials stress the vital role of human relations in business and provide an opportunity for individual growth.

The text consists of 28 chapters organized into nine parts. *Part 1* emphasizes the responsibilities and the opportunities of a secretarial position, as well as the personal qualities requisite for success. *Parts 2* and *3* deal with "word processing," the transformation of ideas into typewritten or printed form, and cover such topics as typing, copying and duplicating, dictating, transcribing, composing, and handling mail. *Parts 4* and *5* cover the use of transmittal services: postal and shipping, telephone and telegraph facilities, and records management. *Parts 6* and *7* encompass a variety of secretarial duties, including such topics as planning travel and arranging for meetings and conferences; collecting, processing, and presenting business data; and handling financial, payroll, and legal responsibilities. *Part 9* examines the wide variety of employment opportunities open to the college-trained secretary, the techniques of job application, and the essentials for achieving professional status. The final chapter of the book discusses the supervisory-administrative role of the secretary.

The Reference Guide at the end of the book will help you to the degree that you allow. It identifies accepted practices for abbreviating and capitalizing words, writing and using numbers, spelling and using plurals and possessives, punctuating, and using words effectively. Following this section are a Communications Guide and a brief Postal Guide. Thus, *Secretarial Procedures and Administration* is both a textbook and a reference book.

At the end of each chapter is a list of carefully selected "Suggested Readings" that enrich the content and broaden the scope of the book.

Each chapter ends with a series of "Questions for Discussion" and several practical problems. As their title implies, the questions are designed to stimulate an exchange of viewpoints. To participate, you will need to draw upon your knowledge of the text, upon reference readings, and upon your own experience. The problems provide a wide variety of challenging secretarial activities. Some problems require information from the Reference Guide of the text, to help you become familiar with it.

Case problems are provided at the end of each part, bringing considerable realism to the course — for many of them are close adaptations of actual office cases. The problems are planned to develop the human relations skills that the secretary's administrative role demands.

Entirely new in concept and in presentation are the supporting materials of the sixth edition: *Simulated Office Situations*, a narration of nine realistic, practical office experiences. Each simulation relates to a particular part of the textbook. The simulations follow the order of the text and interrelate to the extent that you will feel a sense of continuity. The simulations place you in a secretarial position with decisions to make, procedures to follow, work to produce, personnel problems to solve, and challenges to your initiative and creativity. You learn by doing. *Simulated Office Situations* provides a practical test of how well you will perform on the job.

The authors believe you will find this text helpful in your training and, later, useful as a handbook. We hope that you will set the highest professional goals — and that you will achieve them.

**J Marshall Hanna** ● **Estelle L. Popham** ● **Rita S. Tilton**

# Contents

# The Secretarial Profession

*Part* **1**

**A** look at the employment patterns of women precedes an analysis of the secretarial field as a career choice. The many dimensions of secretarial positions—the advantages, the requirements and responsibilities, and the opportunities for supervisory and administrative roles that relate to the career objectives of the college-trained woman—are discussed. This part sets the stage for developing the kinds of operational and managerial competencies that the top-level secretary needs for developing in her professional role.

# Chapter 1

## THE ROLE OF THE PROFESSIONAL SECRETARY

At the beginning of this decade, 31 million women were employed in the labor force. This figure represents the upward trend in the employment of women. Fifty years ago only one out of five workers was a woman. Today, according to the Department of Labor, almost two out of five workers are women. By 1980, it is estimated, the United States will need 101 million workers; and of that number *over* 36 million will be women.[1]

There are many reasons for this increased participation of women in the labor market. Certainly in many cases the most compelling one is economic necessity. Yet, it is true that the life style of the American woman has changed dramatically in the last twenty years. In 1950, for example, a girl might expect to work only a few years, then marry and retire forever from the labor scene. Today the Department of Labor estimates that half of all women between the ages of 18 and 64 are either working or seeking employment. In fact, the profile of the average woman worker shows that she is married, mature (39 years old), and is employed in one of many occupations. As for the number of years that a woman will remain in the labor force, it is currently predicted that 8 out of 10 women will.work for at least 25 years.[2]

To the young woman anticipating a career in the business world, the decade of the 70's offers a new world of professional opportunities. Career doors once labeled "For men only" are now available to the qualified woman. Women are filling many positions needed in the new, expanding industries. Strides have also been made in the area of equal pay for equal work. A woman can expect to be paid more nearly the same salary as her male counterpart. Indeed, the decade of the 70's is an exciting time for the educated, career-oriented woman to enter the labor market!

---

U.S. Civil Service Commission, *Expanding Opportunities . . . Women in the Federal Government* (Washington: U.S. Government Printing Office, 1970), p. 1.
[2] *Ibid.*

One field that may well appeal to the college woman is the secretarial profession. It provides a challenging job after graduation. For the female worker returning to business, too, reentry to the profession is possible with relatively little retraining. No other profession offers to women so wide a variety of occupational areas in which to work.

Even with the advanced technology used in offices today, there is yet to be found a substitute for the secretary. Secretaries are in demand everywhere — in every geographical area and in every type of business, government, or philanthropic organization. Positions are available in all cities — an important factor to one who prefers a certain location or to one who plans to augment the family income.

Today an estimated 2.5 million office workers perform secretarial and stenographic duties, and the market for qualified secretaries continues to grow. Even in times of economic recession, secretarial positions are available. In addition, salaries for secretarial positions continue to be the highest of clerical workers.

Although automation has not changed to any appreciable extent the need for secretaries, it is generally agreed that the secretarial position in the 70's requires more basic intelligence, more formal education, more initiative, and better appearance, in that order. In this decade the secretary's role will become increasingly that of assistant to management. Thus the secretary must bring to the position a higher degree of ability than was formerly the case — in other words, a college education.

This chapter, an overview of the secretarial profession in the 70's, also discusses the personal qualities that are so important for the woman's successful fulfillment in her secretarial role.

## THE SECRETARY DEFINED

The job classification *secretary* is probably the most misunderstood term in office occupations. Almost any woman who works in an office may refer to herself as "secretary," or almost any employer may speak of "my secretary" in describing his clerk. In both cases, the term is used for prestige—prestige to the employee for working at such a high level and to the employer for rating an employee of such importance as a secretary.

RECENTLY, the National Secretaries Association adopted its own definition of a secretary: "An assistant to an executive, possessing mastery of office skills and ability to assume responsibility without direct supervision, who displays initiative, exercises judgment, and makes decisions within the scope of her authority."

## The Secretary's Established Role

Real secretarial work requires high-level performance. The secretary[3] as defined by the National Secretaries Association performs the work within her areas of responsibility for only one individual. She may, however, work for more than one person. According to the *Dictionary of Occupational Titles*, a secretary is one who carries out the following activities:

Performs general office work in relieving executives and other company officials of minor executive and clerical duties

Takes dictation using shorthand or a stenotype machine

Transcribes dictation or the recorded information reproduced on a transcribing machine

Makes appointments for the executive and reminds him of them

Interviews people coming into the office, directing to other workers those who do not warrant seeing the executive

Makes and answers telephone calls

Handles personal and important mail, writing routine correspondence on her own initiative

May supervise other clerical workers

May keep personnel records

A good secretary is a public relations expert, a staff assistant, and the boss's office memory. She is responsible for much of the detail work of the office and is expected to carry out her duties with a minimum of supervision and direction. She represents the company and her employer attractively to the public and generates good human relations in working with all employees in the organization.

A secretary learns how to gain the goodwill and cooperation of her co-workers and the respect of the executives. She identifies her daily business associates as being on a level above her, on her own level, or on a subordinate level; and she applies the best principles of human relations at each level. Examination of problem-personality situations in offices shows same-level relationships to be the most difficult for a secretary to maintain amicably and productively. The secretary is accurate, highly efficient, creative, and sound in judging when to use initiative and when to consult her employer about handling a job. She adjusts flexibly to changing situations, and she can recognize and meet a

---

[3]Because the vast *majority* of secretaries are women, throughout this book the term "secretary" refers to the female gender. (The English language, however, at times compels the use of masculine gender for pronouns in the third person, singular.)

# SAMPLING OF THE AREAS IN WHICH SECRETARIES WORK*

**Accountancy**
  Auditor
  Corporation
  Public
**Advertising**
  Agencies
  Displays, Signs
**Agriculture**
  Equipment and Supplies
  Management Systems
**Appliances**
  Major
  Small
**Automobile**
  Clubs
  Dealers
  Leasing Agents
  Licensing Agents
  Parts and Supplies
  Repair Companies
**Churches**
**Communications**
  Data Processing
    Services
  Magazines
  Newspapers
  Radio
  Television
  Telephone
**Contractors**
  Architects
  Building
  Equipment and Supplies
  Roads
**Cosmetics**
**Cultural**
  Galleries
  Libraries
  Museums
**Education**
  Board of Education
  Administration of
    Colleges and Universi-
      ties
    Elementary and Sec-
      ondary Schools
    Private Business
      Schools
    Technical Schools

**Engineering**
  Aeronautical
  Chemical
  Civil
  Consulting
  Mechanical
**Fashion**
**Finance**
  Banks
  Credit Unions
  Savings and Loan
**Food Products**
  Brokers
  Dairy Products
  Retail Grocers
  Wholesalers
**Food Services**
  Restaurants
**Freight**
  Air
  Motor
  Rail
  Storage
**Industries**
  Gas and Oil
**Insurance**
  Accident and Health
  Automobile
  Aviation
  Life
**Investment Securities**
  Brokers
**Labor Unions**
**Law**
  Attorneys, Corporate,
    Patent, Private Prac-
    tice
**Lumber**
**Manufacturing**
  Chemicals
  Heavy Equipment,
    Light Equipment, Tools

**Medical**
  Chiropractors
  Dentists
  Equipment
  Hospitals, Clinics,
    Nursing Homes
  Physicians and
    Surgeons
**Miscellaneous Organi-
zations**
  Political
  Philanthropic
  Professional
  Social Service and
    Welfare
  Trade Associations
**Office Furniture and
  Equipment**
**Political Offices**
**Printing Companies**
**Publishing Companies**
  Books
  Business Forms
  Periodicals
**Real Estate**
  Agencies
  Management
**Retailers**
  Department Stores
  Mercantile Stores
**Sports**
  Athletic Clubs
  Equipment
  Recreation Areas
**Transportation**
  Bus Lines
  Commercial Airlines
  Private Air Carriers
  Railroads
  Travel Bureaus
**Theater**
**Wholesalers and Job-
  bers**
**Government Offices**
  City
  State
  Federal

*This list is by no means all-inclusive.

deadline. She informs her employer of developments that may affect office efficiency, but she does not bother him with petty problems that she can solve with a little thought or research.

There are, of course, different levels of responsibility in secretarial positions. At the top level is the secretary to the chief executive. He needs a secretary of competence and pleasing personality to assist him with his widespread responsibilities. Such a secretary may have assistants for the routine stenographic and clerical work. When she knows the executive's work thoroughly, has proved her competence, and can — as his *alter ego* — make decisions, she is often advanced to the position and salary of administrative assistant. Secretaries to the presidents or the managing heads of large organizations hold positions at this level — although not all are given the title.

At the next level are secretaries to executives responsible for departmental management. Such an executive works in a narrower, more concentrated field such as that of research director or sales manager. The secretary may supervise other office workers in the department. She learns one branch of the business thoroughly. She may be advanced to be head of a department because of her competence, personality, and knowledge of the company. Her responsibility then is the output of the department and the supervision of the staff.

The system adopted by the Administrative Management Society classifies secretaries into two categories:

### SECRETARY A

Performs secretarial duties for a top-level executive or for someone responsible for a major functional or geographic operation. Does work of a confidential nature and relieves principal of designated administrative details. Requires initiative, judgment, knowledge of company practices, policy, and organization.

> Legend to the contrary, a man's best friend is not his dog. Nor is it his wife, his principles, his good name, or his education. If he's, so to speak, a . . . junior executive with his foot on the first rung of that corporate ladder, his best friend and frequently his only friend is *his secretary*.
>
> — *Business Management* (June), 1971, p. 33.

### SECRETARY B

Performs secretarial duties for a member of middle management. General requirements are the same as for Secretary A (listed above) but limited to the area of responsibility of the principal.

In the text above, the secretary described first is obviously a *Secretary A*; the one described next, either *Secretary A* or *Secretary B*.

## An Emerging Organization Pattern

An emerging organization pattern in some large firms separates the secretarial functions into two parts — typing activities and nontyping activities — with each assigned to a different person, a correspondence secretary or an administrative secretary. The typing functions are handled in a *word processing center.* The executive's machine dictation is transcribed by a correspondence secretary or word processor (the title has not yet been clearly established) who uses power equipment to produce transcripts. The correspondence secretary must be highly proficient technically and highly competent in the use of language. She is a word specialist, and she is paid accordingly. The correspondence secretary may advance through the several grades of her position to Coordinator (proofreading the transcripts) to Word Processing Manager (assigning the work and controlling the center).

The nontyping functions are handled by the administrative secretary. The administrative secretary is able to devote most of her time to administrative tasks, as she is relieved by the word processing center of communication duties involving typing and taking dictation. Thus it is neither impractical nor unusual for her to be assigned to more than one executive. In this organization structure, her classification is generally known as administrative secretary (or assistant). On the other hand, the secretary who is a word specialist is assigned to the word processing center as a correspondence secretary or word processor.

The functions of a word processing center are charted on the next page.

The word processing center concept is an efficient approach to the control of increasing costs in the output of correspondence within a large firm; however, because of the high installation costs of such a system, smaller organizations will likely continue to employ secretaries who perform both functions — administrative assistant and correspondence secretary. Further, it may be that only certain departments of large corporations will create a word processing center. If so, the duties of some secretarial positions in these firms will not change appreciably.

## Secretarial Salaries

Secretarial salaries are among the highest paid for office work. The 1971–72 survey of office salaries conducted by the Administrative Management Society reveals that *Secretaries A* receive higher salaries than *Accounting Clerk A* in every region of the United States.[4]

---

[4]*Office Salaries Directory for United States and Canada* (Willow Grove, Pa.: Administrative Management Society, 1971), pp. 11–13.

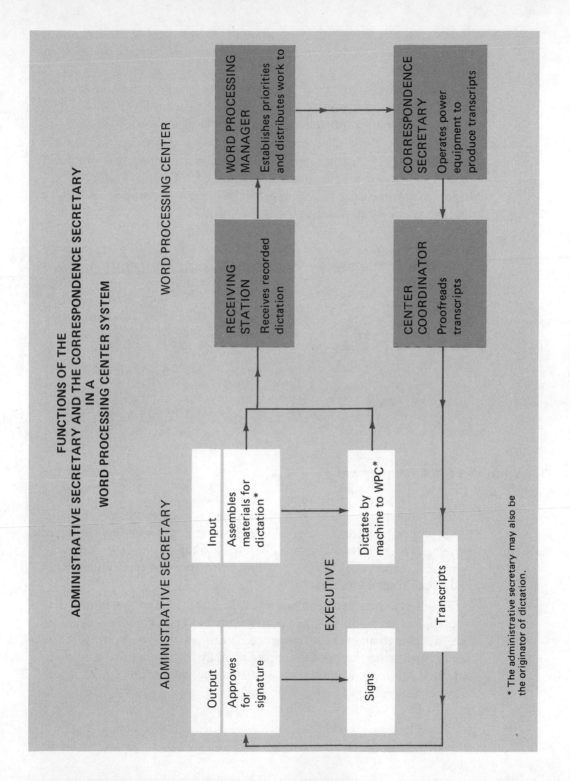

FUNCTIONS OF THE
ADMINISTRATIVE SECRETARY AND THE CORRESPONDENCE SECRETARY
IN A
WORD PROCESSING CENTER SYSTEM

WORD PROCESSING CENTER

WORD PROCESSING
MANAGER

Establishes priorities
and distributes work to

CORRESPONDENCE
SECRETARY

Operates power
equipment to
produce transcripts

RECEIVING
STATION

Receives recorded
dictation

CENTER
COORDINATOR

Proofreads
transcripts

ADMINISTRATIVE SECRETARY

Input

Assembles
materials for
dictation*

EXECUTIVE

Dictates by
machine to WPC*

Output

Approves
for signature

Signs

Transcripts

* The administrative secretary may also be
the originator of dictation.

The survey shows that, in general, *Secretaries A* receive about 15 percent more than *Secretaries B*, and over 30 percent more than *Stenographers*.

Comparative salary figures for various sections of the country will enable readers to evaluate employment opportunities in their own locations. These figures reflect recent growth-of-industry figures.

For the correspondence secretary in the word processing center, the rate of pay currently ranges from $3 to $4 an hour. It is predicted that this position will eventually command a yearly salary of $10,000.[5] In some firms the salaries within grades of the correspondence secretary and the administrative secretary are identical.

## AVERAGE WEEKLY OFFICE SALARIES IN THE U.S.

1973–74 Administrative Management Society's 27th Annual Survey

|  | Total | Eastern | East Central | West Central | Southern | Western |
|---|---|---|---|---|---|---|
| Sec. A | 159 | 164 | 158 | 150 | 151 | 167 |
| Actg. Clerk A | 148 | 151 | 148 | 143 | 145 | 154 |
| Tab. Mach. Op. | 142 | 141 | 149 | 136 | 131 | 156 |
| Sec. B | 137 | 142 | 138 | 127 | 130 | 141 |
| Steno. | 121 | 123 | 124 | 113 | 115 | 129 |

## Opportunities for Advancement

The college-trained secretary finds that advancement in her profession generally comes quickly as she proves her ability in handling the tasks of her position. Salary increments and promotions to higher secretarial posts within a business become available to the secretary who produces quality work and who willingly accepts and tactfully assumes additional responsibilities.

In interviewing businessmen regarding the type of secretary they wanted, Robert J. Gibson, vice president of Norrell Temporary Services, Inc., discovered an overwhelming need for the executive secretary. "The need is great, and the market is growing daily for the high-caliber, well-educated, business woman who wants to become an office executive," Gibson said.[6]

---

[5]"Word Processing," *Administrative Management* (June, 1971), p. 24.

[6]"Are You Hearing Your Boss's Cry for Help?" *The Secretary* (June–July, 1971), p. 18.

In addition to offering a lifetime career to women, in some fields of the secretarial profession the position of secretary is the first rung on the career ladder. For example, women are consistently filling creative positions in such fields as advertising, personnel, television, and journalism after having proven themselves in the secretarial role. Promotion into middle management will undoubtedly become increasingly frequent as the effects of the Equal Rights Amendment, designed to end sex discrimination, are felt.

Further, it is not uncommon to read about the female executive who tells how she reached the top. In most cases, her success story began behind the secretary's desk. Marion Stephenson, the first and only woman vice-president of NBC; Josephine Shaeffer, a top executive in Douglas L. Elliman Company; and Virginia Rehme, vice-president of the Southern Commercial and Savings Bank of St. Louis, are only a few examples of women who "made it big" from the secretary's desk. Isabelle Kirchner, who began her career as a clerk with the Prudential Life Insurance Company, is the first woman officer of the firm, having recently been elected to the post of vice-president and secretary.

As these examples show, the secretarial arena is what the secretary wants it to be. For many women, it is a lifetime profession. For others, it is a stepping stone to another career. For all aspirants to the field, it can be an exciting, rewarding experience.

## Limiting Factors in Secretarial Careers

To be completely fair, this discussion must point out the limiting factors of secretarial work. In the traditional secretarial framework, the secretarial title follows the boss's title — not the worker's ability. The secretary is sometimes rated a *Secretary B* rather than a *Secretary A* because of the status of her superior, not because of her ability.

Another limiting factor is the difference in concept of the word *secretary* held by different organizations and different bosses. An ambitious worker may find herself working for someone who neither knows how nor wants to use her abilities to capacity. There are many ways in which she can change the secretarial image, but sometimes the only way to get ahead is to find a job where the employer's image of a secretary conforms more nearly to the secretary's own.

Still another limiting factor is the necessity for the secretary to submerge herself in her employer's problems. As one secretary said candidly, "If I ever quit, it will be because I'm tired of thinking other people's thoughts and want to work on my own." This theme turns up again and again among college-trained secretaries.

The good grooming expected of an executive secretary or administrative assistant includes not only her outward appearance but also her voice, her manner toward others — even her personality and attitudes.

## THE SECRETARY'S PERSONAL QUALITIES

The secretary has a dual responsibility for the impressions she creates in the office. One is to herself, for she is judged by her personal appearance, personality, behavior, and attitude; the other is to the girls with whom she works, for they tend to pattern their behavior, as well as their appearance, after that of the top-level secretary. She sets the standards for careful grooming, acceptable dress, and approved behavior. Her appearance and actions — both good and bad — are observed, analyzed, and copied.

Most college students try to conform to standards of dress and hair styling that will win the acceptance of their peers. Try just as hard to conform to the standards of business appearance that are acceptable to your new associates. If you take pride in yourself and recognize that you represent your employer to the outside world, you should find it easy to conform to accepted standards of office dress and behavior.

## Personal Appearance

From time immemorial, woman — much more than man — has been judged by her personal appearance. Times have not really changed. A pleasing personal appearance is and always will be an asset to the woman whether she is in the home, in the office, or in school. A pleasant appearance means more than mere physical beauty, however. Good appearance includes being well groomed and appropriately dressed, maintaining good posture, and having a pleasant tone of voice.

Being well groomed and dressing appropriately are important to the secretary because they affect her self-confidence (and thus her competence) and the impression that she makes on others. They are measures of her pride.

> Personal beauty is a greater recommendation than any letter of introduction.　*—Aristotle*

**Grooming.** Good grooming requires regular scheduling of grooming activities and having all garments pressed, cleaned, and ready to wear. The secretary who is well groomed is clean and neat in every detail of her appearance. Her nails are manicured; her hair is tidy and attractively styled. She uses a daily deodorant and oral hygiene preparations for pleasant breath. Her personal appearance makes a favorable impression upon her employer, her associates, and office visitors.

**Appropriate Wardrobe.** Office attire for the secretary has traditionally been labeled conservative. In recent years, however, as women's dress has become more casual, business firms have relaxed their dress codes to include fashion trends in women's clothing. The top-level secretary, nevertheless, is expected to maintain a wardrobe correlative to her salary and status. Her wardrobe reflects good taste and judgment while expressing her individuality.

Gaining in popularity is the use of company "uniforms" for office employees. Banks, credit unions, savings and loan associations, transportation companies, real estate and insurance agencies are but a few examples of business firms utilizing office uniforms.

On the average, the response by female employees has been favorable. Besides being attractive, comfortable, and easily maintained, uniforms can be considered as employee fringe benefits. Money formerly set aside to purchase office attire is made available for other purchases. Companies, too, attest to the benefits of office uniforms. Improved employee morale, rising employee interest in business, and an employee-company identification that results in a sharper company image are but a few of the advantages.

**Good Posture and Good Health.** A requisite of attractive appearance is good posture — a carriage that says that you are proud of yourself, that you *are* somebody. Stand and sit tall; never slump. Walk with a smooth motion, with head balanced and chin parallel to the floor.

Yet another important factor in an attractive appearance, and even more so in the performance of one's job, is good health. Generally (and grammatically), when a secretary doesn't feel *well*, she doesn't look *good!*

The secretary to an executive must be in top physical condition to accomplish the many duties of her position and withstand the many pressures of her job. As the demands upon the executive increase, so do they upon the secretary. To meet capably all the emergencies in a day, the secretary must begin her day well rested and well fed.

**Voice.** College students usually take a speech course — but not very seriously! Yet the personnel officer in charge of work assignments for twenty college students on an internship program between junior and senior years reported that the one universal complaint of the executives with whom they worked was, of all things, *speech*. Ask yourself, "How pleasant is my tone of voice?"

> Her voice was ever soft,
> Gentle, and low, an excellent
> thing in woman.
> —*Shakespeare*
> (KING LEAR)

The best way to determine the effect of your voice on others is to make a tape recording and play it back. If you have never before recorded your voice, the sound may surprise you. You just may want to begin an immediate program of speech improvement!

As you listen to the tape, ask yourself these questions:

**Is my voice too high and sharp?**

**Do I pronounce words clearly and distinctly?**

**Do I maintain an even speed in speaking, without regard to the subject matter?**

**Do I speak at an audible volume?**

The secretary with a low-pitched, well-modulated voice who speaks distinctly at a moderate rate of speed and at an audible volume will find herself highly successful as an office hostess.

## Intangible Assets

Success on every job requires desirable personality traits, and secretarial work is no exception. Many secretaries have met defeat not because of their lack of skills but because of undesirable personal qualities. There are many adjectives to describe the perfect secretary. This discussion centers on four major characteristics essential for the successful secretary; they are her invisible assets.

**The Ability to Get Along with Others.** Seldom does the secretary work alone. Probably the most important ability a secretary can possess is that of working effectively with others. This means the workers in her office and those with whom the company deals. Working in harmony with others requires diligent application of the three C's of effective human relations: *courtesy*, *cooperativeness*, and *cheerfulness*.

**Ethical Behavior.** By her example, the high-level secretary sets ethical standards for the younger office workers to emulate. She avoids and discourages office gossip. She respects the confidentiality of her work. She is loyal to her immediate employer and to her company. She is fair in her use of company time and materials.

**Intelligence.** Another vital characteristic of a successful secretary is basic intelligence. Without it, she is unable to perform adequately the duties of her position. The intelligent secretary can organize her work, yet be flexible in her plan. Her work is accurate and complete. Her decisions are based on logical thinking processes. She shows initiative and resourcefulness in executing her duties. She is her employer's office memory.

**Maturity.** The intangible asset, maturity, involves the mental development of the secretary in her job; therefore, evidence of this asset in the successful secretary may relate not to her age but often to the fact that she has grown during her office experience and has had practice in decision making. The secretary who is mature in her profession is willing to assume responsibility, is dependable, and exercises good judgment in the daily activities of her job. She is objective in her outlook and her approach to problem solving. She is poised and in control of her emotions at all times. She has confidence in her ability, yet continues to search for ways to improve her performance.

> Common sense is the world's most uncommon commodity.

## Personality Development Program

Naturally, you cannot yet measure up to the standards by which top executives rate their secretaries. Nor are desirable traits suddenly acquired when you step into an office; rather, they are developed over a long period of time. The honest uncovering of your weaknesses is the important beginning step.

The rating chart on page 14 can serve as a guide. On each point, rate yourself *excellent*, *so-so*, or *need improvement*. Next, set up a specific program for improvement, pinpointed to your low ratings. Concentrate on one or two traits at a time until the desirable behavior seems to be instinctively yours. Then work on two or three more traits until they are habitual. Repeat the process until you have an attractive, pleasant-to-work-with personality that will score high on this chart.

## A SELF-CHECK ON YOUR SECRETARIAL PERSONALITY

| Performance Components | Human Relations Components |
|---|---|
| **Accuracy**<br>How good am I at finding and correcting errors? | **Consideration**<br>Do I often do kind things without being asked? |
| **Good Judgment**<br>Are my decisions usually thoughtful rather than impulsive? | **Tact**<br>Do I avoid ruffling the feelings of others? |
| **Follow Through**<br>Do I usually see a job through — doing implied as well as specific assignments? | **Discretion**<br>Do I refrain from divulging business and personal information? |
| **Resourcefulness**<br>Do I usually try various possibilities until I solve a problem? | **Loyalty**<br>Do I stand by my family and my friends through thick and thin? |
| **Initiative**<br>Do I often initiate action in my group? | **Objectivity**<br>Can I — and do I — look at personal situations impersonally? |
| **Organization**<br>Can I develop a work plan that, when necessary, can be flexible in its execution? | **Respect**<br>Do I recognize the need for lines of authority as part of a team effort? |
| **Efficiency**<br>Am I aware of the importance of time and the economy of motion in the completion of specific assignments? | **Forbearance**<br>Can I hold my tongue and refrain from petty remarks to a co-worker who is being "difficult"? |
| **Skill Development**<br>Do I make a definite effort to improve the skills in which I am weakest? | **Attitude**<br>Do I accept work assignments cheerfully? |

# SUGGESTED READINGS

## Books and Manuals

Ingoldsby, Patricia, and Joseph Focarino. *The Executive Secretary: Handbook to Success.* New York: Doubleday & Co., Inc., 1969, pp. 247–261.

Lauria, Marie. *How to Be a Good Secretary.* New York: Frederick Fell, Inc., 1969.

Noyes, Nell Braly. *Your Future as a Secretary.* New York: Arco Publishing Co., 1971.

Pogrebin, Letty Cottin. *How to Make It in a Man's World.* New York: Doubleday & Co., Inc., 1970.

Popham, Estelle L., and Blanche Ettinger. *Opportunities in Office Occupations*, Revised 3d ed. New York: Vocational Guidance Manuals, 1972.

Vermes, Jean C. *The Secretary's Guide to Dealing with People.* West Nyack: Parker Publishing Co., 1964.


The following periodicals and subscription services provide current, timely information of help to the secretarial student and to the secretary in the office.


## Secretarial Subject Matter

*Better Secretaries Series.* A monthly 48-page bulletin on the development of secretarial skills, available by subscription from Prentice-Hall, Inc., Englewood Cliffs, New Jersey 07632.

*From Nine to Five.* Twice-monthly pamphlets on specialized topics, available by subscription from Dartnell Corporation, 4660 Ravenswood Avenue, Chicago, Illinois 60640.

*P. S.—A Professional Service for Private Secretaries.* A twice-monthly bulletin on personal relationships, office procedures, and techniques for the secretary. Bureau of Business Practice, Inc., 24 Rope Ferry Road, Waterford, Connecticut 06385.

*The Secretary.* The official monthly publication of the National Secretaries Association (International), 616 East 63d Street, Kansas City, Missouri 64110, containing association news and interesting features.

*Today's Secretary.* A monthly magazine (except for July and August) containing timely and informative articles for all levels of secretaries. Gregg Publishing Division, McGraw-Hill Book Company, Inc., 1221 Avenue of the Americas, New York, New York 10020.

*Word Processing Report.* A twice-monthly technical/management newsletter published by Geyer-McAllister, 51 Madison Avenue, New York, New York 10010.

## Fashion, Beauty, Health, and Careers

*Glamour.* A monthly magazine available at newsstands or by subscription from Condé Nast Publications, Inc., 420 Lexington Avenue, New York, New York 10017.

*Mademoiselle.* A monthly magazine available at newsstands or by subscription from Condé Nast Publications. A list of reprints (at 35¢ each) is available from the College and Careers Department.

*35 Fact Sheets on Careers,* such as *Advertising* and *Publishing,* available from Condé Nast Publications.

## Office Management, Procedures, and Supplies

*Administrative Management.* A monthly magazine available by subscription from Geyer-McAllister Publications, 51 Madison Avenue, New York, New York 10010.

*Modern Office Procedures.* A monthly magazine available from the Industrial Publishing Corporation, 614 West Superior Avenue, Cleveland, Ohio 44113.

*The Office.* A monthly magazine available by subscription from Office Publications, Inc., 1200 Summer Street, Stamford, Connecticut 06904.

*Journal of Systems Management.* A magazine published every two months by the Association for Systems Management, available by subscription from 24587 Bagley Road, Cleveland, Ohio 44138.

## QUESTIONS FOR DISCUSSION

1. In what ways did your study of this chapter change your concept of secretarial work?
2. What factors motivate women to work after marriage and rearing a family? As an undergraduate, should you make initial preparation for such a later career? Why?
3. What might be considered a code of ethics for the secretary?
4. To what extent is a secretary justified in deviating from the established pattern of dress or customs of her office?
5. It is said that a secretary with good office skills can easily obtain a job, but skills alone cannot keep the job for her. How do you interpret this statement?
6. In a supervisory or administrative position, with what problems of training or retraining or readjustment would you be involved in regard to the older woman returning to work?
7. In an interview for a secretarial position in a large company, the interviewer asks you whether you would like to work in a word processing center as a word processor. How would you answer this question?

8. Why do so many executives criticize the speech of college secretarial interns?

9. Name one or more secretarial or supervisory activities that would require:

   (a) **A high level of skill training**
   (b) **Good economic or basic business understanding**
   (c) **Superior supervisory ability**
   (d) **Administrative ability**
   (e) **A high degree of ability in human relations**
   (f) **Initiative**

10. In what ways must today's secretary be superior to the secretary of former years?

11. Give an example of when it is NOT permissible to abbreviate each of the following. Then consult the Reference Guide to verify your answers.

    (a) **The name of a state or territory**
    (b) **Parts of the street address**
    (c) **Publications parts such as column, chapter, and page**
    (d) **A portion of a company's name**
    (e) **Dimensions and weights**
    (f) **The words *Honorable* and *Reverend* when used in connection with a name**

12. Select the correct verb or pronoun from the parentheses in the following sentences so that there is number agreement between related words. Then consult the Reference Guide to correct your work. Compose an example similar to any sentence you missed.

    (a) **Your pair of scissors (is, are) being sharpened; my scissors (needs, need) it, too.**
    (b) **The number of applicants (seems, seem) large; a number (has, have) asked for interviews.**
    (c) **(This, These) data (constitutes, constitute) a comprehensive collection of all the facts and figures available now.**
    (d) **Assignments, and not the examination, (determines, determine) your final grade.**
    (e) **Not only the letter but also the carbons (is, are) messy.**
    (f) **The professor, together with the students, (plans, plan) to go through the main post office.**
    (g) **No book or articles (touches, touch) on this subject.**

## PROBLEMS

■ **1.** Rate yourself according to the chart on page 14. What personality deficiency needs your first efforts for improvement?

■ **2.** Have your voice recorded in the Speech Department and ask for criticism. What realistic improvement plan could help you develop your voice as a more effective tool of communication?

■ **3.** What the secretary or administrative assistant says to others in the office is important in determining the success of her office relationships. For each of the following situations write what you consider to be an appropriate comment or action:

(a) **You have an important airmail, special-delivery letter that needs** to be taken to the post office immediately. You ask an assistant to run the errand.

(b) A stenographer who is under your supervision frequently forgets to return or to pay for stamps that she secures from you. What would you say to her the next time she asks for stamps?

(c) You are preparing for your employer an important, detailed report that must be completed tomorrow. Part of the data for the report must be compiled by the secretary to your employer's partner. She has promised to have the data ready today. When you check with her about it, she informs you that she will not be able to complete the work until tomorrow.

(d) A stenographer completes an unusually difficult assignment in very good form ahead of schedule and submits it to you for your criticism.

(e) You observe that a new calculating machine operator who is under your supervision wastes considerable time making personal telephone calls and writing personal letters.

(f) Another secretary in your office asks you: (a) "Is your employer going to Europe this summer?" (You have already typed his itinerary.) (b) "Who is going to be general manager when Mr. X retires next year?" (You were present when the decision was made.)

(g) During dictation, your employer criticizes one of his superiors and asks you if you agree with the criticism.

(h) Your employer brings you flowers for your desk from his garden at home.

(i) An insurance agent who is attempting to sell your employer a life insurance policy gives you a box of candy.

(j) Your employer unjustly criticizes you in the presence of another employee.

(k) Two weeks ago your employer agreed that you might be away from the office for two days next week to attend the wedding of one of your best friends in a neighboring city. From his dictation you learn that he is now planning a business trip for the same time.

(l) Your employer gets or takes credit for an idea you contributed on a rush job you completed under extremely difficult circumstances.

(m) Your employer, who had a very high regard for the assistant who preceded you, has the habit of saying, "Miss X always did it this way."

(n) You have just been promoted to the position of secretary to the executive vice-president, who passed over several girls who have been with the organization longer than you have.

■ **4.** From a recent Administrative Management Society survey, newspaper advertisements, Bureau of Labor Statistics, or interviews with employment agencies, look for information on salaries for secretaries, including the administrative secretary. Compare, if possible, salary levels in various sections of the country.

# Chapter 2

## THE SECRETARY AND THE OFFICE ENVIRONMENT

This chapter discusses the office divisions and the functions of a typical business firm and describes the location of the secretary's work area in the office of the 70's. It also discusses the organization of time and work for top efficiency and offers techniques which will enable you to plan and execute the duties of your position. Thus, it provides information essential to the top-level secretary.

## THE SECRETARY'S KNOWLEDGE OF THE COMPANY

One of the first things a newly hired secretary must do is to study the organizational structure of the company. She must learn where her employer fits in the management team. For the secretary in a one-girl office or in a small company, the hierarchy is readily apparent. For the secretary in a large company, however, the situation is quite different. She must learn the names of the persons to whom her immediate supervisor reports. Likewise, she must know the names of those who report to her employer and those of status equal to his. Generally, she can get this information from the organization chart or organization manual of the company, by asking specific questions of her employer, by researching the files, and by keeping her eyes open.

To assist you in understanding the functions of the various divisions of a business, a description of an organization typical of a large firm follows, along with an organization chart.

### Company Officers

The top administration of a company usually consists of a president, an executive vice-president, one or more vice-presidents, a secretary, and a treasurer. Each of these officers will have a staff to assist him in his work.

**President.** In most corporations the president is the chief executive officer who is responsible to the board of directors for the profitable operation of the business. He is the liaison between the board of

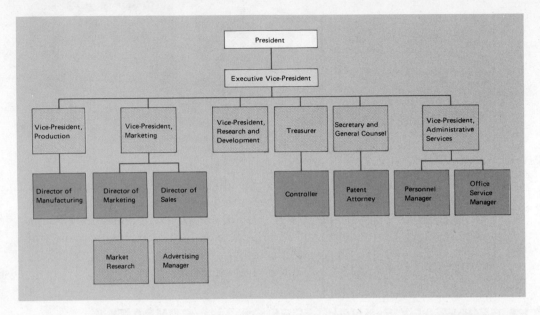

The organization chart for the company described on these pages might look like this. Positions will, of course, vary among companies. This chart clearly identifies the levels of administrative authority in a line structure (one in which authority flows vertically from the top executive to the lowest employee).

directors, on which he usually serves, and management personnel. He interprets board actions to management and management plans to the board. He sees that board resolutions are put into effect.

His duties are often as varied as the activities of the firm. To many persons, he is the company symbol. What he does has a bearing on the reputation of the firm in the community. His leadership ability often determines the type and caliber of management personnel in the organization.

**Executive Vice-President, Vice-Presidents, Secretary, and Treasurer.** The executive vice-president (or senior vice-president) is second in command in the organization. He serves in place of the president and may be selected to succeed as president. Generally, it is his responsibility to suggest any necessary changes in policy and to coordinate the efforts of the vice-presidents in carrying out their specific programs and functions. He also coordinates the work of various departments.

Often there are two, three, or more vice-presidents. Each is a general officer of the company and, with the president and executive vice-president, is involved in achieving the goals of the firm. Each is responsible for a special phase of administration, such as production or marketing, and strives to reach the objectives set for that division.

The secretary of the company is often an attorney, for he is responsible for the legal actions of the business. Typical activities of his staff include scheduling stockholders meetings, drafting resolutions, recording the proceedings of meetings, executing proxies or powers of attorney, and preparing contracts.

The treasurer is the financial officer of the firm, directing all monetary, budget, and accounting activities.

## Divisions of a Company

The office in a large company, such as a manufacturing firm, may be organized around such operational divisions as production, marketing, finance, research and development, and administrative services.

**Production.** The executive in charge of this division is the "vice-president, production"; or in some companies the title may be director of manufacturing, director of engineering, or factory manager.

The production division controls and is responsible for all matters pertaining to the manufacture of the company's products. The objective of this division is to manufacture the product in its desired quality, in the proper quantity, and at the lowest possible cost. This division must cooperate closely with other company divisions such as marketing and finance.

**Purchasing.** The purchasing division is responsible for procuring materials, machinery, and supplies for the entire company. The complexity of the division will, of course, depend on the size of the company. In a very large corporation, the head of the division may be at the vice-presidential level; in a small company, one person (with perhaps some clerical help) can accomplish all purchasing functions. These functions are specialized according to the needs of the organization. One buyer may be in charge of purchasing all raw materials for production, for example, while another may be responsible for the packaging requirements for the corporation's various products, and so on. Further breakdowns in the purchasing procedure occur as necessary.

In general, the procedure is this: A department initiates a purchase requisition, providing as many specifications as necessary. The appropriate buyer locates a source of supply and negotiates the purchase, considering quality, quantity, price, and service.

**Marketing.** Because a business survives only if it sells its products, there must be an effective marketing/sales organization. The marketing division may be divided into two or more departments, the heads of which report to the vice-president, marketing.

*Sales Department.* The sales director (or sales manager) usually directs a staff of salesmen. The department may employ the salesmen, give them special training, assign them to territories, supply samples and literature, introduce new products, and perform myriad other activities.

The selling function, of course, is one of the most important activities of the company. How well this function is performed often determines the company's profit. In addition to the sales department, the sales director may be responsible for developing product policy, approving credit extensions, and preparing a sales budget.

*Advertising Department.* The advertising department, also, is concerned with selling. It is responsible for devising a broad advertising plan appropriate to the overall marketing program and for coordinating this advertising with the selling effort. In some instances it turns over the advertising entirely or partly to an outside advertising agency which plans and executes the program. In this event, the advertising department acts as a liaison, supplying information to the agency about the company products and its marketing goals and approving the agency's proposals.

*Market Research Department.* The work of a market research department is statistical and interpretive in nature. It gathers useful data to guide the business in marketing products or launching new ones. Its scope is extensive. It continuously reexamines and evaluates the market for the company products, evaluates new products of other manufacturers, and provides management with the information necessary for sound business decisions.

**Finance Division.** The finance division handles the moneys and accounting procedures, recording, analyzing, summarizing, and interpreting the financial affairs of the company. Thus the financial division provides a continuous record of company financial transactions. It is also responsible for devising systems and forms and for establishing procedures to summarize company financial activities. This division is involved in formulating company policy.

Often the financial vice-president is in charge, directing the work of the treasurer and the controller.

The *controller* (sometimes spelled *comptroller* but always pronounced *CONtroller*) usually directs all phases of accounting—the general accounting department, cost accounting department, and the combined tax, internal auditing, and procedures department.

**Research and Development Division.** Large companies are increasing their budget allotments for research, recognizing that their survival depends upon success in developing better products.

Scientists and engineers, specialists in their fields, work to develop new and improved products or production methods. They occupy a position of high status in the company cadre.

**Administrative Services Division.** Those departments that serve all others and work almost autonomously are presented here as administrative services departments. These departments generally report to the vice-president, administrative services.

*Personnel Department.* The personnel director or manager directs the work of this department. One function of this department is the interviewing and hiring of employees. This responsibility involves exploring labor sources, processing and filing application forms, organizing and conducting interviews, and administering tests. Some personnel departments also maintain training programs for new employees (perhaps excluding sales trainees), provide employee services and fringe benefits, establish health and safety programs, and accomplish the work involved in transferring, promoting, and discharging employees. The department also develops job descriptions and job analyses.

*Office Services.* Some companies centralize certain office tasks, such as records management, duplicating services, mailing, and word processing systems, by maintaining a specialized staff to perform these office activities. These offices are located where their services are as accessible as individual layouts permit. The company with specialized services relieves the individual office force of performing some of the routine office jobs. For example, a company using word processing centers can conceivably group all secretaries serving one division into a unified location in the division.

In a company without centralized office services, each functional division or department operates as a complete, self-sufficient unit. It handles duties otherwise turned over to a centralized department.

## THE SECRETARY'S OFFICE SURROUNDINGS

Although secretaries in some business organizations are assigned private offices, the trend is to share office space with co-workers.

In expanding business organizations, crowded office conditions and high office allocation costs require the thoughtful reallocation and utilization of office space.

The landscape office design allows office modules, or *work stations*, to be positioned to best fulfill present needs yet allows flexibility as those needs change.

*—Colle & McVoy*

## The Conventional Office Design

In a conventional office design, the secretary may be located in any of three areas: She may share an office with an executive, with her desk immediately inside the door; she may be directly outside the executive's office alongside secretaries to other executives; or she may share a nearby office with several other secretaries. If the secretary is assigned to more than one executive, her desk is placed in a location convenient to each of them. Regardless of the arrangement, the boss-secretary team must be within eyeshot, if not earshot, of one another.

## The Landscape Office Design

A modern approach to office design is the "landscape" method. This approach utilizes movable partitions and screens instead of walls, and open spaces instead of doors and hallways. Colorful, space-age furniture, paintings, thick carpets, sunlight, living or artificial plants, and views of the outdoors typify the new office.

Besides visible changes in the office, the landscape design facilitates work flow and communication between employees and between employees and their supervisor. Employees are positioned according to the flow of work and are visible to their supervisor. Through this office-planning system, employees are made to feel a part of the total process and thus an integral part of the company team. Advocates of this approach say that it increases the productivity of workers and predict that in the future at least 30 percent of the office space will follow this pattern in office design.

A hidden cost in this type of installation is the loss of privacy. Although scientific aids reduce the noise level and the congestion produced by the numerous workers and visitors in a given area, the square footage available per worker is nevertheless reduced considerably and distractions are greatly increased. A secretary housed in this arrangement must develop a power of concentration and show consideration at all times toward others who work around her.

In the landscape office design an office location is a "work station" resembling an office module. For the boss-secretary team, the secretary is in view of her employer, yet cannot be seen by visitors at his desk. Tomorrow's executive office probably will have two sections: an information center (the data input and output devices) and a conference area for informal meetings provided with visual display boards and other visual-audio aids in communication. The secretary will work with input, output, and retrieval equipment and be responsible for projecting the data visually. Even more than now, she will be the facilitator of communication between her employer and his staff members.

## THE SECRETARY'S ORGANIZATION OF TIME AND WORK

An effective secretary makes every minute count. When she works, she works; when she relaxes, she forgets about work and enjoys her free time. She is punctual in all things: in reporting for work, in completing material for the executive, in submitting periodic reports, in relaying messages, and so on. A lackadaisical attitude about time can be a source of irritation in executive-secretary relationships. It can also directly affect other office workers in their attitudes toward time; as in other office-behavior situations, the secretary sets the standard.

### Her Working Day

The secretary to the executive generally does not punch a time clock; neither does she *watch* the clock. She often works on a peculiar time schedule, fitting her hours into the executive's working schedule. He expects her to work late to complete something or to do his banking or other errands on her lunch hour. When a project must meet a deadline, the secretary may even work on the weekends. It is often inconvenient for the secretary to take a short rest break at a scheduled time. She should, however, allow a few minutes' break in her work schedule whenever possible. A short rest period can do wonders in reviving energy and reducing tension.

The secretary, therefore, may find her coming-and-going schedule different from that of other office workers. What she must do is to keep track of her time and give a full week's work, scheduling her time to the executive's convenience. If other office workers comment, she can be confident in her own mind that she has been fair to the company. She is not beholden to account to them for her elastic schedule.

The secretary's vacations, too, may be more irregular than those of other office employees. She must defer to her employer's schedule, remaining on the job when his work load is heaviest.

## THE THREE AREAS OF SECRETARIAL WORK

A secretary works very much on her own, with little or no supervision. True, she does receive instructions occasionally; but after receiving an assignment, she is depended upon to complete it competently. Having a wide area of freedom is very pleasing to one's ego and is one of the real satisfactions of being a secretary.

Secretarial work can be divided into three general areas, (1) assigned tasks; (2) routine duties; and (3) original work.

**Assigned Tasks.** Included among assigned tasks may be such varied items as transcribing a letter, drafting and sending a telegram, making a bank deposit, finding out the flights that leave Sunday night for Washington, making a dental appointment, or getting technical material from the library. In completing these assignments, the secretary may have to adjust her work plan to the emergencies of the moment.

**Routine Duties.** In the area of *routine*, the experienced secretary performs duties such as the following without instruction or supervision: opening the mail, filing, replenishing supplies, preparing periodic reports, collecting time-saving reference materials. She fits these duties into her schedule as time permits.

The president of a large corporation remarked, "The trait that I find most valuable in my secretary is that I can depend on her to do the unimportant, routine jobs as efficiently as she does the bigger, more glamorous ones. Many times an important matter hinges on a record or a document that was part of a routine job."

The executive expects his secretary to be sure that the correlated, executive-secretary work flow is continuous. If he asks for a letter from the files and she has to rummage for it among a stack of unfiled correspondence, he resents the delay. The time spent in keeping his papers well organized is time well spent. The executive will also consider her efficient if, to save time for both of them, she prepares a neatly typed, alphabetic list of frequently called telephone numbers.

**Original Work.** The secretary should use her own initiative in finding original, creative ways to assist the executive. She anticipates his request for certain work and completes it before he asks for it. She notices that having certain information for instant reference would save his time and make it possible for him to work with greater effectiveness; then she compiles that information. If she discovers that certain comparative figures would help him in making a decision, she ferrets them out and sets them up in compact form. If she comes across a pertinent article in a magazine that he ordinarily does not read, she clips the article, mounts it on 8½- by 11-inch paper for easy filing, underlines important points, and adds marginal comments and the source and date of the article. In short, she *thinks*!

The original and creative work of a secretary for her employer is unlimited. It is this kind of work that he particularly appreciates and that she finds most gratifying. The more efficiently she handles the work in the assigned and routine areas, the more time she has for the kind of secretarial service that makes her role truly that of an executive secretary or administrative assistant and earns the attention that leads to promotion.

## The Secretary's Work Plan

The secretary must not only plan her work; she must also work her plan. Work does not come to her in an even flow. There are periods when the executive must turn out important work in a limited time — and so then must the secretary. The secretary's self-analysis of the time and motion spent on routine tasks may free additional time in anticipation of high-priority work. A thorough analysis of all the activities performed by the secretary may provide clues to where time can be conserved. If the secretary anticipates periodic jams and distributes part of the rush-period work to slack days, she can reduce but not eliminate peak loads.

**Work Analysis.** Work measurement is common in offices today. The more repetitive clerical tasks performed by the secretary, such as filing, typing, transcribing, and stuffing and sealing envelopes, have received considerable attention by work analysts. Clerical time standards developed for these tasks can serve as guidelines to the secretary and often are available from the office administrator.

> Schedule more than you can produce; then perhaps you can produce more.

Every secretary should strive to perform her repetitive tasks as efficiently as possible; that is, to work with a minimum of motion, effort, time, and fatigue. The secretary may wish to analyze the factors involved in completing each task to determine where she can reduce motion, effort, time, fatigue, or any combination of them.

For better organization, the secretary may also analyze all her duties over a period of several weeks on a form or a chart designed for this purpose. At predetermined time intervals, the secretary records her current activity, thus providing a daily account of the tasks performed and the proportion of time given to each activity. A careful study of the chart shows where the secretary is not using her time to the best advantage. It may be that she spends too much time on something that she could assign to someone else, such as searching for files that she could have requested from the file clerk.

Certainly, the secretary alone can implement some time-saving practices; for others she may need the cooperation of the employer or even the purchase of new equipment.

**Periodic Peak Loads.** A study of a month's flow of work over the secretary's desk may indicate patterns of fluctuation. For instance, Mondays traditionally bring heavier mail and subsequently heavier dictation, so other Monday plans should be light. A secretary who must issue first-of-the-month statements of account could spread their preparation throughout the month in some organized pattern. Whatever months bring the slack periods, they are ideal for transferring files, typing new card records, bringing address files up to date, and duplicating sets of frequently requested materials.

To help meet the demands of periodic peak loads, the secretary makes whatever preliminary preparations she can. She addresses envelopes, partially completes forms, prepares enclosures, and purchases or requisitions all necessary supplies.

**Real Emergencies.** Even with the best of planning, unavoidable emergencies will occur. An unexpected illness or tragedy may bring the office force below a functional level. The executive may be faced with a

Herculean job and insufficient time in which to perform it. The capable secretary decides which jobs are crisis items, which she can do herself, which she can assign to someone else, and which can be deferred for a day. Through it all, she works calmly and steadily. If necessary, the secretary may suggest employing temporary help.

**Daily Schedule.** As the last routine duty of the day, the secretary prepares her activity plan for the following day, listing the jobs in order of priority. On rare occasions the secretary's plan does not dovetail with her employer's. In that event, the employer's plan has precedence. Remember, HE IS THE BOSS.

## Office Memory Devices

A good memory is basic to office efficiency. The secretary needs a good memory to plan the work for the day and to carry out assignments with the judgment of remembered experience. As noted in Chapter 1, the secretary is her employer's office memory.

**Secretarial Desk Manual.** Every secretary should compile and keep up to date a loose-leaf desk manual. It should cover each duty and procedure of her work while providing a useful place in which to keep often-needed company information. Part 9 of this book explains the contents and organization of such a manual.

**The Tickler.** This efficient office aid derived its name from the accounting term *tick*, meaning to *check off*.

The secretary will enter an item for the tickler to remind herself that an express shipment is due before the end of a week. Notice the abbreviated form of writing memorandums.

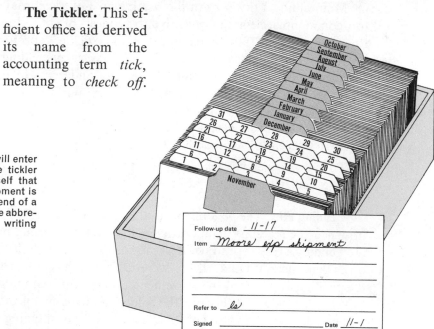

A tickler is an accumulating record, by days, of items of work to be done on future days and then ticked off when they have been accomplished. Items observed in the file beyond the tickler date are effective warning signals if the tickler is checked systematically.

The daily calendar can be used as a tickler for the recording of items to be done on specific dates; however, since calendar-page space is limited, a separate tickler is usually set up and maintained. The most flexible tickler is a file box with 5- by 3-inch guide cards for each month and one to three sets of date guides from 1 to 31. The guide for the current month is placed in the front of the file. A set of day guides is placed behind the guide for the current month and perhaps the next one or two months. An item of future concern is written up on an individual card, and the card is dropped behind the guide for the proper month and for the proper date. If the item is to be followed up several months later, it is dropped behind the month guide; it is filed according to date when that month comes to the front.

Since an item is often forwarded and reforwarded, the follow-up date is written in pencil so that it can be erased and changed. In fact, since this is but a memorandum type of record, the entire item is usually written in pencil. Annual items, such as due dates of taxes, insurance premiums, and wedding anniversaries, are refiled for next year's reminders as soon as ticked off.

Maintaining a tickler is in the routine area of secretarial work; it is too commonplace for the executive to request, organize, or supervise. But if you should fail to remind him of a tickler-type item, he will become *very* provoked—the extent of the *very* depending upon the embarrassment caused him and the dollars and cents involved. The moral is: USE the tickler device as a memory aid in these ways:

1. **To record future-date work**
2. **To remind of work to be done**
3. **To tick off missions accomplished**

To be of dependable help to the executive, you must persistently check a tickler for pending activities.

**Pending File.** The pending file is also a memory aid. It is a file folder in which the secretary temporarily holds mail concerning matters that are pending. It is kept in her desk, in the executive's desk, or in some other place near at hand. If the secretary's desk has a deep file drawer, the pending file can be kept conveniently there. It is not too satisfactory to keep the folder flat, because the folder and its contents often become dog-eared. Making extra copies of incoming and outgoing letters and filing them in their respective files prevents isolating letters that should be available in the regular file. Check through the pending file regularly, or it will grow fat with letters that should have been released to the regular files. The pending file, however, is convenient for the correspondence on *in-process* matters.

**Desk Reference Files.** The secretary can organize her work more efficiently by keeping desk reference files, such as those listing names of important clients, telephone numbers frequently called, addresses of regular correspondents, items that must be followed through before they are placed in the central files, stock identifications and descriptions, and work in process. These desk reference files save much time that would otherwise be lost in hunting for frequently needed facts. The organization of each secretarial desk differs because of the executive's position and type of business. The desk reference files you set up will be those you need most, planned only after you are on the job.

**The Chronological File.** Some secretaries make an extra tissue copy of everything they type, filing it in a chronological file in her desk. Many a day has been "saved" by this ready-reference file. If the secretary is also in charge of the executive's files, she notes on the "chron" tissue the disposition of the file copy.

How long the secretary keeps the chron copies is a matter of preference; for instance, she may wish to keep the past three months' correspondence in her desk and older correspondence in a file drawer.

## Outside Assistance

If the situation warrants, it is good judgment for the secretary to obtain assistance. When there is not sufficient time to complete a sizable office job, the secretary often asks for additional workers. She tries to obtain help within her own office through the office manager, the typing pool supervisor, or from other secretaries, who often help each other in rush situations. If those avenues fail, she may obtain the executive's permission to telephone her request to an agency that supplies experienced temporary help. Among such agencies are Manpower, Inc., Kelly Services, Inc., Olsten Services, and others.

When the work requires professional skills or abilities beyond those of the secretary or when the job is of such size that it can be done more quickly and at less expense outside, the secretary often turns to a special-service agency—after obtaining the executive's permission, of course. She might find it wise to use agencies that prepare multiple copies of original letters and mail them, that obtain hotel and travel reservations, that take full recordings of meetings and prepare transcripts, that handle

A competent supervisor gives clear, concise, and complete directions for a procedure. She then allows her assistant to carry out the directions without the feeling of being under close scrutiny.

*—IBM Corporation*

all or any of the operations of a duplicating job, that furnish and maintain mailing lists, or that provide competent help for other jobs of a specialized or technical nature.

Upon completion of major work or service, the secretary writes in her desk manual a memorandum in which she identifies the agency or the individuals used, records the total cost, and inserts a brief evaluation for future guidance.

## Supervision of Subordinates

The secretary may be assigned one or two full-time assistants or temporary helpers. With relatively young or inexperienced assistants, the secretary may find herself in the role of *teacher*. She must provide opportunities for the employee to work under her supervision to establish proper habits. She should also teach the proper use of equipment and physical facilities, plan the work of the office, and distribute it equitably. She must give thorough directions, leaving no doubt to what she expects the subordinates to do.

Appraise employee's performance in PRESENT ASSIGNMENT. Check ( √ ) most appropriate square. Appraisers are *urged to use freely* the "REMARKS" sections for significant comments descriptive of the individual.

| 1. KNOWLEDGE OF WORK:<br><br>Understanding of all phases of his work and related matters. | Needs instruction or guidance. | Has required knowledge of own and re-    lated work. √√ | Has exceptional knowledge of own and re-    lated work. |
|---|---|---|---|

Remarks: *Is particularly good at research for reports).*

| 2. INITIATIVE:<br><br>Ability to originate or develop ideas and to get things started. | Lacks imagination.   √√ | Meets necessary requirements | Unusually resourceful. |
|---|---|---|---|

Remarks: *Has good ideas when asked for an opinion but otherwise will not offer them. Somewhat lacking in self-confidence.*

| 3. APPLICATION:<br><br>Attention and application to his work. | Wastes time. Needs close    supervision. | Steady and willing worker.   √√ | Exceptionally industrious. |
|---|---|---|---|

Remarks:

| 4. QUALITY OF WORK:<br><br>Thoroughness, neatness, and accuracy of work. | Needs improvement. | Regularly meets recognized    standards. | Consistently maintains highest √√ quality. |
|---|---|---|---|

Remarks: *The work she turns out is always of the highest possible quality.*

| 5. VOLUME OF WORK:<br><br>Quantity of acceptable work. | Should be increased. | Regularly meets recognized √√ standards. | Unusually high output. |
|---|---|---|---|

Remarks: *Would be higher if she did not spend so much time checking and rechecking her work.*

**A Graphic Rating Scale with Provision for Rater Comments**

*Source:* Part of an Appraisal and Development Form used by the Standard Oil Company of California. Reproduced with permission.

At all times, the secretary is a *student* of human behavior. She studies the people under her supervision and reads literature which may prove useful to her in relating to her subordinates. She is responsible for motivating her subordinates to work at their full potential and to take pride in their work. She gives credit and praise when due; but if necessary she uses constructive criticism, discussing the *work* and not the *worker*.

At specified intervals, the secretary formally evaluates her subordinates' performances, perhaps using an evaluation instrument similar to that given above. Note that such an instrument lets the evaluator comment on each factor being rated, an advantage both to the evaluator and to the employee. Remember that the responsibility for objective evaluation goes with this duty.

**The Supervisor's Prayer**

Please, when I am wrong, make me willing to change; when I am right, make me easy to live with. So strengthen me that the power of my example will far exceed the authority of my rank.

—*Pauline H. Peters*

## SUGGESTED READINGS

Anastasi, Thomas E., Jr. *A Secretary Is a Manager*. Burlington, Mass.: Management Center of Cambridge, 1970, pp. 137–146 (supervising).

Becker, Esther R., and Evelyn Anders. *The Successful Secretary's Handbook*. New York: Harper & Row, 1971, pp. 217–227 (appointments and reminders).

Becker, Esther R., and Peggy Norton Rollason. *The High-Paid Secretary*. Englewood Cliffs: Prentice-Hall, Inc., 1967, pp. 45–62 (use of time), 35–44 (supervising), 149–161 (company organization).

Chruden, Herbert J., and Arthur W. Sherman, Jr. *Personnel Management*, 4th ed. Cincinnati: South-Western Publishing Co., 1972, pp. 383–398 (supervising).

Ingoldsby, Patricia, and Joseph Focarino. *The Executive Secretary: Handbook to Success*. New York: Doubleday & Co., Inc., 1969, pp. 83–124 (organizing work).

Lauria, Marie. *How to Be a Good Secretary*. New York: Frederick Fell, Inc., 1969.

*Plan Your Work — A Handbook on How to Work Smarter, Not Harder*. Washington: National Association of Educational Secretaries (1201 16th Street, N.W.).

## QUESTIONS FOR DISCUSSION

1. After considering your interests, abilities, and aptitudes, in which department of a business organization (purchasing, personnel, research, sales, advertising, accounting) would you prefer to work? Give reasons for your choice.

2. You work in an office with a landscape design. What is your responsibility to the workers in your immediate area?

3. For each of the office duties given below, determine whether it is an assigned, a routine, or an original task, and describe the working situation (working with employer, other company employees, things, or outsiders).

   a. Filing a piece of correspondence
   b. Answering the telephone
   c. Looking up a word in the dictionary
   d. Answering employer's buzz
   e. Typing a letter from dictation
   f. Setting up your own chronological file
   g. Proofreading document with another

4. Why plan your work if your employer frequently disrupts the plan?

5. Your employer frequently calls you for rush dictation late in the afternoon so that you must work overtime. With proper reorganization of his work, much of this necessity for overtime work could be avoided. How could you suggest that he change his habits so that both of you could be more efficient and the overtime could be reduced?

6. In what ways can you reduce periodic peak loads? real emergencies?

7. What is the weakness in using a pending file? How can this danger be averted?

8. What would you do first if you were trying to type a telegram which was urgent and the telephone rang, your employer buzzed for you, his superior walked into your office, and your subordinate reported that she had finished her assigned work?

9. The executive may expect that he will need to convert securities to obtain the cash to pay his quarterly income taxes. What kind of item would you put in the tickler? under what dates?

10. Most large business organizations formally evaluate their employees. For what purposes are employee evaluation instruments used? What factors are generally evaluated? What are the weaknesses of some evaluation forms?

11. Capitalize the following sentences. Then refer to the Reference Guide to correct your answers.
    (a) I wonder: is secretarial work as interesting as it sounds?
    (b) The answer is, sell it, even at a loss!
    (c) What other possibilities are there? to start over? to give up? to repeat each experiment?

12. Show how you would type the number *twenty-five* in the blanks in the following sentences. Then refer to the Reference Guide to correct your answers.
    (a) I believe she is about _____ years old.
    (b) Our new address is 6125 _____ Street.
    (c) The premise is based on a _____ year old book.
    (d) _____ replies were received.

## PROBLEMS

■ 1. The following items are on your desk on March 2 to be marked for the tickler file. Before filing these items, you type a card for the tickler file indicating on each card the date under which the card would be filed. Note on the card where the material is filed.

(a) Notes for an article solicited for the September *Journal of Accountancy* (The deadline for the article is April 1.)

(b) A note about setting up a conference with a bank official about a short-term loan to meet the April 1 payroll

(c) A letter accepting an invitation to speak at a meeting of School of Business seniors on May 8

(d) The program of the annual convention of the International Controllers Institute to be held on April 6 in Brussels (Your employer has told you that he plans to attend.)

(e) A notice of a meeting on March 8 of the Administrative Committee of which your employer is a member

■ 2. Your employer is leaving for the airport in twenty minutes. He just requested that you:
(a) Go to the treasurer's office to cash a personal check for him
(b) Call his taxicab

You leave his office, return to your desk to find:
(c) The telephone ringing
(d) Your employer's right-hand man wishing to speak with you

(e) **An office caller, whom you don't recognize**

(f) **The unfinished letter in your type-writer that your employer must sign**

On a sheet of paper, list the order in which you would handle these matters. Explain the rationale behind your decision.

**3.** It is late Friday afternoon and you are fifteen minutes away from your two-week vacation. Your employer is out of town until Monday. You have a number of pending matters on your desk. Decide which of the following items you should handle yourself in the time remaining, which to leave locked in your boss's desk, and which to leave for your replacement to handle. On a sheet of paper, type your decisions and give the rationale behind them.

(a) **Payment of your employer's insurance premium due the following Wednesday (You are authorized to make payment.)**

(b) **Notification of a meeting scheduled for Thursday of the following week**

(c) **Shorthand notes of a letter dictated by one of the staff members**

(d) **Confidential promotion papers concerning a staff member**

(e) **Interoffice memorandum requesting technical data from your employer**

(f) **Chatty letter from your employer's daughter at college**

# Chapter 3

# THE SECRETARY AS OFFICE HOSTESS

The secretary is a public relations representative of her company and of her employer, paid to create a favorable image of both to all visitors and to her co-workers. In few other aspects of her work is the public relations responsibility so heavy or challenging as in her work as office hostess. The more responsibility in this direction that she can assume, the more valuable to her employer she becomes. In the event that the secretary is assigned to more than one executive, she performs the functions of office hostess for all of them.

The secretary must create a pleasant, relaxed office atmosphere that influences visitors to react favorably to the executive's point of view and that enables him to work at top efficiency. From the time she welcomes the visitor until she speeds him on his way, she is the official office hostess, serving as a buffer between the visitor and her employer, interpreting the company's policy and her employer's, and soothing ruffled feelings (however unjustified). When the visitor walks away, he should feel, "That's a good company (or good person) to deal with. I'll come back here."

Such public relations skill is worth uncountable dollars in goodwill. Some is innate, but much skill can be developed on the job. This chapter discusses two aspects of the work of the secretary-receptionist: her duties as an office hostess and her duties regarding the executive's appointments.

## THE SECRETARY'S DUTIES AS HOSTESS

The secretary's responsibility in greeting office visitors varies. In large organizations all visitors go to a reception desk where a trained receptionist screens callers and directs them to the person who handles the phase of work in which they are interested. The company receptionist tells the secretary that the caller is in the outer office, and then the secretary takes over her responsibilities as office hostess.

In smaller companies the caller may first be received by the switch-board operator. In the very small office the secretary is the caller's initial contact with the company. Thus she has a greater responsibility both in determining the use of executive time and in influencing the reaction of the visitor toward her organization. She tends also to handle the problems of many callers herself as they relate to her realm of responsibility.

In her role as official office hostess, the secretary must be confident that she reflects her employer's personal preferences. Moreover, since many of her duties as hostess will occur when her employer is not present, she must contribute to smooth reception procedures on her own initiative.

## The Executive's Preferences

As a new secretary, you should learn how the executive wants you to handle visitors. You should ask your predecessor, or you may ask general questions about his preferences. If you develop sensitivity to the reactions of others, you can learn to discern his preferences through experience.

Discover answers to questions about executive preferences:

| | |
|---|---|
| Does the executive want to see everyone who calls? (Many executives make a fetish of their "open-door policy.") Does he prefer to see callers in a certain category (such as salesmen) at specified times only? | You can get direct answers to these two questions; however, the answers must sometimes be modified. |
| Which of his personal friends and relatives are likely to call, and which should be sent in without announcement? Who else should be admitted without appointments? | Do not ask these questions directly. You will soon sense the answer. Certain persons can always enter the executive's office without first obtaining your permission: top executives to whom your employer is responsible; their secretaries; coexecutives with whom he frequently confers and their secretaries; and his immediate staff. Special-privilege callers come in with confidence. They know they will be welcome, and usually they introduce themselves to the new secretary. |
| How should callers be announced? When should you try to help terminate visits? Are there callers that your employer prefers to avoid? | Watch your employer's reactions to your ways of handling these problems. Sense how he responds to your methods. |

After a cheerful, courteous greeting, the secretary listens attentively to the caller so that she can use good judgment in handling the purpose of his visit. She may need to refer him to someone else, or she may have to decide between interrupting her employer and asking the visitor to wait.

**Welcoming the Visitor.** When a visitor comes to your desk, give him your immediate and undivided attention. To finish typing the line, to file the last three letters, or to continue chatting with another employee is rude.

Your eyes and facial expression can communicate to the visitor that he is indeed welcome. Your greeting should be friendly and cheerful. There are many ways to say "Good morning" or "Good afternoon." A tone of voice can betray the secretary, reveal her mood, and perhaps leave a lasting unfavorable impression upon the visitor.

You must learn who an unscheduled caller is and what he wants. Listen attentively to what he has to say. Smile naturally and greet him by saying, "Good morning. May I help you?" Unless he gives you his name or business card, ask, "May I have your name, please?" or "Who should I say is calling?" You must then get his business affiliation, which usually will explain the purpose of his visit; or your question may cause him to tell you the reason for his call. This is one of the most difficult problems that confronts the receptionist, especially one new in a position; and it requires tact and patience.

If the visitor wishes to see the executive about something out of his scope of duties, the considerate office hostess will try to arrange a meeting with the right person.

*—American Telephone and Telegraph Company*

The legitimate business caller, accustomed to making office calls, will approach the secretary, identify himself, state the purpose of his visit, and ask to see the executive.

A caller may want to see the executive about a matter out of the executive's scope of duties. You will save everyone's time by learning the nature of the visit and referring the visitor to the proper person. Nothing is more annoying than to wait half an hour to see someone only to find that he is the wrong person. The secretary should effect the transfer immediately and skillfully. She can say, "Mr. Lawrence, Mr. Alexander handles that for Mr. Allen. If you wish, I'll be glad to see if he can talk to you now or to make an appointment for another time." Or she can say, "I wonder if you would see Mr. Lane, in Advertising. He is familiar with our handling of that matter and can help you. I'll be glad to see if he is free."

If the caller agrees to see Mr. Lane, the secretary can telephone Mr. Lane or his secretary and explain the situation. She can then say, "Mr. Lane can see you now, Mr. Lawrence. Will you please go to the twelfth floor and tell the receptionist that Mr. Lane is expecting you." In case Mr. Lane cannot see the caller, the secretary might say, "I'm sorry that Mr. Lane can't see you this morning, but he can see you tomorrow at eleven if that is convenient for you."

In most cases the secretary's helpfulness in arranging the appointment will more than offset the inconvenience to the visitor of going to still another office.

If you have the visitor's name and reason for calling and if you are satisfied that the visitor's business is within your employer's province, write the name and purpose of the visit on a slip of paper and take it in to the executive. He will decide whether he wishes to see the visitor. The written memorandum also helps the executive remember to use the caller's name in subsequent conversation.

The secretary will be on the lookout for a person with a scheduled appointment. She will be able to greet him by name, possibly saying, "Good morning, Mr. Lawrence. How are you? Mr. Allen is expecting you. You may go right in."

**Deciding Whom to Admit.** Experienced secretaries, sometimes inclined to become too protective of the executive's time, may turn away too many visitors. A cartoon showing a president's door overhung with cobwebs while the secretary explains, "Oh, nobody ever sees Mr. Jones," dramatizes this secretarial attitude, which antagonizes almost everybody. A good rule to follow is: *When in doubt, ask the executive if he wants to see the visitor.*

If your desk is placed inside the executive's office, callers are inclined to go directly to him, the screening having been done at the receptionist's desk in the outer office. But if your desk is just outside his office, you will probably be responsible for determining who may enter.

Although selected co-workers may enter without your permission, they usually ask courteously if it is convenient for them to go into the executive's office.

The executive's friends and family may have the privilege of going into his office at any time; but if he is busy at the moment, the secretary should ask them to wait, saying that he is busy. She need not go into detail, such as "He is in conference with the general manager," or "He is talking with the vice-president." A statement that he will be free in a few minutes or will return shortly is ample explanation. Learn to know these guests and always try to call them by name. Be friendly with them but not too cordial, because they are a part of the executive's social and home life and you may appear presumptuous if your manner is too personal.

Clients and customers are always accorded cordial and gracious treatment by the secretary. Salesmen of materials and services related to her employer's work are treated with courtesy and listened to attentively. They may provide technical help in ironing out company problems, and the secretary should tell the executive immediately when such a salesman calls.

If the secretary has reason to believe that her company would have no use for the salesman's product, she may say, "Mr. Ward, I don't believe we would be able to use your product, but let me check with Mr. Allen to see if he wants to talk with you," or "We are using another product, and I am not sure that Mr. Allen has time to see you today, but I will ask him. Just a moment, please." She may also find it appropriate to direct him to another office.

Never, never judge a visitor's importance by his appearance; some outstanding people in the artistic, professional, and industrial world are far from prepossessing in appearance. On one occasion the secretary to a college president decided that an early-morning, very ordinary-looking caller was quite unimportant. Therefore, she did not trouble to tell the president that the man was waiting, because the president was busy at the time. Finally the man grew impatient and left. Later she learned — to her chagrin and to the great disappointment of the college — that the caller was a very wealthy alumnus who had intended to give the school a tremendous sum of money. He never came back.

**Remembering Names and Faces.** One extremely valuable secretarial technique is addressing a caller with an easy and natural grace. Unless your caller gives you his business card, write his name and the reason for his call on your daily calendar during the conversation. To remember names requires:

1. *Attention to the name as it is spoken.* Listen carefully when the name is pronounced. If in doubt, ask the person how to pronounce it or how to spell it. Writing the name phonetically in shorthand or in longhand will prevent mispronunciation. Although hearing one's name is pleasant, having it mispronounced is very annoying.

2. *A forceful effort to remember it.* You can train yourself to remember a person's name by: repeating it when you first learn it; using it when addressing the person; recording it, perhaps in a reference notebook or card file; and associating the person's name and face with his business.

Remembering faces is another attribute of the superior secretary. Several devices may be used to develop this skill. The secretary may keep a card file of frequent callers. Or she may file a business card as it is given to her, associating the name on the card with the face of the

An efficient memory aid for the receptionist: Prepare a card for each caller, recording his name, affiliation, purpose and date of visit, subsequent visits, etc. Or make notations directly on the caller's business card. Shown at the right is a business card affixed to a 5-by 3-inch card.

caller. To recognize her employer's colleagues, she should watch carefully for their pictures in company publications, newspapers, or magazines. While reporting a committee meeting, the secretary might draw a seating chart and list some outstanding feature for unknown members so that she could ask for their names later or fill in the names as she hears them mentioned.

Several companies whose success depends upon effective public relations have developed techniques for improving internal relations by helping personnel recognize members of the organization. One, an advertising agency, publishes in its company induction manual an organization chart with the picture and the title of each executive beside his name.

**Keeping a Record of Visitors.** A record of visitors — their names, dates of calls, business affiliations, purposes for calls, and other pertinent information is helpful. Often the secretary uses this record to track down urgently needed facts through its names and dates.

Some offices use a printed form for registering a visitor, asking him to write the required information on the form; or the secretary may secure the information from the visitor and write it on a pad as she talks with him. Later she can transfer the data to the register. If the caller presents his business card, the secretary need only ask the name of the person whom he wishes to see and the purpose of his call.

Professional offices use daily registers such as those used by lawyers and public accountants, because such men usually prepare periodic time reports as a basis for computing costs of services rendered to clients. The register serves as a check list for each period to make sure that the time spent with each client, as recorded, is also entered and charged for on the proper time reports.

| REGISTER OF OFFICE VISITORS | | | | | |
|---|---|---|---|---|---|
| Date | Time | Name and Affiliation | Person Asked For | Person Seen | Purpose of Call |
| 6/8/7– | 9:30 | H. Horton, Cove Lighting Fix. | S.G. | ✓ | Salesman |
| " | 10:30 | L. Alton, Standard Printing | R.B. | ✓ | " |
| " | 11:45 | R. Krause, luncheon appt. | R.B. | – | Merrill cont. |
| " | 1:40 | J. Keller, Flexwood Consultant | S.G. | ✓ | " " |
| " | 3:50 | Flexwood delivery driver | – | – | Brought samp. |

With this ruled register of visitors, the secretary can easily keep a daily record of helpful information about callers, including purpose of the call.

Some offices keep an alphabetic card file of visitors, recording all visits as they occur. A card is filed by a caller's name and is cross-referenced to show his affiliation. Doctors use the card system as a basis for billing patients and as a record of each patient's medical data. Purchasing agents remember the correct names of products and salesmen by using such a file.

If the flow of visitors is small, the secretary can keep her personal record of visitors conveniently and permanently on her daily calendar.

## The Secretary's Contributions

**Pleasant Waiting.** A good office hostess tries to make the visitor as comfortable as possible while he is waiting. She asks him to sit down. She sees that current magazines and an ash tray are close by; she invites him to take off his overcoat, or topcoat, if he has not done so; or she may have coffee available to offer him. If she likes and is not too busy, she may talk with the caller casually about general and impersonal things; but good judgment will tell her never to discuss office business.

**Admitting the Visitor.** After an unduly long wait, the secretary may remind the executive that the caller is still waiting and then report to the caller that it will be only a few more minutes. Of course, the gracious way to deliver a message is to cross the room to the visitor.

Sometimes the executive walks out to greet the caller. Should there be two callers waiting, indicate who is first. If you escort the caller into the private office while other visitors remain near your desk or may enter the office, you may want to cover the work on your desk unobtrusively or put it into a folder.

If this is the visitor's first call, the secretary may take him into her employer's office, leading the way. In most offices she would knock before entering if the door is closed. She would then introduce the caller and leave unobtrusively, closing the door behind her.

In some cases, although she would wish to show the caller into the executive's office, she may have to say: "I am sorry, Mr. Lawrence, but I am busy with a long distance call. Will you please go in now."

**Introductions.** The secretary presents the visitor to the executive. Since the caller has heard the executive's name, the secretary may omit it when making the introduction. It is courteous, however, to address the executive as you introduce the caller.

**This is Mr. Lawrence of Allied Corporation.**
**Mr. Allen, this is Mr. Lawrence, who has an appointment with you.**
**This is Mr. Lawrence.**
NEVER SAY: **Mr. Allen, meet Mr. Lawrence.**

Business position rather than sex or age is usually the determining factor as to who should be introduced to whom. The secretary presents customers or clients to her employer as indicated above. The social rule is reversed in an office; an executive presents his secretary to a man with, "Mr. Lawrence, I should like you to know my secretary, Miss Baer." The secretary usually does not rise unless she is being introduced to an older or notable person such as a chief of state or a clergyman. Neither does she shake hands when she is introduced unless the other person offers his hand first. She acknowledges an introduction merely by saying "How do you do, Mr. Lawrence," being sure to address the caller by name.

**The Difficult Visitor.** Being courteous to certain visitors may require considerable discipline and restraint. Some of them are gruff; some are condescending; some are self-important or aggressive; some, even rude. To be gracious to these persons requires strong willpower.

A visitor who resorts to obvious flattery to get information from the secretary is very obnoxious and usually thick skinned. About the only courteous recourse is to let him know that you intend to remain gracious but will not be bludgeoned. Above everything, the secretary should not answer, except in generalities, the business questions of inquisitive callers. An answer such as, "I really don't know; perhaps Mr. Allen can tell you," will ordinarily stop such questions.

A nuisance visitor such as a peddler resorts to all sorts of dodges to get past the secretary's desk. It is here the secretary needs to exercise tact and firmness. Be wary of a person who, without giving his name, says, "I'm a personal friend; he knows me," or "I want to see him on a personal matter." The caller with important business has everything to gain by giving his name and the reason for his call. You can explain

```
Mr. Blackwell

Your secretary just called and asked that
you call her within 20 minutes for a very
important message.  There is a telephone on
which you can call just outside the confer-
ence room.  (Dial 9 for an outside line.)

                              A. A.
```

```
Mr. Montenegro

The secretary of Mr. Edward Hood is on the
line at my desk and asks that you come to
the telephone for an important message from
Mr. Hood.  I'll wait outside my office while
you talk.  Will you, therefore, please let
me know when you are ready to leave my
office?

                              A. A.
```

Shown above are two acceptable ways in which to handle typical interruptions of business conferences. Before the secretary acts, she decides what procedure will make the interruption as unobtrusive as possible.

that you are not permitted to admit visitors unannounced; if he still refuses to tell you his name and purpose, ask him to sign his name on a card or to write a short note to the executive. You can enclose either of these in an envelope and take it in to the executive, who can then decide whether to admit him.

**Interrupting a Conference.** If it is necessary to give a message to the executive when he is in conference, type it on a slip of paper and take it in to him, usually without knocking if this is less likely to disturb or interrupt the conference proceedings.

When there is a telephone call for the visitor, ask if you can take the message. If so, type it along with the name, the date, and time of receipt. If the one calling insists on speaking to the visitor, go into the conference room and say something like this: "Mr. Lawrence, Mr. Rowett is on the telephone and wants to speak to you. Would you like to take the call here (*indicating which telephone he is to use*),

When a visitor lingers overlong, the tactful secretary can hand her employer a note, the contents of which might read: "Your appointment with Mr. Reynolds is in five minutes. Nod your head if you'd like me to mention it aloud." If the employer needs a graceful way to end the conversation, the note will provide it.

or would you prefer using the telephone on my desk?" She then finds other business away from the phone to afford the visitor privacy.

Some callers stay and stay and stay. Usually the executive rises when he wishes to terminate a conference, but occasionally a caller will not take the hint. The secretary may help the situation by taking to the executive's desk a note which he can pretend contains a request for him to go elsewhere, or by apologetically announcing to him that it is time for him to leave for his next engagement. She should not say where, even though it is a legitimate reminder. She might even telephone from a desk out of range and ask if he wants to be interrupted so that he can send the person away. Often his mere answering of the telephone affords a sufficient break in the conversation to make the caller realize he has stayed too long.

A way to reduce overlong visits is to say before the caller goes into the executive's office, "Mr. Allen has another appointment in ten minutes, but he will be glad to see you in the meantime."

# THE EXECUTIVE'S APPOINTMENT SCHEDULE

Before the secretary can effectively handle the executive's appointments, she should familiarize herself with his connections—the committees on which he is working, the clubs to which he belongs, the speaking engagements he has planned, and the projects in which he is interested. For instance, the president of a large corporation might be a board member of a college or a number of other organizations, a member of several civic clubs or enterprises, president of a professional organization, or author of a book. If the secretary is acquainted with all these activities, she is better prepared to schedule his appointments.

The executive's personality will also affect his appointment schedule. Is he "all business," maintaining a schedule strictly as planned; or is he a warm, outgoing individual, inclined to chat with people? The latter type of executive will often upset a carefully planned appointment schedule.

## Scheduling Appointments

Appointments are scheduled in different ways:

1. The secretary schedules recurring appointments at which the executive's presence is necessary (i.e., regularly scheduled conferences of boards or corporation committees) on his calendar at the beginning of the year and throughout the year as new commitments are made.
2. The executive or secretary may schedule an appointment over the telephone.
3. Either the executive or the secretary may schedule an appointment by mail.
4. The executive may ask the secretary to schedule an additional conference with someone who is then in his office.
5. The secretary may schedule a definite appointment with a caller who just dropped in and found the executive out of the office.
6. The secretary may arrange for an appointment for the executive outside the company offices.

The secretary is depended upon to furnish complete information when scheduling appointments. Even though the executive merely says, "Make it 3:30 Wednesday," she would specify the actual date and the place on the calendar. It is also wise to give a reminder to the person making the appointment. Unless she has the telephone number of the person making the appointment, the secretary exercises wise precaution by recording the number on her desk calendar so that she can cancel the appointment if necessary.

The secretary uses either an appointment book or a desk calendar to record appointments. The executive keeps a pocket diary or a desk calendar and oftentimes so does his wife. As a result, the secretary must

| FEB 19- | MAR 19- | | APR 19- |
|---|---|---|---|

FEB 19-
S M T W T F S
2 3 4 5 6 7 8
9 10 11 12 13 14 15
16 17 18 19 20 21 22
23 24 25 26 27 28

MAR 19-
S M T W T F S
2 3 4 5 6 7 8
9 10 11 12 13 14 15
16 17 18 19 20 21 22
23 24 25 26 27 28 29
30 31

APR 19-
S M T W T F S
1 2 3 4 5
6 7 8 9 10 11 12
13 14 15 16 17 18 19
20 21 22 23 24 25 26
27 28 29 30

*Mr. Peterson*

*Mr. R.L. Cooper*
*Pension Plan*
*Conference*
*Dentist*

*Mr. Hughes - Lamar Hotel*

*Call KLS re. contract*
*Call Calhoun re VA Drive   741-3177*
*Transfer Files*
*Adv. talk in p.m.*

**TODAY**

*Mrs. Victor*

**MEMOS**

*CJV. N.Y. Tickets*
*in safe*
*Pick up Lamps*

Appointments and Reminders For
Monday, April 7, 197-

**TO COME**

*Galley proof*
*from Atlantic*
*Press*

10:00   Staff Meeting

11:00   James F. Bruce, Chamber of Commerce, 829-2300,
        Ext. 509

11:30   Harry Bennington, Mutual Life, 829-4502

12:00   Luncheon Meeting with Frank Snyder, University Club

2:00    Budget Meeting

Today's Reminders:
        Call Frank Snyder, 425-0034
        Follow up on Emerson contract
        License No. 533-429-3001 expires end of month
        Review Andrew's proposal

check daily for possible conflicting dates. In planning future office activities, the executive-secretary team often finds it helpful to maintain a planning guide. Whatever procedure is followed, it is wise to keep appointment records from year to year as a reference source.

In maintaining her executive's appointment record, the secretary concerns herself with the four "W's" of scheduling appointments:

**WHO** the person is—his name and affiliation.

**WHAT** he wants—an interview for a position, an opportunity to sell his product, or a business discussion. Indicate any materials that will be needed for the appointment.

**WHEN** he wants an appointment and how much time he will need.

**WHERE** an appointment away from the executive's office is to be held. Be sure to include the address and room number.

The first thing each morning the secretary, by various means, reminds the executive of his appointment commitments and places on his desk pertinent information and files. Some employers prefer a typed list of the appointments scheduled for the day and other matters that must receive his attention. This list may be on 8½- by 11-inch paper or even on a 5- by 3-inch card. Some executives prefer a separate list of matters to be handled that day with the appropriate files attached. Any matters not handled are carried over to the next day's list.

Another successful practice is to include in the list any questions the secretary may have. The executive writes the answers directly on the sheet, leaving the paper on his desk so that the secretary can get her answers without disturbing the executive.

If the secretary works for more than one executive, she maintains a separate appointment book for each and follows the procedures described above to record appointments and inform her employers.

**The Employer's Preferences.** In selecting the date and hour for an appointment, consider the personal preferences of the executive.

1. Schedule few, if any, appointments on Monday mornings, because the weekend accumulation of mail requires attention.
2. Allow ample time in the appointment schedule to take care of the mail.
3. Avoid late-afternoon appointments so that her employer can complete work of the day.
4. Avoid appointments just before a trip because of the last-minute rush of work.
5. Leave free the first day after the executive's absence of several days because of the accumulation of work.
6. Suggest two alternate times for the appointment, rather than asking, "When would you like to see Mr. Lawrence?"

When the secretary grants an appointment, she explains that it is subject to the approval of the executive and may have to be changed. She enters the appointment on her own calendar, as well as on her employer's calendar. Unless the secretary has been given carte blanche in scheduling appointments, she later explains the appointment and asks the executive to approve it.

In arranging appointments, the secretary has an opportunity to exercise good judgment. A young man from Wisconsin planned to visit an Ohio city to apply for an engineering position. He wrote that he could come to the office of the prospective employer the following Saturday morning. Although the executive would be in his Ohio office on the Saturday morning in question, the secretary knew that her employer would be in a Wisconsin city near the young man's home on the following Monday. She felt the interview could be held there. She asked her employer's opinion, and he directed her to set up an appointment at his Wisconsin hotel any time after 7 o'clock Monday evening. Thus, the applicant saved a great deal of expense and time — and the employer had his Saturday morning free.

**Avoiding Unkept Appointments.** Nothing destroys good relations faster than an appointment not kept. Preventing conflicting appointments is one of a secretary's most difficult problems. Sometimes the executive forgets to tell his secretary about appointments made outside the office. Three suggestions from experienced secretaries may prove helpful:

1. Each morning, try setting aside time to review the executive's calendar with him when you put it on his desk. He may at this point remember an appointment that he forgot to write down.

2. Provide the executive with a pocket diary that he can carry with him. You may ask to see this book until he becomes accustomed to giving it to you for checking.

3. At the end of each day, remind the executive of any unusual appointments such as a very early morning appointment or a night meeting.

If the executive is delayed in keeping an appointment, the secretary should (if possible) notify the next caller by telephone that he should come at a suggested later time. A secretary is most helpful when she can locate the executive for an appointment he may have overlooked. If the executive finds himself involved in an emergency such that he must ask a replacement to keep an appointment for him, the secretary should explain the situation and apologize for the substitution prior to the appointment.

**Saying *No* Tactfully.** Obviously appointments should be refused as tactfully as possible. Refusals should be prefaced by a sincere "I'm very sorry, but . . ." and a logical reason given, such as, "Mr. Allen is out of town," remembering to use your employer's name rather than the impersonal "he." This is a plausible reason and much kinder to the ear than the blunt, "Mr. Allen won't see you." Other tactful refusals would be that the executive is in conference, that he must attend a meeting on that day, that he has a heavy schedule for the next two weeks, or that he is getting ready to leave town. If a caller seems very much disappointed over a refusal, you might offer to talk with the caller yourself and relay a message to the executive or take some other appropriate, helpful action.

## The Actual Appointment

From the record on her own desk calendar the secretary knows when she should be on the lookout for a person coming to keep an appointment. When he arrives, she tells the executive the person is waiting and she talks with him casually if there is a delay. If he is late, it is entirely proper for the secretary to telephone to see if he is on the way.

Often more than one person is involved in an appointment or meeting. If possible, the secretary arranges the executive's office before the meeting and sees that there are enough chairs, comfortably arranged; she also provides pencils, note pads, and ash trays.

When the first conferee arrives, a problem is posed: Shall the secretary tell the executive of his arrival, or wait until the entire group has assembled? There is no hard-and-fast rule; the answer depends on the visitor's status, the executive's activity, and the executive's preference. If the visitor is very important, the secretary may not only inform her employer of his arrival, but telephone the other conferees to come now. Otherwise, she may greet the visitor, make him comfortable, and let him wait until the whole group is assembled before disturbing the executive. A gracious secretary will instinctively introduce the conferees as they assemble.

The secretary should submit before the meeting any correspondence or material that will be helpful in the conference so that the executive can become familiar with the matter. During the conference, the executive may require additional information; thus, the secretary must remain at her desk. When the executive is going out to a conference, she anticipates the papers that he will need and has them in his brief case. One public official, who constantly confers in his office and elsewhere, appreciates his secretary's clever routine. She types on a slip of paper the address of his luncheon appointment and his afternoon program and tucks the slip in her employer's hatband. As he leaves for lunch, he scans it and puts it in his coat pocket for further reference.

## Scheduling Appointments by Letter

Appointments with persons out of the city are frequently made by letter. Answer a request for an appointment promptly and in full. A typical letter granting an appointment follows.

> Dear Mr. Graham
>
> Mr. Andrews will be pleased to interview you on Friday, April 3, at 11 a.m. If you can't be here at that time, please let me know. I shall be glad to reschedule the appointment.
>
> Sincerely yours

When refusing a request for an appointment, include a tactfully phrased explanation. Note the following example:

> Mr. Andrews has asked me to express his regrets that he cannot meet with you on May 8 as you requested. He is preparing to leave the city on a speaking tour and will have no free time until his return on May 15.

## Canceling Appointments

When canceling appointments, the secretary usually writes the out-of-town visitors concerned and telephones the local visitors. In the latter case, the executive often asks the secretary to write a letter confirming the cancellation to prevent embarrassment in case the caller does not receive the telephone message. If possible, schedule a new appointment immediately to take the place of the canceled one. The following is a typical letter of cancellation:

> Mr. Andrews is disappointed that he cannot keep his appointment with you at 3 p.m. on July 19 because he has been called out of town unexpectedly. When he returns, I shall let you know so that we can arrange a new appointment at a mutually convenient time.

## SUGGESTED READINGS

Becker, Esther R., and Peggy Norton Rollason. *The High-Paid Secretary*. Englewood Cliffs: Prentice-Hall, Inc., 1967, pp. 63–74.

Doris, Lillian, and Besse May Miller. *Complete Secretary's Handbook*, 3d ed. Englewood Cliffs: Prentice-Hall, Inc., 1970, pp. 26–35.

Ingoldsby, Patricia, and Joseph Focarino. *The Executive Secretary: Handbook to Success*. New York: Doubleday & Co., Inc., 1969, pp. 125–156 (office visitors).

Klein, A. E. Supervisory ed., *The New World Secretarial Handbook*. Cleveland: World Publishing Co., 1968.

Taintor, Sarah, and Kate M. Monro. *The Secretary's Handbook*, 9th ed. New York: Macmillan Co., 1969.

Wood, Merle, and Margaret A. McKenna. *The Receptionist*. New York: McGraw-Hill Book Co., Inc., 1966.

## QUESTIONS FOR DISCUSSION

1. How would you learn the executive's preferences regarding your hostess duties?

2. Describe the use of a card file for frequent callers, the register of visitors, and the appointment schedule. Which of these three office tools would you regard as most important, and why? Do most offices need all three of these kinds of records? Explain your answer.

3. If you work for more than one executive, would you keep an appointment schedule and visitors register for each employer?

4. If your employer makes appointments without telling you and they conflict with those that you have scheduled, what should you do?

5. In what ways do you think that reception work in the office of each of the following types of businessmen would differ from each other?
   (a) A professional man, such as a doctor or a lawyer
   (b) A bank executive
   (c) The president of a company manufacturing heavy machinery
   (d) An elected government official

6. Insert the proper words in the blanks. Then refer to the Reference Guide to correct your answers.
   (a) Work it out _____ you can. (any way or anyway)
   (b) Let us have your comments _____. (any way or anyway)
   (c) _____ of you can do that. (any one or anyone)
   (d) _____ can do that. (any one or anyone)

■ **1.** What would you do in each of the following situations? When the solution calls for a conversation or a note, indicate exactly what you would say.

(a) A visitor who wishes to see your employer refuses to give you his name or any information about the purpose of the call.

(b) A prospective purchaser of a large order calls when your employer has just gone into a two-hour conference with top executives.

(c) An old friend stops on his way to the airport, but your employer is making a call at a business office not far away.

(d) A frequent caller and good business friend comes to the office and claims that he has an appointment for a particular time, but you have no record of such an appointment. Another appointment is scheduled for that time.

(e) A caller who failed to keep his last two appointments telephones for a third one.

(f) Your employer has given instructions that you are to discourage callers whose business relates to his personal affairs. A representative of an investment company in which your employer owns stock asks to see him. The last time he was in the office, he took over an hour of your employer's time.

(g) An important out-of-town client arrives at the office at twelve o'clock to keep a luncheon appointment with your employer. At 11:30 the president of the company called an emergency meeting of all top executives with instructions that it is to be a closed meeting and that they are not to be disturbed. The meeting will probably last well into the afternoon. You could not reach the out-of-town client by phone.

(h) A salesman of office equipment who is waiting to see your employer continually interrupts your work with personal remarks about your appearance and possible after-office-hours pursuits.

(i) Your employer had an appointment to attend the organization meeting of a committee planning an in-service course for members of the Executives' Club. The president of your company called an emergency meeting on budget at the time of the scheduled appointment. Your employer asks you to get his assistant to represent him at the committee meeting.

■ **2.** As secretary to Mr. Robert L. Stigler of Cleveland Products, you keep his appointment schedule. The following appointments and activities have been scheduled for July 23. Type an appointment schedule in attractive style for Mr. Stigler. Note any reminders at the bottom of the page.

(1) Mr. Stigler made a luncheon appointment at the Erie Hotel with L. W. Rasmussen for 12:30.

(2) A letter from S. T. White, of San Francisco, requested a 10 a.m. appointment, which was granted by return mail.

(3) RLS must appoint a committee by the 25th to handle an outing for the Advertisers' Club.

(4) You made a half-hour barber appointment for 11 a.m. for RLS.

(5) Office conference, which Mr. Stigler must attend, is called for 3:15 p.m.

(6) Mr. T.K. Krause telephoned for an appointment and accepted your suggestion to come in for a 20-minute appointment at 2 p.m.

(7) Mr. White wrote that he is unable to keep the scheduled appointment.

(8) Mr. Thornton, sales manager, requested that RLS come to his office at 9 a.m. for a conference.

(9) Mr. Stigler asked you to verify a 2 p.m. appointment that he believes he made with T. T. Hale. Inasmuch as you have scheduled another appointment at 2 p.m., you called Mr. Hale and arranged for him to come at 10 a.m.

(10) Mr. Stigler asked you to cancel any afternoon appointments that are scheduled to take place before 2:30 p.m. You called Mr. Kraus and arranged for him to come in at 10:30 a.m.

# Part 1

# CASE PROBLEMS

## 1-1  CONFORMITY TO COMPANY POLICY

Although she had a company desk manual that showed adopted letter styles, Helene Williams preferred certain other styles. She felt that they expressed her employer's and her own personality better than the standard forms adopted for company use.

She transcribed and submitted a day's dictation in AMS style (see Communications Guide, page 736). Her conservative employer told her to retype the correspondence in the adopted traditional style and ,that — although he would welcome initiative in Helene's handling of duties for which no prescribed standard existed — in the case of correspondence styles, she had no such freedom.

Helene felt that the AMS letter style was a time-saver and should be used as an indication that her employer was up to date. She sent a questionnaire to the secretary to every executive included on the company organization chart, asking each to express her preference between the letter style prescribed in the company manual and the AMS style.

**What is your reaction to Helene's method of initiating change? How wide should the secretary's area of freedom be? What should Helene have done?**

## 1-2  COPING WITH ENVY

After graduation from Hill College as an office administration major, Mary Alton applied for a secretarial position in the company headquarters of Ashton Brothers in St. Louis. She was told that she would have two weeks of orientation in the training department in the mornings and would work in the stenographic pool in the afternoons. She could then expect to be assigned to a secretarial position, possibly in the personnel office. She was delighted with this arrangement, for she was primarily interested in personnel work and hoped to work into a position of interviewer of applicants for office positions.

Everything went well during the first week. The training department requirements were within her competency; and Mary felt that she was getting excellent exposure to company procedures, realizing that her college background, while helpful, was no substitute for actual experience. She thought that she had made friends with the other trainees and hoped to form a close friendship with one girl whom she liked especially well.

One morning in the women's lounge, she recognized this colleague's voice saying, "How many letters did you get approved this morning?" Another trainee answered, "Four. I was furious because You-Know-Who had seven accepted. Doesn't she just make you sick? She thinks she is so wonderful just because she is a college graduate." The would-be friend replied, "Yes, she *is* mighty superior. Did you hear her say that she wants to be placed as secretary and maybe work into management later? My sister says that all the secretaries are promoted from inside the company and that seniority is what counts. I suppose she wants to be president of the company some day."

Although by now Mary realized that *she* was "You-Know-Who," she decided that revealing her presence at this point would embarrass the girls and antagonize them further. The second speaker continued, "I think that she plays up to the training director, don't you? I guess that's how people get ahead in business. That's what I've always heard."

**When they had left, Mary wondered what action she should take. Should she speak to them about their unfair attitude? Should she discuss the situation with the training director? Should she resign? How can she achieve the relationship toward which she aimed?**

## 1-3  CONFORMITY TO GROOMING STANDARDS

At the end of her college course, Carole Rankin was an honor student; and her secretarial skills were outstanding. She was sent by the Secretarial Department for a job interview for a choice position. Afterward, the interviewer telephoned his friend Dr. Brumage, the chairman of the Secretarial Department, to say that he was offering the job to Carole even though he was doubtful about employing anyone with such unkempt hair and extremely casual dress. He said that he had mentioned Carole's appearance during the interview but asked that Dr. Brumage also discuss this job-related factor with the applicant.

When Carole returned to the college, she told Dr. Brumage about the offer and said rather noncommittally that she had not yet decided to accept. During the conversation, the problem of her appearance was raised. Carole said, "Yes, he did say that I would have to do something about my hair and wear clothes more suitable for the office. But I don't know that I want to work there — or in any other office — if it means that I will have to change my personality."

**What is your reaction to Carole's attitude?**

# Word Processing — Typewriting, Copying, and Duplicating

*Part* **2**

*ven with the many innovations in office equipment, the typewriter remains the basic machine of the secretary and—for that matter—of the office. But typewriters too are changing. New power typewriting equipment, new and improved papers and secretarial supplies are constantly coming on the market; and copying and duplicating processes are undergoing tremendous technological changes. These innovations and changes are having a major impact on office work. The secretary must keep informed, be adaptable, and be constantly alert to developing and adopting new techniques and procedures that increase the quality and quantity of office output.*

# Chapter 4

# WORD PROCESSING —EQUIPMENT AND SUPPLIES

Word processing — the transformation of ideas into typewritten or printed form — is attracting the attention of business and other organizations that are virtually being buried under an avalanche of paper work accompanied by spiraling office production costs. Ways and means of breaking through the paperwork bottleneck and curbing mounting costs are sought. One promising development is the centralizing of new and highly sophisticated "power" (electronic) typing equipment in special operational areas known as word processing centers. Correspondence specialists in these centers type from machine dictation on automated typing equipment most of the letters, memorandums, forms, manuscripts, reports, and statistical tables that constitute 65 to 75 percent of the word processing work of an office. The expensive power equipment, renting for several hundred dollars per month per machine, is not often used for general office work. For this reason, the secretary herself will not be using this automated equipment. Hopefully, though, she will learn how to use it to expedite her work and to assume some of the more routine and time-consuming aspects of secretarial work.

For most secretaries, however, the electric typewriter at her desk is the major word processor at her command. The executive naturally expects his secretary to be the master of her typewriter. He expects and demands superior work. But the quality of typewritten work is influenced not only by the skill and knowledge of the operator but also by the machine, the ribbon, the paper, the quality of forms being used, and the other supplies available to the operator. Most of this chapter, therefore, will be devoted to a discussion of the secretary's typewriter and the supplies and forms with which she works.

## POWER TYPING EQUIPMENT

The use of magnetic or paper-tape media typewriters for correspondence and other routine office typewriting has brought power typewriting into the office. These special-media electronic typewriters

Specialists, using multimedia power typing equipment and located conveniently in word processing centers, can handle most of the letters, memos, reports, and statistical tables generated in the modern office.

are identified as power typing equipment because of the speed with which they can produce errorfree typewritten copy and their potential for increasing typing productivity. They are of two basic types: magnetic-media machines such as the IBM MT/ST (Magnetic Tape Selectric Typewriter) and the MC/ST (Magnetic Card Selectric Type-writer) and the paper-tape-media machines such as the Edityper, Flexowriter, and Quin-Typer.

## Magnetic-Media Machines

Magnetic-media equipment consists of a standard keyboard Selectric typewriter attached to a magnetic tape or magnetic card reading-and-play-back unit. As the operator types each character or space on the Selectric keyboard, the recording unit records it on magnetic tape or card. When the operator makes a mistake, she simply backspaces and strikes over the incorrect letter, word, or phrase. The process of back-spacing and retyping automatically erases the error and replaces it with the new typing on the magnetic medium. New material can be inserted or unwanted copy can be deleted at any point. The process is very much like an audio tape recorder in which the tape can be rewound and played over to erase or to make corrections.

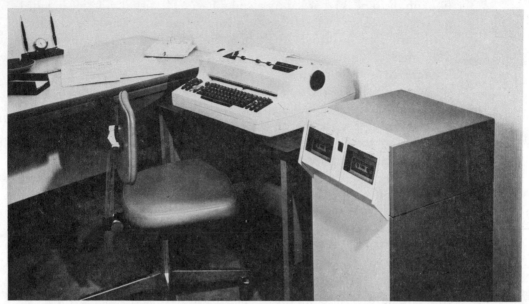

—*Redactron Corporation*

The correspondence secretary in a word processing center uses power typing equipment that allows her to make corrections, insertions, and deletions in rough-draft copy, and then activate the equipment to turn out errorfree material at high speeds.

When the rough-draft typing has been completed (and edited by the originator as required), the typist inserts a letterhead or sheet and any desired carbons into the machine and presses a button on the machine's console. The machine retypes automatically, completely errorfree, at rates of 150 to 175 words a minute. While typing the copy from the magnetic tape or card, the machine makes a number of logical production decisions. These include automatically respacing and repositioning words and sentences, controlling the hyphenation, and determining line and page endings.

A recent development uses the CRT (cathode-ray tube) as a text-editing device. As the operator types, the copy appears on a video-type screen. Corrections, deletions, insertions, and other changes are made by merely typing over the error. Thus, to correct a typing error, the operator backspaces and retypes (rekeys) the material. When the editing is complete, the operator activates the machine, which types the letter automatically with the right margin automatically justified. The copy can be captured and stored on a cassette for reference or reuse. This process, however, is still too expensive for general office use.

The equivalent of a full day's typing will go on one tape cartridge or cassette. The location of each document (letter, memorandum, and the like) on the tape is recorded on a code sheet. The usual practice in word processing centers is to store the medium (the tape, card, or cassette) with hard copy (printout) of the material for a week. If at the end of that time it is not required, the medium is erased and used for new work. Paragraphs and letters that are used repeatedly in replying to correspondence are coded and filed for an indefinite period for reuse as needed.

A time-consuming factor in the operation of machines activated by a magnetic-tape cartridge or cassette is that of searching the tape or cartridge to locate specific copy. To avoid this searching process, the MC/ST machine captures the data on a Mylar magnetic card identical in size to the familiar punched card, placing each typing page (or letter) on a separate card. The card can be filed with the carbon copy for easy and immediate retrieval for reference or playback.

The IBM Selectric Composer, a tape-activated machine, is used to prepare copy for printing. In addition to providing a convenient method of justifying the right margin, it permits the operator to interchange nine different type widths, thus giving the copy an appearance comparable to printer's type. The operator establishes the margins, types the copy manually, glances at a gauge mounted above the keyboard to find the number of spaces needed to justify the line, then sets a dial. The copy is typed a second time automatically with the right margin justified.

## Paper-Tape-Media Machines

Paper-tape-media machines operate very much like the magnetic-tape machines. The copy is punched on paper tape, which makes error correction slightly more complicated. With punched tape, however, it is possible to file each paper tape strip with the hard (carbon) copy. This greatly simplifies the search or scanning process required to locate specific copy on the magnetic-tape cartridges or cassettes.

Variations among makes and models of power typing equipment include the medium on which the copy is stored (cartridge, card, cassette, paper tape), automatic centering, margin monitoring (to produce a tight — relatively even — right margin), justifying the right margin, and speed whereby a medium may be searched to reach editing points after the rough draft has been typed. Further refinements and improvements will certainly come with time.

## Productivity

Power typing equipment increases typing productivity in four important ways, as listed on the next page.

1. It greatly expedites the correction of typing errors. The operator merely backspaces and strikes over the error, avoiding the time-consuming conventional method of correcting an original and a number of carbon copies.

2. It eliminates the manual retyping of an entire letter or page because of editorial changes or noncorrectable typing errors — and studies show that as much as 38 percent of the typist's output is retyping. Power equipment retypes automatically at high rates of speed.

3. It avoids the decrease in typing speed that results from error consciousness in manual typing. Since the typist does rough-draft typing only, the ease and speed of correcting errors gives her the freedom to type at her fastest rough-draft rate.

4. Lengthy reports, manuscripts, and legal and statistical typing usually go through many revisions. With power equipment, only the changed and new material must be typed manually with each revision. The retained material is stored automatically on the medium while additions or corrections are made.

Power typewriting equipment can also duplicate or reproduce a series of similar (form) letters. The operator inserts the letterhead; types the date, inside address, and salutation; identifies the code number of the precomposed paragraphs or letter on the selector for the memory tape; and activates the machine, which types the remainder of the letter automatically. The memory tape or card can be programmed to stop the machine where a fill-in is to be manually inserted. A skilled operator can run four automatic machines, producing form letters that look like individually typed letters — for they actually are typed. Each machine can produce as many as 100 average-length letters a day.

Some power typewriting equipment operates from two tapes, and information from alternate tapes can be merged to produce the finished letter. Names, addresses, salutations, and fill-ins stored on one tape can be combined with the body of a standard letter stored on another tape. The equipment is programmed to alternate playback between the two tapes and thus produce a series of finished letters. When continuous letter forms are used, the machine will operate unattended for long periods of time.

Since power typing equipment is very expensive, 24-hour operation of the equipment is highly desirable, as is now the case with computer installations.

## TYPEWRITERS

Most secretaries prefer the electric typewriter because it produces high-quality work and requires less effort to operate. The secretary has three basic types of electrics from which to select: standard electric, Selectric, and proportional spacing.

The typist can change the pitch (see page 67) on the IBM Selectric II from 10 to 12 characters per inch merely by moving a lever. With the half backspace feature, she can correct errors swiftly and type copy with a justified right margin.

—*IBM Corporation*

## Standard Electric

The standard electric is the most frequently used typewriter in the business office. Although designed primarily for correspondence and general office work, it can be equipped for such special purposes as billing, preparing material for bulletin boards, typing name tags for conventions, and typing statistical material. The movie and television industries use standard model typewriters that produce oversize letters in preparing copy for prompting equipment.

## Selectric

The IBM Selectric, a basic change in typewriter design, eliminates the type bars and the movable carriage. A spherical element the size of a golf ball moves on its own carrier from left to right across the paper. Alphabetic and special symbols are embossed on the surface of the sphere. Striking a key positions the element to type the letter or symbol without jamming the keys and with less vibration and noise. The Selectric II enables the typist to switch from pica type (ten characters per inch) to elite type (twelve characters per inch) simply by releasing a lever and changing the element.

A distinctive feature of the Selectric permits the use of a wide variety of type styles and special symbols. Over thirty interchangeable elements are available, each with a different type style or with different symbols. To change type style, the operator removes an element and in a few seconds inserts one with the desired type style.

E X P A N D E D with one
standard space between
letters

E X P A N D E D with
a proportional space two units
wide between letters

E X P A N D E D with
a proportional space three units
wide between letters

Compare the difference in space consumption
between standard typewriter spacing and proportional typewriter spacing, illustrated at the right.
Shown also are the styles of expanded spacing
that are possible with the proportional spacing
typewriter.

| Proportional | · | iiiii |
| Spacing | · | ooooo |
| Type | · | wwwww |
| Style | · | mmmmm |
| | · | |
| | · | |
| Standard | · | iiiii |
| Spacing | · | ooooo |
| Type | · | wwwww |
| Style | · | mmmmm |

*—IBM Corporation*

## Proportional-Spacing Typewriters

The ordinary typewriter spaces uniformly for each letter of the alphabet. Printing, however, uses proportional spacing; that is, some letters are wider and use much more space than do other letters, as shown by the illustration above.

## Typewriter Variables

Typewriters are available in a wide variety of type styles, line spacings, ribbon mechanisms, cylinder lengths, keyboards, and other special features.

**Type Sizes and Styles.** In addition to the standard type sizes (10 and 12 characters to an inch), type may also be obtained in sizes of 6, 8, 9, 11, 14, and 16 characters to an inch.[1] For specialized work, type sizes and styles are available in wide variety. For example, one typeface is designed for filling in insurance policies; another, for billing work. There are also typefaces that optical scanning equipment can read.

Several type styles referred to as executive typefaces provide a distinctive and formal appearance. Styles also vary from a school-book face resembling printer's type to an informal script that gives

---

[1]The number of characters per inch is frequently referred to as type "pitch," such as 10 typing pitch or 12 typing pitch.

**Imperial**
## Precision built

**Script**
*Your letters are*

**Small Gothic (Condensed)**
clear-cut legibility and

**Letter Gothic**
jobs, especially

**Courier 72**
highly legible.

Various Executive Typefaces

correspondence a personal touch. Light-face, boldface, and italics are other choices. A face consisting of all capital letters is also available.

When the secretary is searching for a distinctive style in alphabet type or in figures, fractions, special characters, or symbols, she has a large variety of type-faces from which to choose. Some acquaintance with the equipment available will help her to carry out supervisory responsibilities and to make her own work both distinctive and appropriate.

**Line Spacing.** Although most typewriters provide the standard six vertical lines to the inch, the line spacing can vary from one line per inch (video type) to eight or more, depending upon the type size, style, and purpose. Included are type styles that use 3, 3.6, 4, 4.5, 5.8, 6, or 8 lines to the vertical inch.

Although single, double, and triple spacing are standard on most typewriters, machines with line-space settings of 1, 1½, 2, 2½, and 3 lines allow flexibility in adjusting to the line spacing on printed forms.

**Special Keyboards.** Special-purpose keyboards can be obtained. These keyboards include symbols and characters common to a type of work. For example, there are keyboards for each of the following uses: billing, legal, chemical, engineering, mathematical, library, and each of several foreign languages. When ordering a typewriter, you may specify the keyboard desired.

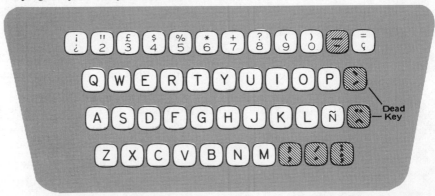

— *IBM Corporation*

Special foreign language keyboards are available for special needs. The trilingual keyboard illustrated above is used for typing in English, Spanish, and French. The "dead keys" for the accents, the dieresis, and the circumflex do not advance the carriage (carrier) when struck.

**Special-Character Keys.** The special characters and symbols available on the typewriter can be supplemented by use of interchangeable type head devices. A wide selection of special characters and symbols for practically any language, profession, or business can be obtained.

**Decimal Tabulator.** A typewriter used extensively for typing financial and statistical reports can be equipped with decimal tabulation by adding a fifth row of keys. These keys (tabulator keys) permit the operator to move to the exact place in a column of figures to align numbers.

**Half-Space Key.** The half-space key or bar moves the carriage only one-half space. It is used for central placement of extra-letter corrections (for example, a four-letter word can be typed exactly centered in the space used by a three-letter word), for expanded headings, and for even distribution of space in justified lines.

**Cylinder (Platen) Length.** Cylinder lengths vary from 11 to 29 inches. The 13-inch cylinder is most commonly used. Some machines have interchangeable carriages whereby the standard carriage can be removed and an extra-long unit set in its place for a special project such as a chart, graph, table, or special display.

**Cylinder Resiliency.** Rubber cylinders range from very soft to extra hard. A soft cylinder can be used for ordinary work involving four or five carbons. When more carbons are needed, the cylinder must be harder. Many typewriters have removable and interchangeable cylinders that can be exchanged easily and rapidly.

**Fabric- and Film-Ribbon Mechanisms.** A typewriter can have either a fabric- or a film-ribbon mechanism, or both.

**Special Attachments.** A number of special attachments can adapt the machine for special uses. Palm tabulators, cardholders, label holders, multiple-form holders and aligners, an attachment for continuous forms, additional repeat controls, automatic paper injectors, and an error-correction tape cartridge are a few of them.

## Selection of Typewriter Ribbons

Typewriter ribbons are of three types: plastic film, carbon paper, and fabric, each with certain properties to recommend it for the specific kind or quality of work desired.  Some electrics are equipped to use all three kinds of ribbons, while others accommodate only a fabric or a reusable film-based ribbon.  Furthermore, with no standardization among typewriter manufacturers, ribbons are wound on some fifty different kinds of spools.  For the proper kind of spool or cartridge, request a ribbon for your specific make and model of typewriter.

**Thinness.**  The sharpness of your typewritten work will depend upon the thinness of the ribbon you use — the thinner the ribbon, the sharper the imprint; also, the thinner the ribbon, the more yardage on a spool. This means longer use and less frequent ribbon change.  Ribbons range from cotton (the thickest), to silk, to nylon, to carbon paper, to coated Mylar or polyethylene film (the thinnest).

**Carbon and Film-Base Ribbons.**  The carbon-paper ribbon is a continuous, narrow strip of one-use carbon paper.  After passing from one spool to the other, it is discarded.  Self-threading carbon ribbons with an adhesive strip attached at the beginning are available.  Pressed onto the end of the used ribbon, the adhesive strip automatically threads the new ribbon through the ribbon guide with the end of the used ribbon.

## TYPEWRITER RIBBON CHART

| | |
|---|---|
| FILM—MYLAR OR POLYETH-YLENE | Highest quality ribbon available. Produces sharp, printlike image. Used for prestige correspondence. Excellent for preparing offset masters. Thinnest and strongest of all film ribbons. Breakfree. Lintfree. Life usually limited to one use; however, reusable Mylar ribbons are available. |
| CARBON PAPER— | Produces good image. Used extensively for correspondence and photocopy work. Breaks easily. Lintfree. Life limited to one use. |
| FABRIC—SILK OR NYLON | Finest quality fabric ribbon. Produces a clear, sharp image that compares well with the film and carbon-paper ribbons. Lintfree. Extra long life. Obtainable in light, medium, and heavy inking. |
| FABRIC—COTTON | Available in a variety of grades. Less expensive and shorter life than silk or nylon. Used primarily for routine correspondence, production typing, and for filling in forms. Deposits lint on keys. Obtainable in light, medium, medium-heavy, and heavy inking. |

Film-base ribbon is made from coated Mylar or polyethylene film and comes in either one-use or reusable form.

Because they print very sharply, do not fill the letters, are the cleanest to handle, and erase easily, carbon-paper and film-base ribbons are generally preferred by secretaries for high-quality work.

**Fabric Ribbons.** Of the fabric ribbons, nylon is the longest wearing and thinnest — then silk, then cotton. All are available in several colors and in various concentrations of ink.

**Special-Purpose Ribbons.** Ribbons designed for special types of work include offset ribbon for typing offset masters, photostat ribbons for preparing copy for photostating, opaque ribbons for photocopy work, correction ribbons with the top half inked and the bottom half white-chalked for speedy corrections, and a number of combinations of bichrome (two-color) ribbons.

## STATIONERY AND SUPPLIES

Most supplies with which a secretary works are available in a wide range of quality. Many factors, particularly the use and quality, must be considered in the selection of supplies.

### Bond Paper

Bond paper is so called because originally it was used for printing bonds, which had to have long-lasting qualities. It can be made from all-cotton fiber (sometimes called *rag*), from all-sulfite (a wood pulp), or from any proportion of the two. High-cotton-fiber bond bespeaks quality and prestige, and it ages without deterioration or chemical breakdown. It has a good, crisp crackle. It is hard to the pencil touch and is difficult to tear. High-sulfite bond is limper, softer to the pencil touch, and easier to tear.

There are excellent all-sulfite papers in crepelike, ripple, or pebble finishes that many companies use exclusively. Letterhead paper is usually made of 25 percent, or more, cotton-fiber bond. Forms for business records usually are made of all-sulfite or high-sulfite bond.

**Watermarks.** Hold a letterhead up to the light. See the design or words? That is the *watermark*. It can be the name or trademark of the company using the paper or the brand name of the paper. Since only better bonds are watermarked, the mark is a hallmark of quality.

There is a right side and a top edge to the plain watermarked sheets. Always have the watermark read across the sheet in the same direction as the typing. Put watermarked sheets in your stationery drawer in such a manner that they will be in the right position automatically when they are inserted into the typewriter.

**Substance.** The weight of paper is described by a substance number. The number is based on the weight of a ream consisting of 500 sheets of 17- by 22-inch paper. If the ream weighs 20 pounds, the paper is said to be of substance 20, or 20-pound weight. Two thousand sheets of 8½- by 11-inch paper can be cut from one ream. Paper is produced in a wide range of weights.

Regular letterheads and envelopes are usually of substance 16, 20, or 24. Airmail stationery is of substance 9 or 13. Other weights, however, are available.

**Erasability.** You can erase typing from some bond papers with exceeding ease. This feature is usually indicated in the brand name of the paper, such as *Ezerase* or *Corrasable*. Ribbon ink or carbon rests lightly on the surface of the paper until it is gradually absorbed into the paper. Thus, you can quickly and neatly remove fresh typing with a pencil eraser. But you can also easily smear or smudge the surrounding typing. The most difficult papers on which to make neat erasures and corrections are the inexpensive all-sulfite ones like those you used in your typing course. A neat erasure can be made without too much difficulty on a 16-pound high-cotton-fiber bond.

## Second Sheets

The thin sheets used for file copies of letters and for multicopy typing are described as *onionskin*, *manifold*, or simply *second sheets*. They are of lightweight paper of substances 7 to 13, in smooth, glazed, or cockle

(rippled) finish. A stack of these sheets can be difficult to control because they tend to slither and slide—mostly onto the floor. To avoid frustration, select a finish that has low "slipperiness." Sheets with cockle finish slip less than others and give the appearance of being of better quality, but they create more bulk in the files than do smooth-finish ones.

*Copy sheets* are used in many offices. They are second sheets with the word COPY printed on them and are used for copies of matter that should be so identified. When necessary, identify a plain sheet as a copy by typing the word COPY conspicuously (in all capital letters, letterspaced, and centered from 7 to 9 line spaces from the top of the sheet).

## Letterheads

Letterheads vary widely and depend upon individual taste and the nature of the company's business. Most large companies have a standard company letterhead designed for use by lower and middle management personnel. These letterheads are produced by offset and are standardized to include the company's name, address, telephone number, (including area code) and name and title of the individual. The letterhead sometimes contains information about the company's products or displays the company trademark. All letterheads may be ordered with matching envelopes and blank sheets for the two-page letter.

Top executives usually have "prestige" letterheads that differ from the standard company letterhead in style, printing process, weight of paper, and cotton-fiber content. The cotton-fiber content usually ranges from 50 to 100 percent, and some exccutives use what is called "101 percent rag," meaning 100 percent cotton fiber of unusually fine quality.

The letterhead of a top executive usually shows only the company name, address (no phone number), and the executive's name and title. In addition, the executive may have a personal letterhead which he uses mainly for outside work with foundations and charity organizations. His personal letterhead may show only his name and address or his name only. In general, as an individual's position becomes elevated in the company, his letterhead becomes more simplified, presenting an appearance of dignity befitting the position.

## Carbon Paper

Conventional typewriter carbon paper is thin, dark-colored tissue, coated on one side with carbon. It is available in a great variety of sizes, colors, weights, finishes, and qualities. It is available in special-purpose packs as well as in single sheets.

**Topcoated Carbon Paper.** Heat and humidity cause carbon paper to curl so that it is frustrating to handle. Most carbon paper now is coated on the uncarboned, or top side, with a metallic, plastic, or varnish finish that makes the sheet curlfree or curl resistant. The top coating reduces wrinkling; wrinkling "trees" or "veins" the copy. High-quality topcoated carbon paper not only is smudgefree but also produces a neater copy and permits more extensive use than does low-quality carbon. Uncoated carbon paper looks worn after a few uses, and a sheet of carbon paper is usually destroyed on the basis of looks—not by scrutiny of the carbon typing it does.

# LETTERHEADS AND ENVELOPES

## Letterheads                    ## Matching Envelopes

**Standard Company Use:**

Business size 8 1/2- by 11-inch          No. 10 (4 1/8- by 9 1/2-inch)
Usually of 16 or 20# bond,               Same weight and fiber content
   25% cotton fiber (rag)           as letterhead

**Top-Executive Use:**

Standard and Monarch size                No. 10 and No. 7 (3 7/8- by 7 1/2-inch)
   (Monarch size: 7 1/4- by 10-inch)

Usually 24# bond, 100% cotton-fiber      Same weight and fiber content
   content                                  as letterhead

## Plain Sheets to Match Letterheads

Same weight, cotton-fiber content, and size as letterhead (*Never use a letterhead for the second or subsequent pages of a letter.*)

## Airmail Envelopes to Match Letterheads

For both standard business and Monarch size, usually 9# or 13#. If bordered airmail envelopes are not available, attach gummed airmail stickers folded around each short edge of the envelope. This will alert the mail sorter even when the mail is "cubby-holed" with the short edges out. If airmail stickers are not available, type *AIRMAIL* below the stamp and border or underline the word conspicuously, preferably in red.

## Interoffice Letterheads

Business size or half size (8 1/2- by 5 1/2-inch); usually of sulphite

## Interoffice Envelopes

Oversize, strong, perforated, reusable envelopes with many ruled lines for the names of successive addressees

## Oversize Envelopes

Strong white or manila envelopes that allow letters and reports to be mailed unfolded; 9- by 12-inch, 10- by 13-inch; gummed flaps with or without metal clasps

# OTHER PAPER SUPPLIES

## Carbon Copy Paper

Thin sheets, usually 8# or 13#, in various sizes, colors, and finishes. Called *second sheets,* onionskin, or manifold paper.

*Copy Sheets:* Sheets imprinted with the word C O P Y

*Carbon Set:* A ready-assembled one-use sheet of carbon paper attached to a plain or copy sheet (available for multiple copies also)

*Carbonless Paper:* Ink-impregnated paper, sometimes called NCR (*No Carbon Required*) The force of the typewriter key releases the ink and reproduces the letter or character.

## Carbon Paper

For description and use, see pages 73–77.

## Duplicator Paper

Business[1] and legal[2] sizes, white and colors, various substances; often called by the process the paper is made for, such as mimeograph paper, offset paper. *Duplicating* paper usually refers to paper designed for use with the direct-process duplicator.

## Forms

Usually in pads to prevent waste. Multicopy forms may be continuous, accordion-folded, and perforated. After the "chain" is inserted in the type-writer to type the first set, the rest feed through automatically. Accordion-folded forms often have spot-carbon coating on the back of each copy exactly where the typing is to appear on the copy underneath, to eliminate handling interleaved carbon.

## Labels, Return Address

Small slips of paper showing company's return address. Are usually gummed on the back.

## Legal Paper

Top-quality legal size[2] bond; plain or with ruled margins

## Manila Sheets

Thin sheets for typing rough drafts or carbons, legal size or business size

## Plain Sheets

Paper 8 1/2- by 11-inch, usually 13# to 16#, most often used for reports and for general typing. May or may not be of easy-to-erase bond.

## Writing Pads

*Ruled Paper:* Legal size or business size, usually yellow
*Scratch:* Assorted sizes. Usually sold by the pound.

---

[1]*Business size:* 8½- by 11-inch
[2]*Legal size:* 8½- by 13- or 14-inch

**Plastic-Base Copying Film.** Although sometimes identified as carbon paper, plastic-base copying film is described more accurately as *copying film* because it employs ink, not carbon; and is made of film, not paper. A sheet of Mylar or polyethylene film is surfaced with a microscopically thin coating of tiny interconnecting cells, each containing liquid ink. The typewriter key forces the cells to release the ink on the typing paper. When the type bar lifts, the ink flows back into the unused area, thus re-inking the sheet, which may be used repeatedly. Since the ink dries immediately, the copy is smudgefree. Copy film is curlfree, easily handled, and difficult to tear. It never trees. It comes in two weights, standard and light. It has a 50- to 60-time usage. Plastic-base copying film is being used increasingly by secretaries for top-quality work.

**Conventional Carbon Paper.** Carbon paper comes in a number of grades, weights, and coatings. Better grades are treated with a wax, varnish, or metallic coating on the uncarbonized side to reduce curling, treeing, and to extend the wear. This coating also prevents the carbon

## GUIDE TO SELECTION OF
## CARBON PAPER FINISH AND WEIGHT

### Finish

| | |
|---|---|
| Soft | USE IF — typewriter has a soft cylinder.<br>USE IF — copies are grayer than desired when using other finishes. |
| | DO NOT USE IF — typewriter has elite or smaller typeface. |
| Hard | USE IF — typewriter has a hard cylinder.<br>USE IF — typewriter has elite or smaller typeface.<br>USE IF — gray copy is acceptable. |
| Medium | USE — for all typing situations not covered above. |

### Weight
FOR MAKING ORIGINAL PLUS:

| | |
|---|---|
| Light | 9 or more copies |
| Medium | 5 to 8 copies* |
| Medium Standard | 2 to 7 copies |
| Standard | 1 to 4 copies |

*Consider weight of copy paper used and adjust weight of carbon.

from going through the tissue and offsetting to the back of the preceding sheet. Special coatings also make the carbon more smudge resistant, cleaner to handle, and capable of producing sharper copies.

Different finishes or coatings are available, from *soft*, which writes like a soft black pencil, to *hard* which writes like a hard gray pencil. The finish to be used depends upon your typewriter (manual or electric), size of type face, hardness of cylinder, number of copies to be made, and "blackness" of copy desired.

Weights of carbon paper range from light (4#) to heavy (10 to 20#). A lightweight carbon paper with a hard finish produces the sharpest impressions.

**Special-Feature Carbon Paper.** Carbon paper may be obtained with special features that contribute to efficiency and convenience. Such features include:

1. **Extended Edges.** An extended uncoated side or bottom edge is provided to permit handling of the carbon sheet without smudging fingers. A cut corner may also be provided to allow the secretary to remove the carbon paper from the copy sheets.

2. **Micrometric Edge.** A numbered guide is printed on a clean, extended right edge of the carbon sheet. The guide shows the unused lines remaining on the page for ease in obtaining uniform top and bottom margins.

3. **Carbon Sets.** A carbon (copy) set is a preassembled sheet of one-time carbon paper affixed to a sheet of copy paper. Two or more sets combine to make a carbon pack. Carbon sets are convenient to use and no time is lost jog-aligning carbons, copy paper, and letterhead. A major disadvantage, however, is that one-time carbon retains a readable stenciled image of what was written, thus producing a "talking wastebasket" — a serious security leak in offices where information must be confidential.

## OFFICE FORMS

American business *runs* on paper forms. In fact, every business function involves some type of business form at some point in its operation: A function is either initiated by a form, authorized by one, recorded on one, or summarized on one. Thus, everyone in a business organization is involved with "paper work," and the secretary is no exception. The secretary spends a significant portion of her time in completing forms, copying information on forms, reading forms, interpreting forms, routing forms, filing forms, using forms for reference, and handling and transmitting forms. Furthermore, the secretary is not only a user of forms, but may be a designer of them.

Modern technology and business ingenuity have provided multiple-copy business forms in different configurations that encompass many time-saving features.

**Unit-Set and Snap-Out Forms.** Unit- or multiple-set forms are preassembled packets with interleaved one-time carbons. Each unit is self-contained, not part of a larger pad. The set is usually bound with a perforated stub at the top or side. This stub permits easy removal of the carbons. Unit-set forms are both timesaving, being preassembled, and convenient, allowing one-motion removal of the carbons.

**Carbonless Forms.** Unit sets are also assembled using carbonless paper (NCR — No Carbon Required) that permits impressions from copy to copy without the use of carbon tissue. An image-forming dye is built into the paper. The dye is released under pressure and reacts with a mating chemical that is built into the paper or coated onto the sheet above. A blue-purple image results from the pressure of typewriter keys or handwriting. Using NCR forms also saves the time required to manipulate the carbon tissues and avoids the smearing and smudging of copies, hands, and clothing that is associated with carbon paper. And eliminating the carbon tissue decreases the bulk of the pack, allowing more copies with one writing.

**Continuous Forms.** With continuous forms, one set of forms is joined to another in a series of accordion-pleated folds. Continuous forms are used to process at one time a large quantity of a specific form (invoices, statements, purchase orders, payroll checks, and the like), saving the time required to feed forms into the typewriter repeatedly.

**Spot-Carbon-Coated Forms.** No-smudge carbon is applied at designated spots on the back of each form in a pack from which reproduction is desired. Thus, typing on the original copy can reproduce on some copies and can leave blank areas on others. This permits the production of a number of different forms in one writing; for example, a packing slip, a shipping order, an address label, an inventory withdrawal slip, and an invoice — each with only the appropriate data thereon.

## Automated Equipment Forms

Automation, and especially the computer, is having pronounced influence on forms design and development. Forms must be designed for use not only by humans but also by machines. The tab card form and the OCR form are two illustrations.

**Tab Card Form.** The tab (punched-card) forms are designed for use with keypunch equipment and for computer input media. They may be assembled in continuous form, for high-speed, continuous processing, or in sets with perforated side stubs for easy snap out.

**OCR Form.** OCR (optical character recognition) equipment can read numeric and alphabet characters printed in a special type style on forms designed for use with this equipment. The overall size and placement of the data field on the form must be compatible with the equipment. The paper must provide the proper background contrast for light-absorbing carbon impressions or ink characters, and the type style must be one that the scanner can be programmed to read.

## Forms Control and Design

As a business expands, the number of forms that it needs seems to multiply at an astonishing rate. Consequently, most large business and government organizations have established systems for forms control. Such systems provide for a periodic review and the discontinuance of any forms that have become useless or obsolete, and for the establishment of definite procedures for the preparation and approval of new forms.

The secretary may be expected to exercise a similar control over the forms originating in her executive's office; namely, systematic review of all forms for possible improvement, the elimination of unneeded forms, and the designing of new forms that will expedite the work of the office. In designing new forms, consider the following factors.

**Necessity.** Is a separate form really needed? Could it be combined with an existing form? In what ways will a new form save time?

**Wording.** Does the title clearly indicate the purpose of the form? Does it contain a code number for filing reference? Does the form contain all necessary information? Does it provide *only* necessary information? (Example: The company name is not needed on intra-company forms.) Does the form mechanize the writing of repetitive data?

**Disposition.** Does each copy of the form clearly indicate its disposition? Is color coding or some other appropriate means used to facilitate distribution?

**Arrangement.** Is the form compatible with the equipment on which it is to be used? (Example: If it is to be filled in on a typewriter, do the type lines conform to typewriter vertical line spacing and require a minimum of tabulator stops? Does the sequence in which the data are to be inserted on the form follow the sequence of the data on the data source? Will the arrangement of the form speed operations?

**Retention.** If the form is to be retained, how and where? Does the form size fit the filing system?

## FULFILLING REQUIREMENTS OF FORMS AND SUPPLIES

The executive usually delegates to the secretary the responsibility of procuring office supplies proper for their use. Unless the executive has a special need or high cost factors are involved, the secretary uses her own judgment in making selections. The procedures for obtaining office supplies differ for the secretary in a large office and the secretary in a small office; however, each one must "know" supplies in order to choose those that best fill particular executive and secretarial needs.

The secretary in the small office is a direct buyer. The secretary in the large office may request forms and supplies from a central stock, or she may requisition from the purchasing department a specific item after she has investigated those available. If she has supervisory responsibilities, she may select and purchase for a department or company. In this case, she must use the sources of product information to learn the comparative factors and to find dependable sources. Then she must follow businesslike purchasing procedures.

### Quality of Supplies

Some businesses feel it is important to use only the highest quality stationery, forms, and office supplies; others find medium quality adequate to their situation. Every office uses a pride factor and an economic factor to determine the level of quality it follows. You will not find this quality level precisely stated or written out for you, nor is it a question you can tactfully ask. You can deduce it by observation of the present supplies and cost records.

A SUGGESTION. To reinforce paper to go into a loose-leaf notebook, attach a strip of tape along the back edge of the paper where the holes will be. Punch holes through both tape and paper.

### Local Sources of Supply

Local office-supply stores cannot carry all varieties of all brands of all office supplies. Each store carries one or two brands of an item (perhaps not your favorite) in the varieties most commonly sold (none of which may exactly fill your need). Therefore, your selection is limited and often you cannot buy as discriminatingly as you would like.

**Salesmen.** Representatives of local office-supply agencies may call on you with samples or catalogs and prices. They, too, limit themselves in brands and varieties, so choice is again restricted. The secretary orders over the telephone from the salesman or from his office. Since you cannot possibly know everything about all supplies, it is helpful to have a dependable salesman of whom you can ask advice. When you are in the market for an item, tell him your exact needs. He is trained to help you make a wise selection.

**Brand-Name Supplies.** Sometimes you want a *specific variety of a specific brand.* If the variety is not sold locally, you can order it from the manufacturer or ask your local office-supply store to order it for you.

Some pieces of equipment, you may decide, produce better results if you use the supplies that are sold by the manufacturer, such as A. B. Dick ink for the Mimeograph, or Gestetner correction fluid for Gestetner stencils. If no local source is listed in the telephone book, order such supplies from the manufacturer.

## Collecting Information

Collect specific information about each kind of office supply you use. Suppliers furnish helpful literature. Descriptive, informative folders are often furnished by salesmen or are given away at exhibits of office equipment and supplies. Collect and file such information by subject. It will help you be a better buyer.

## Choosing Supplies

Choose supplies that are in the quality range of your office. There is no economy in cheap supplies. Unknown brands may contain inferior materials or may be off-size and, consequently, may be more expensive in the long run than the better grades. *Usually you get just about what you pay for.* A carbon paper of good quality gives many more writings. Low-priced duplicating inks of poor quality oils and pigments make fewer copies than high-grade inks. The ingredients in cheap inks often separate when the machine stands idle, and the oil seeps through the mechanism.

There is no reason for shifting from one brand of supply to another as long as the one in use is satisfactory and fair in price. On the other hand, supplies are constantly being changed; a product may now be made of entirely different materials and hence greatly improved since the last time you examined or tested it.

When contemplating a change in brand, get samples of competing products and test them all under the same circumstances. Study the findings of published governmental and technical tests. Compare net prices and quality. Analyze the extra service or added efficiency claimed; if the price is higher, decide whether the difference is justified.

## Overbuying

Some office supplies deteriorate when they are held in stock too long; for example, carbon paper dries and hardens, typewriter ribbons dry out, some paper becomes yellow, liquids evaporate, and erasers harden. New products that come out may be preferable to those you have stocked. It is better, then, to err on the side of underbuying than of overbuying. Repeat orders can always be placed shortly before supplies are needed.

You may want to overbuy because of quantity prices. An item that costs 50 cents a unit in small quantities usually costs appreciably less when bought in larger quantities; consequently, it may seem to be economical to order in large amounts. The monetary saving is not always the prime consideration, however.

Some suppliers of duplicating paper have arrangements whereby a year's supply may be purchased at one time; thus you obtain the price advantage of bulk purchase. The paper is delivered in specific lots at designated intervals through the year. Such a plan provides a price advantage without the storage of paper before it is needed.

## Requisitions and Invoices

In a large company, most of the supplies are kept in stock and are obtained by submitting a supplies requisition. Items not carried in stock must be requested by submitting a purchase requisition to the purchasing department. This form should provide as detailed a description of the item needed as the secretary can provide.

If the secretary or supervisor has the authority to purchase supplies, she has added responsibilities. She must make a careful record of each item purchased or ordered, check out the delivery of the items, and verify the accuracy of the items and extensions of the invoice or bill that accompanies or follows delivery.

When an item is invoiced (included and charged on an invoice) but is omitted, substituted, or defective, the secretary annotates that fact on the invoice and requests an adjustment.

REVISING supply purchasing and control procedures has reduced one company's per year employee cost of stationery supplies over 25 percent.
—*Administrative Management*

## Storage of Supplies

If you wish to determine how neat and orderly a secretary really is, examine her supply storage cabinet. Certainly a storage cabinet that presents an array of boxes, packages, and articles in complete disorder is no recommendation for her efficiency.

The well-arranged storage cabinet has several characteristics. Like materials are placed together. Materials used most frequently are placed to the front at the most convenient level for reaching. Small items are placed at eye level; bulk supplies and reserve stock are placed on the lower shelves. Shelf depths should be adjustable to fit the items and conserve space.

All packages are identified in oversize lettering made with a felt-nub marking pen, or by a sample of the contents affixed to the front. Un-padded stationery items are kept in flip-up, open-end boxes. (There are no carelessly torn-open, paper-wrapped packages.) Loose supplies, such as paper clips, are kept separately in marked open boxes. A list of all supplies by shelves is often posted on the inside of the door.

## SUGGESTED READINGS

"Automatic Typing and Text Editing Devices," *Administrative Management*, Vol. 32, No. 6 (June, 1971), pp. 44–50.

"Forms: New Designs, New Systems," *Administrative Management*, Vol. 32, No. 5 (May, 1971), pp. 52–58.

Kay, R. R. "What We Found Out About Automatic Typing," *Administrative Management*, Vol. 30, No. 11 (November, 1969), pp. 32–34.

"Typing the Best Impression," *Administrative Management*, Vol. 32, No. 2 (February, 1971), pp. 60–61.

Zalkind, Joseph G. "Automatic Typing Keys in New Advances," *Administrative Management*, Vol. 31, No. 11 (November, 1970), pp. 36–44.

## QUESTIONS FOR DISCUSSION

1. Surveys show that stenographers and typists average less than *15 words a minute* when transcribing from shorthand notes or dictation belts and that an average of 38 percent of their typing work is retyping. Manufacturers of power typewriting equipment claim that using their equipment increases the typist's productivity over 100 percent. In your judgment, is this claim exaggerated? Explain your answer.

2. What features would you request for a special-purpose typewriter to be used for typing (a) statistical material, (b) multiple-form invoices, (c) name tags for a convention bureau, (d) foreign correspondence, and (e) general correspondence in the national headquarters of a college fraternity?

3. In what working situations would it be helpful to have a typewriter (such as the Selectric) on which a variety of type styles and symbols could be used?

4. The proportional-spacing typewriter facilitates justifying (making even) the right margin. Some people feel that a letter with a justified right margin looks too symmetrical and gives the initial impression of being a form letter. Express your opinion. For what special type of work would you recommend the use of a proportional-spacing typewriter?

5. You note that a carbon copy produced by your assistant lacks sharpness and is gray in appearance. Upon further checking you find that the carbon you examined was the fifth copy. What are some of the factors you would consider in your effort to improve the quality of the carbons she produces? What procedure would you recommend in your effort to help her improve the quality of her carbon copies?

6. You are aware that your assistant is in the habit of taking paper, stamps, and other office materials for her own personal correspondence and needs. What is your responsibility, and how would you handle the situation?

7. Suppose that the individual described in Question 6 is another secretary over whom you have no authoritative jurisdiction. Is your responsibility the same? What would you do?

8. You are employed as secretary to the manager of the R & D (Research and Development) Division, a highly sensitive area and thus under strict control for security leaks. A major security leak was traced to your wastebasket and to the snap-out forms you have been using. (a) Explain how this could happen. (b) Is there any solution other than discontinuing the use of these forms?

9. Revise the following sentences. Then refer to the Reference Guide to correct your answers.

   (a) It is the consensus of opinion that the buildings are both alike—they have greatly depreciated in value.

   (b) The sum total of my experience leads me to believe that they are both alike.

   (c) It is unnecessary for me to repeat again that we would like to have your payment during the month of October.

   If the executive frequently dictated these redundant terms, would you point out their redundancy? If so, how?

## PROBLEMS

■ 1. You are to be transferred to the position of supervisor of the newly created word processing center in your company. This center will process all correspondence and other typewritten materials. You are asked to submit precise recommendations for power typewriting equipment to be installed in the center. A number of companies manufacture this equipment. Set up the criteria you would use. Gather data on two different makes of automated typewriters, and make your recommendations. Support your selection with reasons for your decision.

■ **2.** Many companies and most government agencies require that detailed specifications accompany a request for the purchase of equipment. In the case of a typewriter, for example, the specifications would cover such items as carriage length, cylinder hardness, line spacing, keyboard, special keys, type face, and special features and attachments.

Assume that you are to be secretary to one of the following departments in your university: mathematics, chemistry, library, engineering. (Select the one with which you are most familiar.) You are asked to submit an order, with accompanying specifications, for a typewriter. Compile the specifications.

■ **3.** A secretary needs to be informed on office supplies. Select one of the following items and make yourself a semi-authority on it — cost, qualities available, and advantages and disadvantages of each brand or type.

(a) **Carbon paper and carbonless paper**
(b) **Paper for letterheads and second sheets**
(c) **Type cleaners**
(d) **Typewriting error correction products**
(e) **Typewriter ribbons**

Prepare a written report on the item and also be prepared to explain and demonstrate to the class the factors to be considered in item selection and how to use.

■ **4.** An examination of your supply cabinet indicates the following items need to be ordered:

**Letterheads for general correspondence**
**Matching plain sheets for the letterheads**
**Matching envelopes for the letterheads**
**Executive-size letterheads (best quality)**
**Typewriter ribbons for your use (IBM Executive Typewriter)**
**Carbon paper**

Type each item on a 5″ by 3″ card, indicating the detailed descriptive data that should accompany your order for each item.

# Chapter 5

## WORD PROCESSING — SECRETARIAL TYPING

The average secretary spends more than 40 percent of her time at the typewriter. Of course, averages can be misleading — and certainly you do not aspire to be just an *average* secretary. But the fact remains that typewriting is part of the stock-in-trade of every secretary; and a beautifully typed letter, with all that this implies, is one of the hallmarks of secretarial success.

Secretarial typing expertise, however, is more than time and production. It is attitude and pride in workmanship. It is economy in the use of time and supplies. It is speed with accuracy. It is the search for ways to increase output and efficiency. It is the ability to show and guide those whom you supervise in their typing assignments.

These qualities come only with time and experience, provided one seeks them out. This chapter is a good place to start. It presents some of the know-how that practicing secretaries and supervisors use in their continual effort to produce high-quality work as efficiently as possible. Practice any techniques new to you and add them to the skills you bring to your work.

## YOU AND YOUR TYPEWRITER

You will quickly become at ease with "your" typewriter if you will, first, *explore and learn its capabilities*; and, second, *give it the care it requires*. Remember the adage: The poor workman quarrels with his tools.

### Instruction Booklets

Every typewriter has a helpful, reassuring booklet of instructions on its use. The booklet accompanies the machine on delivery but often disappears before the machine does. If your predecessor has not left the instruction booklet for you, request one from the manufacturer. It will save you time and give you confident know-how. There is nothing worse than fighting a strange, militant typewriter that has hidden resources.

# FOR A LONGER-LASTING,
# MORE RESPONSIVE TYPEWRITER

1. **Prevent dust from accumulating.** Dust and eraser grit cripple and prematurely age a typewriter.
   - NEVER erase over the type basket. Move the carriage to one side, then erase. (On the Selectric, move the typing element to the right or left.)
   - ALWAYS cover the typewriter when you leave for the day. Clean the cover with a damp cloth occasionally.

2. **Dust the typewriter daily.**
   - Use a long-handled brush to dust the hard-to-reach parts.
   - Brush toward you, away from the mechanism.
   - Dust under the machine.

3. **Clean the keys frequently** — *before* the keys fill up. Clean the keys gently; avoid pushing them out of alignment. Do not use a pin; use one of these ways:
   - Roll a type-cleaning sheet (paper with a chemically treated fiber surface that picks up dirt from typeface) into typing position; set the ribbon for stencil and the pressure control to maximum; then strike each key several times. (This is the cleanest method.)
   - Use a plastic type cleaner. Repeatedly press the plastic firmly against the type until the keys are clean. Knead and fold the plastic as you work.
   - With a stiff, dry, short-bristled brush, use a tapping — not a gouging — motion. Clean the brush as you work by rubbing it on paper.
   - Use a fluid or spray cleaner — sparingly, as excess fluid can carry dirt particles into the mechanism. Some spray cleaners contain dirt-repellent silicone.
   - For the Selectric, remove the element; clean with soap, water, and the special brush that comes with the machine.

4. **Protect the cylinder (platen).** Keep the cylinder clean. Ink and dust on the platen cause it to become shiny and to lose its grip.
   - Clean the cylinder with a soft cloth.
   - If the cylinder is removable, lift it out and dust the trough.
   - NEVER lift a typewriter by the cylinder knobs.

5. **Lubricate sparingly.** Too much oil is harmful. Lubricate only the carriage rail — and oil that only lightly. Keep oil away from rubber parts.

6. **Protect the paper-feed rolls.** Release the paper-feed rolls when the typewriter is not in use. This prevents the rolls from developing flat spots.

7. **Arrange for periodic servicing.** Check the service guarantee. Arrange with a local agency to check and service your typewriter periodically. Investigate the economy of a service contract.

Learn the capacities of your typewriter. It may have features of which you are not aware, such as aids to accurate realignment of typing, scales to determine center positions, fractional spacing devices, and tabulating timesavers. The special features of your typewriter are illustrated and explained in the instruction booklet.

## Typewriter Care

Even though a typewriter is sturdy and almost self-sufficient, it does require a modicum of attention from you. Read the machine-care section of your instruction booklet. Follow it faithfully or follow the recommendations on page 87.

# HANDLING CARBON PAPER

The typing techniques given here may seem commonplace, but the procedures are those used by master typists. They will allow you to produce quality typing and to save motions, time, and material.

## Carbon Sheets

You will find the following practices in using carbon sheets to be paper savers and time-savers:

1. Keep your desk supply of carbon or copy sheets flat, carbon side down to prevent curling, away from heat or dampness, and inside a folder or box.

2. Reverse carbon sheets end for end each time you use them, because the carbon quickly wears off where the date line and other letter-part positions fall.

3. Discard a sheet at once if it becomes wrinkled or treed. It will never be usable.

4. Do not discard a sheet just because it looks worn or because the shine is off the carbon side. Check instead the clarity of the last copy typed. Discard the carbon sheet only when the copy is faint.

5. Use extended bottom-edge carbon paper with cutoff corners for the most efficient removal and reuse. If the carbon sheets are square cornered, lay them carbon side down and cut off one-inch triangles from the top-left and bottom-right corners. This space provides room to hold the set of typed sheets and to remove the set of carbons intact in one quick, clean pull. See the illustrations on page 89.

6. Use carbon sheets with cutoff corners as a visual check of the proper insertion of the carbon pack. With the carbon pack in typing position, the cutoff should be visible in the top left corner. If the cutoff shows at the right, you have inserted carbon side up (which happens occasionally to the best of secretaries).

## Carbon Packs

The number of carbon copies being prepared in the office has been decreasing because of the extensive use of copying machines. Making corrections on multiple carbons is a slow and costly process. Consequently, if a number of copies of a letter, report, or transcript are

TIME-SAVER. Suppose you are typing an envelope and want the address on a card for your address file. You can type the address on the envelope and on the file card at the same time. Simply put the card, with a square of carbon paper backed up to it, inside the envelope before addressing the envelope.

needed, it may be less expensive to type only the original, making swift, visible corrections with opaque correction fluid, and to reproduce the copies with the copying machine. To assume, however, that the secretary will not need to be skilled in handling carbon paper is unwarranted. The copy machine has not eliminated the carbon copy; it has merely tended to reduce the number of carbon copies to be prepared.

**Making Up a Carbon Pack.** Two methods of making up and inserting a carbon pack are the *desk method* and the *machine method*.

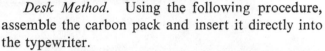

*Desk Method.* Using the following procedure, assemble the carbon pack and insert it directly into the typewriter.

1. Place a sheet of paper on the desk; on top of that sheet, place a sheet of carbon paper, *glossy side down.* Add one set (a second sheet and a carbon) for each extra copy desired. Place a letterhead or a plain sheet of heavier paper on top of the pack for the original copy.
2. Turn the pack around so the glossy sides of the carbon sheets face you.
3. To keep the sheets straight when feeding, use a *leader* — place the pack in the fold of an envelope or in the fold of a narrow folded piece of paper.
4. Straighten the pack by tapping the sheets on the desk.
5. Insert the leadered pack with a quick turn of the cylinder, roll it up, and remove the leader.

*Machine Method.* Using the following procedure, build the carbon pack right in the machine.

1. Arrange the required number and kinds of sheets for insertion into the typewriter.
2. Insert the sheets, turning the cylinder until they are gripped slightly by the feed rolls; then bring all but the last sheet forward over the cylinder.
3. Place the carbon sheets between the sheets of paper with the carbonized surface (glossy side) toward you. Flip each sheet back as you add each carbon.
4. Roll the pack into typing position.
5. When the typing is completed, roll the pack nearly to the bottom of the sheets. Operate the paper-release lever and remove the copy sheets by pulling them out with left hand. The paper fingers will automatically hold the carbon sheets in the machine. Remove with the right hand.

# CARBON-COPY TROUBLE SHOOTING

**Curling**   Curling usually may be traced to changes in temperature or humidity. A curlfree carbon paper or copying film is available. Carbon paper should be stored flat in a box.

**Cutting**   If the typeface is cutting through the carbon paper, check the sharpness of the type face, the hardness of the roller, and the quality and weight of carbon paper being used. Also check the impression regulator on the electric. Use copying film, as it is tougher.

**Illegible Copies**   Illegible copies usually indicate that the carbon paper or copying film is too worn, is too lightweight for the task, or the impression regulator is set too low.

**Roller Marks**   Roller marks on the carbon copies usually indicate that the paper bail is set too tight. Move the rollers off the edge of the paper, using just the paper bail.

**Slippage**   If the carbons tend to slip in the machine, the carbon paper may have too slick a back (frequently the case with plastic-base copying film) and/or the second sheets are too slick (too glossy). Use colored second sheets.

**Smudges**   Smudges on carbon copies usually indicate either carelessly handling the carbon pack or using carbon paper with too soft a finish.

**Uneven Copies**   Dark and light copy on the same page usually indicates that the carbon paper or copying film is too worn or that the typewriter has a faulty impression control.

**Wrinkling or Treeing**   Failure to smooth the carbon when assembling and feeding the carbon pack into the machine, or feeding the pack into the machine unevenly, or using a pack too heavy to feed evenly into the impression rollers can cause wrinkling. When starting a carbon pack into the machine, use the paper release, or a leader, or carbon paper coated to prevent treeing.

**Adjusting Impression Regulator.**   Most electric typewriters are equipped with an impression regulator to adjust the pressure with which the key strikes the paper. This regulator should be adjusted to the thickness of the carbon pack. In general, it should be set at the lowest pressure that will produce the required number of copies. Pressure too high will emboss the letterhead or front sheet, and the carbon impressions will be heavy and lack sharpness.

**Bottom-Line Slippage.**   To control bottom-line slippage, roll the pack back to about midpage. Drop a sheet of paper from the back between the original and the first carbon. Roll the pack forward. As you type near the bottom, the extra sheet will hold the pack securely in place. Steady the top sheet with the left forefinger if necessary.

The master typist folds an envelope or a slip of paper over a carbon pack as a leader for inserting the pack into the typewriter rapidly and evenly.

Correct positioning of the cutoffs at the upper left and lower right corners of the carbon paper permits easy removal of the carbons from the pack.

## CORRECTIONS

Typewriter corrections that defy detection are evidence of the master typist. They are an absolute necessity to quality typing. In fact, if any correction is evident in an otherwise excellent piece of typing, the typescript drops from quality level. The three techniques of making nonevident corrections are careful erasing, perfect positioning, and matched typing.

### Careful Erasing

A neat erasure results from the skillful use of erasing tools. The erasing tools are easily obtained, but erasing skill must be acquired.

**Erasers.** Erasers are available in a variety of textures — art gum, soft, semi-abrasive, abrasive, glass fiber, steel blades — and in many forms and shapes — pencil, wheel, stick. An electric eraser is also available.

For such corrections, use two kinds of erasers — a soft eraser to remove surface ink and carbon that might smear and a more abrasive eraser to remove imbedded ink. Try various brands and shapes of erasers until you find those that you can use most effectively. Clean the erasers by rubbing them on an emery board.

**Erasing Shields.** Erasing shields are basic to neat and complete erasures. A fastidious typist develops the habit of having shields quickly available and of using them automatically whenever erasures are to be made. Erasing shields are of two kinds for two different purposes.

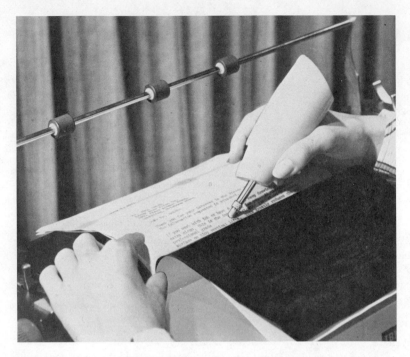

A new cordless, rechargeable electric eraser spot-cleans originals or multiple carbons in the typewriter without the use of an eraser shield.

— *Pierce Corporation*

***An Erasing-Area Shield.*** Unless you use an electric eraser, use a flat metal or plastic shield with letter-height open spaces, in or out of the typewriter, to confine the erasing. It permits erasing to the extreme edge of an error, yet protects adjacent letters. Lightened or fuzzy letters around an otherwise imperceptible correction are telltale and therefore unacceptable in high-quality typing, for the light areas call attention to the erasures.

***A Thick, Pressure-Proof Shield.*** A shield of metal or card stock is used to protect the carbon copies under the page being erased. The shield is placed immediately under the erasing area and on *top*

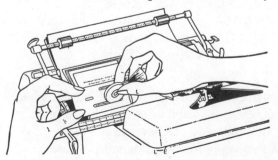

of the carbon. A curved metal shield that hugs the cylinder gives best protection and is easiest to find among papers on the desk.

NEVER use a set of paper slips behind the carbons as erasing shields. They are time-wasters!

**Cover-Ups.** White cover-ups that blend into the paper are often applied over an erasure or error. To fade out an erasure, rub a whitening agent into the paper before typing the correction. You can use a piece of chalk, a direct-process master correction pencil, an aspirin, or a commercial touch-up stick. If you are typing with carbon ribbon and making a carbon copy only for your files, use one of these cover-ups: paint over an error with a white correction fluid that matches the exact whiteness of the paper.[1] Or put a chalk-coated strip of paper, coated side down, over the error and retype the *error* so that some of the chalk transfers and covers it. Then go back and type the correction. A special type of cover-up paper is available for use on carbon copies and with carbon ribbons.

White, self-adhesive correction tape is available in one-line, two-line, and three-line widths. The required length of tape is torn off and placed over the error. Corrections are then typed on top of the tape. Since the correction is obvious, restrict this method to use on copy where appearance may not be important, such as interoffice communications, dummy layouts, and material that is to be duplicated by photographic or offset process.

## Perfect Positioning for Corrections

It is easy to reposition the carriage for an immediate correction unless the error occurs at the very bottom of the page. In that case, do not try to correct it at once, for the sheets almost always slip out of line during erasing and repositioning. Instead, finish typing the page, remove it from the typewriter, and then make the correction on each copy separately.

To save time in repositioning, know the exact relationship of your typing line to your aligning scale. To acquire speed in realigning, look intently as you type a line of words and notice the exact distance *at the typing point* between the bottom of the typed line and the aligning scale. It is the barest fraction of an inch, but memorizing it visually helps you realign more quickly and accurately.

You can find the approximate letter position more quickly by keeping the paper guide set at one spot and using it squarely each time you insert sheets into the typewriter. On a reinserted sheet move the carriage to the first letter of the correction. The typing point will be in almost exact position.

---

[1]Send a sample of your office stationery to the manufacturer of the correction fluid, and the manufacturer will prepare fluid that matches your letterhead perfectly.

# ERASING ON RIBBON AND CARBON COPIES

Some brief but important steps in making a complete and neat erasure are:

1. Erase the original first, then the carbon copies. This sequence could save time should you find that the original cannot be erased satisfactorily.
2. Hold the margin release down and move the carriage to one side to avoid erasing over the type basket. On the Selectric, move typing element to right or left.
3. Turn the copy forward so that the erasure can be made completely. If the error is near the bottom of the page, roll the paper backward to prevent the carbon pack from slipping.
4. Rub a punctuation mark to be erased from a ribbon copy with your thumbnail on the back of the sheet. The mark, imbedded in the paper, erases more completely if pressed outward.
5. Clean the surfaces of the erasers on an emery board.
6. For each copy to be erased, insert a *pressure-proof* shield under the error and on top of the carbon sheet underneath.
7. For each copy to be erased, position the *erasing-area* shield over the error so as to protect adjacent typing. It may take several positionings to complete the erasure.
8. First use plastic type cleaner, if available, to remove as much of the surface ink or carbon as possible. Press the plastic cleaner down on the error and lift off. Plastic cleaner is also good for removing a smudge from carbon copies. If plastic type cleaner is not available, use a soft eraser.
9. Then use an abrasive eraser with light strokes in *one* direction only. Use a "digging-lift" stroke in place of a "scrubbing" action.
10. If necessary, smooth down roughened areas with the thumbnail. Also rub the back of the sheet where the correction was made to smooth the surface and press out any depressions.
11. If ink dye remains in the paper and will not erase, try to fade it out by rubbing with a whitening agent.

## Tests for Exact Positioning

To position a reinserted page for a correction, use the paper-release lever to move the page sideways and the variable line spacer to roll it up or down. Test the exactness of position by the following procedure:

1. Cover the page of typing with a transparent second sheet. Roll the two sheets into the typewriter to the correction line.
2. Test for exactness by typing over a letter near the erased error. Adjust the sheets and type over another letter until the copy is in exact position.
3. Roll the sheets forward a couple of inches. Fold back the thin covering sheet, crease it all the way across, and tear it off. Roll the page into line position, set the carriage at typing point, and type the correction. This method wastes paper but assures exact positioning of corrections and is the cleanest way of correcting reinserted carbon copies.

```
responsible for cordination
responsible for coordination

The data is provided by the
The data are provided by the

the cut-off date for sending
the cutoff date for sending

Not one of them were ready to
Not one of them was  ready to
```

Practice the technique of adding or deleting a letter inconspicuously.

```
The report which you sent last
The report that  you sent last
```

## Fractional-Space Positioning for Correcting

Corrections that require one letter more or one letter less than the error are inconspicuous if they are centered in the space available, as shown above.

**Squeezing and Spreading.** To insert a word containing one letter more than the error, proceed as follows after the erasure has been made:

1. Move the carriage pointer to the space preceding the position of the first letter in the word.
2. Depress and hold down the half-space bar or key, type the first letter of the correction, and release the bar or key.
3. Repeat the process for each letter of the correction.

This procedure will leave one-half space before and after the corrected word.

To insert a word containing one letter fewer than the error:

1. Move the carriage pointer to the space occupied (before erasure) by the first letter of the error.
2. Depress and hold down the half-space bar or key, strike the first letter of the correction, and release the bar or key.
3. Repeat the process for each letter of the correction.

This procedure will leave one and one-half spaces before and after the corrected word.

On machines not equipped with a half-space bar or key, depress the carriage release lever, move and firmly hold the carriage manually in the half-space position, and strike the key. The Selectric element must be held manually. The Selectric II, however, has a half-backspace key.

## COST OF CORRECTING ERRORS IN TYPING*

| ERASURE COSTS | Predetermined Time Study Occurrence Including 16.66% Personal and Fatigue Factor | Total Sec. with 4 Errors per Original | Total Labor Cost Based on 4 Errors per Original* | Total Labor Cost Associated with Copies only** |
|---|---|---|---|---|
| Original Only | 7.6995 sec. | 30.7980 | $.02855 | —— |
| Orig. and 1 Carbon | 16.0990 sec. | 64.3960 | $.05970 | $.03115 |
| Orig. and 2 Carbons | 25.1985 sec. | 100.7940 | $.09346 | $.06491 |
| Orig. and 3 Carbons | 34.2980 sec. | 137.1920 | $.12717 | $.09865 |
| STRIKEOVER COSTS | | | | Labor Cost Associated with Strikeover per Original* |
| Manual Typewriter | .8959 sec. | —— | | $.0008304 |
| Electric Typewriter | .5249 sec. | —— | | $.0004865 |

*Based on estimated average labor cost of $3.34 per hour or $.000927 per second.
**Computed by subtracting labor cost of original only from total labor charge of original with carbon since costs of original will be constant.

—*Administrative Management*

*Adapted from cost figures compiled by the Travelers Insurance Company

**Inserting a Space or Hyphen.** To insert a space or a hyphen between two words, erase the two letters which must be separated. Retype the first letter one-half space to the left of its original position. Retype the second letter by fractional forward spacing. Center a hyphen in the space available by using the backspace key. In this manner, you can make a near-perfect correction.

```
askyou
ask you
```

```
stilllife
still-life
```

**Inserting a Thin Letter in a Word.** In some cases you can insert an *l*, an *i*, or a *t* within a typed word by fractional spacing. Experiment with your typewriter to determine in what instances you can use this method of correcting, recognizing that the correction will be discernible.

```
alignment
insertion
letter
```

```
            to
Time must be of the
essence/permit inter-
linear corrections.
```

```
Time must be of the
         to
essence/permit inter-
```

**Making an Insertion Between Lines.** When time is of the essence, you may have to make a neat insertion between lines. Use the underline and diagonal keys to indicate the insertion. Find the midpoint between the lines for the line of typing. In single-spaced copy type the correction to the right of the diagonal; in double-spaced copy center the correction over the upper end of the diagonal.

### Correcting a Topbound Typescript

Typed pages that are bound at the top can be corrected without unbinding. Feed a blank sheet of paper into the machine in the usual way until the paper shows about a two-inch top margin. Insert the bottom of the sheet to be corrected between the top edge of the paper and the cylinder. Roll the cylinder back to the line to be corrected, position the carriage for the correction, and type it.

### Matched Typing

You will have no problem matching the typing of the correction to the typing on a ribbon copy when using an electric typewriter. On a manual machine, however, type the correction lightly first. Go over it if necessary to match the ribbon typing. Do not use deliberate, forceful strokes; use light, pecking strokes repeatedly until the match is perfect.

**Carbon Copies.** To make a carboned correction on a reinserted page of carbon typing, staple together several slips of paper and a piece of carbon paper, carbon side out. A good size is 1 by 2½ inches. After positioning the carriage for the first letter of the correction, put the pad behind the ribbon with the carbon side against the paper. Type in the correction lightly on a manual machine; retype it if necessary to match the carbon typing on the page.

**Strikeover Corrections.** Certain strikeovers are likely to be almost imperceptible in the specific type style on your typewriter. Experiment and learn those that match and blend into the typing. They may include *d* over *c; h* over *n; o* over *c; E* over *F;* and, *; :* or *?* over the period.

## TYPING SPECIALTIES

Typing specialties that expedite, that control, and that add eye appeal—in short, those that earn praise—are described in this section.

### Special Characters

A number of special characters can be constructed on the typewriter. On the next page is a partial list.

| Brackets | [ ] | *Left Bracket.* Type underline, backspace, strike diagonal, turn platen back one line space, type underline. |
| | | *Right Bracket.* Type underline, diagonal, backspace turn platen back one line space, type underline. |
| Degree sign | 12° | Turn platen toward you slightly; strike lowercase 0. |
| Ditto mark | " | Turn platen forward slightly; strike the quotation mark. |
| Division sign | ÷ | Type hyphen, backspace, and strike the colon. |
| Equal sign | = | Type hyphen, backspace, turn platen forward a bit, strike the hyphen. |
| Paragraph mark | ¶ | Type capital P, backspace, and strike 1. |
| Plus sign | + | Type hyphen, backspace, and strike diagonal. |
| Pound sterling | £ | Type f, backspace, strike t. |

## Multipage Typing

A typing job of many pages, and often of many copies, must be organized in advance and controlled while in process so that it can be carried through to consistent completion. To accomplish this task, formulate the regulations and set them down on paper for both your own reference and the guidance of those who assist you.

**The Job Guide Sheet.** Set up a job guide sheet covering every point of form and typing instruction that may be needed for a long typing job. Try to answer in advance every question that will likely be raised. Include the items below and all others that might apply to the specific job.

1. Kind and size of paper to be used
2. Weight and finish of carbon paper to be used
3. Number of copies to be typed
4. Kind and typestyle of typewriter to be used
5. Page layout:

 Paper-guide scale number

 Left margin—number on typewriter scale

 Right margin—number on typewriter scale

 Top margin—number on line-guide scale (discussion)

 Bottom margin—number on line-guide scale (discussion)

 Single- or double-spaced typing

 Paragraph indention—number of spaces

 Tabulation indention—number of spaces

 Tabulation identification—I, A, (1), (a), etc.

 Tabulation spacing—single-spaced or double-spaced

 Headings—examples and placement

 Subheadings—examples and placement

6. Handling of typed pages awaiting assembly
7. Instructions for proofreading
8. Instructions for collating (see discussion)
9. Instructions for binding
10. Distribution of copies
11. Disposal of original-draft pages

**Top and Bottom Margin Guide.** Use any of several devices to maintain even top and bottom margins.

Turn the paper into the machine until the top edge just catches under the paper bail. Usually, this will provide a uniform one-inch top margin.

Use carbon paper with the line scale printed on extended white edge (micrometric carbon paper).

Make your own numbering line guide by typing line numbers down the extreme right edge of a thin second sheet. Insert this guide at the back of the carbon pack or behind the top sheet with the line numbers showing along the right edge.

```
                                              1
                                              2
                                              3
                      2                       4
                                              5
                                              6
 ven top mar-                                 7
                                              8
 of the paper                                 9
                                             10
 tain even top                               11
                                             12
 r make your                                 13
                                             14
 f the carbon                                15
                                             16
 until they are                              17
                                             18
 paper in a                                  19
                                             20
 se unsight-                                 21
```

Glue a small strip of paper (envelope flap or mailing label) to the side edge of one of the carbon sheets. The strip should protrude from the edge and be approximately two inches from the bottom.

**Treatment of Typed Pages.** Keep the original and the carbon copies of each page together in the same order in which they are typed until they are ready to be proofread and corrected. Never leave the carbon paper in a set of typed pages, because pressure exerted on the pack will cause unsightly offset marks on each copy. Do not fasten each set of pages together with a paper clip because the clip leaves crimp marks. Place the bottom copy on top of the set to protect the choice ribbon copy underneath.

Since the bottom copy is used for proofreading and marking corrections, it will be ready without further handling of the set of pages. If the bottom set of carbon copies is used for proofreading, any illegibility will be revealed, as well, so that an illegible copy will not be passed on and proven to be useless. If you are in doubt about any figures, especially, consider the set unusable.

**Collating.** After the sets of pages have been proofread and corrected, they are ready to be collated. Lay out the copies of the last page across the desk so that hand motions in collating are clockwise. Then lay on the copies of the next-to-last page, original on original, first carbon on first carbon, and so on. When all pages are laid out, check and correct each set for proper page sequence before binding.

For a discussion of automatic collating machines, see pages 120–121. If such a machine is available, use it even for small jobs.

## Display Typing

Very often a secretary must design a typing layout for reproduction. It may be a notice, an invitation, a program, or the like. The finished piece requires that the units of copy, the decorations, and the white space be in pleasing arrangement and that the headings stand out. To achieve this effect, the secretary types blocks of copy and headings in various line lengths, spacing, and styles. She then experiments with their placement on a dummy layout.

**Sample Blocks of Copy.** To find the most pleasing size and shape for the blocks of copy, type one paragraph or short unit of copy in different spacings and line lengths to obtain a set of samples with which to experiment on the dummy layout. You can vary sizes and shapes by:

Single-line spacing or double-line spacing
Different line lengths: full width, three-fourths width, etc.
Copy typed in columnar arrangement
Copy or columns typed with even right margins

**Sample Headings.** To make sample headings with which to experiment, take the longest heading and type it in different styles by:

1. Using uppercase and/or lowercase
2. Using different spacings between letters; using conventional spacing
3. Varying the styles of underlining:  continuous or broken underlining; single or double underlines; use of the underline, the hyphen, or the period key
4. Framing the headings: use of periods, small o's, or asterisks; use of underlines with diagonals; use of hyphens and apostrophes

**Justified Typing with Even Right Margins.**  Even-right-margin or *justified* typing is illustrated below.  To justify copy on a machine with standard spacing:

1. Set the margins for the exact column width desired and type each line of copy in double-spaced form the full column width, filling in each unused space at the end with a diagonal.
2. Pencil in a check mark to indicate where you will insert each extra space within the line.  Try not to use an extra space after the first word in a line or to isolate a short word with an extra space on each side.
3. Retype the copy, inserting the extra spaces.

First Copy to Determine Extra Spaces   Final Copy with Even Right Margin

```
First, set up the column width;///    First, set  up  the  column  width;
then type each line of copy the///    then type  each line  of copy  the
full width of the column filling//    full width  of the column  filling
in each unused space at the end///    in each  unused space  at the  end
with a diagonal.                      with a diagonal.
```

(NONPRINTABLE MARGIN)   (MARGINS AT CENTER FOLD)   (NONPRINTABLE MARGIN)

**PAGE 2**

TO A WINTER WORKSHOP

arranged for all those who
want to be better
secretaries (and that
obviously includes you)!

BY THE PORTLAND NSAI
workshop committee,
who -- remembering the
success of last year's
sessions -- will attempt
to earn your kudos again.

**PAGE 3**

PLEASE BRING ALONG:
A pencil, a pen, a notebook,
and a 9 x 12 envelope.
The other needed items
will be supplied to you
at the workshop.

(PAGE 3) | (PAGE 2)
(PAGE 4) | (PAGE 1)

**PAGE 4**

Please call in your reservation
by Monday, November 8,
to Ms. Holly Stevenson,
621-6879,
or mail the enclosed card.

**PAGE 1**

# You're invited...

This is a dummy for an invitation to be stencil-duplicated on one side of 8½- by 11-inch paper and French-folded: first across, and then up and down with the final fold at the left. The broken lines show the fold lines; the solid margin lines, the limit of the typing area. The copy in the upper half of the layout must be upside down to be in reading position when the sheet is folded. Screened areas indicate the copy that has been fixed in position for a pleasing balance of typed matter to white space. Page 1 was lettered with commercial, transferrable letters.

**Decorative Typing.** Distinctively typed words, designs, and patterns may be used occasionally as "eye catchers" on the cover page of a notice, announcement of a meeting, or an item to be posted on the office bulletin board. The illustrations at the right are a few that can be done by straight typing and spacing. Such decorative typing is rarely used in business work; it requires more time than the results justify and frequently it is out of place on a business document.

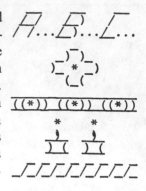

## High-Speed Envelope and Card Routines

You will occasionally have small typing production jobs to do or supervise, such as addressing a hundred or so envelopes or making up a 5- by 3-inch card index. Master the following high-speed routines used in specialized typing assignments.

**Back-Feeding Envelopes.** When you have a number of envelopes to address, you can save time by back-feeding them.

1. Stack the plain envelopes at the left of the typewriter, flap down and bottom edge of the envelopes toward you.
2. Feed the first envelope until only about one half of the bottom of the envelope is free.
3. Place the top of the second envelope between the platen and the bottom of the first envelope. Turn the platen to address position for the first envelope and address.
4. With the left hand pick up the next envelope and drop it into feed position as you turn the platen with the right hand to remove the addressed envelope.
5. With the left hand remove the addressed envelope and stack face down at the left of your machine.

**Front-Feeding Envelopes.** To front-feed envelopes, roll a just-addressed envelope *back* until about one inch of the top edge is free. Have a stack of envelopes at the side of the typewriter flap up with flap edge toward you. Drop one face up between the cylinder and the top edge of the addressed envelope. Roll the cylinder back until the blank envelope is in typing position, then address it. The addressed envelopes stack themselves in sequence against the paper table for occasional removal.

**Front-Feeding Small Cards.** To front-feed small cards, make a pleat a half-inch or less deep straight across the middle of a sheet of paper to form a pocket. The depth of the pleat controls how far down you can type on the cards. Paste or tape the pleat down at the sides to hold it in place. Roll the pleated sheet into the typewriter and align the fold of the pleat with the alignment scale. Place the first card into the pleat and position it for typing. Draw a line on the paper along the left edge of the card to serve as a continuing guide for consistent margins.

**Government Postal Cards.** Government postal cards can be purchased in sheets 4 cards wide and 10 cards long. They can be cut into strips and addressed.

## Fill-Ins

The term *fill-in* refers to the insertion of some typed material in a space provided on duplicated or printed letters, bulletins, or business papers. The fill-in may be an address, a salutation, a word, phrase, or figures. On interoffice correspondence no attempt is made to disguise fill-ins, but on outgoing mail fill-ins should match the body of the message. The procedure is as follows:

> TIME-SAVER. When filling in copy on ruled lines, use the *line finder* instead of the variable line spacer. When you release the line finder, the cylinder returns to the original setting. Adjust the line of typing so that the descenders (portion of letters that extend below the line, as with j, g, q, y, p) just touch the ruled lines.

1. Use a ribbon that matches the body of the message in darkness of color.

2. Set the carriage in position to insert the fill-in. Test the position by typing over a period or comma in the text.

3. When the position has been determined, set the paper guide and margins for use in succeeding fill-ins.

4. Salutations and addresses are placed more accurately if the lines are typed from bottom to top, unless a pinpoint placement dot from the master shows where to begin the first line.

## Typing in the Red

Red typing is used to indicate losses or decreases on financial statements or to give emphasis to part of the text. The red part of a black and red ribbon, red carbon paper, or both may be used. The black part of the copy is typed first, leaving blank spaces where the red copy is to be inserted. Type about three inches of the text at a time, leaving space for the red parts to be filled in. Turn the paper forward slightly and place red carbon in the proper location behind each black carbon. Roll the pages back into position. Shift to red ribbon position, or if the ribbon is all black, place a small piece of red carbon under the card holder of the typewriter and type in the red figures or words. Then remove all of the red slips.

> TIME-SAVERS. Keep a tab stop permanently set for the center of your stationery. You can then center by the backspace method.
> When typing columns of figures with varying digits, set two tab stops for each column, one for 100,000 and one for 100.
> Keep a desk copy of frequently typed reports. Indicate on each the tab-stop numbers and centering positions for all significant lines.

> TIME-SAVER. To bring an address book up to date, type the new address on a gummed label and paste the label over the old address.

## SUGGESTED READINGS

Gavin, Ruth E., and William A. Sabin. *Reference Manual for Stenographers and Typists.* New York: McGraw-Hill Book Co., 1970, pp. 190–194, 228–247.

Klein, A. E., Supervisory ed. *The New World Secretarial Handbook.* Cleveland: World Publishing Co., 1968, pp. 81–87.

Kleinschrod, Walter A. "The 'Gal Friday' Is a Typing Specialist Now." *Administrative Management,* Vol. 32, No. 6 (June, 1971), pp. 20–27.

Whalen, Doris H. *The Secretary's Handbook.* New York: Harcourt, Brace, & World, Inc., 1968, pp. 27–40.

## QUESTIONS FOR DISCUSSION

1. Some office managers feel that it is too expensive to erase and correct typewriting errors. (See table on page 96.) They observe a policy that erasures are not to be made on carbon copies but on the originals of important letters only. What is your opinion of such a practice?

**2.** Assume that you have typed six copies of a five-page, double-spaced report on the subject of dictating equipment. Before assembling the copies, you discover that you have not capitalized the second *s* in *Sound-Scriber*, which occurs on each page. What would you do?

**3.** Suppose the executive has penned-in three corrections on the first page of a letter and two on the second — changes that he made before signing the letter. The time is 4:45 p.m., and he plans to leave promptly at 5 p.m. What would you do?

**4.** If you were assigned the responsibility for typing a long report, what questions would you ask and what items would you decide for yourself before you started the typing?

**5.** Faulty handling of carbon copies can mar superior workmanship. What precautions should you observe in handling carbon copies?

**6.** The *average* cost of a business letter is reported to be over $3 and is rising each year. What factors enter into determining the cost of a letter? Which of these factors, if any, can the secretary control somewhat?

**7.** Fill in the correct word in each of the following sentences. Then refer to the Reference Guide to check your answers.

(a) The letter is (already, all ready) prepared for mailing.
(b) You will have to choose (among, between) the months of June, July and August for your vacation.
(c) The work was divided (among, between) Helen and Ruth.
(d) The change of policy has had a positive (affect, effect) on office morale.
(e) It is not possible to (affect, effect) a reconciliation.
(f) Your attitude will (affect, effect) your promotional opportunities.

## PROBLEMS

■ **1.** A secretary must know how to change a typewriter ribbon. In her role as a supervisor, she may need to demonstrate to those whom she supervises the ribbon-changing process for both film and fabric ribbons. Practice changing the ribbon on your typewriter and also on typewriters of other makes until you feel qualified to demonstrate the technique.

■ **2.** Making undetectable corrections on typewritten material takes practice. This problem will test your skill. Make up a carbon pack of one original and two carbon copies. Type at the top of the page

an exact copy of the following sentences:

(a) How many are coming.
(b) We received your letter of Augst 3 today.
(c) There have been fourty replies so far.
(d) There were both old, and new ones.

While the pack is still in the typewriter, make any necessary corrections on each of the three copies.

Continue by typing these sentences exactly as given.

(e) Our expenses forthe year have increased.
(f) The following is a summary ofour sales.
(g) Only 154 shares of stock were ssued.

Remove the sheets from the typewriter and detach the carbons. Then make the necessary corrections on the original and the two carbons.

■ **3.** Task analysis is a method of determining how to perform a routine with minimum movement. The precise motions made in performing a task are recorded, and each motion is then examined to see if it can be reduced or eliminated.

Prepare a task analysis of each of the following typing techniques. After you have refined the motions, practice each technique until you are competent to demonstrate it before the class.

(a) **Back-feeding or front-feeding of envelopes**
(b) **Front-feeding small cards**
(c) **Assembling and inserting a carbon pack into the typewriter**
(d) **Making a correction on multiple carbons in the typewriter**

■ **4.** There are many techniques that experienced typists use to increase their efficiency, to improve the appearance of the typed copy, or to perform difficult typing assignments. Prepare a short report entitled "A Typewriting Shortcut."

In this report describe a typewriting technique or application that you have learned or read and which is not described in this chapter.

■ **5.** This problem will help you realize the flexibility that is possible in typewritten work. Type the centered heading *Recommendations* in four different ways; type it a fifth time in an original version of your own. (Refer to page 101 and page 102 for ideas.) Indicate your personal preference for use with double-spaced copy on 8½- by 13-inch paper.

■ **6.** Review Chapter 5 to find and try five or more typing suggestions that you have not tried previously.

■ **7.** Style manuals differ in their instructions for certain phases of manuscript typewriting. Compare the instructions given in three reference manuals for secretaries, stenographers, and/or typists for:
**Method of numbering pages**
**Typing of headings and subheadings**
**Margins**

Prepare a report indicating points of agreement and points of disagreement.

# Chapter 6

## COPYING AND DUPLICATING PROCESSES

Technological advancements, reinforced by aggressive competition, have had a tremendous impact on office copying and duplicating. The competition has been not only between copying versus duplicating but also among the many equipment manufacturers, each of whom is seeking a greater share of this *$1.75 billion* industry with its 1.1 million machines producing an estimated 60 billion copies per year.

The secretary continues to be the focal center of much of the research and development in the duplicating area. The objective of each manufacturer is to eliminate the need for specially trained operators for his equipment and to enable the secretary or her assistants to produce high-quality output with greater convenience and speed and at a constantly lower per-copy cost.

In reading this chapter you will need to differentiate between copying and duplicating. Although office copying is not too rigidly defined, in general it is a process that uses an exposing device and an image-forming process to create copies of an existing original. An office copying machine normally is used to make from one to one hundred copies. This limitation, however, is changing because of the introduction of the new copier-duplicators. (See page 113.)

Duplicating, on the other hand, is the use of a device to make copies from a prepared stencil or master. Duplicating machines are used to produce from 10 to 10,000 or more copies.

There are many kinds of office copying and duplicating machines. They vary in the types of written and illustrative materials they will produce, in quality and appearance of the finished work, in the number of copies obtainable, in speed of reproduction, in cost per copy, and in simplicity and ease of operation.

A secretary must be knowledgeable in both copying and duplicating procedures. A supervisor or an administrative assistant should, in addition, be able to make recommendations about the kinds of machines and processes preferable for various purposes, to oversee the reasonable use and care of copying and duplicating equipment and supplies, and to evaluate quality of output.

—*3M Company*

Photocopies are used for the files and for interoffice communication. The copier illustrated here uses the dry photographic process, a modification of the thermographic process.

## COPYING MACHINES

Copying machines are used to reproduce quickly and exactly such materials as original letters, pages from magazines and books, typewritten pages, source documents, financial reports, artwork, charts and graphs, and pictures. The machines may be divided into two major types — plain-paper and sensitized-paper copiers. The plain-paper copier can reproduce on any paper. The sensitized-paper copier requires a specially treated copy paper that is usually provided by the manufacturer of the machine. All copying machines, however, have one thing in common: They produce copies directly from the original; no retyping, master, or stencil is required.

Here are some of the ways in which the use of a copying machine can save the secretary's time and increase her efficiency:

**Copies of an incoming letter can be made and forwarded to several staff members without the delay necessitated by typing copies or routing the letter from one person to another.**

—3M Company

The copying machine is being increasingly used in replying to correspondence. The executive responds in the margins of the incoming letter. After copying the annotated original, the secretary returns it to the sender.

If a sentence or short note can be used to answer a letter, the note can be handwritten or typed on the incoming letter and returned to the sender. The file copy of the original with the answer can be made on the copying machine.

A request for a letter can be accommodated by furnishing a duplicate made on the copying machine, without relinquishing the original letter.

Identical extra copies of accounting papers, statements, statistical reports, tables and statistics from magazines, newspaper clippings, drawings, and illustrations can be made quickly for distribution to departments or individuals.

Copies of incoming orders and other data can be made immediately and routed to the various branches and departments for their use.

File copies can be made of the report itself and of the receipts and other documents that are used to support tax deductions and that are submitted with personal income tax reports.

Mailing lists can be easily updated. The original mailing list is typed once. At each mailing, a copy is made on the copying machine on special label stock. The labels are peeled off and affixed to the mailing piece. Changes in the mailing list can be made directly on the original.

Duplicator stencils, offset masters, spirit masters, and overhead transparencies can be produced immediately from copy without time-consuming retyping.

Manufacturers of copiers using the electrostatic process are highly competitive and offer a wide variety of capacities and speeds of operation. The copier shown here requires no warm-up period, producing the first copy in 15 seconds and 600 an hour thereafter.

*—IBM Corporation*

Most copying machines produce in black only. Colored paper, however, may be used to provide a color contrast with black. One such machine that produces copies in color is currently available, and others will likely follow.

## Copying Processes

Most office copiers use one of three basic processes: (1) electrostatic, (2) thermographic, and (3) diazo. The major expansion and use of copying equipment, however, has been in machines using the electrostatic process.

**Transfer Electrostatic Process (Xerox and IBM).** The electrostatic process is based on the principle that *unlike* electrical charges attract each other, whereas *like* charges repel; and upon the property of amorphous selenium, which will hold an electrostatic charge in the dark but will allow it to be dissipated by exposure to light. A copying camera throws an image of the document to be copied onto a seleniumcoated drum that has been given a positive electrostatic charge. Where the light strikes the drum, the charge is dissipated. The electrostatic charge remains, however, in the image areas. The drum is then treated with a negatively charged powder that adheres to the positively charged lines or letters and thus produces a visible image of the document on the drum, but in reverse. A sheet of ordinary (untreated) paper that has been given a positive electrostatic charge is passed over the drum. The powder image leaves the drum, adhering to the paper, permanently affixed by means of heat.

**Direct Electrostatic Process (Electrofax).** The principle of the direct electrostatic process is basically the same as the transfer electrostatic process. There are three major differences: (1) In the direct method, the electrostatic image is formed directly on the copy paper and therefore does not have to be transferred to it, (2) a liquid toner is required, and (3) a chemically coated copy paper designed for the process must be used.

In addition to copying typewritten, printed, and other materials, most electrostatic copiers can be used to prepare masters for offset duplicating. Some will prepare transparencies for overhead projection.

**Thermographic Process.** The thermographic process is also known as the *infrared* or *heat-transfer* process. The process is based on the physical fact that dark substances absorb more heat than light substances. Material to be copied is placed beneath a heat-sensitive copy sheet. Infrared light is then beamed through the sensitized copy onto the original as both sheets feed through the machine. The dark outlines (words and lines) on the original absorb and hold the heat and turn the sensitized paper dark in the same places, thus producing the image.

Any "faxable" material (material that can be reproduced by the heat process) can be copied. This includes pencil, typing, and printing. Most pen inks and colors will not reproduce.

The thermographic copying machine is used extensively for the preparation of stencils and direct-process masters. In addition, it is used to laminate documents and to prepare transparencies for overhead projection. The original (copy to be projected) is combined with a transparency set and run through the copier. The image is transferred from the original to the transparency in black or in color. Thus, with a combination master/transparency set, the transparency can first be used as a fluid-duplicator master to run off duplicated copies and then used on the projector as the transparency.

A modification of the thermographic process is used in the *dry photographic (3M) process*. In this process the original is transferred to a light sensitized (intermediate) sheet by beaming a light through the original and onto the sensitized sheet. A specially treated copy paper is then put in contact with the intermediate sheet and the image is transferred from intermediate sheet to copy paper by heat and pressure.

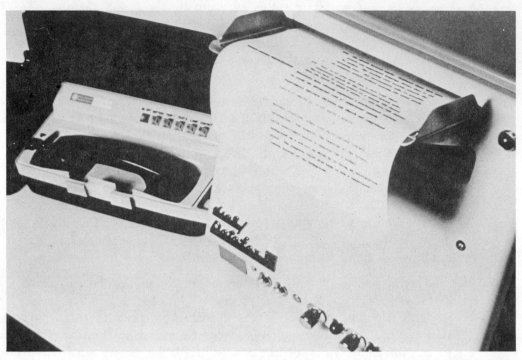

*—American Telephone and Telegraph Company*

This material is being received from a distant point via a conventionally dialed telephone on one that is acoustically coupled to a portable facsimile terminal.

**Diazo Process.** The *diazo process* is an improved form of blueprinting that has been adapted for office use. It produces black-and-white copies, but using colored paper permits other color combinations. Special chemically coated paper must be used for copies. The original is placed over the coated sheet, and the two are exposed to ultraviolet light. The reproduction occurs when ammonia vapor comes in contact with the exposed sheet. Since light must pass through the original, the diazo process cannot copy an original with matter on its underside.

**Telecopier.** By use of a telecopier facsimile device, a copy may be transmitted any distance over the conventional telephone without special wiring or connections. Transmission requires placing the document in a sender, a carbon set in a receiver, the telephone cradle in the coupler unit, and then pressing a button. Upon completion, the machine stops automatically and normal telephone conversation can be resumed. (See page 290.)

The telecopier permits the immediate transfer between two points of accounting data, auditing reports, credit information, financial state-

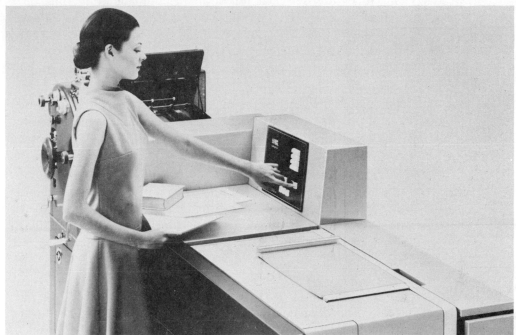

Wholly automated copier-duplicator systems are equipped with programmer controls. They combine the ease of electrostatic master making with the speed and high quality of offset duplicating. The machine pictured makes masters and then copies at a rate of 9,000 an hour.

ments, payroll data, engineering drawings, charts, signatures for verification — in short, anything on paper. The coupler is small and lightweight and can be carried conveniently when traveling. Thus, an executive on a business trip can contact his office and submit and receive data, letters, and other information.

## Copier-Duplicators

In office reproduction, the number of copies to be reproduced can be classified into short runs (up to 10 copies), medium runs (10 to 100 copies), and long runs (over 100 copies). Because of its relatively high per-copy cost and slow speed, the copier has been most economically used for short runs. A duplicating process (stencil, spirit, or offset) has been much faster and more economical for long runs. The medium-run area has represented a grey zone between copying and duplicating. The user has had to weigh the high cost of copying and low cost of duplicating against convenience, simplicity, and urgency.

To fill this gap of the medium-to-long run, several manufacturers are now producing combination machines, called copier-duplicators.

These machines are designed for both medium and long runs on a graduated price scale. They produce copies at a much faster rate (up to 9,000 an hour) than the ordinary copier, and the cost for each copy decreases as the length of the run increases.

There are several types of copier-duplicators. One prominent make is basically a high-speed, high-volume electrostatic copier. The operator merely places the copy in the machine, dials the number of copies desired, and presses a "print" button. Other machines will reduce the size of the copy, trim the copy to the size of the original, and copy on both sides of the paper.

Another approach capitalizes on the convenience of the copying machine yet retains the low-cost feature of the duplicator by combining the copier with the duplicator. The original is transferred to a spirit or offset master or stencil by the copying machine. The master or stencil is then placed on the duplicator and multiple copies produced by duplication.

## Overcopying

The ease with which copies can be made on the copier has led to the tendency of overcopying — that is, making more copies than needed. The urge seems to be almost irresistible, especially on machines that have multiple-copy dials. In addition to overcopying, there is also the cost of unauthorized personal copying — recipes, knitting patterns, bowling scores, and Aunt Maude's letter. While each copy costs only a few pennies, the cumulative total adds many dollars to the monthly copying bill.

To meet the problem of overcopying and unnecessary and unauthorized copying, some companies centralize all copying and assign operators to the machines. A copy-requisition form must be submitted with each original. Assigning an operator has been shown to decrease the volume as much as 20 percent.

Other companies, however, contend that centralized copying increases the time it takes to get a copy, frequently ganging up secretaries at the machines. Thus the time lost far exceeds the saving. The present trend is to decentralize the process by placing copiers in the various departments, readily accessible to the secretaries.

Some companies use key controls: To activate the copier, the operator must have a key. One such lock unit consists of a lock and six nonresettable counters. When any of the six keys is inserted in the lock, the machine operates and the counter corresponding to that key records the number of copies made. This makes possible a count breakdown by departments or individuals to trace excess runs.

Another factor in the mounting copying cost is the temptation, because of its convenience, to use the copying machine rather than the duplicator to produce multiple copies. A multiple number of copies usually can be produced by one of the duplicating processes faster and at a third or less of the cost on a copying machine. Over a period of time, this can amount to a considerable saving.

The secretary will need also to exercise good judgment and restraint against what is frequently called *overcommunicating*. Don't make two copies when one copy, properly routed, will do. Don't use the copier for runs that the duplicator can produce at far less cost.

### Illegal Copying

Because of the ease of making photocopies and the availability of such a machine in the office, there is a temptation to make copies of valuable personal papers and to use or carry the copies in place of the originals. There are rules against, and in some cases penalties for, copying certain papers. Among them are a driver's license, an automobile registration, a passport, a draft card, citizenship papers, naturalization papers, immigration papers, postage stamps, copyrighted materials, and securities of the United States Government.

## DUPLICATING PROCESSES

The amount of duplicating work performed by the secretary varies widely. In a large office that has a special duplicating department, the secretary may be responsible only for preparing the guide copy and selecting the duplicating process to be used. In smaller offices the secretary may be responsible for the entire duplicating process, including the operation of the duplicator. If duplicating is done by an outside agency (a print shop or office-service business), the secretary may need to handle all arrangements. The secretary, therefore, needs to understand the various duplicating processes in order to select the method best suited to the work to be done.

Stencil, offset, and direct processes are the most common for office use. The stencil process and the direct process have been widely used because of their simple operation and low initial cost. Offset duplication for general office use has increased greatly in popularity because of simplified operating controls of offset duplicator machines.

### Stencil (Mimeograph) Process

The *stencil process* is used for the reproduction of all sorts of reports, bulletins, and forms when a number of copies are needed. This process

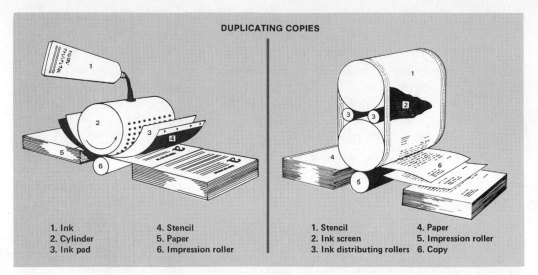

1. Ink
2. Cylinder
3. Ink pad
4. Stencil
5. Paper
6. Impression roller

1. Stencil
2. Ink screen
3. Ink distributing rollers
4. Paper
5. Impression roller
6. Copy

Copies are produced by the stencil process through the meeting of the stencil, the ink, and the paper. The paper is fed, sheet by sheet, between the cylinder and the impression roller. As the paper passes through, the roller lifts, automatically pressing the paper against the stencil. Simultaneously, ink flows through the stencil openings, making a copy on the paper. At the left is a single-drum duplicator; at the right, a twin cylinder.

involves a stencil and an inked drum or twin cylinders. The stencil is a thin tissue, coated with a waxy, ink-impervious substance. A typewriter key or a sharp stylus pushes aside the wax coating, exposing the porous fibers. The stencil is placed around an inked drum or screen, and the ink flows through the exposed fibers to the paper.

Up to ten thousand copies can be made from a stencil, depending upon its quality. Stencils can be preserved and reused. Fast-drying emulsion inks make it possible to print on both sides of the paper without slip-sheeting (inserting a blotting paper between sheets). As many as five colors can be reproduced at the same time by the use of a special multicolor ink pad.

Stencil duplicators are mainly of two types: hollow single-drum machines which generally use a fluid or semi-paste ink and twin-cylinder machines that use a paste ink only. A schematic drawing of each type appears above.

On machines of the single-drum type, the stencil is placed on a hollow revolving drum which has a perforated surface covered with an ink pad. The ink is applied to the inner surface of the drum so that it can pass through the perforations to the pad and the openings of the stencil. Thus, ink impressions are made on ink-absorbing paper as the paper is fed through the machine and comes in contact with the stencil. Automatic inking systems meter the correct amount of ink needed for each copy. Two or more colors can be reproduced by changing the drum and running the sheets through again or by changing the ink pad and hand painting the ink onto the pad.

The twin-cylinder machine covers the closed cylinders with a silk screen; then the stencil goes over the screen. The paste ink is fed onto the surface of the cylinders which, in turn, forces the ink through the screen and the stencil. Multiple colors can be obtained by the simple process of changing the ink and the ink-distribution rollers.

Near-perfect registration (exact position on page, columns, and lines) can be achieved, making it possible to duplicate fill-ins on printed or duplicated forms. Variable-speed controls permit some machines to produce up to 125 copies a minute and to shut off automatically upon completion of a preset number of copies.

The stencil, the key element in quality reproduction, can be prepared on the typewriter, by copying machine, by hand lettering and drawing with styli, and by several other methods. (See pages 125 and 130.)

## Offset Process

The *offset process* is based on the antipathy between grease and water. The outlines on the master hold the greasy printing ink, while the remainder of the surface attracts water and repels the ink. The ink is transferred or offset from the outline to a rubber blanket which, in turn, transfers the copy onto the paper.

This process offers a wide range of possibilities for reproduction, such as printing, pictures, drawings, writing, and typing. All can be put on masters and reproduced. An unlimited number of copies can be run from one master. The masters may be filed and reused. Almost any kind and color of paper can be used. Various colors of ink are usable. Copies can be printed in several colors, but a separate master and a separate run are required for each color. As there is no offset on the back of the sheets, slip-sheeting is unnecessary. A noteworthy advantage of offset reproduction is that copy can be run on both sides of a sheet, thus reducing both paper cost and bulkiness.

A major development in the offset duplicating field is the production of small, table-top, office-size machines designed to produce high-quality work at low per-copy cost. The objective has been to provide a machine that competes with the stencil duplicators for general office duplication. The operation of these machines has been so simplified that they may be operated satisfactorily by the secretary and other members of the regular office staff.

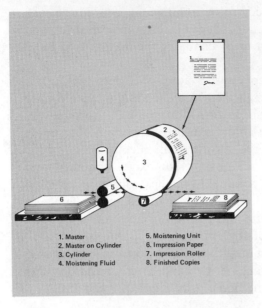

1. Master
2. Master on Cylinder
3. Cylinder
4. Moistening Fluid
5. Moistening Unit
6. Impression Paper
7. Impression Roller
8. Finished Copies

**Masters.** The master may be a paper, plastic, or metal plate. Paper masters are used for short runs and general reproduction work. Plastic plates are used for medium runs; metal masters are used for long runs and for work that is to be of the highest quality.

An offset master may be prepared in a number of ways. The copy may be typed, drawn, traced, or stamped directly on the master. A photographic process may also be used. The most popular method of making masters, however, is to use one of the copying processes. Several of the office copiers will transfer copy to paper plates, and some will also transfer to metal plates.

**Quality Reproduction.** The offset process is capable of producing work of the highest quality. The wide range of paper and variety of colors that can be used make the process especially appropriate where appearance is of major concern, as is the case where materials are going outside the office to customers and to the general public.

## Direct Process

The *direct process*, also known as the *liquid, fluid,* or *spirit process,* is widely used for short runs of material to be used primarily for inside-office distribution. "Direct process" comes from the fact that copies are made directly from the master copy as it comes in contact with sheets of paper. Copy to be reproduced is transferred to the *back* of a master sheet. A sheet of direct-process carbon paper is placed behind the master, and typing is done on the face of the master. Pressure from the typewriter key transfers a small deposit of dye from the carbon paper to the back of the master. The master is then clamped to the cylinder of the machine so that the carbon-typed side comes in contact with the moistened sheets of paper as they pass through the machine.

An alcoholic fluid (hence, spirit duplicator) is used to dissolve and transfer a minute portion of the dye from the master to the paper. This fluid dampens the blank paper as it is fed into the machine. The chemically moistened paper, under pressure, picks up the impression from the master. Copies dry quickly.

Copies can be produced in purple, black, blue, green, or red. Although until recently the best reproduction has been obtained in purple, the improved quality of the black carbon now allows high-quality black-on-white reproduction. Using various colored carbons in producing the master allows several colors to be reproduced at the same time. Since the master is made by carbon, it permits tracing. Charts, pictures, and ruled forms can be traced on the master. A master can also be prepared by typing, printing, thermal imaging, or by writing.

The computer printout can go directly onto direct-process masters and multiple copies run for distribution.

Up to 400 copies can be run from one carefully prepared master. The master may be filed and reused for additional copies when needed. The direct process is an economical, convenient, and rapid method to use in making short runs.

**Blockouts.** Any part of the master may be temporarily blocked out, thus making it possible to produce a number of different forms from the same master. For this reason the direct-process duplicator is widely used in systems work. For example, one master sheet for an order can be drawn up; then by the use of blockout covers, or blockout sections printed on the forms, shipping labels, invoices, work orders, stock-room orders, stock-record cards, back-order sheets, and other forms can be reproduced from the one master. A magnetized metal strip on the drum of some machines permits the easy placement and removal of a blockout mask. Different forms can be reproduced from the same master by merely inserting a blockout mask that meets the requirements of each form.

Have you ever dashed to the duplicator to run off a few copies quickly, only to find that first you need to spend ten minutes cleaning up someone else's mess?

Suggestion: Initiate a sign-up sheet so that each person must register his or her use of the machine. It's amazing how tidy some people become when they know that the next user will definitely know who left the untidiness.

**Azograph.** A disadvantage of the direct process is that the printing dye on the master is easily smudged and rubs off. This problem has been eliminated in the *azograph process* by chemical means. However, copies can be produced in blue color only, and the maximum number of copies obtainable from one master is approximately one hundred. Thus, length of run is sacrificed for cleanliness of operation.

### Addressing Machines

Special equipment addresses mail for repeatedly used mailing lists, as in advertising campaigns. The two basic processes are plate and stencil, but there are more complex units that print from magnetic tape and even from the computer.

In the "plate" process, a machine called a Graphotype embosses the names, addresses, and other information (manually from a keyboard or automatically from punched paper tape, punched cards, or magnetic tape) onto metal plates or plastic cards. Stencil address plates may be produced on the typewriter, teletypewriter, and various data processing equipment. The address plates and envelopes are fed into a machine that addresses the envelopes from the plates. The plates may be indexed to identify selected mailing lists. The addressing machine can be programmed to select only the plates whose addresses correspond to the designated mailing list.

### VariTyper

Offices with a great deal of high-quality duplicating work frequently use a *headliner* (a machine that produces various sizes of type for use in headings) and a VariTyper. The VariTyper differs from the regular typewriter in that the removable type makes possible the use of various typefaces, called *fonts*, in a wide variety of styles and sizes. The Vari-Typer can be adjusted to vary the space between lines and between letters and can justify the right margin, producing copy that closely resembles printing. It is particularly suitable for condensing statistical material into a small space by using a very small typeface. Newspapers, catalogs, and even books can be prepared on the VariTyper.

### Automatic Typewriters

Automatic typewriters produce individually typed material from a master tape or card. For a description of how these machines operate see *Power Typing Equipment*, page 61.

## COLLATING

Collating, the assembling of duplicated pages into sequence to produce multiple sets of a duplicated report, is a time-consuming, inconvenient, and highly routine task — one that few secretaries enjoy. Desk-top collating trays aid but do not eliminate manual collating. A number of mechanical and relatively automatic collators are now available. They are of two types. One type is attached to the duplicating

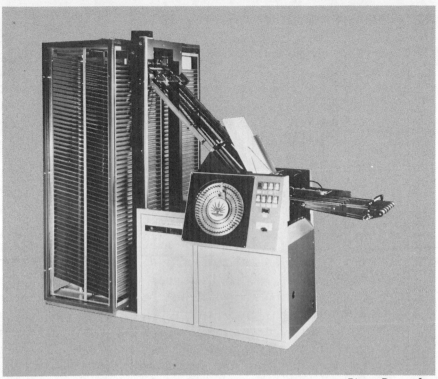

This 200-bin automatic sorter collates independently of the copier or duplicator.

machine. As the first page of the report is being duplicated, the copies come off the duplicator and are automatically separated into a series of bins, one bin for each set desired. The next page is run and the copies go separately into the same bins. Thus, when all the pages have been duplicated, each bin contains a set and the report has been automatically assembled.

Similar collating attachments are available to operate with copying machines. When a collator is attached to an automatic-feed copier, a number of assembled copies of a report can be run without operator intervention. The originals, as many as 200, are placed in the feed tray of the copier and the dial turned to indicate the number of sets desired. As the copies come off the copier, they are assembled automatically by the collator attachment. Thus, the complete production job is done automatically.

A second type of collator operates independently of the copier or duplicator. All the pages are duplicated or copied, and a stack of each page is placed in a separate bin in the collating machine, which automatically or semiautomatically collates the sheets into complete sets.

# PREPARING STENCILS AND MASTERS

Technological developments in the methods of preparing stencils and masters (both offset and direct-process) by copying and electronic methods are significant new developments. Not only do they provide the secretary with a convenient and rapid method of preparing stencils and masters, but they also improve the quality of reproduction, causing major changes in graphic communications.

## Thermal Imaging

The thermographic (heat-transfer) copier produces stencils and spirit masters. The original is prepared by typing, writing, or drawing on paper. Erasers, correction tape, or correction fluid may be used to make corrections. Copy can be cut and a paste-up original prepared. The original is then combined with a *thermal stencil* or *master* and passed through the copier. The heat causes a copy of the original to transfer to the stencil or master, which may be placed immediately on the duplicator and copies reproduced. Any faxable material (see page 111) may be transferred to a stencil or master in a matter of seconds by this method without retyping the material.

One limitation of the thermal process is that certain colors will not transfer, but a copy of a nonfaxable original can be made on an electrostatic copier that will reproduce most inks and most colors. The copy can then be used (in place of the original) to produce the thermal stencil or master.

## Facsimile Imaging

The facsimile process, sometimes referred to as the *electronic scanning method*, is widely used for preparing stencils and offset masters. The process is an adaptation of the principle of the photoelectric cell. Material to be reproduced is placed on one drum of a two-drum machine. An electronic (plastic) stencil or offset plate is placed on the second drum. The drums rotate slowly; and as they do, a photoelectric eye scans each line. The eye responds to light reflected from the copy, creating an electrical current that activates a needle to move across the second drum as the photoelectric eye moves across the first. The needle thus records the image on the stencil or offset master.

Drawings, forms, printed and typed copy, diagrams, and artwork (including photographs) can be transferred to a stencil or master with relatively high-quality detail. A transparency may be prepared simultaneously with the production of the stencil or master. Thus, material can be distributed to a group and also projected on a screen.

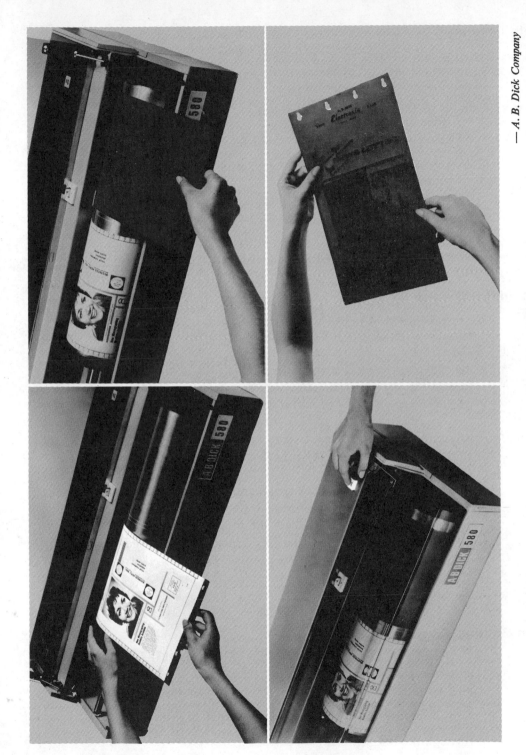

— *A. B. Dick Company*

The four steps in preparing a stencil by the facsimile process are (1) the copy to be reproduced is placed on one drum; (2) an electronic stencil is placed on the second drum; (3) the operation switch is activated; and (4) the completed stencil is removed and is ready to be run on the duplicator.

## Photo Imaging

Small desk-top offset platemakers transfer originals to offset plates within seconds. The original and offset plate are placed on a flatbed window. When the printing button is pressed, a photographic-type lamp automatically exposes the plate. A timer controls the exposure. No film or other intermediate is required, and the process is almost completely errorproof.

## Electrostatic Imaging

This process is nearly as simple and convenient as producing a copy. The original is placed in the copier. A specially sensitized offset plate is substituted for the copy paper, and the image is transferred from the original to the offset plate.

## Die-Impressed Imaging

A business can have stencils, offset, and direct-process masters prepared by the die-impressed or printing method. It is used when a *quantity* of identical stencils or masters is needed. For example, a firm may have a price list on which the prices of the items fluctuate, requiring frequent new price lists for customers. A special printing plate of the *constant* data is prepared and a quantity of impressed stencils or masters are run in reproducing ink from the plate. To prepare a new price list, only the price of each item needs to be typed onto one of the stencils or masters.

Another illustration of the use of this process occurs in handling installment sales contracts where several copies of each contract may be required. From a supply of die-impressed, skeleton contract masters, variable data (names, addresses, and amounts) are inserted on one of the masters and the needed number of copies run off. The outline of the contract is printed on the face of the master to assure correct placement of insertions, thus maintaining the image of careful preparation that is important in all legal papers.

## Form Printing

When stencils or masters are to be used frequently to *insert material on printed forms*, nonreproducing guidelines of the form can be printed on a quantity of stencils or masters. These guidelines aid the typist in positioning copy on the stencil or master and thus assure perfect positioning of the copy on the black preprinted forms as the stencils run through the duplicator.

# TYPING AND RUNNING STENCILS

The quality of stencil duplication depends primarily on the quality of the stencil and the care with which it is prepared.

## Kinds of Stencils

Stencils are produced by a number of manufacturers, each of whom makes several different grades and kinds. Some grades are designed for short runs, others for long runs. Some are recommended for typing work, others for handwriting and art work. They are available, with or without a pliofilm covering, in a variety of colors. The color, however, has no significance except that some stencil manufacturers use color to identify the type or grade of stencil. Each brand carries full instructions on the inside or cover of the box. For best results, read and follow the instructions carefully.

Stencils come in legal, letter, and note size. Form-topped stencils (stencils with outlines printed on the face of the stencil) may be obtained for handwriting, newspaper columns, addressing labels, and four-page folders. There are also continuous stencil sheets for use on the tabulator and computer-printout equipment.

A number of special-purpose stencils are available, such as electronic stencils for use on the electronic scanner, thermal stencils for thermal imaging, and Selectric typewriter stencils. A stencil is available on which writing and sketching can be done with a watercolor brush, using a special solvent ink that dissolves the stencil coating.

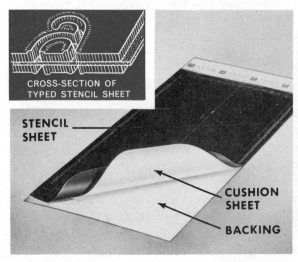

CROSS-SECTION OF TYPED STENCIL SHEET

STENCIL SHEET

CUSHION SHEET

BACKING

—*A. B. Dick Company*

## Special Sheets

A tissue or coated cushion sheet is usually provided with the stencil. It is to be inserted between the stencil and the backing sheet before the stencil is cut. It cushions the impact of the typewriter keys, serves as a depository for the stencil coating which is removed from the underside of the stencil sheet, and broadens the outlines of each stenciled letter. Some stencils have color-coated cushion sheets to facilitate proofreading.

**Typing Plate.** In place of a cushion sheet, a plastic typing plate called an equalizer sheet may be used to produce extra-sharp copies. The equalizer sheet is inserted between the stencil sheet and the backing sheet.

**Transparent Cover Sheets.** When a stencil has a transparent (*plio-film*) sheet over the stencil surface, type right onto it and through it. This film sheet eliminates *type fill*—the accumulation of stencil coating in the keys—and reduces the cutting out of such letters as *o, q, d, b, p*. The film also protects the platen and feed rollers from deterioration resulting from the oils in the stencil coating. If exceptionally sharp copy is desired, use a nonfilm stencil.

## Stocking and Storing Stencils

The coating on some kinds of stencil sheets may deteriorate with age, heat, or humidity. Guard against overstocking. Store unused stencils in a cool, dry place for protection. Weight should be kept off stored stencils; it is best, therefore, to store the boxes on edge rather than flat.

## Preparing the Guide Copy

Until you are experienced in typing stencils, you should prepare a guide copy that is accurate in content and layout. Using a paper sheet the size to be used for running off the copies, you should:

1. Mark on the sheet the limitations or boundary lines shown on the stencil.
2. Indicate the positions of all special illustrations or folds so that the typing copy can be adjusted to the right locations; then type the copy to be reproduced. "Plan before you type" is a basic rule for good stencil reproduction.
3. Check the guide copy with the original copy. Many mistakes in duplicating work can be traced to the omission of this step.

## Placement of Copy on the Stencil

There are several methods to indicate placement of the copy on the stencil. One is to lay the guide copy on the stencil and jot down the line numbers and spaces for each margin and indention according to the scales printed on the stencil. Another method is to lay the guide copy directly under the stencil sheet and mark the places on the face of the stencil by small dots of correction fluid.

Some duplicating machines permit an adjustment of only about one inch to raise or lower copy on the duplicated sheet. Consequently, it is necessary to place the copy carefully for well-proportioned top and bottom margins.

## Typing the Stencil

You will be able to produce good stencils if you observe the following recommended procedures (as well as any special instructions given with the particular brand of stencil that you use):

1. *Clean the type on your typewriter.*

    Unless film-topped stencils are used, it is usually necessary to clean the keys after the typing of each stencil. Letters with less surface, like *i, l, c, e, o,* and *w* (as well as the period), should be watched carefully. It may be necessary to clean them during the course of the stencil typing, especially if the typeface is elite. A liquid type cleaner should not be allowed to spatter on the stencil sheets, nor should a stiff brush come into contact with the coating.

2. *Prepare the typewriter.*

    Set the ribbon lever to the "off," "white," or "stencil" position or the letters will not stencilize completely; only a faint, ragged outline will reproduce. Release card fingers to avoid their hooking into the stencil. Also, move the rolls on the paper bail aside so that they will not roll on the typed stencil surface.

3. *Follow the instructions.*

    Read the instructions provided by the manufacturer or distributor to determine the correct method of assembling the stencil for insertion into the typewriter. When typing lengthwise on the stencil, do not cut off the bottom of the stencil to accommodate reduced carriage width. Merely cut the *backing sheet* to the required length and fold the stencil around the backing sheet.

4. *Type with care.*

    Electric typewriter—Experiment to determine the correct pressure. If the pressure is too light, the copy will be uneven; if the pressure is too heavy, the copy will be dense and lack sharpness. To determine the correct pressure, set the indicator at the lowest registration. Move the carriage to the edge of the stencil outside the printing area; while typing a series of periods and commas, gradually raise the pressure to the point where the periods and commas are reproduced clearly and evenly.

    Manual typewriter—Use a firm, slow, sharp, meticulous, letter-by-letter stroking, with a rhythmic, even, staccato touch. Remember to strike the comma, period, quotation marks, and underline key with a lighter touch and to use a slightly heavier-than-normal touch on compact letters such as *m* and *w*.

5. *Inspect the stencil at the end of each paragraph.*

    See if the typewriter keys are pushing the coating aside properly so that you have clear, evenly stenciled openings. See if any keys need cleaning or if any are making holes in the stencil. Do not roll the stencil backward any more than is absolutely necessary. There is always a chance that it may wrinkle or tear. When it is necessary to roll it back, hold one corner of the stencil firmly.

—*A. B. Dick Company*

There are three steps in preparing a stencil for a correction: (1) turn the stencil forward and separate the film from the stencil sheet, (2) burnish, and (3) apply the correction fluid. After the correction fluid has set, type the correction.

Making corrections on stencils is a painstaking process requiring a light, deft touch. To make a good correction:

1. **Turn the stencil forward in the typewriter so that the line is clear of interference. On film-topped stencils, the film must be detached from the stencil heading, as the correction fluid must be applied under the film.**

2. **When a tissue cushion sheet or equalizer sheet is used, smooth together the edges of the error by rubbing gently with a glass burnisher or the curved end of a paper clip before applying the correction fluid. Lift the stencil away from the cushion or equalizer sheet by inserting a pencil between the stencil and the sheet. This prevents any correction fluid that has leaked through the stencil from adhering to the cushion sheet, which causes a blurred correction. Handle correction fluid with care, as it cannot be removed from clothing. Never use it over the writing plate of an illuminated drawing board. When not in use, correction fluid should be kept tightly corked to avoid evaporation.**

3. **Using a single vertical stroke of the brush, apply a thin coat of correction fluid to the error. The correction fluid should be almost as thin as water for best results. Only a very thin coating of the fluid should be applied over the error—just enough to cover the opening—the less fluid the better, as long as the opening is entirely covered.**

4. **Let the correction fluid set about half a minute and remove the pencil. Test with the finger for dryness.**

5. **Type the correction. On an electric typewriter, lower the pressure adjustment slightly.**

When removing the stencil from the typewriter, use the paper release to insure the least damage to the stencil. Then examine the stencil for scratches, unnecessary marks, or holes. All of these should be covered with correction fluid. If other blemishes show up after the stencil is on the machine, paint them out with correction fluid.

## Proofreading the Stencil

Every stencil should be checked paragraph by paragraph while being typed and also read in its entirety after it is taken from the typewriter. Accuracy is paramount in duplicating work.

If the proofreading must be done alone by the secretary, the stencil should be read back phrase by phrase in comparison with the guide copy (if the guide copy has already been checked with the original). The safest method is to have another person read aloud slowly from the guide copy while you check the stencil, holding it up to the light or against a light table, or from the copy that offsets onto the cushion or backing sheet. Circle each error conspicuously so that you can locate it easily when you make the correction.

A surprising amount of stencil patching and rearranging is possible. This salvaging work can be done before or after the stencil has been run on the duplicating machine. Experiment with a discarded stencil.

The correction or new material to be inserted is typed on an unused section of a spoiled stencil sheet that is still attached to its backing sheet. The piece to be discarded is cut out and the opening neatly trimmed. The new copy is cut with a margin around all sides and placed on the face of the stencil sheet over the opening. Make sure the patch is in proper alignment and that the edges do not cover up any other copy on the stencil sheet. The patch is then anchored with patching cement and sealed all around the edges with correction fluid to prevent leakage at any point.

Small sections of the stencil can be blocked out by placing a piece of carbon paper over that portion of the stencil. The adhesive action of the ink will hold the blockout paper in place.

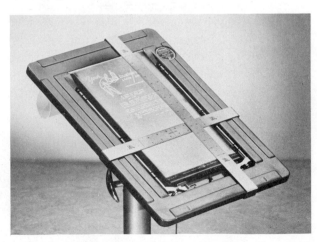

Placing the typed stencil on a light table similar to that at the right facilitates the steps of proofreading, correcting, and aligning patches and blockouts.

Dots of correction fluid at starting and stopping points of copy areas locate paragraphs, lettering, illustrations, and so forth.

—*A. B. Dick Company*

## Guide Points for Salutations and Addresses

When typing a stencil for letters that are to have the inside addresses inserted individually on the typewriter, indicate the beginning position of the address by making a tiny dot on the stencil with a pin at the point where the inside address or salutation should start. This is an efficiency aid to the person who will fill in the addresses. These small dots are almost invisible after the fill-ins are made. They can also be used to indicate folding, cutting, or stapling positions.

## Handwork on Stencils

The drawing of lines, forms, and illustrations; hand lettering; and other artistic work on stencils require the skillful use of styli, lettering guides, screen plates, and the illuminated drawing board. Best results are obtained when a flexible writing plate is used instead of the cushion sheet under the stencil.

The selection of the correct stylus is very important. In general, the wire-loop stylus should be used for solid-line work and signatures, a wheel stylus for charts, graphs, and ruled forms, ball point for fine detail work, and a lettering guide stylus for lettering. Books and packets are available with headings, cartoons, and the like, for tracing on stencils.

## Running Off the Copies

There are a number of different models and makes of stencil duplicating machines in use in business offices. A detailed instruction booklet accompanies each machine, describing how it should be operated. If you will study this instruction booklet, you will be able to operate your machine satisfactorily. If additional help is needed, call on the company servicing your machine. These companies are always glad to assist users of their machines to obtain the best duplicating results possible.

The stack of duplicated copies should be lifted out of the tray without joggling or straightening and laid aside until the copies are dry. Paper used in stencil duplicating is more absorbent than regular correspondence paper; but, even so, the ink may smear unless the sheets are allowed to dry before they are handled.

## Cleaning and Filing Stencils

Only those stencils which may be reused are cleaned and filed. Cleaning may be done by placing the stencil between two sheets of newspaper and rubbing the surface of the newspaper to remove the ink from the stencil, using fresh newspaper until all ink is removed. When water-based contact-drying inks are used, wash the stencil with soap in lukewarm water before filing it.

There are special stencil wrappers made of absorbent paper stock for filing stencils that are used with oil-base emulsion (or paste) inks. With these wrappers it is not necessary to clean a stencil before filing it; merely place the stencil in the wrapper, ink side up. The wrapper is then closed, and the entire surface is rubbed with a smooth hard object such as the bottom of an ink bottle or a paper weight. Leave the stencil in the folder from five to sixty minutes; then open the folder, loosen the stencil, and turn it over. Close the folder. A new wrapper should be used each time a stencil is reused. The stencil is left in the wrapper and filed as you would file a regular folder. While there are special file cabinets in which to file used stencils, they can also be filed in empty stencil boxes and stored on edge.

A plan should be followed for identifying stencils for future use. When a stencil wrapper is used, one of the duplicated copies may be attached to the wrapper; or the wrapper itself may be run through the duplicator before the stencil is removed, thus reproducing on the wrapper a copy of the stencil. To avoid excessive handling of stencils, a numbering system is frequently used. The stencil and a duplicated copy are identified with the same number. The copies are then filed in a folder or punched and inserted into a notebook. Thus when a stencil is to be rerun, its number is obtained from the filed copy, and the stencil is located by number.

## TYPING OFFSET MASTERS

Typing an offset master is no more difficult than preparing a stencil. In some ways it is easier; penciled-in guidelines for copy placement will not reproduce, the copy is clearly readable for proofreading while it is being typed, and corrections are easy to make.

Typing on an offset master can be done with the regular carbon-paper or film-base (Mylar or polyethylene) ribbon. A *fabric* ribbon must be a special offset-process ribbon that contains a grease-based ink. If you prepare offset masters regularly, use the offset ribbon for all work, avoiding the inconvenience of changing the ribbon to type a master.

When it is impractical to use a carbon-paper, film, or offset ribbon, use offset carbon. Place the carbon sheet face down on the master and type directly on the back of the carbon sheet.

As in all other duplicating processes, keep the typeface clean and the paper-bail rollers positioned to ride on the master but *outside* the usage area. Type directly on the face of the master, using normal typing pressure. Too heavy a pressure may dent the surface of the master slightly and cause poor reproduction.

For best results, allow an interval of fifteen to thirty minutes between the typing and the running of the master. This permits the image to set.

To reinsert a master into the typewriter, place a sheet of paper over the master while inserting it to prevent damage by the feed rollers.

A nonreproducing pencil may be used to help plan the placement of the copy on the plate. With this pencil, markings can be made directly on the master as guide lines in typing the copy. The pencil marks will not reproduce.

### Writing, Drawing, and Tracing

Writing, lettering, drawing, and rulings may be made directly on the offset master. An offset ink, crayon, or pencil that will adhere to the master and leave a film must be used.

An offset carbon paper must be used to trace a form or sketch directly on the master. The carbon paper is placed over the master, carbon side down, and the drawing on top of the carbon. The tracing is done with a ball-point pen, hard pencil, or stylus.

Another method of tracing is to use a very thin, translucent tracing paper with a yellow wax coating. The copy to be traced is placed under the master and the tracing paper on top. An illuminated drawing board or scope is used, and the copy is traced with a sharp pencil or stylus. This method eliminates the extra thickness, gives a sharper outline, and protects the original from tracing marks.

You can brush on a drawing fluid for heavy lettering and use a rubber stamp with an offset-ink stamp pad for signatures and other data.

### Making Corrections

Corrections are made by erasing the error and retyping. A special eraser is produced for this purpose, but any soft (nongritty) eraser may be used. Only a few light erasing strokes are necessary, as the deposit comes off readily. A faint "ghost" image will remain, but it will not reproduce. Clean the eraser by rubbing it on paper after each stroke to prevent ink on the eraser from rubbing into the surface of the master. Avoid touching any other spot as you erase, as it will smudge and the smudge will reproduce. Use a normal touch to type in the correction. A second correction cannot be made in the same spot.

To reinsert a typed master into the typewriter, lay a clean sheet of paper over the master to prevent the typewriter rollers from smudging the typing.

When proofreading, hold the master along the edges to avoid fingerprints on the surface, for they will reproduce.

## Cleaning and Storing Masters

A properly cleaned and filed master can be rerun any number of times. After a run, moisten a cotton pad with water and gently clean the surface. Remove any ink or solution left along the edges of the master. Cover it with a thin coating of a preservative (gum solution). When it has dried, store the master in a plain, nonoily paper folder in a file drawer. Separate the masters with a sheet of paper or a folder, or they may pick up traces of oil or ink from the back of the adjacent master and reproduce these traces on the finished copy when rerun.

# TYPING DIRECT-PROCESS MASTERS

The master sheet for the direct-process duplicator is prepared by typing, writing, or tracing on a master sheet backed by a direct-process carbon. (See page 122 for preparation of masters by copying machine.) The coated side of the duplicating carbon paper is against the back of the master sheet. Thus, the impression is made *in reverse on the back of the master*.

Master sheets are packaged in sets with carbon attached; interleaved with tissue that must be removed before use; and for long, medium, and short runs. A number of colors of duplicating carbon paper can be used to prepare the master. These different colors can go close together with little or no problem. For variety, simply place small pieces of various colors of carbon in certain areas on the master.

Although duplicating carbon is now highly smudge resistant, it needs to be handled carefully, and special cleansing cream that removes the dye should be kept available. (Creaming the hands before using the carbon makes stains easier to remove.)

## Typing the Master

The typing, done on the front of the master, is always visible because the ribbon remains engaged.

If the length of a run exceeds the number of copies possible from the kind of master you have, prepare two masters at the same time by placing one master sheet and carbon over another master sheet and carbon, adjusting the touch regulator for the extra copies. In one operation you will have prepared two identical masters.

Until your employer can sign a direct-process master, keep it clean by replacing the tissue (with the signature area cut out) between the carbon and the master.

## Drawing on the Master

Artwork and ruled lines can be traced directly on the master by laying the copy on top of the sheet and tracing over the copy. The impression will be transferred to the back of the sheet by the carbon underneath. A pencil, stylus, or ball-point pen can be used. Halftone effects can be obtained by using a shading plate beneath the carbon copy and rubbing over it. Multicolored drawings can be made by using the different colors of carbon paper.

## Making Corrections

Corrections can be made by blocking out the error on the back of the master sheet (the front surface is not corrected) with a wax blockout pencil as follows:

1. **Separate the master sheet from the carbon. (Some secretaries prefer to insert a master set into the typewriter with the bound edges at the bottom so that it is not necessary to detach the carbon in making corrections.) Care must be exercised not to wrinkle the set in placing it in the typewriter.**

2. **Lay back the master sheet so that the error rests on the flat part of the typewriter, or put a rigid shield underneath it.**

3. **Scrape the carbon dye from the error with a razor blade or knife or the special stylus with a small blade made for this purpose. Remove remaining carbon with a soft typewriter eraser.**

4. **Cover the error with a wax block-out pencil. (This step may not be necessary but is an extra precaution and recommended to assure a perfect correction.)**

5. **Roll the sheet and carbon into approximate position for typing. Slip a small piece of unused carbon paper in back of the error and type the correction. Remove the carbon slip immediately.**

To produce many copies of a letter or report, put a direct-process master behind the letterhead and file carbon. You can then run off a large number of clear copies.

You can make corrections by using a self-adhesive correction tape with the same surface as the master sheet. Cut off the length needed and press it on the back of the master over the incorrect copy. You need not remove the carbon dye first; merely type the correction. This method is best where more than several letters must be corrected.

A small area can be permanently blocked out by cutting out the area with a razor blade or by covering it on the carbon side with plastic tape. A convenient tool for making neat, precise cutouts is an X-ACTO knife, available at stationery and art supply shops.

## Reuse of Masters

Masters can be rerun. A master, however, can reproduce in total only a limited number of copies. Additions, changes, or corrections can be made on a master even after it has been run. For example, it is possible to run a dozen copies from a master, to insert additional information on it, and then to run more copies. Instead of removing the carbon paper from the master copy sheet, fold the carbon sheet under the master and leave it attached when placing the master on the machine for the first run. This method keeps the unit set intact and holds the carbon paper in its original position for making the addition and retaining the original alignment.

A SAFETY HINT! Keep the single-edge razor blade you use for corrections in an empty matchbook, sharp edge inserted where the matches used to be. If you use a double-edge blade, wrap several thicknesses of adhesive tape around the center. Leave the corners free for scraping.

## PAPER FOR COPIERS AND DUPLICATORS

The secretary or supervisor may be assigned the responsibility for buying paper for the office copier and duplicator. The purchasing problem is complicated because several of the office copiers use sensitized papers, and each duplicating process requires its own type of paper.

An important consideration in buying copier paper is to avoid overstocking. Most copier papers have a "shelf life" which should be checked before buying in quantity.

Paper used in duplicating is usually wood sulfite. It comes in a wide variety of colors. The three standard weights for mimeo and duplicating paper are 16, 20, and 24 pounds. Offset paper may carry these same weight identifications or different weights such as 50, 60, or 70 pounds. A 50-pound offset paper weighs slightly less than a 20-pound bond.

Offset paper comes in two general types—coated and uncoated. The coated paper is designed for high-grade work, and offset enamel is the very highest quality. Uncoated paper is used for the majority of in-house work which does not require a high quality reproduction.

Paper for stencil duplicating, unlike that for spirit duplicating, is unglazed and absorbent. Since moisture affects the quality of reproduction and the ease with which the paper is handled by the machine, duplicating paper should be kept wrapped in the moisture-proof covers in which it is received, stored in a dry place, and stacked flat.

Duplicator paper, like other paper, has a top and a bottom side. The best results are obtained by using the paper top side up. The printed label on the package usually indicates the correct printing side.

## COMMERCIAL DUPLICATION

In every city there are commercial shops that make a specialty of duplicating work. These businesses are usually listed in the *Yellow Pages* of the telephone directory under such headings as "Letter Service and Addressing" or "Letter Shops." They will prepare the stencil or master, run the copies, address the envelopes, fold and insert the enclosures, and so on. They will do any one phase or the entire job.

If the office does not have adequate duplicating equipment or if time is short, the secretary or supervisor may need to turn to an outside shop. She will then investigate the service offered and the rates charged, place the order, and follow up to see that the work is completed as directed and on time. She should keep a file of information about the shops with which she has worked.

## SUGGESTED READINGS

"Copiers." *Administrative Management*, Vol. 32, No. 12 (December, 1971), pp. 34–50.

*How to Use the Stencil Duplicating Process.* Yonkers, New York: Gestetner Corporation.

*Mimeograph and Fluid Techniques.* Chicago: A. B. Dick Company, 1971.

*Stencil Typing Hints.* Yonkers, New York: Gestetner Corporation.

1. Three types of machines are used in office reproduction: copier, duplicator, and copier-duplicator. In what ways do these three types of machines differ, and what factors would determine which type would best fit the reproduction needs of an office?

2. What is meant by "overcopying"? Why is it a major problem in the office?

3. Which reproduction process would you recommend for each of the following projects, assuming that all types of copying and duplicating processes are available to you?
   (a) 2,000 copies of a form letter to be sent to sales prospects
   (b) 6 copies of an order to be distributed to department heads with the least possible delay
   (c) 300 copies of a notice to be sent to all salesmen, announcing the annual contest
   (d) 15 copies of a two-page report to be sent to department heads
   (e) 600 copies of a four-page house newspaper that is issued monthly and contains pictures and illustrations
   (f) 55 copies of a one-page announcement showing the route to be followed to reach the annual picnic grounds (The notices are to be placed on bulletin boards throughout the plant.)
   (g) 5 copies of the secretary's minutes of the directors' meeting
   (h) 120 copies of a price list duplicated each week (The list covers 72 standard items arranged in alphabetical order. As the prices fluctuate, a new price list is prepared, duplicated, and distributed weekly to all sales employees.)
   (i) 800 preprinted time cards to be titled each week—one time card for each company employee (The title on the card shows the employee's number, his name, address, social security number, and number of income tax exemptions.)

4. For what purposes would the addressing machine be used in each of the following types of offices or business:
   (a) Publishing company
   (b) Advertising firm
   (c) Payroll department of a large manufacturing company
   (d) Billing and shipping department of a wholesale firm

5. How many lines of copy could you get on a stencil or master to be run on
   (a) 8½- by 11-inch paper with 1½-inch top and bottom margins, single-spaced?
   (b) 8½- by 14-inch paper with 2-inch top margin and 1½-inch bottom margin, double-spaced?

6. List the criteria you might use to evaluate the appearance of duplicated copies of material.

7. By what methods can you personalize a duplicated letter?

8. One of your assistants duplicated a report on a stencil machine. Upon examining the copies you note the following:
   (a) On some copies, the image at the left is lighter than that at the right.
   (b) The letters are not evenly sharp and are rather broad and heavy.
   (c) The center of some of the circular letters such as *o* and *p* and *d* are all ink.
   What would you suggest that your assistant do to improve the quality of her duplicating work?

9. Find the words that have been converted in these sentences to unconventional parts of speech; find more suitable words. Then refer to the Reference Guide to evaluate your answers.

(a) **They constantly interrupt the program to give a commercial.**
(b) **People in the know suspect a seasonal upswing.**
(c) **He gets paid for being an extra each day he is on the set.**
(d) **Observance of company policy is a must in every office.**

## PROBLEMS

■ **1.** Because of the many types of office copying and duplicating machines available, the selection of a machine that will best meet the needs of a particular office requires careful study.

List the factors to consider in selecting a copying machine and those to consider in selecting a duplicating machine. Type your lists in the form of a report to your employer.

■ **2.** Be prepared to demonstrate one of the following:

(a) **Planning the placement of the guide copy on a stencil or offset master**
(b) **Typing the stencil or offset master**
(c) **Correcting errors on a stencil, direct-process master, and offset master**
(d) **Using a copying machine to produce a stencil, offset master, direct-process master, or a transparency**

■ **3.** To help employees you are supervising, prepare an instruction sheet clearly explaining procedures for one of the following activities, illustrating your explanation, if possible:

(a) **Placing the master copy on a direct-process duplicator and running the copies**
(b) **Placing the stencil on a stencil duplicator, running the copies, and removing and preparing the stencil for filing**
(c) **Placing the master on the offset duplicator, running the copies, and removing and preparing the master for filing**
(d) **Using a copying machine**

(e) **Using a heat transfer copier to produce a direct-process master or stencil**
(f) **Using a copying machine to produce an offset master**
(g) **Preparing a liquid duplicating master and making five copies**

■ **4.** Follow Steps (a) through (d), below, to prepare a stencil or direct-process or offset master and run ten copies of the vertical bar graph shown in Chapter 20. Below the graph, type the five suggestions for preparing bar graphs shown in Chapter 20.

(a) **Prepare a guide copy.**
(b) **When you are satisfied with the accuracy and form of the guide copy, plan your stencil or master placement.**
(c) **Type the stencil or master and draw lines.**
(d) **Run ten copies.**

■ **5.** You are asked to establish a policy as to whether the stenographers under your supervision should type carbon copies of letters or should type only the original and reproduce copies by the copying machine that is immediately available. You make a study and find that (1) each stenographer makes an average of two corrections a letter, and (2) the cost of reproducing a copy on the copying machine is 6½¢ a copy (including labor cost). Refer to the table *Cost of Correcting Errors in Typing* on page 96. Write your recommendation and support it with figures.

# Part 2

# CASE PROBLEMS

## 2-1 INTRAOFFICE RELATIONSHIPS

Theresa Moss had been executive secretary to Mr. Robert Johnson, president of Moln Products, for five happy years. One Monday morning Mr. Johnson said, "I want you to meet Fred Abbott, my new administrative assistant. You will continue to do my confidential secretarial work, and Mr. Abbott will assume some of your responsibility for contacts both inside and outside the office. He was recently graduated from the University of Michigan where he majored in business administration. I am sure you will be glad to help him learn the ropes around here."

Naturally, Miss Moss was disturbed. She usually knew Mr. Johnson's plans for personnel changes, but she had heard nothing of his adding an assistant. In the back of her mind was the remembrance of a talk which stressed that women cannot usually aspire to management status and that they should reconcile themselves to the fact that men win most of the promotions. She had worked long enough with Mr. Johnson to sense that he was slightly embarrassed and on the defensive. The change was obviously not to be further discussed with Mr. Johnson. Theresa also decided against discussing Fred Abbott's role with him. She felt that it was not her responsibility to train someone in secretarial techniques who showed that he felt superior to secretaries.

Fred seemed to be getting along well with Mr. Johnson. It developed that they belonged to the same college fraternity. Soon Fred was calling Mr. Johnson "Bob," although nobody else in management did so. He greeted all callers and tried to handle their business. He reached for the telephone before it stopped ringing. A typical conversation follows:

Hello. No, Mr. Smith, this is Fred Abbott instead of Miss Moss. Just a minute and I will look it up. (Aside in a stage whisper: "Theresa, what is the regulation on overtime for supervisory personnel?" Miss Moss icily gives the information.) They get nothing above their 35 hours unless it is specifically authorized on a Form 11 by Bob. Bob has to sign it. Oh, you're welcome. Any time I can help, just let me know.

The crisis came after six weeks when Fred Abbott stopped at Miss Moss's desk and said, "Theresa, I'm working on some budget figures. I can't seem to locate the file on administrative salaries. Will you get it for me, please." Miss Moss said, "Mr. Abbott, that is a confidential file. Nobody but Mr. Johnson ever sees that file."

Fred Abbott walked away muttering, "Oh, well, if that is the way you want to cooperate! Just keep that chip on your shoulder and see where it gets you." Miss Moss burst into tears and rushed into Mr. Johnson's office and said, "Mr. Johnson, it is either Fred Abbott or me. I will NOT work with that clod any longer." Mr. Johnson put down his papers and said, "Why, Miss Moss, what is wrong? I had no idea you felt this way."

In dealing with this situation, you are to concentrate only on Miss Moss's behavior, not on that of the administrative assistant.

What should Miss Moss have done when Fred asked for the file?

In what ways should she have modified her behavior during the six weeks?

Can she do anything about the situation now, or does the correction lie with Mr. Johnson? Ideally, what should he do?

## 2-2 GETTING COOPERATION FROM SUBORDINATES

Inez Potter was secretary to Howard Brownlee, advertising manager in a computer manufacturing corporation. The day before the annual national business equipment show, Mr. Brownlee discovered that his display manager had not followed through on the work for the display. Before starting to direct the assembly of the display himself, he telephoned Inez from the exhibition hall and told her to get the other members of his staff to help her with the following rush work:

Design and reproduce 15,000 forms to be filled out by salesmen manning the booth, giving the name, address, business connection, and specific interest of each visitor to the booth.

Take the 15,000 forms to the exhibition hall personally and deliver them directly to Mr. Brownlee. (He does not want to trust a delivery service.)

Send by company truck 5,000 copies of Pamphlets 67, 81, and 89.

Take an inventory of the supply in the office of Pamphlets 67, 81, and 89. If the supply is below 1,500 copies, rush order from the printer 1,500 more copies of each pamphlet for delivery to the exhibition hall by noon on Tuesday.

Deliver to Mr. Brownlee 10 yards of cloth with which to dust the display during the day.

Inez typed a schedule of the work to be assigned to others, reserving for herself the items above the routine level. Her first request was to Roberta, whom she asked to get money from the petty cash fund to buy some cloth in the Woolworth store in the next block. Roberta replied, "Oh, no, Miss Potter. I'm a clerk-typist, not an errand girl."

How might Inez have secured staff cooperation in this emergency situation?

## 2-3 INTEROFFICE COOPERATION

Adele Perry was secretary to Harold Painter, the person responsible for assembling material for the annual report. Together Adele and Mr. Painter worked out the procedures to be followed and established December 28 as the deadline for submitting last-minute data.

On December 29 Adele discovered that Mr. Watkins, the general sales manager, had not sent his material. She telephoned his secretary, Marcia Bundy, who was known to be ungracious. The following conversation ensued:

Adele: Marcia, we don't seem to have Mr. Watkins' final sales figures for the report.

Marcia: No, they're not ready yet. Mr. Watkins has been too busy.

Adele: Mr. Painter has asked me to get them by noon today so that I can fill in the sales figures and have the report ready for the printer by Friday.

Marica: He'll do them if he gets to it. The President wants something special today, too. Mr. Watkins has his own work, you know.

Adele: Thank you very much. I'm sure Mr. Watkins will understand the urgency and will cooperate if you'll tell him the problem, Marcia. Goodbye.

How better could Adele have secured Marcia's cooperation? What should Adele have done next if she had not received the data by noon?

# The Secretary's Responsibilities for Written Communications

*Part* **3**

**M**ore than a hundred written or printed communications may be delivered to the executive's office in one typical day. Obviously the secretary helps her employer cope with this tremendous load. She organizes incoming mail. She ferrets out information needed for the replies. Then starts the word processing routine: The executive dictates a reply to a machine or to the secretary. She transcribes the dictation, sometimes so skillfully that the finished product represents what he wishes he had said rather than what he did say. Or, if she has proved her communications skill, she composes letters and memorandums based on her employer's instructions.

# Chapter 7

## PROCESSING MAIL

Making it easier for the employer to act on his myriad piles of incoming mail is a challenging secretarial duty. The first, and heaviest, mail of the day is followed by subsequent deliveries. Special-delivery and hand-delivered mail create additional volume, as do the innumerable interoffice memorandums circulated through the company — some of which are more important than the letters and must be evaluated and handled.

All of this mail must be *processed* — prepared for efficient executive action. This chapter deals with the procedures that the secretary follows in handling her mail-processing role. Naturally, when new mail arrives, she drops all but the most urgent tasks and begins the mail-handling cycle again.

## MAIL-PROCESSING PERSONNEL

The first step in the handling of mail is opening the envelopes and sorting the contents into groups for expeditious handling. The personnel involved differs according to the way the mail is addressed and, of course, the size of the company or firm.

### The Mail Room

If a letter is addressed to the company and not to an individual in the company, the envelope is opened in the mail room, which is prepared for quantity handling of mail and contains equipment more elaborate than that in the individual offices. The mail clerk follows established procedures for assigning the mail to appropriate departments for action. He also makes a record of the receipt of the mail and the routing assigned to it. It is then delivered by pneumatic tube or by messenger to the designated offices.

The mail room, too, accumulates outgoing mail, completes its final processing, and dispatches it.

### The Secretary

If letters are addressed to specific employees or departments, the mail room delivers the envelopes unopened. The secretary then gives the unopened envelopes to the addressees, except her employer's mail. She opens his mail and sorts it, but she also takes further steps to expedite its handling before she gives it to him.

In a small office, the secretary opens all mail not addressed to a specific employee, assigns it to the appropriate person for answering, and prepares her employer's mail for his action.

## PROCEDURES FOR PROCESSING MAIL

Steps to follow in opening, reading, and expediting the handling of incoming mail are discussed here. The processing of outgoing mail is described in later chapters.

### Opening the Mail

You need special supplies for opening mail. Lay them out before you start to work, arranging them within convenient reach.

| *You need:* | *You may also need:* |
|---|---|
| An envelope opener | A date or time stamp |
| A stapler, pins, or clips | A routing stamp or slips |
| Pencils | An action stamp or slips |
| The tickler | Cellophane tape for mending |

**First Sorting.** The mail may be sorted three times if it is received in considerable volume. On the first sort, pull out only the *important business and personal mail for immediate processing.* Lay aside all envelopes that look as if they might contain letters of importance to the executive. How, you ask, can the envelope tell you that the letter is important? Two clues can guide you in sorting: the *source* and the *kind of mail service used.*

1. The sender's name, address, or the postmark tells you the source or gives you a clue to it. You will soon learn to recognize those business and personal correspondents of high interest to the executive because you will become familiar with his business activities and certain facets of his personal and family life.

2. An airmail letter, a special-delivery letter, or a certified letter signals "Important." An airmail package takes precedence over a parcel-post package. After completing the first sorting, stop and process the important mail according to the steps given on pages 149–150. Keep in mind that including something unimportant is preferable to missing something important. Unless you are authorized to open personal mail, leave personal letters unopened (even though they are not marked *personal* or *confidential*) and submit them with the processed mail.

**Second and Third Sortings.** Lay out the mail by kind in a second and a third sorting. (Because of their bulkiness, put aside the publications; later on, open, scan, and perhaps stamp or initial them as your employer's copy.) First, sort the envelope mail into these three groups: business, personal, and advertising.

The bulk of each mail will be *business mail* — that which relates to the purposes of the office. You will quickly learn that business mail has a pattern. Follow this pattern in sorting the group once more into like kinds — envelopes from branch offices, from the home office, from customers or clients, from traveling associates, from suppliers, and so on. Group the first-class window envelopes that, usually, contain invoices or statements. Put a large *X* on the back of any incorrectly addressed or odd-looking envelope to remind you to attach it to the letter for the executive's attention.

*Personal mail* also has a pattern. If there is enough volume, sort it again according to the executive's outside activities and his financial interests. Open and process the activities mail from the societies to which he belongs, his clubs and organizations, sources of items that he collects, and so on. Separate the financial mail into like kinds — such as the bills, the bank letters, investment-house letters, and stock-ownership letters.

*Advertising mail* comes in envelopes of all sizes, shapes, and colors — for attention value. You can easily spot it, although the advertisers try hard to fool you. The envelopes rarely, if ever, carry first-class postage. They almost always have open ends with sealed flaps. They have pre-cancelled stamps or printed permit numbers and are not postmarked. Open these when you have time, perhaps after the other mail is processed and handed to the executive. Organize the contents of advertising mail (it is always full of floating, loose pieces, it seems) and give them to the executive at your convenience sometime during the day. Do not destroy them. The executive likes to keep up on *direct mail* — as it is called in the advertising profession. He likes to know what is being advertised and how, and sometimes he returns the enclosed postcards. He may also keep special files of materials of particular interest to him. (This type of file is discussed in Chapter 14.)

**Opening the Envelopes.** Keep the sorted groups intact for convenient handling of the letters later. For the easiest removal of contents, open the envelopes along the top edges. The efficient placement of envelopes and the movements differ with the kind of opener used. An efficient routine for a right-handed person using scissors or a letter knife is described on the next page.

The secretary knows that of utmost importance in processing the executive's mail is extreme care not to damage contents of an envelope. The letter opener shown at the left slices a hairline edge from the top of the envelope.

*—Pitney Bowes, Inc.*

1. Keep forearm working area free.
2. Place stack of envelopes to the left, flaps up, with top edges to the right.
3. Hold envelope with left hand; slip the knife under the flap and with one quick stroke open the edge or cut off a narrow strip along the flap edge with the scissors.
4. Lay the opened envelope down with the left hand, in the left-side area. Keep the cut edges to the right.

When using a lever-operated letter opener (as illustrated above):

1. Stack the envelopes with the top edges parallel to the letter opener.
2. Insert one envelope, press the lever, and lay the envelope to the left side without changing position of the envelope.

The letter opener illustrated is hand operated, but a small electric opener is available for desk use. Mail rooms use electric openers that operate at high rates of speed, sometimes processing more than one hundred envelopes a minute.

**Removing the Contents.** To remove the contents, again keep the forearm working area free. Place the stack of opened envelopes to the left, open edges to the right, flap sides up. Pull out the contents with the right hand. With the left, hold the envelope up to the light, glance to see that everything has been removed, and lay it to the far left, still with the same side up. Use both hands to unfold and flatten the letter and attach enclosures. As you open the letter, scan to see if it contains the sender's address; if not, retrieve the envelope and attach it to the letter. Scan also to see if the letter mentions enclosures and whether those you found agree with the letter. If not, after checking inside the envelope again, underline the reference notation of the enclosure or the mention of the enclosure in the letter and write *No* nearby. Attach any marked envelope to its enclosed letter to be given to the executive.

Mend any torn material. Lay the unfolded letters *face down* in a stack to the right to keep them in the same order as the envelopes in case a letter and envelope have to be rematched later.

It may be a rule in your office to staple the envelope to the back of each piece of mail received. If not, save the envelopes for a day, in case you need to identify the sender, to determine the sender's address, to investigate the reasons for delayed receipt, to recheck for missing enclosures, to establish legality of time of mailing, and so on. Specifically, these include situations in which:

1. **An envelope is incorrectly addressed.** When the executive dictates his answer, he may want to mention the correct address for the future guidance of the correspondent, or as explanation of why the letter was not answered more promptly.
2. **A letter was missent by the post office and had to be forwarded.** This information is needed to explain the reason for a delayed answer.
3. **A letter does not contain a return address.**
4. **The return address in the letter differs from that on the envelope.** Sometimes an individual uses business, hotel, or club stationery and does not indicate his return address, even though the answer to his letter should not be sent to him at the address given in the letterhead.
5. **The date of the letter differs too much from the date of its receipt.** A comparison of the letter date with the postmark date will reveal whether the fault lies with the sender or with the postal service.
6. **Neither a handwritten nor a typewritten signature appears in the letter.** The name of the sender may appear as a part of the return address on the envelope.
7. **A letter specifies an enclosure that was not attached to the letter nor found in the envelope.**
8. **A letter contains a bid, or an offer or acceptance of a contract.** The postmark date may be needed as legal evidence.

**Registering, Dating, and Time Stamping.** It is often desirable for the secretary to keep a *mail register* of important mail for follow-up or tracing purposes. The mail register is used to record special incoming mail (such as registered, certified, special delivery, or insured mail), expected (separate-cover) mail, and mail that is circulated to the executive's associates. For expected bulk mail it may be necessary to give the mail or receiving clerk a memorandum that a package is incoming. Telegrams and cables are also logged in.

Name _Connie Armstrong_

Dates this page _3/14 —_

| RECEIVED | | FROM | DATED | ADDRESSED TO | | DESCRIPTION | SEP.COV. | REFERRED | | WHERE |
| Date | Time | Name/Address | | Dept. | Person | Kind of Mail/Enc./Sep.Cov. | RECEIVED | To | Date | FILED |
|---|---|---|---|---|---|---|---|---|---|---|
| 3/14 | 9:15 am | F. Stevens, N.Y. | 3/12 | Adv. | | Adv. pamphlet - layout | — | Adv. | 3/14 | Adv. |
| 3/18 | 9 am | Steel Equipment Co., Chicago | 3/11 | | M.L.A. | Expected catalogs — file cabinets | 3/21 | Purch. | 3/22 | Purch. |
| 3/20 | 1 pm | D. H. Sims, New York | 3/19 | | M.L.A. | ACA Banquet tickets | | | | |
| 3/22 | 3 pm | L. Cox Lima, Ohio | 3/18 | Adv. | | Book - type faces | 4/10 | Adv. | 4/11 | Adv. |
| 3/23 | 2 pm | D. Ellis, Chicago | 3/22 | | M.L.A. | Special delivery — rush order | — | Sales | 3/23 | |
| 3/24 | 9 am | I.R.S. - local | 3/26 | | K. Logan | Quarterly taxes - forms enclosed | — | KL | 3/23 | |
| 3/26 | 2 pm | Jones, Inc. - local | 3/26 | Acctg | | Registered Ck. #345 | — | Cashier | 3/26 | |
| 3/28 | 9:20 am | R. Keith, Denver | 3/26 | | O. Miller | Insured package | — | Sales | 3/28 | |

Secretaries say that the mail register is "worth its weight in gold" as a protective record that verifies the receipt and disposition of mail. Only a few minutes are needed to record the entries, since abbreviations are used freely. A ruled form similar to the one illustrated above may be used. The blank space in the "SEP. COV. RECEIVED" column, for example, indicates to the secretary that the executive's banquet tickets have not yet arrived.

Another precaution in keeping track of incoming mail is to record the date and time of receipt on the face of each letter between the letter-head and the body, either with date-and-time stamp or in longhand.

For several reasons it is important to know the date on which each piece of mail is received:

1. It furnishes a record of the date of receipt.

2. It furnishes an impetus to answer the mail promptly. (Each reply should be regarded as a builder of goodwill, but no reply that is unduly delayed — no matter how courteous or affable it may be — will promote good public relations.)

3. A letter may have arrived too late to take care of the matter to which it refers. The date of receipt authenticates that inability.

4. The letter may be undated. The only clue to its date is the date of receipt. (You may find it hard to believe, but undated letters are frequently mailed—even letters typewritten by secretaries.)

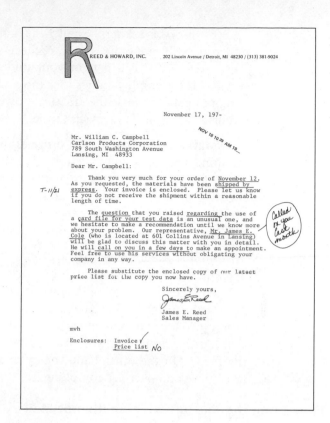

The annotations and the date-time stamp indicate that this letter is ready for presentation to the executive.

## Reading, Underlining, and Annotating

After opening the envelopes and dating the contents, you begin the interesting, secretarial part of handling mail. It involves three steps:

1. Read each letter through once, scanning for important facts. Make necessary calendar notations.

2. Underline those words and phrases that tell the story as you read the letter again. Be thrifty with underlining. Call attention only to the necessary words and phrases.

3. Annotate (write in a margin) any necessary or helpful note to the executive.

Marginal annotations come under two headings:

1. Suggested disposition of routine letters, such as "File," "Ack." (for acknowledge), and "Give to Sales Department." (The secretary anticipates the executive's decision and saves his time, but he may disagree with her suggestion and retain the letter for his own handling.)

2. Special notes, such as "See our last letter attached" (which the secretary will have removed from the files and attached to the annotated letter), or "When Mr. B. was here, you agreed to make this talk." (Such notes are usually reminders, although some may be of a helpful identifying type — this is, a brief "who's who" of the writer or the company.)

You may be asking, "Shall I, as a new secretary, read, underline, and especially annotate, if my predecessor did not?" The answer is *Yes*. Act as if it is a part of your understanding of a real secretary's service. If the employer questions the routine, abide by his decision. He is more likely to praise the practice, however, than to question it; if it is intelligently done, it saves him time.

**Notations for Filing.** Save processing time by adding, at this point, the filing notations on any letters that require no replies. For example, if Clyde Crawford's reply to your letter can be filed without further correspondence, the filing notation should be put on the letter during processing. (Methods of determining where to file letters and when and how to make filing notations are presented in a later chapter.)

**Limiting Annotations.** Since original letters are sometimes copied on machines and sent outside the organization, an executive may request you to avoid all writing on the face of letters and ask you to add annotations only on the back of them. Some copying processes will not, however, reproduce ink or colored pencil. If you are using a copying process that has this limitation, you need not worry about making notations on the face. On the other hand, many executives want notations copied to achieve compact yet comprehensive records.

## Expediting the Executive's Handling of Mail

You can expedite the executive's handling of specific letters by anticipating and preparing for certain procedural steps that he will take. You can be of help to him for the mail services described below.

**Letter Requiring Background Information.** In many cases a letter cannot be answered unless additional information is at hand. For instance, suppose you are a secretary to a sales manager who receives a letter canceling an order because the customer is tired of waiting for delivery. You would look up and attach all the pertinent information about the order, its date of receipt, its present whereabouts, and the cause of holdup. You may have to judge how much background information you should supply. If the executive will ask you for it anyway, anticipate his request. If it only *might* prove useful, weigh the amount of time required to get it, the amount of time you have to give to it, and the executive's probable attitude.

**Letter Referring to Previous Correspondence.** When there is need to refer to previous correspondence, get it and attach it to the letter. Write *See attached* in a margin. With a bound file, put the letter on the file, and insert paper markers in the file at the pertinent points.

DATE_____

TO _____

*Refer to the attached material and*

☐ Please note.
☐ Please note and file.
☐ Please note and return to me.
☐ Please mail to _____
☐ Please note and talk with me
    this a.m._____; p.m._____.

☐ Please answer, sending me a copy.
☐ Please write a reply for my signature.
☐ Please handle.
☐ Please have _____ photocopies made
    for _____
☐ Please sign.
☐ Please let me have your comments.
☐ Please RUSH —immediate action desired.
☐ Please make follow-up for _____
_____

REMARKS:


*Signed* _____

---

Please read the attached material and pass it on to the persons indicated.

| Refer to: | Date Received | Date Passed on |
|---|---|---|
| Mr. Adams | _____ | _____ |
| Mr. Beckel | _____ | _____ |
| Miss Bergold | _____ | _____ |
| Mr. Caldwell | _____ | _____ |
| Mr. Carmichael | _____ | _____ |
| Mr. Davidson | _____ | _____ |
| Mr. Gerhardt | _____ | _____ |
| Mr. Good | _____ | _____ |
| Mrs. Hesoun | _____ | _____ |
| Mr. Holmes | _____ | _____ |
| Mr. Kerr | _____ | _____ |
| Mr. Pineault | _____ | _____ |
| Mr. Robinson | _____ | _____ |
| Mr. Rodriguez | _____ | _____ |
| Mr. Smith | _____ | _____ |
| Mr. Swillinger | _____ | _____ |
| Mr. VanDerbeck | _____ | _____ |
| Mr. Wanous | _____ | _____ |
| Mr. Williamson | _____ | _____ |
| Mr. Zwick | _____ | _____ |

Return to:

---

A secretary devised this check-off slip to save the executive's time in distributing information to and requesting action from his assistants. She provided room for his signature or initials at the bottom because an initialed or signed request is more gracious than a printed name.

One of these duplicated slips is attached to mail to be distributed to others. The secretary or executive checks in pencil or ink the names of those to receive it. Since routing slips must conform with changes in personnel, they are often office-duplicated rather than printed.

**Letter Requiring Follow-Up.** When a letter refers to mail that will follow, or contains a request that requires additional action besides the routine answer, or when a letter must be answered within a certain time, or if other time factors are involved, follow these steps:

1. Select the earliest date in the future when the action should be accomplished.
2. Write that date on the face of the letter with a key (like *T* for *Tickler,* or *FD* for *Follow-Up Date*) so that the executive and you know that a reminder has been recorded.
3. Make a tickler entry under the selected date.
4. If material is expected in a separate mail, write a note on your calendar page, or send a memo to the mail department describing the mail expected. Indicate such notifications in the margin of the letter. (See also Mail Register, page 148.)

**Letter to Be Referred to an Associate.** Often an executive passes along to one of his associates a piece of mail for either action or information. He may want it acknowledged, answered, or followed up; or he may want a report on the subject matter. He may also pass along for-your-information mail. In preparing this mail for an employer whose action you can anticipate, you might attach a routing slip or an action slip similar to those illustrated, lightly penciling in both the individual's name and the action needed. If the suggested action is approved, you may attach the slips to the letter; or, if there is any possibility that you may need later follow-up, photocopy the letter and indicate on the original the name of the persons to whom you sent the copies, the action to be taken, and your own follow-up date, if any. Photocopying is superseding the routing slip because it speeds up dissemination of information. If you send an original copy out of the office, KEEP A RECORD OF WHERE YOU SENT IT.

**Letter Misaddressed to the Executive.** When a letter addressed to the executive actually should have been sent to another person, annotate the correct name in the top margin and put the letter with the other mail for the employer. He will probably ask you to send it on, but he should see it first because it is addressed to him.

**Personal Letter Opened Inadvertently.** If you should inadvertently open a personal letter addressed to your employer, stop reading the letter as soon as you discover that it is personal and not business. Refold the letter, replace it in its envelope, and attach a short note to the face of the envelope, "Sorry, opened by mistake—K. A."

**Enclosed Bill or Invoice.** When an envelope contains a bill or an invoice, if possible compare the prices and the terms with those quoted. Always check the mathematical accuracy of the extensions and the total. Then write "OK" on the face of the bill or the invoice if it is correct, or note any discrepancy. Any arithmetic computations in a letter should be checked for accuracy as well.

**Enclosed Check or Money Order.** Compare the amount of a check or money order enclosed in an envelope with the amount mentioned in the letter of transmittal or the copy of the statement or invoice. If it has been mailed alone, check it with the file copy of the bill to verify the correctness of the amount. Handle the remittance according to the procedure of your office. If it is to be turned over immediately to a cashier, indicate the amount in the margin of the letter or invoice, or prepare a memorandum for the executive, reporting the amount and the date of receipt.

**Publications Received.** Identify each publication permanently with the executive's name or initials. Scan the table of contents and indicate any item he will probably want to read. If an article is of especial interest, underline the salient points and paper clip all the preceding pages together so that he will turn to it as soon as he opens the publication; or attach a note to the front cover telling him about the article.

### Final Arrangement of the Mail

Arrangement of processed and personal mail for presentation to the executive depends on his preferences, his daily schedule, or even his mood. In general, though, the mail is separated into these four groups:

1. **For immediate action**—Possible order of precedence: telegrams, unopened personal letters, pleasant letters, letters containing remittances, important letters, unpleasant letters
2. **To be answered**—Routine letters having no great priority
3. **To be answered by secretary**—Letters that are usually turned over to you for handling (Don't preempt his right to make this decision.)
4. **To read for information**—Advertisements, publications, routine announcements

One successful secretary recommends the use of a four-pocket organizer for submitting mail, with each pocket clearly identified as to contents. This organizer keeps the mail confidential, even from those who seem able to read letters upside down. In any case, the mail should be covered if the executive is not at his desk when you present his processed mail.

On a day when the employer has only limited time for the mail, you may wish to submit items from Category 1 only. On a day when he seems to be marking time waiting for the mail, send in the first half as soon as it is ready, and take in the rest when it is processed. If you know that he expects a specific piece of mail, take it in as soon as it arrives.

## HANDLING MAIL DURING THE EMPLOYER'S ABSENCE

Executives spend a great deal of their time in travel. When they are away from the office, crises occur in handling the mail. Simply forwarding personal mail or sending photocopies of incoming business mail will not always meet the situations that arise. The secretary is in a decision-making role and *must* evaluate each piece of mail before giving it routine treatment.

For instance, an employer may be out of the country when his quarterly income tax is due. He must have the necessary state and local forms to mail with his payment. If they have not arrived before he leaves, he can alert the secretary to open mail from these sources and enclose the forms with his checks, thus meeting the deadline. He may be on an extended trip when the rent, telephone, or utilities bills arrive.

```
                DIGEST OF INCOMING MAIL

Date      From                    Description
4/29    J. B. Moore       Requests material for press
                          release on Project 75 by
                          5/15.

4/29    Rice Univ.        Invitation to be guest
                          speaker on 8/4.  No conflict
                          with present schedule.

5/2     Knoxville         Asks for raw-material bud-
        office            get approval by 5/9.

5/2     Business          Request for more informa-
        Week              tion on Project 75 for news
                          release.  Referred to JMM.

5/3     Ted Wolfe         Requests an appointment to
                          discuss packaging needs for
                          Project 75.
```

These bills should not be forwarded to a foreign country. The secretary should get explicit prior instructions for such contingencies.

The same caution holds for business mail. The employer should not receive a photocopy, forwarded and reforwarded, of a letter about a major reorganization that affects him personally. Yet at times he may need information by the most rapid transmission service. The secretary must assume high responsibilities in processing mail in her employer's absence.

**The Executive's Business Mail.** The executive will expect you, in handling his business mail, to:

1. Communicate with him immediately if mail of vital importance arrives that no one else can handle. Executives on business trips may telephone their secretaries regularly, but occasions arise when the secretary must initiate a call.

2. Set aside those letters that can await his return, but acknowledge their receipt if his answer may be delayed for several days.

3. Give to associates or superiors those letters which must have immediate executive action. Make a photocopy or typewritten copy of each one for the executive's information, noting to whom you gave it, to inform him of the action taken.

4. Send copies (not originals) of those letters that contain information of interest or importance or that require the executive's personal attention, if they will reach him in time.

5. Answer or take personal action on letters which fall within your province.

6. Prepare a digest of mail and either send it to the executive or hold it for his return, depending on circumstances. (See illustration on this page.)

7. Collect in a mail-received folder: (a) all the original letters awaiting attention; (b) copies of all letters given to others for action; (c) both the originals and answers of letters you have answered. Before giving the file to the executive, sort the letters into logical sequence, with the most important on top.

**The Executive's Personal Mail.** Before he leaves, ask the executive what, if any, personal mail he wants you to open and attend to. Do NOT, however, open his personal mail unless he expressly asks you to do so. Hold it for him in the mail-received folder. If he is to be away sufficiently long for mail to reach him if it is forwarded, send it to him. It is often easier to retrieve a letter if it is forwarded in a fresh envelope with your business return address than under a corrected forwarding address.

Keep in the mail-received folder a running record of all letters mailed to an out-of-town address. Identify each forwarded letter by its postmark date and sender's name or by the postmark city if that is all that is shown.

**The Executive's Advertising Mail.** Hold the advertising mail in a separate large envelope. Sort and give it to the executive when the press of accumulated work has lessened after his return.

## WORKING FOR MORE THAN ONE EXECUTIVE

When the secretary is working for more than one executive, the routine is basically the same. Probably a higher level of decision making is required because she must keep each employer's preferences and sphere of responsibility in mind and must keep materials flowing to each of them.

She will, of course, sort the mail into separate piles for each executive. If she sees that one of them is waiting while she completes her classifications, she will take him the first few communications.

The value of the mail register increases when she is responsible for mail to several addressees, for it is proof that material was received.

When one executive is more demanding than the others, the secretary's tact is called into play. Her employers must share in her services, and she may find herself challenged in maintaining an impartial distribution of attention.

## SUGGESTED READINGS

Cook, Fred S., and Lenore S. Forti. *Professional Secretary's Handbook*. Chicago: Dartnell Corporation, 1971, pp. 41–42.

Klein, A. E., Supervisory ed. *The New World Secretarial Handbook*. Cleveland: World Publishing Co., 1968, pp. 165–167.

Mayo, Lucy Graves. *You Can Be an Executive Secretary*. New York: Macmillan Company, 1965, pp. 51–56.

Neuner, John J. W., B. Lewis Keeling, and Norman F. Kallaus. *Administrative Office Management*, 6th ed. Cincinnati: South-Western Publishing Company, 1972, pp. 246–260 (handling incoming mail in large offices from management standpoint); pp. 677–681 (correspondence cost reduction).

## QUESTIONS FOR DISCUSSION

**1.** If you were secretary to an executive who did not utilize your services in processing the mail as suggested in this chapter, what would you do?

2. In processing a morning's mail for the president of a corporation, decide what you would do if—

(a) A letter refers to a letter the executive wrote nine months ago
(b) A customer's letter complains about the actions of a salesman
(c) A letter asks that certain material be prepared and sent before the first of the month
(d) A letter requests a photograph, the responsibility of which is in the public relations department
(e) A letter contains information of importance to three department heads
(f) The envelope obviously contains a bill from an engraver who recently supplied personal stationery for the executive
(g) The letter requests duplicated materials available through your office
(h) The letter refers to a package being sent as a separate mailing

3. The executive is away on a two-week trip. Decide what you would do with a letter that—

(a) Asks him to give a talk five months from now
(b) Requires immediate management action
(c) Is from his mother, whose handwriting you recognize

4. What steps could you take to obtain the address of a person who inquired for information and prices on your product when the request was typed on a plain sheet of paper with no address given on either the letter or the envelope?

5. If the executive is out of town but expects to return tomorrow, what action would you take to record receipt of the following communications? How would you handle each situation?

(a) An airmail, special-delivery letter requesting an estimate on a large quantity of coated paper
(b) A telegram from one of your salesmen sending in a rush order for one of his customers
(c) A letter about a shipment of card stock complaining that one fourth of the blue is two shades lighter than the rest (Samples are enclosed as proof.)
(d) A letter asking the length of time a Mr. Edwards was employed as a salesman by your company and his reason for leaving, and requesting a reference

6. Fill in the correct spelling in the following sentences. Then refer to the Reference Guide to verify or correct your answers.

(a) The executive made a special ——————— of his secretary. (confidant, confidante)
(b) He is a handsome ———————. (brunet, brunette)
(c) Alice is a natural ———————. (blond, blonde)

## PROBLEMS

1. Criticize each of the following steps in a secretary's procedure for handling incoming mail. Type your comments for each step.

(a) The secretary arranges all of the mail in a stack and proceeds to open it and to remove the contents of each envelope in sequence.
(b) She flattens out the letters and enclosures and discards the envelopes.
(c) After all the letters have been removed, she checks the letters for

stated enclosures. Pertinent enclosures she separates from the letters and sends to those concerned (such as orders for the order department). She discards the advertising.

(d) She then time stamps, reads, underlines, and annotates all letters. She prepares a routing slip for letters requiring the attention of more than one person, and she fastens each routing slip to the proper letter with a paper clip.

(e) She then places the letters, in the order in which they were processed, on the executive desk face up for his immediate attention.

■ **2.** Arrange the model desk in your secretarial practice room for opening and sorting incoming mail. Prepare a list of supplies needed. Have the instructor check the list and your demonstration of letter-opening and sorting techniques.

■ **3.** What action would you take to prepare the following three letters for Mr. Richard Stanley's desk? Where would you locate the necessary information? Exactly what underlines and annotations would you make in each of the three cases?

---

# hollander corp.

MANUFACTURERS OF AIR CONDITIONERS
1201 GRAND AVENUE / WADSWORTH, OHIO 44301

*date-time stamp → ← airmail*

March 16, 197-

Mr. Richard Stanley
Auto-Tool Mfg. Co.
320 Euclid Avenue
Cleveland, OH  44102

Dear Dick

In your talk at the meeting yesterday, you referred to a 1971 book that would be helpful to those of us involved in records management, Design of Sequential Filing Systems. We are hoping to revise our entire filing system this fall, and this book may be just what we need as a starting point.

Could you please give me the name of the publisher, the author, and the price? It would be helpful, also, to have the address of the publisher.

Any help you can give me, Dick, will be appreciated. You may know of other books to suggest, for I know that you are especially interested in this field.

I am enclosing a stamped, addressed envelope for your reply.

Cordially yours

*Martin Klaus*

Martin Klaus
Records Manager

mc:da

Enclosure

---

EASTMAN

AND

DURST          801 EAST MARKET STREET • AKRON, OH 44281


March 17, 197-


Mr. Richard Stanley
Auto-Tool Mfg. Co.
320 Euclid Avenue
Cleveland, OH  44102

Dear Mr. Stanley:

Several times today I tried to telephone you but was unsuccessful.
I wanted to tell you that you can buy the 500 shares you want in
the newly organized First Investors Fund for Growth, a mutual fund,
at approximately $10 if you place your subscription by March 19.

To make this change of investments, it will be necessary to sell
either your General Foods (bought at 28) or your Standard Oil of
California (bought at 52 1/2).  I suggest that you refer to today's
market quotation on both stocks as a basis for your decision; and
then telephone me on March 18, if possible.

                         Sincerely yours,

                         *David Grimes*

                         David Grimes
                         Investment Counselor


*[handwritten margin notes: march 19 · 28 · 52 1/2]*

---

the **emporium**          fourth & vine streets
                          washington, ia 52353


March 17, 197-


Auto-Tool Mfg. Co.
320 Euclid Avenue
Cleveland, OH  44102

Attention Mr. Richard Stanley, General Manager

Gentlemen

As you will note, I have replaced Carson Lawrence as manager.  Since I do
not yet know the names of individuals on your staff, I'm directing these
several points to you.  Please pass them on to the appropriate persons.

1.  We are enclosing our check for $209.25 in payment of your invoice of
    February 6 for $212.50, less 2% discount.

2.  Do you have sufficient stock on hand to send us 2,000 units of #68912?

3.  Do you have a new catalog?  If so, please send one.

Yours very truly

*K. Edward McGowan*

K. Edward McGowan, Manager

ep
Enclosure:  Check No. 437

# Chapter 8

# WORD PROCESSING —TAKING AND GIVING DICTATION

Although the word processing center (page 61) is gaining considerable acceptance, the secretarial student should prepare herself to take dictation in shorthand, to transcribe her notes, and to transcribe matter from voice-writing equipment — for that is what she probably will do. At least, in 1971 Western Girl, Inc., a national temporary office help service, found that 40 percent of their job orders required transcription skills, 28 percent specifying shorthand experience and 12 percent requiring transcribing-machine experience. Dictators showed a strong preference for face-to-face dictation (74 percent) rather than dictation to a machine (38 percent). A few use both, as you can see by the discrepancy in the percentage total.

Thus, this chapter considers first the traditional ways of taking shorthand dictation. Then are discussed the various dictation systems used in a word processing center and also individual and portable dictation units.

Finally, because the secretary herself probably will dictate to machines (either in the Center or in her office), instructions for giving easily transcribed dictation are included. Covered also is the role of the administrative secretary when her employer's dictation is relayed to the word processing center.

## PREDICTATION RESPONSIBILITIES

Several of the secretary's predictation responsibilities apply regardless of how she will receive the dictation. Among them are preparing a list of items for today's attention and replenishing the executive's supplies.

### Attention-Today Items

The first preliminary to dictation is the collection of *attention-today* items that the secretary prepares for the executive early each morning.

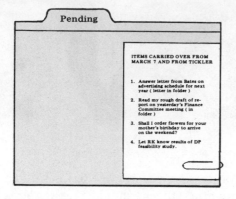

The secretary prepares a folder containing any carry-over correspondence. She attaches to the edge of the folder a list of:
1. Any carry-over items in the folder
2. Items for the day from her employer's desk calendar and her own and from her tickler file.

Some of the items will require dictation, while others may consume some of the executive's available dictation time. Overtime letters, reports, and shipments or letters and reports that must meet deadlines — all will require dictating attention. The day's appointments, conferences, and meetings will also affect the time available for dictation.

Type in brief form, in duplicate, the attention-today items, retaining a copy from which to take unfinished carry-over items each day. Clip the note (or separate notes for each item) to the edge of a portfolio or file folder. When the executive has attended to an item, he can either tick it off the list or discard its note. Take the collection of items to his desk as early in the day as possible — definitely before he begins dictation to you or to dictation equipment.

## The Executive's Dictation Supplies

Another predictation responsibility is the daily checking and replenishing of the executive's supplies to see that he has:

*Sharpened pencils*—An executive often dictates with pencil in hand. He jots down reminders to himself on the letter he is answering; he enters items on his calendar as he commits himself to certain dates; and he may even doodle.

*A scratch pad*—He often uses scratch pads for auxiliary notes.

*Filled stapler, paper clips, pins*

*Ash tray, matches, cigarettes*—If your employer smokes

If the dictation will be given to a voice-writing machine, also include:

*A supply of discs, belts, cassettes, or tapes,* as appropriate

*An empty file folder* or portfolio in which the dictator can insert items related to his dictation as he progresses

*A wax pencil* with which to date and identify the dictated units

*A supply of printed forms* for listing the material dictated on a unit, for special instructions regarding transcription, or for indicating any changes to be made

*A supply of the special envelopes* required for mailing a completed item

**(This item applies when the executive will be dictating on the road.)**

If the executive is dictating directly to the Center, supply him not only with the usual pencils, paper, clips, and staplers, but also with a number of empty folders for the material related to the dictation. These folders of material do not go to the Center. Retain them in your area for reference by you and your executive. Also provide him with the appropriate printed forms for listing special instructions to the Center.

## The Secretary's Dictation Supplies

If you take shorthand dictation, keep your supplies ready and waiting for instant pickup. To avoid unnecessary clutter at the executive's desk, take adequate — but not excess — supplies.

*A notebook*—If you have a choice, use a notebook that has:
   a. Green pages ruled in green (easiest on the eyes, especially for transcription)
   b. Spiral binding so that the pages lie flat
   c. Stiff covers so that the book will stand alone for transcription. Take in only one book unless you are near the end of the current one.

*A filled pen*—Notes written in ink are easier on your eyes at transcription time. Violet ink is reputed to dry quickly and to be the easiest to read under fluorescent lights. A fine-point pen — not a ball point — is best. (An administrative secretary can insist on a high-quality pen.) The objections to using a pen are its running out of ink at crucial moments and the messiness of filling it.

*Pointed pencils*—Choose your favorite kind for holding and for softness or hardness. Some secretaries prefer automatic, thin-lead pencils.

*A colored pencil*—The executive most often uses red or blue.

*Possibly an empty folder or portfolio with pockets on each side*—Some secretaries clip notes to the portfolio as reminders to discuss the contents with the executive. If the executive wishes to put each answered letter in a file folder or portfolio, present it at each dictation session.

## Answering the Call to Dictation

If the executive tries to dictate at approximately the same time each day, stay at your desk awaiting this call. Whenever you leave your desk, tell a co-worker or roll into your typewriter a note of your errand and the expected time of your return so that you can be located if necessary.

Before leaving your desk to take dictation — or for any extended time for that matter — cover, put away, or hide all confidential papers and those of more than general interest and ask someone nearby to take care of your telephone calls and visitors.

You may resent being called to dictation when you are engrossed in other work; but when a call to dictation comes, do try not to act annoyed at being interrupted. Go to the executive's desk with an attitude of willingness and helpfulness.

## PERSON-TO-PERSON DICTATION

The new secretary *may* have faced a classroom "I-dare-you-to-get-the-dictation" situation and hesitate to ask questions of the dictator about unfamiliar words or unclear statements. She often is reluctant to make a tactful suggestion even if she thinks that she can improve the end product—the transcript.

Yet for best results, dictation must be a cooperative effort. The secretary complements the dictator by catching omissions, errors, and ambiguities, and by either correcting them herself or calling them to his attention in a helpful way. Each has a role to play. His is the major, decisive one; hers, a supporting but very important one.

### At the Executive's Desk

During actual dictation periods, the secretary should adopt certain accepted practices. Seemingly unimportant details that often affect the success of the dictation period are the secretary's location, her grooming, and her poise.

**The Dictation Chair.** In the give and take of dictation, the executive and secretary work together at close range. Your dictation chair will be placed conveniently for him. If you have a choice, sit where you have a generous-sized writing area. If he paces the floor while dictating, try not to fence him in.

**Grooming.** Your grooming at dictation time is under casual but close scrutiny, and your hair, makeup, eyeglasses, hands, neckline — all should be equal to it.

**Unobtrusiveness.** As a thoughtful, considerate secretary, you need to be as unobtrusive as possible during the executive's dictation. He can do his most productive concentrating and effective phrasing when he is able to forget your presence. Self-effacement requires the ability to take dictation with confidence, to manage your supplies and papers with as few motions as possible, to refrain from all unnecessary movements, and to avoid any indication of critical reaction to the dictation.

### Enlarging Your Dictation Vocabularies

A secretary has to experience only once the embarrassment of using *elegant* for *eloquent*, *dentures* for *indentures*, or *ingenious* for *ingenuous* to learn the meaning, spelling, and pronunciation of each such pair of words that sound somewhat alike in dictation and look somewhat alike in shorthand.

To learn the executive's vocabulary quickly, read file copies of his recent letters and the trade magazines that apply to his field. From them make a list of words new to you. Alongside each one write its shorthand equivalent. Learn the meanings of the words, their spellings, and their pronunciations. In other words, compile your own glossary.

The several secretarial handbooks in the special fields of law, accounting, medicine, real estate, and so on, have word lists which can hasten the enlarging of those vocabularies.

## Types of Dictation

In addition to business communications, the secretary's dictation probably includes instructions, reminders, requests, and mail to answer. She may be given first a letter, then an interoffice communication, then a telegram, then a request to go to the bank at lunch hour to get a check cashed, then another letter, then instructions on a tabulation of sales costs, then a request to copy certain paragraphs from a magazine article, and then a memorandum to get an appointment for the employer with the mayor. One of the annoying faults of an inexperienced secretary is her reluctance to take notes of anything except transcription items. Instead of recording the instructions in black and white, she relies on her memory to carry them out — and sooner or later gets into trouble.

Dictation falls into the two broad categories of communications and instructions.

**Communications.** The bulk of dictation is in the category of communications. It includes all the dictation to be transcribed—letters, memos, telegrams, outlines, drafts, and so on.

**Instructions.** During the dictation period, numerous instructions are given to a secretary. *Take down all of these in your notebook:*

*Directions for Transcribing.* The dictator gives a direction for transcribing the communication, often at the end of an item; however, you should place it at the beginning if it:

Pinpoints the item for rush handling
Affects the kind of stationery used
Indicates the number of copies to be typed
Refers you to another person before transcribing an item

Use short abbreviations of your own devising and print them in oversized capitals, such as *RUF* for a rough-draft request, *AM* for an airmail letter that requires airmail stationery, and *5 CCs* to indicate that six copies must be typed. For fast finding at transcribing time, turn back corners of pages that contain rush items.

*Directions for Composing.* The executive often delegates the composing of a letter to the secretary. It may be a letter answering one at hand, or a letter to be originated at the secretary's desk. For the former he will usually hand you the letter and say, "Tell him thus and so. . . ." Take such directions in shorthand verbatim, either in the notebook or on the letter itself. For an originating letter, take down the directions verbatim in the notebook. It is imperative to have complete, exact directions for each letter or memo to be composed in order to cover the points that the executive requested.

*Specific Work Instructions.* Take in shorthand in your notebook any specific instructions, such as to cancel one of the executive's appointments, to plan an itinerary, or to write and cash a check, conspicuously keyed for easy finding. One secretary draws a rough box around each work instruction; another writes each one in the right column, which she leaves blank for instructions and insertions.

*General Work Instructions.* Take in shorthand in the notebook all instructions or explanations of office routines and executive preferences in procedure. Transcribe them when there is time and insert them in your desk manual for reference use.

## Good Dictation Practices

Each of the dictation practices recommended below is a *good* one because it promotes efficiency. See how some of them are followed in the illustrated notes on page 167.

1. Write the beginning date of use on the notebook cover—the month, the day, and the year. When the notebook is filled, add the final date and keep the notebook for six months.

2. Reserve one place in or on your desk for the notebook. Keep an extra notebook and pencils in the employer's office too, just in case he decides to dictate while you are with him on another job.

3. Keep a rubber band around transcribed pages to help you find the first blank page on which to write.

4. Keep a filled pen, sharpened pencils, and one colored pencil under the rubber band around the notebook ready for instant use. While transcribing, keep these items together *in one specific place* where they can be quickly reached when a call to dictation comes.

5. Keep a few paper clips around the edges of the notebook cover for possible use during the dictation session.

6. When the executive receives a personal telephone call, leave his office quietly; stay nearby so that you can return as soon as he is finished. When a visitor comes in who will undoubtedly stay for a while, take your materials to your desk and start transcribing. When dictation is resumed, read the last several sentences in your notes without being asked, to help the dictator regain the thought.

7. During interruptions, write transcribing instructions in colored pencil and circle implied instructions, such as *attached* or *enclosed*. Use pauses and interruptions to read your notes, improve outlines, insert punctuation, and write transcribing instructions in red pencil.

8. Date each day's dictation on the first page with the month and year *in the lower right corner in red pencil*. Dictation notes are often the only source of valid reference. If the dictation load is heavy, add a.m. or p.m. to the bottom-of-page notation.

9. If you take dictation from more than one executive, add the dictator's initials to each date or use a different notebook for each dictator.

10. Leave several lines between items of dictation or leave the right column blank to provide room for insertions, changes, and instructions. If the executive makes frequent or lengthy changes and insertions, leave six or eight lines or the full right column. If he rarely does this, leave only three or four lines.

11. Should there be no lines available in which to write a transcribing instruction, print it in oversized capitals in abbreviated form diagonally across the beginning of the notes.

12. If there is the slightest possibility of inability to transcribe proper names, write them out during dictation.

13. Write uncertain words and unfamiliar terms in longhand if necessary.

14. To remind yourself to clear up an error, a question, an omission, an ambiguity, a redundancy, or the repeated use of words that occurred during dictation, put down some conspicuous signal such as a king-sized X.

15. Indicate the end of each item of dictation, *be it a communication or an instruction*, in some conspicuous way, such as with a quick swing line across the column or with a cross. You need a visual aid to assure your transcribing the item completely or your carrying out the instruction.

16. Put each letter that the dictator hands you face down on top of the last one to keep the letters in the same order as the dictation.

17. If the executive assigns a number to each letter being answered (so that he does not have to dictate the name and address of the recipient each time), write only the number in the notebook. At transcription time, pair your numbered notes with the same-numbered letter; and write the name of the addressee in your notebook *above the numbered item* for later identification if necessary.

18. Tape a small calendar on the back cover of your notebook for quick reference during dictation.

# KEY TO THE PAGE OF DICTATION →

(1) A transcribing instruction is inserted as soon as possible in shorthand, in longhand abbreviations, or in king-sized capitals. Later, it is circled or underlined with a colored pencil for attention value.

(2) The swing line across the column indicates the end of an item.

(3) All instructions for composition are written in full so that they can be followed carefully.

(4) The personally devised abbreviation HW is used for Honeywell.

(5) This instruction signals that a tickler notation must be made.

(6) A transcribing instruction to make two carbon copies is inserted at the beginning of the item and later circled in color.

(7) The circled X indicates a question: Should the regional sales manager also get a copy?

(8) The corner is turned back to help locate quickly the page containing the rush item.

(9) The right column is left available for work instructions and insertions.

(10) A work instruction is always identified by a rough box.

(11) The initials of the executive, JR, are used instead of his whole name.

(12) The abbreviation *Ins C—3b* identifies the notes as Insert C to be used three pages back.

(13) Lines are drawn through notes to be deleted.

(14) *Hospitalization* was written in longhand because there was a mental block on the shorthand form. Rather than leave it out or waste time struggling to write it in shorthand, it was written in longhand.

(15) Slash lines are used to segregate an insertion from the surrounding notes.

(16) The date of dictation is always written at the *bottom* of the page.

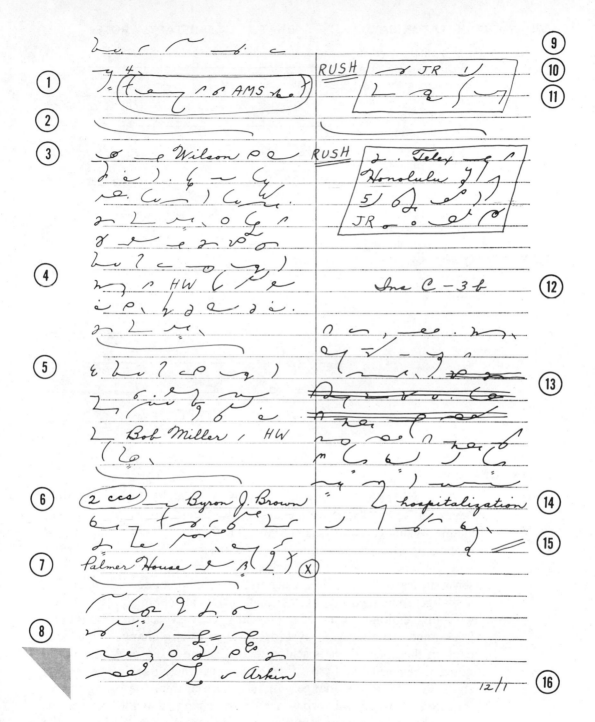

These notes are keyed and signaled for efficient and accurate completion. The practices followed by this secretary are numbered and explained on the opposite page.

Take a letter to Phillips over at Central Tool and Die. We will have our schedule of machine tool requirements completed by — call Carl Johnson in Engineering and see when he'll have it — and in the meantime we need to know approximately how long it will, you *estimate* it will take you to make the fixtures, *jigs* and fixtures, for our subcontract with GE for the jet engine Model so-and-so, be sure to use the right number, as we outlined in our letter to you last week.

## Making Changes

You will have to recognize changes of thought during dictation. An executive often starts to dictate a sentence and, after a pause, begins again. Watch carefully to determine whether it is a new thought or a rephrasing of a previous one. An executive who habitually rephrases is a trial and worry to a beginning secretary, but through some sixth sense she learns to recognize which phrases are bona fide. When making a change, some men say, "Cross that out," and then begin to rephrase without mentioning what to cross out. They expect the secretary to know, and she almost always does. When a long change is made far back in the notes, there is seldom enough time to go back, locate the notes to be deleted and cross them out; nor is there likely to be enough room to write in the change. In such a case, treat the change as an insertion, taking down verbatim both the change and the instructions as to what is to be crossed out so that you can go back and make the deletions later. *Do not rely on your memory to handle changes.*

The point has been made that you should be unobtrusive at dictation time. There are, however, at least three situations when interruptions may be helpful or even necessary.

1. When the executive is so far ahead of you that the thread of dictation is being lost, you must interrupt! Look up inquiringly and repeat the last words that have been taken down. He much prefers that you get complete notes, interrupting if necessary, rather than leave his desk with words and phrases missing or incorrect.

2. When the executive repeats a conspicuous multisyllable word or root word, call it to his attention—if you find he appreciates your help. If the executive said *"elaborate* plans" and then dictated "They have *elaborated* upon this idea," mention impersonally, "We just used *elaborate*." He will then substitute another word, or he may just say, "You fix it up." From then on you would "fix it up" and make the substitution when you go over the notes.

3. When a question comes to your mind about the dictation, insert a clear-up signal at the end of the line. Some men prefer to be interrupted immediately about such a question, others at the end of each item, and still others prefer to wait until all the dictation is completed. The executive will quickly learn your clear-up signal and at a propitious moment will often ask to what it refers.

## Unusual Dictation

A secretary is often asked to take unusual kinds of dictation, such as those discussed below.

**Highly Confidential Dictation.** Transcribe highly confidential dictation when there is little likelihood of anyone's being around. Give the original and carbon copies to the executive as soon as possible and destroy the dictated notes. If the carbon paper retains an imprint of the typescript, destroy it also.

**Telephone Dictation.** In taking telephone dictation, you have the use of only one hand and may have to ask for phrases to be repeated. Since the dictator cannot see how fast you are taking notes, it helps him if you say *Yes* after you have completed each phrase. To avoid errors, read the entire set of notes back to the dictator.

Occasionally the executive may request you to monitor a telephone conversation and take notes. Unless you are usually speedy, you cannot hope to get every word, but you can take down the main points in the way one takes lecture notes. Transcribe such notes at once while they are still fresh in your mind.

Both sides of a telephone call can be recorded on a dictating machine placed near the telephone. Legally, however, the other person must be told. The recording may be kept for reference, or you may be asked to transcribe the entire conversation or abstract the important points.

In the midst of a conference, the executive has asked her secretary to come in and record comments on an advertising layout under consideration.

**On-the-Spot Dictation.** At times it is necessary to take dictation within a split second, while standing or working at a desk where there is no cleared space. You may even have to take the notes on scratch paper. Practice taking dictation with a notebook on your knee or while standing using a scratch pad, in order to become accustomed to the awkwardness of such rush work. The idea is to get it done quickly without fuss or commotion. After transcription, date the notes, fold them to less than page size, and staple them to the first blank page in the dictation notebook.

**Dictation at the Typewriter.** Occasionally the executive may ask you to typewrite something as he dictates it to you. It helps to ask before starting whether it will be long or short, to determine the placement of the item on the page. A retyping, however, is often required, because in the majority of cases the placement is unsatisfactory and insertions or corrections have been necessary. Do not stop to erase errors as they are made. It is better to correct the errors or retype the page when the executive has finished dictating and has left your desk.

**Printed-Form Dictation.** The answers to questions on a printed form are frequently dictated. The executive usually holds the form in his hands; therefore, the information given will seem sketchy and incomplete. If the dictator does not give the identifying numbers or letters of the items, ask him to include them so that you can type the information on the proper lines.

If only one copy is furnished, it may be well to make a photocopy of the completed form for the files.

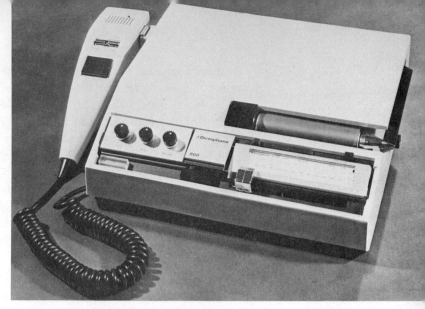

This dictating machine has a magnetic belt and a carriage that returns automatically when the belt is removed. Three controls in front select (1) input (dictation or conference), (2) tone, and (3) volume. The microphone features a continuous backspace with which to review the entire dictation.

—*Dictaphone Corporation*

## MACHINE DICTATION

In some companies all communications are dictated to receiving equipment in a word processing center. There the communications are transcribed by qualified correspondence secretaries or *word processors* (page 61). Dictation involving technical vocabulary is handled by specialists in technical vocabulary. Confidential dictation is given to operators who have been cleared for confidential work.

In companies with word processing centers, the administrative secretaries as well as executives will dictate material to the word processing center for typed output. Secretaries in companies with the traditional organizational pattern will be involved, too, in both giving and transcribing machine dictation.

### Dictating Equipment

Dictation may be recorded on magnetic tapes, belts, cassettes, or discs. Four basic types of equipment are used for machine dictation.

**Centralized Telephone Systems.** Access to this system is through Bell telephone. In some installations it is even possible to record long distance dictation. The dictator pushes the appropriate button on his telephone to make contact with the dictation equipment at the terminal word processing center. When he hears the dictation signal, he speaks into the recording attachment. He can play back his dictation and make corrections at any point. With one type of equipment the dictator can attach a simple, inexpensive device to a public telephone, from which he can then dictate to equipment in his office. It is also possible for the word processor to start transcribing immediately, without waiting for the dictator to complete his input.

**Endless Loop or Tank Systems.**  Dictators use non-Bell lines in a manner somewhat like a revolving carousel during a three-hour revolution.  Dictation enters the magnetic-tape loop at one point and can be picked up by the transcriber at another.  *Transcription* can be done at any time: after, during, or simultaneously with another person's dictation; however, *dictation* can be done by only one person at a time — if someone is dictating to the equipment, no one else can use it until he releases it.  Because of this disadvantage, several systems connected to a "mother" distribution unit are required for volume dictation.

**Desk Units.**  The majority of dictating equipment in use today fits on the dictator's desk.  Dictated material on belts, cassettes, or discs can be sent to the word processing center; or it is transcribed by the secretary or her assistant, where no word processing center exists.

**Portable Dictating Machines.**  This equipment is especially useful to the traveling executive or to the person who works at home.  It is battery powered and accommodates up to thirty minutes of dictation on one cassette, belt, or disc.  The recorded dictation can be mailed in special envelopes usually provided with the equipment so that the material can be transcribed by the time the dictator returns.  The portable dictating machine is regarded as a satellite to a larger word processing system.

## Relationship of the Administrative Secretary to the Word Processing Center

In the organization of a typical word processing center, the administrative secretary will have responsibilities for input and output from the Center.  These are some of her responsibilities:

She assembles Attention-Today items that require dictation.
- researches special names and addresses, sending them to the Center to supplement their records.
- keeps the backup materials from which the dictation originated, organized for possible reference.
- receives the completed work, which she inspects to the extent of her employer's wishes, possibly even proofreading.
- presents the work to the dictator for signature.
- provides all appropriate enclosures and mails the material.
- returns to the Center any material to be corrected or revised.
- photocopies and distributes copies of signed material when the regulation number of copies provided is inadequate.
- follows up if the *turn-around* time (the elapsed time between dictation and delivery of transcript) is too long, requesting the completed material from the Center.
- records and files the code numbers assigned to any material stored on permanent tape.

## Machine Dictation by the Multifunction Secretary

The multifunction secretary, too, finds it efficient to use machine dictation of materials that an assistant or she herself can transcribe.

## Learning to Dictate

A deterrent to using dictating equipment is the reluctance of the dictator to organize his thoughts and materials before he starts to speak. He also fears that he will dictate imperfect items, although all equipment provides for playback, correction of dictation, and an index slip with which to alert the transcriber to a transcription problem. Some secretaries, accustomed to transcribing and to speaking slowly and distinctly with logical phrasing, have less difficulty in dictating efficiently than do some executives.

To prepare for giving easily transcribed dictation, first study the instruction book for the equipment until you can operate all the controls. Dictate a practice item that contains tricky words and figures; wait until a later time; then see whether you can distinguish every word and figure.

An outline made before the dictation is a useful device in producing dictation of which you can be proud. And the more complex the letter, the more necessary the outline.

A large insurance company asked its transcribers to make a list of desirable dictation manners that were lacking in those from whom they took dictation.

Here are a few of their requests:

*Before you start dictating*
Identify the rush items and dictate them first.
Indicate immediately if it is a RUSH item.
First, mention the item to be dictated — letter, memo, report, and so on.
State the number of copies needed and to whom they are to be sent.
Give instructions about typewritten form — if it is unusual.

*During the dictation*
Spell out proper names and technical words.
Dictate figures very clearly.
Enunciate precisely.

*After the dictation*
Be gracious when the transcriber has a question.
Give praise once in a while.
Reject substandard work so that the transcriber keeps up her level of quality.

# SUGGESTED READINGS

Aurner, Robert R., and Morris Philip Wolf. *Effective Communication in Business*, 5th ed. Cincinnati: South-Western Publishing Co., 1967, pp. 169–192 (how to dictate).

Bellotto, Sam, "Dictating Machines Sound Off Four Ways." *Administrative Management*, Vol. 32, No. 6 (June, 1971), pp. 36–43.

Gregg shorthand textbooks. (The four high school textbooks and the four college textbooks have hints on techniques for handling dictation.) New York: McGraw-Hill Book Co., Inc.

*How Much Do You Know About Business Letter Writing?* (40 questions and answers about using dictating machines) New York: Dictaphone Corporation, undated and unpaged.

Huffman, Harry, Donald Mulkerne, and Allien Russon. *Office Procedures and Administration*. New York: McGraw-Hill Book Co., Inc., 1965, pp. 191–201 (dictation procedures).

Neuner, John J. W., B. Lewis Keeling, and Norman F. Kallaus. *Administrative Office Management*, 6th ed. Cincinnati: South-Western Publishing Co., 1972, pp. 77–78 (dictating equipment).

Simpson, George. A monthly column on word processing in *Administrative Management*.

## QUESTIONS FOR DISCUSSION

1. In what ways would your predictation responsibilities for supplies differ if your employer (a) dictates directly to you, (b) dictates to a desk dictation unit, or (c) dictates to a remote dictation terminal?

2. Would it be better for the secretary to give her employer a list of attention-today items when she goes in for dictation instead of making a special trip the first thing in the morning?

3. Robert Benchley once confessed, "It makes me nervous to have a young lady sitting there waiting for me to say something so that she can pounce on it and tear it into hieroglyphics." What could his secretary have done to allay his fears of the dictation period?

4. Suppose your employer on a two-week trip used dictating equipment available during a plane flight and sent it to you at the beginning of his journey. When you put the cartridge on your machine, the dictation is so garbled that you cannot transcribe it. What would you do?

5. What would you do if you were called to take dictation—
   (a) At 11:45 and you had a luncheon engagement at 12:10?
   (b) Just as you were in the midst of giving instructions to an assistant who would have no other work to do unless you finished the explanation?
   (c) As you were putting the finishing touches on an important report that the executive had instructed you to complete before doing anything else?
   (d) As you were in the midst of reorganizing your card file?

6. What would you do if the executive uses many stereotyped phrases of which you do not approve? makes obvious errors in grammar? coins unattractive words? repeatedly uses a conspicuous word? mumbles? dictates obvious punctuation? consistently uses passive voice?

7. How does the secretary record shorthand notes involving (a) transcribing directions, (b) composing directions, (c) specific work directions, and (d) general work directions?

8. As the new secretary to the research director of a chemical company, how would you familiarize yourself with his highly technical vocabulary?

9. What would you do if during dictation the executive—

    (a) Hands you a letter of application and tells you to acknowledge it, explaining that there are no openings at present but that the application will be considered if such an opening occurs? He wants you to check the references.
    (b) Dictates a telegram?
    (c) Asks you to arrange an appointment for that afternoon with Mr. Webster, the executive vice president?
    (d) Dictates a long report letter? He asks you to rough it out.
    (e) Asks you to insert a paragraph near the beginning of a letter?
    (f) Dictates a word you do not understand?

10. Give the preferred plural for each of the following words. Then use the Reference Guide to verify or correct your answers.

| | | | |
|---|---|---|---|
| attorney general | coming in | handful | spoonful |
| basis | court-martial | higher-up | trade-in |
| bill of lading | editor in chief | Jones | trade union |
| Chamber of Commerce | formula | knight-errant | trades union |

## PROBLEMS

1. Twenty letters and the following instructions were given during a dictation period. (a) How would you treat the following items in your notes? (b) What precedence would you give these items? During the dictation period, the dictator said:

(1) "On that Ohio State letter back there, send a copy to Flynn, too."

(2) "Better airmail-special the letter to the Executive Office."

(3) "Remind me Tuesday to order flowers for Mother's birthday."

(4) "See what you can dig up on summer camps or work programs for high school boys Jim's age."

(5) "Make an appointment with the club barber for tomorrow at 9."

(6) "Draft a note of congratulation for me for Dave in the Sales Department. It's wonderful—his being made president of the Sales Executives' Club at 29."

(7) "Call the department store and ask them to pick up that abstract painting I had them send over here on approval."

(8) "My wife wants to go to Miami for spring vacation. Give me a list of flight schedules and rates for leaving on Saturday morning in two weeks and returning the following Saturday in the afternoon."

(9) "Make a rough draft of this and bring it in so I can work on it to send out at 2 today."

(10) "Call Parker Williams in New York for me when we finish here."

2. As a multifunction secretary, you usually rough out your compositions before typing a final copy. Your firm changes to a word processing center, and you fear you are unable to dictate "perfect" communications to the Center. Outline a plan of action for becoming more confident.

3. Take office-style dictation from your instructor or from a tape prepared by your instructor until you feel that you have mastered the special techniques required. (Dictation material is in teacher's manual)

# Chapter 9

## WORD PROCESSING —PRODUCING QUALITY TRANSCRIPTION

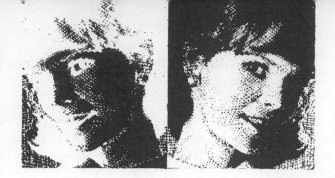

To dictate, type, mail, and file a business letter in 1973 cost the astronomical figure of $3.31, we are told by Dartnell Office Administration Service. When you compare this cost with the $1.83 of 1960, only twelve years earlier, you can see the necessity for economy in word processing.

One way to reduce costs is the use of power typing equipment, which enables a transcriber to more than double her daily typing output. A word processor or correspondence secretary performs only the function of transcription into rough draft with subsequent correction and playout on automated typewriters. The elimination of interruptions caused by administrative duties thus increases her production potential; and, by performing only one function, she achieves maximum utilization of the very expensive equipment required for a word processing station. In addition, the word processing center standardizes format and improves the quality of output by using power typing equipment.

While some secretarial trainees will undoubtedly either join a word processing center or become nontyping administrative secretaries, most of you will transcribe shorthand or machine dictation as part of your total secretarial responsibilities, not separated by function into word processing or administrative categories.

This chapter will, then, be concerned with transcription (1) at the conventional typewriter by the multifunction secretary and (2) on power typing machines by the word processor. As you read the chapter, keep in mind that systematizing your transcription practices in either situation is vital to output of the highest quality and quantity. You can contribute to the reduction of the $3.31 cost of the business letter.

## YOUR FUNDAMENTALS

The secretary's tool of the trade is her facility with the English language—her spelling, punctuation, word usage, typewriting style, and use of reference books. She must master the fundamentals so that she can transmit the dictator's ideas flawlessly. She—not necessarily the dictator—is the expert in this area; on her devolves the responsibility for perfection in letter mechanics.

Language skills are especially important to the correspondence secretary in a word processing center. In fact, applicants for positions as word processors are tested for mastery of English, punctuation, spelling, judgment, and visual acuity rather than for typewriting speed. Every company with organized word processing centers is concerned with in-service elementary and advanced training programs that will develop language specialists capable of improving the quality of the material dictated, not just transcribing as an automaton. The multifunction secretary, too, is a word processor and shares responsibility with the dictator for letter-perfect output.

## Spelling, Punctuation, and the Dictionary

A secretary must know how to spell—everything from common business words through the troublemakers.

**Spelling Aids.** To master your spelling difficulties, compile and maintain your own list of troublesome words, perhaps using the blank inside-cover pages of this book. If you will persistently write down each misspelling that occurs in your writing and each uncertainty that you have to check in a dictionary, you will have a custom-made list for instant reference.

It may help you also to develop your own mnemonic devices. Many a secretary has clinched correct spellings by word associations or parallelisms that are easy to remember: *calendar* ends with the *a* of *day*; *privilege* has the *leg* that comes from *legal; all right* parallels *all wrong*, and so on.

**Punctuation.** A secretary must know the rules of punctuation as they apply to formal writing. Some of her work is at that level. A paper that is to appear in print or a report to the board of directors must be punctuated with formal correctness. In routine business writing there is a trend to reduce the amount of punctuation, especially those marks which indicate pauses. Such punctuation is often omitted in the customary places in sentences which are clear in meaning. But whenever you are in doubt, punctuate fully. Comprehensive punctuation rules are given in the Reference Guide.

**The Dictionary.** Dictionaries vary—from the very British and formal *Oxford English Dictionary* to *Webster's Third New International Dictionary of the English Language*, which aroused a great furor among scholars of the English language when it appeared in 1961. It contains new words that have crept into the language through usage but have never before been listed. Those willing to accept such words as "finalize" and who see a dictionary as a descriptive record of living language will approve the new *Third*, being guided by the designations *slang*, *substandard*, and *nonstandard* in their choice of a word. Those who look at a dictionary as a source of what the language *ought* to be and who believe that language should be a pure body of words revealed from on high, among which workaday forms are out of place, will choose a more traditional reference.

The *Random House Dictionary of the English Language*, 1966, made the best-seller lists for a reason; for it puts a wealth of authoritative reference materials at the user's fingertips. Other recommended desk dictionaries are *Webster's New Collegiate*, *American College Dictionary*, *Webster's New World Dictionary*, and *Funk and Wagnalls' New College Standard Dictionary*. A desk dictionary should be replaced every five years or so with a current edition.

Turning to the dictionary at transcribing time, you want to learn:

1. **The correct spelling of a word—such as** *neophyte*
2. **The correct spelling of an inflectional form—such as the past tense of** *benefit*
3. **The preferred form of variant spellings—such as** *acknowledgment* **or** *acknowledgement*, *judgment* **or** *judgement*
4. **Whether to use one word or two words—such as** *high light* **or** *highlight*
5. **Whether to treat a word as a foreign one and underline it—such as** <u>bon voyage</u> **and** <u>carte blanche</u>
6. **How to divide a word at the end of a line—**committal**, for example**
7. **Whether to use a hyphen with a suffix or prefix, to join the suffix or prefix to the word or to treat it as a separate word=such as** *pre-Socratic* **and** *preview*; *selfsame* **and** *self-control*; *businesslike* **and** *droll-like*

Unfortunately, each of these seven situations is usually indicated in different ways in the entries in different dictionaries. The key to how they are indicated in your dictionary is given in the Explanatory Notes at the front of the dictionary. (See page 180.) (Sometimes this section has a more explicit title, such as "Guide to the Use of the Dictionary.")

When you do locate the explanation, underline it or enclose it in a frame with pencil for easy finding the next time. You thus save considerable time on repeat hunts. One secretary hyphenated numerous words, positive that she was right, because she misinterpreted a mark denoting separation of syllables as a hyphen. She had neither studied nor checked back to the Explanatory Notes.

(Boldface numerals refer to corresponding numbered paragraphs in the Explanatory Notes of Webster's Seventh New Collegiate Dictionary, beginning on page 7a.)

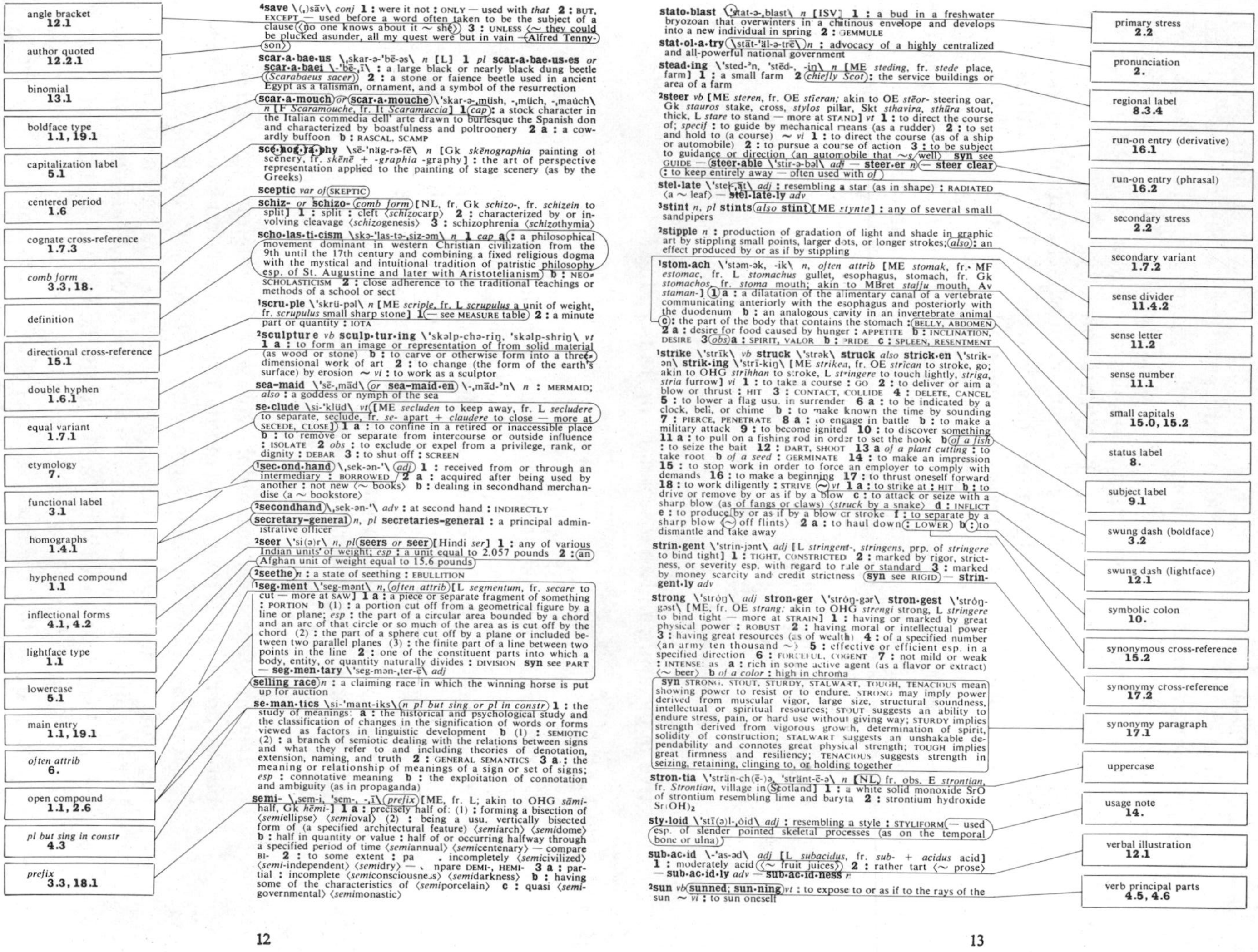

| Label (left column) |
|---|
| angle bracket **12.1** |
| author quoted **12.2.1** |
| binomial **13.1** |
| boldface type **1.1, 19.1** |
| capitalization label **5.1** |
| centered period **1.6** |
| cognate cross-reference **1.7.3** |
| comb form **3.3, 18.** |
| definition |
| directional cross-reference **15.1** |
| double hyphen **1.6.1** |
| equal variant **1.7.1** |
| etymology **7.** |
| functional label **3.1** |
| homographs **1.4.1** |
| hyphened compound **1.1** |
| inflectional forms **4.1, 4.2** |
| lightface type **1.1** |
| lowercase **5.1** |
| main entry **1.1, 19.1** |
| often attrib **6.** |
| open compound **1.1, 2.6** |
| pl but sing in constr **4.3** |
| prefix **3.3, 18.1** |

**⁴save** \(,)sāv\ conj **1** : were it not : ONLY — used with that **2** : BUT, EXCEPT — used before a word often taken to be the equivalent of a clause ⟨no one knows about it ~ she⟩ **3** : UNLESS ⟨~ they could be plucked asunder, all my quest were but in vain —Alfred Tenny-son⟩

**scar·a·bae·us** \,skar-ə-'bē-əs\ n [L] **1** pl **scar·a·bae·us·es** or **scar·a·baei** \-'bē-,ī\ : a large black or nearly black dung beetle (Scarabaeus sacer) **2** : a stone or faience beetle carved in ancient Egypt as a talisman, ornament, and a symbol of the resurrection

**scar·a·mouch** or **scar·a·mouche** \'skar-ə-,müsh, -,müch, -,mäch\ n [F Scaramouche, fr. It Scaramuccia] **1** (cap) : a stock character in the Italian commedia dell' arte drawn to burlesque the Spanish don and characterized by boastfulness and poltroonery **2 a** : a cowardly buffoon **b** : RASCAL, SCAMP

**sce·nog·ra·phy** \sē-'näg-rə-fē\ n [Gk skēnographia painting of scenery, fr. skēnē + -graphia -graphy] : the art of perspective representation applied to the painting of stage scenery (as by the Greeks)

**sceptic** var of SKEPTIC

**schiz-** or **schizo-** (comb form) [NL, fr. Gk schizo-, fr. schizein to split] **1** : split : cleft ⟨schizocarp⟩ **2** : characterized by or involving cleavage ⟨schizogenesis⟩ **3** : schizophrenia ⟨schizothymia⟩

**scho·las·ti·cism** \ska-'las-ta-,siz-am\ n **1** cap **a** : a philosophical movement dominant in western Christian civilization from the 9th until the 17th century and combining a fixed religious dogma with the mystical and intuitional tradition of patristic philosophy esp. of St. Augustine and later with Aristotelianism **b** : NEO-SCHOLASTICISM **2** : close adherence to the traditional teachings or methods of a school or sect

**¹scru·ple** \'skrü-pəl\ n [ME scriple, fr. L scrupulus a unit of weight, fr. scrupulus small sharp stone] **1** (— see MEASURE table) **2** : a minute part or quantity : IOTA

**²sculpture** vb **sculp·tur·ing** \'skəlp-chə-riŋ, 'skəlp-shriŋ\ vt **1 a** : to form an image or representation of from solid material (as wood or stone) **b** : to carve or otherwise form into a three-dimensional work of art **2** : to change (the form of the earth's surface) by erosion ~ vi : to work as a sculptor

**sea-maid** \'sē-,mād\ or **sea-maid·en** \-,mād-'n\ n : MERMAID; also : a goddess or nymph of the sea

**se·clude** \si-'klüd\ vt [ME secluden to keep away, fr. L secludere to separate, seclude, fr. se- apart + claudere to close — more at SECEDE, CLOSE] **1 a** : to confine in a retired or inaccessible place **b** : to remove or separate from intercourse or outside influence **2 obs** : to exclude or expel from a privilege, rank, or dignity : DEBAR **3** : to shut off : SCREEN

**¹sec·ond·hand** \,sek-ən-'\ adj **1** : received from or through an intermediary : BORROWED **2 a** : acquired after being used by another : not new ⟨~ books⟩ **b** : dealing in secondhand merchandise ⟨a ~ bookstore⟩

**²secondhand** \,sek-ən-'\ adv : at second hand : INDIRECTLY

**secretary-general** n, pl **secretaries-general** : a principal administrative officer

**²seer** \'si(ə)r\ n, pl **seers** or **seer** [Hindi ser] **1** : any of various Indian units of weight; esp : a unit equal to 2.057 pounds **2** : (an Afghan unit of weight equal to 15.6 pounds)

**²seethe** n : a state of seething : EBULLITION

**¹seg·ment** \'seg-mant\ n, (often attrib) [L segmentum, fr. secare to cut — more at SAW] **1 a** : a piece or separate fragment of something : PORTION **b** (1) : a portion cut off from a geometrical figure by a line or plane; esp : the part of a circular area bounded by a chord and an arc of that circle or so much of the area as is cut off by the chord (2) : the part of a sphere cut off by a plane or included between two parallel planes (3) : the finite part of a line between two points in the line **2** : one of the constituent parts into which a body, entity, or quantity naturally divides : DIVISION **syn** see PART — **seg·men·ta·ry** \'seg-mən-,ter-ē\ adj

**selling race** n : a claiming race in which the winning horse is put up for auction

**se·man·tics** \si-'mant-iks\ n pl but sing or pl in constr **1** : the study of meanings **a** : the historical and psychological study and the classification of changes in the signification of words or forms viewed as factors in linguistic development **b** (1) : SEMIOTIC (2) : a branch of semiotic dealing with the relations between signs and what they refer to and including theories of denotation, extension, naming, and truth **2** : GENERAL SEMANTICS **3 a** : the meaning or relationship of meanings of a sign or set of signs; esp : connotative meaning **b** : the exploitation of connotation and ambiguity (as in propaganda)

**semi-** \,sem-i, 'sem-,-,ī\ prefix [ME, fr. L; akin to OHG sāmi-, Gk hēmi-] **1 a** : precisely half of: (1) : forming a bisection of ⟨semiellipse⟩ ⟨semioval⟩ (2) : being a usu. vertically bisected form of ⟨a specified architectural feature⟩ ⟨semiarch⟩ ⟨semidome⟩ **b** : half in quantity or value : half of or occurring halfway within a specified period of time ⟨semiannual⟩ ⟨semicentenary⟩ — compare BI- **2** : to some extent : pa . incompletely ⟨semicivilized⟩ ⟨semi-independent⟩ ⟨semidry⟩ —. npare DEMI-, HEMI- **3 a** : partial : incomplete ⟨semiconsciousne.s⟩ ⟨semidarkness⟩ **b** : having some of the characteristics of ⟨semiporcelain⟩ **c** : quasi ⟨semigovernmental⟩ ⟨semimonastic⟩

**stato·blast** \'stat-ə-,blast\ n [ISV] **1** : a bud in a freshwater bryozoan that overwinters in a chitinous envelope and develops into a new individual in spring **2** : GEMMULE

**stat·ol·a·try** \stat-'äl-ə-trē\ n : advocacy of a highly centralized and all-powerful national government

**stead·ing** \'sted-'n\ n [ME steding, fr. stede place, farm] **1** : a small farm **2** (chiefly Scot) : the service buildings or area of a farm

**²steer** vb [ME steren, fr. OE stieran; akin to OE stēor- steering oar, Gk stauros stake, cross, stylos pillar, Skt sthavira, sthūra stout, thick, L stare to stand — more at STAND] vt **1** : to direct the course of; specif : to guide by mechanical means (as a rudder) **2** : to set and hold to (a course) ~ vi **1** : to direct the course (as of a ship or automobile) **2** : to pursue a course of action **3** : to be subject to guidance or direction (an automobile that ~s well) **syn** see GUIDE — **steer·able** \'stir-ə-bəl\ adj — **steer clear** (to keep entirely away — often used with of)

**stel·late** \'stel-,āt\ adj : resembling a star (as in shape) : RADIATED ⟨a ~ leaf⟩ — **stel·late·ly** adv

**³stint** n, pl **stints** (also **stint**) [ME styntte] : any of several small sandpipers

**²stipple** n : production of gradation of light and shade in graphic art by stippling small points, larger dots, or longer strokes ⟨also⟩: an effect produced by or as if by stippling

**¹stom·ach** \'stəm-ak, -ik\ n, often attrib [ME stomak, fr. MF estomac, fr. L stomachus gullet, esophagus, stomach, fr. Gk stomachos, fr. stoma mouth; akin to MBret staffu mouth, Av staman-] **1 a** : a dilatation of the alimentary canal of a vertebrate communicating anteriorly with the esophagus and posteriorly with the duodenum **b** : an analogous cavity in an invertebrate animal **c** : the part of the body that contains the stomach (BELLY, ABDOMEN) **2 a** : desire for food caused by hunger : APPETITE **b** : INCLINATION, DESIRE **3** (obs) **a** : SPIRIT, VALOR **b** : PRIDE **c** : SPLEEN, RESENTMENT

**¹strike** \'strīk\ vb **struck** \'strək\ **struck** also **strick·en** \'strik-ən\ **strik·ing** \'strī-kiŋ\ [ME strikea, fr. OE strican to stroke, go; akin to OHG strīhhan to stroke, L stringere to touch lightly, striga, stria furrow] vt **1** : to take a course : GO **2** : to deliver or aim a blow or thrust : HIT **3** : CONTACT, COLLIDE **4** : DELETE, CANCEL **5** : to lower a flag usu. in surrender **6 a** : to be indicated by a clock, bell, or chime **b** : to make known the time by sounding **7** : PIERCE, PENETRATE **8 a** : to engage in battle **b** : to make a military attack **9** : to become ignited **10** : to discover something **11 a** : to pull on a fishing rod in order to set the hook (of a fish) **b** : to seize the bait **12** : DART, SHOOT **13 a** : of a plant cutting : to take root **b** : of a seed : GERMINATE **14** : to make an impression **15** : to stop work in order to force an employer to comply with demands **16** : to make a beginning **17** : to thrust oneself forward **18** : to work diligently : STRIVE ~ vt **1 a** : to strike at : HIT **b** : to drive or remove by or as if by a blow **c** : to attack or take with a sharp blow (as of fangs or claws) ⟨struck by a snake⟩ **d** : INFLICT **e** : to produce by or as if by a blow or stroke **f** : to separate by a blow ⟨~ off flints⟩ **2 a** : to haul down (LOWER b) **b** : to dismantle and take away

**strin·gent** \'strin-jənt\ adj [L stringent-, stringens, prp. of stringere to bind tight] **1** : TIGHT, CONSTRICTED **2** : marked by rigor, strictness, or severity esp. with regard to rule or standard **3** : marked by money scarcity and credit restrictions ⟨a ~ market⟩ (syn see RIGID) — **strin·gent·ly** adv

**strong** \'strȯŋ\ adj **stron·ger** \'strȯŋ-gər\ **stron·gest** \'strȯŋ-gəst\ [ME, fr. OE strang; akin to OHG strengi strong, L stringere to bind tight — more at STRAIN] **1** : having or marked by great physical power : ROBUST **2** : having moral or intellectual power **3** : having great resources (as of wealth) **4** : of a specified number ⟨an army ten thousand ~⟩ **5** : effective or efficient esp. in a specified direction **6** : FORCEFUL, COGENT **7** : not mild or weak : INTENSE **a** : rich in some active agent (as a flavor or extract) ⟨~ beer⟩ **b** : of a color : high in chroma

(SYN) STRONG, STOUT, STURDY, STALWART, TOUGH, TENACIOUS mean showing power to resist or to endure. STRONG may imply power derived from muscular vigor, large size, structural soundness, intellectual or spiritual resources; STOUT suggests an unshakable ability to endure stress, pain, or hard use without giving way; STURDY implies strength derived from vigorous growth, determination of spirit, solidity of construction; STALWART suggests an unshakable dependability and connotes great physical strength; TOUGH implies great firmness and resiliency; TENACIOUS suggests strength in seizing, retaining, clinging to, or holding together

**stron·tia** \'strän-ch(ē-)ə, 'stränt-ē-ə\ n (NL), fr. obs. E Strontian, fr. Strontian, village in ⟨Scotland⟩ **1** : a white solid monoxide SrO of strontium resembling lime and baryta **2** : strontium hydroxide Sr(OH)₂

**sty·loid** \'stī(ə)l-,ȯid\ adj : resembling a style : STYLIFORM — used esp. of slender pointed skeletal processes (as on the temporal bone or ulna)

**sub·ac·id** \'-'as-əd\ adj [L subacidus, fr. sub- + acidus acid] **1** : moderately acid ⟨~ fruit juices⟩ **2** : rather tart ⟨~ prose⟩ — **sub·ac·id·ly** adv — **sub·ac·id·ness** r

**²sun** vb **sunned**; **sun·ning** vt : to expose to or as if to the rays of the sun ~ vi : to sun oneself

| Label (right column) |
|---|
| primary stress **2.2** |
| pronunciation **2.** |
| regional label **8.3.4** |
| run-on entry (derivative) **16.1** |
| run-on entry (phrasal) **16.2** |
| secondary stress **2.2** |
| secondary variant **1.7.2** |
| sense divider **11.4.2** |
| sense letter **11.2** |
| sense number **11.1** |
| small capitals **15.0, 15.2** |
| status label **8.** |
| subject label **9.1** |
| swung dash (boldface) **3.2** |
| swung dash (lightface) **12.1** |
| symbolic colon **10.** |
| synonymous cross-reference **15.2** |
| synonymy cross-reference **17.2** |
| synonymy paragraph **17.1** |
| uppercase |
| usage note **14.** |
| verbal illustration **12.1** |
| verb principal parts **4.5, 4.6** |

—G. and C. Merriam Company

## Grammar and Usage

English grammar comprises the relatively fixed standards used in communicating at a formal or educated level. Since much of the executive's writing is at a formal level, *the secretary must have a confident knowledge of grammar*. She is expected to know grammatical construction inside out and upside down. She is expected to speak correctly and is depended upon to write correctly.

There are some points of grammar on which authorities do not agree. As a student and as a secretary, you may follow the authority of your choice—an English textbook, one of the accepted handbooks on English grammar, or the Reference Guide at the end of this book. Should your employer be one who concerns himself with the fine points of grammatical construction and who has decided opinions, always defer to his preference. He, too, has the privilege of following his favorite authority.

Good English usage is that which is appropriate to the situation, to the writer, and to the reader. It has no fixed standards but has a propriety. As a part of this chapter read *Usage—Words and Phrases* in the Reference Guide. Were you aware of the differences between grammar and usage and the latitude these differences give to an executive in dictating and to a secretary in transcribing?

## Reference Books

A current and comprehensive secretarial handbook will be of frequent and valuable help to you. At the end of this chapter several preferred ones are listed. You will also find it helpful to take this textbook to the office for reference use, since you are familiar with its format and content and will be able to find reference items quickly.

There are also secretarial manuals for special fields: law, medicine, science and technical work, accounting, and so on. These, too, are listed at the end of the chapter for your aid in case your work involves a specialization.

If your office does not supply you with the minimal desk reference books, do buy your own. Find out the titles of the latest books by watching for announcements that come over your employer's desk or appear in the professional magazines in his or your field. You may also go to the library and look in the current year's edition of *Subject Guide to Books in Print*. Examine the various books available in several different bookshops. Comparison-shop before you make a selection. You can make sure you are getting the latest editions of the books you select by checking the current *Books in Print*, which lists books by title and author.

To control the turn-around time, which most companies try to limit to six hours, the transcriber time-stamps a control slip to show when she obtained the dictation. She stamps the slip again when the transcription is released.

*—IBM Corporation*

## TRANSCRIPTION PROCEDURE

To assure efficient transcription, first make certain that all is in readiness: the typewriter keys clean; the ribbon in good condition; the supply of letterheads, envelopes, and carbon paper adequate and carefully arranged for a flow of work without waste motion; reference books within reach; a pencil for use in editing the notes and a colored pencil for identifying or emphasizing instructions at hand; and erasing and correcting supplies nearby. To hold your notebook in an upright position, attach a large button or tie a large knot at each end of a piece of string so that you can set the opened notebook between the buttons or knots.

If machine dictation is being processed in a Center, the transcription unit is placed on a table adjacent to the MT/ST or MC/ST typewriter, within easy reach when the operator adjusts the controls. Behind the operator are three reference sources for each dictator to whom she is assigned: a name-and-address file of frequent correspondents, a file of technical or unusual words used by the originator, and a file of his preferences as to letter mechanics such as salutations and closing lines.

The kind of executive who requests rough drafts so that he can edit and improve them may also appreciate improvements the secretary makes during transcription.

— *Olivetti Corporation*

## Order of Transcription

Transcribe the rush and top-priority items in the order of their immediacy — as indicated by your notes or the machine index slips. In general, give telegrams first priority. The executive may like to read a telegram before you send it, or he may make you responsible for its accurate transcription. If he does not mention his preference, have him check the telegram. The first time you might casually ask him (with telegram in hand), "Would you like to read this telegram before I send it?" and be guided by his reply in the future. Special-delivery and air-mail letters should be attended to next and, if urgent, taken in immediately for signing and mailing. When time is a factor, give early precedence to providing instructions for subordinates. They can be working while you are busy with other matters.

Store in one regular place any transcription items that must be carried over until the next day.

## Editing and Completing Dictated Items

Before starting to type an item, read intently through it; then edit until it is letter-perfect and ready for smooth, continuous transcription. To read and rework her notes does not indicate a secretary's incompetence but rather her efficiency. As you read through each item:

| Insert punctuation. | Make substitutions for repeated words. |
|---|---|
| Indicate paragraphs. | Rewrite poor sentences. |
| Correct errors in grammar. | Verify facts—prices, names, etc. |
| Correct errors in fact. | Write out difficult spellings. |
| Eliminate redundancies. | Fill blanks left by executive. |
| Clarify ambiguities. | Find and insert needed information. |

The final step before actual transcription of each item is to check any instructions in your notes, on the index slip, or at the beginning of a machine-dictated item as to number of copies, distribution, additions on certain copies, enclosures to be prepared, and under-separate-cover shipments to be initiated.

When you feel that a whole paragraph should be changed, type the dictated text on a piece of paper with your revision underneath it. Take it in to the executive and say something like, "I roughed out a paragraph here. I thought you might want to change it because . . . ." Do not try to sell your revision. If he prefers his own, accept it matter-of-factly.

If the dictated sentence does not make sense to you, it probably will not be clear to the addressee. When in doubt, ASK. If the dictator is in the next room, interrupt him only at a propitious time. If he is in another area, and if your superiors in the Center cannot clear up a transcription problem, telephone him.

## Rough-Draft Transcripts

A *rough draft* is an accurate transcription of notes on inexpensive paper to permit editing and polishing. The executive may request a rough draft in any transcription set-up where there is reason for a carefully written communication — such as an important letter, a report to a superior, a speech, or a paper to be published. Type only one copy unless your employer requests more. Strike over and mark out; in fact, final-draft care on a rough draft is inefficient.

Most transcription in a word processing center is rough draft, not submitted to the dictator unless he requests it. The transcriber then edits the rough draft. Later, as the tape or cassette plays out, she stops the automatic typewriter at the appropriate points and inputs the correction or change.

Single-space a rough draft of a *letter* on letterhead-size paper in exact letter form so that the draft will also serve as a guide to final placement. Type a rough draft of a *report* or *paper* on legal-size substandard paper or on business-size colored sheets, thus getting both attention and reminder value among the other papers on the desk. Use margins of only an inch or so, and double- or triple-space the lines to provide room for editorial changes.

# VALID, SENSIBLE CHANGES

| What the Executive Said: | What the Secretary Typed: |
|---|---|
| Let's meet in Chicago Wednesday morning, January 24. I'll fly in late the night before and back right after the meeting. Please make a reservation for me at the Conrad Hilton for the 24th. | Let's meet in Chicago Wednesday morning, January 24. I'll fly in late the night before and back right after the meeting. Please make a reservation for me at the Conrad Hilton for the 23d. |
| Deciding on the terms of the contracts are the first order of business. | Deciding on the terms of the contracts is the first order of business. |
| The entire order must be received by the 4th. It is entirely possible that we will lose the entire contract unless . . . . | The entire order must be received by the 4th. It is possible that we will lose the contract completely unless . . . . |

# CHANGES MADE BY WHIMS OF TASTE

| What the Executive Said: | What the Secretary Typed: |
|---|---|
| The finalization of the deal will depend on several factors: (1) | Several factors will determine the finalization of arrangements: (1) |
| Kurt Johnson will be in charge of the company display at the International Trade Fair next month. | Mr. Kurt Johnson has been put in charge of the company display at the International Trade Fair next |
| We are sending you a selection of samples of our line. | A selection of samples of our line is on its way to you. |
| The need for selectivity in our next order is apparent in that | Apparently, we need to be selective in our next order because |
| Please enumerate for me the procedures used in completing Project KL-2. | Please give me an enumeration of the procedures used in the completion of Project KL-2. |

The secretary should move slowly in making changes in the dictated material when she transcribes. She should call any inaccuracy to the executive's attention, and she should avoid changes based merely on her whims in taste.

## Secretarial Changes in Dictated Matter

A beginning secretary is concerned about making changes in the executive's dictation. To edit or not to edit depends upon what is to be changed and the executive's attitude about tampering with his communicative endeavors; however, two kinds of changes must always be made:

1. **Always correct a mistake in fact or grammar.** No executive wants a letter to go out with *Monday, July 7,* if it is *Monday, July 8*; nor does he want *the set of illustrations show that*—when it must be *shows that.* Be sure, however, that it is in error before making a change. Avoid the embarrassment of the secretary who changed *criterion is* to *criteria is* because she was not familiar with the singular form and did not check the dictated word in the dictionary.

2. **Always make a change when a conspicuous word or root word is repeated within the same paragraph.** Should the executive dictate *we communicated with him* and then a few sentences later say *as soon as we receive his communication,* change the second clause to *as soon as we hear from him.*

Another secretarial alteration approved by many companies seeking to improve communications is to change sentences in the passive voice to the more dynamic active voice. (See pages 202–203.)

Choice of words or phraseology is often a matter of personal preference; the secretary should change the words only if she is positive the executive approves. Make minor changes at first. Progress to major changes only if he reacts favorably to the minor ones.

## Transcription Techniques

You may not transcribe items in consecutive order. As you complete each item, draw a diagonal line through your shorthand notes. In machine transcription mark the indicator slip according to instructions when each item is finished.

When shorthand transcription is interrupted, insert a conspicuous signal at the cutoff place in your notes, or you may reread the whole page to find your place.

In machine transcription, try for larger and larger bits of dictation at a time, with the ultimate goal of typing without stops to listen for copy.

## Stationery

Give some thought to what is the most efficient arrangement for your stationery so that you can locate the right letterhead quickly.

**Choice of Letterheads.** More than likely you will use a variety of letterheads. There will be at least the regular business one, the interoffice one, and the executive's personal letterhead. If the employer serves as an officer or member of the board of an outside organization, he will probably correspond on that letterhead, too.

**Waste of Stationery.** Letterheads are expensive, and the waste of them is appalling. Office wastebaskets are full of letterheads discarded because of careless work and slovenly corrections. Transcribe carefully and become skillful at correcting. One company reduced the cost and waste of hasty transcribing with a huge sign like that shown at the left.

IT TAKES LESS TIME
TO BE RIGHT
THAN TO REWRITE!

## Number and Kinds of Copies

Some companies require two copies of every letter, one for the individual correspondence file, and another for a bound reading file of all letters mailed each day. In order to save filing space and supplies, other offices have a carbon copy typed on the back of the incoming letter. The majority, however, have one copy made on a second sheet for a correspondence file.

You will be asked to make and furnish certain individuals and departments with carbon copies of every letter you type that relates to subjects of mutual interest. List in your desk manual the persons who should receive copies for each general subject. You can then make the correct number of copies and distribute them properly each time.

## The Matter of Dating

Date every paper. Use the date of transcription if it differs from that of the dictation. It may be necessary to edit the dictation to make it conform, as "your visit *yesterday*," rather than "your visit *this morning*." On casual typewritten matter use the abbreviated form, as *8/28/—*.

## Diacritical Marks

Add any diacritical marks needed (in pencil or ink) after removing the sheet from the typewriter.

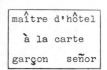

maître d'hôtel
à la carte
garçon    señor

## Letter Placement

If you have difficulty estimating letter length by eye and getting attractive placement on the letterhead, here is a backward approach to setting up placement guides.

Go to the files and remove carbon copies of the executive's letters. Select a short one, a medium one, and a long single-page one. Copy each one on a letterhead in perfect style and attractive placement. Then write each one in shorthand in your notebook. Be guided by a page of your notes taken from dictation to approximate your usual spacing of notes. Remove the pages of notes and attach each set to its own letter. Put them in your desk manual as models for style and placement and as guides with which to measure the length of letters.

## Letter and Envelope Styles

Many companies furnish form and style manuals for use with their correspondence. If you do not receive one, compile your own models from previous correspondence and from style authorities. Model letters and envelopes are shown on pages 736–737 of this book.

A secretary who works with confidential matters should form the habit of casually covering the work on her desk whenever someone approaches. She can do it so unobtrusively that the caller is unaware of her action.

### Keeping It Confidential

In a word processing center one or more operators are cleared for confidential work, and they observe safeguards to insure that nobody else sees the work.

There are always several persons in a large office who are inquisitive as to what is currently happening in the executive offices. Transcripts on the secretaries' desks are often fruitful sources of information: finished letters waiting to be signed, the letter being typed, and carbon copies openly in view. If someone comes to your desk while you are transcribing, roll the letter back into the typewriter, making your action as unobtrusive as possible. Keep the group of transcribed letters covered with a sheet of paper, or in face-down order, or inside a file folder. Carbon copies are just as informative as originals, so treat them with the same respect. Many executives now use an electric wastebasket that shreds paper that might reveal company secrets.

### Proofreading the Transcript

Proofread each page before removing it from the typewriter, using the bail as a line guide and a ruler to follow your notes. Check carefully the address and any numbers or calculations. Watch for omissions or repetitions. Do not rely on your editing of the shorthand notes to preclude errors in grammar or sense; many errors passed over in the editing process stand out clearly in the transcript. As you read, jot down any enclosures mentioned or any special instructions that you could forget.

In a word processing center, the correspondence secretary or word processor proofreads all her work. If she is not yet qualified as a language specialist, the Center coordinator proofreads the material again before returning it to the dictator's administrative secretary, who proofreads a third time, attaches the necessary enclosures, and submits it for signature — a regrettable amount of proofreading, but necessary until time brings more efficient use of power equipment.

## Reference Initials

There are certain situations in which it is poor public relations to indicate that the executive delegated a letter to the secretary or an associate to compose.

Reference initials may be treated in a variety of ways:

1. **If the executive's name is typed in the closing lines, his initials may be omitted and only the transcriber's initials used.**
2. **The reference initials may be put on only carbon copies; the letter recipient is not aware that a *blind* carbon copy was sent.**
3. **Reference initials follow a carefully worked-out pattern whenever others compose letters for the executive's signature.**

## Enclosures

Whenever an enclosure is mentioned in a letter, there is an implied instruction that you are to obtain the enclosure and attach it to the letter before presenting the letter for signature. If possible, collect all enclosures at the same time. Do not take for use as an enclosure either the file copy of a letter or the original copy of a letter received. Instead, prepare a copy on a copying machine; or typewrite a plain, identified copy.

If an enclosure is small enough not to cover the body of the letter, it is attached to the face. If larger, it is put at the back. To enclose a check or currency, pin or staple it to the face of the letter. To enclose coins, tape them to a card and fasten the card to the face of the letter and mark the envelope *Handstamp*. To enclose stamps, paper clip them to a corner of the letter or enclose them in a small cellophane envelope. Place an envelope to be enclosed so that no fold, or a minimum number of folds, is required. Put page-size enclosures behind a letter and paper clip or staple them to it. Some companies, however, disapprove of fastening page-size enclosures to a letter. They believe the folds are sufficient to hold letter-size sheets together and that folding is made more difficult when the enclosures are fastened to the letter.

Should it be necessary to send in a letter for signature without its enclosures, clip a note to it listing the enclosures missing. The note will serve a dual purpose: it will inform the executive that you have not forgotten the items to be enclosed and it will remind you not to mail the letter until the enclosures are at hand.

October 16, 1973

Mr. W. R. Brooks
236 Brockdorf Drive
Cincinnati, OH 45215

Dear Mr. Brooks

I am writing to you to apologize for my tardiness
in transferring the 1,220 shares of Albemarle, Inc.,
stock from the name of the trust to the original
grantor, Mr. Albert R. Edgerton.

The certificate of transfer is enclosed. Please
let us know whenever we can be of help to you.

Sincerely

Bartley R. Johnson
Account Executive

sc

Enclosure

*Enclose certificate of transfer*

If an enclosure will be bulky or difficult for the signer to handle, the secretary attaches a note to the letter as a signal that she is aware of the enclosure and as a reminder to herself at mailing time.

## Separate-Mail Items

Prepare or obtain material to be sent in a package or a mailing envelope and get it ready for mailing. If someone else is responsible, give complete instructions in writing to the person or department, and prepare a typewritten address label. Make a tickler item to check later on the material.

You may enclose a letter with a parcel-post package, seal the package, put the parcel-post postage on it, add on the front a notation *First-Class Letter Enclosed*, and add a first-class stamp to the other postage to cover the letter put inside. This procedure saves sending out a great deal of under-separate-cover mail and keeping track of it by tickler items.

## Envelopes

Before removing a letter from the typewriter, drop its envelope between the letter and the platen. When you remove the letter, the envelope will be positioned for addressing. After addressing the envelope and before removing it from the typewriter, check it against the original source document for accuracy. Then slip the addressed envelope, flap up, over the top of the letter and its enclosures. The accumulated stack of correspondence is easier to handle, and your employer will find it easier to read and sign the letters.

## Identifying Copies

With a letter addressed to several persons but typed in one writing, type all the names in the address position. Treat each copy as an original, individual letter as indicated below.

1. **Put a check mark above or beside the name of the person to whom the copy will be sent.**
2. **Address an envelope for that name; slip the envelope over that copy.**
3. **Present each checked letter and addressed envelope for signing with the rest of the mail.**

When carbon copies of a letter to a single addressee are to be sent to others for their information, type the names or initials of the carbon-copy recipients following the *cc* reference notation. Such copies are handled the same as multiple-addressee letters except that the sender does not sign each one.

When *blind copies* of a letter are to be sent, use the reference notation *bc* in the usual position for noting carbon copy distribution. Type the names or initials of the recipients on all copies *except the original letter* and handle them as if they were regular carbon copies. To reduce handling, use a piece of paper to cover the notation position on the original; type the notation before removing the carbon pack from the typewriter.

## Submitting Correspondence for Signature

As a last-minute touch before sending in the correspondence, erase any fingermarks or smudges. Carefully read all the correspondence written by assistants and have it corrected before approving it for signing. Take a rush letter in as soon as it is ready and mail it immediately after it has been signed. Submit the rest of the correspondence upon its completion. If there has been a great deal of dictation, it may not be possible to get it all transcribed by mail-signing time. In that case, take in all that is finished. Some men like to sign at noon the mail that is ready and sign the rest just before leaving for the day. Learn and follow the executive's preferences. The correct arrangement of transcribed material is the letter and its envelope, extra carbons, and file copy with its notations.

If the executive is at his desk, present the letters face up. If he is away from his desk, turn the top letter face down to keep it clean and to prevent its being read.

Most secretaries arrange to be at the executive's desk when he signs the communications. He often has questions and comments about these items and the work ahead.

A frequent point of irritation between an executive and a transcriber is the difference between what the executive thinks he dictated and what has been transcribed. A young worker on her first job almost had the executive tearing his hair over her "That's-what-you-said" habit. On reading a letter to be signed, he would say, "I didn't say this"; and she, bristling, would answer, "Yes, you did! It's in my notes!"

There is only one gracious secretarial way of handling these differences of opinion as to who is at fault. The secretary should take the blame, when she is at fault and when she is not! It really does not make any difference who made the mistake. The important thing is to go about correcting it at once, cheerfully and willingly.

## Secretarial Signatures

Do develop a good business signature—readable and generous in size. A dainty signature is not fitting for business mail. If you are a man, spell out your first name to indicate that fact. If you are a woman, indicate whether you are *Miss* or *Mrs;* otherwise, correspondents are not sure how to address you and must use the indeterminate but increasingly popular form *Ms.* (Some secretaries prefer this form.) The customary ways for a secretary to sign mail in the executive's absence or at his request are:

| Signature | Explanation |
|---|---|
| Sincerely yours<br>*Jonathan Hais* *ia*<br>President | Sign the executive's name in your own handwriting and add your initials. |
| Sincerely yours<br>*Jonathan Hais*<br>President | Imitate the executive's signature. |
| Very truly yours<br>*Dan Donaldson*<br>Dan Donaldson<br>Secretary to Mr. Hughes | A male secretary should spell out his first name so that the correspondent can address his reply to Mr. _____ . |
| Very truly yours<br>*Connie Armstrong*<br>Miss Connie Armstrong<br>Secretary to Mr. Ford | For a woman, *Miss* or *Mrs.* may be included or omitted in either the typewritten or the longhand name. |
| Very truly yours<br>*(Miss) Connie Armstrong*<br>Connie Armstrong<br>Secretary to Mr. Ford | If the title is included, it is enclosed in parentheses only when used with the signature. *Miss* or *Ms.* is used if no title is provided. If the name is commonly used by men, the *Miss* or *Mrs.* is helpful to the reader, who may need the information for a reply. |

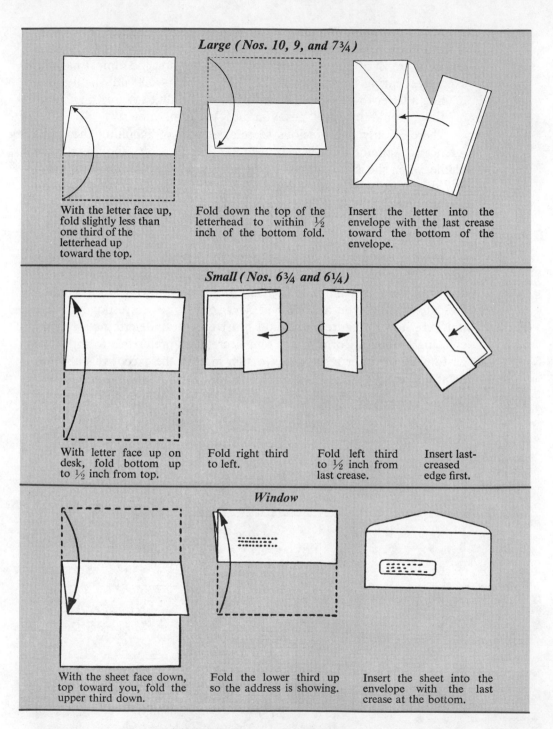

## Large ( Nos. 10, 9, and 7¾ )

With the letter face up, fold slightly less than one third of the letterhead up toward the top.

Fold down the top of the letterhead to within ½ inch of the bottom fold.

Insert the letter into the envelope with the last crease toward the bottom of the envelope.

## Small ( Nos. 6¾ and 6¼ )

With letter face up on desk, fold bottom up to ½ inch from top.

Fold right third to left.

Fold left third to ½ inch from last crease.

Insert last-creased edge first.

## Window

With the sheet face down, top toward you, fold the upper third down.

Fold the lower third up so the address is showing.

Insert the sheet into the envelope with the last crease at the bottom.

Letters are folded in such manner that they can be removed from the envelope and opened easily and quickly in position for reading.

### Readying the Correspondence for Filing

All transcribed correspondence must now be readied for filing. Staple the carbon copy of each reply to the top of the incoming letter it answers. Staple the carbons of letters originating at your desk into sets if the letters are longer than one page. Place pertinent letters in the pending file or make tickler items from the carbon copies, and write each follow-up date on the carbon copy of the letter itself to show that the date has been set and recorded. Add the filing notation before laying the correspondence aside. The matter of designating *where* to file each letter is taken up in Chapters 14 and 15.

In a word processing center the correspondence secretary files tapes with a carbon copy in her desk for one week. Tapes to be used again are coded and placed in the Center's files.

## SENDING THE SIGNED MAIL

In some large offices secretaries are relieved of the final work of sending out correspondence. Mail clerks collect the signed letters and the envelopes and fold, insert, seal, and stamp them. In smaller offices the secretary attends to every step of the routine.

Modern office equipment, such as the folding machine shown on the next page, makes the routine faster and easier, but the secretary should know the most efficient manual procedures as well.

### Folding and Inserting Letters Manually

A letter is ready for mailing when it is signed and all enclosures are assembled. A secretary often folds and inserts the letters while she waits at the executive's desk for him to read and sign the rest of the mail. Every letter should be folded in such a way that it will unfold naturally into reading position. The proper methods are illustrated on page 192.

You can fold and insert a stack of letters very quickly at your own desk by developing a routine based on these steps.

1. Have a cleared space on the desk.
2. Then take a letter from the stack of signed mail; place it before you on the desk and fold it neatly; insert it into the envelope at once.
3. Lay the envelope aside in a stack with the flap out flat (not folded over the envelope) and with the address side downward.

The routine that proves most efficient for you must be worked out. Experiment with some twenty or thirty large and small dummy envelopes and letters until you have developed a routine free of waste motions.

This folding machine can be set to fold sheets automatically at rates up to 18,000 an hour. The machine can also be set to perforate or score the sheets, as well as to fold in standard and non-standard folds.

— *Michael Business Machines Corp.*

### Sealing Envelopes

When all the letters are enclosed, joggle the envelopes into a neat stack. All of the address sides will be down and the flaps will be opened out. Now pick up the stack, grasp the flaps, and bend them back in order to make them flatter. Holding the short edges of the stack of envelopes between the two hands, drop the envelopes off the bottom of the stack one at a time, on to the desk, so that only the gummed part of the flap of each envelope is visible. Then take a moistening tube, and with one swing of the arm start at the bottom and moisten all of the flaps at once. Lay the tube aside on a blotter and start sealing the envelope nearest you by folding over the flap. Continue up the column. As you seal each envelope, pick it up in your left hand and lay it in a stack to the left, flap side up.

In the ceramic wheel type of moistener, a wide wheel passes through a shallow reservoir of water at the bottom. To use this moistener, turn the stack of envelopes over so that the address sides are up. Take the top envelope and, with both hands at the short edges, pull just the gummed part of the flap over the rotating wheel. With the forefingers, fold the moistened flap down over the envelope and lay it aside, address side up.

### Stamping

If the sealed envelopes are to be stamped by hand, first remove all those that require special stamping. Lay the rest of them out in columnar form with the address side up, leaving depth enough for the stamps to be pasted. Take a strip of stamps that are joined with the horizontal edges together, moisten a stamp at a time on a nearby sponge or moistener, and affix it to an envelope, working from the top envelope down. For

The secretary in a small office can process mail conveniently with this desk-model mailing center. It opens incoming mail and weighs, seals, and stamps outgoing mail in one operation. The device uses real stamps and combines a stamp affixer and postage scale with a ball bearing letter opener, letter sealer, and pull-out cash drawer.

— *Data-link Corporation*

strip stamps that are attached at the vertical edges, as rolled stamps are, lay the envelopes across the desk.

Envelopes requiring special stamping should be given individual attention. Those that are sent airmail, special delivery, or to other countries and those that are too heavy for the minimum postage should be handled separately. Write in the stamp position the amount of postage needed. This penciled figure is later covered by the stamps.

Because of the considerable loss incurred from using excess postage and because the recipient has to pay the postage due, every office should have some kind of postal scale. Weigh every piece of mail that may be overweight. "When in doubt, weigh!" Small scales for first-class mail are sensitive to fractions of an ounce. Incidentally, have your scales checked for accuracy periodically.

## Routine Mailings

You may be responsible for regular mailings to a specified list— 40 branch managers every Thursday, for instance. You can save time by following this routine:

1. Type stencils of the addresses, 10 to the page.
2. Run off 52 copies from each stencil, using gummed-back paper.
3. Cut individual labels from each sheet and affix them to the envelopes.

Envelopes for the year's mailings are ready in three operations.

With certain types of power typing equipment you can store addressee material on magnetic tape for a large mailing list if you observe certain limitations. The first name must not exceed six letters, the middle initial cannot be more than one letter, and the last name can consist of no more than 13 letters — for a total of 20 characters in the first line of the address.

# SUGGESTED READINGS

A basic reference that should accompany you to your first position is this textbook, with its valuable reference section. The references below will help the secretary in self-development.

## General Secretarial Manuals

Becker, Esther R., and Evelyn Anders. *The Successful Secretary's Handbook.* New York: Harper & Row, 1971.

Doris, Lillian, and Besse Mae Miller. *Complete Secretary's Handbook*, 3d ed. Englewood Cliffs: Prentice-Hall, Inc., 1970.

Engel, Pauline. *The Executive Secretary's Handbook.* West Nyack: Parker Publishing Co., 1970.

Hutchinson, Lois. *Standard Handbook for Secretaries*, 8th ed. New York: McGraw-Hill Book Co., 1969.

Klein, A. E., Supervisory ed., *The New World Secretarial Handbook.* Cleveland: World Publishing Co., 1968.

Parker Editorial Staff. *Secretary's Desk Book.* West Nyack: Parker Publishing Co., 1970.

Schweiger, Twyla. *Modern Secretary's Complete Guide.* West Nyack: Parker Publishing Co., 1971.

Taintor, Sarah, and Kate M. Monro. *Secretary's Handbook*, 9th ed. New York: Macmillan Co., 1969.

## Technical Secretarial Aids

Adams, Dorothy, and Margaret Kurtz. *The Technical Secretary: Terminology and Transcription.* New York: McGraw-Hill Book Co., Inc., 1968.

Freedman, George. *Handbook for the Technical and Scientific Secretary.* New York: Barnes & Noble, Inc., 1967.

Laird, Eleanor. *Engineering Secretary's Complete Handbook*, 2d ed. Englewood Cliffs: Prentice-Hall, Inc., 1967.

## Medical Secretarial Aids

Agnew, Peter L., and Phillip S. Atkinson. *Medical Office Practice*, a practice set. Cincinnati: South-Western Publishing Co., 1966.

Bredow, Miriam, and M. G. Cooper. *Medical Assistant*, 3d ed. New York: McGraw-Hill Book Co., 1970.

Miller, Besse May. *Medical Secretary's and Assistant's Handbook.* Englewood Cliffs: Prentice-Hall, Inc., 1960.

Root, Kathleen Berger, and Edward E. Byers. *Medical Secretary*, 3d ed. New York: McGraw-Hill Book Co., 1971.

## Legal Secretarial Aids

Blackburn, Norma D. *Legal Secretaryship.* Englewood Cliffs: Prentice-Hall, Inc., 1971.

Leslie, Louis A., and Kenneth B. Coffin. *Handbook for the Legal Secretary,* New York: McGraw-Hill Book Co., Inc., 1969.

Miller, Besse May. *Legal Secretary's Complete Handbook*, 2d ed. Englewood Cliffs: Prentice-Hall, Inc., 1971.

National Association of Legal Secretaries. *Manual for the Legal Secretarial Profession.* St. Paul: West Publishing Co., 1965.

Sletwold, Evangeline F. *Sletwold's Manual of Documents and Forms for the Legal Secretary.* Englewood Cliffs: Prentice-Hall, Inc., 1965.

1. Should a secretary be expected to buy her own reference books?

2. Would any of the three following practices suggested in the chapter be unnecessary time-wasters for an experienced, competent secretary?

   **(a) Prereading and editing notes before transcribing**

   **(b) Making a reading file of the day's transcription**

   **(c) Making rough drafts of items to be corrected as they are played out**

3. Give your opinion of the following secretarial signature:

   *Lee Whitson*

   (Mrs.) Lee Whitson
   Secretary to Mr. Wilbur Metcalf

4. Some executives dictate at the end of an item the number of extra copies wanted. How can the transcriber for such an executive assure herself that she will not find herself short of requested copies? Do you have a suggestion for changing his dictation habits?

5. In what ways do the administrative secretary's and the word processor's responsibilities for a dictated item differ?

6. Do you think that a secretary should be expected to correct and improve the employer's dictation?

7. What implied directions would you follow in transcribing:

   **(a) A proposed contract for the construction of a new plant?**

   **(b) A personal letter to Henry Wilson?**

   **(c) An acceptance of an invitation to represent a college at the inauguration of a new president?**

   **(d) A reply to a letter of complaint about the service given to a customer by a branch office?**

8. Type the first lines of letter addresses to Mark Alan Nolte, using the:

   **(a) Abbreviation of *honorable* before the name**

   **(b) Words *the honorable* before the name**

   **(c) Abbreviation of *esquire* following the name**

   **(d) Roman numeral *II* after the name**

   **(e) Word *professor* or its abbreviation before the name**

   Refer to the Reference Guide to verify or correct your answers.

## PROBLEMS

**1.** On the inside cover of your own collegiate dictionary paste a typewritten listing showing exactly:

(a) *How* the following are shown in the dictionary:

Foreign words
Hyphened words
Inflectional forms

Parts of speech
Preferred spellings
Syllabication

(b) *Where* the following can be found in the dictionary:

Abbreviations
Adjective-and-noun phrases (such as *blind alley*)

Biographical names
Place names
Prepositional phrases (such as *on hand*)
Punctuation
Noun-and-noun phrases (such as *band wagon*)
Rules of grammar

Having such a reference will save you much time in using a dictionary.

■ **2.** Be prepared to set up and demonstrate: (a) speed sealing of envelopes, using as many types of manual moisteners as possible; (b) speed stamping.

■ **3.** Skill in the use of secretarial publications is part of the necessary equipment of the secretary. Prepare in typewritten form answers to the following questions; then correct your answers, using the reference books designated in the chapter and citing your authority.

(a) What are synonyms for *agent, integrity, mediocrity?*

(b) What is the correct salutation for a clergyman?

(c) What are the approved regular and ZIP Code abbreviations for *Oregon? Connecticut? Nebraska?*

(d) Is there a space after the first period in writing *Ph.D.?*

(e) How should the following sentence be punctuated?
    Did he say Are you going

(f) Should *cooperate* and *reread* be hyphenated?

(g) What is the distinction between *majority* and *plurality?*

■ **4.** One of your greatest assets in producing quality transcripts is your ability to proofread accurately. As a pretest of your competency in this area, reproduce this letter and check the errors, retyping a mailable copy if instructed to do so by your instructor. (You may need to refer to the Reference Section.) Can you locate 15 errors?

Johns & Simon
1 Wall Street
New York, NY   10005

Gentlemen

We have no way of determining from your letter of February 10 you needs for additional display equiptment.

We have asked our salesman, Walter Johnson to telephone you for an appointment before Fridays conference opens, and see whether we can assist you in setting up your booth or in supplying other display materials.

You should be warned that a city ordnance prohibits exhibitors from obstructing the street during the hours between ten a.m. and four p.m.; these being the hours of heaviest traffic.

Last year several companies were fined for traffic violations; and we don't want you to meet the same fate.

Yours Cordially

# Chapter 10

## COMPOSING ASSIGNMENTS

During dictation every day you will probably have some letters handed to you with either the oral or written notation, "Tell him . . . ." Your employer may say, "Ask Kansas City why in blazes their request for raw materials isn't in," and expect you to translate this instruction into a courteous request that he will be proud to sign. Or he may be away from the office for a protracted period and you will have to carry on without direct supervision of your letters.

Every day that a letter remains unanswered, the gulf widens between the writer of that letter and the person or company to whom it was addressed. No letter, no matter how ingratiating its tone, can build maximum goodwill if the letter is overdue.

> EVERYONE appreciates promptness. For that reason . . . we're taking the liberty of an informal reply to your letter. It's the only way we can adhere to our rule of pleasing you by answering each day's correspondence the day of its receipt, for volume sometimes inundates us.
>
> You'll understand, we're sure, for you must face the same problem. In the meantime, if you write again on this subject, be sure to return all correspondence.

Recognizing the necessity for promptness, many companies have a policy of answering every day's correspondence the day it arrives, even if the quality of the reply may suffer. For example, a reply to a request for information addressed to the Administrative Management Society was typed on the incoming letter with the notation at the left clipped to the top of the letter. The recipient appreciated the manner of handling chosen. Notice, too, how this procedure reduces the filing volume.

Whether you compose letters for your employer's signature or write them for your own signature (and each day will bring occasions for both), you will want to become "letter perfect." This chapter presents, in capsule form, the principles of composing various kinds of business communications in a tone that produces favorable reader reaction and the desired response.

# THE "HOW TO" OF COMPOSING

Writing ability is nine tenths perspiration and one tenth inspiration. Your employer knows this, so do not worry about the time you must spend in composing a letter; worry about how well the letter represents your employer. If you are unsure of your first draft, read it aloud. A phrase or a word that might antagonize the reader is quickly discernible after an oral reading. When composing a crucial letter, lay your first effort aside for a while; then revise and edit it until it is precise in meaning and diplomatic in tone.

> LETTERS, like people, have personalities which attract or repel.
>
> —*Lord Chesterfield*

Most business letters should be less than a page in length. Remember the famous quotation, "I wrote a long letter because I didn't have time to write a short one." Take time to eliminate unnecessary words, to polish, to "write a short letter."

The best aid to good tone is to visualize the reader as you write. If you know him, visualizing is easy. If you don't, try to picture the kind of person who would hold his position—such as the head of an enterprise, a junior executive, a department head, or a clerical worker. The tone of a letter to a clerk about a routine order could be different from that of a letter to an executive about office systems.

It helps, too, to put yourself in his place. What would be your reader reaction to the facts you are telling him? What would be your reaction to the way you express them? This is writing with the YOU-attitude uppermost in your mind. The techniques of writing for this positive reader response are analyzed in the next pages.

## Tone and Reader Response

Tone is the manner of writing that shows a *certain attitude on the part of the writer*. You want the tone of every letter you compose to result in friendly reader response, one of good feeling toward your office. You don't want any letter of yours to create a feeling of annoyance, frustration, confusion, or short-shrift treatment.

**Writing in Anger.** Never write a letter in anger. To "blow your top" orally is bad enough, but to provide written evidence of lack of composure is a luxury that no business, no person, can afford. Cool off, and then try your hand at composition. (If the employer violates this principle, maybe you, as his administrative assistant, can hold up his letter for a few hours. He knows, too, this rule of thumb; and when he calms down, he will follow it and thank you for making him see its importance without your ever uttering a word of criticism.)

**The Matter of Style.** If you are writing something for your employer to sign, try to make it sound like him, not like yourself. His letters reflect *his* personality, and your goal is to capture his style. Study his dictation and letters in the files; become his *alter ego* in his letter-writing activities, maybe occasionally even surpassing his skill so that you write what he *wishes* he had said.

If you are writing letters to be signed "Secretary to . . . ," you, too, can develop a style compatible with your business personality—a step beyond the effusive communication of the novice.

## Ways of Composing

You can draft a communication in a number of ways. The methods most commonly used are:

1. Compose carefully in longhand. This method is the slowest.
2. Compose in shorthand in the dictation notebook. This method permits you to write as fast as thoughts are formulated, provides opportunity to change and to improve the draft, and furnishes a notebook record. It is the method used by most secretaries who do not have dictating facilities.
3. Compose as you type. This method requires facility of expression and does not allow as easily for changes of mind. It is of help to those who are visual-minded and must see what they write.
4. Compose as you dictate. This method requires the ability to compose orally and takes practice to become skillful.

## Preparing to Write

The effective writer doesn't just sit down and begin to write. He prepares to write. When you are asked to answer a letter, do these things before you put down one word:

1. *Read* the letter you are to answer, in its entirety. If it is a letter originating at your desk, read through the instructions you are to follow. Know what action you want the reader to take, and *plan* how to make it easy for him to take it.
2. *Decide* on the answers to the questions asked and the information necessary to answer them. *Verify* all data you are going to include. *Collect* information needed before you start writing, so that you can give *complete* information.
3. *Make notes* of what you want to say. Organize the points you want to cover into the best sequence for reader understanding and response. Keep these points in plain sight as you compose.

## Sentence Quality

Your writing will improve if you determine to let each sentence express one idea.

**One-Thought Sentences.** Letter-writing experts place much emphasis on simple, clear, direct writing. Such writing is achieved partly by writing sentences of but one thought. The New York Life Insurance Company, which carries on a continuing program to help its executives and secretaries write better letters, stresses this point in succinct sentences:

Put only one idea in each sentence.

Stop at the end of an idea and add a period.

Take a few simple words and arrange them into simple sentences.

Simple sentences are the mainstay of simple writing—a single clause with one subject and one predicate.

A letter of all one-clause sentences could, however, become monotonous, even though it is easy to follow. It could imply low reader intelligence and limited writing ability. Keep the reader in mind as you write.

**Clarity.** Clarity is a goal in writing the first draft, but it is usually achieved by rewriting. Rarely is a new secretary so skillful that she can achieve 100-percent clarity on a first try. For this reason alone it is wise for the secretary to draft an important letter and then edit it for clarity.

One-thought sentences make for clarity. Exact, descriptive words help. Rephrasing confusing statements helps. Leaving nothing to be taken for granted helps. Clarity, then, is often the result of a cleaning-up step to make each sentence crystal clear.

**Conciseness.** A sentence that expresses a thought briefly and clearly is concise, stripped of superfluous words.

Conciseness is a mark of finesse and skill. It is important because it is a saver. It saves time—the writer's, the typist's and the reader's—and it can save paper. To achieve it, state a fact but once. Cut out the superfluous words and phrases in each sentence. Beware, however, of the brusque tone that can be created through *abrupt* conciseness. For instance, "Be here at five," lacks the graciousness of "I'm looking forward to seeing you at five."

In examples that follow, notice where conciseness is an asset and where it is a liability.

**Forceful Sentences.** To make a forceful impression, writers have found that the active rather than the passive voice is helpful. Passive voice tends to weaken a sentence. When *forcefulness* is not a factor, however, and the writer wants to concentrate on the *you* attitude, passive voice may be used to avoid *we* and *I*. A verbal phrase at the beginning of a sentence may weaken the sentence. Substituting strong verbs enables you to write forceful sentences.

|             Less than Forceful             |             Forceful            |
| ------------------------------------------ | ------------------------------- |
| Learning your reaction to our timer will be of great interest to us. | We are interested in your reaction to our timer. |
| Your letter is being forwarded today to Mr. Crane who is in Memphis this week. | We airmailed your letter today to Mr. Crane in Memphis. |

**First Sentences.** The tone of the letter is almost always set by the very first sentence. It is best then to start with thoughts that reflect the *you*-attitude, a genuine interest in the reader. Be gracious and courteous, and use words that are pleasant to the reader, such as those at the right. In the first sentence, establish friendly contact with the reader. The letter-writing situation is similar to a social meeting with a friend. On first meeting him, you do not start by

> Thank you, Miss Adams, for telling us . . . you will be glad to know that . . .
>
> You are right. We did . . .
>
> Thank you, Mr. Graves, for asking us . . .

talking about yourself. You talk about him, or of something of interest to him. Note the letter openings at the right below.

| | |
| --- | --- |
| I searched our records both in this department and in Sales to locate the information requested in your letter of June 6. I find that . . . . | Your request was a real challenge. But I have the information you want. Here it is . . . . |
| We have your letter of April 10 asking for a copy of our new folder. It was mailed to you. | The folder you requested is on its way. . . . |

## Importance of Words

The choice of words is important in all writing. In business letters words are vitally important because of their effect on the reader. Letter-writing authorities have examined the impact of specific words and kinds of words and make the following recommendations.

**Short Conversational Words.** The trend in business letters is toward short words that are used in conversation. They usually create a friendly, personal relationship between the writer and the reader; and they help the writer to relax and write just as naturally as he talks.

If a word is long or erudite, chances are you should change it to a shorter, common one. There are readers, however, who are dignified, scholarly, intellectual. You should not write to them in a folksy tone; perhaps it would be in poor taste. Visualize the reader and use the kind of words suitable to him, to his position, or to his probable education.

In the list that follows, look over the commonly used words in business writing, and their short, conversational counterparts. Would you say that the short ones are always preferable to the long ones? That the long ones are always preferable to the short ones?

| | | | |
|---|---|---|---|
| ameliorate | improve | endeavor | try |
| ascertain | learn | equitable | fair |
| cognizant of | aware of | initiate | begin |
| commitment | pledge, promise | modification | change |
| communication | letter | procure | get |
| consummate | complete | remuneration | pay, salary |
| determine | learn | submitted | sent |
| disseminate | spread | utilization | use |
| effectuate | bring about | verification | proof |

**You, I, and We.** The letter reader, being human, is interested most of all in himself. Each *you* and *your* and each word of direct address he reads is pleasant when it is used in a natural, easy way. If, on the other hand, a sentence has been tortuously twisted to bring in the personal tone, the reader becomes annoyed. It is also wise to avoid beginning the letter, and most paragraphs, with *I*—although using *I* as the first word in a paragraph *can* help the writer achieve simple, direct writing in many situations. Unnatural style might result if you rigidly follow the now outdated rule.

There is a technical point of interest to the secretary in choosing between *I* and *we* in her letters. If a letter is signed THE JONES COMPANY, followed by the writer's signature and title, and *we* is used throughout, the legal responsibility of the writer is reduced. Today the letter writer frequently uses *I*, *my*, *we*, *our*, *me*, and *us* in correspondence, thus showing his personal interest in the reader, as illustrated at the right.

> We are pleased that you wrote us about the error we made in . . .
> You will be pleased to know that we will be able to send you . . .

**Negative Versus Positive Words.** In every kind of letter, words of negative connotation are to be avoided. Negative words can cause the reader's hackles to rise; or, as one correspondent put it, they can turn a letter into a brink-of-war communiqué. Negative words in their kindest usage still have an unpleasant tinge. A starting list of negative-reaction words is given here. You can undoubtedly add others — and should!

| | | | |
|---|---|---|---|
| alibi | cheap | evict | reject |
| allege | claim | failure | scheme |
| biased | complaint | fault | so-called |
| blame | defend | impossible | useless |

Words of positive connotation are tone helpers. Use them whenever possible. Compiling your own reference list of positive-reaction words will help you to become alert to using them. Here are a few.

| | | |
|---|---|---|
| ability | good | please |
| advantage | gratifying | prominent |
| benefit | kind | recommend |
| effective | lasting | responsible |
| fitting | pleasant | thoughtful |

**Phrases or Words?** Business-writing authorities recommend reducing wordy and hackneyed phrases to single-word or short equivalents. Oft-repeated phrases like those below make a letter commonplace. They imply that the writer is too indolent to find short, apt replacements by using a dictionary, thesaurus, or book of synonyms.

| | |
|---|---|
| for the purpose of | for |
| preparatory to | before |
| in order to | to |
| make inquiry regarding | ask about |
| afford an opportunity | allow |
| for the simple reason that | because |
| at the present time | now |
| due to the fact that | because |
| experience indicated that | we learned |
| in a position to | can |
| meets with our approval | we approve |
| this day and age | today |
| until such time as | until |
| reason is because | because |
| in the course of | during |
| by means of | by |

With but one possible exception, limit your use of such phrases because they are trite and tiresome. The possible exception is in a refusal letter, discussed later in the chapter.

**Redundant Expressions.** Avoid redundant expressions, those using two or more words when one will do. Their use indicates that the writer doesn't know better or doesn't care. Build a *Watch List*.

| | |
|---|---|
| baffling and puzzling | reiterate again |
| invisible to the eye | the only other alternative |
| new innovation | joined together |
| matinee performance | small in size |
| one and the same | true facts |

## Length of Letter

*Write a short letter instead of a long one* when you can.  Make a word do the work of a phrase; a phrase, the work of a clause.

The speaker, ~~who was~~ *known for his verbosity,* attracted only a few listeners.
*(Past participial phrase in place of adjective clause)*

~~Anyone who is in Congress~~ *(Any Congressman)* would have studied the problem.
*(Noun replacing pronoun modified by adjective clause)*

~~When you read~~ *(In)* the recommendations, you will find a surprising innovation.
*(Prepositional phrase replacing a clause)*

Mail early ~~so that you may~~ *(to)* be sure of delivery before Christmas.
*(Infinitive replacing a clause)*

He approached his new assignment ~~with a great deal of caution~~ *(cautiously).*
*(Adverb replacing an adverbial phrase)*

## SPECIAL LETTERS AND PUBLICITY

Letters are written for many purposes: to complete records, such as acknowledgments and covering letters; to make simple requests for material or information; to serve as reminders, such as follow-up letters. Because of their simplicity and brevity, these somewhat routine letters are usually the first ones turned over to a new secretary; however, the executive and the administrative assistant should not lose sight of the importance of such letters.

Negative letters such as complaints and refusals, letters of business courtesy such as congratulations and sympathy, and formal acceptances and regrets require great skill and knowledge.  But they, too, are often given to the secretary or administrative assistant to compose; or she drafts them on her own initiative and gives them to the executive for editing.

## Acknowledgments

In general, every letter should be *answered* or *acknowledged* promptly, preferably on the day it is received.  In *answering* a letter, one discusses the points raised.  In *acknowledging* a letter or material, one merely tells of its receipt and adds any other necessary information.  An effective letter of acknowledgment is courteous and complete, and it sounds personal.  Read the following examples as if they were addressed to you. Notice how their tone affects your own reader reaction.

This will acknowledge receipt of the package of printed letterheads and bill for it.  Payment will follow before the tenth of the month.

Thank you for your good work in meeting our deadline for new letterheads.  You will receive our check before the tenth of next month.

We acknowledge receipt
of your letter of
November 19 and thank
you for it.

This is to acknowledge
receipt of your request
of June 6, which will
have Mr. Bender's at-
tention upon his return
to the office.

Thank you for your help-
ful letter of November 19
about Mr. Smith's credit
experience with you.

Mr. Bender is out of
town until next week.
I am sure he will answer
your letter of June 6
shortly after his return.

## Covering Letters

A universal business practice is to inform the recipient when money
or material is sent to him. Such a covering letter tells, with a little dash
of personal interest, what is being sent, why, when, and how.

Under separate cover we
are sending you a sam-
ple case of file
folders. When they have
served your purpose,
will you please return
the case, as they are
difficult to replace.

Today by REA Express
we sent you a full stock
of our samples of file
folders in a convenient
sample case. We are glad
to lend these materials
to you and hope you will
find something that will
exactly fit your needs.

When you are ready to
return the case of sam-
ples, just use the en-
closed address label.

## Requests and Inquiries

Every request or inquiry should be phrased courteously and contain
complete information. The following example is typical:

Will you please send me literature about movable
office partitions. We plan to remodel our
offices soon using movable partitions to provide
greater flexibility in our office layout.

Since our plans are still in the "idea" stage,
please do not send a representative. When we
near the point of decision, however, we shall ask
you to have a representative call.

## Reminder Letters

Every secretary keeps a tickler of items that have to be completed.
Answers awaited, reports due, goods to be received—all are recorded.
When an item is overdue, the secretary sends a reminder. She usually

writes it without being instructed to do so. She uses tactful phrasing, for no one likes to be reminded of his negligence or lack of promptness. Here is an example:

> On June 18 we asked you to send us detailed information about several of your recent quotations. We are eager to receive these details so that we can write directly to the contractors.
>
> Can you possibly send the data by the first of next week? We don't want to impose a hardship upon you, but we do need to complete this transaction soon.

## Negative Letters

Often a letter must be written on an unpleasant subject: *complaints* or *claims*, *refusals*, *mistakes*. These require special care in composing.

**Complaint Letters.** A complaint letter can be such a bitter tirade that it is pushed aside by the recipient with a shrug that some crackpot wrote it, or the complaint can helpfully point out a weakness or an area in which improvement is needed. Usually the person or company does not even know there is a reason for dissatisfaction, so complaint letters are generally appreciated.

You have just received delivery of a repeat order of the executive's personal letterheads, many of which are soiled with greasy fingerprints. As his secretary, you can keep quiet and ignore the poor job, discard the worst ones, and try to clean up the rest with an art gum eraser. Instead, you write a letter of complaint similar to the one given below:

> Mr. Stanley's repeat order of engraved letterheads was received today, but we are sorry that they are not satisfactory. Many have greasy fingerprints on them and are completely unusable.
>
> Can you duplicate the shipment early next week? I hope that the replacements will be as carefully and immaculately engraved as always before.

**Refusal Letters.** Banks often have to reject loans, insurance companies have to refuse life insurance, employers have to turn down applications for positions, individuals must sometimes refuse to grant favors. All such refusals require tactful phrasing.

In a refusal letter, you will have to say *No*, but try to say it nicely. If possible, open with an alternative. If there is none to offer, start with a positive *you*-approach sentence. Try to convince the reader that you do have his interest at heart. Use *I* with the *we's* to indicate that you have a personal concern, as in the following opening paragraph:

```
It was very gracious of you to invite Mr. Howard
and me to show our slides of Alaska at your March
meeting.  Unfortunately, I have loaned them for
two months to a friend in Idaho.  We cannot,
therefore, show them again until late May.  If
you wish to select another date, we shall try
our best to come.
```

If you must apologize, do it in a few simple words—once. "We are sorry that . . . ." "We sincerely regret that . . . ." Nothing is gained by reiterating apologetic phrases.

A *No* letter should be longer than the usual concise letter that communicates facts. A short *No* letter is like a curt dismissal. An executive's wife lost a mink stole. The executive reported the loss to his insurance company, explaining that his wife had no idea when or how the loss occurred. Shown below is the entire letter he received, which, incidentally, cost the agency his future business.

```
As to your wife's mink stole—your floater policy
does not cover "mysterious disappearance," which
this is.  We regret we cannot reimburse you
for its loss.
```

**Mistake Letters.** When you must write a letter about a mistake—one of omission or one of commission—admit that it was your fault. Do not beat about the bush with pompous phrases and long words.

Occasionally and unfortunately, mistake letters have to be written by the secretary. If, for example, she has neglected to put in an enclosure with a letter and discovers the oversight the next day, she drafts and types a note of explanation, attaches the omitted enclosure, and sends the message in with the rest of the day's mail to be signed so that the executive learns about her error. Psychologically, you want to help a person when he openly admits a mistake. Compare your reactions to the following:

| | |
|---|---|
| We find on checking our shipping records that through an unavoidable combination of circumstances we inadvertently delayed shipping the special gear you wanted. It has gone out today by airmail.<br><br>We hope you have not been inconvenienced. | This morning, when we discovered that the special gear you requested had not gone out with yesterday's shipment, we immediately had it packaged and sent to you by airmail.<br><br>We are sorry for the inconvenience and delay. |

## Letters of Business Courtesy

A secretary can, without being told, do much to make the executive appear thoughtful and gracious. She can draft letters for him to his business friends, recognizing their special accomplishments, congratulating them on promotions, extending sympathy when there is need, expressing appreciation for kindnesses to him, and so on.

**Recognition.** The secretary will come to know many of her employer's friends and will recognize their names when she sees them in print. If one of them has an article in a current magazine, she can scan the article and draft a letter complimenting the friend, using the executive's writing style, as in the following example:

```
I have just read your interesting article in the
current issue of Dynamics. The article is in-
formative and shows your skill in organizing
usually confusing ideas into a clear, pro-and-
con presentation that allows valid conclusions
to be drawn. Your readers, I know, will commend
you for your treatment of this complex subject.
```

**Congratulations.** If there is publicity about the promotion or professional achievement of one of his friends, she will draft a letter of congratulations in his writing style, such as:

```
Congratulations, Bob, on your appointment to the
vice-presidency. I should like to add my sin-
cere good wishes to the many others. From our
years of association I know that you will bring
to the position the keen intellect and the fine
personal qualities that the office requires.
```

**Sympathy.** If death or tragedy occurs in the family of one of the executive's friends, the secretary can draft a sympathy note for him to write in longhand. Such notes are sincere, and usually brief. The words *die* and *death* are seldom used in sympathy notes, for they seem to be lacking in consideration. Euphemistic phrases such as *your bereavement, fatal illness, tragic happening,* and *the obituary in the paper* are kinder.

```
I was very sorry to        I cannot find words to
read in this morning's     express my sympathy for
paper of your mother's     yesterday's events.
passing away. My           Please know that my
thoughts are with you.     thoughts are with you.
```

## Formal Acceptances and Regrets

When an invitation is received by letter or in formal style from an organization, the answer should be made by letter or by telephone. A formal invitation, however, must be answered in handwriting in a similarly formal style on folded stationery. When her employer receives a formal invitation, the secretary can help him by drafting his answer in the proper wording and form. Center each line of his answer, and use attractive vertical spacing.

In answering, repeat only the last name (not the initials) of those who extend the invitation. In an acceptance include the day, date, and time as an assurance that they are correctly observed. In a regret it is obviously not necessary to include the time.

| **Formal Acceptance** | **Formal Regret** |
| --- | --- |
| | The reason in Line 3 may be omitted. |
| Mr. David Bender accepts with pleasure Mr. and Mrs. Edwards' kind invitation for dinner on Tuesday, the tenth of May, at seven o'clock. | Mr. David Bender regrets exceedingly that, because of a previous engagement, he is unable to accept Mr. and Mrs. Edwards' kind invitation for dinner on Tuesday, the tenth of May. |

## Guide Letters

The secretary soon discovers that situations repeat themselves and that many of the letters she composes cover the same circumstances. When she finds an especially effective phrase or sentence, she should preserve it for the next letter. For instance, most adjustment letters from an exclusive ladies' specialty shop close with, "We hope that we can serve you more effectively next time." This sentence suggests further association with the customer, stresses the service motive, and makes a positive rather than a negative approach in admitting error. A gem like this is worth using again and again.

For help in developing guide letters that reflect your employer's language and typical reactions, you may compile a guide-letter reference manual. Although the preparation of such a book takes time, it will be one of your office's greatest timesavers.

Here is how to do it:

1. Keep an extra carbon copy of all outgoing letters for a month.

2. Reread them at the end of the month, all in one sitting. As you reread them objectively, you will recognize words, phrases, and ideas that recur.

3. Separate the letters into categories, making extra copies of those that fit several classifications; underline pet phrases and other keys to your employer's ways of handling situations; and set up a file folder for each group. Ask yourself the reasons for variations among the letters in the amount of detail used, degree of cordiality, language, tone, and style.

4. Make an outline of the points usually covered in a letter in each category.

5. Pick out the best opening and closing sentences and the best key points tailored to specific situations.

6. Compile a letter guide, using a loose-leaf notebook. Type the model outline for the category on a heavy sheet to be used as the divider between categories of letters. Type model opening and closing sentences for the category on a separate sheet and model paragraphs on other sheets.

7. Code the index tabs for each section. For instance, "Congratulations" could be C and an especially good paragraph could be C4.

8. When you compose a letter, compare it with the outline to be sure that you have included all necessary parts.

9. Keep a record of the form used for each letter sent so that you will not again send the same letter to a person.

In word processing centers, letters can be built from a variety of standard paragraphs stored on magnetic tape or on mag cards. The operator can personalize such a letter by stopping the automatic typing at an appropriate point and manually typing a personalized insertion or addressing the recipient by name.

## Letters to Non-Americans

Most of our corporations now do business abroad. Letter style for foreign correspondence is much more formal and traditional than for domestic correspondence. Although you will probably not compose many foreign letters (too important!), remember if you do: Choose a formal, more "flowery" style of writing. Always observe the social amenities meticulously. Many a business deal has fallen through because the citizen of another country thought the American "direct" style brash and rude—both in personal contact and in correspondence.

When addressing a letter to a foreign correspondent, copy the address *exactly* as it is given. Here, too, style differs. In European and South American countries the street number *follows* the street name, as Nassaustraat 7, not 7 Nassaustraat. In Japanese addresses there are many other designations in addition to the street name and number with which to locate the prefecture and the section of the city; all are essential.

## News Releases

If, in your company, publicity is not the responsibility of an advertising department or agency, you will at times be asked to compose or type brief articles for publication. They will probably cover such subjects as new products, new personnel, or new services of your company; or they may relate to activities of organizations in which the executive is interested. These brief articles are called *news releases*.

**Content.** News releases are unsolicited and are sent to editors in the hope that they will be used. Editors are flooded with them and only a small percentage are published. A news release, therefore, must be newsworthy in an editor's eyes. It must contain news (not veiled advertising) and be of interest to the readers of the publication.

**Style.** A good news item contains all the facts clearly stated *without* opinion. The italicized words in these expressions are opinions of a writer: *dire* emergency, everyone *should*, *noted* attorney, *signally* honored.

In composing a news release, answer the five W's—*who*, *what*, *when*, *where*, and *why*—plus the *how*. Get the most vital facts into the first sentence, the second most vital into the second, and so on. Such is journalistic style. It is for the convenience of the busy reader and the busy editor. If the release has to be shortened, the editor cuts out sentences beginning with the last one and works upward. This leaves the important news intact without rewriting.

**Typewritten Form.** A company that submits numerous releases uses a special letterhead form such as that shown on page 214. Otherwise, an item is put on a regular letterhead or on an 8½- by 11-inch sheet of good-weight paper (editors dislike handling small, odd-size, or thin onionskin sheets). If a plain sheet is used, the name, address, and telephone number of the company are typed across the top. In every case a person whom the editor can call for additional information should be named. If the news stems from an outside activity of the executive, the secretary uses a plain sheet of paper and gives the executive as the contact. Other practices to observe are given on page 214.

# A B·DICK ®

BURSON-MARSTELLER
PUBLIC RELATIONS

NEW YORK . . . . . . . 866 Third Ave., (10022)
(212) Plaza 2-8610
CHICAGO . . . . . . . . One East Wacker Drive, (60601)
(312  329-9292
LOS ANGELES . . . . . 3600 Wilshire Blvd., (90005)
(213) 386-8776
PITTSBURGH . . . . . One Oliver Plaza, (15222)
(412) 391-5454
WASHINGTON, D.C. 1776 K Street, N.W., (20006)
(202  833-8550

TORONTO · BRUSSELS

LONDON · PARIS

GENEVA · STOCKHOLM

## NEWS FROM A. B. DICK COMPANY

Manufacturer and distributor of copying, duplicating, electronic
printing and display equipment and related products.
5700 West Touhy Avenue, Chicago, Illinois 60648

FOR RELEASE:  AT WILL

CONTACT:  Walter Bilitz-
Chicago
312/329-9292

### NMA SHOW WILL SEE NEW MICROFICHE
### READER/PRINTER FROM A. B. DICK

A new, heavy-duty microfiche reader/printer that produces high-

quality copies and electrostatic offset masters with ease and

economy will be exhibited by A. B. Dick Company at the annual

National Microfilm Association Show in Detroit's Cobo Hall, April

10-13.

The unit, Model 810, is designed for the microfiche user whose

requirements are typically for 30 or more copies per day.  According

---

Give the date that the news may be published—the release date.

Type the release date near the top.  Express it in either of these ways: *FOR IMMEDIATE RELEASE;* or *FOR RELEASE TUESDAY, FEBRUARY 2, 19--.*

Give the article a title if possible.  This gives the editor an idea of the contents at a quick glance.  He will probably not use the title, but it is helpful to him.

Double-space the text.  Leave generous margins for editorial use.  Confine the release to one page, if possible.

Number each page after the first one at the top center.

Type—*more*—at the bottom of all pages but the last one.

Type # # # at the end of the release.

Send an original copy and type "Exclusive to . . ." on the release if it really is exclusive.  A carbon copy indicates you are sending the same release to other publishers, and the editor may be one who uses only what he assumes is an exclusive.

Mail the release direct to the department editor so that it reaches his desk promptly.  Go to the trouble of finding out his name and the correct spelling by telephone or from the listings of the editors in the front part of the publication.

# SUGGESTED READINGS

Aurner, Robert R., and Paul Burtness. *Effective English for Business Communication*, 6th ed. Cincinnati: South-Western Publishing Co., 1970.

Bernstein, Theodore M. *Miss Thistlebottom's Hobgoblins, The Careful Writer's Guide to the Taboos, Bugbears, and Outmoded Rules of English Usage.* New York: Farrar, Straus and Giroux, 1971.

Buckley, Earle A. *How to Write Better Business Letters.* New York: McGraw-Hill Book Co., Inc., 1971.

Eddings, Claire N. *Secretary's Complete Model Letter Handbook.* West Nyack: Parker Publishing Co., 1970.

Krey, Isabel, and Bernadette Metzler. *Effective Writing for Business.* New York: Harcourt, Brace & World, Inc., 1968.

Parkhurst, Charles C. *Business Communication for Better Human Relations.* Englewood Cliffs: Prentice-Hall, Inc., 1971.

## QUESTIONS FOR DISCUSSION

1. If your employer were promoted to a position involving international trade, how could you help him write overseas business letters that build goodwill for your company?

2. What is your reaction to the practice of the Administrative Management Society of typing the reply directly on the letter being answered and attaching the printed notation quoted in the chapter? For what kinds of letters would AMS adopt this practice?

3. The executive says, "Subscribe to *Business Week* for me, please." These are the only details he gives you. How would you handle this task?

4. If your employer asked you to send a "bon voyage" note to the ship on which one of his friends is sailing, how would you get the sailing date, the name of the ship, the city of embarkation, and where mail should be addressed for embarkation delivery?

5. What is your reader response to these first sentences in letters?

    (a) **This is in answer to your letter of July 10. Your ideas . . . .**
    (b) **We cannot send the merchandise you wanted until we receive payment for the last shipment.**
    (c) **Your ball-point pens are lousy, and we are sending back the whole kit and caboodle of them express collect!**
    (d) **It is with extreme pleasure that we send you the catalog you so graciously requested in your welcome letter of May 7.**
    (e) **We want action! In fact, we demand it. You promised delivery of our machine the first of this month. Where is it?**
    (f) **We cannot give you credit for the dress because it had been worn.**

6. The following clauses have the fault of wordiness. Try to reduce them to the most concise phrases possible:

    (a) **It is also of importance to bear in mind the following . . . .**
    (b) **Consideration should be given also to the possibility of . . . .**
    (c) **It is the consensus of opinion of the group that at the present time we should not endeavor to ascertain the reason for the change.**
    (d) **We will all join together to make inquiry about the other possible alternatives.**

7. Your company has just employed a new sales manager. As secretary to the vice-president in charge of marketing, you are gratified when your employer hands you a data sheet from the new employee's personnel file and asks you to rough out a news release to be sent to the three local newspapers about the new appointment. Naturally, you want your first effort to meet with approval. What steps would you take in preparing the release? What matters of style would you follow?

8. Revise the following sentences to make them more euphonious. Then use the Reference Guide to correct your answers.

(a) The letter was too abrupt and tactless.

(b) The job was just a job to her.

With what euphemisms would you replace the italicized words in the following sentences?

(c) Her secretarial work is satisfactory, but she *is irritating* to others.

(d) He *was discharged* last August.

(e) He came from a *poor* neighborhood.

## PROBLEMS

▪ **1.** At a recent secretarial workshop the participants were asked to reduce the text of the following letter to the smallest possible number of words. One secretary got it down to eight words. Can you do as well?

Gentlemen

A copy of your pamphlet of "The Human Side" has been handed to the undersigned and in reading the contents we have been very much impressed and are wondering if this pamphlet can be secured by subscription and if so, what are the charges for such subscription. Might we hear from you in this regard at your earliest convenience.

Yours truly

▪ **2.** Mr. Stanley intercepts the following two letters written by his assistant. He asks you to write acceptable replacements for them. Type each on a half-sheet simulated letterhead.

(a)

Dear Mr. Williams

Replying to your letter of the 21st, we are sorry to advise that we cannot fill your order due to the fact that our factory has been on strike for the past three months.

As soon as possible after work is again resumed, we hope to be able to let you know when we can take care of your valued business.

Be assured that we appreciate your order and will do everything in our power to serve you again just as soon as we get back on our regular schedule.

Yours respectfully

**(b)**

Dear Mr. Rosenthal

We are sending you a copy of our catalog, and it should reach you by about the day after tomorrow. Mr. Henderson, our new salesman in your territory, will visit you this month.  We trust that you will give him orders to fill your requirements.  X—Tray Products can meet your packaging needs for a long time, we are sure.

You failed to place an order with us in December. We want your business.  Please let Mr. Henderson demonstrate to you again the high quality of goods and services offered by our company.

Yours truly

■ **3.** As a secretary you will be expected to decide upon the order in which you will perform the many duties incident to your work. Prepare a form containing the following columnar headings:

| To Do At Once | To Do Soon | To Do When Time Permits |
|---|---|---|

List on the form the following duties in the columns under which the duties would normally fall. Consider as duties "To Do Soon" those which would be done sometime during the day after the "At Once" items were taken care of. (List each duty by number instead of writing it out.)

(1) Transcribe a telegram.

(2) Address notices of a meeting to be held a month from today.

(3) Prepare a manuscript for mailing to a trade magazine.

(4) Write up the minutes of a board meeting held yesterday.

(5) Transcribe a letter telling an applicant that there is no vacancy.

(6) Transfer material to the dead files.

(7) Clean out your own desk.

(8) Make a routine bank deposit.

(9) Deliver pay checks to members of your department.

(10) Type a new organization chart for the department.

(11) Locate and file the telephone numbers of all the members of the Kiwanis Club, of which Mr. Stanley is secretary.

(12) Transcribe a recorded telephone message.

(13) Send a form letter to a group of customers regarding a special price offered them on an overstocked item.

(14) Remind Mr. Stanley of an important appointment.

(15) Prepare Mr. Stanley's income tax payment and transmittal record for the quarter ending tomorrow.

(16) Make a hotel reservation for a trip which begins tomorrow.

(17) Prepare an inventory of office furniture for insurance records.

(18) Type the lease for a property that Mr. Stanley has just rented to a man whose occupancy begins in two weeks.

(19) File all the materials transcribed today.

(20) Confirm a speaking date for Mr. Stanley for a meeting to be held two months from today.

(21) Renew the subscriptions to all the office magazines.

(22) Pay the insurance that is due within a week.

(23) Type an annual report to be presented tomorrow.

(24) Duplicate the agenda for a sales meeting to be held three days hence.

(25) Pick up tickets for Mr. Stanley's trip next week.

(26) Correct the page proof for the revised edition of the office manual.

(27) Post payroll items to the personnel cards of the employees in your department.

(28) Clip an item about an honor conferred on Mr. Stanley and paste it in his scrapbook.

(29) Read an article about the development of a new process by your company.

(30) Complete an evaluation of the work of your assistant for her personnel record.

(31) Transcribe the dictation of answers to a questionnaire from a graduate student writing a thesis about office procedures.

(32) Telephone a client that Mr. Stanley will not be able to see him tomorrow morning.

(33) From the monthly telephone bill, charge the long distance calls to the proper departments.

(34) Develop a list of short forms for words occurring frequently in your dictation.

# Part 3

# CASE PROBLEMS

## 3-1 DELEGATION OF RESPONSIBILITIES

Alice Barry, secretary to Edwin New, president of a large manufacturing company, was overworked. Her employer gave her heavy responsibility and regarded her as his strong right arm, never giving part of his work to others. Alice stayed long after 5 p.m. to finish each day's work and always felt hurried during the day as she tried to meet the expectations of her boss. Also, feeling indispensable, she carried in her mind much of the burden of her job after she finally left for the night.

She decided to discuss the situation with Mr. New, but three weeks passed before she could broach her problem. One evening just before five, she started to describe the problem and ask Mr. New's advice for its solution. After one sentence Mr. New broke in with, "Yes, Alice, I know you have too much to do. Why don't you get some of the girls in the stenographic pool to help you on some of the routine jobs? I certainly don't want you to work so hard that you get ill. Just work things out and anything you do will be fine with me. I want to catch the 5:25, so I'll have to hurry."

With that Mr. New took his briefcase and rushed from the office. In fact, Alice felt that he was somewhat annoyed that she had brought up the problem.

The next morning Alice went to two young stenographers who had impressed her as competent and assigned 50 form letters to be completed by 4 p.m. Rather than being flattered to work directly for the president, they seemed annoyed and indicated that they would do the work — but only as a favor to Alice. At 4:30 they left the letters on her desk. In her usual check she found many errors that made the letters unmailable. She stayed after five to retype the letters, took a pill for her ulcer, and grumbled, "Well, *that* didn't help matters; I had to do the work myself after all. I don't know why these kids that we get in here can't do anything right."

**What principles of supervision had Alice Barry violated?**

**How *could* she have solved her problem?**

## 3-2 ERROR RESPONSIBILITY

As supervisor of a ten-employee office, Marion Winton always prided herself on the principle that one can delegate authority but not responsibility. She checked all work meticulously, devoting so much time to rechecking the work of others that she was often forced to work overtime.

When she proofread a table prepared by May Botsford, an experienced worker, she found an incorrect total. She called May to her desk and said, "May, look at this error. I just can't understand how you could submit work like this, especially when I saw you and Helen proofread it together."

May replied, "Well, Miss Winton, I am going to tell you how such a thing could happen. I have decided that I am going to transfer out of this department. Maybe what I have to say will help those foolish enough to stay on and try to please you. It's no fun working for you. You don't trust anybody to do anything. You are always snooping around to find our errors. No wonder we get careless. We don't need to find our mistakes; you'll find them anyway. I'm interested in getting promoted myself and have been taking a course in supervision in night school. I've learned that a worker should be given 'areas of freedom' as long as he gets the job done right. Some freedom with you!"

Marion said, "I am sorry that you feel this way. Just make the correction so that I can get it to Mr. Smith by noon. Suppose you see me tomorrow at ten to discuss this situation further. Let me think about it until then."

After her initial resentment at the criticism and lack of respect, Marion asked herself, "Could I or should I make the girls responsible for their own errors? How can I make untrustworthy people trustworthy? Do 'areas of freedom' refer to the way the work is performed or to the final result?"

**How would you advise Marion if she asked you for help?**

## 3-3  YOU CAN'T TRUST ANYBODY AROUND HERE

As state president of the National Secretaries Association (International), Helen Sillman took Friday off for the state convention. She left Mary Malone in charge of her desk, with the responsibility for mailing 200 notices for a monthly dinner meeting of the American Records Management Association, of which her employer, Mr. Knowland, was chapter secretary.

Returning to the office Monday morning, she faced a barrage of telephone calls asking where the meeting was to be held. Although the notice said the Park Avenue Restaurant, an announcement had been made at last month's meeting that a new meeting place was to be selected.

Helen distinctly remembered having shown Mary last month's notice and also having told Mary that the current dinner would be held at the Colony Inn. Helen herself sent a new mailing of the notice, Mr. Knowland was furious, and Mary was in tears. When the furor subsided, Helen announced that she would never again take time off from work for a professional meeting.

**What principle of supervision is illustrated in this case? How could Helen have improved her supervisory skills? Could Mary have improved her efficiency?**

# Secretarial Use of Transmittal Services

*Part* **4**

*he technological progress being made in the transmission of products and information is phenomenal. The postal service is being completely reorganized. Not only can the voice be transmitted more clearly and swiftly all the time; but pictures, drawings, and volumes of word and number data can be sent at dizzying speed—often without the sender's leaving his office. New uses for telegraphic equipment multiply the opportunities for communicating business information. Vast networks involving the interchange of data are developing so fast that it seems impossible to keep up with developments. Yet—if her company is to get the optimum return on its communications dollars—the secretary-administrative assistant must be familiar with the multiplicity of services available.*

# Chapter 11

## POSTAL AND SHIPPING SERVICES

It is estimated that by 1980 about 110 billion pieces of mail will be processed every year. Approximately 75 percent of this volume is business mail, for which, naturally, business wants to keep costs as low as possible. Another heavy business expense involves costs of shipping goods. Postage and shipping charges are big items in any firm's budget — even in a small company.

The secretary, closely associated with preparing and sending business mail, can greatly reduce postage expense by learning the relative costs of the different mail classifications and services. But there can be other considerations even more important than economy. If she is familiar with the wide variety of services offered by the post office, REA Express, and other shipping agencies, she can choose the type of service that best fits each situation and handle unusual postal and shipping problems as they arise.

## REORGANIZATION OF THE POSTAL SERVICE

Because of the tremendous growth in demand for postal services along with deterioration of transportation services, the post office has experienced severe difficulties. A new, less politically oriented postal system was needed, one that could adopt modern management techniques and create modern facilities.

### United States Postal Service Corporation

In 1971 the cabinet-level position of Postmaster General was eliminated and postal service for the United States was transferred to the United States Postal Service Corporation, a government-owned corporation similar to the Tennessee Valley Authority. The corporation is under the control of a President-appointed board of directors, with a separate rate commission that recommends to Congress the rates to be charged. Congress reserves ultimate control of rates and classifications of mail. The Postmaster General is elected by the board of directors.

## Innovations

The country is divided into five administrative regions. The position of local postmaster is no longer a patronage plum. The new corporation aims to become a self-sustaining service eventually. Bonds are being floated to build modern mail-processing facilities near centers of high population density.

During the transition period, changes in rates and mail classifications may occur as scientific cost studies are completed. Initial rate changes are being phased in over a period of several years to ease the effects of making all changes immediately. The secretary will need to be especially alert to changes in current rates and services during this time.

Considerable experimentation with new equipment, new services, and new methods is going on in selected post offices before changes are adopted nationally.

## Sources of Information

A booklet, *Instructions to Mailers*, contains most of the information from Chapter 1 of the larger and more expensive *Postal Service Manual*, and is the secretary's best postal reference. It is available from the Superintendent of Documents, Government Printing Office, Washington, DC 20402, for $3.

The United States Postal Service also publishes excerpts from the *Postal Service Manual* and other pamphlets as needed, such as:

*What Mailers Should Do to Get the Best Service* (No. 153)
*Domestic Postage Rates, Fees, Information* (Notice 59)
*International Postage Rates and Fees* (No. 51)
*How to Prepare Second- and Third-Class Mailings* (No. 21)
*How to Address Mail* (No. 28)
*How to Pack and Wrap Parcels for Mailing* (No. 2)
*Refunds of Postage and Special Service Fees* (No. 5)
*Express Mail Service* (No. 163)
*ZIP Code — Abbreviations for Use with ZIP Code* (No. 59)

Post offices in locations large enough to justify the job title have *customer service representatives* who go into locations of large mailers and analyze their mailing problems. The service representatives show films designed to improve mailing practices and hold employee seminars (including secretaries) to help implement the results of their analyses.

Changes in rates and services are always widely publicized in the press, which the secretary should scan for relevant items.

The Alphabetical telephone directory lists telephone numbers to call for various kinds of postal information. (Look under *United States Government* and then *Post Offices*.)

# DOMESTIC MAIL CLASSIFICATIONS

*Domestic mail matter* includes mail transmitted within, among, and between the United States and its territories and possessions; Army-Air Force (APO) and Navy (FPO) post offices; and mail for delivery to the United Nations in New York City.

The Postal Service divides mailable matter into the following general classes: *first class, second class, controlled circulation publications, third class, fourth class, airmail, official and free mail, mail for the blind,* and *mixed classes.* (Refer to the Postal Guide in Part 10 of this book for detailed descriptions of classes, services, rates, and fees.)

## First-Class Mail

Among the kinds of mail sent by *first class* are: letters in any form (typewritten, handwritten, carbon copy, or photocopy); post cards; business reply mail such as that shown at the bottom of this page; and matter partly in written form, such as bills and checks. Pieces less than 3 inches wide or $4\frac{1}{4}$ inches long are nonmailable. Airmail up to 8 ounces (sealed or unsealed) is called first-class airmail matter. For methods of sending first-class mail in combination with a larger envelope or parcel of mail of another class, see pages 229–230.

Much first-class mail that was formerly transported by rail is now carried by plane. It is not, however, guaranteed space on the plane as is airmail but goes on a space-available basis.

## Second-Class Mail

*Second-class mail* includes printed newspapers and periodicals. Publishers and news agencies are granted second-class rates if they file the proper forms obtained from their local postmasters, pay the required fees, and comply with the regulations. Such mail must bear notice of second-class entry and be mailed in bulk lots periodically.

The postage for such a business reply envelope is guaranteed by the addressee and is paid when the envelope is returned to him. No postage is paid for envelopes not returned.

No Postage Stamp Necessary If Mailed in the United States

Postage Will Be Paid by Addressee

**BUSINESS REPLY MAIL**
First Class Permit No. 53, Minneapolis, Minnesota

**HONEYWELL**
**2701 Fourth Avenue South**
**Minneapolis, Minnesota 55408**

Newspapers and periodicals that are mailed unsealed by the public are sent at a "transient rate." (See Second-Class Mail, Postal Guide, Part 10 of this book.)

### Controlled Circulation Publications

Publications of 24 or more pages circulated free, or mainly free, come under a special class called *Controlled Circulation Publications*. Since only a limited number of secretaries will work with this class of mail, it is recommended that when information regarding such mailings is needed, the secretary study *Instructions to Mailers*.

### Third-Class Mail

*Third-class mail* is used for matter that cannot be classified as first- or second-class mail and that weighs up to 16 ounces. The same matter in parcels of 16 ounces and over is considered fourth-class mail.

All sealed pieces mailed at the third-class postage rates must be marked THIRD CLASS (or BULK RATE if bulk rate has been authorized). This notation may be printed anywhere on the envelope (front or back), except in the permit imprint or meter stamp. Third-class mail which is unsealed does not require any endorsement.

Mail that may be sent third class includes merchandise, printed matter, keys, and so on. Special rates also apply to books, manuscripts, music, sound recordings, films, and the like.

### Fourth-Class Mail

The more common term for *fourth-class service* is *parcel post*. It includes all mailable matter not in the first, second, or third class and with weight of 16 ounces or over.

Parcel-post rates are scaled according to the weight of the parcel and the distance it is being transported. Every local post office charts the country into eight zones. Zone charts showing the parcel post zone of any domestic post office in relation to the sender's post office may be obtained free from the sender's post office.

There are both weight and size limits for fourth-class packages according to delivery zones. Size limits are given in total inches of length and girth combined, as shown in the illustration at the top of the next page. There are also special rates according to weight and zone for catalogs and similar printed advertising matter weighing 16 ounces or over. Refer to the Postal Guide in Part 10 for fourth-class zone rates. Size limits vary by class of post office at the destination. Consult your local postmaster.

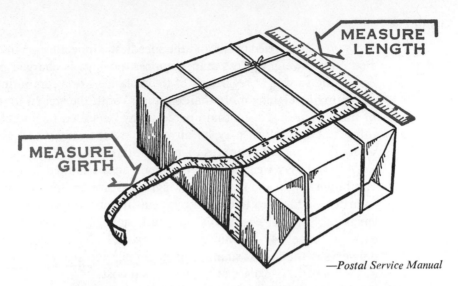

—*Postal Service Manual*

To determine the size of a parcel, measure the longest side to get the length; measure the distance around the parcel at its thickest part to get the girth; and add the two figures together. For example, a parcel 10 inches long, 8 inches wide, and 4½ inches high measures 35 inches in length and girth combined (length, 10 inches; girth, 25 inches: 4½ inches + 8 inches + 4½ inches + 8 inches). A free pamphlet on "Packaging and Wrapping Parcels for Mailing" may be obtained from your post office.

Third- or fourth-class packages may be sent unsealed or sealed. Sealing implies that the sender consents to inspection of the contents. This silent assent replaces the old written endorsement: MAY BE OPENED FOR POSTAL INSPECTION. A sealed package is treated as parcel post by the postal sorters no matter what rate of postage has been paid unless the package is conspicuously marked FIRST CLASS.

Certain kinds of packaged mail are given special low rates as follows:

**Special Fourth-Class Mail.** Books without advertising that contain at least 22 printed pages are eligible for a preferential rate. (See *Special Fourth-Class Mail*, in the Postal Guide in Part 10.)

**Library Materials.** The *Library Rate* applies to materials sent to or from libraries, schools, and certain nonprofit organizations. The secretary is concerned with this rate when, as a borrower, reader, or member, she is returning qualifying material to any of the organizations that are permitted to use this rate. The rate is the same to all zones and applies to books, periodicals, theses, microfilms, music, sound recordings, films, and other library materials. (See the Postal Guide in Part 10.) The package may be sealed, but it must be marked LIBRARY RATE.

It is recommended that the sender consult the local postmaster before mailing special fourth-class mail or library materials.

## Airmail

*Airmail* is carried by air and the speediest connecting ground carriers. For matter weighing less than 8 ounces, postage is charged on airmail according to weight regardless of the distance. For computing postage for airmail weighing more than 8 ounces, both the weight and the zone of address are used. Airmail parcels may be sealed or unsealed. Anything not hazardous may be airmailed except that which is liable to damage at low temperatures or high altitudes.

Airmail may weigh up to 70 pounds and is limited to 100 inches in combined length and girth. The weight and size limitations do not apply to articles addressed to certain overseas military post offices. Generally speaking, it is less costly to send small packages by airmail than by air express (page 247) or air freight (page 249). Airmail, plus special delivery, is the fastest small-package air service available. Letters may be enclosed in packages at no additional cost.

Special mailboxes are placed outside post offices in most cities for the deposit of airmail and special-delivery mail. The post office has as its goal next-day delivery of such mail if the destination is no more than 600 miles distant. In fact, it is expected that next-day delivery will be possible for at least 95 percent of all airmail.

The secretary in a city with limited air service should get from the postmaster a schedule showing airmail dispatch schedules for the cities to which she frequently sends airmail.

Envelopes banded in red, white, and blue are best; if you must use a plain envelope, place airmail stickers around *both edges* to identify it as airmail even in a stack of mail.

Fourth-class mail sent by air is called *priority mail* and requires higher postage rates than regular parcel post.

## Official and Free Mail

Federal government offices and personnel send out official mail without affixing postage. There are two kinds of official mail: franked mail and penalty mail.

A *franked* piece of mail must have a real or facsimile signature of the sender in place of the stamp and the words PUBLIC DOCUMENT— FREE on the address side. Only a few persons are authorized to use the frank, such as the Vice President of the United States, members and members-elect of Congress, Resident Commissioners, the Secretary of the Senate, and the Sergeant of Arms of the Senate.

*Penalty mail* is used for official government correspondence. It travels in penalty envelopes or under penalty labels.

Notice the difference between an official franked envelope and a penalty envelope. A franked envelope must show a real or facsimile signature and carry the words OFFICIAL BUSINESS. A penalty envelope must carry the penalty warning and the words OFFICIAL BUSINESS under a return address.

Free mail—mail sent without postage by the general public—is limited to a few items such as matter addressed to the Register of Copyrights, census mail, immigration and naturalization service mail, and absentee ballot envelopes from members of the Armed Forces. For further details, see *Instructions to Mailers.*

## Mixed Classes of Mail

Sometimes it is expedient and reflects better judgment to send two pieces of mail of different classes together as a single mailing to assure their arrival at the same time. A first-class letter may be attached to the address side of a larger envelope or parcel of mail of another class; or it may be enclosed in the larger envelope or parcel. Postage is paid on the two parts at their respective rates. When a first-class letter is *attached*, the correct postage is affixed to each part separately. When a first-class letter is *enclosed*, the postage is computed on each part separately but is affixed together on the outside of the package. The words FIRST-CLASS MAIL ENCLOSED must be written, typed, or stamped below the postage and above the address. A piece of combination or mixed-class mail is handled and transported by the post office as mail

To enclose a letter, invoice, or other first-class mail inside a third- or fourth-class sealed or tied package, mark the outside of the package FIRST-CLASS MAIL ENCLOSED and add the extra first-class postage required to the regular postage. Place the words RETURN POSTAGE GUARANTEED below the return address. An invoice, instructions, order form, reply envelope, catalog, or other *printed* matter (not typewritten or handwritten) may be enclosed in a package without additional postage.

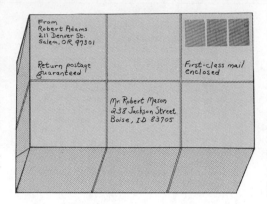

matter of the class in which the bulky portion falls—not as first class. (If airmail service is desired, airmail rates must be paid on both parts.)

A piece of mail of mixed classes may be sent special delivery or special handling by paying one additional fee. It may also be insured or sent *COD*.

## Mail for the Blind

Some kinds of mail to and from the blind may be mailed free; other kinds may be mailed at nominal rates. If, as a secretary, your work involves sending letters and parcels to or from the blind, you will want to study *Instructions to Mailers*.

## SPECIAL MAIL SERVICES

In addition to transmitting mail, the post office provides many special services.

## Registered and Insured Mail

A piece of important or valuable mail can be registered or insured, depending on its nature.

**Registering Mail.** Only first-class mail can be registered. The full amount of the value must be declared on a piece of mail being registered because the fee charged is based on the full value. There are two sets of fees. The one used depends upon whether the sender has commercial insurance covering the matter being mailed. The rates are slightly lower for values above $1,000 if the sender has such insurance. When the maximum liability of the post office is less than the value of the shipment, special private insurance is usually taken out by the sender for the specific shipment during transit.

Each piece of mail to be registered must be tightly sealed along all edges (transparent tape cannot be used) and bear the complete addresses of both the sender and addressee. The sender takes it to the registry window where the postal clerk computes the fee.

The sender of the registered mail may instruct the post office to change the address should it be necessary. For example, if you sent a registered letter to a company salesman in St. Louis and then learned that he moved on to Kansas City, you should telephone the St. Louis post office and request that the address be changed.

**Insuring Mail.** A piece of third- or fourth-class mail, or airmail containing third- or fourth-class matter, may be insured up to $200. The package is taken to the post office window where the clerk makes out a receipt for it, stamps the package INSURED, and puts on it the receipt number, if any. An unnumbered receipt is given if the package is insured for $15 or less. After placing the regular and insured postage on the package, the clerk gives the receipt to the sender for filing. If the package is lost or damaged, the post office reimburses the sender according to the amount of the fee. The insurance limits and corresponding fees are given in the Postal Guide in Part 10 of this book.

If a business frequently sends several insured packages at one time, it may be more convenient to use a mailing book rather than filing a separate receipt for each package. Mailing books will be issued by the post office on request that provide pages for entering the description of parcels insured. The sheets of this book are officially endorsed at the time of mailing and become the sender's receipts.

**Return Receipts and Restricted Delivery.** The sender is always furnished with a receipt showing that the post office accepted the piece of insured or registered mail for transmittal and delivery. However, the sender often wants legal evidence that the piece of mail was also actually received by the addressee. For an added fee the sender may obtain a signed receipt, commonly called a *return receipt*, on any piece of certified or registered mail or on any piece of mail insured for more than $15. This service is helpful when the address used is one of several years' duration or when there is reason to believe that the addressee may have moved. The fees for return-receipt and restricted delivery services are given in the Postal Guide in Part 10.

For an added fee delivery may be *restricted to the addressee* only if the piece of mail is registered, certified, or insured for more than $15.

When the sender wants a return receipt, he fills in the number of the receipt and his name and address on a postal-card form supplied by the

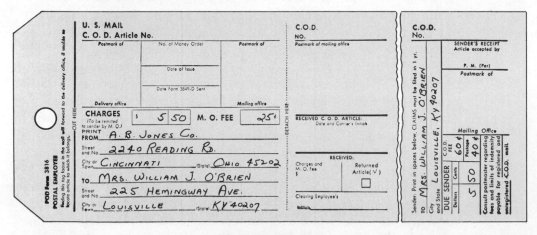

Ungummed Side — Gummed Side

post office and illustrated above and writes RETURN RECEIPT REQUESTED on the front of the mail.

This card is pasted (face down) along its two gummed edges to the back of the envelope or package. At delivery the postman removes the card, obtains the addressee's signature on the ungummed (reverse) side, fills in the information required, and mails the card to the sender.

## COD Service

Merchandise may be sent to a purchaser *COD*—that is, *collect on delivery*—if the shipment is based on a bona fide order or on an agreement made with the addressee by the mailer. The sender prepays the postage on the shipment and the COD fees, but they may be included in the amount to be collected if agreeable to the addressee. Otherwise, the addressee pays the amount due on the merchandise, plus the fee for the money order to return the money collected to the sender. The maximum amount collectible on one parcel is $200. Information on mailing COD parcels is available from the local postmaster. Three sections of the form are shown below.

Sender's COD Forms

## Certificates of Mailing

For 5 cents a sender may obtain a very simple proof of having taken a piece of mail to the post office for dispatching. It may be used for any kind of mail. The sender fills in the information required on a certificate blank and pastes on it a 5-cent stamp. This certificate he hands to the postal clerk with the piece of mail. The clerk cancels the stamp and hands it back to the sender as evidence that the piece of mail was received at the post office.

POST OFFICE DEPARTMENT
**CERTIFICATE OF MAILING**
Received From:
Miss Mary Elaine Owen
530 Elberon Avenue
Cincinnati, Ohio 45205
One piece of ordinary mail addressed to:
Mrs. D. R. Watson
2249 Westchester
Cleveland, Ohio 44122
MAY BE USED FOR DOMESTIC AND INTERNATIONAL MAIL, DOES NOT PROVIDE FOR INSURANCE. — POSTMASTER
POD FORM 3817
NOV. 1963          ☆ GPO 1963 : OF—712-835

Certificate of Mailing

This is an economical service for one who is mailing something that is of value to the addressee but who has no obligation or responsibility to pay the extra expense of having it insured, registered, or certified. It also furnishes a sender with an inexpensive proof of having mailed tax returns.

## Special Delivery and Special Handling

The delivery of a piece of mail may be expedited by use of either special-delivery or special-handling service.

**Special Delivery.** *Special-delivery service* provides the fastest handling—from mailer to addressee—for all classes of mail. Mail must be marked SPECIAL DELIVERY above the address. Immediate delivery is by messenger during prescribed hours to points within certain limits of any post office or delivery station. Do not send special-delivery mail to post-office-box addresses, military installations (APO, FPO), or other places where mail delivery will not be expedited after arrival.

**Special Handling.** Most people are not aware of *special handling* for fourth-class parcels—a service that is less expensive than special delivery. It provides the most expeditious handling and ground transportation practicable. Parcels move with first class, but they do not receive special delivery at the destination post office. When airmail is used, special handling is unnecessary because airmail also receives priority ground handling.

Since all special delivery mail (including packages) is handled and transported in the same manner as first-class mail, it is not necessary to include SPECIAL HANDLING on a package being sent *special delivery*.

## Certified Mail

Airmail or first-class mail that has no real value (such as a letter, bill, or nonnegotiable bond) may, for a 30-cent fee, be certified. The sender is issued a *Receipt for Certified Mail*, like that illustrated above. If at any time within six months after mailing he needs proof that the letter was delivered, he may use the receipt to obtain a delivery report.

Certified mail has the following advantages: (1) It provides the sender with a means of checking on the delivery of the letter. (2) It provides official evidence of mailing if a postmarked receipt is obtained. (3) It gives the letter the appearance of importance and urgency, and for that reason it is frequently used by collection agencies.

## Insufficient Postage

Mail received at the post office without sufficient postage will be forwarded to the addressee and postage collected at the time of delivery. It is a breach of business etiquette, however, to send mail without sufficient postage, thus making the recipient pay for your negligence.

## Slugs for Hand Stamping

Bulky mail, called *slugs*, should be marked *Hand Stamp* in large red letters on both front and back of the envelope. Unmarked slugs are often ruined during mail processing; and, unless clearly marked for separation from other mail, slugs may be routinely placed in the canceling machine and cause serious damage to it.

## Stamps and Stamped Envelopes

Ordinary postage stamps are available in sheet, coil, or booklet form. Everyone is familiar with the 100-stamp sheet from which the postal clerk sells stamps at his window and the little booklets of bound stamps for home use. Coiled stamps are often used in business because they can be quickly affixed to envelopes and packages and because they are less likely to be lost or mutilated than are individual stamps. They are coiled either sidewise or endwise. Postage stamps can be exchanged at full value if stamps of the wrong denomination were purchased or if damaged stamps were received.

**Precanceled Stamps and Envelopes.** Precanceled stamps and pre-canceled stamped envelopes may be used only by those persons or companies who have been issued a permit to use them, and then only on matter presented at the post office where the precanceled stamps or envelopes were purchased. Their advantage is the saving of canceling time at the post office.

**Stamped Envelopes and Cards.** Stamped envelopes in various sizes, kinds, and denominations may be purchased at the post office individually or in quantity lots. For a nominal amount the post office will have the sender's return request and name and address imprinted on them when the envelopes are ordered in quantity lots.

First-class postal cards are available in single or double form, the latter kind being used when a reply is desired on the attached card. Airmail postal cards are available only in single form. To facilitate in-company printing, government postal cards are available in sheets of 40.

Unserviceable and spoiled stamped envelopes and cards (if uncanceled) may be exchanged. Such envelopes are exchangeable at postage value; postal cards are exchangeable at 85 percent of their value. Such exchanges are made in stamps, stamped envelopes, or postal cards.

## Metered Postage

One of the quickest and most efficient ways of affixing postage to mail of any class is by means of a *postage meter* machine. The postage meter prints on each piece of mail the postmark and the proper amount of postage. Consequently, metered mail need not be canceled or post-marked when it reaches the post office. As a result, it often catches earlier trains or planes than does other mail.

The meter machine may be fully automatic, not only printing the postage, postmark, and date of mailing, but also feeding, sealing, and stacking the meter-stamped envelopes. The imprint is usually red and may carry a line or two of advertising. Some models also print the postage on gummed tape which can be pasted onto packages. The meter registers the amount of postage used on each piece of mail, the amount of postage remaining in the meter, and the number of pieces that have passed through the machine.

This desk-model postage meter has a push-button keyboard that closely resembles the new telephone keyboards. After the operator enters the correct amount of postage, the meter electrically prints the postage (including a meter ad, if desired) and seals the envelope. For packages, the meter prints gummed postage tape.

*— Pitney Bowes, Inc.*

The machine itself is purchased outright, but the meter mechanism is leased. In order to use a postage meter, a company must first obtain a meter license by filing an application with the post office where its mail is handled. The application must tell the make and model of the meter. A record of use must be maintained in a *Meter Record Book* supplied by the post office.

The meter is taken out of the machine to the post office where the meter is set and locked for the amount of postage bought. When that amount of postage is used up, the meter locks; and it is necessary to take it to the post office again and pay for more postage. Additional postage may be purchased before the meter locks. The operation is very simple, but the meter must be reset each time before it locks.

## Forwarding, Returning, and Remailing

Unfortunately, mail does not always reach its final destination upon first mailing. Some pieces must be forwarded, returned to the sender, or remailed. Additional postage may or may not be required.

**Forwarding Mail.** The secretary is often required to forward mail. The following information indicates the extra postage or fee required.

*First-Class Mail Up to Thirteen Ounces*—No additional postage required. Change the address and deposit in mail.

*First Class Forwarded by Air*—Change address, affix postage equal to difference between first-class postage (already paid) and airmail postage, and deposit in mail.

*Second-Class Publications*—Full postage must be paid at transient rate. Change address, affix postage, endorse SECOND-CLASS MAIL and deposit in mail.

*Third-Class Mail*—Full postage at single-piece rate must be paid. Change address, affix postage, and deposit in mail.

*Fourth-Class; Airmail over Eight Ounces*—Additional postage at applicable rate is required. Change address, affix postage, and deposit in mail.

*Airmail of Eight Ounces or Less*—No additional postage is required. Change address and deposit in mail.

*Registered, Insured, COD, and Special-Handling Mail*—Forwarded without payment of additional fees (*registry, insurance, COD, special handling*); however, ordinary forwarding postage charge, if any, must be paid.

*Special-Delivery Service*—This mail will not receive special-delivery service at second address unless a change-of-address card has been filed.

**Return of Undeliverable Mail.** A piece of undeliverable first-class or airmail up to eight ounces (with the exception of post cards and postal cards) will be returned to the sender free of charge by ordinary mail.

Undeliverable airmail over eight ounces will be returned to the sender by surface transportation and with return postage due. An undeliverable third- or fourth-class parcel is returned postage due if the parcel is of obvious value.

To assure that postal and post cards and third- and fourth-class packages are returned, place RETURN POSTAGE GUARANTEED conspicuously below the return address.

Undeliverable letters and packages without return addresses are sent to the dead-letter office where they are examined. They may be opened for finding return addresses, so it is wise to enclose a completed address label in a package being mailed. Whenever an address is found, the mail is returned for a fee. Undeliverable dead mail is destroyed or sold.

**Remailing Returned Mail.** The secretary is always chagrined when mail lands back on her desk. Any piece of mail returned with the "pointing finger" rubber stamp RETURNED TO WRITER, with one of six reasons checked, must be put in a fresh, correctly addressed envelope, and postage paid again.

## Change of Address

The post office serving you must be officially notified by letter or by one of its forms when you change your address. The old and the new address and the date when the new address is effective must be given. Correspondents should be notified promptly by special notices or by stickers attached to all outgoing mail. The post office will supply new address cards free for personal and business use.

## Recalling Mail

Occasionally it may be necessary to recall a piece of mail that has been posted. This calls for fast action. Type an addressed envelope that duplicates the one mailed. Go to the post office in your mailing zone if the letter is local or to the central post office if the letter is an out-of-town mailing. Fill in Form 1509 (*Sender's Application for Withdrawal of Mail*).

If the mail is an undelivered local letter, on-the-spot return will be made. If the letter has left the post office for an out-of-town address, the post office will wire or telephone (at the sender's request and expense) the addressee's post office and ask that the letter be returned. If the mail has already been delivered, the sender is notified; but the addressee is not informed that a recall was requested.

## Presorting Mail

Before depositing mail, separate it into major categories such as local, out-of-town, air, precanceled, and metered. It can then bypass one or more preliminary handlings in the post office. Types of presorting vary with the types of individual mailings. For instance, if most of the mail goes to in-state addresses, this mail may be kept separate and identified as "all for (*State*)," eliminating one sorting operation and permitting immediate placement with the mail for that state.

**Metered Mail.** Postal regulations require bundling and identifying five or more pieces of metered mail.

**Presorting by ZIP Code.** Mail presorted by *ZIP Code* moves faster. Large mailers can presort and forward mail to a specific *ZIP Code* or to a specific company in one bag. The post office furnishes trays for presorting in preparing mail for deposit at the post office.

## MAIL COLLECTION AND DELIVERY

A number of plans have been inaugurated by the Postal Service to cope with the increasing volume of mail, to improve service, and to reduce operational costs.

## ZIP Code and Optical Character Reader

The five-digit *ZIP* (Zone Improvement Program) *Code* was designed to speed mail deliveries and facilitate use of automated equipment to reduce costs. The first digit represents one of ten large geographical areas

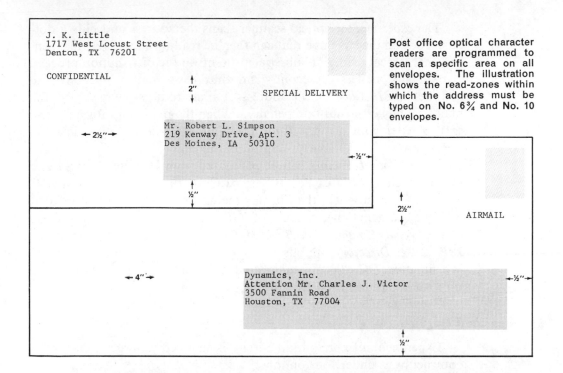

J. K. Little
1717 West Locust Street
Denton, TX 76201

CONFIDENTIAL

2"

SPECIAL DELIVERY

2½"

Mr. Robert L. Simpson
219 Kenway Drive, Apt. 3
Des Moines, IA 50310

½"

½"

Post office optical character readers are programmed to scan a specific area on all envelopes. The illustration shows the read-zones within which the address must be typed on No. 6¾ and No. 10 envelopes.

2½"

AIRMAIL

4"

Dynamics, Inc.
Attention Mr. Charles J. Victor
3500 Fannin Road
Houston, TX 77004

½"

½"

of the United States. For example, 0 represents the New England States, 1 represents the Middle Atlantic States, and so on. The second two digits represent sectional centers or large cities. The last two digits stand for either a particular postal zone in a city or a particular post office in a small community or rural area. (See the local telephone directory for postal zone numbers for street addresses in your city.)

Type the *ZIP Code* without a comma two spaces after the state name. To permit the use of addressing equipment with limited line length for bulk mailings, the postal service has designed and approved a two-letter abbreviation for each state and abbreviation for cities with long names. The two-letter abbreviations can be used *only with a ZIP Code*. The list of approved abbreviations is presented on page 751 of this book.

Machines (optical character readers) that electronically read addresses are used in post offices in several major cities and will be used increasingly as more locations add new equipment.

Post office optical character readers are programmed to scan a specific area on all envelopes; so the address must be completely within this read-zone, single-spaced, blocked in style. The state abbreviations shown on page 751 (typed in uppercase) must be used. Acceptable placements for a No. 10 and a No. 6¾ envelope are shown above.

The experimental optical scanner scans the address and puts a dot-dash code on the envelope that can then be read by a relatively inexpensive mechanical reader at subsequent points in the distribution process.

All bulk mailers of second- and third-class mail are required to include the *ZIP Code* on the address. Failure to do so may subject the mail to a higher-postal-rate penalty. When the mail is up for a second sort, a letter with no *ZIP Code* goes into the reject slot, a delaying operation.

A *ZIP Code Directory* can be purchased from Headquarters Service Division, United States Postal Service Corporation, Washington, DC 20402. The cost is less than it may seem, for the directory is updated without charge. Other sources of *ZIP Codes* are: the current edition of the *World Almanac and Book of Facts*; a paperback edition of the *ZIP Code Directory*, published by Norman Publishing Company, Washington, DC 20005, and available at stationery stores; and the directory placed in the lobby of most post offices.

## Express Mail Service

Experimental Express Mail Service is supplied to large mailers on a contract basis under four options:

1. **On a regularly scheduled basis a postal driver picks up dispatches, takes them to a special airport agent, who dispatches them on the next aircraft to the destination city, where another special postal agent gives them to a postal driver for delivery.**
2. **The same service except that the addressee picks up the mail at the receiving airport.**
3. **The same service except that the mailer takes the dispatches to the airport.**
4. **The same service except that the mailer and the addressee handle delivery to and from the airport.**

Under Option 5 (available without contract) the mailer delivers the dispatches before 5 p.m. to a designated downtown outlet, which guarantees delivery to the destination post office for pickup by 10 a.m. the following morning.

## Mailgram

The *Mailgram* (described and illustrated on pages 274–275) is a marriage between the postal service and Western Union. Western Union owns and installs in post offices equipment that receives messages on a continuous roll of paper. A post office employee tears off the message, inserts it into a window envelope, and dispatches it for guaranteed delivery with the next morning's mail.

## Facsimile Mail

Facsimile mail is being sent experimentally between New York and Washington. Copies of letters, charts, graphs, blueprints, and other printed matter are transmitted electronically with a four-hour target delivery time. Like Mailgrams, facsimile copies can be mailed after receipt by the post office, or the addressee can save time by picking up transmissions in person.

## VIM

*VIM (Vertical Improved Mail)* is a mail distribution system installed in many new large office buildings. In essence, *VIM* is the reverse of the familiar mail chute that drops mail from the upper floors into a collection box. Under *VIM* all incoming mail is delivered to a central mail room in the building. There postal employees sort it into lockboxes by floors. These boxes are then placed on a conveyor belt and keyed by dial to be ejected automatically to the right floor. There the office personnel pick up and deliver the mail. By this process the offices on each floor of the building can have continuous delivery of incoming mail.

## General Delivery

Mail may be addressed to individuals in care of the *General Delivery* window of main post offices. This service is convenient to transients and to individuals who have no definite address in a city. Such mail is held for a specified number of days and, if uncalled for, is then returned to the sender.

The executive on a touring vacation or a sales representative who is driving for several days and does not have hotel addresses frequently asks to have his mail addressed in care of *General Delivery* to a city en route. The address can also include the words *Transient* or *To Be Called For*. This is the way the envelope address would look:

The secretary should not overlook the convenience of *General Delivery* to reach a traveling executive whose schedule is somewhat uncertain.

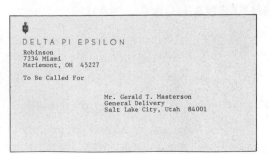

```
DELTA PI EPSILON
Robinson
7234 Miami
Mariemont, OH  45227

To Be Called For

                        Mr. Gerald T. Masterson
                        General Delivery
                        Salt Lake City, Utah  84001
```

Such a letter would go to the main post office in Salt Lake City and be held at the *General Delivery* window for Mr. Masterson for 10 days or up to 30 days if the envelope bore such a request. If not picked up within that time, the letter would be returned to the sender.

### Private Mail Service

Private mail services charging rates below those of the United States Postal Service are springing up and may become increasingly important, particularly for sending business mail and direct mail (advertising) between cities in this country. Such services can be located in the *Yellow Pages Directory* in the larger cities.

## MONEY ORDERS

Money may be transferred from one person or business to another by use of a *money order*. There are instances in which money orders are the requested form of payment. They are also a convenience to individuals who do not have a checking account.

### Domestic Money Orders

Postal money orders may be purchased at all post offices, branches, and stations. The maximum amount for a single *domestic money order* is $100. However, there is no limit on the number of money orders that may be purchased at one time.

### International Money Orders

Money may be sent to a foreign country by means of an *international money order* procurable at the local post office. When buying such an order, you are given only a receipt for it by the postal clerk, who then arranges for sending the money order abroad. Exact information is required about the payee and his address; if the payee is a woman, she must state whether she is single, married, or widowed.

## INTERNATIONAL MAIL

Information regarding the rates, services, and regulations covering international mail may be obtained from the local post office or from *The Directory of International Mail*.

### Classifications of International Mail

International postal service provides for *postal union mail* and *parcel post*. Parcel post is a separate category from postal union mail.

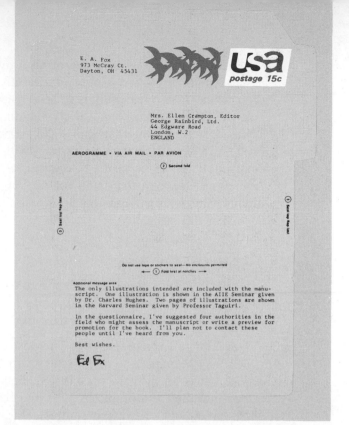

A message that will fit into the space available on the aerogramme form (1⅓ pages) can be sent at a rate lower than the regular international airmail rate. No enclosures are allowed. An aerogramme that is found to contain an enclosure is sent at the regular airmail rate.

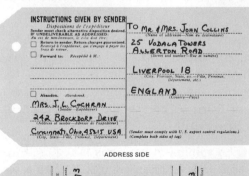

ADDRESS SIDE

CUSTOMS DECLARATION SIDE

**Customs Declaration Label**

**Postal Union Mail.** This mail is divided into *LC Mail* and *AO Mail*.

**LC Mail** (Letters and Cards)—letters, letter packages, air letters (aerogrammes), and postal cards

**AO Mail** (Other Articles)—printed matter, merchandise samples without salable value, commercial papers, small packets, matter for the blind

The postage for letters and postal cards mailed to Canada and Mexico is the same as for the United States.

To all other countries the rates are higher and weights are limited. Letter packages (small sealed packages sent a letter rate of postage) are given letter treatment if they are marked LETTER. A customs label identifying the contents must be attached to each letter or letter package containing dutiable merchandise.

**Parcel Post.** Parcels for transmission overseas are mailed by *parcel post* and must be packed even more carefully than those delivered within the continental United States. These packages may be registered or insured. Special-delivery and special-handling services are also available. There is now no international *COD* service. A *customs-declaration* form must be attached to the parcel with an accurate and complete description of the contents. As rates, weight limitations, and other regulations are not the same for all countries, the secretary should obtain information from the post office about requirements for her particular shipment.

## International Air Postal Services

Rates on letters by air to foreign countries are charged at a fixed rate for a *half* ounce (except to Canada and Mexico where rates are the same as in the United States—a one-ounce basis for fixed rate).

**Air Letters (Aerogrammes).** The post office sells an *air-letter* sheet which may be mailed to any country with which we maintain airmail service. It is an airmail, prestamped, lightweight, single sheet that is folded into the form of an envelope and sealed. No enclosures, either paper or other kinds, are permitted. Firms engaged in international trade may print, subject to prior approval of the Postal Service, their own aerogramme letterheads.

**AO Mail by Air.** Many concerns are not aware of the cheapest and fastest of all international postal services—*AO Mail by Air*. No export forms are required for most shipments. This service is restricted to samples of such items as merchandise, maps, printed matter, and drawings, but it is ideal for shipping small articles and should be investigated by those companies using other air services.

**International Air Parcel Post.** A minimum of forms is required in shipping by *international air parcel post*. This service is available to nearly all countries of the world and is rated on the first four ounces and each additional four ounces according to the country of destination.

## Reply Postage

To enclose reply postage with mail going out of the country, use an international reply coupon, called *Coupon-Response International*. It is purchased at the post office and is exchanged for stamps by the addressee in the country where it is received, whose stamps are then used for postage on mail addressed to this country.

# SAVING POSTAGE PENNIES

- Send letters by airmail only when fast delivery is really important. First-class letters *may* get there just as soon. On Friday airmail usually represents waste.
- Maintain up-to-date address lists, continually correcting all lists that may involve changes in addresses.
- When unsure of the correct amount of postage, weigh the mail to avoid wasted postage or mail delayed by insufficient postage.
- Obtain up-to-date rate charts from the postal authorities.
- Use special-delivery service to small towns judiciously, as small post offices do not always provide such service or may give it only during post office hours.
- Except for urgent items, combine in one mailing at the end of the day all mail addressed to the same person or the same branch office.
- Type airmail material and memos to branch office on paper of lighter weight than letterheads.
- When sending reply-requested mail, use business reply envelopes rather than stamped envelopes, thus paying postage only on the envelopes actually returned.
- Use Special Handling rather than Special Delivery for packages except in case of emergency.
- Sending packages that weigh less than eight ounces by airmail costs less than by third-class mail.

# SPEEDING MAIL DELIVERY

- Type addresses within the OCR read-zone. Use single spacing and keep the address to three lines or, at the most, four.
- In addressing mail to multiunit buildings, type the room, suite, or apartment number on the second line, *after* the street address.
- *ZIP Code* all mail.
- When the volume justifies the nominal expense, use the services of the post office to correct mailing lists and to add ZIP Codes (even on EDP tapes).
- Bypass one or more preliminary handlings at the post office by presorting mail before depositing it. (See page 238.)
- Mail early and often rather than all at once at the close of the business day. Establish an afternoon cutoff for low-priority first-class mail (usually 2 or 3 p.m.) and send it to the post office before the evening rush. Low-priority first-class mail readied after this cutoff is then scheduled for deposit the following morning.
- Investigate the desirability of renting a *post office box*. Box holders can obtain mail more often and at irregular hours. Mailgrams can be obtained by the start of the working day.
- When urgency is indicated, consider Express Mail Service, Mailgrams, or facsimile mail (if available).

## SHIPPING SERVICES

Shipments are made by means other than the various postal services —by air, rail, ship, bus, and truck. Even pipelines pumping oil and gasoline to refining centers may be considered a type of shipping service. The secretary does not need to know every detail; but she does need to know the kinds of services rendered, the advantages of each, and the sources to turn to for current information. The following discussion deals with two shipping services—*express* and *freight*.

### Express Service

Packages may be shipped by rail, air, or bus express. Each service offers advantages. The service to be used would depend upon the specific shipping needs.

**Railway Express.** *Railway express* service—a widely used shipping service—is provided by REA Express (formerly Railway Express Agency, Inc.). Speed is an important feature, and there are practically no limitations as to the character or size of shipments—from ladybugs to elephants—from an ounce to a carload. Each shipment is given the care and protection required.

Railway express is picked up and delivered with no additional charge. REA shipments receive space priority on carriers. They are automatically insured for a certain amount, and additional coverage may be purchased. Armed-guard protective service can be arranged for highly valuable shipments at reasonable cost. Animals are cared for, and refrigerated cars are provided for perishable commodities.

*Charges.* The express charges are computed on the weight of the shipment, the distance it is to be transported, and the kind of items that are being shipped.

The local office of REA Express will, upon request, furnish the secretary with a copy of the classification index of items and the rate scales applying to her locality. The local office is also glad to answer telephone inquiries about rates and to look over and estimate charges for a shipment.

*Shipping Procedures.* An express package should be securely boxed, wrapped and sealed, and addressed on two sides. A third copy of the address should be included on the inside. The address should be as complete as possible, giving street, number, building, room, department—any information that would be helpful to the expressman delivering the package.

The shipping forms which accompany the package may be made out ahead of time by the secretary, or the expressman will make them out when he picks up the parcel. A supply of the forms is furnished to frequent users of REA Express service. Shipping charges may be fully or partly prepaid, or fully or partly collected from the consignee on delivery of the shipment.

**Air Express.** *Air express* is a joint venture of the airlines in cooperation with the Air Express Division of REA Express. Service is provided to some 1,800 airports. In addition, over 20,000 off-airline communities are served by combining air service with the trucks and rail facilities of the REA Express.

Air express has priority after airmail on all passenger and cargo planes and thus provides the fastest means available for transporting packages. Overnight delivery is provided between airport cities and to many off-airline points. Next-day delivery is assured to most points in the United States. Pickup and delivery service is provided (at no extra cost) with a pickup guaranteed within two hours after your call.

When making a rush shipment, the secretary should compare the rates and services of the various air services—*airmail, air express, air freight*. She may discover that air express would be the least expensive and the most convenient.

The local post office, local express agent, and air cargo representative, will be glad to give detailed information about their services. Such references as *Leonard's Guide* and the *Official Air Express Guide* might also help.

The relative popularity of the three types of air cargo is indicated on the chart shown here.

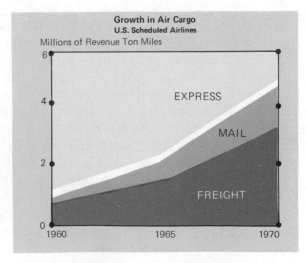

*— Air Transport Association of America*

**Bus Express.** If the executive wants speedy delivery of a package to a small town in another part of the state, the secretary should consider *bus express*. This service is particularly useful when destination points are located where there are no airports. Round-the-clock service is offered, including Sundays and holidays—and between many points, same-day service. Pickup and delivery is available at an extra charge. Most bus lines offer this type of shipping, the most widely known being the *Greyhound Package Express*. Items such as films, optical supplies, foodstuffs, medicines, glass, and auto parts are insurable (free up to $50) with a weight limit up to 100 pounds a package and with a size limit of 24 by 24 by 45 inches.

## Freight Services

*Freight* is generally thought of as a shipment sent by any method other than mail or express. It is the most economical service used to transport heavy, bulky goods in large quantities. Because freight shipping is the most complex of all methods, the secretary will probably not be required to select the carrier and to route the shipments. She should, however, know a few of the salient facts.

**Railroad Freight.** Ordinarily when goods are shipped by *railroad freight*, they must be delivered by the shipper (consignor) to the local freight office. When the shipment arrives at its destination, the addressee (consignee) must arrange for delivery or must call for the shipment. Many railroads, however, have instituted store-door delivery with trucks operated by the railway company in order to meet the competition of the door-delivery service of trucking companies. More and more, the shipper loads the goods into containers at his location and takes them to the carrier, who transports and delivers the shipment to the consignee with no further handling. Containerized shipping offers the advantage of better security, also.

A service called *piggyback* is offered by the railroads to trucking firms for long-distance hauls. Here loaded truck trailers are driven to the railway depot in one city, detached from the trucks and placed on railroad flatcars, and moved by rail to another city where they can be unloaded and driven to their destinations. Thus towns and areas not on the regular railroad lines can be reached by this service.

To provide a less-than-carload freight service at a special rate, *freight-forwarding companies* assemble from several consignors shipments that are less than carload and that are going to the same destination. This service allows shippers of small quantities to gain a carload rate from the railroads.

The volume of freight being moved by cargo planes is growing rapidly as businesses discover this way to reduce costs of inventory, warehouse space, and packing.

*— American Airlines*

**Motor Freight.** *Motor freight* is used for both local and long-distance hauls. Truck companies operate coast-to-coast service and have connecting services with local trucking lines. As described above, they often work in conjunction with railroads. Sometimes shipments are held by trucking companies until they have a paying load destined for the same locality. Specialized trucks also carry single commodities such as milk, gasoline, new cars, chemicals, sand, and gravel in truck-load quantities.

**Air Freight.** Businessess find that the higher cost of air freight is partly offset by reduced costs in inventory and in warehouse space. There is also a saving in packing costs, as air shipments do not require the sturdy crating that surface shipments frequently demand.

Delivery service is provided without charge; however, there is a small charge for pickup service.

**Water Freight.** *Water freight* is usually considerably cheaper than any other means of freight transportation. River barges and other vessels on the inland waterways of the United States carry such commodities as lumber, coal, iron ore, and chemicals. Bulky items for overseas shipment are carried in freighters, while passenger liners carry mail and items packaged in crates. Information on services and rates can be obtained from shipping companies.

**Bills of Lading.** For every freight shipment—no matter what kind of freight carrier—a bill of lading must be made out. Two types are used: the *straight bill of lading* and the *order bill of lading*.

When the freight shipment is sent on open account to the consignee, the straight bill of lading is used. It is also used when the freight carrier is to act as the collection agency for a COD shipment. The letters COD and the amount to be collected are written on the face of the bill of lading.

If a bank at the destination of the shipment is to act as the collection agency, an order bill of lading and a sight draft are used. In this case, the consignee pays the bank the amount of the sight draft and obtains transfer of the bill of lading. He then presents the bill of lading to the carrier and receives the shipment.

## International Shipments

The market for American products is worldwide. International air cargo service makes it possible to deliver goods to most places in the world within a matter of hours. The bulk of tonnage to foreign markets, however, still moves via *surface* (ships).

International shipments present problems—special packing, complicated shipping procedures, marine insurance, foreign exchange—usually not encountered in domestic trade. The mere handling of communications with a foreign business firm can be a problem in itself. (See pages 212–213.)

**Shipping Documents.** A foreign shipment involves the preparation of a number of documents, such as forms to obtain an *export license* (some commodities), *ocean bill of lading, consular invoice* or *certificate of origin*, and *export custom declaration*. Large manufacturers doing extensive business abroad usually establish export departments: (1) to market the products, (2) to execute the required export and shipping forms, and (3) to arrange for the actual shipments.

Many smaller firms use the services of an export broker or CEM (Combination Export Management) firm. This firm performs the same functions as an export department; namely, marketing, processing, and shipping of goods.

Some businesses prefer to use the services of a Foreign Freight Forwarder or Cargo Agent, which specializes in processing foreign shipments. The agent executes the required export and shipping documents and arranges for the actual shipment.

International airlines and steamship companies also maintain departments that assist customers with their overseas shipments.

**International Air Cargo.** To send a shipment by *international air cargo*, whether one package or a carload, contact the office of an international airline. The airline will provide instructions on packaging and addressing the shipment and completing the necessary documents such as *bill of lading* and *customs declaration*. In many cases, air freight or even express is less expensive than international parcel post.

## SUGGESTED READINGS

*Administrative Management*, Vol. 33, No. 9 (September, 1972), pp. 37–53 (various articles on mail and mail handling).

"Big Changes in Mail Services." *U.S. News and World Report* (April 26, 1971), p. 43.

"Case for Postal Reform." *Nation's Business* (July 5, 1969), pp. 52–54.

"Postal Service Gets Down to Business." *Business Week* (June 26, 1971), pp. 78–80.

"What New Mail Service Means to You." *U.S. New and World Report* (July 5, 1971), pp. 46–51.

"What's Wrong with the Mails." *Nation's Business* (March 31, 1969), pp. 40–41.

## SUGGESTED REFERENCES

*Instructions to Mailers.* Washington: U.S. Government Printing Office.

*National ZIP Code Directory.* Washington: U.S. Government Printing Office.

*Postal Service Manual.* Washington: U.S. Government Printing Office.

*World Almanac and Book of Facts*, published annually by Newspaper Enterprises Association, 230 Park Avenue, New York, NY 10017.

(The ZIP Code for the U.S. Government Printing Office is 20402.)

## QUESTIONS FOR DISCUSSION

1. What is the correct way to readdress mail for forwarding to a new address?

2. Why should mail be presorted before it is deposited? Into what categories should it be presorted?

3. How does use of the ZIP Code speed mail not only through the postal system but also before the mail goes to the post office?

4. What five sources of information about postal rates and services could a person responsible for business mail consult?

5. If much first-class mail is transported by plane, why would the secretary choose the more expensive airmail for an important letter?

6. How should an envelope be addressed to insure that it can be read by an optical character reader?

7. Why has air cargo service increased proportionately faster than air express or airmail?

8. What are the advantages of containerized shipping?

9. Your employer hands you an addressed and sealed envelope for stamping and mailing and says that it contains his income tax return. How would you go about obtaining for him legal evidence that the income tax return was mailed? (The federal government prosecutes a taxpayer whose return is not received, even though the taxpayer has in his files a carbon copy of the return and makes a verbal claim that the return was filed by mail.)

10. A stenographer who is under your supervision frequently forgets to return or to pay for stamps that she gets from you and uses for personal mail. What would you do the next time she asks for a stamp?

11. What would you do if you assigned to your assistant the job of enclosing, sealing, weighing, stamping, and posting each day's mail and in the morning you found for the third time in two weeks that she had left the mail lying on her desk, ready for mailing but not posted?

12. Mail from the home office reaches your city post office around 2 a.m. each morning. However, it is not delivered to your office until the time of the regular mail delivery at 10:30 a.m. Your employer would like to have the home-office mail as early as possible so that district salesmen can be told of price changes. What would you suggest to solve this problem?

13. You are sending a request for a free brochure published in Norway. How can you arrange to enclose with your request adequate postage for mailing the brochure?

14. There are three ways of sending a letter about a parcel-post package being mailed out: separately, enclosed with the contents, or in an envelope fastened to the outside of the package. Which do you think is preferable and why?

15. The executive to whom you are secretary is president of a small company that sends out about a hundred letters a day. Each employee keeps and affixes his own postage to his own mail. Discuss whether or not a postage meter (machine) would be worth the rental fee.

16. Your employer asked you to mail an important letter to Germany. You are chagrined when it is returned for insufficient postage. The letter weighed one ounce, and you had affixed domestic airmail postage. For what two reasons was it returned? How can you prevent the recurrence of such an error?

17. See how many of the following questions you can answer. Then refer to the Postal Guide in Part 10 of this book to verify or correct your answers.

    (a) **What is the maximum weight of a package that may be sent by airmail to an APO address?**

    (b) **Uncovered hotel keys may be mailed to the hotel by what class of mail?**

    (c) **What is the difference in pounds between the maximum weight of a package going to a local-zone address and one being sent to an APO address?**

    (d) **How much more is the special delivery fee for a 15-pound package than for a 1-ounce letter?**

**18.** Fill in the blanks in these sentences. Then use your Reference Guide to verify or correct your answers; tell which Reference Guide subheading entry applies to each point.

(a) It occurred in the _____ century. (8)

(b) Refer to page _____. (1,016)

(c) It happened in the _____. (nineteen forties)

(d) The trend started in the _____. (mid-60s)

(e) They now have a _____ workweek. (3 day)

(f) There are _____ users of gas in the area. (186,000)

(g) It cost _____ last month. (876 dollars and 75 cents)

(h) They cost _____, _____, or _____, depending upon grade. (8¢, 18¢, 20¢)

## PROBLEMS

**1.** Assume that your employer is out of the city on a business trip. How would you go about forwarding each of the following unopened pieces of mail? State whether additional postage is required.

(a) A personal letter

(b) A 1-ounce airmail letter which you wish to forward by airmail

(c) A piece of registered mail requiring a signed return receipt

(d) A letter mailed by your office to the employer but returned because of an insufficient address

(e) A special-delivery letter you wish to have forwarded by special delivery

(f) A parcel-post package

**2.** Set up a 3-column table with each column head indicating the information requested in (a), (b), and (c), below. In the appropriate columns, enter the information required by Items 1–31.

(a) The class of postal service that should be used. If parcel post is chosen, indicate the zone,

(b) The kinds of fees that must be paid in addition to postage, and

(c) Special requirements or secretarial procedures:

(1) A carbon copy of a letter

(2) A pen-corrected copy of a printed price list

(3) A 14-ounce bound copy of a typewritten thesis addressed to a library

(4) A library book you are returning by mail

(5) A letter addressed to a relative of the executive, enclosing bonds valued at $500 and registered for full value. Return receipt required showing address where delivery was made

(6) A magazine addressed to a city 30 miles distant and sent at the request of the executive

(7) An 18-ounce sealed package containing a printing plate and addressed to a city 550 miles distant, with special-handling service

(8) A 480-page textbook weighing 2½ pounds and sent to a city 800 miles away

(9) A 26-ounce sealed parcel containing a gear and measuring 8 inches by 2 inches by 4 inches addressed to a city 700 miles away

(10) A 7-ounce unsealed package of candy sent special delivery

(11) A $20 money order addressed to a city 20 miles distant

(12) A box 3 feet long, 1½ feet wide, and 1½ feet high, weighing 40 pounds, addressed to a city 400 miles distant

(13) A sealed parcel weighing 5 ounces sent airmail

(14) A box of bulbs weighing ½ pound

(15) A monthly statement of a department store to a local customer

(16) An airmail, special-delivery letter weighing 2 ounces

(17) A postal card to a city 300 miles distant

(18) A 1-pound parcel containing clothing sent to a city 95 miles distant and insured for $15 with a return receipt requested at the time of mailing

(19) A check for $8.92 to a city 300 miles away

(20) A 1-pound sealed package containing samples of soap sent special delivery to a city 750 miles away

(21) Sixty individually addressed unsealed envelopes containing 1-page mimeographed price lists

(22) Copyright matter addressed to Register of Copyrights in Washington, registered for $5

(23) A 20-pound box (2 feet long, 10 inches high, and 14 inches wide) containing automobile parts addressed to a city 250 miles distant

(24) A letter sent by certified mail with a postmarked receipt wanted

(25) A 1-pound parcel containing costume jewelry valued at $75 but registered for only $50, being transmitted 2,500 miles

(26) A 1-pound sealed parcel containing costume jewelry insured for $75 and being transmitted 2,500 miles

(27) A certified letter containing notice to an heir of an estate, with return receipt requested showing where envelope was delivered

(28) Thirty mimeographed invitations in unsealed envelopes addressed to out-of-city members

(29) A 5-ounce box of stationery addressed to a town 700 miles distant

(30) A sealed 6-inch by 4-inch by 3-inch parcel containing stationery weighing 12 ounces, addressed to a city 350 miles away

(31) A magazine weighing 10 ounces and sent by an individual to a city 1,500 miles distant.

■ 3. Determine the total postage and fees for mailing each of the following: (Use the Postal Guide in Part 10.)

(a) An airmail letter weighing 2½ ounces sent special delivery return receipt requested, showing the person, time, and address for delivery

(b) A merchandise package weighing 7¼ pounds sent to an address 1,100 miles away to be insured for $60 and to receive Special Handling.

(c) A package containing 16-mm film being returned to a library located 350 miles away (The package weighs 12½ pounds and is to be sent special delivery.)

(d) An aerogramme to Rome, Italy

# Chapter 12

## BASIC TELEPHONE AND TELEGRAPHIC SERVICES

The business telephone can provide some of the day's most frustrating moments, perhaps interrupting you as you try to finish a rush job under pressure. People who would not be rude in face-to-face conversation can be extremely inconsiderate over the telephone. Mistakes bring wrong numbers, misunderstood messages, premature disconnections, or misdirected referrals from other telephones.

The telephone, though, is a vital link between you and the public and you and your co-workers. It speeds up communication, often supplanting personal visits or letters. It is a way of knowing and serving many people and should challenge you to master its operation. You will need to choose the type of service to use in different situations, so you should know about the telephone equipment and services available.

Telegrams and cablegrams, too, are media for accelerating business action. They often get results impossible with slower means of communication. You must know how and when to compose and send telegraph messages and how to choose the appropriate service.

This chapter will improve your basic telephone and telegraph communication techniques.

## TELEPHONE CONVERSATION

To save time and to build goodwill, many executives answer their own telephones although you will, of course, answer when your employer is away from his desk or obviously too busy to answer. He may dial many of his own calls, but you will also initiate many calls for him and for yourself. Naturally, you will want to master good *business* telephone techniques; for being able to represent your employer and your company attractively over the telephone has real dollars-and-cents value.

Some phase of at least 90 percent of all business transactions is conducted by telephone. That is why many personnel officers check the telephone performance of applicants before hiring them. It is also why companies frequently provide in-service telephone training for all office employees.

The secretary with the phonogenic voice will sound friendly and interested. She will treat every call as important.

*— American Telephone and Telegraph Company*

What the secretary says in carrying on the telephone conversation is important: tactful choice of words in contrast to blunt statements; offers of help in contrast to plain *No's*. Ease in conducting pleasant, effective conversations comes with experience and training.

## The Phonogenic Voice

Just as your appearance determines whether you are photogenic, your voice determines whether or not you are *phonogenic*. In business your telephone voice must sound pleasing and friendly because the impression you make is formed largely from the sound of your voice.

A telephone ring is an anonymous thing. The secretary does not know who is calling. It may be an important client, the employer's wife, or the president of the company. It is wise to assume that whoever is calling *is* important and deserves one's best telephone personality.

Here are a few simple rules to follow in developing the "voice with the smile" over the telephone:

1. Speak at a normal speed, with rising and falling inflections that avoid monotony.
2. Use a tone suitable for face-to-face conversation, keeping the voice low pitched.
3. Speak directly into the transmitter, which should be between half an inch and an inch from the lips.
4. Try to visualize the caller and speak *to* him—not *at* the telephone.
5. Try to convey a friendly, intelligent interest.

### Terminating Conversations

Sometimes a secretary is required to terminate a conversation suddenly for any of several reasons. Use a plausible excuse—the truth, tactfully worded—for example, "I'm sorry, Mr. Allen has just buzzed for me to come into his office"; or, "I'm sorry, someone is waiting for me in the reception room"; or, "I'm sorry, I must get out a rush letter for Mr. Allen."

### Accuracy Technique

It is often necessary to give or take accurate information over the telephone—names, addresses, amounts, dates, and code words. Sounds do go wrong as they travel over the wires. *F* and *S* are often confused, as are *P* and *B*, *T* and *D* and *M* and *N*. *Five* and *nine* often get mixed up; and strange as it may seem, so do *zero* and *four*.

When word accuracy is needed, telephone spelling is used. To prevent mistakes, use any simple, easy-to-understand word to identify a letter, such as *D as in David*, *A as in Alice*, and so on. It is particularly important that the listener understand any numbers used in telephone conversation. The speaker should slightly exaggerate the enunciation, as "Th-r-ee" (strong R and long EE). Repeat the number; or, if there is still a question about one digit, give its preceding sequence, as "Three, four, FIVE," emphasizing the final proper number.

## INCOMING CALLS

To handle incoming calls effectively, the secretary must understand the equipment she uses and techniques for answering, screening, and transferring calls, as well as for taking messages.

### Equipment

The secretary will probably operate some kind of switchboard and possibly several types of desk telephones.

**Switchboards.** Calls come into the office over a private branch exchange (PBX) or a private automatic branch exchange (PABX), which is discussed on page 290. Although some switchboards require the operator to plug in cords to make connections, most are cordless with keys or push buttons for controlling calls.

In a small office with a simple board, the secretary's duties may include relieving the switchboard attendant during the day, although this practice is probably becoming outmoded with the adoption of new equipment.

The Call Director telephone enables the secretary to answer many telephones in an office from one location. Associated with other equipment, the Call Director may be used for interoffice communication, to arrange conference calls, to "add on" stations, and so on. Square plastic buttons light up for an incoming call, when a line is in use, or when a call is being held. The buttons are identified in the windows.

*— American Telephone and Telegraph Company*

**The Call Director.** The Call Director is practically a small desk switchboard, equipped with up to 29 lines, all controlled by the secretary. It can be connected to the larger switchboard, and lines can be reserved for tie-line calls (see page 292) or for an intercom system. Optional equipment is available by which a Speakerphone (see page 293) or intercom conference equipment can be added.

**Key Telephones.** The secretary will probably use a desk telephone equipped with two to six lucite push buttons below the dialing mechanism. This *key* telephone enables her to make or take a number of calls simultaneously from both inside and outside of the office. A key telephone in the hands of an inefficient secretary can create havoc with office procedure.

To answer a call:

1. Determine the line to be answered by the location of the ring, the tone, or the signal light on the bottom.
2. Depress the key for the line to be answered, remove the receiver, and speak.

To place a call:

1. Choose a line that is not in use (unlighted).
2. Push down the key for that line, remove the receiver, and make your call.

*— American Telephone and Telegraph Company*

3. If you accidentally choose a line that is being held, depress the hold key to reestablish the hold.

To hold a call:

1. Ask the person to hold the line.
2. Depress the hold key for about two seconds to assure holding; both the line key and the hold key will return to normal position (with the light on).
3. Place or answer another call on another line. The person being held cannot overhear your other conversation.

To transfer a call:

1. To transfer the call to another telephone in your button system, depress the key for the line wanted.
2. When you hear the called person answer, replace your receiver.

The desk telephone may also be connected with the central transcription facility so that the executive can pick up his telephone and dictate an item to a voice-writing machine.

**Centrex.** One of the frustrations of the modern office is the difficulty of getting through the switchboard to the extension wanted. To circumvent this problem, many companies are changing over to *direct in-dialing* to the specific extension wanted (Centrex). The frequent caller is given the extension number and the company number; he can then dial the extension from his outside telephone. Unanswered calls automatically go to the switchboard for handling. To save time on subsequent calls, *record the Centrex number*.

## Techniques

The secretary develops two simple but effective habits in handling incoming calls. First, she answers her telephone before the third ring, benefiting everyone concerned. Delayed answering can be a source of irritation to the executive, for when he hears the secretary's telephone ringing several times, he wonders if she is at her desk and whether he should answer. Unfortunately, a call often comes at the busiest possible moment; but the person who answers must avoid implying by tone of voice any feeling that the call is an intrusion.

Secondly, she is ready to take notes. As she answers the telephone, she picks up a pencil and pushes a pad of paper into place.

**Identification.** The words with which the secretary answers her telephone depend upon whether it is connected directly to an outside line or to the company switchboard; but she always identifies her company or office and herself. If her telephone is on an outside line, she may answer, "Allen and Lovell—Miss Baer." If the call comes through the company switchboard, she will answer, "Mr. Allen's office, Miss Baer," because the PBX operator has already identified the company when she answered. In no case does the secretary say only "hello" or "yes."

For the secretary to recognize his voice and use his name in a telephone conversation is complimentary to the caller. As soon as the caller identifies himself, use his name in speaking with him.

The third or fourth time an individual calls, the secretary may be able to recognize his voice and should then address him by name. In case of any doubt, however, the secretary should not risk the possibility of offending a caller by using the wrong name.

**Screening Calls.** His personal preference, the nature of the office, and time available determine whether the executive answers his own calls. When the secretary answers a call from among those she learns to recognize as VIP's, she automatically puts it through without question.

When a caller does not identify himself or the secretary is unable to recognize the voice, she may be required to find out who is calling. This procedure requires skillful questioning. The abrupt question, "Who is calling?" sounds rude and discriminating. Tactful secretaries phrase their questions somewhat like these:

May I know who is calling, please?      *or*      May I tell Mr. Allen who is calling, please?

When she does not let the caller talk with the executive, she needs to give a plausible reason and to suggest a substitute person or time. A typical turn-down explanation might be:

Mr. Graham, Mr. Allen is holding an important conference. Perhaps I can help you or transfer you to somebody who can.

**Executive Unavailable.** The secretary has three responsibilities regarding incoming calls when the executive is not available for answering the telephone:

1. Giving helpful but not explicit information to the caller about the executive's time schedule and activities
2. Getting information from hesitant callers
3. Taking messages and keeping a record of incoming calls

*Giving Information.* When the executive is not available, the secretary is discreet about giving information. Definite information may be exactly what the executive does not want told to certain callers. *When in doubt, DON'T* be specific. Unless there is a known reason for being specific, the secretary tries to be helpful but not explicit. Note the differences in the responses on the next page.

| Specific | Helpful But Not Explicit |
|---|---|
| He is in conference with the president. | He isn't at his desk just now. I expect him back soon. |
| He is in Chicago on business. | He is out of the city today. |
| He left early this afternoon to play golf. | He won't be in again until tomorrow morning. |

*Getting Information.* The telephone caller is sometimes reluctant to give information to the secretary. Often he just says, "I'll call back," and hangs up without identifying himself. A secretary can often learn both the identity of the caller and the reason for the call by using an oblique approach. The conversation might develop along these lines: "Mr. Allen is away today. I am his secretary; perhaps I can help you." Notice she does not ask who is calling or what he wants. If the caller is still reluctant, the secretary might ask, "May I have him call you tomorrow?" If he answers, "Yes, will you? This is Ed Fox, 621-6412," she can then ask, "Shall I give him any special message, Mr. Fox?"

Or she might ask, "Will Mr. Allen know what you are calling about?" A positive answer to any such question necessitates the caller's divulging his name or the purpose of his call.

*Taking Messages.* Always offer to take a message when your employer is out. Ask the caller to explain any details which you do not understand. Take time to repeat the message and verify all spelling and figures. Afterwards, complete the record by adding the date, the time the call came, the name and identity of the caller, and your initials. Some firms use small printed slips for this purpose. It is possible to buy books of telephone message forms interleaved with carbon sheets so that the original message can be put on the executive's desk and the carbon copy retained in the book for reference.

Even if there is no message to report, make a record of the call. Actually, when the executive is away, a helpful secretary keeps a complete telephone diary of all calls received and messages recorded. National Cash Register prints a book of three-to-a-page Phone-O-Grams on NCR carbonless stock. Copies are made automatically as the message is recorded and can be bound for future reference and follow-up.

*Transferring Calls.* When a call comes that someone else can handle better, transfer the call to him. The caller, however, may be justifiably annoyed if he has already been transferred to you. Several techniques can be used that demonstrate that you and your organization want to be helpful. First, be sure that the person to whom you transfer the call can actually give the information sought. Second, tell the caller that you are transferring the call but if you are disconnected, he can call you back at ————. Stay on the line until you are sure that he has reached someone else. Third, consider the possibility of getting the information for the caller and returning his call. Nothing is more important than your company's image — nor more exasperating than the "I-couldn't-care-less-I-have-my-own-work-to-do" attitude.

## Receiving Long Distance Calls

Occasionally when your employer is absent, you will have to take long distance calls. If so, listen carefully and repeat your understanding of the message. Type a full report of the call immediately, so that there will be a correct and complete record for the employer when he returns.

If your employer is not available to answer a person-to-person call, give the long distance operator full information as to when he will be back at his desk. The operator will ask you to have the executive call her and will give you those details of the call that will help her to complete it quickly when he calls back; such as, "Please have him call Operator 18 in Detroit, and ask for 971-1380, Mr. Smith calling."

If the executive can be reached at another telephone, either locally or in another city, and you believe he would not object to receiving a call there, you should tell the operator where he can be reached.

## Message-Taking Services

New devices and services that are available assure that telephone calls are always answered, even when the telephone is not covered.

**Answering, Recording, and Switching Devices.** Automatic answering equipment can deliver any message that the user records. Before leaving the office, the businessman (or his secretary) turns on the machine and makes a recording to tell callers when he will return and asks them to leave a message. The person calling in hears the announcement and then records his message. An innovation made possible by electronics is equipment that enables the businessman to call in and revise his recording. Small businesses, such as real estate and insurance offices, find this service especially advantageous. This equipment has been expanded to attract larger users. For instance, up to six hours of recorded messages capture overnight orders for a meat wholesaler.

With a *Call Diverter*, a thumb wheel is set with the number where the owner-subscriber will be, and incoming calls are automatically transferred to that telephone.

**Telephone Answering Service.** Unlike the automatic recording device which merely recites impersonal messages, the operator in a telephone answering service is able to exercise judgment and understanding in personally assisting the caller. Many business firms invest in such service as a way of personalizing their offices during the hours they are not open. The secretary who finds herself in an office using such service should establish friendly relations with the answering service, check with the operator immediately upon coming into the office after it has been closed, and provide complete information when the office is to be covered by an answering service.

**Taped Announcements.** Almost every telephone user is familiar with taped announcements that may be dialed: time of day, weather, flight information during inclement weather, market information, movie schedules, and even prayers. It is possible for a telephone user to develop such announcements.

## Special Reverse-Charge Toll Service

A business can make its services easily available by telephone in cities where it has no office with a special listing in the telephone directory of each of the desired cities. These listings permit the caller to make the call as a local one, and the toll charge is billed to the listed number. For instance, a Yonkers company would have a New York City number listed in the New York City directory as follows:

Acetate Box Co
263 AshbrtnAv Ynkrs...........NYC Tel No--292-2435

On such incoming calls, the secretary provides complete and cordial help — without waste of long distance time. (See page 265 also.)

## OUTGOING CALLS

In addition to answering the telephone, you will place local and long distance calls. To do this well, you must know how to get maximum service from your telephone directories and telephone operators and how to make the appropriate choices of service.

### Using Telephone Directories

Before placing a call, the secretary must locate the telephone number, and sometimes that takes quite a bit of skill. The telephone directory has two parts: the *Alphabetical Directory* (white pages) which contains a complete list of subscribers, their addresses, and telephone numbers; and the *Yellow Pages* (*classified directory*) containing the alphabetic listings of names of businesses under headings which are also arranged alphabetically by product or service offered.

Both directories print, in the upper outside corner, the first and last names or headings listed on each page. The conspicuous location of these guide words makes it possible to locate the proper page quickly.

The telephone directory is a mine of information, especially one for a metropolitan area. For instance, the New York City alphabetical directory contains in its introductory pages: emergency numbers; instructions for dialing *Directory Assistance* (*Information*) in any locality; instructions for telephoning locally, nationally, and overseas; special services such as marine and mobile service; a map showing area-code distribution; a local postal-zone map; information about setting up conference calls; explanations of billing; descriptions of available Picturephone service; and restrictions on the use of customer-provided equipment.

A corporation may find it advantageous to keep in a central location a collection of telephone directories from cities in which it conducts a large volume of business. It is also possible to find out-of-town directories from the larger cities in some hotels and major travel terminals.

**The Alphabetical Directory.** In the *alphabetical directory* the numbers are usually located quickly, but the exceptions make it necessary for the secretary to know the rules followed in arranging names in alphabetical sequence in filing. For example, there are twenty-one columns of the surname *Miller* in one metropolitan directory. Alternate spellings are suggested as, *Also see MILLAR*.

Locating the various government offices and public services also requires a knowledge of the alphabetical listings. They are generally listed under their proper political subdivisions—city offices under the name of the municipality, county offices under the name of the county, state offices under the name of the state, and federal offices under *United States Government*. Public schools are usually listed under the municipality and then under *Board of Education*. Parochial schools are individually listed. Addresses of identical listings are in the alphabetical order of street names followed by numbered streets in numerical order. (*Eighth Street* would follow rather than precede *Second Street*.)

**The *Yellow Pages* Directory.** The *Yellow Pages* directory of business listings is a very helpful source of reference to the secretary. In metropolitan areas a separate *Yellow Pages* directory contains all classified listings. The executive may want to talk with "that air-conditioning firm on Church Street," but neither he nor his secretary knows its correct name. She looks in the *Yellow Pages* directory under *Air Conditioning Equip & Supls* and finds that he wants *Tuttle & Bailey, Inc.*

An efficient secretary will circle every frequently called telephone number in the directory so that she can find it more quickly the next time. She may jot the number down on a slip of paper just in case she gets a busy signal the first time she dials it.

When a new number is obtained, it should be listed on the proper directory page or in a desk telephone directory.

**Personal Telephone Directory.** Every secretary keeps a *personal, up-to-date telephone directory*. In it she lists alphabetically the names of frequently called persons and firms and their telephone numbers. A thoughtful secretary types a condensed list of such numbers for the executive and places it in some convenient spot, such as the back of his daily calendar pad, or inside his office directory of extension numbers.

Some kind of card listing or tab-insertion scheme is preferable to a solid-typed list which makes no provision for the addition of names and changes of personnel or telephone numbers. Any list becomes out of date quickly unless some system is devised that provides for additions and deletions.

The time-and-motion-conscious secretary will be interested in the analysis of the telephone company: You can look up a number in your personal telephone directory in 10 seconds, about a third of the time required for a search of the large directory. A personal telephone booklet may be obtained from the local telephone company for the asking.

Some people prefer not to have their telephone number listed in the directory. This may cost them 50 cents a month because of additional administrative costs. Usually, Directory Assistance (Information) will not have the number in its records. Only in exceptional circumstances, and with the customer's consent, will the telephone company arrange to complete the call. Keeping unlisted numbers in the personal directory becomes doubly important, since they cannot be looked up. Telephone numbers of frequent correspondents may be taken from letterheads and entered in the personal telephone directory for possible use.

**Special Reverse-Charge Listings.** To stimulate business or to provide wider service, a corporation may make a special listing in the directory of a city in which it does not maintain an office. The listing looks like this:

LeChateau Inn&Country Club Inc WhiteHavenPa
No Charge To Calling Party
Ask Operator For.............Enterprise 6969

Charges are automatically billed to the called party; no acceptance of the charges is requested.

The Area Code 800 numbers, largely adopted by hotel-motel reservation services, is another special reverse-charge toll call. It looks like this and is explained on page 292.

**DENNIS HOTEL/MOTEL**
Boardwalk&SMichiganAv AtlanticCityNJ
No Charge To Calling Party . . . . . . . . . . . . . 800 257-7908

## Placing Local Calls

The procedure in placing calls varies with the kind of telephone equipment. If the desk telephone is a direct outside line, give the number to the telephone operator or dial it. If the line goes through the office switchboard, you either dial 9 for an outside line or ask the PBX attendant for a line by saying "Outside, please." When you get a dial tone, you dial the number.

You will regularly be making two kinds of local calls—reaching someone whom the employer will talk with on his extension and placing your own calls.

In the first case, after getting the number desired, ask for the person wanted and immediately identify your employer as the caller, saying something like:

Mr. Norman, please. Mr. Allen of Allen and Lovell calling.

To avoid making the person wait on the line, always determine if the executive is ready to take the call before placing it.

If the answering operator or secretary asks you to put your employer on the line before she puts hers on, be gracious and follow her request. The person who must waste a few seconds waiting for the other to respond should be the one who originated the call.

In making your own calls, you will find it advisable to jot down what you want to say before you get the person on the line in order to avoid the embarrassment of having to call back for a point forgotten. You will speak with more confidence and effectiveness and you will make a better impression by knowing in advance what you are going to say.

Introduce yourself properly. Upon being connected, give your own name, and, if desirable, your firm name. For example, "This is Miss Baer, Mr. Allen's secretary, of Allen and Lovell." Making a good impression on people whom you telephone is just as important as is making a good impression on those who call at your office.

## Message Units

Within a metropolitan area, calls between widely separated locations are not considered local calls or long distance calls but are individually charged as *message-unit calls*.

A message unit is a telephone term describing a standard base rate used in determining the cost of a call. The table of rates in the front of the directory shows the *number* of message units chargeable between telephone exchanges and the length of the overtime period which is charged as a message unit. For instance, from Manhattan Zone 3 to Westchester Zone 6 is four message units (four times the base rate of 5 cents) or 20 cents. Message units are automatically charged and billed in total—not itemized.

## Types of Long Distance Calls

There are two general types of long distance calls—*station-to-station* and *person-to-person*. Even person-to-person calls can now be dialed, as discussed on pages 270-271. The secretary is expected to know the relative costs, the recommended and permissible practices, and the situation in which to use each type.

**Station-to-Station.** Because of the time and money saved through Direct Distance Dialing on *station-to-station calls*, business will probably tend to use this type of service more and more except in cases where there is a question of whether a specific person can be located readily.

Station-to-station calls are now Direct Distance Dialing calls. The procedure for learning a distant telephone number is discussed on page 270. The secretary dials station-to-station when she is willing to talk with anyone who answers the call or when she is reasonably sure the person wanted is within reach of his telephone. Charges begin at the time the called telephone or switchboard answers even if the person desired is not available. No charge is made if no one answers the telephone called.

Sometimes several valuable minutes are wasted by the efforts of the answering attendant to locate the person wanted. If a secretary were trying to reach a company salesman registered at a hotel, the hotel operator might have to page him in the lobby and the hotel restaurants. If she was unsuccessful in finding him, the call would be fully chargeable; or if it took her two and a half minutes to get him on the line, there would be little of a three-minute initial period left.

**Person-to-Person.** A *person-to-person call* is made when you must talk to a particular person or extension telephone. Charging begins when the called person or extension answers. The procedure for dialing a person-to-person call is given on pages 270-271.

| | STATION-TO-STATION | | | | | | PERSON-TO-PERSON |
|---|---|---|---|---|---|---|---|
| | DIRECT DISTANCE DIALED (paid by calling person) | | | | OPERATOR-ASSISTED | | ALL DAYS |
| | DAY Mon.-Fri. 8 am to 5 pm | EVENING Sun.-Fri. 5 pm to 11 pm | NIGHT All Days 11 pm to 8 am | WEEKEND Sat. 8 am to 11 pm Sun. 8 am to 5 pm | DAY Mon.-Fri. 8 am to 5 pm | EVENING Mon.-Fri. 5 pm to 8 am All Day Sat. & Sun. | ALL HOURS Lower overtime rates apply from 5 pm to 8 am weekends and all day on weekends and holidays |
| | Initial 3 Min. | Initial 3 Min. | Initial 1 Min. | Initial 3 Min. | Initial 3 Min. | Initial 3 Min. | Initial 3 Min. |
| Atlanta, Ga. | 1.05 | .65 | .20 | .50 | 1.45 | 1.10 | 2.40 |
| Atlantic City, N. J. | .60 | .40 | .15 | .35 | .70 | .70 | 1.05 |
| Boston, Mass. | .75 | .55 | .20 | .48 | .85 | .85 | 1.35 |
| Chicago, Ill. | 1.05 | .65 | .20 | .50 | 1.45 | 1.10 | 2.40 |
| Cleveland, Ohio | .95 | .60 | .20 | .50 | 1.25 | 1.05 | 1.90 |
| Denver, Colo. | 1.25 | .75 | .25 | .65 | 1.70 | 1.30 | 3.10 |

This table shows the relationship in cost between station-to-station calls that are dialed direct and those that are operator assisted and between station-to-station and person-to-person calls.

## Relative Costs

The station-to-station rate is lower than the person-to-person rate between the same points because the connection can be made in less time. The time of day and day of week affect station-to-station rates, as shown above on calls from New York City to six cities.

A table of long distance rates to many cities is given in the front of every telephone directory. Rates to places not listed are obtainable from the long distance operator.

The secretary must often decide whether to use person-to-person or station-to-station service. She can arrive at the better choice only by considering carefully every factor, including cost and whereabouts of the person called.

If you were asked to reach a salesman at his home office, it would not be good judgment to place a station-to-station call. More likely he would be out in his territory. On the other hand, if you were asked to call the manager of the New York branch office who is usually at his desk, you might place a station-to-station call.

The Bell system is trying to decrease the number of operator-assisted calls by emphasizing the advantages of direct dialing. An advertisement in a business magazine features a prominent businessman saying, "On long distance calling, I play the percentages. I've learned I'm ahead when I dial direct rather than call person-to-person, even if the odds are only 50-50 that my party will be there."

This map shows telephone areas, area codes and time zones (Standard Time) in the continental United States and Canada.

## Telephone Systems

More than 90% of the nation's telephones belong to the regional telephone companies that comprise the Bell system. In addition, there are 1,850 independent telephone systems. The telephone network is truly a giant. It is possible to make long distance calls to all telephones in the various domestic systems, as well as to most other countries and territories throughout the world. Most Bell systems, and many of the others, have Direct Distance Dialing (DDD). (See page 270.)

## Time Zones

Time zones are important to the secretary in placing long distance calls. A New York office would not call San Francisco before 12 noon because there would be little likelihood of reaching anyone in the San Francisco office before 9 a.m. Conversely, a secretary in Los Angeles would not place a call for Boston, Massachusetts, after 2 p.m., for very likely the office in Boston would be closed very shortly after 5 p.m. During summer months, of course, areas on Daylight Saving will be an hour later. If placing overseas calls is part of the secretary's job, she should learn the time differences for the cities called.

The map that appears at the top of this page indicates time zones in the continental United States and adjacent Canadian Provinces so that the person placing a long distance call can plan his calls to coincide with the business day in the place called. The time-zone map shows the code number to be used with the desired long distance number. The time at the place where the call originates determines whether day, evening, or night rates apply. Daylight Saving may affect some points during the summer.

### Placing Long Distance Calls

Long distance calls may be made by Direct Distance Dialing or through the long distance operator.

**Direct Distance Dialing (DDD).** Station-to-station long distance calls are dialed direct, without assistance from an operator except in case of difficulty. Usually, the caller dials *1\** plus a three-digit *area code*, then the telephone number desired, except when he is dialing a number with his own area code number.

Specific directions for DDD may be found in the front section of the telephone directory. The general procedures to be followed are described in the next two paragraphs.

Secure the area code from the company letterhead (where it is often included with the address), from your desk telephone directory, the front of the telephone directory, or the operator. If you have the area code but do not know the telephone number of the person to be called, dial the prefix 1 (where necessary), the area code, and the number 555-1212. After you identify to the information clerk the city you wish to call, she can give you the number. There is no charge for this service. If there is even a remote possibility of later calls, record both the area code and the telephone number in your personal directory.

Dial the number carefully, but if you reach the wrong number on any DDD call, obtain the name of the city you have reached and promptly report this information to the operator to avoid charges for the call. If you are cut off before completing a call, inform the operator so that the charges can be adjusted. If it is evident that for some reason your call is not going through, dial the operator for help. Sometimes you get a recorded message telling you that your call has not been completed and asking you to initiate it again.

**Operator-Assisted Calls.** If you know the area code and telephone number to be called but you wish to call person-to-person, collect, on a credit card, or with the call to be charged to another number, you need only routine operator assistance. Follow this procedure (known as *Expanded Direct Distance Dialing*):

---

*Some areas do not require dialing the prefix *1*. Learn and follow your local usage.

1. Dial *O* (zero), the area code, the telephone number.
2. When the operator answers, for a:

  *Person-to-person call*, give the name of the person you are calling.

  *Collect call*, say "Collect" and give your name.

  *Credit card call*, say "Credit card call" and give your credit card number.

  *Call charged to another number*, say "Bill to" and give the area code and telephone number to which the call is to be billed.

If you require some special assistance from the operator, dial *O*. When she answers, state your problem and give her whatever information you have. One secretary had to call an official in Washington, D.C., at two o'clock for her employer, who expected to be in the local courthouse near another telephone at that time. She explained the situation to the operator, who placed the call at two o'clock to the courthouse telephone but charged the call to the employer's office telephone. Another secretary was asked to get in touch with Mr. A. J. Dearing, who was staying at a Pittsburgh hotel. The secretary told the long distance operator that her only clue to Mr. Dearing's whereabouts was that he would be staying at one of the better hotels. The operator checked the hotels until she located Mr. Dearing. The secretary need not hesitate to ask for this kind of service.

## Paying for Long Distance

The secretary may be responsible for accepting long distance charges, accounting for them, reversing them, or securing her employer's credit card on which he charges calls.

**Obtaining Charges on Toll Calls.** Charges for long distance calls are referred to as *toll charges*. If you need to know the cost of a call, request the operator *at the time the call is placed* to report the charges. She will then notify you after the call has been completed and the cost has been calculated. This service is not available on DDD calls.

**Cost Records of Toll Calls.** For accounting purposes most companies charge toll calls in their records to specific departments, clients, or jobs. With memorandum records kept at the secretary's desk showing the date, point called, and the person calling, the correct toll charges can be checked against the bill and charged to the proper departments.

The federal government levies on long distance calls an excise tax which the telephone company collects from the subscriber. The tax rates are shown on the customer's bill. If the secretary is required to keep a cost record of each long distance call for accounting purposes, the tax must be computed and added to the toll charge.

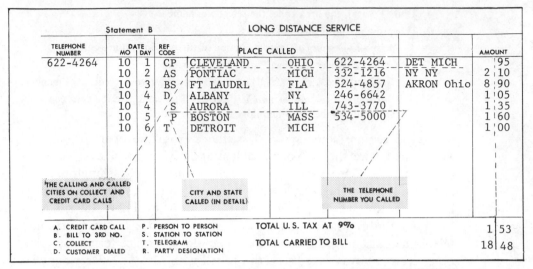

From this statement it is possible to allocate toll charges to the proper account. Notice that the calls involved the use of the credit card, direct dialing, a telegram charged to the telephone, and reverse charges. The number of the telephone called is included on each listing as an aid in allocating the charges and verifying the accuracy of the bill.

**Collect Calls.** A long distance call (toll call) can be made *collect*. Charges on person-to-person and station-to-station calls can be reversed —that is, charged to the telephone called rather than to the one placing the call. The request to reverse the charges, however, must be made at the time of placing the call so that the receiving number can have an opportunity to accept or refuse the charge. Because collect calls are operator assisted, they are more expensive than automatic calls.

**Telephone Credit Cards.** Your employer may carry a telephone credit card that entitles him to charge his long distance calls to his home or business number while traveling. It shows his code number, name, and business affiliation. When making a call, the employer tells the long distance operator that it is a credit card call and gives her the code number and the number of the party he wants to reach. Credit card calls are identified as such on the monthly statement.

## SECRETARIAL RESPONSIBILITY FOR TELEGRAMS

Once a telegram presaged only disaster. Then it became largely a business tool, the quickest and cheapest method of relaying abbreviated business information. It is still widely used to dramatize the urgency of a situation—to solicit an overdue check or manuscript, to stop an

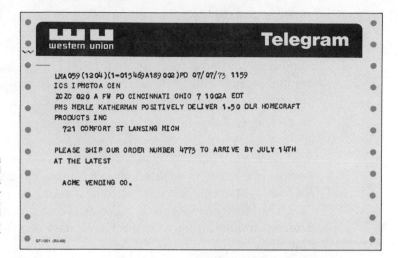

western union

# Telegram

LMA 059 (1204)(1-015469A189 002)PD 07/07/73 1159
ICS IPMSTOA CSN
ZCZC 020 A FW PD CINCINNATI OHIO 7 1002A EDT
PMS MERLE KATHERMAN POSITIVELY DELIVER 1.50 DLR HOMECRAFT
PRODUCTS INC
 721 COMFORT ST LANSING MICH

PLEASE SHIP OUR ORDER NUMBER 4773 TO ARRIVE BY JULY 14TH
AT THE LATEST

 ACME VENDING CO.

SF-1201 (R5-69)

When for some reason a telegram must be delivered by messenger, there is a charge of $1.50 for the service. Note the words "Positively deliver" and the delivery charge notation, 1.50, immediately after the addressee's name.

unwanted action, to influence political action, to serve notice of eviction, to relay congratulations, to get attention that might otherwise be denied, and to transact business rapidly when a record of notification is needed. It is still important, therefore, that the secretary learn to use telegraph services for the right occasion and to choose appropriate service.

## Domestic Telegraph Services

A secretary works primarily with domestic messages—those communicated within the continental United States. Techniques for sending telegrams to Canada and Mexico, however, are practically the same as those for the continental United States.

The classes of telegrams and other services are standardized; but rates and regulations occasionally change, so it is advisable to secure up-to-date information from time to time from your local Western Union office.

**The Three Classes of Telegrams.** Just as the Post Office has various classes of mail services, Western Union offers a choice of telegraphic services. The three classes of domestic messages are regular telegrams, overnight telegrams, and Mailgrams.

Rates for all classes of telegrams are determined by whether the telegram is to be received intrastate (within the same state) or interstate. The rate for an interstate message is somewhat higher than that for an intrastate message.

An additional charge of $1.50 is made for delivery by messenger of a telegram, a well-justified expense when fast delivery is urgent. The service, however, *must be requested.*

*Regular Telegrams.* A *regular telegram* is sent immediately at any time, day or night, and takes precedence over all other classes of domestic service. The minimum charge is based on 15 words exclusive of address and signature; an additional charge is made for each additional word. Although deferred service is available at lower rates, the regular telegram is used most frequently.

*Overnight Telegram.* An overnight telegram can be sent at any time up to midnight for delivery the next morning. It is a less expensive class of service. The minimum charge is based upon a message of 100 words. For longer messages a charge is made for each additional word. An overnight telegram is used when next-morning delivery is acceptable.

The overnight telegram is especially attractive to West Coast companies communicating with the East Coast because of the three-hour time difference. An overnight telegram originating on the West Coast after the East Coast office is closed will be delivered by the time the receiving office opens the following morning.

*Mailgram.* The Mailgram combines telegraph and postal services. Western Union installs its telegram-receiving equipment in the local post office. A postal employee receives the up-to-100-word messages on continuous rolls of paper (from late afternoon through the night), tears each message off the roll, and mails it in a window envelope for guaranteed delivery in the first delivery of the morning. The Mailgram is relatively low in cost.

Mailgrams can be input into the computerized equipment that provides post office reception by TWX and Telex only (see page 289). Public filing is possible in only a limited number of cities; however, the Mailgram represents a combination of public service facilities that will probably expand in usage.

**Selecting the Proper Class of Service.** The common practice in a company with a communications manager is to type the message on a standard company form similar to the one illustrated here. The communications manager notes whether the message is for immediate delivery or whether it can be sent at a cheaper rate for later delivery and chooses the class of service to use.

A secretary without the services of a communications manager chooses the appropriate service. When time is of the essence, she will send a regular telegram. For a message to be delivered at a certain time (at a dinner honoring a friend, for example), she will still choose a regular telegram. If a message of 16-100 words can better serve the purpose of the sender, she will choose the overnight telegram or (where available) the Mailgram.

# MAILGRAM

```
MAILGRAM NEWARK

VIA WU ISCS (CH091NN305163) 05/30/71
FROM: XYZHQS NYK
ZCZC 001 NEW YORK NY 16
ZIP 07020




A. B. JONES, EXECUTIVE VICEPRESIDENT
CLARKE PAPER BOX COMPANY
411 2ND STREET
NEWARK NEW JERSEY 07020



BT
   DEAR MR. JONES:

COMPANIES ACROSS THE COUNTRY ARE NOW BENEFITING FROM A FASTER,
YET ECONOMICAL, MEANS OF HANDLING THEIR WRITTEN COMMUNICATIONS
THAN EVER BEFORE BY USING WESTERN UNION'S MAILGRAM SERVICE.

FOR THE FIRST TIME, A CUSTOMER CAN BE ASSURED THAT HIS MESSAGE
WILL BE DELIVERED TO ANY MAILBOX IN THE CONTINENTAL UNITED STATES,
EXCEPT ALASKA, ON THE NEXT BUSINESS DAY, ELIMINATING A GREAT DEAL
OF DELAY AND FRUSTRATION BECAUSE OF SLOW AND UNPREDICTABLE MAIL
DELIVERIES.

   JIM JONES
   WESTERN UNION
NNNN (1129A EST)

MAILGRAM NEWARK
```

```
                              TELEGRAM
                              Regular
                              January 31, 197-

   Mrs. Dorothy Jacobs         Phone:   (815) 761-4399
   Jacobs Realty Company
   379 Parkside Drive
   Sycamore, Ill.

   Mr. and Mrs. Raymond Anderson would like to buy the house at 742

   Hill Street.  Please make firm offer of $48,900 to owner today if

   possible.

                              Phillips, Relocations Dept.
                              Electronics Development, Inc.

   sf
```

If her company has a communications department, the secretary types the appropriate number of copies of a telegram on plain paper and sends the original to the communications department for filing.

To aid in deciding which class of service to use, the secretary can obtain printed rate folders and relationship-of-rates tables from her local Western Union office.

**Addressing Telegrams.** The telegraph company makes no extra charge for long addresses except in unusual cases. For instance, there is no extra charge for "George Harrison, care of Henderson Manufacturing Company, 1 William Street, New York, N.Y." or "Mr. and Mrs. William Schwartz and family" or for the inclusion of a telephone number that will expedite delivery. There is a charge for "or Harry Miller" in the address "John Smithson or Harry Miller."

Sometimes people address a telegram to "Robert Smith, Empire State Building, New York City," forgetting that there are thousands of people employed in that building. Use company or firm names and room numbers. The address "24 Fifty-Second Street, New York City" may necessitate attempts at delivery on both East and West Fifty-Second Street. If, however, the telegram is addressed to a well-known national or local figure, or a nationally known business or bank, it is unnecessary to give the room number, building, and street address.

**Typing the Telegram.** Telegrams can be typed on plain paper labeled *Telegram* or perhaps provided with a box for indicating type of service, relative urgency, and the like. The number of office copies varies among business organizations. If there is a communications manager, his department files a copy. You will certainly need at least one file copy, and you may also need an accounting copy and a verification copy.

If the message is very important or contains technical information, the verification copy can be mailed to the addressee to make certain that the telegraph message was transmitted correctly. The sample telegram on page 281 provides a model. Paragraphs and punctuation are transmitted without charge and should be typed in the telegram to be sent.

**The Message.**  The message should be complete but concise, including only words necessary for clarity. It is better to say, "Arrive International Airport at 8:30 p.m. daylight saving, Thursday, United Flight 241; please meet plane," than "Arrive New York Thursday 8:30 plane. Please meet me." With the latter message, the recipient does not know which airport is meant, whether the plane left the sender's airport at 8:30 or will arrive in New York at 8:30, whether 8:30 in the morning or at night is intended, and at which terminal to expect his guest.

Unnecessary words such as "the," "and," "that," "a," and "I" and minor adverbs and adjectives can be omitted without loss of meaning. Abbreviations, groups of figures, and combinations of letters not forming a dictionary word are counted at the rate of one word for every five letters or fraction of five letters.

A signature identification, such as "Sales Manager," may clarify the message and costs no more than a single name. Any street address needed by the addressee should be included below the signature line.

Below the complete message, type the dictator's initials and your own, followed by the sender's street address when it is not to be transmitted but included only for reference.

If the addressee is a passenger on a train, bus, or airplane, the telegram can be delivered to him if all the essential information is given:

```
MISS DELIA CRAIG
TWA FLIGHT 402, EASTBOUND
DUE KENNEDY INTERNATIONAL AIRPORT, JULY 6, 8:15 P.M.
NEW YORK
```

When the message is in answer to a telegram for which the street address of the sender is unknown, write after the name of the addressee the date of his telegram which you are answering, as "Answer May 29," meaning you are answering his telegram of May 29. Then the originating office will be able to locate the original telegram to facilitate delivery of the answer. Use the city and telegraph office from which the original telegram was received, in place of the regular address. The originating telegraph office is the main office in the city unless the identifying letters for a branch office precede the city name. In the following answer address, *MS* identifies the branch office.

```
SCOTT DORNER, ANSWER MAY 29 MS NEW YORK, N.Y.
```

When you want to wire a person who intends to call at a Western Union office for the message or money order, address the message:

R. C. ROBERS, CARE WESTERN UNION, COLUMBUS, GEORGIA

When sending a telegram to a person who will register at some later time at a hotel, indicate this information by adding to the message: *Hold for Arrival.*

A "rush message" takes precedence over other typewriting and can be typed without removing material that is already in the typewriter. If you have a carbon pack in your typewriter:

1. Roll the material backward until one inch or so is left in front of the platen.
2. Drop a plain sheet or a Western Union blank against the paper table and another behind each carbon. Add carbons if necessary.
3. Roll the material forward to position the blank for typing the message.
4. Roll the material backward and remove the original and carbon copies.
5. Position the material you were previously typing and continue.

**Code Words.** For fewer chargeable words and as a measure of privacy in some cases, code words are devised for names of specific products, stock numbers, titles of publications, names of clients, and so on. It would be quite costly to write these names, numbers, and titles in full each time. Code words are usually of five letters or less, but they may be longer if they are dictionary words.

A public accounting office would not refer to a client by name in a telegram because such identification might divulge confidential information. A code name for the client tells nothing. For example:

SATAB INVENTORY $3,250,000. SURPLUS $950,000.
TREW PAPERS WILL BE SHIPPED FRIDAY.

Code systems are classified as private and public. Private code systems are those devised by private business concerns for use in messages with others who are supplied with copies of the code. Public code systems are provided by certain publishers. Messages using code words may be translated by anyone who has a copy of that code system.

## Filing a Telegram

In telegraph parlance, *filing* a telegram means to get it into the hands of the transmitting agency. A telegraph message can be filed:

Over the telephone
By your Desk-Fax
At the communication manager's desk in your company
Over the counter at the telegraph office

In filing a telegram over the telephone, the secretary asks the operator to read the message back to verify its accuracy. She should always specify the type of service wanted: regular, overnight, Mailgram, or messenger delivery.

**Canceling a Filed Telegram.** When the executive wants to cancel a telegram that has been filed, call the transmitting telegraph office immediately. If it is possible to do so, that office will comply with the request. If the message has not left the local office at the time of cancellation, no charge is made. Charges stand for messages received at the destination office, as well as an additional charge for the message of cancellation; and, since the cancellation message can go no faster than the original message, cancellation is sometimes impossible.

**Precautionary Measures.** Two special services (repeat-back and report-delivery) can be requested on the foregoing types of messages.

*Repeat-Back Service.* If *Repeat Back* is typed above the address on a telegraph blank, the destination office of the telegraph company will (for an additional charge equal to one half the unrepeated message rate) repeat the message back to the sending office to be checked for possible error. If an error is discovered, the corrected message is then sent at no additional charge. The liability of the telegraph company is increased when this service is used. Although this service is not frequently used, it is advantageous when the message contains technical terms, stock numbers, amounts of money, or code words. The words *Repeat Back* are counted as chargeable words in computing the cost of the message.

A precautionary measure which Western Union provides without charge to business customers such as brokerage houses is to repeat at the bottom of the message received all numbers included. For instance, a telegram notifying a customer that he must pay for 50 shares of stock costing $1343.12 by two o'clock on October 2 would show typed at the bottom of the message "50, $1343.12, 2PM, and 2."

*Report-Delivery Service.* If the sender wishes the telegraph company to notify him when and to whom delivery of a message is made, *Report Delivery* is typed immediately after the addressee's name, as "Donald W. Eastman, Report Delivery, Wayne Manufacturing Co., 6012 West . . . ." and counts as two chargeable words. The report stating to whom and when the telegram was delivered is wired collect from the destination office of the telegraph company to the sender. This service is particularly valuable in trying to reach a person who is traveling.

**Methods of Paying Telegraph Charges.** Several methods of paying for telegraph services are used. Usually those who use these services infrequently pay cash for each message when it is filed. For those who make frequent use of telegrams, the telegraph company keeps a record of the charges and submits a monthly statement. When messages are sent by telephone, they are billed on the telephone company's toll statement. Payment can be made either through the telephone company or directly through a personal or company account with Western Union.

The telegraph company permits a person to send messages collect —that is, the recipient pays for the sending of the message. A firm may request its customers and sales representatives to send messages collect, in the first instance as a courtesy, and in the second to eliminate handling the charge on the salesmen's expense accounts. Western Union offers a liberal credit policy. A customer need only give his address or telephone number—home or business.

Whether the telegraph charges are billed on a Western Union statement or on the telephone toll statement, the secretary checks them with the file copies of the telegrams. The Western Union accounting office will help in resolving discrepancies.

## Handling Incoming Telegrams

When a telegram comes to your desk, it requires special and prompt handling, for its very use indicates urgency. Therefore, attach to it any pertinent information and give it to the executive at once.

A telegram will come to your desk by one of four ways:

**By office teleprinter and delivered to you**
**By telephone from the Western Union office**
**By Desk-Fax**
**By Western Union messenger**

If the telephone operator says, "I have a telegram for you," take the message down on your note pad and transcribe to a telegraph blank immediately afterward for easy later identification. It is always wise, however, to ask for a file copy to be sent by mail so that you can verify the message, especially if figures are involved.

If the telegraph company fails to deliver a message or makes an error in the transmission of the message, it is liable for damages. A maximum liability under each of the different circumstances is stated on the back of the telegraph blank. The liability is much larger when a message is sent at the "repeat back" rate (page 279).

A delivered telegram is illustrated on page 281. From the second typed line you can ascertain the city from which the message was sent, and the date that the message was filed. If it is other than a fast telegram,

```
 ШШШ                                       Telefax
 western union
 CALL                      CHARGE
 LETTERS   MAZ _____    TO 24764  Akron Construction Co.

                           Akron, Ohio, April 22, 197-

 Harry De Marco
 Buffalo Supply Co.                    APR 22 197— 3 P.M.
 624 Delaware Ave.
 Buffalo, N.Y.  14209

 Please call me tomorrow before noon with final
 figures on the Landon job.  We need to revise our
 completion date and must have your data.

                  Al Ebert
```

**SENDING BLANK**

*Send the above message, subject to terms on back hereof, which are hereby agreed to*

**PLEASE TYPE OR WRITE PLAINLY WITHIN BORDER-DO NOT FOLD**

WU I269 (R9/69)

There is no extra charge for an identifying title with the sender's name; therefore, the secretary includes the title unless her employer and the addressee are well acquainted, as was the case in this telegram.

the type of service in code precedes the name of the city. The first numbers in the line refer to the wire number of the message. The receiving telegraph office time-stamps the message, showing the full date and the exact time the message came into the office.

## Other Western Union Services

Western Union renders a number of services other than the transmission of messages. The telegraph company will serve as an intermediary in the transmission of money by means of a *telegraphic money order*. The sender gives the money to the telegraph office, which wires the destination office to pay that amount to a certain person in American Express Travelers' Checks, if desired. The recipient must be able to identify himself. The rates are the same as for a fifteen-word, fast telegram plus a money-order fee. Overnight money orders are charged at telegram rates. At a small extra charge a message may be included.

It is possible to get messenger and errand service by calling Western Union. Gifts such as Candygrams are available from and delivered by Western Union.

The secretary may be responsible for sending telegrams of congratulations, condolence, greetings of various kinds, or political endorsement or dissension. Some of these may be the special-rate standard-form telegrams for which the suggested messages are available in Western Union offices.

The words *Will call* can supplant the address on a telegram. When a traveler knows in advance that a telegram will be sent to him *will call* in a specific city, he calls for the message at the Western Union office there. Telegraphic money orders are often sent with a *Will-call* designation. After 72 hours a message is sent without charge to report that the message has not been called for.

## SUGGESTED READINGS

Cook, Fred S., and Lenore S. Forti. *Professional Secretary's Handbook.* Chicago: Dartnell Corporation, 1971, pp. 95-106.

*The Executive Secretary's Desk Manual.* Waterford: Bureau of Business Practice, 1968, pp. 13-15.

Griesinger, Frank K. "Ma Bell Interconnects," "All That New Telecommunications Equipment," and "Facsimile Units: They Transmit What Voice Can't." *Administrative Management*, Vol. 33, No. 10 (October, 1972), pp. 35-50.

Klein, A.E., Supervisory ed. *The New World Secretarial Handbook.* Cleveland: World Publishing Co., 1968, pp. 203-223.

## QUESTIONS FOR DISCUSSION

1. Think of business telephone calls in which you have engaged. Describe the techniques used by the other party that have pleased you and those that have annoyed you.

2. Examine your local telephone directory. What information is found in the introductory pages? in the Yellow Pages?

3. If your office is located in Philadelphia, between what office hours (yours) would you try to reach an office in Salt Lake City by long distance? If your office is in Salt Lake City, between what office hours (yours) would you try to reach a Philadelphia office?

4. What class of long distance service would you use in trying to reach each of the following persons?
   (a) A buyer in a department store
   (b) A lawyer who is pleading an important case
   (c) A politician who is staying in a hotel at which you made his reservation
   (d) Your employer's son who lives in a college dormitory not equipped with Centrex

5. When a call between two executives is being connected by their secretaries, the question may arise as to which executive should be placed on the line first to await the answer of the other executive. What is your opinion?

6. What precautionary measures can the secretary take to assure more effective telegraph services, both sending and receiving?

7. Would you suggest establishing a rule that a verification copy be sent to the address of every telegram? Explain your answer.

8. What considerations would affect your decision to send a full-rate message rather than an overnight telegram?

9. What class of telegraphic service would you use in each of the following situations:

   (a) At 3 p.m. a secretary in Seattle, Washington, is given a 30-word telegraphic message to send as quickly as possible to an office in Boston, Massachusetts, which closes at 5 p.m.

   (b) At 11:30 a.m. a secretary in Albany, New York, has a 40-word message to be sent to a firm in Butte, Montana. The message should be delivered the same day.

   (c) At 3:30 p.m. a secretary in Oklahoma City is instructed to send a 120-word message to a firm in Salem, Oregon. Delivery the same day is not important.

   (d) At 3:30 p.m. a secretary in Minneapolis is given a 15-word message to be sent to a firm in Montgomery, Alabama. It is important that the message should be delivered as quickly as possible.

10. What instructions would you include, or what service would you request, in sending these telegrams?

    (a) To a person who will register at a hotel at some later time

    (b) To either of two persons at the same address

    (c) To a person traveling by automobile who is expecting a message at a Western Union office in a specific city

    (d) On which you wish to know when delivery was made

    (e) Which *must* be transmitted exactly as filed

11. Assuming that the following words came at the ends of typewritten lines, indicate those words that you could correctly divide and show where you would make the divisions. Then use the Reference Guide to verify or correct your answers.

| | | |
|---|---|---|
| freight | profit-taking | science |
| Anderson | forgotten | February 26 |
| half-brother | holiday | mailable |
| foundation | selling | into |

## PROBLEMS

■ 1. Locate in the alphabetic section of your local telephone directory the numbers for the following. Type in tabular form a list showing for each item the organization or department wanted, the name under which the telephone is listed, and the telephone number.

(a) City hall
(b) Western Union
(c) Fire department
(d) Park or recreation department
(e) Police department

(f) Post office
(g) Public library
(h) The nearest hospital
(i) Your college or university
(j) The local office of the state employment service
(k) Telephone repair service
(l) Weather information
(m) Local ZIP Codes

■ 2. The purpose of this problem is to familiarize you with the organization of your Yellow Pages.

Type a list showing the heading in the Yellow Pages under which you would find the names of subscribers for each of the types indicated in the following list:

(a) Agents for calculating machines
(b) Certified public accountants
(c) Dealers in advertising stickers
(d) Dealers in traveling bags
(e) Dealers in window displays
(f) Dealers in window shades
(g) Income tax specialists
(h) Interior decorators
(i) Lawyers
(j) Ministers

■ **3.** Type the following excerpts of conversation in acceptable form. Then use the Reference Guide to verify or correct your answers.

(a) **The opening part of a telephone conversation which occurred this Monday, shortly before noon. Mr. Lawrence Bell called Mr. Thomas Green.**

Bell—Tom, have you come to a decision yet? Green—No, I'd like a day or two more to think it over. Bell—Time is getting short, Tom. I have to know by Wednesday at the latest. Green—I'll sleep on it and let you know the first thing in the morning.

(b) **A confidential memorandum to the president of the company, reporting on a conversation which occurred in the executive's office two weeks ago today between Steve Douglas and Charles Duncan:**

This is the conversation as I recall it. Steve said I talked it over with Nelson, very confidentially of course, and he thought he could arrange a meeting before the end of this month. Charles said do you think it was wise to expose our hand. Steve said I don't think talking it over with Nelson can be called exposing our hand. He's trustworthy. Charles said well it's done now. What about the meeting?

■ **4.** Rewrite each of the following telegraph messages, using not more than 15 words so that the message may be sent as a regular telegram.

(a) THERE WILL BE A SALES MEETING SATURDAY MORNING IN THE OFFICE AT TEN O'CLOCK. PLEASE ARRANGE TO BE THERE. BRING REQUESTED ESTIMATES.

(b) MR. WILCOX WIRED SAYING HE WOULD BE HERE TOMORROW. IS IT POSSIBLE FOR YOU TO COME BACK? MUST KNOW BY THREE O'CLOCK.

(c) IN ANSWER YOUR TELEGRAM SUGGEST YOU OFFER A 40% DISCOUNT TERMS 2% 10 DAYS. DELIVERY TO BE MADE FOB NEW YORK.

■ **5.** The following incoming telephone calls were received while your employer, Mr. Simpson, was out of the office. Prepare a brief memorandum for Mr. Simpson on each call.

(a) **Mr. Kiley called at 3:25 p.m. and left a message that he would pick up your employer at 5:10 p.m. at the front entrance to the building.**

(b) **Mr. Mellon, of the District Sales Corporation, called at 3:30 p.m.; he said he would call back at 4:30 p.m.**

(c) **Mr. Wilcox, of National Products, Inc., called at 4 p.m. about their order for equipment and wants you to call him back. His number is 243-4891.**

(d) **Mr. Roberts, of the Cleveland office, called long distance at 4:10 p.m. to tell you that the Fuller Implement Company order is to be canceled. A letter of explanation will be mailed tonight.**

■ **6.** Miss Mary Holmes, secretary to Harry Miller, handled the following telephone calls:

(a) Mr. Miller was attending a Kiwanis luncheon meeting at the Terrace Hotel and expected to be back at his desk at 1:30 p.m. At 12:15 a long distance call came in from his superior, who was in Boston. Miss Holmes said, "Mr. Miller will not be back until 1:30 and cannot be reached until then."

(b) At closing time the long distance operator had not reached a person with whom Mr. Miller must talk before the next morning. Mr. Miller was going to dinner at his brother's home but would be at his own home until 7 p.m. Miss Holmes said, "Operator, try that number again and keep trying until seven o'clock. Mr. Miller will be at 734-8973 in half an hour and will be there until seven."

(c) Mr. Miller was playing golf. The long distance operator informed Miss Holmes that she had a call from his New York broker, Mr. Adams, who wanted to talk to him as soon as possible. Miss Holmes said, "Mr. Miller is out of the office for the afternoon. If you will tell me where Mr. Adams can be reached, I will try to get in touch with Mr. Miller and ask him to call back immediately. I should be able to reach him within an hour."

(d) Mr. Miller was writing copy for an advertising circular and told Miss Holmes that he did not wish to be disturbed under any circumstances before four o'clock. A call came in from George Herman, his assistant, who was in Baltimore attending a sales conference. Mr. Herman was to leave Baltimore on a three o'clock plane. Miss Holmes said, "I am sorry, but Mr. Miller can't be reached this afternoon. Ask Mr. Herman if I can help him. I am Mr. Miller's secretary."

(e) Mr. Miller wanted to make a long distance call from the office telephone, 623-2219, to Dr. L. K. Nelson of New Orleans on a personal matter. Miss Holmes did not know Dr. Nelson's number but knew that he was a noted ophthalmologist. She dialed the operator and said, "Operator, this is 623-2219. I want to call Dr. L. K. Nelson in New Orleans. I do not have the number, but he is a well-known eye specialist. Will you give me the code and the number, please, so that I can dial him direct."

(f) Mr. Miller wanted to call Mr. Houston in the purchasing department of the Acme Company in White Plains, New York, Area Code 914. Mr. Miller wished to say that on Friday afternoon he would call on either Mr. Houston or his assistant about the new service contract. Could one of them be available for a conference? Miss Holmes made an operator-assisted call.

(g) Mr. Miller wanted to call his wife, who was visiting in Akron, Ohio. Her number was 864-0753 and the Area Code 216. He said that it need not be a person-to-person call; but he wanted the call charged to his home number, 266-7106. Miss Holmes said, "Operator, this is 263-2219, Extension 62. I want to place a call to 864-0753 in Akron, Ohio. Don't charge the call to this number. It should be charged to 266-7106."

(h) Mr. Miller wanted to call Lawrence Taylor of the Lenox Supply Company in Los Angeles about the cancellation of an order. The number was 823-6501; the Area Code number, 213; the charges were to be reversed. Miss Holmes said, "Operator, this is 263-2219. I want to place a call to Lawrence Taylor of the Lenox Supply Company in Los Angeles. I don't know the number. Tell the switchboard operator there that Mr. Miller won't pay for the call because it is about an order he plans to cancel. Ask Mr. Taylor to pay for it.''

(i) While Miss Holmes was on the button telephone, a second call came through. She excused herself and answered the second call, which was for Mr. Miller. She depressed the local button to ask Mr. Miller if he would take the call and then transferred it to his wire. When she returned to the first caller, he had been disconnected.

(j) Mr. Miller asked Miss Holmes to call the Research Center at the State University. She dialed *Information*, obtained the number, and then made a direct (DDD) dialing of the number. Upon connection, she found that she had the wrong Research Center; but they gave her the correct number to call. Miss Holmes thanked them, hung up, listened for the dial tone, and dialed the correct number.

(k) Mr. Miller asked Miss Holmes to get Harry Stokes of the Eastern Publishing Company in Boston on the phone. Miss Holmes checked the letterhead of the Eastern Publishing Company, obtained the telephone number, and dialed the number direct (DDD). When Eastern Publishing Company answered, Miss Holmes said, "Mr. Stokes, please." Miss Holmes then waited patiently for approximately six minutes before her connection at the publishing company came back on the line to say, "Thank you for waiting. I am unable to locate Mr. Stokes. He is in the building somewhere; I am still trying. Do you wish to wait?"

Miss Holmes was surprised when Mr. Miller told her that he had arranged for her to take a five-hour course to improve her telephone techniques. She had always thought that she was unusually proficient in this area.

Criticize Miss Holmes's handling of the eleven calls described above. Indicate what you would have done in the cases that were poorly handled.

# Chapter 13

## SPECIAL TELEPHONE AND TELEGRAPHIC SERVICES

The breakthroughs in electronic word-and-number transmission are revolutionizing telephone and telegraph services. The potential for sending voice, pictures, typed or longhand messages, and other data has increased vastly. Telephone and telegraph systems are being challenged by newcomers who are also introducing new machines and devices into an increasingly competitive field.

Until recently, branch business offices controlled their individual departments, compiling and sending operating reports weekly, monthly, or annually to headquarters for use as the basis for decision making. Improved business communications have, however, reduced the communicating time between branches or plants and their headquarters from days to seconds as information flows freely and constantly among all units of the organization. No part of the organization is isolated from any other part. Management can base its decisions on information more current and complete than before and can better control and coordinate its operations.

> By 1980, the U. S. will be rewired for a new era in the communication of sight, sound, and data. Virtually all the experts see the same broad-brush panorama: the growth of computer networks and the promise of the cashless-checkless society; the development of the picturephone and the commuting-free office far from the city; the use of broad-band cables and laser-bright wall-sized TV pictures in the home; the creation of worldwide satellite-linked distribution systems for information and education. And more. The technology seems ready, only a short step from production. — "The Revolution in the Phone Business," *BUSINESS WEEK*, November 6, 1971

## THE NATURE OF TODAY'S COMMUNICATION SYSTEMS

With appropriate sending equipment, all forms of information can be transmitted from a point of origin to any distant point equipped with appropriate receiving equipment: handwritten or typed messages, processed or unprocessed data, pictures, or voice.

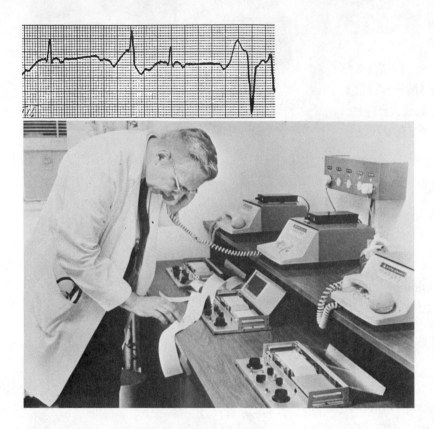

Reproduced at the left is an electrocardiogram transmitted through Bell System Data-Phone service to a cardiac specialist for his diagnosis.

—*Western Electric*

## Teleprinting Machines

Western Union and others have for many years used the teleprinter for sending messages. The operator types the message, which is reproduced on perforated tape. The paper tape is then fed into an automatic transmitter that sends a message to a high-speed message center in a nearby central city. There an electronic "brain," acting on codes previously punched into the tape, routes the message through the proper circuits. The words travel across the country at the speed of light. Seconds later another tape—a duplicate of the original one prepared in your local telegraph office—is punched automatically in the destination switching center, where it is quickly translated back into regular characters on the receiving teleprinter and delivered.

New uses for teleprinters have developed, and businesses have installed teleprinters suited to their own needs. Teleprinters have improved as technology has improved; so messages can now be sent not only by keyboard but by other means, such as data on punched tape and cards sent via electromagnetic waves. The output item can be page copy, printed tape, or punched tape.

A fast, efficient way to communicate in written form, the Telex or TWX dial service gives your business versatile and reliable written communications on a message-rate basis. Messages can be transmitted at more than 100 words a minute.

—*Western Union*

Teleprinters or teletypewriters are used by large companies for intercompany and intracompany communication. A teletypist calls the other operator in another location. Once the connection is established, operators at the two machines converse by typing back and forth or by feeding paper tape to the equipment for automatic transmission of the message. Teletypewritten communication is similar to a telephone conversation, except that the message is written instead of oral, providing the advantage of printed records of the messages sent and received.

For years Western Union used the Telex teleprinter. In 1971 it bought the rival TWX teleprinter. The two systems integrated into one network serving virtually every major business location in the United States, Canada, and Mexico.

Western Union teleprinting is placed in post offices for use in printing out Mailgrams. (See page 274.)

## Tone Transmission

Words and numbers can be sent long distances by transmitting *tones* to a terminal point on equipment that reconverts the sound signals into words and numbers.

**The Touch Telephone.** The telephone companies have developed a telephone that can be used for both regular service and long distance tone transmission of business information to compatible equipment that converts the electronic signals into printouts. In contrast to the ordinary dial telephone, the touch telephone provides small business with access to an entire communication system. The touch telephone inputs business information into either a company's own transmission system or a network used by numerous subscribers. (See pages 423–446 for a more complete discussion of data communication systems.)

**The Data-Phone.** The telephone companies also install the Data-Phone, which transmits data over the regular telephone network.

**Foreign Attachments.** The Federal Trade Commission's 1968 Carterfone decision, a potent motivation to telephone equipment innovations, struck down the American Telephone and Telegraph's restriction against all "foreign attachments" (devices not owned by the telephone company) to the telephone system. Now a user can own his plug-in hardware. Keen competition is introducing many new devices, with a resultant need for technical standards for design and maintenance.

A number of manufacturers produce private automatic branch exchanges with special features for the hotel-motel market and others. Some PABX's (private automatic branch exchanges) substitute a "beep" on the busy line for the busy signal. With this system, one can either press a *hold* button and answer a new call or allow the switchboard to ring a nearby telephone automatically if the first telephone ignores the ring, thus salvaging calls that may mean increased profits.

Many of the small PABX's have cordless or plugless consoles, so receptionists can operate them easily. Conference calls can be set up also. It is also possible for an important caller or an incoming emergency call to break into busy lines. Most PABX's can be tied into paging and dictation systems.

## Xerography

Equipment for the transmittal of facsimile copies of documents through regular telephone circuits is available, with which the operator dials the recipient, places a document in the long distance facsimile unit, and places the transmitting device on the unit. Six minutes later a clear facsimile is reproduced 3,000 miles away by *Long Distance Xerography* or other facsimile equipment.

Incidentally, the suffix *Fax* refers to transmittal of facsimile copies. For instance, *Desk-Fax* is Western Union equipment designed for the desk of the secretary for receiving and sending messages to the local Western Union office. *Intrafax* is an interoffice transmittal system for sending pictorial, written, typed, or printed matter. *Ticket-Fax* reproduces an airplane or railroad ticket at a receiving center in eight seconds. *High-Speed Fax* can send a whole 20-page magazine, including illustrations, in a few minutes.

## Microwave Radio Transmission

The relaxation of Federal Trade Commission controls subsequent to the Carterfone decision has led to the development of customer-owned telephone systems that can interconnect with existing telephone facilities. Microwave Communications, Inc., built the first link in the first customer-owned telephone system, between Chicago and St. Louis. It is a common-carrier system that provides both voice- and data-grade communication by radio beams of ultrashort wavelengths. The great advantages of microwave transmission are economy, high quality, and the choice of purchasing a system or leasing lines for private use. For instance, a renter could lease enough voice-grade channels to meet its needs during business hours and switch to broadband data channels at night. (Broadband exchange service automatically links two subscribers over bands of greater width than are required for voice transmission, thus providing greater speed and capability for handling various nonvoice data.) Microwave Communications, Inc., expects to extend its system into a national network that will serve all of the communication needs of its customers.

## EXTENDED SERVICES

The preceding section describes technical developments that are to a large extent informational to the secretary. These developments have, however, provided her with extended services which she should be able to handle capably.

## Wide Area Telephone Service (WATS)

WATS service enables the user to place an unlimited number of calls within a specific radius of his place of business for a flat-rate monthly fee, unlimited in either number or length of calls. A measured-time service is also available that provides ten hours of unlimited calls.

The country is divided, for WATS service, into six geographic areas ranging in size from Area I, which usually covers only neighboring states, to Area VI, which extends from coast to coast.

One type of company may need expanded long distance service to only one or possibly two zones, while another may need WATS service covering all six areas. One company may want unlimited calls, while another may need only a limited number of calls and may want to restrict the length of calls. With WATS, abuses of the long distance privilege sometimes occur, so each subscriber develops its own means of controlling calls. The secretary should be exemplary in her use of the WATS privilege.

WATS service has been extended to *Inward WATS*. A company that has already purchased WATS service advertises a telephone number beginning with 800 and states that there is no charge to the calling party. (See page 266.) Since the call has already been paid for, there is no further billing.

### Extended Area Service (EAS)

The concept of Extended Area Service (EAS) reflects the larger community of interest that exists in metropolitan areas. A business located in Washington, D.C., that wishes "local" service to suburbs (such as Alexandria, Virginia, and Silver Springs, Maryland) could purchase reduced-rate EAS at a flat monthly fee. The extent of use of such service is shown by the fact that more than a third of the calls handled as long distance calls 20 years ago now go through as local.

### Leased Lines

It is possible for a company to lease from the telephone company or from a private company telegraph and telephone lines for its exclusive use.

The tie-line connects the various locations of a business complex in different parts of the same city or in different cities, providing direct, voice contact between separate units of a business and also transmitting data. The tie-line can connect switchboards, Call Directors, key telephones, and regular telephones. It provides unlimited calling at a fixed monthly charge and is always reserved for the exclusive use of the subscriber.

### Foreign-Exchange Service (FX)

A local telephone number in a site remote from a plant or company headquarters can be listed so that a call made to the listed number goes

The use of a Speakerphone (page 295) adds greatly to the efficiency and convenience of conference calls.

—*American Telephone and Telegraph Company*

through as a local call: The New York City directory might carry the number of a firm located in New Brunswick, New Jersey, as New York City Tel. No. 987-6604. (See page 263.)

## Conference Call

A *conference call* is placed when the caller wants to talk simultaneously with several persons at different locations. An executive may want to get a group opinion on an idea or to announce design or price changes or a policy decision. The secretary calls the number for long distance, asks for the conference operator, and gives the locations and names of persons to be included, sometimes specifying the time the call is to be put through. From three to fourteen long distance points can be connected for a *two-way* conference call. With specialized equipment such as a Speakerphone shown in the picture above or a loudspeaker, several persons may listen in on a call at any one location. Up to 49 points can be connected for a *one-way* conference call (one in which the voice of only the caller is transmitted).

With recent innovations in equipment, it is sometimes possible to set up conference calls without the services of the operator. Also, with the *Add-On* feature, a caller already engaged in a two-way conversation can add a third person to the call.

An improved mobile telephone service provides all the features of regular telephone service. Users can dial directly over the nationwide network and continue their business uninterrupted by air or surface travel. This mobile service is being extended rapidly.

—*H. Armstrong Roberts*

## Mobile Service

More than 25,000 customers have mobile telephone service. These customers include trucks, news services, private automobiles, buses, planes, trains, and many other mobile users. Anyone can make a call to mobile equipment from any telephone, and any telephone can receive a call from mobile equipment. To place a call to a mobile telephone, either dial the number (which is listed in the telephone directory) or contact the mobile service operator. The conversation travels part way by radio and part way by telephone wire.

## Overseas Service

The extension of American business to foreign countries and the increased interaction between American and foreign companies has made overseas service increasingly common.

**Telephone.** To call almost any point in the world by telephone, the caller dials the operator and gives the country to be called, the name of the company wanted, and the name of the person to be reached. Of course, it is essential to consult the time zone (page 295) and to check with the local operator or directory for the times during which the various rates apply and for the charges.

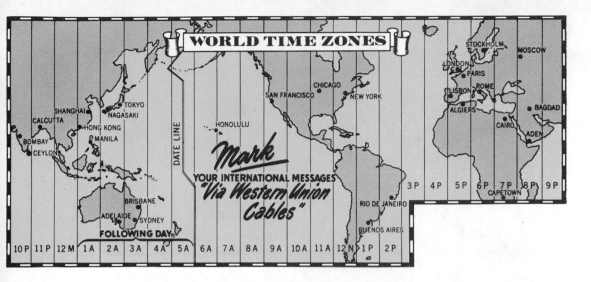

This world time-zone map will help the secretary in planning overseas communications. Refer also to page 269 for a time-zone map of the United States.

**Telegraph.** Increased capabilities are available through Western Union International, Inc., which provides *Datel* services, high-speed combined message and data communications; *Telex* worldwide service between correspondents in 100 countries; and leased-wire voice data circuits.

**Ship-to-Shore Messages.** A "ship-to-shore" (actually, *shore* to *ship*) radiogram should give the name of the addressee, the name of the ship, the name of the coast station through which it should be reached, with DOM or FOR following the address to indicate whether the vessel is of domestic or foreign registry.

## NEW SERVICES

Special equipment of many types is available so that the telephone can be tailored to the user's needs. In addition to items discussed previously, the following supplementary services may be obtained from the telephone company for a surcharge or purchased from the vendor.

### The Speakerphone

The *Speakerphone* has built-in transmitter and volume control so that both sides of a conversation can be amplified. The secretary can leave the telephone, walk to the opposite side of the office, look up information in a file, and read it to the caller from this location. The

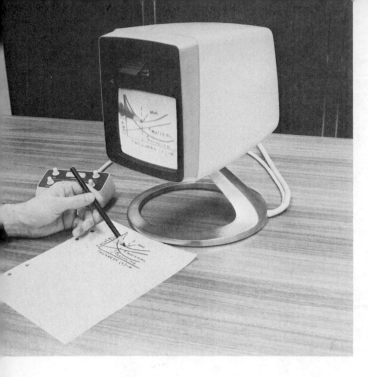

The Bell System's Picturephone set can be used to transmit drawings or charts by setting the camera focus at one foot. In the photograph, the "self-view" option is being used to position the graph while it is being transmitted.

*—American Telephone and Telegraph Company*

caller can be heard in various parts of the room; and vice versa, the caller can hear comments and discussions with others in the room. This equipment expands opportunities for full communication during conference calls. It is also possible to telephone lectures that may be amplified for delivery to class and conference groups. The Speakerphone is illustrated on page 293.

## Picturephone

Picturephone booth service has been introduced between New York, Pittsburgh, Washington, and Chicago with which people can make see-while-you-talk calls from certain locations. With Picturephone, illustrated above, it is possible to have face-to-face discussions, demonstrations, and presentations. Some commercial service has been added to booth service.

## Bellboy Service

Bellboy is a personal signaling service. A salesman, for instance, can put the compact, lightweight unit in his pocket. When his associates wish to get in touch with him, they merely dial his Bellboy number as they would dial any telephone number. Bellboy begins to buzz. The salesman goes to a nearby telephone and calls his office for a message.

## AIDS TO DIALING

A number of automatic dialing conveniences have been introduced.

### The Card Dialer

The Card Dialer enables a user to reach frequently dialed numbers by placing a punched-hole plastic card into the telephone and pushing the start bar. Cards are stored at the back of the telephone within easy reach of the user.

### Magicall

Numbers are stored on magnetic tape. The user presses a tape drive key which brings the correct alphabetic group forward. A selector wheel positions the desired name between guide lines. The caller waits for the usual dial tone and presses the *Call* button. The call has been automatically placed.

### Individualized Equipment

Color telephones, lightweight Princess telephones, Trim-line telephones with the dial embedded in the handset (especially attractive to those who see poorly) are available to the user who wants individualized equipment. With the influx of new equipment that permits individually owned telephones, we can expect a flood of new designs.

## INTERNATIONAL TELEGRAPH SERVICES

A secretary who uses international service frequently should get from the nearest telegraph offices their literature concerning their services. Overseas telegraph communications are sent either by underwater cables (cablegrams) or by radio (radiograms). International messages may be sent by Western Union International, Radio Corporation of America, French Cable, and International Telephone and Telegraph. Undoubtedly data communication services will develop rapidly.

### Classes of International Service

Classes of international services include full-rate telegram, letter telegram, cable money orders, and IMCO service.

**Full Rate; Letter Telegram.** There are two basic classes of international service—*Full Rate* (*FR*) and *Letter Telegram* (*LT*). These services are summarized in the table on page 299.

**Cable Money Orders.** Cable money orders are sent in the same way that Western Union money orders are sent. The money is deposited with the local office for payment abroad. Only full-rate service is available.

## Codes and Ciphers

Because one code word may mean several plain-language words, code language is frequently used in cables. Code words are composed entirely of letters. They may be real or artificial words, but they must not contain more than five letters. In an international message the use of code words lowers the cost of the message. For example, the one code word KALOP may be used to cover the statements "We authorize you to act for us. Will confirm this by mail."

A.B.C., Acme, Bentley's, and the Western Union codes are used most frequently. If you decide to use a private code, check with the telegraph company used to determine whether this code will be acceptable in the country to which the cablegram is sent.

Cipher words, used for secrecy, are usually composed of figures or of letters exceeding five per group, not fulfilling the requirements of code or plain language. In a message that contains a combination of code, cipher, and plain language, the code and cipher words are charged at the rate of five characters to the word, while plain language is charged at the rate of fifteen letters to the word. Codes and ciphers are permissible only in the address and signature of a letter telegram but may be used in all parts of full-rate messages.

## Counting Words in International Messages

The basic principles in counting chargeable matter in international messages are as follows:

1. **Count each word in address (except country of destination and routing designation for which there is no charge), text, and signature.**
2. **Count each plain language dictionary word at the rate of 15, or fraction of 15, characters to the word.**
3. **Count each secret language nondictionary word at the rate of 5, or fraction of 5, characters per word. (Not admitted in letter telegrams or press messages)**
4. **Count groups of figures, letters, signs, or a mixture of them where authorized, at the rate of 5 characters per word.**
5. **Place names:**
    (a) **In address—if destination point is a compound name, join it and count the name as one word, regardless of length.**
    (b) **In text and signature—count at the rate of 15 characters per word as written by sender.**
6. **Punctuation:**
    (a) **In figure or letter groups—count as 1 _character_ each.**
    (b) **In normal sense in text—count as 1 _word_ each (transmitted only on specific request of sender).**
    (c) **Acceptable signs are: . , : ? ' - — ( ) " /**
7. **Special characters or symbols should be spelled out because they cannot be transmitted: ¢ $ @ & # £**

|                                 | **Full Rate (FR)**                                                                              | **Letter Telegram (LT)**                                                            |
| ------------------------------- | ----------------------------------------------------------------------------------------------- | ----------------------------------------------------------------------------------- |
| *Indicator Preceding Address*   | No indicator necessary                                                                          | LT                                                                                  |
| *Charge for Indicator*          | ——                                                                                              | LT chargeable as 1 word; position immediately preceding the address                 |
| *Precedence of Transmission*    | Takes precedence over all other messages                                                        | Delivery at destination next morning                                                |
| *Language*                      | Plain language, secret (cipher or code), or a combination                                       | Plain language, but code may be used in address and signature                       |
| *Word Length*                   | Plain language: 15 letters to a word Cipher or code language: 5 characters to a word            | 15 letters to a word                                                                |
| *Minimum Number of Words*       | 5                                                                                               | 22                                                                                  |
| *Relationship of Rates*         | Based on distance message is sent                                                               | One half of full rate                                                               |

## Cable Addresses

Except for the destination country, each word in the name, address, and signature is counted as a chargeable word in a cablegram; therefore, a one-word cable address saves words in both incoming and outgoing messages. For a small annual charge cable address may be registered at any telegraph office. It cannot duplicate another already on file.

Frequently a firm in this country and its foreign correspondent will register an identical cable address and restrict its use to the exclusive exchange of messages between themselves. This procedure is known as a reversible address and obviates the need for a signature on messages, thus saving the cost of one word.

## QUESTIONS FOR DISCUSSION

1. What factors led *Business Week* to forecast a "telephone revolution?"
2. What capability does the Touch-Tone telephone have over the regular dial telephone?
3. What innovation has occurred in tie-line service?
4. What is the difference between EAS and WATS?
5. What is the relationship between WATS service and 800-number services?
6. How does a rural or suburban company, wishing to pay toll charges for incoming calls from prospective customers handle its telephone listings?
7. What considerations would affect your decision to send a full-rate international message rather than a letter telegram?
8. Name two types of business information that might advantageously be transmitted between each of the following business communication points: department to department, branch to headquarters, company to company, and company computer to computer service center.
9. What equipment innovations have speeded up telephone service?
10. In what ways is the secretary involved in data communication?

## PROBLEMS

■ **1.** If you were employed by a well-equipped corporation headquarters, which type of communication would you probably choose in the following situations? Tell why you chose the medium you did.

(a) A message to a governor asking that he sign a bill that is on his desk

(b) A message to three sales managers in different locations (A reaction is necessary from each of the three.)

(c) A message informing the payroll department in a branch office that data required for issuing paychecks have not been received

(d) A message containing detailed information about production schedules of a branch factory for the next two months

(e) A message to inquire about prices of a well-known office machine manufactured in a nearby suburb

(f) A message (about an important interview in London) to the president of the company en route to Europe by ship

(g) A message to a salesman 500 miles away, asking him to call on a prospective customer

(h) A message to the production manager in a distant branch factory

(i) A request for information from a bank in Englewood, New Jersey (across the Hudson River from your Manhattan office)

(j) A message that must reach 12 salesmen in different locations within three hours

(k) A message to the president of the company en route to Europe by ship (The message requires an immediate answer.)

(l) A message to the manager of a restaurant for which you supplied building materials, expressing good wishes on opening day.

(m) A message that will be received after closing hours but must be available when the office opens the following morning

(n) A graph to be used tomorrow in a national sales meeting

■ **2.** Develop a bibliography of ten articles published within the past six months describing innovations in data communication. Of what value was this investigation?

■ **3.** Visit the teletypewriter, Telex, TWX, or Data-Phone installation in one company and report on its equipment usage to the class.

# Part 4

# CASE PROBLEMS

Katherine Denton was secretary to the personnel manager. At lunch with a group of co-workers, she heard a boy from the mail room say to his friend, "Mary, I'm going to take this afternoon off. You sign out for me at five o'clock. Remember, I did the same for you on Monday."

Katherine had suspected that the mail department was loosely administered, but she had not believed it was possible to leave work without the absence being detected.

Since she worked in another department, she wondered about her responsibility.

**Should she report the conversation to her employer? to the head of the mail department? Should she speak to the young employees herself? Not wanting to tattle, should she ignore the situation entirely because it does not involve her?**

## 4-2  RESPONSIBILITY WITHOUT AUTHORITY

Eva Green was secretary to Larry Feeser, manager of a small branch office that operated in an exemplary way when he was there; however, he was frequently away for several days at a time, leaving Eva in charge. The rest of the staff — several young men and their secretaries — regarded his absence as a time to vacation. They came in late, took two hours for lunch, and left early.

Eva was the only one who covered the office. She arrived on time, had a sandwich at her desk so that she could answer the telephones, and worked overtime to finish her own work.

Although Eva was theoretically in charge, she had no real authority. She needed the cooperation of the staff but was reluctant to tell her employer the situation, knowing that they would resent her action.

**What should Eva have done?**

## 4-3 THEY CAN SPARE IT!

Joan Seagle was having a cup of coffee after work one evening with an office colleague, Harry Fleckman, who was studying for a master's degree in business administration. When they left the coffee shop Harry forgot a package. He retrieved it and, as he rejoined Joan, said, "Glad I found it. It's a ream of paper from the office and goodness knows I'll need it — with three term papers due in the next month."

**What is your reaction to Harry's behavior? Had Joan any responsibility in this social situation?**

## 4-4 FLEXITIME OR GLIDING TIME

Adele Norton was taking the minutes of the weekly staff meeting of the personnel department. Dan Darby, director, discussed a new idea, "flexitime," which has been adopted by a number of European corporations and is attracting considerable attention in America.

Flexitime allows an employee to choose — within guidelines — his own starting and finishing times. It is not the same as staggered hours in which an entire office or department adopts an earlier or later starting time in recognition of the difficulties in traveling to work. Rather, an employee may come to work, say, between 8 a.m. and 10 a.m. and adjust the rest of his day accordingly within a 35-hour, five-day week. Week-to-week schedules are usually submitted in advance for approval and may be rejected by a supervisor if too many people request the same time off. In some companies workers sign in and out on an honor system; in others everybody punches in and out on a time clock.

The advantage claimed for the plan is better company morale. Workers accept the responsibility for adhering to the schedules they choose. Some companies also report higher productivity.

Mr. Darby suggested that a plan be developed for soliciting company reaction to such a proposal and asked that each staff member should comment on the idea. Then he turned to Adele and said, "Miss Norton, you are our authority on secretarial problems. Will you too write your reaction in terms of our problems of lateness and absenteeism. Is there any particular problem posed here because of the relationship of executive to employee?"

**(In planning your statement, perhaps you should review Part 1.)**

# Secretarial Management of Records

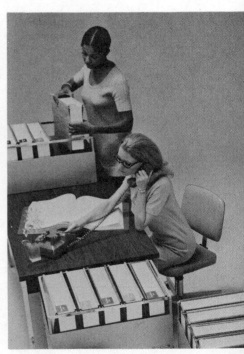

*Part* **5**

*Indexing, storage, and retrieval of business information are, of course, fundamental to records management. Perhaps as important to good records management, however, are setting up filing systems, deciding what to file and what to discard, determining what to retain in an executive's files—and how long to retain it. Records management also includes special filing systems and various filing procedures—releasing, indexing and coding, cross-referencing, sorting, requisitioning, charging out, and following up. This section will discuss each of these topics.*

# Chapter 14

## CONTROLLING OFFICE FILES

The cost of operating a standard four-drawer file in today's office is estimated by one manufacturer of filing equipment to be $596 a year. Another company reports that locating a misfile can cost as much as $61.23. These are impressive figures. Yet of all the skills she needs on the job, the new secretary usually knows least about filing.

The purpose of keeping business correspondence and records is to have them available when needed; this is why files are maintained. Obviously, unless material can be found when needed, the business system breaks down. But filing is done by people, thus creating many opportunities for error. A paper may be put in the wrong folder, or inadvertently attached to material in an unrelated file, or removed from a folder with no record of its withdrawal, or buried in the mass of papers on the executive's desk (or the secretary's), or stacked in the file clerk's work-to-be-done area. The secretary's responsibilities involve using a filing system for her personally supervised files that will minimize error potential. In addition, she must cooperate efficiently with the supervisor of the central files. The secretary is also responsible for observing good filing practices and for insisting that others with access to "her" files observe those practices.

## THE SECRETARY'S FILING RESPONSIBILITIES

Files are the memory of a business. They may be *centralized* in one location or *decentralized* in various departments or branches. The secretary will probably maintain a decentralized executive file and also send materials to and secure materials from a larger central file. She and her employer must plan together the executive file if it is to work well, but she will follow company procedures for borrowing and returning documents to central files.

If the company in which she works has a strong records management program, she will probably receive instructions about how to maintain her current files efficiently and how long to keep certain records before

One of the major contributions that a secretary can make to her employer is that of a well-organized, up-to-date filing system. She may be responsible for selecting the most efficient, appropriate filing methods and equipment for her employer's particular needs.

—*Oxford Filing Supply Co., Inc.*

destroying them or sending them to a low-cost storage area. Records managers are primarily concerned with reducing the amount of paper to be filed. Since it costs over 1½ cents a year to keep a piece of paper in the files, they want to prevent filing anything without reference value, to reduce duplication of copies in several locations, and to insure that superseded material will be destroyed when a current replacement is filed. To save space, they frequently try to reduce executive files. On the other hand, the executives, fearing that they cannot refer to items easily once the records have left their hands, build "little empires" that take unnecessary space and increase the expense of paperwork.

The better the background in filing procedures that the secretary can acquire, the more intelligent and helpful will be her judgment in deciding what to discard, what to file, and how to file it.

### Designing and Supervising the Files

The *secretary* must reconcile with her employer's habit of keeping almost everything the need for reducing his files without reducing the accessibility of materials that he will actually need.

She must follow accepted filing practices in her office and must understand the central filing system so that she can readily secure materials not available in her own files. Frequently she supervises, rather than does the filing, in the executive's office. She must create and/or maintain various kinds of files suitable to the needs of her employer and herself, for every situation is different. Possibly she will need card or strip name files, project files, files of catalogs frequently consulted, tickler

Particularly at the end of the work day the secretary should see that important papers are safe against fire and prying eyes. Confidential papers must be safeguarded at all times.

files involving upcoming events, geographic files, and files for storing engineering blueprints or other outsize materials, in addition to traditional drawer files with alphabetic or numeric captions. She will certainly need that very important round file, the wastebasket, to which many, many papers should be consigned, for executive files should be reduced to a minimum of space. She would do well to base file-planning decisions on factors of findability, confidentiality, and safety.

**Findability.** Unfortunately, files are thought of first as places to *put* papers, not places to *find* papers. Yet the criterion for judging any file system is findability, and the efficient secretary makes her decisions about where to put material after asking herself, "How will it be requested?" or "How can I find it?" She must locate materials with dispatch, selecting from a complete file only the papers actually wanted. To do this, she must understand her employer's need for a file so that she will not burden him with 250 pages when he wants only 10 — but the *right* 10.

**Confidentiality.** The secretary is also responsible for the confidentiality of her employer's files. The degree of security required varies from the tight surveillance over top-secret documents required by the aeronautical engineer to the careful protection needed for the less sensitive work of the typical executive. Yet it can safely be said that the records of any high executive are confidential and should be kept so.

**Safety.** Allied to the need for security is the secretary's ultimate responsibility for the safety of the records in her office. Many of them are irreplaceable, so it behooves her to take especial care of those she handles. Before leaving at night, she should lock all folders in a filing cabinet or vault as a safeguard against prying eyes or fire damage.

```
                        FILE INDEX
                          NO. 89
                        CHEMICAL

                                        Location
                               ┌─────────────────┬─────────────────┐
                               │    File No.     │    Drawer No.   │

        Correspondence
            Company                    2                 1
            Government                 2                 2
            Patents                    2                 3

        Personnel Work
            Applications               1                 2
            Medical                    1                 3
            Security                   1                 6

        Reports
            Company                    5                 1
            Outside                    5                 3
```

## Developing an Index

The secretary in a new position may find in her procedures manual a *table of contents* for her employer's personal file. Chances are, though, that she will have to develop her own index telling *where* in the files to look for materials. Even after the secretary has become familiar with the file, she will find the preparation of such a guide advantageous, for it will help anyone (including the executive or a new assistant) to locate material. A simple table of contents that indicates where to look for all types of records is shown above. Do not underestimate its value.

Communication between secretary and executive seems particularly bad in the filing area. The secretary feels that she is the one who has to get the material from the file so she should not bother her employer with questions about *her* system. Yet, it is *their* system; and if they work together in planning it, a continuity can be developed that will not be destroyed with the transfer of either of them. Certainly the new secretary should not reorganize the files until she has developed considerable insight into the nature of the office. Equally so, no executive objects to intelligent questions that will improve performance.

The secretary can sometimes get ideas for setting up files appropriate to her type of work from professional organizations and publications. For instance, she may find suggestions in an engineering magazine for filing blueprints. An educational secretary might find a model for pupil attendance records in publications of the National Association of Educational Secretaries. The Life Office Management Association has made studies of office systems for insurance records. Likewise, manuals

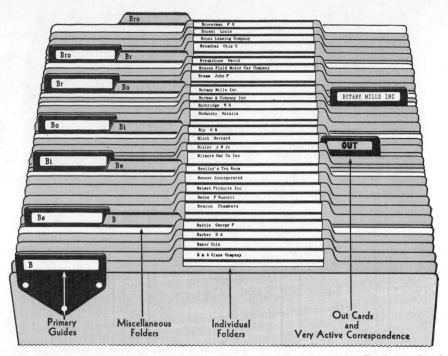

Bro

Bro · Br

Br · Bo

Bo · Bi

Bi · Be

Be · B

B

Broverman F S
Brossi Louis
Bronx Leasing Company
Broadnax Otis C

Breakstone David
Braves Field Motor Car Company
Braam John F

Botany Mills Inc
Borman & Company Inc
Borbridge W R
Bodansky Natalie

Bly H B
Black Bernard
Bixler J W Jr
Bilmore Hat Co Inc

Bentley's Tea Room
Benner Incorporated
Belmet Products Inc
Beebe F Russell
Beacon Chambers

Battle George F
Barber D A
Baker Cole
B & A Glass Company

BOTANY MILLS INC

OUT

Primary
Guides

Miscellaneous
Folders

Individual
Folders

Out Cards
and
Very Active Correspondence

—*Remington Rand*

In this illustration of an alphabetic file, four positions are used for the captions.

of the legal profession give directions for developing numeric legal files. The American Municipal Association has developed a list of subject headings peculiar to municipal activities and problems. The American Institute of Architects has created a standard filing system and alphabetic index for information on the materials, appliances, and equipment used in construction and related activities.

It is also possible to buy prefabricated subject file systems for certain types of offices. For example, Shaw-Walker manufactures a prefabricated Administration file containing main subjects and subclassifications printed on guide and folder tabs. The manufacturer claims this system will provide indexing applicable to 90 percent of all basic executive data.

## FILING METHODS

Material should be filed according to the designation by which it will be sought and according to a method with an established procedure and set of rules understood by all who use the files. There are four basic filing methods — *alphabetic*, *subject*, *numeric*, and *geographic*.

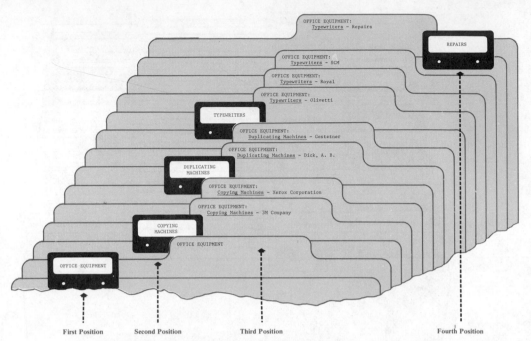

OFFICE EQUIPMENT:
Typewriters - Repairs

REPAIRS

OFFICE EQUIPMENT:
Typewriters - SCM

OFFICE EQUIPMENT:
Typewriters - Royal

OFFICE EQUIPMENT:
Typewriters - Olivetti

TYPEWRITERS

OFFICE EQUIPMENT:
Duplicating Machines - Gestetner

OFFICE EQUIPMENT:
Duplicating Machines - Dick, A. B.

DUPLICATING
MACHINES

OFFICE EQUIPMENT:
Copying Machines - Xerox Corporation

OFFICE EQUIPMENT:
Copying Machines - 3M Company

COPYING
MACHINES

OFFICE EQUIPMENT

OFFICE EQUIPMENT

First Position          Second Position          Third Position          Fourth Position

This subject file would be suitable for the purchasing agent or the office manager.

Manufacturers of filing equipment have devised and patented improvements upon these four fundamental methods, such as color schemes to expedite sorting, filing, and finding procedures — or techniques for grouping names spelled differently but pronounced alike. Trade names such as *Variadex*, *Tell-I-Vision*, *Amberg-Nual*, or *Safeguard* refer to commercial systems available. The word *system* is reserved for any filing plan devised by a filing equipment manufacturer.

## Alphabetic Filing

Most, possibly as high as 80 percent, of all the filing done in the office is alphabetical; that is, the files are sequenced alphabetically. Alphabetic filing is popular because it is based on a sequence understood by everyone and the filing is *direct* (meaning that it is not necessary to consult a subordinate file before filing or finding). The method is based on the strict observance of the guides for alphabetic indexing that are presented in Chapter 15.

## Subject Filing

The nature of some executives' work makes logical the filing of most of the correspondence, reports, and documents to be retained in the office under *subject headings* arranged in an alphabetic sequence in the files (actually, an alphabetic file except that all captions refer to subjects or topics rather than to names of people or organizations.)

Each piece of material is filed under *one subject caption*, but a *relative index* is prepared to support the subject file. The index is basically a cross-reference system. It lists all captions under which an item *may* be filed. To obtain an item from a subject file, the searcher first consults the relative index to identify all possible headings under which the item may be stored.

The executive and his secretary may profitably spend time in developing the relative index—time that will be saved later when the executive asks for the material under a number of captions. If the executive asks for the file on wage incentive plans of a rival company, the Green Corporation, the secretary may have it filed under (1) fringe benefits, (2) incentive plans, (3) personnel, or (4) Green Corporation. Reference to the relative index will help her locate the pamphlet.

A description of a portion of the subject file pictured on page 310 will perhaps best illustrate the principles. This illustration shows only one of the major headings with its subdivisions.

Each main heading has a number of subheadings. For instance, OFFICE EQUIPMENT is subdivided into several categories such as:

```
OFFICE EQUIPMENT:   Copying Machines
OFFICE EQUIPMENT:   Duplicating Machines
OFFICE EQUIPMENT:   Typewriters
```

Some of these subdivisions are further subdivided. For example, OFFICE EQUIPMENT: Typewriters is subdivided into:

```
OFFICE EQUIPMENT:   Typewriters - Olivetti
OFFICE EQUIPMENT:   Typewriters - Royal
OFFICE EQUIPMENT:   Typewriters - SCM
```

The subdivision Typewriters is further subdivided by the special classification guide REPAIRS in the fourth position.

Subject filing presents special retrieval problems because material may be requested under any one of many titles. For this reason one management consultant said, "To do subject filing well, the secretary must think like her executive." No area of filing requires the exercise of better judgment on the part of the secretary than does arranging materials by titles that best indicate their content.

## Numeric Filing

Lawyers, architects, engineers, accountants, and contractors may assign a number for each project; and that number becomes the basis for the numeric file. Case records and confidential material where anonymity is desired are commonly filed numerically.

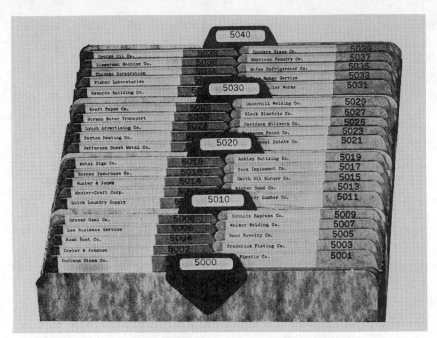

—*Shaw Walker Company*

A numeric filing plan has four parts:

1. **Alphabetic card index**
2. **Main numeric file**
3. **Miscellaneous alphabetic file for correspondence**
4. *Accession* **or number book, a record of the numbers already assigned**

In the numeric file, the alphabetic card index is first consulted to obtain the file number. The item is then located by number in the main numeric file. For a name or subject not shown in the card index, the miscellaneous alphabetic file is searched. Numeric filing is an *indirect* system, as one must refer to a card index before referring to the main numeric file.

**Advantages and Disadvantages.** Numeric filing has both advantages and disadvantages. It is easy for file clerks to learn. Misfiling is reduced because individually assigned numbers are less confusing than are similarly spelled names. Furthermore, extensive cross-referencing is possible in the alphabetic card index. A disadvantage is the necessity of consulting the card index before locating the material—a time factor. And when misfiling does occur, it is usually more difficult to locate the misfile than is true with an alphabetic file.

**Terminal-Digit Filing.** In straight numeric filing, as the files increase, the numbers assigned to them become higher. Because most of the filing work deals with the most recent dates, the work involves the

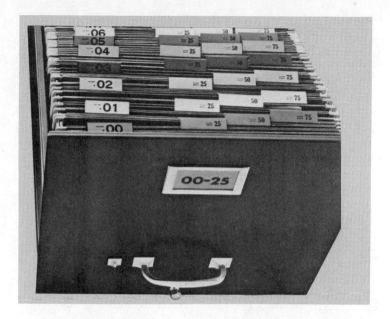

This illustration shows a portion of the 25 drawer of a terminal-digit file. The terminal-digit system assures easier filing and finding.

*—Oxford Pendaflex Corporation*

highest numbers. In a numeric file of insurance policies, for instance, the most recent policies would be the highest numbers. Chances are that the file clerk would work mostly with the higher-numbered files.

*Terminal-digit filing* avoids concentrating the bulk of the filing action in a small section of the files. This indexing method divides a number into pairs of digits. For example, insurance policy No. 412010 would be identified as 41 20 10. The last (terminal) digits would identify the drawer number; the second pair of digits to the left would indicate the guide number in the drawer, and the remaining digits would indicate the sequence of the folder behind the guide. Thus, policy No. 41 20 10 would be filed in Drawer 10, behind Guide 20, and in 41st sequence behind the guide (between policy No. 40 20 10 and No. 42 20 10).

To appreciate the advantage of terminal-digit filing, visualize 100 file drawers, each labeled with a two-digit number (00, 01, 02, and so on through 99). Policy No. 2 12 00 would go in Drawer 00, while policy No. 2 12 01 would go in Drawer 01, and so on. As consecutive new policy numbers are assigned, the policy materials will be distributed throughout the 100 drawers.

This system has been adapted and modified into systems such as the triple-terminal-digit system (using the last three digits) and the middle-terminal-digit system (using the two middle digits as the drawer number).

Research shows that terminal-digit filing saves up to 40 percent of file-operation costs by assuring a uniform work load, better employee relations, unlimited expansion facilities, and fewer misfiles.

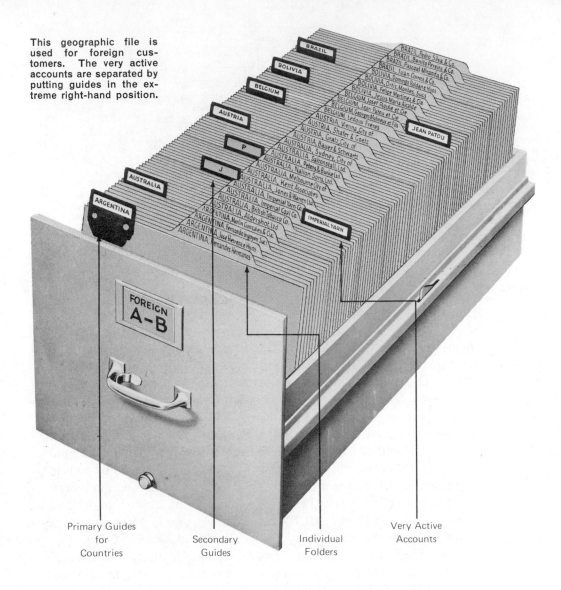

This geographic file is used for foreign customers. The very active accounts are separated by putting guides in the extreme right-hand position.

Primary Guides for Countries

Secondary Guides

Individual Folders

Very Active Accounts

## Geographic Filing

Geographic filing keeps records by geographic units or territories. Divisions are made in some logical sequence: nations, states or provinces, cities, and so on. Guides are used for the larger divisions and subdivisions. Behind each guide, material is filed in miscellaneous folders alphabetically, usually by name of city and then by name of correspondent. Individual folders are filed alphabetically by location, then by name.

The secretary who compiled this chronological file used the inside front cover as a convenient place to fasten a check list of items of particular importance to her.

Each month the secretary removes and discards the filed materials for the earliest month involved (those in the back of the file).

## The Secretary's Chronological File

A secretary who must send her material to a centralized file usually keeps a chronological file as a ready in-office reference. This file, sometimes called a *reading* file, consists of a copy — carbon or photo — of each *outgoing* item of the day, filed in chronological order in a ring binder or topbound folder. Such a file can answer many questions: Was a letter mailed, to whom was it addressed, when was it mailed, what price was quoted, and was an enclosure mentioned — all without the delay of consulting the central file. The secretary retains materials in this file for a limited time only, perhaps six months to a year, each month discarding the materials for the earliest month.

## FILING EQUIPMENT

Improved filing equipment and supplies are the result of the intense competition among manufacturers. Some of the new developments have significance for the secretary's files; others are important mainly to the larger centralized filing department.

## Vertical Files

The most-used type of filing equipment is the vertical file (with papers filed on edge vertically) available in one- to six-drawer units in a wide range of colors. Opening the drawers of these units requires a minimum of three to four feet of space in front of the cabinet.

**Rock-a-File.** This is a variation of the vertical file in that the drawers rock or tilt open sideways, requiring less floor space in front. The rock-a-file may meet space requirements in special situations.

In *open-shelf filing* the complete folder is removed when material is needed. Tabs on both sides of the guides and folders permit reading from either the left or the right.

*—Republic Steel Corp.*

**Roll-Out File.** The drawer in a roll-out file rolls out flat but sideways, thus exposing the entire contents of the drawer. It requires half the aisle space needed for a conventional vertical file drawer. A roll-out file is shown on page 306.

**Open-Shelf File.** The folders are placed vertically on open shelves with no drawers involved. Access to the folders is from the front. Since the shelves can extend to the ceiling, they can accommodate more material per square foot of floor space than can the drawer file; they require less floor and aisle space; they cost less; and they require less time to file and find records.

**Mobile File.** Mobile files allow what is known as close-support filing — putting the records at the point of use. The concept is to bring the highly active file unit to the operations area rather than forcing the worker to go to the file. Some mobile files are single units that are pushed around like tea carts. Others are multiple modules that roll on a suspension system from the ceiling. Some are stationary, like the tub file, with trays rotating to give operators access to needed material.

This visible file makes personnel data quickly available. The lower border of each card extends below that of the card above it and shows the information necessary for easy findability.

*—Remington Rand*

## Horizontal Files

Horizontal files store in a flat position materials such as maps, drawings, or blueprints, that normally are much larger than the materials filed in a vertical drawer file. They are most commonly found in engineering and architectural offices.

## Visible Card Files

In a visible card file, cards filed in a shallow metal tray or on upright stands show only the lower edge of each card. Flipping up the preceding card reveals the card desired. Cards can easily be inserted into and removed from holders that are so fastened that the backs of cards can also be used for record keeping.

Visible card files are used extensively for perpetual inventories, accounting records of sales and purchases, personnel histories — those situations in which information must be available quickly, as in answer

A circular, motorized file like this one can make available to four desks large amounts of data, such as accounts receivable, production control, and inventory information.

*—Wassell Organization, Inc.*

to a telephone inquiry. Colored signals provide a visible means of control; for example, a blue signal attached to the visible edge of a credit card may mean "Watch credit closely."

## Rotary Card Files

The rotary wheel file is designed to make a limited amount of information available within arm's reach of the operator. The wheel can be small for desk use or motorized to hold large trays of cards, such as accounts receivable, credit information, and data processing keypunched cards.

## Keyboard Access Files

Several highly mechanical or electronically controlled filing systems bring a high degree of automation to filing. In most of these systems, each stored item is coded. The operator enters the code number on a keyboard. The equipment either mechanically or electronically searches, locates, and retrieves the item bearing the code number. The most sophisticated equipment will find and deliver a document from a room-sized storage area within seconds.

To use the microfilm reader, the secretary selects the cartridge from the film file on the left, inserts it into the reader, and keys the code number of the desired projection on the machine at the right. The projector electronically scans the film, locates the desired frame, and projects it onto the screen. Hard copies can be made of the projected image. (See page 213.)

—*Eastman Kodak Company*

### Tape Files

Tape files use specially designed folders to hold punched tape, edge-punched cards, and magnetic tape.

### Microfilming

Microfilming involves transferring correspondence and records to film, destroying the correspondence and records, and storing only the film. The film is viewed with a microfilm reader but a full-sized hard copy can be produced or the image can be inserted into a plate enlarger to make an offset plate for duplicating. The system was used initially to record inactive and semiactive files that would normally be stored; however, it is being used increasingly for current-record storage.

Microfilming reduces filing space requirements in a ratio of 98 to 1. But it is an expensive process — often more so than the space saved.

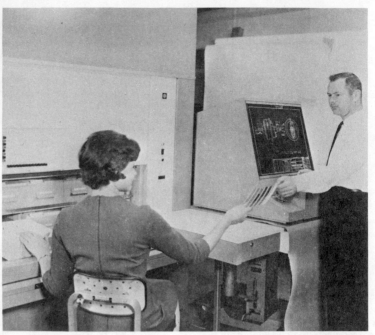

—Remington Rand

There are four major methods of filing microfilm — rolls, transparent jackets, aperture cards, and microfiche cards. Chips are also used frequently. The secretary at the left is using an aperture card. The secretary above is handing her employer a transparent jacket of microfilm.

—Mohawk Industrial Laboratories, Inc.

The four major methods of filing microfilm are *rolls*, *transparent jackets*, *chips*, and *aperture cards*.

Microfilmed chronological or sequenced data such as sales slips, deposit slips, checks, newspapers, magazines, and lengthy reports are usually stored in rolls (reels) in specially designed boxes or drawers indexed by content or inclusive dates.

Transparent jackets and aperture cards comprise what is called "unitized" microfilm, in which individual frames or clips cut from a microfilm roll are inserted into the jacket or mounted on the aperture card. Indexing information is added to each jacket or card before filing.

**Microfiche.** A miniature version of microfilm is called *microfiche* (pronounced micro*feesh*). "Fiche" is a French word meaning a card or slip of paper. Sixty pages can be recorded on a card. Thus, a 60-page report can be recorded on one 6- by 4-inch card. Microfiche cards can be filed in a card file or in a specially designed book-type binder.

A number of systems provide almost immediate access to a desired aperture or microfiche card from storage. When the cards are keyboard coded, electronic devices can retrieve the card from the file.

By means of a cathode-ray tube, the output of a computer can be projected on a screen and photographed onto microfilm or microfiche.

**Computer Output Microfilm (COM).** The output of a computer can go, by several methods, directly onto microfilm or microfiche. One method involves a cathode-ray tube. The computer projects the information onto the tube, from which it is then photographed onto microfilm. The advantages of this process are:

1. The information can come off the computer at a rate much faster than that of an electronic printer.

2. There is a tremendous saving of space. For example, 200 feet of microfilm can carry the same amount of data as approximately 4,000 sheets of computer printout paper.

3. Additional copies can be made from the microfilm without tying up the computer.

# FILING PROCEDURES

Many papers are filed that should have been destroyed. Letters of acknowledgment, letters of transmittal, announcements of meetings (noted on the desk calendar), forms and reports filed in another location, duplicate copies, and routine requests for catalogs and information fall into this category. (In some well-run organizations the original request is returned with the material.)

Any document that is superseded by another in the file should be removed. When filing a card giving a change in telephone number, remove the old one. When a new catalog is filed, destroy the old one.

A temporary file may be kept for materials having no permanent value. The paper is marked with a *T* and destroyed when the action involved is completed.

The government has developed this technique to a high level. In many departments of the government every document receives a date-of-destruction notation before it goes into the file. By continually purging the files of outdated material, the secretary can reduce the volume of material and keep her files up to date.

## Preparing Materials for Filing

Routines for preparing materials for filing should proceed by the following steps.

**Conditioning Materials.** All pins, brads, and paper clips are removed, and related papers are stapled or welded together for material to be filed. Clippings or other materials smaller than page size should be attached to a regular sheet of paper with paper cement. Damaged records should be mended or reinforced with tape. If they are not filed in special equipment, oversize papers should be folded to the dimensions of the folder and labeled to make it unnecessary to unfold them for identification.

**Releasing Materials.** When the secretary places an incoming letter in her filing basket, it should bear a *release mark* indicating that it has been acted on and is ready for filing. This mark may be the executive's initials, a FILE stamp and the secretary's initials, or a diagonal mark across the sheet. A check of all attachments will indicate whether they belong to the document. A release mark is not necessary on a carbon copy of an outgoing letter or on an original to which a carbon copy of a reply is attached. The file copy is usually of a distinctive color.

**Indexing and Coding.** The term *indexing* means deciding where to file a paper; *coding* refers to noting that decision on the face of the paper either by underlining the name or words that are to be used as a basis for filing, or by writing the appropriate name, words, or number in a prominent place. A colored pencil is commonly used for this purpose.

In alphabetic filing, correspondence is usually filed according to the most important name appearing on it. A letter to or from a business is usually coded and filed according to the name of that business. If a correspondent is an individual, his name is ordinarily used in coding. If, however, he is writing as an agent of a business and the name of that business is known, the business name is used instead. Similarly, if a business letterhead is used by an individual to write a personal letter, the name of the individual is coded rather than the name of the business. Complete rules for alphabetic-filing sequence are given on pages 337–349.

In subject filing, the subject title must be determined from the body of the letter; the letter is then coded according to that title or a number that represents that subject. In numeric filing, the number to be used as a code is determined from a card index file. In geographic filing, coding is done by underlining the city and state in the heading of an incoming letter or in the inside address of an in-house carbon copy.

**Cross-Referencing.** For correspondence or material that could be filed under more than one name, a cross-reference sheet or card should be prepared and filed. For instance, a letter from Allen Rothmore Company poses the problem: Is Allen a given name or a surname? In such a case a used file folder should be cut apart and only the back half used for the permanent cross-reference folder with the caption ALLEN ROTHMORE (*See* ROTHMORE ALLEN) and filed under *Al.* The regular file should be set up for ROTHMORE ALLEN and filed under *Ro.*

A letter may be received from the Modern Office Equipment Co. regarding an exhibit at the Eastern Office Equipment Association meeting in Atlantic City. The file clerk might file all correspondence about this meeting under EASTERN OFFICE EQUIPMENT ASSOCIATION; however, she should also make a cross-reference sheet like the one at the right and file it under MODERN OFFICE EQUIPMENT CO. Indicate that you have cross-referenced by an *X* (for cross-reference) near the name on the letter.

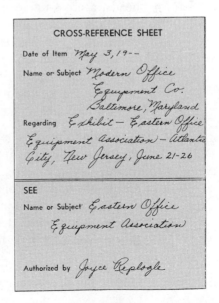

CROSS-REFERENCE SHEET

Date of Item *May 3, 19--*

Name or Subject *Modern Office Equipment Co. Baltimore, Maryland*

Regarding *Exhibit — Eastern Office Equipment Association — Atlantic City, New Jersey, June 21-26*

SEE

Name or Subject *Eastern Office Equipment Association*

Authorized by *Joyce Replogle*

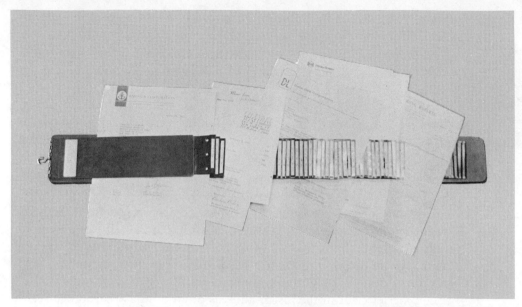

Speed up the sorting process with a sorting device like the one shown here.

A photocopy or an extra carbon copy of the letter (usually in a color different from the file copy) can also be used as a cross-reference. In this case, it would be filed under MODERN OFFICE EQUIPMENT CO. and the cross-reference sheet would not be prepared.

Perhaps a letter should be cross-referenced by subject. If inquiries have been mailed to several printers asking for quotations on new letterheads, a cross-reference sheet labeled "Letterhead Quotations," listing the firms written, may be filed under *Le*, and the correspondence with the printers may be filed alphabetically according to firm names.

Cross-reference forms may be colored sheets imprinted with blanks that are to be filled in; or they may be tabbed colored cards on which the reference information is listed. A good secretary follows the rule, "When in doubt, make out a cross-reference."

**Sorting.** Sorting is arranging the papers, including cross-reference sheets, in order for filing. When sorting material, the secretary should first make one or two preliminary sortings before the final one. For example, she may first place the A-E, papers in one group and then in the second sort put them into A, B, C, D, and E order. It is a simple matter then to put each of these letter groups in correct alphabetic sequence. Sorting for a numeric file should follow a similar efficient procedure.

**Typing Labels.** Pressure-sensitive labels are easier to attach than others, but the secretary should be sure to press the label down securely at all corners. When using rolls of labels, type the label before tearing it off. To prevent captions from being hidden in the file, type the caption uniformly two spaces in from the left edge of the label as illustrated below. Keep the captions in perfect alignment; do not stagger them. Type the primary reference in all capitals on the top line. Type the secondary reference such as the city and state (if any) in caps and lowercase on the second line blocked on the first line.

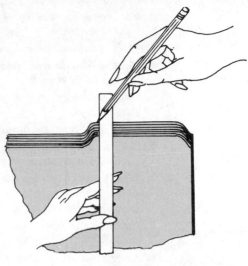

Achieve uniform placement of labels by premarking the folders.

### Techniques for Drawer Filing

Use an *individual folder* for letters and other materials to, from, or about one correspondent or subject. For each section, use a *Miscellaneous* folder for those individuals and businesses with whom correspondence is infrequent. When five records relating to a person or topic have accumulated in the *Miscellaneous* folder, open an individual folder. File material in the *Miscellaneous* folder in alphabetic order; then, within the alphabetic order, file in chronological order with the most recent date first. Adopt the time-saving guides listed on the next page.

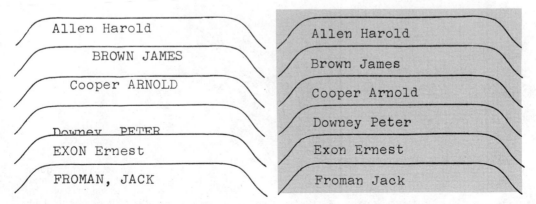

The captions at the left are inconsistent in style, punctuation, capitalization, and placement. Captions may be typed in all capital letters or as shown at the right.

1. Set a definite time for filing every day.
2. File records face up, top edge to the left, with the most recent date to the front of the folder.
3. Place individual folders immediately *behind* the guides.
4. Place a *Miscellaneous* folder at the end of each section of the file, just in front of the next guide.
5. Use a guide for every 6–8 folders (1 inch of drawer space), about 20–25 to each drawer.
6. Leave one fifth of the drawer for expansion and working space.
7. Keep no more than 20–25 sheets in one folder. With heavy loads, use scored (creased-at-the-bottom) folders for expansion.
8. "Break" the files when the folder becomes crowded. Underscore the caption on the old folder in red so that all new material will be placed in the new folder. Date each folder and keep the folders filed together.
9. Use specially scored and reinforced folders for bulky materials such as catalogs.
10. Avoid accidents by opening only one file drawer at a time and closing it when the filing has been completed.
11. Lift the folder an inch or two out of the drawer before inserting material so that the sheets can drop down completely into the folder.
12. Do not grasp guides and folders by their index tabs, or they become dog-eared.

## Requisitioning Materials from the Files

When the secretary releases to the central files materials that will be needed at a definite future time, she can mark or stamp the item with the notation "Follow-up" or "Tickler" and the date on which she will need the material. Frequently, however, she will not know just when she will need the material again. In these cases she will make her request for such materials when she needs them, following the usual

Date Due *April 6, 19--* Charge Date *April 3, 19--*

MATERIAL REQUESTED FROM FILES

Name or Subject *Mohawk Supply Co.*
Address *Boston, Mass.*
Regarding *adj. on Feb. statement*
Date of Material *Latter part of Feb.*
REQUESTED BY

Name *James Morris*
Department *Auditing* Date of Request *4/3/--*

The secretary may request material from the central file on a standardized form such as this. The filing department records the two dates at the top of the card.

*Part 5* • SECRETARIAL MANAGEMENT OF RECORDS

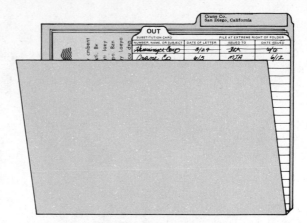

OUT or substitution cards like this one are commonly used to replace one paper or a few related papers removed from a folder.

routine — by telephone, in person, or by *requisition card* sent to the filing department. She may request the entire contents of a folder or specific items in a folder. A telephone request is faster than a requisition, especially if the information sought can be given verbally.

The secretary should return materials to the files as soon as she has finished using them. A special problem arises when files that the secretary has received are transferred to someone in another department before they are returned to the filing department. In some companies the secretary reports such a transfer to the filing department on a special form. In any case she must inform central files of the location of the file.

**Charge-Out Methods.** When an entire folder is taken from the files or when separate items are removed from a folder, a record should be made so that others will be able to locate the materials.

Several charge methods are in common use. When an individual item is removed from the folder, a *substitution card* is usually put in its place in the folder. This card indicates the nature of the material, the name of the person who has the material, and the date it was removed. When an entire folder is removed, an *out guide* may be substituted for the folder; or an out folder with a *substitution card* may be placed in the drawer to take the place of the regular folder. Sometimes the regular folder is retained in the file drawer, and the contents of the folder are transferred to a special *carrier folder*.

In many companies the original requisitioned material never leaves the central filing area. A photocopy is sent to the person making a requisition, and he may destroy the copy when he has finished with it.

**Follow-Up Methods.** A secretary frequently uses her daily calendar pad as a memory aid or follow-up to filing. She anticipates the due date of a letter and jots down such a notation on the future-date page of her calendar. See page 326 for follow-up steps.

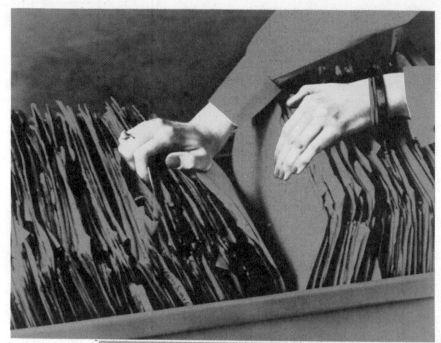

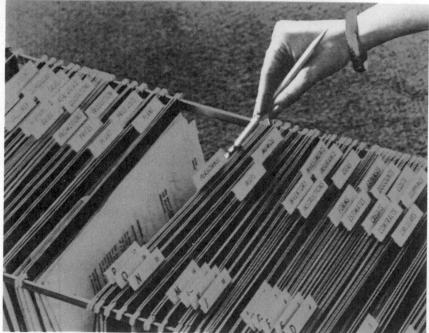

The upper picture shows a crowded, untidy file drawer of the conventional design. In the lower picture is a suspension file drawer in which the folders hang from, and slide along, metal bars at each side of the drawer. It is easy to imagine how much more pleasant and efficient the use of the suspension file drawer would be, compared to the one above it.

## MECHANICS OF GOOD FILING

### Reducing Misfiles

The secretary should vow to avoid expensive misfiles. One cause of misfiles is carelessness—placing a record in a folder without scanning its contents to see if they are related to the paper being filed, fastening materials together with paper clips which often also pick up unrelated papers, or putting one folder inside another one. Another cause for misfiles is not using supplies and equipment as recommended—too many or too few guides, overcrowded folders that sag so much that their tabs are hidden, drawers so overstuffed that there is inadequate work space, and miscellaneous folders crowded with papers for which individual folders should have been opened. The final cause of misfiles lies in coding—captions that are not mutually exclusive, the choice of a wrong title, or too few cross-references.

## Places to Search

If only one paper is lost, it is probably in the wrong folder. Check the folders in front and in back and check the bottom of the drawer. Look in Charge-Outs and in file baskets, and don't overlook the boss's desk and your own. Look in the index of files transferred to storage areas. Look under similar names, numbers, or titles. For instance, if the name is Brooks Allen, look under Allen Brooks. If 2309 is lost, look under 2390. Look in the relative index for other possible captions.

If an exhaustive search does not locate an item, type on a sheet of paper all the information known about the missing item and the date on which the loss was discovered. File the sheet (perhaps in a folder labeled *Lost*) where the missing item should be. This practice forestalls a later search for the same item. Consider the possibility, also, of obtaining a copy of the lost item from its sender or source.

## FILING SUPPLIES

Some secretaries purchase their own filing supplies; some requisition them from the stock room. In either case, a secretary needs to know what is available and how to describe each item correctly when ordering.

### File Guides

File guides are stiff sheets somewhat deeper than the folders. They come in a variety of tab widths (tab *cuts*). A *one-fifth cut* means that the tab occupies one fifth of the top edge of the guide, permitting five tab positions. The positions are identified from left to right as *first position*, *second position*, and so on. An order for guides must specify the cut position or positions, as "one-fifth cut in second position" or "one-third cut in staggered positions."

Some guide captions are printed directly on the tab (frequently the case with alphabetic systems), or the tab may be a metal or plastic holder into which small typed or printed captions can be inserted.

Alphabetic guides with printed captions are available in sets ranging from the 23-units sets used by small businesses to the sets of several hundred units used by large businesses.

### File Folders

File folders come in various styles, weights, cuts, colors, and materials. Tab cuts range from full width to one fifth with *single* or *double* captions (depth of the cut). At the bottom front of the folder two or more horizontal scores or creases permit folding the folder to form a flat bottom surface to adjust to the thickness of the contents.

Folders come in light, medium, heavy, and extra-heavy weights; 11-point paper stock (a point is .001 inch) is medium weight. An innovation is folders of thin, durable plastic. For bulky papers, pressboard folders with cloth expansion hinges at the bottom are best.

Also available are folders with built-in fasteners, with metal hooks for suspension from frames within the file drawer, with printed captions, and in a wide range of colors for color coding. A suspension file drawer is shown in the lower picture on page 328. Folders with pockets for holding punched tape, punched cards, or standard-size sheets can also be obtained.

Orders for folders must specify weight and color of stock and size, position, and depth of cut.

## Folder Labels

Folder labels for captions come in continuous perforated rolls or in self-adhesive strips in a range of colors and in various widths to fit the tab cuts.

## Cross-Reference Sheets

Cross-reference sheets should be lightweight to conserve space and in a color for easy identification in the folder. The secretary can purchase them or have them duplicated in the office.

# GOOD RECORDS MANAGEMENT PRACTICES

Practices recommended by records-management specialists should be helpful to the secretary in controlling her files and in understanding the management aspects of records control, including retention and transfer.

## Retention Schedules

The most efficiently operated companies have an overall file retention plan which the secretary should follow. The retention schedule of a company specifies how long a document can remain in the office flow; if and when it is to be removed to a separate, low-cost records center; and when it should be destroyed.

From among the various professionally organized retention plans that are available, an adaptation of recommended practices is presented.[1]

---

[1]Records Controls, Inc., Chicago, Illinois.

1. File one month:
   General correspondence requiring no follow-up

2. File three months:
   Incoming and outgoing correspondence with customers and vendors on routine, promptly settled business
   Bank statements
   Stenographers' notebooks
   Expired insurance policies

3. File two years:
   Work sheets for financial statements
   Internal reports and summaries, including printouts from data processing equipment, and all punched cards and tapes
   Physical inventories

4. File to comply with the statute of limitations in the states affected:
   Cancelled payroll checks and summaries
   Invoices to customers and from vendors
   Employee data, including accident reports
   Completed contracts and leases, as well as other legal papers
   Duplicate deposit tickets and checks, except as noted below

5. File permanently:
   Books of accounts and minutes
   Capital stock ledgers and transfer records
   Cancelled checks, vouchers, and cost data on capital improvements
   Tax returns and related papers
   Perpetual agreements about pensions, group insurance, and other fringe benefits
   All property records
   Maps, specifications, plans

## Transferring Materials

Plans for storing files are made in relation to the importance of the material and the reduction of costs effected by storing infrequently called-for material in cheaper filing equipment and in cheaper rental areas. Possibility of destruction of vital records by nuclear attack has caused concern for safe storage—in mountain vaults and caves in some instances and in widely dispersed units in others. Some companies have built storage centers, and others have rented file storage space from companies that specialize in providing ready access to stored materials.

Certain types of files can be handled under a perpetual transfer plan. When a case is closed or a project finished, the file is closed and transferred. In other cases periodic transfer is made. By the one-period method all material is taken at a designated time from the active files and sent to transfer files. Although active files are established, it is all but impossible to avoid consulting some old records. With a two-period transfer, however, the middle drawers are used for current materials;

the upper and lower drawers, for semiactive materials. The semiactive materials are transferred in turn.

A variation of this plan is the maximum-minimum transfer. Only the inactive material is transferred at regular intervals. For instance, with a transfer date of June 30, 1973, materials filed from January, 1973, through June 30, 1973, would not be moved (they would remain in the active files). Materials dated from January 1, 1972, through December 31, 1972, however, would be transferred to storage. New materials would go into the active file until June 30, 1974. Then the files from January 1, 1973, through December 31, 1973, would be transferred, leaving the files for January 1, 1974, through June 30, 1974, in the active files. The secretary labels each transfer file with its contents, inclusive dates, and in some firms, the discard date.

## SUGGESTED READINGS

Dickinson, A. Litchard. *The Right Way to File*. New York: Geyer-McAllister Publications, 1971.

Griffin, Mary Claire. *Records Management, A Modern Tool for Business*. Boston: Allyn and Bacon, Inc., 1964.

Johnson, Mina M., and Norman F. Kallaus. *Records Management*. Cincinnati: South-Western Publishing Co., 1967.

Kahn, Gilbert, Theodore Yerian, and Jeffery Stewart. *Filing Systems and Records Management*, 2d ed. New York: McGraw-Hill Book Co., Inc., 1970.

Place, Irene, and Estelle L. Popham. *Filing and Records Management*. Englewood Cliffs: Prentice-Hall, Inc., 1966.

Place, Irene M., Estelle L. Popham, and Harry N. Fujita. *Fundamental Filing Practice*, 3d ed. Englewood Cliffs: Prentice-Hall, Inc., 1973.

Weeks, Bertha. *Filing and Records Management*. New York: The Ronald Press, 1964.

## QUESTIONS FOR DISCUSSION

1. In what ways has your concept of the filing work of a secretary changed since reading this chapter?

2. What factors should be considered in determining whether or not an item should be retained or discarded and, if retained, the length of the retention period?

3. In some companies the executives are permitted only two filing drawers for their personal files. What advantages do you see in this blanket rule? what disadvantages?

4. What procedures can you adopt to insure that the executive's files contain only material needed for reference?

5. If you were employed as secretary to the head of research projects in a chemical company, what steps would you take to develop an understanding of a subject file already in operation?

6. If you were working for a company with no records-retention schedule, how would you proceed to establish one?

7. If you started to work in a position during a peak period and discovered that many materials were misfiled, the folders and drawers were overcrowded, the materials were not arranged chronologically in the folders, and the miscellaneous folders contained materials for which individual folders should have been opened, what would you do?

8. Suggest situations in which each of the following types of files would be advantageous:

| alphabetic | subject | visible card file |
|---|---|---|
| numeric | geographic | chronological |

9. While dictating a letter addressed to Mr. V. C. Hogan, your employer interrupts the dictation to say that he vaguely remembers a Mr. Hogan in Cedar Rapids or Muscatine, Iowa, who formerly dealt with the company and who had a bad credit record. He asks you to get any information available from the central files about such a person. How would you state your request to the central file department?

10. Type the following sentences in correct form. Then use the Reference Guide to verify or correct your typing of *yes* and *no*.
    (a) The answer is no we are sorry to say.  (b) On second thought, we will say yes.

11. There is some feeling that quoting an unusual word choice is uncomplimentary to the intelligence of the reader, and in some cases is sarcastic. Discuss the following italicized words. Would you use quotation marks with any of them in a business letter? Would you revise any of the sentences? Is any one of the italicized words an acronym?
    (a) We have your *so-called* revised chapter.
    (b) He is a *VIP*—an extremely important one.
    (c) The situation is completely *snafued* now.
    (d) Your *complaint* can be taken as a compliment too.
    (e) To save time we are sending you a rough draft in which deletions have been *X'd* out.
    (f) It looks as if we *goofed* on your order.

    Refer to PUNCTUATION; *Quotation marks*; *Words different in tone* and to WORDS: COINED in the Reference Guide to check your answers.

# PROBLEMS

■ **1.** You are secretary to the sales manager, Bert Henderson. The following items have been seen by Mr. Henderson and are ready for action. Indicate what disposition you would make of each one. For instance, a notice of an interoffice meeting would be entered on the desk calendar and destroyed. If an item is retained, indicate under what name or subject it would be filed. (A separate file is kept for Mr. Henderson's personal items.)

(a) A reminder notice for the next weekly meeting of the Sales Executives Club

(b) A new catalog from Brown and Brown, a firm that services sales-incentive plans (The old catalog is in the files.)

(c) An application for a sales position from William Ainsworth

(d) Copy for the *Weekly Sales Newsletter*, which is sent to the sales manager by Bob Miller, editor, for final approval before it goes to the reproduction department

(e) A letter from an applicant for a sales position thanking Mr. Henderson for his initial interview

(f) An announcement of fall courses at a local college (The company reimburses employees who take job-related courses for their tuition costs.)

(g) A notice that Mr. Henderson's subscription to *Sales Management* has expired

(h) A letter from James Miller asking to change his appointment from Wednesday to Friday at the same hour.

(i) A completed chapter for a book on *Prognosis of Sales Ability* (The name of the chapter is "Psychological Testing.")

(j) A carbon copy of Mr. Henderson's expense account for the preceding week

(k) A requisition for a new Norelco dictating unit for Mr. Henderson's use on the road

(l) A car-rental contract covering rental of salesmen's automobiles in the Chicago area

(m) A quarterly report of Xerox Corporation in which Mr. Henderson holds stock

(n) An interoffice memo from the president of the company approving Mr. Henderson's request to hold a sales training conference at Lake Crystal on September 18–20

(o) A letter from an irate customer complaining about the treatment he received from the Little Rock area salesman, Herman Beckwith

(p) A catalog from Hertz Company about its blanket quarterly service contract for company rentals

(q) Safety regulations applying to all departments in the home office

(r) A computer printout summarizing sales in each district for the preceding quarter

(s) Sales projection figures which you submitted to the Administrative Committee Monday

■ **2.** Your employer, J. B. Hamm, dictates the letter given below. He then tells you to follow it up in ten days with Form Letter 6 if the account is still unpaid. If no action has been secured in twenty days, you are to send Form Letter 9.

(a) Type the letter and one carbon copy in good form so you can prepare the carbon copy for filing

(b) Prepare a cross-reference sheet (see page 323) and cross-reference the letter

(c) Release the letter for filing

(d) Prepare the follow-up card for the tickler file.

July 18, 197-

Mr. John R. Lowell
415 North Center Street
Lima, Ohio 45801

Dear Mr. Lowell

On June 4 you wrote us that you had purchased the L. J. Bees firm in Lima and that you would assume all his obligations. At that time Mr. Bees owed us $36.15 on invoice No. 5301. On June 13 you ordered more goods for $42.81 at 2/10, n/30.

The old bill incurred by Mr. Bees is now sixty days overdue and your own order of $42.81 remains unpaid. We wonder if something is wrong, Mr. Lowell. You know, we are sure, the importance of having good credit relations with your suppliers.

Won't you write us at once, either enclosing your check for the two invoices or letting us know when we may expect payment?

Sincerely yours

*J. B. Hamm*

J. B. Hamm, Credit Manager

lbe

# Chapter 15

# ALPHABETIC INDEXING

Imagine what would happen if everyone made and used his own rules for placing material in the office files. Obviously, there would soon be utter chaos. The alternative is equally obvious: a set of rules that everyone must observe — rules that provide a clear guide of how items should be indexed for entry into the files.

A secretary or a file supervisor, as well as a file clerk, must understand thoroughly principles and rules of filing.

—*Remington Rand*

There is general agreement on most of the rules for alphabetic indexing; but, unfortunately, they do not cover every filing situation. Occasionally an item may be filed under either of two rules. Thus, in addition to mastering the alphabetic indexing rules, the secretary must be able to handle the exceptions. She is responsible for seeing that variations in the rules are clearly written down and consistently observed. When either of two rules may be followed, she must select the rule that best fits the needs of the particular office or organization. Consequently, the secretary must be a master of filing and, in a large organization, must work very closely and cooperatively with the filing supervisor.

> To be useful, a stockpile of relevant records must be *organized* so that any item can be found when it is needed. Therefore, records in big stockpiles, such as we find in business and government today, have to be classified, housed, managed, and systematized for quick retrieval — instant use.
>
> — *Fundamental Filing Practice*

On the following pages are rules for alphabetic indexing. The examples under each rule are listed in correct alphabetic order. In each example the underline indicates the first letter or letters used in determining the indexing sequence.

## NAMES OF INDIVIDUALS

### (1) Basic Order of Indexing Units

Each part of the name of an individual is an indexing unit. Consider the surname (last name) as the first unit, the first name or initial as the second unit, and the middle name or initial as the third unit. Arrange all names in A–Z sequence, comparing each letter in order until a point of difference is reached. *The letter that determines the order of any two names is the first letter that is different in the two names.* Consider first the first unit of each name. Consider the second units only when the first units are identical. When further indexing is necessary to determine the relative position of two or more names that have exactly the same coding units, the relative position of the two or more names is determined by a further *identifying element*, such as *junior* or *senior*, or a part of the address. In such cases, the coder places a check mark above or at the left of the identifying element.

| Name | Index Order of Units | | | Identifying |
|---|---|---|---|---|
| | Unit 1 | Unit 2 | Unit 3 | Element |
| [1]John Ander | Ander, | John | | |
| John E. Ander | Ander, | John | E. | |
| Louis Ander | Ander, | Louis | | |
| Adam Anders | Anders, | Adam | | |
| John C. Anderson, Jr. | Anderson, | John | C. | Junior |
| John C. Anderson, Sr. | Anderson, | John | C. | Senior |
| Aaron Andersson | Andersson, | Aaron | | |
| David Lee Andrews | Andrews, | David | Lee | |
| E. Bennett Andrews | Andrews, | E. | Bennett | |
| [2]Soo On Bee | Bee, | Soo | On | |
| Eli J. Dorman, II | Dorman, | Eli | J. | II |
| Eli J. Dorman, III | Dorman, | Eli | J. | III |

**Note 1:** *Ander* precedes *Anders* because the *r* in *Ander* is not followed by any letter. This is an example of the rule that *nothing precedes something.*

**Note 2:** An unusual or foreign personal name is indexed in the usual manner, with the last word considered to be the surname and therefore the first indexing unit.

## (2) Surname Prefixes and Hyphened Surnames

(A) A surname prefix is considered to be a part of the first indexing unit. Among the common prefixes are *D', Da, De, Del, Des, El, Il, La, Le, Les, Los, Mac, Mc, O', Van,* and *Von.* In some cases the first letter of a prefix is not capitalized, and spacing of the surname is not significant. (B) When compound (hyphened) surnames, such as *Martin-Ames,* occur in filing, each part of the surname is considered a separate unit.

| Name | Index Order of Units | | |
|---|---|---|---|
| | Unit 1 | Unit 2 | Unit 3 |
| Charles Lemate | Lemate, | Charles | |
| Francis LeMate | LeMate, | Francis | |
| Ruth Martin-Ames | Martin- | Ames | Ruth |
| Wallace Martin | Martin, | Wallace | |
| Raymond O'Bonner | O'Bonner, | Raymond | |
| Albert Odell | Odell, | Albert | |
| [1]Edith St. Marner | Saint | Marner, | Edith |

**Note 1:** Even though *St.* is abbreviated in the name *Edith St. Marner,* it is indexed as if it were spelled in full and is considered to be the first unit. (A variation of this rule is to consider the prefix *Saint* and the part of the surname that follows it to be one unit.)

**Note 2:** A variation of Rule 2B above is to consider hyphened surnames as one unit.

## (3) Initials and Abbreviations

(A) An initial in an individual's name is considered as an indexing unit and precedes all names in the same unit beginning with the same letter as the initial.  (B) An abbreviated first or middle name or a nick-name is considered as if it were written in full.

| Name | Index Order of Units | | |
|------|--------|--------|--------|
|  | Unit 1 | Unit 2 | Unit 3 |
| Paul Cameron | Cameron, | Paul | |
| D. D. Crawford | Crawford, | D. | D. |
| Dale Crawford | Crawford, | Dale | |
| Wm. E. Dackman | Dackman, | William | E. |
| Willis Dackman | Dackman, | Willis | |
| [1]Bob L. Davenport | Davenport, | Bob | L. |
| Robert Davenport | Davenport, | Robert | |

**Note 1:** When the brief form of a given name is known to be used by an individual in his signature as his given name, this brief form name is treated as a unit.

## (4) Titles

(A) A personal or professional title or degree is usually not con-sidered in filing.  When the name is written in index form, the title is placed in parentheses at the end of the name.  (B) A title is considered as the first indexing unit only when it is followed by given name only or by surname only.

| Name | Index Order of Units | | |
|------|--------|--------|--------|
|  | Unit 1 | Unit 2 | Unit 3 |
| Miss Mary J. Fatam | Fatam, | Mary | J. (Miss) |
| [1a]Father Delbert | Father | Delbert | |
| Rev. A. O. Hanson | Hanson, | A. | O. (Rev.) |
| Ralph Hanson, D. D. | Hanson, | Ralph (D. D.) | |
| [1a]Father Robert O. Hanson | Hanson, | Robert | O. (Father) |
| Madame Mavis | Madame | Mavis | |
| Capt. Orrin Mason | Mason, | Orrin (Capt.) | |
| Mrs. Ann Jones Milton | Milton, | Ann | Jones (Mrs.) |
| Dr. Alfred Miltson | Miltson, | Alfred (Dr.) | |

**Note 1:** For names including the religious titles *Father, Brother,* and *Sister,* Rule 4B may be modified as follows:

(a) To group together within a filing system all names bearing one of these titles, consider the titles themselves of first importance in indexing, regardless of the names that follow them. Names that do not include a surname are indexed in the order written: *Father Delbert.* Names that include one or more given names and a surname are transposed after the title, as explained in Rule 1: *Hanson, Robert O. (Father).*

(b) To set up a separate section to include all such names in the files, consider the name or names following such titles as of first importance, and *disregard the title.*  Names that do not include a surname are indexed in the order written. Names that include one or more given names and a surname are transposed. Indexing order for Father Delbert in such case would be *Delbert (Father)*; for *Father Robert O. Hanson* would be *Hanson, Robert O. (Father).*

## (5) Names of Married Women

The name of a married woman is indexed according to her legal name (her first name, either her maiden surname, or her middle name or initial, and her husband's surname). The title "Mrs." is disregarded in filing, but it is placed in parentheses after the legal name. The husband's name, if known, may be given in parentheses below a woman's legal name; but legally she assumes only the surname when she marries.

| Name | Index Order of Units | | |
| --- | --- | --- | --- |
| | Unit 1 | Unit 2 | Unit 3 |
| Mrs. Robert (Becky Mae) Fritts | Fritts, | Becky | Mae (Mrs. Robert) |
| Mrs. Lucien (Becky Smith) Fritts | Fritts, | Becky | Smith (Mrs. Lucien) |

## (6) Identical Names

When the names of individuals are identical, their alphabetic order is determined by their addresses, starting with the city. Names of states are considered when the names of the cities are also alike. When the city and the state names as well as the full names of the individuals are alike, the alphabetic order is determined by street names; next, house and building numbers, with the lowest first. When it is used, the address is treated as an identifying element.

*city, state, St name, no.*

| Names | Index Order of Units | | | Identifying Element |
| --- | --- | --- | --- | --- |
| | Unit 1 | Unit 2 | Unit 3 | |
| John Hess 314 Elm Street, Toledo | Hess, | John | | Elm |
| John Hess 92 Plum Avenue, Toledo | Hess, | John | | Plum |
| Edward Horton, Akron | Horton, | Edward | | Akron |
| Edward Horton, Columbus | Horton, | Edward | | Columbus |
| Edward Horton, Dayton | Horton, | Edward | | Dayton |
| Edward B. Horton | Horton, | Edward | B. | |

# NAMES OF BUSINESSES AND GROUPS

## (7) Basic Order of Indexing Units

(A) Usually the indexing units of a business or group name are considered in the order in which they are written. (B) An exception is made to the usual rule when a business name includes the full name of an individual. In that case the units in the individual name are considered in the same order as if the individual name appeared independently, as shown below.

| Names | Index Order of Units | | |
|---|---|---|---|
| | Unit 1 | Unit 2 | Unit 3 |
| S. Martin Hats | Martin, | S. | Hats |
| Sam Martin Garage | Martin, | Sam | Garage |
| Nelson Lumber Company | Nelson | Lumber | Company |
| [1]Newsweek | Newsweek | | |
| John Nobee News Corner | Nobee, | John | News |
| World Almanac | World | Almanac | |

**Note 1:** The name of a magazine or book may be indexed according to these basic indexing rules for the name of a business.

## (8) Articles, Conjunctions, and Prepositions

(A) Such words as *the, and, &, for, on, in, by,* and *of the* are generally disregarded in indexing and filing. However, they are placed in parentheses for coding purposes. An initial *the* is placed in parentheses after the last unit. (B) A word normally classified as a preposition but used as the first word in a business name, or a modifying word, or part of a compound name is considered to be a separate indexing unit.

| Names | Index Order of Units | | |
|---|---|---|---|
| | Unit 1 | Unit 2 | Unit 3 |
| By the Lane Inn | By | Lane (the) | Inn |
| Charles of the Ritz | Charles (of the) | Ritz | |
| Committee on Departmental Reorganization | Committee (on) | Departmental | Reorganization |
| Emery & Frank Shoes | Emery (&) | Frank | Shoes |
| End of the Mile Tavern | End (of the) | Mile | Tavern |
| The Favorite Music Shop | Favorite | Music | Shop (The) |

## (9) Initials, Abbreviations, and Titles

(A) An initial or letter that is not a common abbreviation precedes a *word* beginning with that letter. (B) A known abbreviation, even though the abbreviation consists of a single letter without a period, is treated as if it were spelled in full, except *Mr.* and *Mrs.*, which are filed alphabetically as they are written. (C) A business name including a title followed by a given name, a surname, or a coined name is indexed in the order in which it is written.

| Names | Index Order of Units | | |
| --- | --- | --- | --- |
| | *Unit 1* | *Unit 2* | *Unit 3* |
| BB Brakes | B | B | Brakes |
| Ball Crank Co. | Ball | Crank | Company |
| B & O Railroad | Baltimore (&) | Ohio | Railroad |
| Bayard Co. | Bayard | Company | |
| C and C Dress Shoppe | C (and) | C | Dress |
| City Cleaners | City | Cleaners | |
| Dr. Footeze | Doctor | Footeze | |
| Monsieur Antoine Beauty Salon | Monsieur | Antoine | Beauty |
| Mr. Jim's Steak House | Mr. | Jim's | Steak |
| Mrs. Della Knits | Mrs. | Della | Knits |

## (10) Numbers and Symbols

(A) A number in a firm name is considered as if it were written as one word. It is indexed as one unit. Four-place numbers are expressed in hundreds (not in thousands) in order to consider a smaller number of letters in the index unit. (B) A symbol with the number is considered separately as a word.

| Names | Index Order of Units | | |
| --- | --- | --- | --- |
| | *Unit 1* | *Unit 2* | *Unit 3* |
| A 1 Garage | A | One | Garage |
| 8th St. Bldg. | Eighth | Street | Building |
| 1110 Choices Store | Elevenhundredten | Choices | Store |
| $5 Bargain Store | Five | Dollar | Bargain |
| Ft. Evans News | Fort | Evans | News |
| 40th Avenue Laundry | Fortieth | Avenue | Laundry |
| Fortilair Food Shop | Fortilair | Food | Shop |

**Note 1:** Some file manuals omit the words *hundred* and *thousand* in considering the indexing unit—examples: fiveten for 510 and twelveseventy for 1270.

**Note 2:** When several names differ only in numeric designations, the order of those names may be based upon the numeric sequence instead of the alphabetic order of those numbers written in words. For example, if several branch stores of the same company are numbered, it might be more convenient in an office to have the names arranged in numeric sequence.

## (11) Hyphened Names

The hyphened parts of business names (including coined parts) are indexed and filed as separate words.

An exception is made to this rule when the hyphened parts are shown in the dictionary as a single word or as a hyphened word. Both parts of such a word are considered together as one indexing unit.

| Names | Index Order of Units | | |
|---|---|---|---|
| | Unit 1 | Unit 2 | Unit 3 |
| A-1 Retail Markets | A- | One | Retail |
| Read-N-Sew Studio | Read- | N- | Sew |
| Ready-Built Shelf Shop | Ready- | Built | Shelf |
| Reedy-Adam Corp. | Reedy- | Adam | Corporation |
| Charles A. Reedy Corp. | Reedy, | Charles | A. |
| Reedy-Miller Studios | Reedy- | Miller | Studios |
| Adam D. Reedy-Smith Corp. | Reedy- | Smith | Adam |
| Self-Service Laundry | Self-Service | Laundry | |
| Self-Study Society | Self-Study | Society | |
| Selfton Voice Studio | Selfton | Voice | Studio |

## (12) One Versus Two Units

When separate words in a business name are shown in the dictionary as one word, the two should be treated as one indexing unit.

| Names | Index Order of Units | | |
|---|---|---|---|
| | Unit 1 | Unit 2 | Unit 3 |
| Semi Trailer Rentals, Inc. | SemiTrailer | Rentals | Inc. |
| Semi Weekly Cleaning Service | SemiWeekly | Cleaning | Service |
| Semiweekly Communication Review | Semiweekly | Communication | Review |
| Southwestern Machine Products | Southwestern | Machine | Products |
| South Western Office Supplies | SouthWestern | Office | Supplies |
| South-Western Publishing Co. | SouthWestern | Publishing | Co. |
| Southwick Drug Service | Southwick | Drug | Service |
| Southwick Drug Store | Southwick | DrugStore | |
| Stephan's Super Repair Shop | Stephan's | Super | Repair |
| Stephan's Super Market Displays | Stephan's | SuperMarket | Displays |

## (13) Compound Geographic and Location Names

(A) Each English word in a compound geographic or location name is indexed as a separate unit. (B) A prefix or foreign article in such names is not considered as a separate indexing unit but is combined with the word that follows.

| Names | Index Order of Units | | |
| | Unit 1 | Unit 2 | Unit 3 |
| --- | --- | --- | --- |
| Le Mont Food Products | LeMont | Food | Products |
| Los Angeles Actors' Guild | LosAngeles | Actors' | Guild |
| New York Central R. R. | New | York | Central |
| North Dakota Curios | North | Dakota | Curios |
| Old Saybury R. R. Station | Old | Saybury | Railroad |
| St. Thomas Island Home | Saint | Thomas | Island |
| Saintbury Publishing Co. | Saintbury | Publishing | Company |
| [1]San Diego Greenhouses, Inc. | San | Diego | Greenhouses |
| [1]Santa Clara Lithographers | Santa | Clara | Lithographers |

**Note 1:** The words "San" in San Diego and "Santa" in Santa Clara mean "Saint," and are therefore indexed separately according to their spelling.

**Note 2:** When it is part of the actual name of a city (as *The Dalles*), *The* is considered to be the first unit.

**Note 3:** Some plans of filing treat each geographic name as one word regardless of the number of words in the name. *New Orleans* would be considered as one unit in such a filing system.

## (14) Possessives

When a word ends in *apostrophe s* ('s), the final *s* is not considered as part of the word for filing purposes, except as part of a contraction. When a word ends in *s apostrophe* (s'), however, the final *s* is considered.

| Names | Index Order of Units | | |
| | Unit 1 | Unit 2 | Unit 3 |
| --- | --- | --- | --- |
| Girl Scouts of America | Girl | Scouts (of) | America |
| Girl's Sportswear | Girl('s) | Sportswear | |
| Girls' Short Stories | Girls' | Short | Stories |
| Harper's Restaurant | Harper('s) | Restaurant | |
| Harpers' | Harpers' | | |
| Harperston's Apparel | Harperston('s) | Apparel | |
| Harperston Bank | Harperston | Bank | |

## (15) Identical Business Names

(A) Identical names of businesses are arranged alphabetically by address, with address parts treated as identifying elements. (For this reason the word "City" should not be used in place of the name of the city.) (B) If the names of the cities are alike, filing arrangement depends upon names of states. (C) When two or more branches of a business are located in the same city, the names of the branches are arranged alphabetically by streets.

| Names | Index Order of Units | | | Identifying Element |
|-------|---------|---------|---------|------------|
| | Unit 1 | Unit 2 | Unit 3 | |
| Jones Stationers, Decatur | Jones | Stationers, | | Decatur |
| Jones Stationers, Eureka | Jones | Stationers, | | Eureka |
| Jones Stationers, Sterling | Jones | Stationers, | | Sterling |
| Kastner's, 531 Main Street | Kastner('s), | | | Main |
| Kastner's, 1024 Oak Street | Kastner('s), | | | Oak |

**Note 1:** The name of the building in which the firm is located should not be considered unless the name of the street is not provided or is identical for both branches.

## (16) Banking Institutions and Newspapers

(A) When only local banking institutions are involved, their names are indexed as written. (B) When banks from several cities are involved, however, the names of the cities in which the banks are located are considered as the first indexing units with the words in the names of the banks following. If the name of the bank contains the name of the city or state, that geographic location is not repeated in the indexed form. If several states are involved, the names of the states should be considered after the name of the city, as identifying elements. (C) Newspapers follow the same indexing rules as those used for banks.

| Names | Index Order of Units | | | Identifying Element |
|-------|---------|---------|---------|------------|
| | Unit 1 | Unit 2 | Unit 3 | |
| Bloomington Trust Co. Bloomington, Illinois | Bloomington | Trust | Company | Illinois |
| Bloomington Trust Co. Bloomington, Indiana | Bloomington | Trust | Company | Indiana |
| Third National Bank Duluth, Minnesota | Duluth: | Third | National | |
| Wenatchee Times Wenatchee, Washington | Wenatchee | Times | | |
| Times Herald Williamsport, Pennsylvania | Williamsp't: | Times | Herald | |

## (17) Elementary and Secondary Schools

A public elementary or secondary school name is indexed first by the name of the city and then by the name of the school. An individual's name within a school name is transposed in the usual manner. If a school name begins with a city name, the city name is considered only once. State names are treated as identifying elements if a city name is alike in two or more states. A parochial school is indexed by name.

| Names | Index Order of Units | | | Identifying Element |
|---|---|---|---|---|
| | Unit 1 | Unit 2 | Unit 3 | |
| Crispus Attucks High School Indianapolis, Indiana | Indianapolis | Attucks | Crispus | |
| Modesto Elementary School Modesto, California | Modesto | Elementary | School | |
| Muncie Central High School Muncie, Indiana | Muncie | Central | High | |
| Muncie Southside High School Muncie, Indiana | Muncie | Southside | High | |
| Newport Beach High School Newport Beach, California | Newport | Beach | High | |
| Newport High School Newport, Rhode Island | Newport | High | School | Rhode Island |
| Newport High School Newport, Washington | Newport | High | School | Washington |

## (18) Colleges, Universities, Special Schools, Hotels, Motels, and Other Organizations

(A) When common usage makes one part of a name more clearly identify the organization, that part is used as the first indexing unit. Otherwise, names of such organizations are indexed as they are generally written. (B) A city or state name as part of the organization name is considered an indexing unit or units. When the name of an organization is the same in two or more cities, city names are considered last as identifying elements.

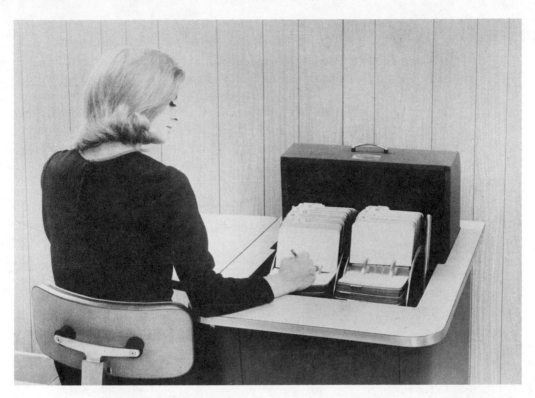

*—Wheeldex, Inc.*

This secretary has discovered that a rotary (wheel) file allows her to make entries of continually changing data with speed and ease, thus providing her employer with the current facts that he must have.

| Names | Index Order of Units | | |
|---|---|---|---|
| | Unit 1 | Unit 2 | Unit 3 |
| [1]Howard Johnson's Motor Lodge | Howard | Johnson's | Motor |
| University of Idaho | Idaho, | University (of) | |
| Indiana University | Indiana | University | |
| Hotel Jolee Florists | Jolee, | Hotel, | Florists |
| Priest River Kiwanis Club | Kiwanis | Club, | Priest |
| Los Angeles City College | Los Angeles | City | College |
| Association of Lumbermen | Lumbermen, | Association (of) | |
| First Methodist Church | Methodist | Church, | First |
| [1]Martha Nelson Beauty College | Nelson, | Martha, | Beauty |
| [2]WLBC | Radio | Station | W |
| Venovich Motel | Venovich | Motel | |

**Note 1:** An individual's name within the name of the organization is transposed in the usual manner unless the name is always considered as a unit.

**Note 2:** Preferable way to index a radio or television station is to consider *Radio Station* or *Television Station* as the first two units, followed by each call letter as a separate unit.

*(dep. bureu, division)*

The name of a federal government office is considered for indexing in the following order: (1) United States Government, (2) principal word or words in the name of the department, (3) principal word or words in the name of the bureau, (4) principal word or words in the name of the division. Such words as *Department of*, *Bureau of*, and *Division of* are transposed, with the word *of* disregarded and so placed in parentheses.

| Names | Index Order of Units | | | | |
| | Unit 4 | Unit 5 | Unit 6 | Unit 7 | Unit 8 |
|---|---|---|---|---|---|
| **Bureau of the Census U.S. Department of Commerce** | Commerce | Department (of) | Census, | Bureau (of the) | |
| **Weather Bureau U.S. Department of Commerce** | Commerce | Department (of) | Weather | Bureau | |
| **Social Security Administration U.S. Department of Health, Education, and Welfare** | Health | Education (and) | Welfare | Department (of) *Unit 9:* Security *Unit 10:* Administration | Social |
| **Office of Indian Affairs U.S. Department of the Interior** | Interior | Department (of the) | Indian | Affairs | Office (of) |
| **Federal Bureau of Investigation[1] U.S. Department of Justice** | Justice | Department (of) | Federal | Bureau (of) | Investigation |

**Note 1:** The Federal Bureau of Investigation is so well known by its full name and initials that the name is often filed as known.

## (20) Other Government Offices

(A) The name of any other government office is considered in the following order: (1) principal word or words in the name of the political subdivision, followed by its state, county, or city classification, (2) principal word or words in the name of the department, board, or office. Such words as *Department of* and *Bureau of* are transposed, with the word *of* placed in parentheses.  (B) If two or more political subdivisions within a state have the same first indexing unit, the state name as an identifying element is considered immediately after the first principal word in the political subdivision, to determine relative placement of the items with identical first units.

| Names | Index Order of Units | | |
|---|---|---|---|
| | Unit 1 | Unit 2 | Unit 3 |
| Department of Public Safety California | California, | State (of) | Public |
| Board of Health Cincinnati | Cincinnati, | City (of) | Health |
| Tax Collector Cook County | Cook, | County | Tax |

## (21) Foreign Governments

Foreign-language names are translated into English for indexing, and the distinctive English name of the foreign country is considered first.  Next, divisions are considered in the same manner as are United States governmental units.

| Names | Index Order of Units | | |
|---|---|---|---|
| | Unit 1 | Unit 2 | Unit 3 |
| Republique Francaise Armée de l'Air[1] | France | Air | Force |
| Estados Unidos Mexicanos Secretaria de Industrio y Commercia | Mexico Secretary (of) | Industry (and) | Commerce, ←— Unit 4 |

**Note 1:** The names of foreign countries may be uniformly filed according to the native spelling, rather than the English translation.

## GENERAL GUIDES

The student of alphabetic indexing rules may find it helpful to think in terms of general guides and then to note variations of these general guides.  The following items would be among those most important:

1. An individual's full name is transposed, in either a personal or a business name; otherwise a business name is indexed as written.

2. Articles, conjunctions, prepositions, apostrophe addition in possessives, and titles are disregarded and placed in parentheses except where (1) a preposition or modifying word is a coined major part of a business name, or (2) a title is followed by a given name only or by a surname only.

3. Numbers and known abbreviations are spelled in full as one word, except *Mr.* or *Mrs.* or a nickname used as part of the individual's official signature.

4. Initials, hyphened parts of names, and separated words are treated as individual units except where hyphened or separated words are shown by the dictionary to be acceptable as one word.

5. A special organization is indexed first by that part of the name which common usage causes to stand out most clearly in identifying that organization.

6. Elementary and secondary schools, newspapers, and banking institutions may be indexed first by the name of the city.

7. Governmental offices are indexed first by the major governmental unit of which the particular office is a part.

The secretary or the file supervisor, in determining which of several possibilities of filing rules will best fit her office or her organization, should keep in mind major criteria of serviceability: (1) What indexing procedure will provide for filing or refiling of materials with the least amount of error? (2) What indexing procedure will provide for filing or withdrawing materials and refiling materials with least time waste?

Once such a decision is made, definite steps must be taken to assure that, through the manual and whatever other means might be helpful, the procedure will be communicated successfully to all concerned and followed consistently.

## QUESTIONS FOR DISCUSSION

1. For what purposes other than filing may the secretary make use of the rules for alphabetic indexing?

2. Why do rules for filing government units, banks, schools, churches, and other organizations differ from the other rules for alphabetizing?

3. Can you think of a good reason why the rule for filing hyphened individual names differs from the rule for filing hyphened business names?

4. In what order are the units of an individual name considered in indexing?

5. Why should the word "City" not be used instead of the city name for local correspondents?

6. In what order are the units of a federal governmental office considered for indexing?

7. Refer to the Reference Guide. What salutation would be correct to use in a letter addressed to each of the following persons?
   (a) The wife of the President of the United States
   (b) The Vice President of the United States
   (c) An American ambassador
   (d) A member of the President's Cabinet
   (e) A priest in the Catholic Church

**1.** You are to set up a portion of a file for the Sales Promotion Department of Ohio Bell Telephone, which is planning solicitation of all business organizations in a small Ohio city for a new type of push-button telephone. Arrange the following names in the correct filing form and order:

1. First National Bank of Athens
2. Saint Joseph's Church
3. Martins' Service Station, Third Street
4. South-Eastern Ohio Freezer Co.
5. Bank of Ohio, Xenia
6. First Baptist Church of Xenia
7. Agricultural Extension Service (Federal Office)
8. Board of Education, Xenia, Ohio
9. Ohio University
10. Vocational Rehabilitation Service (Federal Office)
11. Athens Chamber of Commerce
12. State Highway Department
13. C & O Railway
14. Martin's Drive-in Theater
15. Third National Bank of Athens
16. Aaron Jones Retail Outlet
17. Martins' Service Station, Elm Street
18. Aaron-James Production Credit Corporation
19. Cartinson Dress Shoppe

**2.** Rewrite the following business names in index form. Underline the first unit of the name once and the second unit of the name twice.

1. Stoke's Paper Company
2. Mr. Tom's Fur Salon
3. The Las Vegas Novelty Shop
4. Tom & Joe's Bait Shop
5. Top of the Mount Restaurant
6. Russell Stone Camping Equipment
7. 8th Street Garage
8. John Stokes and Sons
9. S & T Delicatessen
10. Bureau of Labor Standards U.S. Department of Labor
11. Stone's Grocery, No. 1
12. South West Auto Supplies
13. San Bernardino Rest Home
14. Stone's Grocery, No. 2

**3.** The purpose of this project is to bring your card filing to a skill level. You will need 75 cards (5- by 3-inch).

*Standards to Try for:*

Type the cards in 15 minutes (approximately 15 words per minute—15 *wam*).

File the cards in 30 minutes—not more than 2 errors.

With practice, reduce your time to 20 minutes—no errors.

Type each of the following names in index form at the top of a file card. (a) Place the number of each name in the upper right-hand corner of the card. (b) Arrange the cards in correct alphabetic order.

1. Paramount Theater
2. K & D Statistics Bureau
3. Mrs. Carl (Ann L.) Sailor
4. El Dorado Saddle Shop
5. Brother Edward Burke
6. N.Y.C.R.R.
7. Internal Revenue Service Treasury Department U.S. Government
8. Richard Donaldson Camera Shop
9. No-Run Hose
10. North Western Printing Company
11. W. Walter, Jr.
12. Union Trust Company Dallas, Texas

13. National Savings Bank
    Newark, New Jersey
14. Joseph Hall, LL.B.
15. Water Works Department
    City of Glendale
16. Nordell, Inc.
17. Yecch Sandwich Counter
18. National Park Service
    Dept. of Interior
    U.S. Government
19. Acacia Mutual Insurance Co.
20. Mt. Carmel Welfare Center
21. Jas. Le Doux
22. South Eastern Carloading Co.
23. Department of Health
    City of Rockdale
24. A & B Welding Co.
25. 19th Hole Restaurant
26. Walter-Woody, Attys.
27. C. C. Walter
28. Adam Salter
29. Paramount Shops, Inc.
    1000 Vine
    Cincinnati, Ohio
30. A 1 Letter Service
31. Edith Marie Beauty Shop
32. KDKA Radio Station
33. Bureau of Nursing Service
    City of Birmingham
34. Town of Ft. Mitchell
35. Wm. Walter
36. Employment Service
    Department of Labor
    U.S. Government
37. Phillip St. Clair
38. John W. St. Clair
39. Bureau of Public Relief
    City of Rockdale
40. Paramount Shops, Inc.
    918 Glenway
    Cincinnati, Ohio
41. A B Furniture Co.
42. Jerome Rice Newman
43. La Mode Frocks
44. G. Laderman
45. East Hyde Park Market

46. Edith's Dancing Studio
47. Advance Laundry
48. Paramount Shops, Inc.
    Elder and Race
    Springfield, Ohio
49. Commission of Public Utilities
    City of Rockdale
50. South Norwalk Delicatessen
51. Civil Aeronautics Authority
    Dept. of Commerce
    U.S. Government
52. Carl Walter
53. Ann Sailor
54. Paramount Shops, Inc.
    2719 Erie Avenue
    Springfield, Ohio
55. Dr. H. F. Newman
56. Rev. Wm. J. Lekwin
57. J. A. Eckerle
58. Ad-Sales Corp.
59. Mountain Valley Water Co.
60. Newman-Rice Institute
61. B. A. Walterman
62. Fire Department
    City of Rockdale
63. The J. H. Albers Co.
64. Paramount Shops, Inc.
    133 East 5th Street
    Springfield, Massachusetts
65. St. Charles Hotel
66. Charles G. Walter
67. A & P Food Shoppe
68. Southern Pacific Lines
69. B. A. Walters, Sr.
70. The Abstract Co.
71. 9th St. Baptist Church
72. William E. Walter
73. Paramount Shops, Inc.
    4220 Glenway
    Cincinnati, Ohio
74. Mrs. Anna Adams
75. B. A. Walters, Jr.

■ 4. Group I is arranged alphabetically. File each Group II name in its proper position in Group I by placing the letter at the end of the line of the name it follows.

## Group I

1. AAA Answering and Office Service
2. A & A Window Corporation
3. ABC Vending Corporation
4. A-1 Taxi Service
5. Abbey Floor Waxing Company
6. Abbott, A. C., Company, Inc.
7. Abraham & Straus
8. Abrahamson's Pharmacy
9. Abrams, Norman J. (Dr.)
10. Abrantes, Anthony (Jr.)
11. Academy Auto Wreckers
12. Accessory Shop
13. Ace Auto Service
14. Ackerman, Mary E.
15. Ackermann, Andrew J.
16. Acme Excavating Corporation
17. Acme-Standard Supply Company
18. Acorn Landscape Service
19. Acousticon of White Plains
20. Adam, Mary T.
21. Adams, Leonard C., Company
22. Addressograph-Multigraph Corporation
23. Adelman, Murray P.
24. Adelson, Marvin
25. Air Dispatch Incorporated
26. Air-Way Travel Service
27. Al & Nick's Restaurant
28. Albanese's Eastchester Inn
29. Albert Studio (The)
30. Alert Employment Agency
31. Alex's Radio & Television Service
32. Alfredo, A., Nurseries
33. Alitalia Airlines
34. All County Electric Service
35. Allen Brothers Incorporated
36. Allen-Keating Corporation
37. Allen's Supply Company
38. Allevi, Lillian (Mrs.)
39. Allied Van Lines, Incorporated
40. Allis-Chalmers Manufacturing Company

## Group II

A. Accounting Associates
B. Addressing Machine & Equipment Company
C. A & A Automotive Company
D. Abrahamson Dress Shop
E. J. B. Allid
F. A-B-K Electric Company
G. Adler Shoes for Men
H. Acme Steel Company
I. Joseph H. Alleva
J. Academy of Aeronautics
K. Air-Step Shoe Shop
L. Mrs. Elizabeth Abbott
M. Alexander Carpet Company
N. A & P Food Co.
O. Al's Glass Service
P. Paul Allen Incorporated
Q. Aladdin's House of Beauty
R. Julian B. L. Allen
S. First National Bank of Alden, New York
T. The Alice Ackermann Shop
U. The Allen-Andrews Mailing Co.

■ **5.** The following letters are filed in the individual folder for Mary Young. Indicate the order, from front to back, in which the letters should be placed in this folder.

(a) A letter of recommendation from Mr. Wilson, dated April 23.

(b) Our request, dated April 7, to Harry Watson for a reference for Miss Young.

(c) A cross reference dated March 27 to a letter with five suggestions for candidates, including Mary Young.

(d) Our reply to her on April 6.

(e) A letter setting an appointment for Miss Young's interview, dated April 27.

(f) Mr. Watson's recommendation for Miss Young, dated April 10.

(g) Mary Young's application for a position, dated April 4.

(h) Our second request to Mr. Wilson for a reference, dated April 20.

(i) Our request to William Wilson for a letter of reference, dated April 7.

■ 6. Rewrite the following names of individuals in index form. Underline the first unit of the name once and the second unit of the name twice.

1. Wm. Mier, 381 Shady Lane, Louisville, Kentucky

2. J. L. Meyers

3. Jas. C. Naber

4. John L. Meyer

5. Mrs. Robt. (Debra L.) O'Brien, Akron

6. Tom M. O'Connell, Sr.

7. T. Kenneth MacNabb

8. Wm. Mier, 29 Parkland Avenue, Louisville, Kentucky

9. Mrs. J. Clarence Naber

10. Sister Norita

11. Mrs. Robt. (D. Lucille) O'Brien, Springfield

12. Tom M. O'Connell, Jr.

13. Thomas McNamara

14. John Meyers

15. J. L. Meyer, Ph.D.

# CASE PROBLEMS

## 5-1 I'D RATHER BE RIGHT

Late one afternoon, Lowell Hayes, a busy young executive, was reading the transcribed letters placed on his desk for his signatures. Suddenly he buzzed for his secretary, Opal Schmidt, and said, "Something is wrong in this Allied letter. I didn't say that."

Opal felt annoyed but decided to say nothing until she could prove her point. She searched through her shorthand notes until she located the sentence in question; then she said resentfully, "I'm sorry, Mr. Hayes, but that is exactly what you said. I have it right here in my notes that way. I wondered about the meaning at the time, but that *is* what you said."

**What is your reaction to Opal's response? What should she have said or done? What is the principle involved in handling this situation?**

## 5-2 CONTROLLING THE FILES

Randall Kerr, Anne Taylor's employer, often bypassed company rules that mited access to the files to secretaries only. He took folders and single items from the files without telling Miss Taylor or charging them out. He left material on her desk for refiling or in his desk or attache case until a search located the material.

One day, after being embarrassed by Mr. Kerr when she couldn't locate the file on the preliminary budget (*Budget, Preliminary*) she found it filed behind "P." Hoping that Mr. Kerr would get the hint, she posted a KEEP OUT sign on the front of the file cabinet.

**Evaluate the way Miss Taylor handled the situation. How would you have handled it?**

## 5-3 "TRAINING" THE EMPLOYER

Vera Carter had a long conference with Edgar Barney's secretary, whom she was replacing. To prepare Vera for her new duties, the secretary told her:

"You will love Mr. Barney, but you won't always love working for him. In fact, I was never able to solve one of the problems caused by his generous nature. Maybe you will be able to do a better job of training him than I did. He is a very impulsive person, and he expects everybody else to be as interested in the company as he is. Whenever he is discussing a problem with a colleague — or even with someone outside the company, for that matter — he will give or lend a brochure, a file, a letter, or even a book about the problem. And he never makes a record of the loan or gift.

"Mr. Barney is forgetful, too. When he wants the material later, he will ask me to locate it in the files, forgetting that he ever gave it away. Then he gets annoyed when I can't find it and thinks that I am inefficient.

"Maybe a new secretary who is forewarned can prevent this embarrassing situation. Think it over before you start. I hope that you can devise a plan that will reform him and save yourself trouble. Naturally, I expect you to respect the confidentiality of my criticism. I only want to help you."

**Can or should a secretary "train" her employer, or is her function merely to follow his bidding?**

**What plan can you suggest?**

## 5-4 WHAT'S IN A NAME?

Karen Cranmer, a new secretary, was learning the routine for retrieving filed materials. She telephoned Central Files and said, "This is Karen Cranmer, Mrs. Hellman's secretary. Is this the head file clerk?" An icy voice responded, "This is Records Management, and I am Mrs. Grayson, supervisor of Central Files. May I help you?"

Karen had been warned about office protocol but had not willfully violated it.

**How could she have avoided antagonizing Mrs. Grayson in her first telephone encounter?**

# Assistance
# with Travel and
# Conferences

*Part* **6**

oday's business executive seems to be constantly on the wing—going from an interoffice meeting to a local community leadership committee meeting, from a branch visit to a headquarters policy-making discussion, from a national or international convention to a meeting with the administrators of an overseas plant. Consequently, the executive secretary spends an increasing amount of time in planning and following through on travel arrangements, in helping the executive organize the meetings that he chairs, and in assisting with the reports of those meetings. The secretary will enjoy this work and can say contentedly, with Emerson, "I've traveled a good deal in Concord."

# Chapter 16

# HANDLING TRAVEL ARRANGEMENTS

Today is the age of the branch office or factory, the conglomerate, and the international corporation. Businessmen responsible for the interlocking activities of their organizations are truly "on the go." In fact, they spend more than a third of their time out of their offices, averaging more than 40 one- or two-day domestic trips and one or two foreign trips of about two weeks a year.

The secretary to the traveling executive has responsibilities of three kinds concerning his frequent trips: preparing him for the trip, taking care of the office while he is away, and following up after the trip by completing the details. Transportation is a highly competitive field; and changes in equipment, services, and fares are being announced constantly. You cannot handle travel arrangements efficiently unless you keep up with these changes and incorporate them into your arrangements for your employer's travel. You will also need to know your company's policies about travel arrangements, which may change often too. You will want to learn your employer's preferences as to airlines, hotels, rented automobiles, and all facilities that will make his strenuous but necessary trips as pleasant and relaxing as possible.

## COMPANY POLICIES REGARDING TRAVEL ARRANGEMENTS

The secretary's first concern in handling travel arrangements is to learn her company's policies. Who handles this responsibility? What airline, hotel, and other credit cards are issued? and what procedures are authorized for their use? How are tickets paid for? How are employees reimbursed for travel expenses? What restrictions does the company have as to per diem travel expenses? How are travel funds obtained?

Travel arrangements may be handled by a traffic department within the company, by an outside travel agency, or by the secretary herself.

## Travel Department

In a very large office actual reservations for travel are expedited by a *traffic department* or *central travel service* that maintains close contact with all carriers; has on hand complete official guides for airlines, railroads, and steamships; and deals with special reservation clerks (at unlisted numbers) serving only such volume buyers. Here, the secretary informs the special department of a proposed trip; the department then suggests possible schedules to be approved by the executive and his secretary. When their decision is made, the department obtains the necessary tickets. The travel department also secures and distributes credit cards for authorized personnel.

## Travel Agencies

In recent years the business world has turned increasingly to travel agencies. Some agencies now work with business travelers exclusively. The know-how of the reputable agency is especially helpful to an overseas-bound customer; moreover, it is a convenience to the domestic traveler.

A travel agency charges the customer no fee; the transportation lines "pick up the tab." The agent plans the entire itinerary, handles all ticketing, and at times provides unusual services, such as car rentals, special discounts, and the like. The secretary gives the name, business and home address, business and home telephone, the cities to be visited, the hour at which the traveler must be in each city and the hour at which he can leave, any hotel preferences, and any cost requirements.

## The Secretary

If a business organization provides neither the services of an intracompany special travel department nor the regular services of a travel agency, the secretary is "on her own" in handling all travel arrangements. She will deal directly with the transportation companies, or she may enlist the services of a travel agency.

The alert secretary arranges travel facilities that conform to the executive's personal preferences. She will soon discover the hotel chain he likes best, the airline he prefers, and whether he prefers the section reserved for nonsmokers. By consulting the executive about his preferences or by remembering them from trip to trip, she can alleviate some of the mental and physical stress of his traveling and leave him free to concentrate on his work.

# AIR TRAVEL

Most businessmen prefer to fly, especially on long trips, because they save time. Today, a passenger can breakfast in Chicago, lunch in San Francisco, and dine in New York. The jet age has given the executive the advantage of keeping close contact with operations without being away from his desk for too long a time. Air travel, however, has an element of uncertainty with the possibility of a canceled flight due to weather conditions, particularly during the winter. When an executive has a speaking engagement or a meeting where his presence is imperative, the efficient secretary will provide him with a list of flights scheduled from alternate airports that may be open.

## Classes of Flights

Some people like to fly the jumbo 747's that connect the large cities of the United States with each other and with foreign cities. These planes are equipped with large away-from-seat lounges for both coach and first-class passengers and have in-flight movies, recorded entertainment, and — on de luxe flights — even live entertainment. Other travelers prefer smaller planes, which also may boast movies and recorded entertainment.

The major airlines are supported by regional lines that fly to cities too small for jet runways. A passenger from a large city to a small one will probably fly on both jet planes and those of the regional airline.

Most planes have both a first-class and a coach section. Generally, the classes of flight are:

*First class.* **Serves complimentary meals during conventional mealtimes and generous refreshments. Has several attendants. Seats are wider, farther apart, and provide more leg room than those in the coach section. Special airport lounges and in-flight meals at reserved tables are recent innovations designed to attract the affluent passenger.**

*Coach.* **Serves a complimentary meal when the plane is aloft at mealtime and a snack at other times.**

After-dinner coach flights originate after nine o'clock and are considerably cheaper than daytime flights. A few airlines still operate night coach flights between midnight and dawn at reduced fares, but some airlines have abandoned them in the interest of noise abatement. A limited number of airlines schedule de luxe flights for extra-fare passengers.

Meal services are diversified by competing airlines. Choices of up to three entrees in coach class are offered on certain domestic flights. Meals to accommodate special diets can be ordered in advance.

Among other special services, some airport lounges are equipped to give stock quotations when the operator presses the button appropriate for the stock in which he is interested.

For shuttle service between certain cities (as New York/Boston and New York/Washington), passengers board the plane without reservations; the flights then leave at frequent intervals or as soon as the plane is filled. Passengers pay aloft with either cash or credit card. Carry-on luggage only is accepted on these flights.

Businessmen sometimes travel on first-class flights, but for a short flight a coach reservation may be adequate. On a long trip the executive may prefer more luxurious facilities. His executive status and company policy will determine his travel status.

On domestic flights each passenger is allowed two pieces of luggage, one measuring not more than 62 inches in girth, the other measuring not more than 55 inches. The passenger may carry some luggage aboard without charge. The size and nature of this luggage varies among airlines, as does the extra charge (from $2 to $5) for extra luggage.

## Air Fares

Most air schedules show one-way fares on the schedule between cities. (See the schedules on page 363.)

A schedule of sample one-way first-class and coach fares between major cities is also given in the back of the timetable folder. The cost of limousine service is also indicated.

Currently an 8 percent federal tax is added to the cost of domestic airline tickets.

## Flight Schedules

Airline flight schedules are not uniform in structure among airlines. Two sample schedules (not intended to be valid) are given on page 363 to illustrate the ease with which they can be read.

First is the schedule of all Delta Air Lines flights from Kansas City, Missouri, to Atlanta, Georgia.

Only two flights are nonstop, one at noon and one in the late afternoon. The 4:40 p.m. flight is scheduled for the convenience of the businessman. He can spend almost an entire day in Kansas City and still reach Atlanta in the early evening. Lunch or dinner is served on these flights to both coach and first-class passengers. Flight 606 flies on Saturday only and supplants Flight 604. A nonstop flight between

| Leave | Arrive | Flight Number | Stops or Via | Meals | Remarks |
|-------|--------|---------------|--------------|-------|---------|
| **KANSAS CITY, MO.** | | | **To** | Reservations 471-1828 | |
| | | | | Air Freight 471-7612 | |
| **ATLANTA, GA.** | | | | | |
| 1 15a | 5 21a | 788 | Two | | ★ |
| 8 00a | 11 40a | 300/845 | Memphis | B -S | |
| 11 55a | 2 28p | 918 | NONSTOP | L -L | |
| 1 55p | 5 26p | 606 | One | S - | 6 |
| 1 55p | 5 26p | 604 | One | S - | X6 |
| 4 40p | 7 13p | 908 | NONSTOP | D -D | |
| 6 00p | 10 49p | 460 | Three | S -S | |

## REFERENCE MARKS

**MEALS:** Royal Service. Flights with prestige catering appropriate to the time of day in First-Class section.

D Dinner   br Brunch
L Lunch   m Munch (Same idea as Brunch but in the afternoon/evening)
B Breakfast   S Snack
(A single meal symbol indicates service to First-Class or Deluxe Night Coach only)

**FREQUENCY CODE** All Flights Daily Except as Noted

| 1 — Monday | 4 — Thursday | 7 — Sunday |
|---|---|---|
| 2 — Tuesday | 5 — Friday | X — Except |
| 3 — Wednesday | 6 — Saturday | |

**MISCELLANEOUS SYMBOLS**

★ Money-saving Early Bird morning flights or Owly Bird evening flights offering Deluxe Night Coach and Night Coach service.
o Jet Economy service available. (no meals)
/ Separates flights on connecting service.

---

**From DENVER, Colo. (MDT)**

Limousine 30 Min. $1.50

**RESERVATIONS: Domestic:** 292-6620
**International:** 292-6353   **Freight:** 398-3611

**To: CHICAGO, Ill. (CDT)**

F-$87.00   Y-$67.00   K-$60.00
**AIRPORTS: M**-Midway   **O**-O'Hare

| | | | | | | |
|---|---|---|---|---|---|---|
| 8 00a | O | 1058a | 276 | NON-STOP | Ex Su | Twin Seat |
| 9 20a | O | 1218p | 214 | NON-STOP | Daily | Twin Seat |
| 12 00n | O | 301p | 278 | NON-STOP | Daily | Twin Seat |
| 12 00p | O | 301p | 908 | NON-STOP | Daily | |
| 1 25p | O | 426p | 116 | NON-STOP | Daily | Twin Seat |
| 5 30p | O | 834p | 366 | NON-STOP | Daily | Twin Seat |

**SYMBOLS**

Music
Meal
* Change of airport

**CLASS OF SERVICE**

F First Class
Y Coach Economy
K Economy/Jet Commuter

---

Kansas City and Atlanta takes about one and a half hours. A convenience provided by this timetable is the inclusion of the Kansas City telephone numbers for Delta Air Lines passenger reservations and freight shipments.

A simulated schedule of flights on the Trans World System from Denver, Colorado, to Chicago, Illinois, above, differs considerably.

This table shows that Denver is on Mountain Daylight time, and Chicago is on Central Daylight time (one hour later). The time required to reach the airport and the limousine fare ($1.50) are shown, as well as the local telephone numbers of the various TWA services. All flights between Denver and Chicago are nonstop, and only one operates fewer than seven days a week. All flights serve meals, and one provides music. The one-way fare (without tax) is given for first-class (F), coach (Y), and economy/jet (K) passengers. None of these planes provide K service (which is available on commuter flights and on which a meal can be purchased if desired). All of these flights go to O'Hare Field; none to Midway airport. Flight time between Denver and Chicago is about two hours.

## Flight Information

Because air fares, services, and times of departure change frequently, the secretary must be certain she is using an up-to-date schedule. She can telephone the Reservations and Information number lised for a particular airlines. The reservations clerk will willingly help with planning a flight and can give information on the flights of airlines other than his own. For infrequent travel planning, this is a quick, convenient method.

An executive who travels regularly, however, will profit by subscribing to one of the airlines guides published by the Reuben H. Donnelly Corporation of Chicago: the monthly or semimonthly *Official Airline Guide*, the monthly *OAG Pocket Flight Guide*, or the quarterly *Travel Planner*. Subscribers receive updated materials automatically. With one of these publications at hand, the secretary can research the most convenient flights available and present alternative plans for her employer's approval before she initiates the actual reservations. These publications (according to their individual completeness) also give information about the airport facilities, the distance from the airport to the center of a city, limousine service (time, fares, and pickup points), hotels (Mobil ratings and rates), car rentals, and air taxi services available. The guides are simple to use, once you understand the general method of presentation. The opening pages provide keys to the abbreviations and symbols used. Flight information is listed alphabetically by the *destination* city, then alphabetically by the cities from which flights to that city are available. A brief discussion of using the *Official Airline Guide* follows.

Include in your list of frequently called numbers those of the Reservations and Information desks of the airlines you are likely to use in your travel assistance duties.

Suppose your employer is to fly from Boston to Phoenix. You would turn to the *To Phoenix* section (listed alphabetically under *P*). Under *To Phoenix*, you would then locate the *From Boston* listings (listed alphabetically under *B*). There you would find a flight schedule similar to that shown at the top of page 365.

Reading from the top of the table, you learn that:

| To PHOENIX, ARIZ. | | | | | MST | PHX | |
|---|---|---|---|---|---|---|---|
| From BOSTON, MASS. | | | | | EDT | BOS | |
| | F | 175.93 | 14.07 | 190.00 | 380.00 | | |
| | Y | 140.74 | 11.26 | 152.00 | 304.00 | | |
| X6 10:30a | 5:40p | AA 239 | F/Y | 72S | SD | 5 | |
| 11:30a | 4:35p | AA 85 | F/Y | 72S | LS | 3 | |
| 1:55p | 5:35p | AA 385 | F/Y | B7F | SD | 2 | |
| 5:00p | 8:25p | AA 115 | F/Y | 72S | D | 1 | |
| **CONNECTIONS** | | | | | | | |
| 7:50a | 11:52a | TW 193 | F/Y | 72S | B | 0 | |
| 9:03a ORD | 10:40a | TW 315 | F/Y | 72S | L | 0 | |
| 10:10a | 2:16p | UA 977 | F/Y | 72S | L | 0 | |
| 12:20p DEN | 1:45p | WA 473 | F/Y | 72S | S/ | 0 | |
| 10:45a | 5:36p | NE 327 | F/Y | D9S | S | 0 | |
| 12:00n DCA | 12:50p | DL 623 | F/Y | D9S | * | 3 | |
| | | DL 623 * MEALS LSD/LD | | | | | |
| 11:45a | 3:15p | TW 265 | F/Y | 72S | L | 0 | |
| 12:55p ORD | 2:00p | TW 149 | F/Y | 727 | L | 0 | |
| 3:00p | 7:02p | TW 435 | F/Y | 727 | | 0 | |
| 4:13p ORD | 5:50p | TW 403 | F/Y | 727 | D | 0 | |
| 4:30p | 8:35p | UA 163 | F/Y | 727 | D | 0 | |
| 6:35p DEN | 8:00p | WA 479 | Y | 737 | | 0 | |

- Phoenix is on Mountain Standard time (currently with this schedule).
- PHX is the City/Airport code for Phoenix.
- Boston is on Eastern Daylight time.
- BOS is the City/Airport code for Boston.
- The first-class (F) and jet coach (Y) fares are shown.

Under the flight schedules, you learn that for the first *direct* (no change of plane) flight of the day:

- **Except on Saturday (X6), you leave Boston at 10:30 a.m.**
- **You arrive in Phoenix at 5:40 p.m. (Phoenix time).**
- **It is American Airlines Flight 239.**
- **First class and jet coach classes are available.**
- **The aircraft is a Boeing 727 super fan jet (72S).**
- **You will be served a snack and a dinner enroute.**
- **The flight will make five stops.**

Looking under the heading *Connections*, you learn that if a change in planes enroute is acceptable, you can:

- **Leave Boston (every day) at 10:10 a.m. and arrive in Phoenix at 2:16 p.m., (Phoenix time).**
- **You leave Boston on United Airlines Flight 977, first class or jet coach, on a Boeing 727 jet, and will be served lunch on this portion of the flight, which is nonstop to the connecting point.**
- **You arrive at the connecting airport at Denver at 12:20 p.m. (Denver time).**
- **You leave Denver at 1:45 p.m. on Western Airlines Flight 473, first class or jet coach, on a Boeing 72S super fan jet, will be served a snack, and will fly nonstop to Phoenix.**

Using these facts and assuming that the departure times suited your employer, you would probably decide that the amount of time saved on the nondirect flight would offset the inconvenience of changing planes.

## Flight Reservations

Reservations for air travel must be made (by telephone or in person) at the airport terminal, a ticket office, or a travel agency. After the traveler chooses a flight, he asks the airline reservations clerk to check

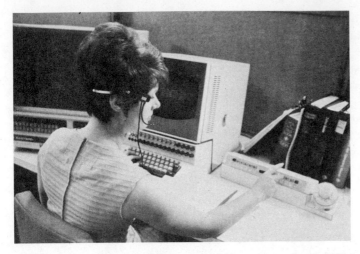

Using the Bell System's voice-grade data set, this operator is entering an airline reservation into the equipment that will inform all other ticketing stations that the space has been reserved.

—*American Telephone and Telegraph Co.*

the availability of space in the desired section. This is done with electronic equipment that records and stores reservations made for a flight from all ticketing stations.

A ticket for an in-person reservation is issued at once; otherwise, it is issued and mailed to a specified address or held for pickup at the ticket office or airport. Messenger service is also available (for a fee) for ticket delivery and fare collection. Payment can be made by cash, by check, or with an acceptable credit card for later billing.

Even with a trip involving several destinations and airlines, only one ticket is issued (by the airline on which the flight originates). A passenger who does not know the flights he will subsequently need can purchase an *open* ticket and make reservations later. Data for any changes in ticketed flights are merely attached to the original ticket.

When a passenger checks in for some flights, he may reserve an exact seat location or choose an aisle seat or a window seat; the smoking or nonsmoking section; or the front, back, or center section of the plane.

## Ticketing Plans

*Tickets-by-Mail* service enables the customer to make a telephone reservation and then pay the invoice mailed with the ticket in time for his check to clear before the actual flight.

Air travel credit cards are issued to key personnel by many organizations. Other companies maintain charge accounts with the airlines and are billed regularly for authorized travel by employees. Some airlines have special credit-card ticketing plans that allow a passenger to fill in his own ticket after making a telephone reservation. A passenger who travels often between the same two cities may buy commuter books of tickets to use for confirmed reservations between the two points.

## Reconfirmations

Although reconfirmation on domestic flights is not *required*, it is always wise to reconfirm reservations for each part of a continuing air trip after the first. This can be done on arrival at the airport. By giving the telephone number at which he can be reached in that city, the passenger is assured of a contact with the airline.

## Redemption of Unused Plane Tickets

Unused or unused portions of plane tickets can be redeemed by submitting them to the airline ticket office. Usually a check is mailed later.

## Airport Transportation Services

An *airport limousine* is available for transportation between downtown locations and the airport, usually at a lower rate than taxi service. In some cities the limousine calls for passengers at key hotels; in others it leaves from either a downtown ticket office or a downtown airline terminal. The ticket often shows the location of the limousine pickup point and departure time for the airport. Sometimes it is necessary to reserve limousine space when making a plane reservation. If the limousine leaves from a downtown airport terminal, the passenger checks in at the terminal (checks in his baggage, which then becomes the airline's responsibility, and checks in for the flight); when he arrives at the airport, he has only to board the plane. If the limousine leaves from a point other than a terminal, the passenger checks in at the airport.

Limousine service is also supplied between airports serving one city.

The airline timetable indicates whether *helicopter service* is available between airports in cities served by more than one facility or from the airport to downtown points. While the cost may be included in long distance flight fares, it is more expensive than taxi or limousine service.

## Rent-a-Plane Service

Either *taxi-plane service* (with pilot) or *fly-yourself service* is available in some cities. The automobile rental services can provide information.

## Company-Owned Planes

Many corporations own one or more planes. Business is taking to the air in its own craft to reduce travel time for executives even more than is possible by commercial aviation. Many companies, however, observe the precaution of limiting the number of top officials who can fly in the same plane (private or commercial) to protect continuity of management in case of an accident. Charter planes are also increasingly important, especially to areas not served even by regional airlines.

# TRAIN TRAVEL

Train travel for long distances is less and less attractive to business-men because of the time required and the reduction of services. Train travel may, however, improve: In 1971, the 22 different passenger rail-roads were merged into the *Amtrak* system which has as its motto, "We're making the trains worth traveling again."

*Metroliners* are available between Boston and Washington, D.C. and points between, offering improved services and fast schedules that enable the railroad to compete with airlines. On these special trains all seats are reserved when the ticket is purchased. Because of heavy de-mand, tickets must be bought well in advance. On some trains parlor seats can also be reserved.

Overnight trains between East Coast points and Florida and between Chicago and Florida are available with various kinds of sleeper service; and extra-fare, extra-service trains are added during the winter season. Sleeper and dining car service is also available between Chicago and the West Coast.

The secretary can become familiar with the rail services by consulting the *Official Guide of the Railways*, which contains schedules of all rail-way and steamship lines in the United States, Canada, Mexico, and Puerto Rico.

A railway timetable is simple to read, as can be seen from the fol-lowing condensed schedule of the Penn Central Railroad showing trains operating from New York City to New Haven, Connecticut.

### NEW YORK TO NEW HAVEN

Schedule symbols should be checked carefully against
"REFERENCES" at the right.

**REFERENCES**

X—Does not stop at 125th Street.
S—Saturdays and Feb. 15 only.
G—Runs Friday & Saturday nights Only.
H—Sunday and Holidays only.
E—Express.
U—Departs from upper level, G.C.T.
L—Departs from lower level, G.C.T.
Holidays are Nov. 26, Dec. 25, Jan. 1, and Feb. 15.

#### MONDAY THRU FRIDAY except HOLIDAYS

| Leave G. C. T. | Due New Haven | Leave G. C. T. | Due New Haven | Leave G. C. T. | Due New Haven |
|---|---|---|---|---|---|
| U4:40AM | 6:45AM | U2:05 | 3:51 | L6:25 | 8:27 |
| U6:05 | 7:53 | L3:05 | 4:51 | U7:05 | 8:55 |
| U7:05 | 8:51 | U4:05 | 5:49 | U8:05 | 9:51 |
| U8:05 | 9:55 | L4:38 | 6:28 | U9:05 | 10:51 |
| U9:05 | 10:51 | UX4:57E | 6:35 | U10:05 | 11:51 |
| L10:05 | 11:51 | U5:00 | 7:03 | U11:05 | 12:51AM |
| U11:05 | 12:51PM | UX5:21 | 7:17 | U12:05AM | 1:51 |
| U12:05PM | 1:51 | LX5:39 | 7:33 | UG1:05 | 2:51 |
| GXU1:05 | 2:51 | U6:05E | 7:47 | .... | .... |

#### SATURDAYS, SUNDAYS, AND HOLIDAYS
##### Upper Level

| | | | | | |
|---|---|---|---|---|---|
| 6:05AM | 7:51AM | 4:05 | 5:51 | 8:05 | 9:51 |
| 8:05 | 9:53 | S5:05 | 7:00 | 10:05 | 11:51 |
| 10:05 | 11:51 | 6:05 | 7:51 | 12:05AM | 1:51AM |
| 12:05PM | 1:51PM | 7:05 | 8:51 | G1:05 | 2:51 |
| 2:05 | 3:51 | .... | .... | .... | .... |

The schedule shows the time of departure from Grand Central Station, the level (*U* or *L*) from which the train leaves, the trains that do not stop at 125th Street, the holidays on which certain trains will not operate, the one express train (at 4:57 p.m.) that is especially attractive to commuters, and the time of arrival in New Haven. Morning hours are shown in lightface type, and afternoon hours are shown in boldface type.

## Rent-a-Car Travel

At times a businessman finds it convenient to travel by air or train and then to rent a car at his destination. Both airline and railroad timetable folders indicate those cities with rent-a-car service. Automobile rental companies publish directories of their rental agencies both here and abroad, giving daily rates and mileage charges of each station. Reservations for rental cars, specifying the make and type wanted, can be made along with the travel reservation or with the rental agency office at point of departure or pickup point.

Upon arriving at the pickup point, the traveler presents his driver's license and makes financial arrangements for renting the car. An especially attractive feature is the "rent-it-here-leave-it-there" policy of the agencies. The rental costs can be charged to any of a number of credit cards, a desirable feature because the deposit required can involve a heavy outlay of cash.

Rental agencies will help with local routes, where to eat and stay, and what to see.

The American Automobile Association provides its members with travel guides for any contemplated trip. Several oil companies will map routes on request. Many handy dining and lodging guides are available at book stores and travel agencies.

> One thoughtful secretary sends expected visitors an area map showing her employer's office location and the location of recommended hotels, motels, and restaurants nearby. She also includes the approximate driving time.

# INTERNATIONAL TRAVEL

"Last week when I was in Rome . . ." is as common in business conversation today as a casual reference to a trip to a neighboring state used to be. A secretary to a top executive will probably plan his international—as well as his domestic—travel and will need to understand its many ramifications.

## General Considerations

Planning for foreign travel differs in several ways from planning for shorter domestic trips. For instance, time changes can take a great toll on the executive. (See time zones, page 295.) Air Force medical experts suggest that important decisions should not be made either shortly before or after a long jet flight, so the businessman who travels by plane should try to allow one day on arrival in Europe and two days on return to the United States to adjust both physically and psychologically to time differences. Leaving here on a morning flight which arrives overseas at night will force the traveler to rest before he starts his negotiations, and flying home on the first day of a weekend will provide rest before going back to the office.

Another difference between domestic and foreign travel is in arranging appointments. Both because of possible difficulties in getting around in a foreign city and because of the slower pace at which European business is conducted, the American visitor will want to keep his appointments to two or three a day.

Fares are standard, so an airline can attract the lucrative American business travel only by providing special services. One airline arranges for conference rooms at the international airport and coordinates flight schedules of participants so that they can meet conveniently, sometimes without ever leaving the airport and going through customs. Other lines help to make business contacts, arrange for secretarial services and conference rooms, or make hotel reservations if they are given at least two weeks in which to provide these special accommodations and services.

The business card is an important adjunct to the business call, perhaps one with English on one side and the appropriate foreign language on the reverse side. A card is always presented by a caller; therefore, a business visitor can easily use up a supply of 200 cards if he is attending a business fair. The European business fair has no counterpart in this country. An entire year's output of a product may be sold during such a fair.

Learning the mores of the countries to be visited is important to the success of a business visit. Most of the international airlines now publish guides for conducting business in Europe. These and *Business Week's Businessman's Guide to Europe* are useful references when planning a trip. In them are found dates of important trade fairs, holidays in each country, hotel and restaurant information, addresses of important business contacts in each country, currency information, and invaluable hints for improving business contacts.

Abroad it pays to bring gifts — judiciously. There are as many subtleties to the art of international gift giving as there are differences in customs and business methods around the world. What pleases a customer in London may be offensive to his Tokyo counterpart. A present to the wife of a business contact in Europe would be accepted gratefully, but a present to the wife of a Near Easterner would be most unacceptable. Asking advice of a resident of the country being visited may pay dividends.

## Services of a Travel Agency

A company's travel department or a travel agency can be of great help in planning a foreign trip. In fact, without a well-established company travel department, the secretary will find the services of a travel agent almost indispensable to:

- Make hotel and rent-a-car reservations
- List available transportation
- Suggest an itinerary or itineraries and procure tickets
- Notify you of the required travel documents and how to obtain them
- Give currency information and secure enough foreign currency for entering the first country on the itinerary
- Explain baggage restrictions
- Secure insurance for traveler and baggage
- List port taxes levied (Most international airports charge from $1 to $3. An international transportation tax of $3 is imposed on each international passenger departing from the Continental United States.)
- Give information as to time limitations for visits
- Supply free literature and services
- Arrange for the traveler to be met by a travel representative or a limousine
- Get visas, give advice about vaccinations and inoculations required in each country to be visited, and supply blanks for International Certificates of Vaccination

## Foreign Business Contacts

Half the work of a successful trip abroad will take place before the executive boards the jet. Locating business contacts and other data must precede the trip.

The United States Bureau of International Commerce (350 Fifth Avenue, New York, New York 10001) will give information about any foreign country regarding economic developments, regulations, and trade statistics; costs and channels of distribution; key persons to contact both in the United States and in the foreign country; methods of protecting patent, copyright, and trademark rights; import and export restrictions; and national holidays, which can affect adversely an entire business trip. Field offices of the United States Commerce Department are also a source of last-minute information on such matters if the request is submitted on a special form, Request for Assistance by American Businessmen Traveling Abroad.

Businessmen traveling to South America can get background information for their trips by consulting the Council of the Americas (680 Park Avenue, New York, New York 10021), which is run by United States corporations with South American holdings. The Council maintains local offices in virtually every South American location of economic significance. Dun and Bradstreet's reference service will provide subscribers with a card authorizing the holder to request credit information from any one of their foreign offices. The *Foreign Trade Handbook* (Dartnell Corporation, Chicago) covers foreign trade organizations, management, finance, technical procedures to follow, and legal considerations. A visit to the commercial attachés of the countries to be visited may uncover valuable data.

## Passports

The first requisite for foreign travel is a *passport* issued by the Department of State. A passport is an official document granting permission to travel to the person specified in it and authenticating his right to protection. For travel in most countries outside the United States, a passport is necessary; but it is not required in Canada, Mexico, Bermuda, the West Indies, and Central American countries, although proof of citizenship may be requested. A visitor to Mexico who plans to stay longer than three days must secure a travel permit at the port of entry.

Passport application forms can be obtained from the travel agent or from passport offices (Department of State) in Boston, Chicago, Los Angeles, Miami, New Orleans, New York, San Francisco, and Washington or from passport office in local Federal buildings. An applicant for his first passport is required to appear *in person* before an agent of the passport office or a clerk of a federal court or a state court authorized by law to naturalize aliens, with the following papers:

- **The completed application**
- **Proof of United States citizenship (birth certificate, baptismal certificate, or certificate of naturalization) If these proofs are not available, he submits a notice by appropriate authorities that no birth record exists and such secondary evidence as census records, newspaper files, family Bibles, school records, or affidavits of persons with personal knowledge of the applicant's birth. An identifying witness may also appear with him.)**
- **Two signed duplicate photographs *taken by a photographer* within the past two years**
- **The passport fee (currently $10) in cash**

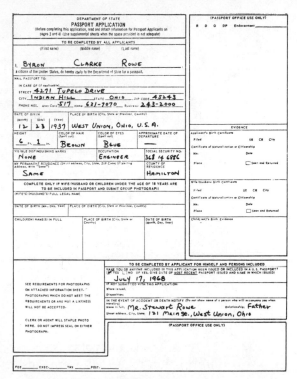

Within the form image:

DEPARTMENT OF STATE
PASSPORT APPLICATION
(Before completing this application, read and detach information for Passport Applicants on pages 3 and 4) (Use supplemental sheets when the space provided is not adequate)

(PASSPORT OFFICE USE ONLY)
R    D    O    DP    Endorsement

TO BE COMPLETED BY ALL APPLICANTS

(First name)    (Middle name)    (Last name)

I, BYRON    CLARKE    ROWE
a citizen of the United States, do hereby apply to the Department of State for a passport.

MAIL PASSPORT TO:

IN CARE OF (if applicable)
STREET 4271 TUPELO DRIVE
CITY INDIAN HILL    STATE OHIO    ZIP CODE 45243
PHONE NOS. Area Code 517 Home 631-7070 Business 243-2000

DATE OF BIRTH
(Month) (Day) (Year)
12  23  1937
PLACE OF BIRTH (City, State or Province, Country)
WEST UNION, OHIO, U.S.A.

HEIGHT 6 ft. 1 in.
COLOR OF HAIR BROWN
COLOR OF EYES BLUE
APPROXIMATE DATE OF DEPARTURE

VISIBLE DISTINGUISHING MARKS NONE
OCCUPATION ENGINEER
SOCIAL SECURITY NO. 368 14 6886

MY PERMANENT RESIDENCE (Street address, City, State, ZIP Code) (If sending Address, write "Same")
SAME
COUNTY OF RESIDENCE HAMILTON

EVIDENCE
Applicant's Birth Certificate
Filed    SR    CR    City
Certificate of Naturalization or Citizenship
No.    Date
Place    □ Seen and Returned

COMPLETE ONLY IF WIFE/HUSBAND OR CHILDREN UNDER THE AGE OF 18 YEARS ARE TO BE INCLUDED IN PASSPORT AND SUBMIT GROUP PHOTOGRAPH)
(WIFE'S) (HUSBAND'S) FULL LEGAL NAME

DATE OF BIRTH (Mo., Day, Year)
PLACE OF BIRTH (City, State or Province, Country)

Wife/Husband Birth Certificate
Filed    SR    CR    City
Certificate of Naturalization or Citizenship
No.    Date
Place    □ Seen and Returned

CHILD(REN) NAME(S) IN FULL
PLACE OF BIRTH (City, State or Country)
DATE OF BIRTH (Month, Day, Year)

Child(ren)'s Birth Evidence

SEE REQUIREMENTS FOR PHOTOGRAPHS ON ATTACHED INFORMATION SHEET. PHOTOGRAPHS WHICH DO NOT MEET THE REQUIREMENTS OR ARE NOT A LIKENESS WILL NOT BE ACCEPTED.

CLERK OR AGENT WILL STAPLE PHOTO HERE. DO NOT IMPRESS SEAL ON EITHER PHOTOGRAPH.

TO BE COMPLETED BY APPLICANT FOR HIMSELF AND PERSONS INCLUDED
HAVE YOU OR ANYONE INCLUDED IN THIS APPLICATION BEEN ISSUED OR INCLUDED IN A U.S. PASSPORT?
□ YES □ NO (IF YES, GIVE DATE OF MOST RECENT PASSPORT ISSUED AND NAME IN WHICH ISSUED)
JULY 17, 1968
IF NOT SUBMITTED WITH THIS APPLICATION:
Where issued:
Disposition:
IN THE EVENT OF ACCIDENT OR DEATH NOTIFY (Do not show name of a person who will accompany you when traveling)
Name in full: MR. STEWART ROWE    Relationship: FATHER
Street address, City, State: 121 MAIN ST., WEST UNION, OHIO

(PASSPORT OFFICE USE ONLY)

FEE _____ EXEC. _____ TWS _____ POST. _____

At the right is the first page of the four-page application for a United States passport (Form DSP-11). The secretary should obtain an application and study it in advance to learn what documents, dates, and other data her employer should take along when applying for his passport.

If the applicant is going abroad on a Government contract, a letter from his employing company is required showing his position, destination, purpose of travel, and proposed length of stay.

A person holding a previous passport issued in his own name within the past eight years may renew his passport by mail in one of two ways: Form DSP-11 may be completed and the applicant go before a designated official before mailing his application; Form DSP-82 allows any applicant who meets the requirements stated on the back of the form to mail his application directly, without appearing in person before any officials. The secretary can obtain copies of each form from the nearest passport office to see which form is appropriate. Then the applicant completes the form, signing and dating the application, and attaching two signed duplicate photographs taken within six months of the date of the application, the expired passport, and the passport fee. These materials are mailed to the nearest passport office.

A passport is valid for five years from date of issue. Since processing a passport application may take three or four weeks, anyone contemplating foreign travel should keep his passport in order. The secretary to a traveling executive can be of assistance by noting the expiration dates in her tickler file.

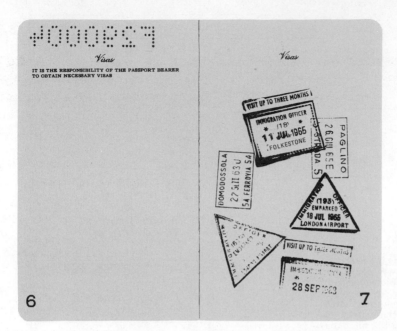

When a traveler enters a foreign country, an immigration officer of that country may stamp the immigrant's passport with a visa stamp (date of entry and allowable length of visit) and with an embarkation stamp when the visitor leaves the country.

As soon as the passport is received, it should be signed and the information requested on the inside cover must be filled in. It should always be carried during overseas travel. The business traveler should also carry a letter from the business organization represented — stating the where, when, why, and duration of the proposed visit.

**Visas.** A *visa* is a permit granted by a foreign government for a person to enter its territory. It usually appears as a stamped notation in a passport indicating that the bearer may enter the country for a certain purpose and for a specified period of time. Anyone in doubt as to the necessity of obtaining a travel visa for travel in any foreign country should consult the consul or a travel agent before leaving the United States. Consular representatives of most foreign countries are located in principal cities, and their addresses can be found in the *Congressional Directory*, or in the *Yellow Pages* under "Consulates." If the traveler intends to work in the country to be visited, he should check to see whether he needs a work permit.

**Vaccination and Inoculation Requirements.** The travel agent or the consulate of the country to be visited can give information about vaccinations and inoculations required by the country visited and by the United States upon reentry. Records of these vaccinations and inoculations are signed by the physician and validated by the local or state health officer on the International Certificates of Vaccination obtainable from the travel agent, the passport office, or some physicians.

## Overseas Flights

International plane travel is basically the same as it is for domestic flights, with a preponderance of jumbo jets that seat more than 200 passengers. Innovations in services include large passenger lounges, a choice among several entrees at mealtime, and containerized baggage compartments in which baggage is always stored in an upright position and unloaded swiftly by bringing the containers to the customs area.

There are two classes of flights on most planes — *first class* and *tourist*. Gourmet meals and beverages catered by world-famous chefs such as Maxim's of Paris are served in first class. Beautiful china, crystal, and silver are used; and the service of stewards and hostesses is outstanding. In tourist class meals meet a lower quality standard, but the passenger has a choice among entrees on some flights. First-class passengers are allowed 66 pounds of luggage on overseas flights, and tourist-class passengers are allowed 44 pounds.

Fares vary with the season of year. They are constantly changing because of the competitive nature of the airline business. During the peak period (eastbound during June, July, and August and westbound during July, August, and September) fares to and from Europe, the Middle East, and Africa are higher than they are during the rest of the year. Fares are sometimes higher for weekend travel than for during the week. Fares differ according to the length of the stay, with the differential being 17 days, 28 days, 45 days, and longer than 45 days. The only way to keep abreast of air fares is to consult the airline reservation clerk or the travel agent for any available special excursion rates.

An international flight schedule is as easy to read as is a domestic one. For instance, a secretary in Pittsburgh planning a flight to London for her employer could refer to the TWA table on page 376.

She would note that there are two direct daily flights and would choose, if possible, the one leaving at 6:45 p.m. because it stops only once; and although it leaves one hour and forty minutes later than the earlier flight, it arrives in London only thirty minutes later (8:15 a.m.). By referring to the world time zone map on page 295, she would realize that this is 2:15 a.m. in Pittsburgh.

Timetables for foreign airlines are usually based on the 24-hour clock (illustrated and explained at the left).

### 24-Hour Clock

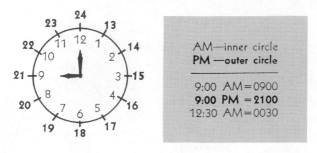

AM—inner circle
PM —outer circle
___
9:00 AM = 0900
9:00 PM = 2100
12:30 AM = 0030

From PITTSBURGH, Pa. (EDT)

RESERVATIONS: Domestic: 391-3600    International: 391-2277    Freight: 771-4000

Limo. 50 min. $2.00

To LONDON, England

| | | | |
|---|---|---|---|
| 505p | 754 | Two-stop | Daily |
| 645p | 756 | One-stop | Daily |
| 7 45a | 754 | | |
| 8 15a | 756 | | |

## EXAMPLES OF TRANSATLANTIC FARES

MANY OTHER SPECIAL LOW COST FARES ARE AVAILABLE TO/FROM POINTS IN EUROPE, MIDDLE EAST, AFRICA AND ASIA FOR INFORMATION CONTACT YOUR NEAREST TWA OFFICE.

Fares in U.S. Dollars

| BETWEEN / AND | | NEW YORK | | BOSTON | | CHICAGO | | DETROIT | | KANSAS CITY | | LOS ANGELES SAN FRANCISCO | | PHILADELPHIA | | PITTSBURGH | | WASHINGTON D.C. | |
|---|---|---|---|---|---|---|---|---|---|---|---|---|---|---|---|---|---|---|---|
| | | ONE WAY | ROUND TRIP | ONE WAY | ROUND TRIP | ONE WAY | ROUND TRIP | ONE WAY | ROUND TRIP | ONE WAY | ROUND TRIP | ONE WAY | ROUND TRIP | ONE WAY | ROUND TRIP | ONE WAY | ROUND TRIP | ONE WAY | ROUND TRIP |
| LONDON | First Class | 391.00 | 782.00 | 382.00 | 764.00 | 445.00 | 890.00 | 424.00 | 848.00 | 482.00 | 964.00 | 570.00 | 1140.00 | 402.00 | 804.00 | 427.00 | 854.00 | 415.00 | 830.00 |
| | Peak Period Economy | 276.00 | 552.00 | 271.00 | 542.00 | 319.00 | 638.00 | 301.00 | 602.00 | 348.00 | 696.00 | 419.00 | 838.00 | 284.00 | 568.00 | 306.00 | 612.00 | 292.00 | 584.00 |
| | Basic Period Economy | 226.00 | 452.00 | 221.00 | 442.00 | 269.00 | 538.00 | 251.00 | 502.00 | 298.00 | 596.00 | 369.00 | 738.00 | 234.00 | 468.00 | 256.00 | 512.00 | 242.00 | 484.00 |
| | 17 - 28 Day Excursion | — | 322.00 | — | 315.00 | — | 409.00 | — | 379.00 | — | 466.00 | — | 536.00 | — | 335.00 | — | 382.00 | — | 347.00 |
| | 29 - 45 Day Excursion | — | 272.00 | — | 265.00 | — | 337.00 | — | 329.00 | — | 416.00 | — | 457.00 | — | 285.00 | — | 332.00 | — | 297.00 |
| MADRID | First Class | 413.00 | 826.00 | 413.00 | 826.00 | 473.00 | 946.00 | 461.00 | 922.00 | 504.00 | 1008.00 | 592.00 | 1184.00 | 424.00 | 848.00 | 449.00 | 898.00 | 437.00 | 874.00 |
| | Peak Period Economy | 298.00 | 596.00 | 298.00 | 596.00 | 346.00 | 692.00 | 336.00 | 672.00 | 370.00 | 740.00 | 441.00 | 882.00 | 306.00 | 612.00 | 328.00 | 656.00 | 314.00 | 628.00 |
| | Basic Period Economy | 248.00 | 496.00 | 248.00 | 496.00 | 296.00 | 592.00 | 286.00 | 572.00 | 320.00 | 640.00 | 391.00 | 782.00 | 256.00 | 512.00 | 278.00 | 556.00 | 264.00 | 528.00 |
| | 17 - 28 Day Excursion | — | 353.00 | — | 353.00 | — | 440.00 | — | 410.00 | — | 497.00 | — | 567.00 | — | 366.00 | — | 413.00 | — | 378.00 |
| | 29 - 45 Day Excursion | — | 297.00 | — | 297.00 | — | 362.00 | — | 354.00 | — | 441.00 | — | 482.00 | — | 310.00 | — | 357.00 | — | 322.00 |
| MILAN | First Class | 459.00 | 918.00 | 450.00 | 900.00 | 513.00 | 1026.00 | 492.00 | 984.00 | 550.00 | 1100.00 | 638.00 | 1276.00 | 470.00 | 940.00 | 495.00 | 990.00 | 483.00 | 966.00 |
| | Peak Period Economy | 330.00 | 660.00 | 325.00 | 650.00 | 373.00 | 746.00 | 355.00 | 710.00 | 402.00 | 804.00 | 473.00 | 946.00 | 338.00 | 676.00 | 360.00 | 720.00 | 346.00 | 692.00 |
| | Basic Period Economy | 280.00 | 560.00 | 275.00 | 550.00 | 323.00 | 646.00 | 305.00 | 610.00 | 352.00 | 704.00 | 423.00 | 846.00 | 288.00 | 576.00 | 310.00 | 620.00 | 296.00 | 592.00 |
| | 17 - 28 Day Excursion | — | 398.00 | — | 391.00 | — | 485.00 | — | 455.00 | — | 542.00 | — | 612.00 | — | 411.00 | — | 458.00 | — | 423.00 |
| | 29 - 45 Day Excursion | — | 315.00 | — | 308.00 | — | 385.00 | — | 372.00 | — | 459.00 | — | 500.00 | — | 328.00 | — | 375.00 | — | 340.00 |
| PARIS | First Class | 413.00 | 826.00 | 404.00 | 808.00 | 467.00 | 934.00 | 446.00 | 892.00 | 504.00 | 1008.00 | 592.00 | 1184.00 | 424.00 | 848.00 | 449.00 | 898.00 | 437.00 | 874.00 |
| | Peak Period Economy | 298.00 | 596.00 | 293.00 | 586.00 | 341.00 | 682.00 | 323.00 | 646.00 | 370.00 | 740.00 | 441.00 | 882.00 | 306.00 | 612.00 | 328.00 | 656.00 | 314.00 | 628.00 |
| | Basic Period Economy | 248.00 | 496.00 | 243.00 | 486.00 | 291.00 | 582.00 | 273.00 | 546.00 | 320.00 | 640.00 | 391.00 | 782.00 | 256.00 | 512.00 | 278.00 | 556.00 | 264.00 | 528.00 |
| | 17 - 28 Day Excursion | — | 353.00 | — | 346.00 | — | 440.00 | — | 410.00 | — | 497.00 | — | 567.00 | — | 366.00 | — | 413.00 | — | 378.00 |
| | 29 - 45 Day Excursion | — | 297.00 | — | 290.00 | — | 362.00 | — | 354.00 | — | 441.00 | — | 482.00 | — | 310.00 | — | 357.00 | — | 322.00 |
| ROME | First Class | 484.00 | 968.00 | 475.00 | 950.00 | 538.00 | 1076.00 | 517.00 | 1034.00 | 575.00 | 1150.00 | 663.00 | 1326.00 | 495.00 | 990.00 | 520.00 | 1040.00 | 508.00 | 1016.00 |
| | Peak Period Economy | 352.00 | 704.00 | 347.00 | 694.00 | 395.00 | 790.00 | 377.00 | 754.00 | 424.00 | 848.00 | 495.00 | 990.00 | 360.00 | 720.00 | 382.00 | 764.00 | 368.00 | 736.00 |
| | Basic Period Economy | 302.00 | 604.00 | 297.00 | 594.00 | 345.00 | 690.00 | 327.00 | 654.00 | 374.00 | 748.00 | 445.00 | 890.00 | 310.00 | 620.00 | 332.00 | 664.00 | 318.00 | 636.00 |
| | 17 - 28 Day Excursion | — | 429.00 | — | 422.00 | — | 516.00 | — | 486.00 | — | 573.00 | — | 643.00 | — | 442.00 | — | 489.00 | — | 454.00 |
| | 29 - 45 Day Excursion | — | 320.00 | — | 313.00 | — | 390.00 | — | 377.00 | — | 464.00 | — | 505.00 | — | 333.00 | — | 380.00 | — | 345.00 |

The table of transatlantic fares shows the price advantage of the 29- to 45-day economy trip ($332) over the peak period economy fare ($612). In planning a business trip, however, one may not always find price to be the determining factor in the final choice.

## Travel By Ship

Many travelers go to Europe one way by plane and the other way by ship so that they can combine business with vacation. An executive would choose either luxurious first-class or less glamorous but still very comfortable cabin-class passage rather than tourist class. There is a trend today toward one- or two-class ships.

On many ships there are two seatings for dinner, so the travel agent should be told the passenger's preference in this matter as well as in the number of other diners he prefers at his table. The agent can make the necessary arrangements before the ship sails.

## Train Transportation

Most foreign railroads provide three classes of service: (1) *first-class* accommodations with four to six persons in a compartment, (2) *second-class* accommodations with six to eight persons, and (3) *third-class* where passengers sit on wooden, unupholstered seats. Seat reservations are necessary for first-class travel.

Sleeping cars are of the compartment type. The class of service indicates the number of passengers per compartment. Reservations well in advance of the trip are recommended, for it is often difficult to obtain sleeping-car (*wagon-lit*) accommodations. Extra-fare trains carrying first- and second-class sleepers only are available on the most important international routes. These de luxe trains with individual seats are also available for day travel.

Restaurant cars are attached to most express trains. Before the meal, the dining-car conductor comes through the train and takes reservations. The meal is served at an announced time at one seating only in most countries.

It is possible to buy a Eurail Pass *in this country only* that entitles the holder to unlimited train travel in European countries during the length of time specified on the ticket. Several foreign railway systems maintain ticket and information offices in major cities in America.

## Hotel Reservations

Hotel reservations can be made through the travel agent either in this country or abroad or through the airline used. Businessmen's guides indicate whether secretarial services or meeting rooms are available in listed hotels. Breakfast is included in the hotel charge in Great Britain and frequently in The Netherlands. In other countries in Europe a "continental breakfast" consisting of a hot beverage and a roll is included.

### Automobile Rentals

Rented automobiles are as readily available in larger foreign cities as in the United States. Flight schedules indicate whether this service can be secured at the airport. Rental can be arranged by the travel agent here, and it is usually possible to leave the car at a designated point rather than return it to the place of rental.

In most countries a United States state driver's license is sufficient; but to be on the safe side, the traveler may obtain an American International Driving Permit from the American Automobile Association either here or in Europe for a small fee.

## TRAVEL DETAILS HANDLED BY THE SECRETARY

The groundwork for planning a trip will probably be laid during a conference between the executive and the secretary. The executive will mention the places to be visited and the dates, and perhaps he will specify names of hotels. For example, he may tell the secretary that he plans to be in New York on November 2; visit the Upper Darby plant on November 3; spend the weekend with his sister in Paoli; attend a convention in Philadelphia from November 6–8; visit customers on November 9 and 10 (for which definite appointments must be arranged in Pittsburgh and Baltimore); spend the weekend back home in St. Louis, and be back in the office on the morning of November 13.

### Planning the Trip

Planning a trip requires checking transportation schedules and making necessary reservations. In the case just given, the secretary must route the executive to New York, Philadelphia, Baltimore, Pittsburgh, and back to St. Louis.

First, she would obtain and study current timetable folders of airlines and railroads to determine *convenient* times and accommodations for the St. Louis to New York trip, New York to Philadelphia trip, and so forth. From these she would list the convenient flights and trains that could be used, giving departure and arrival times, and other pertinent information. She would select only those flights and trains that

| ST. LOUIS TO NEW YORK SERVICES* | | | | | | |
|---|---|---|---|---|---|---|
| *Via* | *Flight* | *Leave St. L.* | *Ar. NY* | *Terminal* | *Type of Service* | |
| TWA | 700 | 3:00 p.m. | 6:26 | JFK | Non-Stop | Meal |
| TWA | 56 | 4:00 | 7:05 | LaGuardia | Non-Stop | No Meal |
| TWA | 108 | 5:00 | 8:10 | LaGuardia | Non-Stop | Meal |
| Amer. | 382 | 4:50 | 8:00 | LaGuardia | Non-Stop | Meal |

*No flights leaving St. Louis before 3 p.m. or arriving in New York after 9 p.m. are listed. Only one flight to Kennedy International airport and no flights to Newark, New Jersey, are listed because of the shorter travel time into the city from LaGuardia.

fit into the executive's particular business schedule. Especially important would be the location of the airport and its distance from the city. Such a schedule is illustrated above.

## Making Reservations

When the executive has selected the flights he will use and the accommodations he prefers, the secretary can make the reservations. She is usually asked to make the hotel or motel reservations. If a rented automobile is to be used, a motel may be preferable. In many cases the executive will provide the names of the hotels or motels, or the secretary may know which ones he prefers. When she is expected to select the accommodations or to provide information about suitable ones, she uses one of the directories, such as the *Hotel and Motel Red Book* (published annually by the American Hotel Association Directory Corporation), or *Leahy's Hotel Guide and Travel Atlas of the United States, Canada, and Mexico*, or regional directories published by the American Automobile Association or the oil companies. These directories give the number of rooms, the rates, and whether (in the case of a hotel) the lodging is operated on the *European* or the *American plan*. Under the European plan the rate represents the cost of the room only. Under the American plan the rate includes the cost of meals as well as the cost of the room. Most commercial hotels are European plan.

Room rates quoted in a directory are for one night's lodging. Many hotels offer a reduced rate for occupancy of a room during the daytime only. This service is desirable for use as daytime headquarters when the traveler will be in the city for only a few hours. Since the time of arrival is often early morning, the executive may want to "register in" a night earlier to be assured of accommodations before the midafternoon checkout hour.

Requests for reservations should be specific, indicating the items listed below and on page 380.

- *Kind of Room Desired*—one room or a suite (location away from elevator, above a certain floor, with a view, etc.)
- *Kind of Accommodations*—twin beds; studio; tub or shower bath

- *Approximate or Relative Rate*—medium-priced room—$15 in small cities to $30 in large cities
- *Number of Persons in the Party*
- *Date and Approximate Time of Registration (If Known)*— after 6 p.m.; 9 p.m. (If the executive may be late in arriving, a "guaranteed-arrival" reservation can be made. The room will be held, but the guest will be billed even if he does not come.)
- *Type of Transportation*—because of uncertainty of time of arrival if by plane
- *Probable Length of Time Accommodation Is Needed*

There are several ways of making a reservation. Hotels and motels in a chain such as Hilton or Sheraton have communication systems for making reservations with other member hotels with confidence. A telephone call to the local hotel-motel assures the reservation in a member hotel. Out-of-town hotels sometimes maintain in major cities local offices where the reservation can be made. Once again, check the Yellow Pages, where numbers can even be found for making reservations for hotels in Japan and Europe. The secretary may call 800-AE8-5000 free from *any* location and receive immediate confirmation of a reservation in hotels and motor inn chains serviced by The American Express Space Bank. A free world-wide directory can be obtained from American Express Reservations, Inc., Box G-10, 770 Broadway, New York, New York 10003. Most airlines also make hotel-motel reservations for their passengers. Some of them have a business tieup with hotel chains. (Examples are United Airlines and Western International Hotels; TWA and Hilton Hotels.) The secretary in a company with teletypewriter equipment may ask its operator to request reservations; large hotels have teletypewriters. The secretary can write for a reservation if there is sufficient time, or she can telephone or telegraph if not.

In requesting a hotel-motel reservation, it is important to mention the business connection, as a special commercial rate may be involved. (Special rates are usually available to guests attending a convention.)

Confirmation policy differs; however, it is always safe to request a confirmation that the executive *can have in his hands when he registers*. Rooms are at a premium in many cities, and a confirmed reservation is a good precaution.

To simplify their accounting, some hotels and motels request that a deposit *not* be sent. Smaller operations may require a deposit.

## Preparing the Itinerary

The secretary can give real secretarial service by preparing a comprehensive itinerary for the executive shortly before he leaves. The usual itinerary covers *when*, *where*, and *how* the traveler will go. An itinerary

ITINERARY FOR JON JANOSIK
November 1 - 10, 197-
New York - Upper Darby - Philadelphia - Baltimore


WEDNESDAY, NOVEMBER 1 (ST. LOUIS TO NEW YORK)

5 p.m.      ·Leave St. Louis airport on TWA 108 (tickets in TWA
             envelope)

8:10 p.m.  ·Arrive LaGuardia (Guaranteed-arrival reservation at the
             Waldorf-Astoria, confirmation attached)

THURSDAY, NOVEMBER 2 (NEW YORK)

10 a.m.     ·See Mary Parker, Sales Manager, Largo Products
             2431 Seagram Building, 243 Park Avenue
             (Go out Park Avenue entrance for taxi)

1 p.m.      ·Lunch at New York Athletic Club, 61 Central Park South,
             with Arthur Pfahl and Beth Bardell of J. Walter Thompson
             Advertising promotion of Multiflex (Folder in briefcase)

4 p.m.      ·Interview in your room at the Waldorf with Roger Ball
             for position of production manager (Application and
             job specifications in folder marked Ball, Roger in
             briefcase)

7 p.m.      ·Dine at the Hargroves, 42 East 62 Street (Mrs. Hargrove's
             first name is Mildred.  Children:  Holly and Michael--
             at college)

FRIDAY, NOVEMBER 3 (UPPER DARBY PLANT AND WEEKEND IN PAOLI

9 a.m.      ·Leave Penn Station on PRR (No reservation; buy coach
             ticket at station)

10:30       ·Arrive Philadelphia, 30th Street Station
             Pick up Hertz car (arranged for) and drive to Upper Darby
             plant (File on plant proposals will be mailed to you at
             the plant. Call your sister if you'll be late for dinner.)
            ·Drive to Paoli (Turn in car whenever you're ready at
             Hertz, 39 West Lancaster Pike, Paoli.)

MONDAY, NOVEMBER 6 (PHILADELPHIA CONVENTION)

            ·Arrive Sheraton Hotel (Confirmation of reservation attached)
             Ask at desk if charts to illustrate talk have been received--
             will be mailed November 1 (Return wrapping, postage, and
             labels are in the package.)

10 a.m.     ·Convention opens

2 p.m.      ·Your speech (in briefcase; duplicate in package with
             charts)

7 p.m.      ·Banquet (White tie; convention secretary will give you
             your dais ticket)


This first page of an itinerary contains all the details of the executive's travel and appointments, together with reminders on procedure. Note that the secretary has relieved him of many details.

APPOINTMENT SCHEDULE

| City | GMT* Date/Time | With | Telephone | Address of Appt. | Remarks |
|---|---|---|---|---|---|
| London | Thursday, Aug. 6, 9 a.m. | Phillip Morse | Mansion House 3312 | To be arranged | Telephone Mr. Morse on arrival. Folder A contains papers for meeting. |
| | "   1 p.m. | Hubert Poling | Waterside Savoy 1113 | " | Mr. Poling is arranging meeting with possible patent lawyer. Folder B contains patent information. |

*Greenwich Mean Time

For an overseas (or extended) trip the executive may find it desirable to have two separate forms—(1) a travel itinerary prepared by a travel agent, and (2) an appointment schedule.

serves also as a daily appointment calendar. It contains helpful reminders and shows the tickets and business papers taken along. The executive may have his secretary make a number of copies for his associates and his family so that mail or messages can be forwarded to him and so that he can be reached immediately in an emergency. Foresight and analysis are required to be able to prepare this type of itinerary.

A good way to start is to set up a file on the trip as soon as it enters the planning stage. In it, place the memorandum prepared on convenient flights and trains, the purchased tickets, the reservations made, confirmations received, the appointments obtained, the factual material needed for scheduled meetings and appointments—in fact, everything that pertains to the trip. When it is time to prepare the itinerary, the items and notes can be sorted into chronological sequence according to the day and time each will come up. It is then an easy matter to list and describe each item in order. The first page of an itinerary on page 381 shows the detail and thoroughness with which it should be prepared.

On an extended or foreign trip it may be desirable to separate the actual travel schedule from the appointments and prepare two separate forms. Suggested headings for the travel portion are: DEPARTURE POINT, DEPARTURE TIME, DESTINATION, ARRIVAL TIME, TRANSPORTATION (including airline and flight number), HOTEL RESERVATIONS.

## Carrying Travel Funds

Often the executive relies on the secretary to remind him to obtain ample travel funds. She can ask if he wants her to get money from the company's cashier or the bank. If it is an overseas trip, she determines whether there are any restrictions to the amount of currency he can take into the countries to be visited. She orders a $10 packet of local currencies through his bank or reminds him to purchase one at the automatic vending machine in the international airport. She supplies him with a number of convenient $1 bills.

**Travelers' Checks.** If he plans to carry *travelers' checks* (which, of course, he *must* purchase himself), she can remind him of that need. These are usually bought at the bank or at American Express. American Express Company travelers' checks are sold in denominations of $10, $20, $50, and $100; they cost $1 per $100. If the executive intends to take $500 on his trip, he may purchase $400 worth in the denominations he wishes, say $50 and $100. Each check is numbered and printed on a special kind of paper. The purchaser signs each check on a line near the top before an agent of the Express Company. To cash one of the checks, he takes it to a business concern, bank, hotel, or American Express office and signs the check again at the bottom in front of the person paying out the money. Such checks are as acceptable as cash and constitute almost personalized money, because anyone other than the purchaser must forge the purchaser's name on each check in the presence of another person in order to cash it. The secretary should prepare a record in duplicate of the numbers and amounts of the checks issued, one for her files and one for the executive to carry so that reimbursement can be immediate in case the checks are lost or stolen.

As a hedge against a decline in value of American currency while he is out of the country, a traveler can now buy American Express travelers' checks in some foreign currencies, such as Canadian dollars, pounds sterling, Swiss francs, and West German Deutsche marks.

**Money Orders.** Sometimes the secretary acts as an advance money agent who supplies the traveling men of the firm with company funds through *express money orders*. Travelers' checks cannot be used for this purpose because they must be signed at the time of their purchase by the person who is to use them. In order to facilitate the cashing of express money orders, American Express Company furnishes identification cards which include the signature of the bearer.

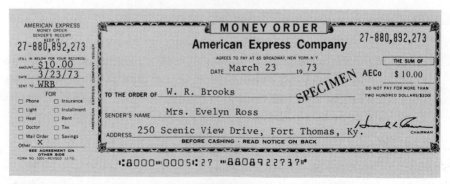

An express money order can be cashed only by the designated payee or by someone to whom the payee has endorsed the money order. The sender retains the stub as his receipt.

If the executive should find himself without funds, he can always wire his secretary to send him a *money order by telegraph*. She takes the cash, cashier's check, or money order to the Western Union office, which in turn telegraphs the distant office to pay that amount to the executive when he has met their identification test.

**Letter of Credit.** Sometimes a *letter of credit* is used when extensive travel is involved or when the amount of travel funds required is relatively large. The cost for a large amount of money through a letter of credit is considerably less than the cost of travelers' checks. This travel fund can be obtained from the local bank. It indicates the person to whom issued, who is identified by his signature on an identification card. It also states the amount the holder is entitled to draw on the issuing bank. To obtain funds, the holder presents the letter of credit to any one of the designated banks in the city where he is traveling. The amounts drawn are recorded on the letter of credit so that the balance that can still be drawn is always known.

**Credit Cards.** A recent trend is toward extensive use of multipurpose credit cards. Airline, railway, telephone, hotel, American Express, BankAmericard, MasterCharge, Diner's Club, and similar credit cards permit the holder to charge practically any service or goods to his own or his company's charge account. With some cards, he can even cash small checks. Credit cards must be carried and ready for presentation when needed. Usually the executive keeps his credit cards in his wallet, and the secretary's only responsibility is in requesting renewals on those which expire and in keeping the serial numbers on file. (See page 534 for credit card statements.)

Credit card charges help the secretary in preparing expense reports and enable the executive to verify expenditures.

## Securing Insurance

The employing company sometimes buys blanket insurance policies covering executives while they are traveling for their companies. In addition, it has rules governing the purchase of trip insurance at the airport. The secretary is expected to inform herself of company policy about travel insurance and follow through to see that the executive is appropriately covered.

## Speeding the Executive on His Way

The secretary is frequently charged with packing the briefcase that accompanies the executive, an important responsibility — for the effectiveness of any business trip is determined by the accessibility of relevant material when it is needed. When the secretary becomes aware that a trip is "in the making," she should start immediately to assemble materials to be taken along and to procure tickets and other papers necessary for the trip. She also checks the appointment book and asks her employer how he wants to handle any scheduled appointments. She checks on any personal items, such as rent, insurance, or income tax payments, that may fall due before his return and gets his instructions for handling them. She writes any preliminary letters that will increase the effectiveness of the trip. She and her employer decide any special handling to be given to expected mail. She finds *who* is responsible for *what* while he is away.

Just before his departure, the secretary hands the executive all the documents that she has obtained, prepared, and kept safe:

- **His travel tickets (also a schedule of alternate flights to remote spots)**
- **Notes about reconfirming reservations for foreign flights**
- **Hotel and motel confirmations**
- **Travel funds (money packet of foreign currency for first stop, travelers' checks) and an American International Driving Permit (unless the secretary has determined that a United States driver's license is sufficient).**
- **Car rental arrangements**
- **Itinerary (both a detailed one and a thumbnail copy on a card)**
- **Address book (including addresses of any people he wishes to see in the area)**
- **Passport, International Certificates of Vaccination, and baggage identification labels for foreign travel**
- **Papers to be taken along. Bulky materials may be sent air express on the same plane. A separate envelope for each appointment is recommended, including carbon copies of previous relevant correspondence, lists of people to be seen and their positions in their companies, and memorandums about matters to be discussed.**
- **A personal checkbook and expense-account forms**
- **A supply of business cards for foreign calls**
- **Personal items such as medication or extra eyeglasses**
- **Typed address labels which he can easily attach to letters for known correspondents, such as his wife, his secretary, or the president of the company**

## WHILE THE EXECUTIVE IS AWAY

While the executive is away, the secretary assumes greater responsibility for smooth operation of the office. But she need not shoulder this role alone. Sometimes it is better to discuss some of the problems with a colleague he has named. Routine matters, of course, should be taken care of promptly by the secretary.

The executive who wants to keep in touch with home base usually telephones his secretary daily, especially if his company uses WATS service. (See page 291.) If the secretary expects to hear from the executive by telephone, she should keep notes about events she wishes to discuss with him.

Her performance while the executive is away is just as important as when he is present. While other employees are quick to notice whether she keeps busy or fritters away time, the capable, mature secretary will *automatically* be busy with her work — not merely to make a good impression.

When the executive returns, he will be grateful and pleased if she has taken care of the routine matters, has kept records of office activities for his review, and has arranged the matters that need care in the order of their importance. The material accumulated for him should be separated into two groups:

1. **Matters already taken care of by the secretary or others**
2. **Matters to be handled personally by the executive**

The secretary places the first group in a folder and marks it "Information Only." The second group she puts in a folder marked "Important." Just before the executive's return she sorts the material in each folder into logical order, placing the most important items on top.

The executive also likes to know who telephoned or visited him during his absence, although in some instances it may be of more interest than importance. A list of appointments and engagements made for him should obviously be included in the "Important" folder.

When he is away for some time, he may wish the secretary to send him copies of letters that require his personal attention (refer to pages 153–154 for proper processing of the mail). And an executive always appreciates a letter telling him of interesting developments in the office.

Two copies of mail may be sent to the traveler — one to the destination at which the secretary expects to find him and one to his next destination, in case mail service is slower than expected.

## FOLLOW-UP ACTIVITIES

After the executive returns to the office, a flurry of activity is required to wind up the trip. First are the expense accounts.

### Expense Reports

Some firms advance funds to a traveling executive. Periodically or on his return, he submits a complete report of his travel and the expenses incurred. In other companies executives advance their own funds and are reimbursed later in accordance with the expense report submitted and approved. In either case the executive must keep an accurate record of the dates and times of travel, the conveyances used, and the costs. He sometimes must submit receipts for hotel and other accommodations. His word is usually taken for the amount of taxi fares, meals, and tips; but they must usually be listed or itemized.

If she realizes that it takes $100 a day to keep a company salesman on the road today (and even more to finance an executive's trip), the secretary will understand the importance of this facet of her work.

Expense account forms are usually provided by the company and need only be filled in correctly and completely and totaled. The secretary should, however, check the executive's present accounting with previous reports to make sure that his amounts for such items as taxis and meals are reasonable and that the flight and rail fares are correct. Reimbursement is frequently held up until all items are in line and approved by the auditor's office.

## Letters

Thank-you letters must be sent to show appreciation for favors during the trip. The need for other letters will be generated by the nature of the trip.

## Files

Materials will be unpacked and returned to the files. Duplicate files can be destroyed. Files will be updated by the secretary to reflect any changes originated by the trip.

## SUGGESTED READINGS

Any of the airlines' special periodicals, such as Pan American's *Clipper Cargo Horizons* or Japan Air Lines's *JAL Trade Courier*, are available without charge to possible business customers. Practically every major airline publishes a handbook on business travel and international trade as a service to prospective customers in this highly competitive market. For instance, TWA's handbook is *TWA's Business Travel Tips—Europe*, 190 pp. JAL publishes *JAL's Business Man's Guide to Japan* and *Hong Kong for the Businessman*. American Express, American Airlines, and Hertz jointly publish *The Meeting Planners Guide*.

Cook, Fred S., and Lenore S. Forti. *Professional Secretary's Handbook*. Chicago: Dartnell Corporation, 1971, pp. 109–16.

Engel, Pauline. *The Executive Secretary's Desk Manual*. West Nyack: Parker Publishing Co., 1970.

Finney, Paul. *The Businessman's Guide to Europe*. New York: McGraw-Hill Book Co., 1965.

# QUESTIONS FOR DISCUSSION

1. How can the secretary find out her company's policies about travel arrangements? How can she find out her employer's preferences?

2. Compare the first page of an itinerary and appointment schedule on page 381 with the appointment schedule on page 382. Which was prepared by the more efficient secretary? Why do you say this?

3. Report any recent plan for airline or railroad ticketing that is not described in the chapter. Compare it with the methods described, in terms of convenience to the customer.

4. If your employer were going to Europe to visit an affiliate of your company, how would he probably carry his funds? Why?

5. If your employer found himself without cash while on a trip, what would he probably do?

6. Who should receive copies of itineraries?

7. Your employer is visiting a dissatisfied customer in a distant city. He telephones you to mail him at once the entire correspondence file relating to his customer. There is a strict company rule that no files can be taken from the building. What would you do?

8. What criteria should the secretary use in determining what mail should be forwarded to her employer while he is away on a business trip? What procedures should she follow in forwarding the mail?

9. Just after your employer left on a somewhat lengthy business trip by plane, you discover that he has forgotten to take along his itinerary, reservation letters, and appointment schedule. What would you do?

10. If an employer is dilatory about submitting his expense reports, how can his secretary make it easier for him to meet deadlines for such reports?

11. What suggestions could you offer an executive who flies frequently and complains that he cannot keep up with the recurrent changes in airline schedules?

12. You are asked to write either of your two senators to request a certain report. How would you type the address and salutation? Refer to the Reference Guide to check your answer.

13. Type the following sentences correctly. Then refer to the Reference Guide to verify or correct your answers. Tell which Reference Guide entry you used for each reference.

    (a) The Case Western Reserve library is closed on Mondays.
    (b) Go to room 10 of the library this noon, please.
    (c) U.S. route 4 is within a half mile of our office.
    (d) All we know is: he is a negro who upholds democracy.

# PROBLEMS

1. Your employer, Mr. Robert Stanton, raises the following questions. The answers can be found in schedules on pages in this chapter. Write the answer to each question in memorandum form; that is, in a brief and clear presentation for Mr. Stanton.

(a) What flight would you suggest that I take to Atlanta from Kansas City for a speaking engagement at 8 p.m. on Wednesday? I have an appointment in Kansas City that morning at 10.

(b) What flight should I choose to Chicago from Denver for a luncheon speech on Monday?

(c) I'll be in New York and want to spend the weekend in New Haven with my brother. What trains can I take up there on Friday?

(d) I'll be in Pittsburgh when I have to leave for London. Which flight should I take for that trip?

(e) We're thinking of restricting first-class flights to our Rome office to the president and the senior vice-presidents. What other classes are available and how much would we save on each class for a round-trip fare?

■ 2. Prepare a schedule of available services for a business trip from your community to the capital and the largest city of each of three neighboring states. Insofar as possible, traveling should be scheduled after office hours and at least six hours in each city should be available for office calls. Include the airplane and train services that might be used.

■ 3. Prepare what you consider to be the best itinerary based upon the schedule of available services that you prepared in the preceding problem. Assume that all appointments will be typed on a separate schedule.

■ 4. Jeanne Kistner is secretary to Bill Murray, sales manager for General Products, a national corporation located in Newton, Massachusetts, selling packaged frozen foods. The six division sales offices have the following number of regional salesmen doing the following amounts of business:

|  | No. of Salesmen | % of Volume |
|---|---|---|
| Houston, Texas............. | 16 | 25 |
| San Diego, California........ | 12 | 21 |
| Tacoma, Washington........ | 12 | 16 |
| Kansas City, Missouri....... | 9 | 15 |
| Columbia, South Carolina.... | 8 | 13 |
| Newtown, Massachusetts..... | 3 | 10 |
|  | 60 | 100 |

Last year the annual sales conference was held in Boston and included a visit to Newton because Mr. Murray wanted the salesmen to see the new methods of processing food which had been developed. No startlingly new processes, however, were introduced during this year. Mr. Murray decides to hold this year's conference in Houston to "give a shot in the arm" to the lagging sales force there. Six weeks before the conference, however, he receives this memorandum from the president: "Last year's conference costs were exorbitant. Remember our austerity budget. Cut expenses by 40 percent, but don't give the boys a cheap conference."

Mr. Murray decides to visit all sales offices at once so that he can plan a more effective conference. He wants to visit the one with the poorest record first and plan the most economical itinerary from there on. Assume that you are Miss Kistner and comply with his request that you suggest his itinerary for the sales trip.

He also asks you to recommend a conference location that would reduce expenses and also provide attractive facilities, easily accessible.

# Chapter 17

## EXPEDITING MEETINGS

Meetings, meetings, meetings. Regular meetings of the executive committee, the employees' continuing education committee, or the safety committee. Meetings of special committees charged with one specific responsibility, such as implementing a new state regulation, studying the feasibility of initiating a cooperative education program with a local community college, or making recommendations for standardization of forms used throughout the company. Small informal meetings at which policy and strategy are hammered out before they are introduced to a larger group. Meetings to familiarize colleagues with new products or procedures. Meetings with businessmen and -women from other companies to exchange experiences and gain insight into trends. Conferences for the assessment of new concepts and organizational patterns. Annual conventions of people with similar interests to learn new developments in their field and to develop policy for their professional organizations. Annual meetings of corporations, where management accounts to the stockholders for its performance.

Much of the executive's time is spent in meetings. His prestige and effectiveness partially depend on the number of intracompany and outside committees to which he is elected or appointed.[1] His secretary can expect, then, that she too will be constantly involved in preparing for meetings, reporting them, and completing the follow-up work generated by them.

## COMMITTEE MEETINGS OR INFORMAL OFFICE CONFERENCES

Many office meetings do not involve complicated arrangements. The secretary, however, may have to spend considerable time on the

---

[1]The typical business executive is involved in one or more organized activities that are not a part of his regular job, and 72 percent are leaders of such organizations, a survey by Dartnell Institute reveals.

Informal meetings (joint meetings of committee chairmen, special committees, subcommittees, and the like) may follow no protocol. The secretary takes notes on all items of discussion and then summarizes them, as illustrated on page 405.

telephone with the secretaries of other executives in trying to schedule a possible meeting time. After the time is agreed upon, it is still a precautionary measure to send a confirming note reminding those who are to attend of the time and place. If the meeting takes place in the executive's office, the secretary makes sure that the room is in good order with enough chairs available for all members and that all the materials needed are assembled.

She and her employer may provide a gracious gesture by stocking supplies for serving coffee: styrofoam cups, plastic spoons, powdered coffee, cream, and sugar.

During the meeting the secretary may be asked to take notes. Recommended conference procedure suggests that the chairman summarize the actions and consensus of the meeting. If the secretary is reporting a meeting for such a chairman, she is lucky. Many office conferences, however, are informal discussions where opinions are exchanged, conclusions are reached, and recommendations are made with no observance of protocol. In these cases the secretary herself is expected to make the summary—subject to the executive's revision, of course—to be distributed to all participants. Certainly, if during the meeting it is agreed that certain conferees take specific action, as a reminder the secretary should send each a copy of the report *underlining the agreed-upon action*.

# FORMAL MEETINGS

Just as soon as you know that a meeting is to be called, you should set up a file folder, listing on the caption the name of the meeting and its date. Into this folder goes every bit of relevant information that crosses your desk during the planning stages. When you prepare the agenda or later attend the meeting, you will derive much help from this folder.

If you are involved in planning a local meeting, the hotel personnel will make useful suggestions about facilities. For out-of-town meetings, various airlines and hotels provide planning services. For instance, one airline advertises that it will provide a planning consultant to help in choosing the most convenient and economical location and in planning the conference. Other airlines and hotels will coordinate the flight arrangements of the conferees and provide rooms, meals, and meeting rooms equipped with such necessary facilities as lecterns, chalkboards, or flip charts. Another (international) airline provides conference facilities at airports for its passengers' convenience.

A hotel in which a convention is held customarily provides a complimentary bedroom suite for the president of the organization.

## Reserving the Meeting Room

The first detail to be taken care of by the secretary in making arrangements for a meeting is that of reserving the meeting room. This must be done before notices are sent out. What usually happens is something similar to this. The executive says, "Will you call a meeting on budget requests for next Wednesday afternoon at two." He does not say, "It will be held in the conference room." He always holds his meetings there, and he takes it for granted that the secretary will see that the conference room is available for his use. It is the secretary's responsibility to make sure the room is not being used that afternoon by another group. It is very embarrassing to the executive — and it is the secretary's fault — if the executive's group tries to gather in a room that is already in use.

In case the meeting is to be held in a hotel, the secretary should be sure also that the meeting place and hour are posted correctly on the announcement board in the lobby and in the elevators. Usually, all participants have traveled a distance to the meeting, and nothing is more annoying than to reach the hotel at the last minute and be unable to locate the meeting. Even though she has checked with the hotel about the time and place, the secretary must make a final check to see that any last-minute changes appear in all the announcements throughout the building.

## Notices of Meetings

The secretary's responsibility for taking care of the notices of a meeting frequently involves the five steps listed below:

1. Making the calendar notations
2. Preparing the mailing list
3. Composing the notice
4. Typing and sending the notices
5. Handling the follow-up work

**Making the Calendar Notations.** The secretary must make follow-up notations on the calendar to remind herself to prepare and send the notices. Make the notations on dates far enough ahead to allow time for the notices to be composed, reproduced, and delivered several days before the meeting. Notices that are too late reduce attendance; those that are too early may be forgotten. And while the notice for an office conference of staff men could be delivered the day before the meeting, an office conference of traveling men might require two weeks' notice. You should also make a calendar notation for several days before the date on which you must confirm room reservations.

**Preparing the Mailing List.** For notices sent out periodically to the same group, prepare a mailing list of names and addresses on loose-leaf sheets in a notebook or desk manual or on 5- by 3-inch cards. Type the addresses in either of two ways: Invert the name for easy filing (and follow with the address as it will appear on the notice), or type the entire item exactly as it will appear on the notice, perhaps underlining the last name as a filing aid. Type some sort of identifying signal beside each address, such as *AMS* to indicate that the addressee belongs on the Administrative Management Society list. List or file by the last name of the addressee, using a systematic arrangement — straight alphabetic or alphabetically under geographic area, committee, group, or team.

Preparing addressing-machine plates for those who receive frequent notices will expedite the notifying process. These plates are classified and filed in drawers marked for easy selection. For instance, tabs on plates for the total membership of an organization might be white; and tabs on plates for the chairmen of committees might be pink. An entire drawer is inserted into the addressing machine, and the entire list of notices can be quickly addressed. The machine can also be programmed to select only the pink-tabbed plates from among those in the drawer, thereby controlling a mailing to committee chairmen. The plates are automatically replaced in the drawer after usage. Also, envelopes or cards can be addressed during slack periods so that one set is always ready for use. Where addressing-machine plates are impractical, run master copies of lists on a duplicator.

This notice is part of a double post card.  The return portion is preaddressed to the secretary and provides spaces for the recipient's name and the number of reservations he requires for himself and his guests.

An address list MUST be kept up to date.  Once a year the secretary should send out double postcards for the membership to use in reporting their current addresses.  When a change of address occurs, the secretary corrects her mailing list or has a new addressing-machine plate made and inserted at the proper position in the drawer.

**Composing the Notice.**  Simple notices can be composed by the secretary for approval by the executive.  The notice of the previous meeting is a good model to follow if it specifies the day, the date, the time, the place, and either the purpose of a special meeting or the fact that it is a regularly scheduled one.  If the secretary is required to prepare an agenda of items to be discussed at the meeting, she should include a request for agenda items in the notice of the meeting.

Before a notice of an official meeting is sent out, the legal department should check the organization's bylaws for any stipulations of certain information necessary for an item to be acted upon at the meeting.  For instance, the bylaws may require that the notice include a statement that no dividends can be voted upon until the question of dividends is discussed at the meeting.  Even in a less formal situation, it is desirable to indicate the agenda of the meeting.

In case the secretary is preparing a notice of a corporation meeting, she should enclose with the notice a form on which the shareholder may execute a proxy, giving someone else authority to vote his stock in case he does not plan to attend. As this notice must include a detailed list of the business to be transacted, the reasons for soliciting the proxy, and other information specifically required by law, it is usually prepared by the legal department.

**Typing and Sending the Notice.** For small groups the notice is either typewritten or telephoned. For large meetings the notice is printed or reproduced by some duplicating process.

Post-card notices should be typed attractively, with the message neatly displayed. A simple, double-spaced form is acceptable for short notices. Some secretaries underline the important words.

If the secretary is sending notices of regular meetings, a form may be printed or duplicated at the beginning of the club year so that the date, program topic, or other pertinent information is all that need be filled in to complete the form.

Some meetings or conferences are of such importance that the announcement is typed or duplicated on letterhead paper. If only a few names are involved, a tabular listing of the names of those to receive the letter may be typed, in place of the usual single name, address, and salutation. With the tabular listing the salutation then is a general one, such as "Dear Member," "Dear Committee Member," or "Dear Mr. . . . . . . . . . .," with the name to be filled in later. Modern usage permits the omission of the salutation entirely. An individual letter to each person is sometimes used, but that is a time-taking procedure unless power typing equipment is available.

Keeping a copy of the notice and the date of mailing is a precautionary measure that the secretary should adopt.

## Handling the Follow-Up Work

The secretary's follow-up duties consist chiefly of recording who and how many will or will not attend the meeting. If return post cards have been furnished, the notice follow-up is merely a matter of sorting the cards into the *will's* and *will-not's*. But usually it means also telephoning several persons for a definite *Yes* or *No*.

The executive who is secretary of a civic luncheon club in a large city sends out multigraphed notices one week before the monthly meeting. Two days before the meeting his secretary telephones each member who has not responded to ask whether he plans to attend. She records attendance plans on a three-column sheet (one wide for names and two narrow for acceptances and refusals). As soon as responses are in from all the members, she telephones the hotel, giving the exact number of reservations. A quick method is to use a duplicated form that includes the names and the telephone numbers of members. Each name can be checked off as an answer is obtained. The frequency of meetings determines whether or not the preparation and duplication of a special form of this kind is justified.

A helpful secretarial service, especially with a fairly small group, is to make reminder telephone calls to all persons expected. Early in the morning of the meeting day the secretary calls each person, or preferably the secretary, and tactfully mentions the meeting. A diplomatic way to do this is to inquire of the secretary if the executive plans to attend such and such a meeting called for such and such a time, adding in explanation that you are making a final check on probable attendance. Some members may be unable to attend for last-minute reasons; others may explain that they will be late. Fortified with such knowledge, the chairman can call the meeting to order promptly.

## Preparing the Order of Business

Every meeting follows some systematic program, which is planned and outlined before the meeting. In organized groups, this program is usually called the *order of business*. It is called the *agenda* in academic and business meetings and conferences. *Calendar* is the term used at meetings of some legislative bodies, such as a city council.

If the executive is to be the presiding officer, the secretary should remind him to prepare the order of business several days before the meeting. If she knows the purpose of the meeting, she can probably prepare this agenda in rough-draft form so that he will merely have to complete and rearrange it to his liking. It is definitely a secretarial duty to see that the order of business is ready on meeting day. A review of the bylaws and the minutes of previous meetings (properly indexed for easy cross reference) will be of invaluable aid in preparing the order of business and in helping the presiding officer to carry out the agenda in an effective manner.

In small discussion groups each person receives a copy of the order of business or program. This is an especially helpful secretarial service in office conferences because it gives those attending the conference time to arrange their thoughts on the questions to be discussed. If the meeting has been called to discuss a proposed plan, the secretary can distribute copies of the proposal prior to the meeting to facilitate action at the meeting.

The order of business may be set forth by the organization in its bylaws. If not, the usual order is:

- **Call to order by presiding officer**
- **Roll call—either oral or observed by secretary**
- **Announcement of quorum (not always done)**
- **Reading of minutes of previous meeting (Sometimes the minutes are circulated before the meeting, and the body approves them without their being read orally.)**
- **Approval of minutes**

- **Reports of officers**
- **Reports of standing committees** } *Copies usually are given to the secretary.*
- **Reports of special committees**

- **Unfinished business (taken from previous minutes)**
- **New business**
- **Appointments of committees**
- **Nominations and elections**
- **Date of next meeting**
- **Adjournment**

A group that is meeting for the first time appoints a temporary chairman to preside and also a temporary secretary. The group then elects permanent officers or appoints a committee to nominate officers and to draw up the constitution and bylaws.

## Last-Minute Duties

The secretary's first duty on meeting day is to check on the meeting room to see that the air in the room is fresh; that there are enough chairs, ash trays, matches, paper, pencils, clips, and pins; and that any requested equipment such as a portable chalkboard or a tape recorder has actually arrived.

She should next assemble materials in a file folder for the executive, arranging them in the order in which he will refer to them as indicated on the agenda.

This secretary is preparing the conference room of a building of the Indianapolis Power and Light Company. Just before the meeting she will adjust the lighting to a level that is correct for comfort and good vision and check the heating controls for a comfortable temperature.

—*General Electric Company,*
*Nela Park*

She should take to the meeting minutes of previous meetings, a list of those who should attend, a copy of Robert's *Rules of Order* for her employer's reference, the bylaws, a seating chart, blank ballots, and aids similar to those illustrated on page 401 for taking minutes.

Many small business meetings and conferences are recorded on tape. If this is the case, the secretary should make arrangements for setting up the recording machine. One of her responsibilities at the meeting may be to operate the tape recorder.

Unless she has previously done so, the secretary's next job is to gather together all the material that will be needed at the meeting — notebooks, pencils, a filled fountain pen, the minute book, reports to be distributed to participants, or perhaps a list of those attending, the companies they represent, and their addresses. It is most embarrassing to the secretary to leave the meeting room several times for things that she should have provided. It advertises that she is not very thorough. On the other hand, offering to get records or material on subjects that arise unexpectedly shows her willingness to please. Before leaving a meeting room, however, the secretary must first get permission from the executive or the presiding officer. She is there to record data for the minutes, either through her own notes or through verbatim recordings of a professional reporter or a tape recorder (supplemented by her own notes that she takes as an aid in later abstracting the important points from the mass of material).

The secretary should study the minutes of previous meetings to acquaint herself with the usual procedure and make an analysis of techniques used in television or radio round-table discussion. She may also familiarize herself with parliamentary procedure by reading Robert's *Rules of Order* (now in paperback) or other references named at the end of this chapter. She should know the requirements for a quorum, without which business cannot be transacted.

If she has noted beforehand from the order of business the names of those who are to present topics, she can record the names and topics easily on the day of the meeting. She can also bring to the meeting a seating chart on which to fill in names as she hears them, and thus will be able to match names with motions or discussions.

Before the meeting opens, the secretary may have to make introductions, acknowledge introductions, or help the executive on some last-minute arrangements.

## Parliamentary Procedure

The secretary can better report a meeting if she understands parliamentary procedure. She can also unobtrusively call the attention of the chair to any violations of parliamentary rules, such as voting on a motion before voting on an amendment to the motion. Therefore, she should review important points of parliamentary procedure before going to the meeting.

Parliamentary law has been defined as "common sense used in a gracious manner." Its purpose is to arrive at a group decision in an efficient and orderly manner. Parliamentary procedure is based on four principles:

1. **Courtesy and justice must be accorded to all.**
2. **Only one topic is considered at one time.**
3. **The minority must be heard.**
4. **The majority must prevail.**

Most business is transacted through main motions, which require a majority vote for adoption. A member addresses the chair, is recognized, and makes a motion. Another member seconds the motion. After the motion has been made and seconded, the chairman states the motion, names both the one who made it and the one who seconded it, and calls for discussion. When the discussion ends, a vote is taken, usually by voice. The Chair announces the result, "The motion is carried (or defeated)." If anyone calls "Division," the chair asks for a show of hands or a standing vote. If a majority demands it, the vote must be taken by ballot.

After a main motion has been made, a member of the body can propose an amendment to the motion. If the proposal is seconded, it is discussed. The proposed amendment must be voted upon before the main motion can again be considered. After the chairman announces the action on a proposed amendment, he says, "The motion now before the house is . . ." and states the original motion plus the amendment, if the amendment carried. If the amendment loses, the original motion is acted upon.

If a motion involves two actions rather than one, a member can move that the question be divided for voting; then each part becomes a separate motion.

If a motion is so bogged down that further discussion would seem to be a waste of time and if two thirds of the voting members support him, a member can "move the question," an action that forces an immediate vote. If the motion loses, discussion of the original motion continues.

A motion can be made to *table* a motion (to delay further discussion or action). A seconded motion to table must be voted on at once. A successful motion to table permits the group to consider more important business and sometimes allows a motion to die — although a tabled motion may be taken from the table by a majority vote. (An even surer way to kill a motion is to move that the motion be postponed indefinitely.)

When it becomes obvious that further information is needed, a motion can be made to refer a matter to a committee, which is then named by the chairman.

By unobtrusively calling the attention of the chairman to a violation in parliamentary procedure, a secretary may avoid embarrassment to her employer occasioned by a member saying, "I rise to a point of order," at which time the presiding officer must decide, without debate, whether the person raising the question is correct in claiming that the rules are being broached, or must rely on the parliamentarian for advice. An error or omission in procedure can be pointed out by a brief reminder note tactfully phrased.

*Privileged* motions have precedence over others. One of these is "to call for orders of the day," a motion that, without debate, forces the chairman to follow the agenda.

```
Number present _____          Motion _____
                                        _____
Excused (names):
                                 Proposed by _____
_____
                                 Seconded by _____
_____
                                 Vote:    For _____
_____
                                        Against _____
Absent (names):
                                 Summary of discussion:
_____
_____


Things to do after the
meeting:
1.
2.
3.
```

During the meeting the secretary may use skeleton forms similar to those above to aid her in taking minutes. If she wishes, she can put all items on one page for easy handling. Or she may prefer slips that can be clipped to the shorthand minutes. She can type an agenda on large sheets, leaving ample space for notes covering each item and varying the space given each item according to past experience.

## The Secretary at the Meeting

The secretary's first duty at the meeting may be to report to the chairman when a quorum is present. If the secretary is to take full notes, she concentrates on taking minutes as unobtrusively as possible. She should, however, ask to have everything repeated that she does not hear distinctly or that she is unable to get into her notes. She may say, "I did not get that," or she may give a prearranged signal to the Chair, such as raising her left hand slightly. Then the chairman will ask that the point be repeated. The bylaws of some organizations require that the person making a motion submit the motion to the secretary in writing so that it will be exactly phrased in the minutes. Even here, though, the secretary would be well advised to take the oral motion down verbatim to be sure that the written motion conforms to the motion made on the floor.

Too many notes are better than too few. No one turns to the secretary in a meeting and says, "Take this," or "You need not take this." The secretary is simply held responsible for getting everything important in her notes. She must remain alert for motions, amendments, and decisions. If she is afraid to decide at the instant whether remarks are important, she should record them. (If they are not important, they can be omitted from the final draft.)

*Mr. Tillas requested this addition to the minutes: Mr. Baker left the meeting at 11:25.*

MEETING OF THE FOOD PRODUCTS STAFF

June 27, 197-

Time and
Place of
Meeting

The regular monthly staff meeting of the Food Products Division was held on Wednesday, June 27, 197-. The meeting was called to order by the Director, Mr. Thorne.

Roll Call

Twenty-two members were present. Absent: McCarton, Vogt, Thiele, and Brown.

Committee
Reports

Mr. Ordway, chairman of packaging requirements, reported that five suppliers had been furnished with artwork for the Product X7-3 package and that quotations would be submitted by July 15.

Mrs. Lippman, chairman of testing, reported that final results of tests on the formula containing no preservatives would be submitted at the next regular meeting.

The presiding officer may ask for corrections or additions after the secretary reads the minutes. The secretary then adds these changes to the minutes as they were originally written.

Some essential parts of the minutes may not be specifically recorded at the time of the meeting. The date, time, and place of the meeting and the name of the presiding officer may not be stated. The roll may be called; but if not, the *secretary is expected to observe and to record* all the details of attendance — who attended, who did not attend, who arrived late, and who left early. The last two items of information are important in recording action on measures voted upon. (Those not wishing to go on record with their votes may absent themselves from a part of the session for just that reason.) To report the attendance of a person at the entire meeting when he attended only a part of it could have serious consequences.

If the secretary is depending on a verbatim report of the meeting as her source of minutes, she will need to make notes *of items that are not likely to appear in the record:* the names of those attending, the official title of the speaker, the time of meeting and adjournment, the names of those voting *Yes* and *No* to motions, the names of those coming in late and leaving early and possibly any difficult names and words that may cause confusion in transcription. If she outlines the proceedings during the meeting, she can more easily make necessary insertions when she works with the verbatim report.

If it is the secretary's duty to read the minutes of the last meeting, she should read them in a meaningful manner and in a voice loud enough that everyone in attendance will be able to hear what matters were considered and what decisions were made.

After the minutes are read, the presiding officer asks for corrections and additions to them. Usually this is a mere formality, and the vote approves the minutes as read. In some cases, however, corrections or additions are made. When this happens, the minutes should not be rewritten. The changes should be made in red ink on the copy of the minutes as they were originally written; and, of course, the corrections and additions become a part of the minutes of the meeting at which they are made. To save meeting time, some organizations have a *Minutes Committee*, whose function is to examine the minutes before the next meeting and report to the membership whether the minutes are in order or what changes should be made.

An illustration of a typical addition to minutes is shown on page 402. Events of the meeting might lend significance to the absence of Mr. Baker.

The order of business follows the agenda. The story of every motion, passed or defeated, must be recorded in the minutes. The name of the person making the motion, the complete motion exactly as stated, the name of the person seconding it, a summary of the pro's and con's given during the discussion, and the decision by vote — all must go into the secretary's notes. Motions written out by their originators and written committee reports are important source documents.

After the business of the meeting is completed, the date of the next meeting is announced, usually just before adjournment. After the meeting has been adjourned, the secretary collects copies of all papers read and all committee reports so that she can make them a part of the minutes. (The committee reports are attached to her minutes.) Before leaving the meeting room, the secretary should check and verify all doubtful or incomplete notes, such as the correct spelling of names and the correct phrasing of a motion.

## Follow-Up Work after the Meeting

A lot of work for the secretary always follows a meeting, aside from putting the meeting room back in order and writing the minutes or proceedings. Items that require future attention must be listed on both the executive's and the secretary's calendars. Individual letters must be

A resolution is usually presented as a formal statement. Each paragraph begins with
**WHEREAS** or **RESOLVED** typed in capital letters or underlined.

written to those elected to membership and to those appointed to serve
on committees or requested to perform certain tasks — even though
they were at the meeting and are aware of the appointments or assignments. For expenses of participants to be paid by the organization, the
secretary should see that necessary forms are completed and reimbursement made as soon as possible. (Many executives send a summary
of the meeting to the entire group.)

**Resolutions.** Often an organization wishes to send an expression of
its opinion or will (such as a resolution expressing sympathy on the
death of a member or concurrence in a stated objective) in the form of a
resolution to a person or an association. A resolution may be presented
at the meeting in writing, or the secretary may be instructed to prepare
an appropriate resolution. After the meeting the secretary is responsible
for composing or typing the resolution, having it signed and sent out,
and incorporating it into the minutes.

**Reporting the Meeting.** The secretary finds herself confronted with a
problem in reporting what is *done* in a meeting, for she has learned to
record only what is *said*. To winnow from the discussion the pertinent
facts to serve as a record of *what has been decided* and as a guide to *what
needs to be done by whom* challenges her best efforts.

MEETING OF THE EDITORIAL COMMITTEE

September 4, 19--

The Editorial Committee met in the office of the Chairman,
Mr. Perry, at 10 a.m. on Friday morning, September 4, 19--, for
its regularly scheduled semimonthly meeting.  Those present were
Mr. Perry, Mr. Harrison, Mr. Solkol, and Miss Henry.  Mr. Richman
was absent.

The following decisions were reached:

New Books.  The manuscript submitted by Lawrence LeMar will
be published in May without major change.  The manuscript submitted
by Alice Lewis was rejected with the recommendation that she col-
laborate with James Allison in a revision.

Personnel.  The Committee voted unanimously to request that a
new editorial assistant be employed to work on the reading series.

Schedules.  Mr. Perry discussed at length the necessity for
revising publishing schedules for school textbooks.  He stated that
it is necessary for a book to be available in January if September
adoption is planned.  Miss Henry suggested that every member of the
Committee submit to her by September 10 a written and detailed progress report on every book on which he is doing editorial work so
that she can make a report to the Committee at its next regular
meeting.  The Committee voted to follow this suggestion, Mr. Solkol
dissenting.

Cover Designs.  Cover designs were submitted for E67 and M14.
It was decided to use Murray Brown's design for E67.  The Committee
voted to reject all designs submitted for M14.

The meeting was adjourned at 12:30.

*September 18, 19--*
Date

*Alex Harrison*
Alex Harrison, Secretary

The secretary merely summarizes the major actions
of a meeting that follows no formal order of business.

```
            P E R S O N N E L    C L U B
            MEETING OF MARCH 10, 19--

Time and              The regular monthly meeting of the Dayton
Place of       Personnel Club was held on Tuesday, March 10, 19--,
Meeting        in the Regis Hotel.  The meeting was called to
               order at 8:10 p.m. by the President, Mr. Walker.

Roll Call             There were thirty-four members present.

Reading of            The minutes of the February meeting were
Minutes        approved as read by the Secretary.

Treasurer's           The Treasurer presented his monthly report
Report         showing a balance of $51.32.  This report, a copy
               of which is attached, was accepted.  Two small
               bills, amounting to $8.15, were presented and
               approved for payment by the Treasurer.

Committee             The President called for special committee
Reports        reports that were ordered for this meeting.  The
```

Minutes of a meeting follow the order of business given on page 397. They indicate whether the meeting was a regular or a special one.  Marginal headings aid in locating items.

Reports of meetings vary with the degree of formality required. For an office conference, the proceedings are compact and simple. For a meeting of an organization, the report customarily recognizes the efforts of individual members or refers to letters from former members, as well as recording the formal actions taken. The final minutes may not record the events in chronological order if the secretary finds that regrouping around a central theme is clearer. For *official minutes* of a formal nature, however, the proceedings are recorded in the order of occurrence in complete detail, including the exact wording of all motions or resolutions.

Sometimes the secretary records the minutes in the secretary's book only. In other cases, however, it may be desirable for her to duplicate and distribute the minutes after they have been officially approved by the chairman. If the minutes are to be referred to at subsequent meetings, duplicated minutes are often prepared with the line numbers typed at the left margin. It is then easy for a speaker to refer to *Page 3, Line 17*, and have the entire group follow him easily.

The secretary can aid the reader in locating each motion by typing in either of the following ways:

Professor Scott moved THAT A SPECIAL COMMITTEE BE ESTABLISHED TO RECOMMEND —

or

Professor Scott moved that a special committee be established to recommend —

The minutes should answer the journalistic questions: What? Where? When? Who? Why? The following suggestions apply to writing minutes of all kinds.

1. Capitalize and center the heading which designates the official title or nature of the group which met, as *Committee V*; *Student Personnel Services*; *Recruitment, Guidance, and Placement*.

2. Single- or double-space the minutes and allow generous margins. There is a preference for double-spaced minutes.

3. Prepare the minutes with marginal subject captions for the various sections to expedite locating information. Record each different action in a separate paragraph.

4. Establish that the meeting was properly called and members notified properly. Indicate whether it was a regular or a special meeting.

5. Give the names of the presiding officer and the secretary.

6. Indicate whether a quorum was present, and provide a roll of those present. At official meetings and committee meetings, list those absent.

7. Rough out the minutes with triple spacing for approval by your employer before preparing them in final form.

8. Transcribe notes while they are still fresh in your memory. If that is impossible, you may find it desirable to take the notes home and read them through, getting them in mind for accurate transcription the next day. If minutes for a meeting which you did not attend are dictated to you, be sure that you get all the pertinent data from your employer at the time of the dictation and that he interprets his notes to you properly.

9. Capitalize such words as *Board of Directors, Company, Corporation*, and *Committee* in the minutes when they refer to the group in session.

10. Send official minutes to the secretary of the organization or presiding officer or both, for signatures. At the end of the minutes type a line for recording the date of their approval. *Respectfully submitted* or *Respectfully* may be used on formal minutes.

11. Do not include personal opinions, interpretations, or comments. Record only business actions, not sentiments or feelings. Such phrases as *outstanding speech, brilliant report*, or *provocative argument* are out of place in the minutes. Where gratitude or appreciation is to be expressed, it should take the form of a resolution.

12. Try to summarize the gist of the discussion about the motion, giving reasons presented for and against its adoption. A recently formed organization interested in improving business records for historical purposes decries the lack of helpful information contained in the minutes of company meetings at all levels. This organization stresses the value of such summaries when later discussions of similar proposals are held.

```
SALARIES

Appointment of Committee for
Recommendations

1946 - p. 63
1953 - p. 11
1957 - p. 59
1961 - p. 81
1965 - p. 23
1973 - p. 30
```

```
SALARIES

Increases approved

1952 - p. 26
1954 - p. 35
1959 - p. 56
1963 - p. 47
1969 - p. 34
1973 - p. 38
```

These sample cards from an index to minutes show the years of action and page references to actions taken on the subject of salaries. Both cards follow the subject guide *Salaries*.

**Indexing the Minutes.** Because the composition of committees and organizations is constantly changing, sometimes groups find themselves in embarrassing situations because they do not know the regulations which they, as a body, have previously passed. They may take an action contrary to required procedure; they may violate their own regulations; or they may pass motions that contradict each other. The presiding officer may look at old minute books, which have been preserved since the beginning of the organization, and decide that it will be impossible to ferret out the separate actions on recurring problems. Nothing that you could do for the harrassed officer could be more helpful than the preparation and maintenance of an index of the minutes by subject, giving the year and page number of each action taken. Sometimes a separate volume is used for the minutes of each year.

Writing captions in the margin of the minute book beside the motions passed will facilitate preparing file cards for the index.

**Other Duties.** The secretary should be especially diligent in processing all forms necessary for prompt payment of honoraria, fees, and expense accounts to those who performed and those who attended the meeting. She would also check to see that appropriate thank-you notes and notifications of committee responsibilities resulting from the meeting are written.

## Minutes of Corporations

Corporations are usually required by law to keep a minute book for recording the minutes of meetings of stockholders and directors. Stockholders usually meet once a year, but directors' meetings are held more frequently. Minute books are extremely important legal records. Recorded decisions must be carried out, for they constitute the regulations to which the management must conform.

The records of a corporation are kept by the corporation secretary, a full-time officer of the company, whose duties differ greatly from those of the secretary discussed in this book. He is a company executive and will probably employ a secretary whose duties approximate those described here. He also issues proxies for shareholders who do not plan to attend the annual meeting but who wish to vote.

Auditors who examine the accounting records of a corporation read the minutes carefully to see that all financial decisions have been executed. They observe whether all transactions entered into by the corporation—those that are of a nature required by law or by the company's charter to be passed upon by the board of directors or stockholders—are authorized or approved in the minutes. For instance, an item in the minutes to pay a dividend of $1 a share on common stock as of a certain date makes it legally mandatory that such a dividend be paid.

One large company whose success and continued operation depended upon a certain process patented by its founder learned upon his death that the heirs were claiming royalty rights to the patent. The founder had stated verbally his intention of passing the patent rights on to the company itself. A statement to that effect, which was found in the minutes of a meeting held fifteen years previously, was upheld by the courts.

**The Minute Book.** Two separate books are frequently used for corporate minutes, one for stockholders' meetings as illustrated on the next page and one for meetings of the board of directors. If only one book is used, a portion of it is assigned to each group so that each set of minutes can be entered in consecutive order. A corporate minute book may also contain a copy of the certificate of incorporation and a record of the bylaws adopted.

The minute book may be bound or loose leaf. The latter is preferable, for it permits the typing of the minutes. In order to prevent substitution or removal of sheets, one of the following types of loose-leaf books is used:

One with prenumbered pages, with each page signed by the corporation secretary and carrying the date of the meeting

One with pages watermarked with a code symbol

One with keylock binder, making it impossible to remove or insert sheets without the use of a key

Papers are seldom made a part of corporate minutes; but if so, they are pasted into the book. The final copy of the minutes is signed by the

MINUTES OF FIRST MEETING OF STOCKHOLDERS
THE ATOMIC POWER COMPANY

Held March 3, 19--

Pursuant to written call and waiver of notice signed by all the incorporators, the first meeting of The Atomic Power Company was held in the Board Room of the Company's offices at 25 Mission Street, San Francisco, California, at 2:15 p.m., March 3, 19--.

There were present in person:  J. A. Barnes, D. E. Barnes, W. J. Howe, H. A. Lomax, and M. A. Miller.  Mr. J. A. Barnes called the meeting to order and was elected Chairman by motion unanimously carried.  Mr. D. E. Barnes was elected Secretary.

The Chairman reported that the certificate of incorporation had been filed with the Secretary of State on January 16, 19--, and that a certified copy had been filed with the County Recorder on February 7, 19--.  H. A. Lomax made the following resolution, which was duly seconded and unanimously carried:

> RESOLVED, That said certificate of incorporation be accepted, the Directors named therein be approved, and the Secretary be instructed to cause a copy of such certificate to be inserted in the minute book of the Company.

The Secretary presented bylaws prepared by counsel, which were read, article by article.  Upon motion duly made by W. J. Howe, seconded by H. A. Lomax, and unanimously carried, the following resolution was adopted:

> RESOLVED, That the bylaws submitted be, and the same hereby are, adopted as the bylaws of this Corporation, and that the Secretary be, and he hereby is, instructed to cause the same to be inserted in the minute book of the Company immediately following the copy of the certificate of incorporation.

The Chairman announced the date of the next meeting to be April 6, 19--, to be held in the Board Room of the Company's offices at 10:30 a.m.

There was no further business.  Upon motion made and seconded, the meeting was adjourned.  The time of adjournment was 4:30 p.m., March 3, 19--.

*J. A. Barnes*
_____
J. A. Barnes, Chairman

*April 6, 19--*
_____
Date

*D E Barnes*
_____
D. E. Barnes, Secretary

Formal minutes of a corporation are shown above.

officers required to do so. Corrections are written in and the incorrect portions ruled out in ink. These changes are initialed in the margin by the signers of the minutes.

**Contents of Corporate Minutes.** The following information is recorded in corporate minutes:

1. **Membership of group—directors or stockholders**
2. **Date and place of meeting**
3. **Kind of meeting—regular or special**
4. **Names of those attending**
5. **A complete record of the proceedings of the meeting**

Ordinarily the responsibility for formal minutes is given to the official secretary of the company. His secretary may help in the routine work of typing the minutes; but he carries the full responsibility of their completeness, accuracy, and legality.

# CONFERENCES AND CONVENTIONS

The executive is likely to participate in numerous conferences and conventions. A *conference* is a discussion or consultation on some important matter, often in a formal meeting. A *convention* is a formal meeting of delegates or members, often the annual assembly of a professional group. The executive's secretary is often involved in planning these events. Much of her work precedes and follows the actual meeting.

## Secretarial Preplanning Responsibilities

Some conferences and conventions require the full-time efforts of a secretary for an entire year. Weeks and months of painstaking work are required to:

1. **Secure speakers and tell them explicitly what they are to do and how long a time they will have for their presentations**
2. **Obtain biographical material from speakers**
3. **Mail publicity material to prospective participants**
4. **Prepare menus and plan social activities**
5. **Prepare or maintain up-to-date mailing lists**
6. **Provide for the distribution of name tags**
7. **Iron out the thousand-and-one details necessary for a smooth-running conference**
8. **Possibly secure registrations by mail**
9. **Publicize the conference or convention**

With all of these details and more, the secretary is expected to assist.

## AMERICAN RECORDS MANAGEMENT ASSOCIATION

Suite 823 — 24 North Wabash, Chicago, Illinois 60602

*Providing for Leadership in Data and Information Management*

**NATIONAL OFFICERS**

**PRESIDENT**
Thomas G. Doyle
New England Telephone Co.
Braintree, Massachusetts

**EXECUTIVE VICE PRESIDENT**
Miss Helen R. Harden
Frito-Lay, Inc.
Dallas, Texas

**TREASURER**
William H. Williams
North American Rockwell Corp.
Aerospace & Systems Office
El Segundo, California

**SECRETARY**
Mrs. Olive R. Surgen
Management Consulting Division
Gilbert Associates, Inc.
Reading, Pennsylvania

**VICE PRESIDENTS**
**Region I**
Miss June Astley
Elliott Company
Division, Carrier Corporation
Jeannette, Pennsylvania

**Region II**
Richard E. Matyn
Ford Motor Company
Dearborn, Michigan

**Region III**
Edward N. Johnson
Bureau of Archives and
Records Management
Florida Department of State
Tallahassee, Florida

**Region IV**
Gerald F. Brown
Missouri Pacific Railroad Co.
St. Louis, Missouri

**Region V**
Mrs. Gisela Robinson
Union Texas Petroleum Co.
Division, Allied Chemical Corp.
Houston, Texas

**Region VI**
Stan M. Sammarcelli
IBM Corporation
San Jose, California

**Region VII**
Bruce D. Carswell
M & T Chemicals, Inc.
Subsidiary—American Can Co.
Rahway, New Jersey

**Region VIII**
Donald T. Barber
Datafile, Limited
Scarborough, Ontario, Canada

**Region IX**
Joseph H. Santone
Cleveland Electric
Illuminating Company
Cleveland, Ohio

**IMMEDIATE PAST PRESIDENT**
Donald F. Evans
Union 76 Division
Union Oil Company of California
Palatine, Illinois

**EXECUTIVE SECRETARY**
William Benedon
Lockheed Aircraft Corporation
Burbank, California
213: 847-6507

September 28, 197-

Dr. Estelle Popham
210 East 68 Street
New York, New York 10021

Dear Doctor Popham

Many thanks for accepting our invitation to speak and lead
a seminar on Training and Motivating Records Management
Personnel at the Region VII one-day conference at Great
Gorge, McAfee, New Jersey, on Monday, April 24 of next year.

As a seminar leader, you will be expected to give a formal
presentation of approximately 40 minutes from which to evolve
the participation of the attendees. The remaining time will
be devoted to a dialogue with participants on such questions as:

Is on-the-job training adequate in most operations today?
If not, why not?

What formal training programs for records personnel are available?

How do you upgrade clerical help and prepare them for middle-
management positions?

What standards do you have for selecting employees for filing-
records management positions?

What standards do you use for selecting employees in our field?
What tests do you use?

Based on a registration of 70-90 people, we would expect each
session to total 20-25 attendees in the morning and the same
number in the afternoon.

Four of our six speakers have already accepted, and we expect
confirmation of the other two this week. As plans develop,
you will be kept informed. Again, many thanks.

Yours very truly

*Bruce D. Carswell*

Bruce D. Carswell
Vice President Region VII

cc to W. L. Bishop
T. C. Doyle

This letter illustrates excellent preconference planning. It was written approximately five
months before the event. It identifies the date and location, lists specific questions to be
covered, and shows the division of time to be made by the leader. It estimates the size of
the audience, enabling the speaker to prepare the correct number of handouts. Equally
important, it transmits the enthusiasm of the writer.

The letter was preceded by an invitation giving full details as to topic and financial arrangements. It was followed by a letter a month later indicating that the expected attendance was
now double the figure estimated in the preplanning sessions, requesting biographical
material, and describing plans for publicizing the conference. This sort of communication
brings the speaker into the circle of those working for the success of the conference.

## Duties at the Meeting

During the meeting the secretary is responsible for seeing that an *opaque* projector requested by a speaker is available—not an *overhead* projector. It is the secretary who determines whether the hotel uses AC or DC current and checks the compatibility of the equipment with the wiring. She sees that the projectionist is on hand at the very minute the speaker wants to show his slides. Above all, it is she who sees that the microphones are operating and that repairmen are on hand during any presentations. (Who can't remember at least one meeting that was ruined by failure of audio-visual equipment because nobody bothered to check it before the meeting started?) She is the one who remembers to send complimentary tickets for the wife of the luncheon speaker, to have ice water at the lectern, to check the number of chairs on the platform, and to provide place cards for the speakers' table and arrange them with some sense of protocol. It is she who must follow through with the gracious gestures that send the participants home happy.

## Conference Reporting

At many conferences, the proceedings are of such value that they are preserved in permanent form. For example, the American Management Association may hold a conference on employee appraisal and later publish the proceedings as a service to its entire membership and outside purchasers of the report. These meetings are usually reported by specially trained reporters. Here the secretary's function changes from reporter to coordinator. If she works in a situation where outside conference reporters are regularly used, she is expected to locate persons who can do excellent work. Keeping a file of possible reporters, printers, lithographers, and artists—along with an appraisal of the quality of their services—will aid her.

The secretary is responsible for all the conference groundwork and probably for all the follow-up work, just as she would be for any other meeting. She should not, however, be concerned with the writing of the conference report—only with the processing of it.

Often registrants at the conference want a copy of the proceedings. This service might be paid for by the registration fee, or an additional charge might be made. In any case the secretary may be responsible for securing mailing addresses of those entitled to the publication.

If papers are read at the conference, each speaker is usually asked to submit his paper prior to (or at) the meeting so that it can be either printed in its entirety or abstracted. It is the secretary's responsibility

Only the executive in charge of a conference — and his secretary — can know the countless hours spent in preparing for, executing, and following up the myriad details of a successful conference.

—*Bell & Howell*

to obtain a copy of this paper for publication. The conference reporter needs to report only the discussion following the presentation of the paper—either from tape recording or from summary notes. Sometimes the speaker is asked to prepare the summary himself. Then the reporter has to organize the material; edit it for uniformity of style; and write proper introductions, conclusions, or recommendations.

A last task for the secretary might be to compose recommendations for subsequent meetings, based on experience gained from this one.

## SUGGESTED READINGS

Augur, Bertrand Y. *How to Run More Effective Business Meetings.* New York: Grosset & Dunlap, 1964.

Cook, Fred S., and Lenore S. Forti. *Professional Secretary's Handbook.* Chicago: Dartnell Corporation, 1971, pp. 164–74.

Cruzan, Rose Marie. *Practical Parliamentary Procedure*, 3d ed. Bloomington, Ill.: McKnight and McKnight, 1962.

*The Executive Secretary.* Waterford: Bureau of Business Practice, 1968, pp. 72–75.

Klein, A. E., Supervisory ed. *The New World Secretarial Handbook.* Cleveland: World Publishing Co., 1968, pp. 368–386.

Robert, Henry Martyn. *Rules of Order*, Revised ed. Chicago: Scott, Foresman and Co., 1970.

1. In what ways could an efficient secretary have improved the last organized meeting you attended?

2. When should you send notices for each of the following meetings:

    (a) A monthly luncheon meeting for which reservations must be received not later than the day preceding the meeting

    (b) A meeting of the board of directors of a large corporation. All committees must present full reports

3. What duties must the secretary perform before a meeting is held?

4. While taking notes at an office conference, you feel that the subject being discussed would be clarified by reference to a report filed in your employer's personal file in the next room. Would you (a) write a note to him asking if you should obtain the report? (b) leave the room to obtain it? (c) do nothing?

5. If the telephone in the meeting room rings during the meeting, should the secretary answer it?

6. How can the consensus of a meeting be reflected in the minutes without subjectivity on the part of the secretary?

7. Is a motion voted on before the amendment to a motion? Can an amendment to a motion be amended?

8. What should the secretary do (a) if an unidentified person makes a motion? (b) if a person makes a motion that lacks clarity and that is changed several times in phraseology before it is voted on? (c) if the Chair entertains a new motion before the motion on the floor has been disposed of?

9. If a conference is being reported by a professional organization, what is the secretary's responsibility for the summary of the proceedings?

10. Why are strict rules followed for keeping corporation minutes? What precautions are taken to avoid substitution of pages in the minute book?

11. What follow-up work should be done by the secretary after the meeting?

12. Capitalize words as necessary in the following sentences. Then use the Reference Guide to verify or correct your answers.

    (a) Attendance declines in the summer.

    (b) The atomic age brings its own wonders—its own terrible fears.

    (c) Mr. Lawson is the new president of our company.

    (d) We heard an address by president Lawson.

    (e) He hopes to become a professor of marketing.

    (f) The professor of mathematics spoke, too.

    (g) I know professor Lawson well.

■ **1.** Your employer, H. C. Campbell, is secretary of the Pittsburgh Credit Managers Association. The regular monthly meeting of that organization was held on Thursday, June 22. The week before, you had mailed notices of that meeting to be held at 6:30 p.m. at the Hotel Pittsburgher.

Mr. Campbell gives you the following notes for the minutes of that meeting. You are to type the minutes in good form, using marginal or side headings for each paragraph. Mr. Campbell also instructs you to do these things as follow-up work: (a) Notify Harry Shorten of his nomination, as he was absent; (b) Write a note of appreciation to the speaker, enclosing a check for $27.50 which the treasurer drew for his expenses. (Since Mr. Campbell does not have any stationery of the Pittsburgh Credit Managers Association, use plain stationery.)

Called to order—8:05 p.m.

Mr. Riopelle, Pres., absent—Mr. Bavin, V.P., presided.

No. present—16. Minutes of May meeting read by secy.—approved.

Treas. report—present bal.—$572.68. Accepted (copy of report given to you by Mr. Steiner). No bills presented for payment.

Budget Com.—Betz, Chairman. Acceptance moved and seconded. Discussion. Motion carried.

Membership Com.—Herbert, Ch., introduced 2 new members—T. E. Gary and R. C. Taylor.

Nominating Com.—Overly, Ch. Officers nominated for year beginning Aug. 1.
President—Shorten, Clevelle

Vice President—Horgan, Steer
Secretary—Bruck, Anderson
Treasurer—Murphy, Hartline

Acceptance of report moved, seconded, and passed. No nominations from floor. Nominations closed by motion. Bavin announced election of officers to be held at next regular meeting as provided in the constitution.

Clevelle, Ch. of Program Com., reminded members of golf tournament and dinner—Oakdale Country Club, afternoon and evening of June 29.

Steer introduced Mr. Donald Durst of Atlanta as speaker. Subject—"Trends in Installment Credit." Question and answer period.

Mr. Bavin announced July 27—date of next reg. meeting.

Motion for adjournment carried—9:37 p.m.

■ **2.** You have been appointed chairman of a committee in the local chapter of The National Secretaries Association (International) to prepare a resolution of appreciation of the services of Miss Janet Godfrey, who founded the local chapter and is retiring as president after serving two terms. Miss Godfrey is also a member of the State Board of the organization and has contributed two articles to the national magazine.

Draw up the resolution to be presented at the meeting.

■ **3.** Prepare the following notices of meetings, sending them in the name of your employer, Ms. Jane Tully, who is secretary of both organizations:

### (1)

Send a double postcard notice of a luncheon meeting of the Metropolitan Club at one o'clock at Yeatman's Tearoom, on June 24, to Mr. Charles Steele, 816 East Third Street, Des Moines 50309. The topic of a panel discussion that will constitute the program is: "How to Make Des Moines Schools Better." The return portion of the double postcard will include space for the member to state his intentions about attending the meeting, any plans to bring a guest, and his signature. Experiment with the organization of the material until you feel that you have designed the notice in the most effective and attractive way so that you can use it as a model for each monthly meeting.

### (2)

Also send Mr. Steele a notice of the monthly social meeting of the Hobby Club to be held Friday night of next week at 8:30 p.m. at the home of the president, J. C. Garson, at 6118 Grand Vista Avenue. Mr. Garson would like to know how many are planning to attend because refreshments are to be served. Ask that Mr. Steele call your office, 351-6866, by Monday evening. There will be a special display of woodworking projects.

■ **4.** Compose and type an interoffice communication notifying the key men in the factory of a conference to be held on safety measures. There have been four accidents in the past month, one fatal. Each man is to come prepared with specific suggestions on safety measures and ways to improve the safety record. The meeting will be held in the Foremen's Dining Room at 3:45 p.m. ten days from today. The following men are asked to attend:

| | | |
|---|---|---|
| N. A. Daniell | John Whitford | James Rahn |
| Paul G. King | Carl Gates | Clyde Richardson |

■ **5.** A secretary involved in planning an annual sales meeting searched the files relating to last year's meeting and discovered that:

One salesman arrived at the Boston hotel at the last minute and could not locate the meeting room.

One salesman asked to be excused because he and his wife had completed all travel arrangements for a trip to Europe during his month's vacation before he found out the date of the conference.

The charts her employer wanted to use in illustrating his opening talk were not delivered to him in the meeting room because he was not registered at the hotel but commuted from Cambridge.

Considerable effort was needed to get expense reports from two salesmen.

Something happened to the tape recorder, so no record was made of the report on new products to be marketed.

Some of the salesmen paid for their rooms themselves, and the hotel inadvertently charged the company for them again.

Some of the salesmen could not get into their rooms until 4 p.m. on the first afternoon of the conference although they arrived at 8 a.m.

**In preparation for this year's conference, the secretary is asked to submit a plan for handling the details before and during the conference (which she will attend) so that everything will run smoothly.**

■ **6.** The director of research at American Chemical Company assigned his secretary, Mary Johnson, to supervise the preparation of the proceedings of a special national conference on enzymes. The conference was attended by scientists from industry and education. At the conference the research director asked that each of the fifteen participants who had read papers give Miss Johnson a two-page summary of his paper for the conference records.

Miss Johnson finished the necessary post-conference chores and opened her brief case to start her editorial work. She found that she had:

   8 summaries that required very little work
   3 summaries that were written in first person
   1 summary that was in outline form
   1 summary that filled 15 pages
   1 summary with neither name nor title
 18 unmarked reels of tape (recording the complete program)
 60 conference registration cards with no addresses

She remembered that the German participant whose summary was missing planned a three-month sightseeing trip in the United States and Canada.

**What is your evaluation of Miss Johnson's preplanning? How can this year's experience be utilized in planning for next year's conference?**

# Part 6

## CASE PROBLEMS

## 6-1 CONFIDENTIALITY OF OFFICE INFORMATION

As secretary to the president of a small service company, Mildred McGuirr supervised the 15 members of the office staff. She was aware that Eileen Barton, a 20-year-old girl in charge of the files, gossiped about office matters, usually those involving the personal conduct of colleagues.

She was surprised, however, when one of the older and more responsible members of the staff made the more serious complaint to her that Eileen had revealed confidential information about salaries, company negotiations with other groups, and proposed changes in personnel. The woman cited proof of her statements.

Mildred decided to have a conference with Eileen in which she would stress the importance of keeping confidential information confidential, especially in the case of an employee having ready access to company business materials.

**What approach should Mildred have taken during the interview? Can you simulate the conversation?**

## 6-2 HANDLING A SUPERVISORY PROBLEM

The office of the Regal Manufacturing Company has grown from a small office of three employees supervised by Mr. Thompson, president of the company, to an office staff of 20 employees. Up to now, the office staff was responsible to certain officials of the company; that is, certain staff members were responsible to the sales manager, others to the production manager, and so forth. Mr. Thompson has decided to reorganize the office and place the entire staff under the direct supervision of an office manager. Mary Adams has been Mr. Thompson's secretary for the past ten years and has grown with the company. She knows almost all of its operations and policies; she is company-minded and loyal. She knows all of the employees well and is well liked. Mr. Thompson decides that she would be the logical one to place in the newly created position of office supervisor. Mary accepts the position.

Mary's attitude is that she has not changed merely because her title has changed; therefore, she will continue her very close personal friendships with certain members of the office staff. It is Mary's plan to continue to identify with the secretarial and clerical staff, and not with the supervisory staff of the company. Thus, she will continue to eat lunch with the girls in the office and be concerned with their personal problems as she has in the past. The one thing she isn't going to be is high-hat or basically changed in her relationship with her fellow workers.

When a new employee comes to the office, Mary always makes it clear that, although she is technically the office supervisor, she wants to be treated and considered just as a member of the office gang. Her function is to help them, not to supervise them.

Mary is very hesitant to delegate difficult or unpleasant duties to other members of the staff. She feels that she should not ask others to do things that she herself would not like to do; as a result, she herself does many of the really tough jobs and more unpleasant chores. Whenever she assigns responsibilities, she always does it in the name of some other company official, such as "Mr. Thompson would like you to do this"; or "Mr. Franklin asked me to ask you to do this."

Working on the assumption that most problems will take care of themselves, if just given time, she plans to avoid becoming involved in arbitrating personality problems that arise among the office staff except when the situation becomes extremely serious. She is determined that she is not going to meddle in the petty frictions that are certain to arise when people work together.

**How successful do you think Mary Adams will be as a supervisor?**

**Is Mary the kind of person for whom you would like to work?**

**Can a supervisor maintain close personal friendships with her working staff?**

**Should a supervisor ask a subordinate to do a task that she would not wish to do herself?**

**To what extent should a supervisor become involved in attempting to solve the petty personality problems of the office staff?**

## 6-3 SNOOPING

When Elizabeth Jacobs returned to her desk from a dictation session with her employer, she surprised John Billings, a young assistant treasurer, while he was rummaging through the folders on her desk in which she kept confidential materials.

Obviously embarrassed, John said, "Oh, Elizabeth, I tried to call you; but nobody answered your telephone. I wanted some information about the Higgins announcement because I must plan to reproduce and mail it before the first of the month. I couldn't seem to find it."

**What principle should govern Elizabeth's handling of the situation?**

**What should she say to someone who outranks her? What should she do?**

# Collecting, Processing, and Presenting Business Data

*— Allstate*

*Part* **7**

*R*eliance upon the speedy processing of the tremendous bulk of incoming and outgoing data is a reality of today's business. Without the aid of electronics as applied to data processing, our largest business organizations would be unable to function: Without information essential for management decisions; without instant communications between the main office and its branches; without meaningful reports, tables, charts, and other graphic presentations of facts, business couldn't function. Involvement in the presentation of data gives the secretary a splendid opportunity to prove her value as an administrative assistant.

# Chapter 18

# DATA PROCESSING AND COMMUNICATION

The office has been aptly described as the nerve center of the business —the center for planning, recording, and communicating activities. Budgets must be compiled; production schedules developed; raw materials, equipment, supplies, and labor purchased; orders processed; payrolls prepared; records with customers and creditors maintained; costs computed; and financial information communicated to stockholders and others. Most of these activities involve data processing— that is, the recording, coding, sorting, calculating, summarizing, storing, and communicating of data for more effective management of the business. Information is processed manually, electromechanically using the punched-card system, or electronically through the use of the computer.

High-speed data processing systems have become essential because of rapid expansion of business and markets and because of the need for better production control and increased office efficiency. In addition, more and more immediate data are required by management in order to keep businesses competitive. Responsible management decisions require that voluminous data be processed and reported in time for action. These requirements have necessitated the constant search for faster and more efficient ways to handle data, so that decisions may be formed on the basis of up-to-date, accurate information.

The modern office uses many machines and facilities in *processing data*. Some—typewriters, duplicators, copiers, and calculators—the secretary uses regularly in her work; others, like punched-card equipment, tape-activated machines, and the electronic computer, she may or may not operate—but they are important to her work. The computer and the telecommunication system are revolutionizing office work and present an entirely new method of operation for the executive. Undoubtedly, in tomorrow's office, the computer will be as commonplace as is today's electric typewriter and copying machine.

The secretary is not expected to be a specialist in office automation. As a key person on the office staff, however, she must understand the concept of office automation, the functions involved, and the various methods of processing data.

## COMMON MACHINE-LANGUAGE MEDIA

The volume of paper (forms, statements, reports, communications) in business has been growing at a fantastic rate and will undoubtedly continue to do so. Billions of pieces of paper are processed annually on a vast array of key-depression machines such as typewriters, teletypewriters, calculating and adding machines, payroll machines, checkwriters, and bookkeeping machines found in most large offices. They are called key-depression machines because they are activated by an operator who depresses keys.

In processing data the identical information may be written many times; thus the identical key strokes are repeated over and over. For example, a sales order sets in motion the preparation of a variety of other pieces of paper. These include inventory forms, sales-record forms, production forms and reports, shipping orders, bills of lading, customer invoices, accounts receivable records, and company reports. Some identical information is written on each of these.

In one firm a count revealed that in processing a sales transaction, identical information was recorded nine times; thus nine repetitions on key-depression machines were required; and *each had to be checked for accuracy*.

### Work Simplification

Several means have been devised to decrease the manual writing of the same information on different forms and in different offices in the same company and thus keep the business from being drowned in a sea of paper work. Carbon-interleaved multipurpose forms, pegboard one-write systems, window envelopes, embossed metal plates for names and addresses, and multiple forms produced via duplicating machines (as explained on page 119) permit one writing or one typing to produce several different forms required to process the information. Edge-notched cards have simplified sorting applications.

These methods have reduced, but have not eliminated, repetitive writing. Furthermore, they do not save time and labor in processing repeat orders—orders from the same customer for the same items which comprise the bulk of the business of many firms. The basic need for large-scale paper work production, therefore, is to capture the data on one machine and then reproduce the same data, when needed, by mechanical or electronic means on other machines. This procedure requires the use of common machine-language media—a code system that can communicate between machines—that is, a language that machines can read and use to activate other machines. Punched-card code and channel code (tape) are forms of common machine language.

## Common-Language Tape

Punched or perforated tape was initially developed to communicate between machines used in telecommunication. It was later adapted for use in other office operations.

**Teletype Machine (Teleprinter; Teletypewriter).** The *teleprinter* and the *teletypewriter* are equipped to produce punched tape and also may be activated (operated) by tape. When connected through the facilities of the telephone or telegraph company, these machines transmit written conversation to a distant point just as the telephone transmits vocal conversation. Although transmission may be direct from machine to machine, it is frequently done via paper tape, as the tape may be sent at a much faster rate. As the message is typed on the teleprinter or teletypewriter, a five-channel paper tape is produced. The tape is then used to transmit the message over the wire. The receiving teleprinter or teletypewriter reproduces the communication in page copy in multiple copies if desired. It can also produce a tape as a by-product.

**Automatic Typewriters.** The automatic typewriter was the first machine to use punched tape for the handling of routine correspondence. Many businesses have a certain number of form letters—letters of acknowledgment, sales letters, letters of credit standing, collection letters. Standard paragraphs can be recorded on punched tapes or perforated rolls and fed into an automatic typewriter as needed. The operation can be so planned as to provide for an automatic halt of the typewriter at appropriate places to permit manual insertions of the date, inside addresses, salutations, appropriate figures, and other entries necessary to personalize the letter. The finished letters look like individually typed letters, for they are.

**Tape-Activated Office Machines.** Punched tape is now used to operate other office machines. Typewriters, adding, calculating, billing, payroll, bookkeeping, and other machines can produce tapes as by-products of their normal operations. These machines are also activated by paper tape. Punched tape thus has become a *common machine language*—that is, the tape produced by one office machine can be read by a number of different types of office machines. The holes punched in the tape represent letters, numbers, and special characters. The punches appear to run in channels the length of the tape although the machine reads the punches *across* the tape.

To process a sales order, for example, a tape-reading typewriter reads punched tape by sensing the difference between the punched holes

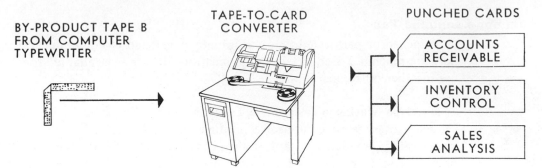

BY-PRODUCT TAPE B
FROM COMPUTER
TYPEWRITER

TAPE-TO-CARD
CONVERTER

PUNCHED CARDS

ACCOUNTS
RECEIVABLE

INVENTORY
CONTROL

SALES
ANALYSIS

Shown above is a schematic drawing of the automated processing of a sales order.

and the unbroken tape. From master tape files, two tapes—one containing customer information such as the firm name, location, salesman, shipping instructions, and terms and the other containing stock information—are located and fed into the tape-reading typewriter to type the shipping order. The operator makes manual insertions where necessary. The machine that types the data on the order form automatically prepares a punched tape as a by-product. The by-product tape is used to operate a computer-typewriter that performs the calculations and types the invoice from the tape, the next step in the operation. The computer-typewriter prepares a by-product tape which is used in the preparation of account records, inventory controls, and reports. Note that the tape produced in the one recording of the data could be used repeatedly, thus eliminating the manual typing of such details as names, addresses, descriptions, and prices.

**Reading Tape.** The tape developed by the communication industry for use with the Teletype machine was five-channel tape. The following illustration shows the coding that is used. A single hole punched into the top channel represents the letter *E* or the figure *3*. *A* and the hyphen (-) are coded by holes in the first and second channels.

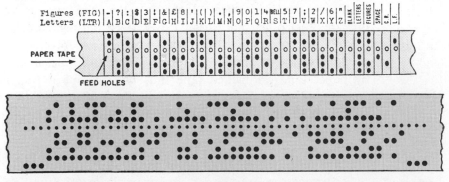

The lower tape is the coding for the title of this book, *Secretarial Procedures and Administration*.

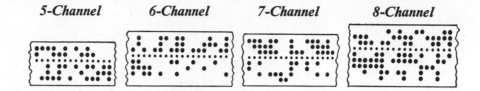

| 5-Channel | 6-Channel | 7-Channel | 8-Channel |
| --- | --- | --- | --- |

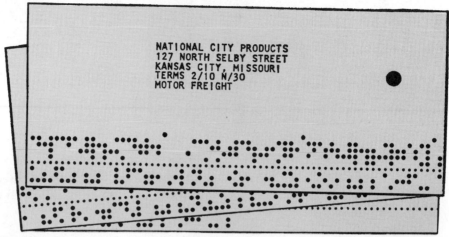

NATIONAL CITY PRODUCTS
127 NORTH SELBY STREET
KANSAS CITY, MISSOURI
TERMS 2/10 N/30
MOTOR FREIGHT

*—Friden, Inc.*

This common-language card has been edge-punched in eight-channel tape. The cards are sectioned for folding in seven-inch lengths. As many sections as necessary for all the desired data may be used and retained as one unit. The printed information appears in readable position when the card is filed and the lower edge of the card is punched.

The number of different letters, figures, special characters, and tabulations that can be coded on five channels is restricted. This limitation led to the development of six-, seven-, and eight-channel tapes illustrated above. The increased number of channels enables the coding of upper- and lowercase letters and additional special characters. An extra channel also permits a mechanical method of checking accuracy of the tape.

Tape can be used to communicate between offices. It can be transmitted by wire, or it can be mailed. Thus, tape used in preparing an invoice can be sent to the warehouse in a distant city where it can be used to prepare such forms as the shipping order and bill of lading.

## Edge-Punched Cards

In addition to tape, edge-punched cards are also used as a common-language medium. Data are punched along the edge of the card in channel code. Edge-punched cards offer the advantages of easy filing

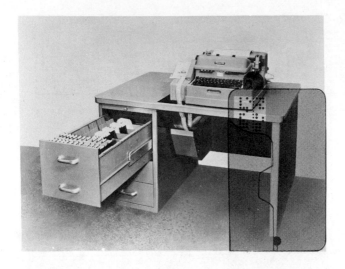

Punched paper tape and edge-punched cards are filed in a number of ways. One common method is to label and file each tape alphabetically or numerically in a small jacket or pocket card. The jacket can also indicate what is on the tape. The operator removes the jacket just as he might take a letter from a file folder.

—*Shaw Walker Co.*

and location, durability, and visible reproduction on the card of the punched data. Many machines can handle both tape and edge-punched cards. The cards can vary in width and can be punched on either edge or on both edges.

## PUNCHED-CARD (UNIT-RECORD) SYSTEM

The principle of the punched-card system is that data (words and figures) are "written" in the form of holes punched in cards according to a predetermined code and location plan. Machines that sense the location of the holes read and act upon the information as the cards are run through. They can sort the cards into desired groups; they can perform required calculations, such as additions, subtractions, multiplications; and they can decode the information back to written words and figures.

Although the punched-card system is fast becoming obsolete, computer installations often use these machines as auxiliary facilities. For this reason, a basic understanding of the system is desirable.

### Punched-Card Equipment

There are four basic machines used in the process: the keypunch, the sorter, the calculator, and the tabulator.

**Keypunch.** The *keypunch* is the initial machine used to process the data. It is operated manually by depressing keys set upon a typewriter-like keyboard. The operator takes the data from the original document

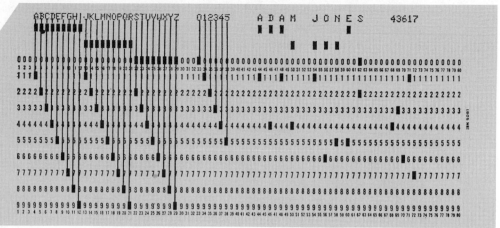

—IBM Corporation

This card illustrates the meaning of the punched holes. Each letter has its own combination of two punches in one vertical column: one punch in one of three positions at the top of the card and the other punched in one of the figures in the same column. Note that the letter *A* is represented by a punch in the top position plus a punch in the figure *1* (in Column 4). The letter *W* is represented by a punch in the zero row (the lowest position at the top of the card) and in the figure *6*. A column with only one punch represents the actual figure punched, as shown in Columns 68–72 on this card. The cards feed through the machine and activate the equipment electrically.

—a sales order, an invoice, or a payroll sheet—and "types" the keys according to an established sequence to enter the data upon cards in the form of holes.

Since there is always the possibility of the operator's making an error, the punched cards are checked for accuracy by using either an *interpreter* or a *verifier*. The machine referred to as the *interpreter* reads back the data recorded by the holes on the card and prints the data on the card where they can be verified by reading. The key *verifier* is similar to a keypunch machine. The original data are again punched on the verifier. A comparison of the results with the first card will reveal any error that may have been made on the card.

A recent development is a keypunch with a memory unit. This machine speeds the punching of the cards by making it possible to key data into the memory unit rather than directly onto the cards. Thus, errors can easily be corrected by the keypunch operator by merely backspacing and correcting the characters before the cards are actually punched.

A *reproducer* is used to read all or part of the data in an existing punched card and punch the desired data into duplicate cards automatically. Data from two or more cards also can be combined and punched into one card by the reproducer.

**Sorter.** The punched cards can be sorted in numeric or alphabetic sequence or classified into groups or sequences by a machine called a *sorter*. The sorter consists of a reading device (to pick out holes on the card), a rack of pockets, and a mechanism to shunt the cards into their appropriate pockets. If the sales manager, for example, wished to know the total sales made by a salesman, all the sales orders (on punched cards) would be run through the sorter. This machine would pick out those cards (orders) which had a hole or holes in a certain coded location designating the salesman. All cards with holes in this coded location would be directed by the machine into a separate pocket and thus separated from the rest of the orders.

A *collator* is a special type of sorter that is capable of taking two batches of cards and combining them into one sequenced deck.

**Calculator.** The *calculator* reads the information on the punched card, performs the calculations required, and produces the result in punched holes on the card.

On a sales invoice, for example, the calculator will multiply the unit price by the number of units for each item, record the extension amount for each item, the total for the order, the amount of discount, and net amount of the invoice.

**Tabulator.** The principal elements of the *tabulator* are a reading unit, a printing device, and a series of accumulators.

The reading unit senses the holes in the cards and activates type bars which print the data on sheets of paper forms fed through the machine. The accumulators add, subtract, and produce totals. The three components—reading unit, printer, and accumulator—are interconnected through the control panel or wiring unit. The tabulator may be wired to accumulate, summarize, and print all or part of the data for all or part of a group of cards.

The principle of the punched card system is illustrated on page 426 in the processing of a sales order.

## Limitations of the Punched-Card and Punched-Tape Systems

Punched-card and -tape systems greatly increase the speed of processing certain types of data. They also increase accuracy and eliminate a great deal of manual effort. They are, however, restricted in the extent to which they can take alternative courses of action in the processing operation. Each of these systems, therefore, must be conducted in sections, not as one continuous process. The operator makes required decisions between steps and transfers the cards or tape manually from one machine to the next. Although they are rapid as compared with strictly manual methods, they are exceedingly slow when compared with electronic data processing which is described in the following section.

## ELECTRONIC DATA PROCESSING

The electronic data processing system (EDP), consisting of input equipment, a central processing unit (the computer), and output equipment, offers a number of advantages over the punched-card or punched-tape systems. In the electronic system, data are processed several hundred times faster than with the punched-card system; the processing is a continuous chain of operations performed within the system; information can be stored for immediate or future use in the computer's memory component; operations are performed by reading a program of instructions into the computer system; and decisions and alternate courses of action are possible through the logic unit of the computer.

This section discusses the basic elements of the electronic data processing system—the input media and devices, the central processing unit, output media and equipment, and computer applications.

### Input Media and Devices

The term *input* describes the act of introducing data into an electronic data processing system. The input data may be any data upon which one or more of the basic data processing functions are to be performed—recording, coding, sorting, calculating, summarizing, storing, and communicating. An *input medium* is the machine-language form used by the system. An *input device* is equipment used to read the input medium into the computer system. Input devices vary with the types of input media used.

**Punched Tape and Punched Card.** The punched tape and punched card discussed earlier can be used to introduce source data to the computer system. High-speed readers convert the punched holes into coded electrical impulses which in turn are transmitted to the central processing unit.

To carry out its work, the central processing system must be given specific, step-by-step instructions as to what it is to do. These instructions are called the *program*. The program is usually recorded on punched cards or tape and fed into the central processing unit by the input equipment.

The activities surrounding the secretary's desk often correspond to the basic elements of a computer system. Here the secretary combines several data sources (dictation and research notes) into a report. She follows the form and style set forth in her operating procedures manual.

**Magnetic Tape.** A more sophisticated computer-system input medium than the punched-card or paper tape is magnetic tape. Besides being a high-speed input medium, magnetic tape has the additional capabilities of erasability and storage capacity for much more information.

Magnetic tape is plastic, coated with a metallic oxide, and comes in widths of ½ to 1 inch and lengths of 2,400 to 3,600 feet per reel. Data are recorded on the tape as invisible magnetized spots that, when read into the system, create electrical impulses. As on punched tape, data are recorded in channels. A tape drive unit is used to read the magnetized spots to the computer.

Magnetic tape is considered a sequential access medium; that is, what is first on the reel is read first, what is second is read second, and so forth. In other words, in order to locate information halfway through the tape, all the preceding material must be read first. For some business operations, such as periodic updating of customer accounts, the magnetic tape is ideal; but where information is scattered throughout a tape, the computer access time necessary to reach the desired data can delay the processing.

Error detection on magnetic tape is comparatively difficult; some installations, therefore, record source information on punched cards and then convert the cards to magnetic tape for reading into the computer system, thus combining the advantages of both media.

A recent trend is keying data directly to magnetic tape for reading to the computer, using a keyboard similar to that of an electric typewriter. Further, with recent technological advances, the operator can key data on miniature magnetic tapes in tape cassettes, which the computer can then convert to run-size tape for processing. This operation can even be a by-product of the original business typing.

Key-to-tape input, with no time for converting cards to tape, cuts processing time as much as 20 percent.

**Magnetic Disc.** Magnetic discs are thin, circular metal plates, coated on both sides with ferrous oxide. In appearance, a file of magnetic discs resembles a stack of phonograph records. Information is recorded and stored as magnetic spots on both sides of a disc, using various key-to-disc devices, and can be transferred from the disc to a tape for processing by the computer.

While magnetic tape is a *sequential-access* medium (the computer must search from the beginning of the tape for desired data), magnetic discs are a *random-access* medium (the computer can go directly to any disc in the file and retrieve desired data). Thus access time to retrieve information is shorter with magnetic discs than with magnetic tape; and the discs, like the tape, are durable and erasable. This equipment is used in computer installations for large-volume storage capacity.

**Magnetic Ink and Optical Character Recognition.** Symbols and numbers imprinted in magnetic ink can be read and processed electronically by a Magnetic Ink Character Recognition (MICR) reader. This process is used mainly in the banking industry where customer checks and deposit slips are numbered with magnetic ink in a standard type *font* ( a complete assortment of type in one size or style). The use of magnetic ink has greatly automated banking transactions.

The Optical Character Recognition (OCR) reader reads and translates printed or handwritten characters into machine language and transfers the data directly into the computer system. Since no special ink is required, large billing companies like the petroleum industry, catalog houses, and utility companies commonly use this process for their credit account numbers.

MAGNETIC INK CHARACTER RECOGNITION CHART — E-13B type font

| 0 | 1 | 2 | 3 | 4 | 5 | 6 | 7 | 8 | 9 |
|---|---|---|---|---|---|---|---|---|---|
| ZERO | ONE | TWO | THREE | FOUR | FIVE | SIX | SEVEN | EIGHT | NINE |

AMOUNT SYMBOL    ON US SYMBOL    TRANSIT NUMBER SYMBOL    DASH SYMBOL

# INPUT DEVICES: WHAT THEY ARE AND HOW THEY WORK

| The Way It Works | | Advantages |
|---|---|---|
| **Keypunch:** A keyboard-operated electromechanical device punches holes in the cards according to a prearranged code. |  | Most efficient system for straight forward, standard data. Inexpensive. Easy to operate. |
| **Buffered Keypunch:** By storing two card records in a small core memory, it actually punches one card while the operator is keying the next. |  | Verifying and punching can be combined in one unit. Duplication and skipping at electronic rather than mechanical speeds. Backspace and strikeover capabilities. |
| **Key to Tape:** Allows recording data directly onto magnetic tape in the format in which they were entered. Can be immediately processed by the computer. |  | Eliminates card-to-tape conversion and hardware needed for that conversion. Can record up to 120 characters per line. |
| **Key to Cassette:** Data are recorded directly on a small magnetic-tape cassette, converted later to full-size mag tape for acceptance by the computer. |  | Eliminates need for separate verifiers. Works at electronic speeds. Can be used anywhere data are originated. |
| **Optical Scanning (OCR):** Reads documents printed or handwritten in an alphanumeric font, transmitting the data directly to the computer, bypassing human data preparation. |  | Keyboarding errors eliminated. Faster input of data. Economical for extremely heavy data-entry loads. |
| **Shared Processor:** Also called "key to disc." Data are keyed onto a random access storage disc or drum built around a dedicated central processor. Output is on computer-compatible mag tape. |  | Up to 64 keystations can be handled per system. Edits and validates off-line. Unlimited record lengths and formats. Data can be re-formatted before going to mainframe. |

*Source:* Administrative Management © Geyer-McAllister Publications, Inc.

Input data is stored in a buffer area while the operator verifies the data visually on the televisionlike display screen that is possible with cathode-ray tube equipment.

—*Mohawk Data Sciences Corporation*

**Cathode-Ray Tube.** The cathode-ray tube (CRT) displays input data in much the manner of a television set. The unit contains a keyboard, a display screen, and a buffer storage area in which input information is retained while the operator verifies the information. Input data are submitted to the computer by using the keyboard or a light pen or by activating by touching sensitized points on the tube.

**Console Typewriter.** Although the console typewriter keyboard *can* introduce data directly into the system, it is too slow for volume input and is used primarily for direct communication with the central processing unit, such as asking questions.

## Central Processing Unit

The heart of the electronic data processing system is the *central processing unit*. It consists of (1) an internal storage or memory file, (2) an arithmetic-logic component, and (3) a control unit.

**Storage or Memory File.** *Storage* (frequently called memory, or memory file) is where data and programs are stored magnetically.

Storage is organized into thousands of individual locations, each with a unique address by which it can be located in the same manner that a house can be located by a street address. The speed with which the processing unit can locate an address in the storage or memory file and transfer the amount in the computer's "address" to the arithmetic component is referred to as *access time*. Since large processors can perform several hundred operations per second, the access time to stored data is critical; that is, slow access time uses up valuable computer time.

Most computers have two types of storage, internal and bulk (external). The internal storage is quick-access storage. The quick-access storage holds the program and the data that are being used at the time.

**Arithmetic-Logic Component.** The arithmetic section of the computer is like an electronic calculator, electronically performing addition, subtraction, multiplication, and division. It can also make certain logical decisions concerning the data being processed.

*Arithmetic Ability.* This component has two sections, the adder circuits and the accumulator registers. The calculations are performed in the adder section at lightning speed measured in *microseconds* (millionths of a second) and sometimes in *nanoseconds* (billionths of a second) of time. Naturally, this time varies with the size and complexity of the unit. A small computer might require .001 second to multiply a four-digit number by a five-digit number (a thousand microseconds).

The *accumulator* is that portion of the arithmetic unit where results (answers) of the arithmetic operation are temporarily stored until the calculation is complete. The instructions may direct the equipment to:

(1) Copy a number from a storage location into the accumulator.
(2) Get a second number from a storage location and add it to the number in the accumulator.
(3) Multiply the sum of the two numbers (in the accumulator) by 25 and return the answer to storage.

*Decision-Making Ability.* One of the distinctive qualities of the computer is its ability to select among alternate courses of action. This is frequently referred to as decision-making ability. The computer can be programmed to examine a figure and determine if it is above or below a certain amount. If it is above, the computer will follow one set of instructions. If it is below, the computer will follow another set. This decision-making ability makes it possible, once data and a program have been fed into the system, for the computer to complete a sequence of operations automatically. For instance, it can process a payroll without any further human intervention after data on the individual time cards are fed into the computer. It calculates the wage for each employee, searches out his payroll information and obtains the number of withholding tax exemptions and then determines the withholding tax and social security tax, makes other approved deductions, determines the net pay, and prints the paycheck. In addition, it stores the payroll information and produces complete payroll information on each employee and prints the W-2 forms (Withholding Tax Statements). A payroll for several thousand employees can be completed within a few hours.

**Control Unit.** This unit directs the many functions of the computer system. It seeks instructions from the storage files, interprets, and executes them; it internally controls operations of the input devices, the storage unit, the arithmetic-logic unit, and the output devices.

An operator may communicate with the computer through the console typewriter keyboard. For example, the operator may use the keyboard to ask the balance of an account. The typewriter then receives and types the computer's responses.

## Output Media and Equipment

*Output* refers to information processed by the computer. The *output medium* is the form on which the processed information appears. The *output device* is the equipment connected to the system that records or displays the processed data. The information can be in the form of punched cards, tape, or magnetic tape for use in further data processing, or records, reports, visual displays, or voice responses for people to use.

**Punched Tape, Cards, Magnetic Tape.** Data can be printed out on tape, cards, or magnetic tape and stored; and it can be transferred by telecommunication to a central computer, later to be read into the same computer. Output devices include card punches, tape punches, and magnetic tape units.

**Records and Reports.** Processed information in the form of records and reports are printed on high-speed printing equipment that usually prints a whole line of characters at one time. Printers are of two types, *impact* and *nonimpact*. Impact printers print by means of a type bar that presses against a paper and ribbon. Nonimpact printers print information photographically. In terms of speed, many line (impact) printers can print at 1,000 lines a minute while nonimpact printers can produce up to 5,000 lines a minute. The printing requires no special paper and can be used with business forms and gummed labels.

The end product may be a sales analysis, payroll checks, utility bills, statistical reports, invoices, cost distribution, and the like.

**Visual Display.** The cathode-ray tube (CRT) serves as both an input and an output medium. (See page 435.)

**Voice Response.** For businesses like airlines, transportation companies, and banks, the most convenient means of data retrieval are voice-response terminals. For example, a salesman can dial directly into the computer system and submit data orally by merely placing a telephone receiver on the unit's adapter or interface. To check the credit reference of a customer, a bank representative can dial into the computer and a voice will respond with the requested information. The words come from a vocabulary stored in the system and are generally restricted to the basic type of information processed.

# A GUIDE TO DATA PROCESSING TERMS

**Access Time.** The time required for the computer to locate data in its memory or storage section

**Binary Number System.** A number system using the base 2 (There are only two symbols: 1 or 0 — zero. In the electronic data processing system this is represented by "on" or "off" pulses.)

**Common Language.** A term used to describe punched paper tape, edge-punched cards, punched cards, or magnetic tape which may be read by and used to activate various office machines

**Control Console.** A panel through which the operator regulates the flow of data and instructions to the computer

**Erase.** To remove information stored on a magnetic drum, magnetic tape, magnetic disc, or other storage device

**Hardware.** The components or configuration of machines (such as input, output, or power units) which make up a system of equipment

**Input.** Information (data) being transferred into the computer

**Instruction.** A coded symbol or word which tells the computer to perform some operation

**Memory.** Devices used for the internal storage of data such as magnetic tapes, magnetic drums, magnetic discs, and magnetic cores

**Microsecond.** One millionth of a second

**Millisecond.** One thousandth of a second

**Nanosecond.** One billionth of a second

**Off-Line and On-Line Operation.** The operation of peripheral equipment that is not in direct communication (off-line) or in direct connection (on-line) with the central processing unit of the computer

**Output.** Information produced by the computer

**Peripheral Equipment.** Equipment used in conjunction with a computer but not a part of the computer itself; that is, a converter, optical scanner, tape reader, printer

**Printer.** The machine that prints the output from the computer

**Read, Read In, Read Out.** The operation of transferring information from one location to another.

**Software.** Programming aids, such as routines, applications, programs available to the computer

**Storage.** A general term used for the ability of the machine to hold information (This is frequently referred to as the memory.)

**Write.** The operation of storing a number on the surface of a magnetic tape, or drum, transferring information to an output medium

**Updating.** The process of bringing data stored in the computer memory unit up to current value

## Minicomputers

With the development of the minicomputer, it is almost certain that within this decade every business concern will either own a computer or have access to one. Although the minicomputer has a smaller capacity and slower speeds than the larger computer systems, it has definite advantages. Minicomputers are flexible: They can form the entire computer system for a firm or can supplement a larger system; and they can be programmed at the user's office. In addition, "minis" are comparatively low in cost and have attractive rental and leasing possibilities.

## Computer Applications

Since the computer is capable of making routine decisions, it is being successfully used as an accounting device to perform many types of routine jobs which formerly required clerical workers. Computer installations perform payroll calculations, update accounts receivable and payable, control inventories, process insurance data, prepare dividend checks, keep depositors' checking accounts, distribute costs and expenses, make out bills for telephone and electric utilities, and analyze personnel data. The ability of the computer to do routine work is causing major changes in the office structure and in the clerical occupations.

The computer can help to eliminate part of the guesswork in long-range business planning. The projected activities of a business for one, two, or three years in advance can be simulated and fed into the computer. Within minutes, the computer can report the results, completing calculations that would take a man with pencil and paper many years to do. On the basis of the computer's reports, management can proceed with or modify its projected activities.

## Developments in Data Communication

Coupled with the development of the computer have been significant developments in the area of data communication—the transmission of data from one point to another. These developments have made possible transmitting large volumes of data, at high speeds, over long distances, at relatively low cost. Thus it is possible and economical to communicate data from their point of origin to a central data processing center and then to transmit the processed data back to the point of origin.

The telephone connection that permits voice transmission over distances is now being used to transmit data in other forms. The telegraph circuit, microwave, and broadband telephone lines are other services commonly used for data transmission.

To transmit information, however, the data must be converted into a medium that not only can be carried over the telephone wire or microwave system but also can be understood by the receiving computer. Conversely, data from the computer must be reconverted to a medium acceptable at the remote facility. Descriptions of several devices follow.

The use of the telephone to communicate with the computer is a major advance in data processing technology. The telephone equipment generally used to connect with a computer and to send and receive information is the *Touch-Tone telephone*, although the dial telephone is used in some installations. The pushbuttons on the Touch-Tone telephone facilitate the transmission of data. Keying the code number of the distant computer facility sends *tones* over the regular telephone lines. Contact is made with the computer, and data are sent and received.

In addition to the telephone devices at the originating location and at the remote computer facility, it is necessary to have a telephone attachment that converts the *tones* into business machine signals at the computer terminal and, in reply, changes the business machine signals to tones for transmission to the originating station. This device is the *modem*, an acronym for Modulator-demodulator (also known as a *data set*). In effect, the modem is a translator. It is the equipment that hooks an EDP terminal to the telephone lines. Although the American Telephone and Telegraph Company manufactures and leases modems to business users, other companies also manufacture data sets.

The *Data-Phone* is a trademark of the American Telephone and Telegraph Company to identify its equipment used for data transmission over regular telephone lines. This equipment includes a telephone-like device and a data set, or *modem*.

While this discussion has focused on the use of the telephone as the primary input-output device in data communication, actually a wide range of communication terminals, with or without the telephone, can be used. Depending on the type of terminal used, it is possible to communicate with a distant computer by paper tape, punched cards, magnetic tape, visual display, graphic plotter, or any combination of these.

## Impact of EDP upon Business Management

The advent of electronic data processing has made absolutely necessary the "systems approach" in all phases of business operations.

Several alternatives to computer *ownership* are available to business. It is now possible to purchase time-sharing units from a large computer installation, to lease a computer, or to buy service from a data processing center. These alternatives are discussed in this section.

**Information Flow.**  Formerly it was impossible to communicate data from one location to another without an appreciable time interval.  Because the flow of information was restricted to one physical segment of an organization (one plant, one location), it was necessary to decentralize operations and management.  Decision making had to be delegated to management at the local level.

Improvements in the computer and telecommunication allow the flow of information through the entire business organization.  Corporate branches, regardless of geographical location, can be connected "on line" with a central computer.  Thus, each branch has a direct connection and can feed data into and receive answers back from the computer.

An illustration of the on-line process is the reservation system used by some airlines.  Each ticket sales office of the airline throughout the United States has an on-line connection with the computer center.  In a matter of seconds, a ticket agent can question the computer on space available on any flight, receive the reply, and ticket (reserve) the space.

In one company payroll, records are typed into a teleprinter and transmitted to a teleprinter at the central accounting center, where the data are converted to punched cards and processed.  At the end of the weekly payroll period, the processed data are transmitted to the local plant and automatically printed on checks that have been inserted into the keyboard printer.  Then they are signed by authorized personnel.

A department store with several branches accumulates data from the cash register in each department into a central processing center.  When a sale is recorded on any register, it is automatically and simultaneously transmitted to the processing center.  The center answers with voice response all requests for credit information, provides management with a daily report of sales in each department plus a comparison with last year's figures for the same day, analyzes sales trends, and compares the daily performance of each sales person with his previous records.

**Centralization of Management.**  Telecommunication is bringing about important changes in management operational patterns.  First, it is making all relevant facts immediately available to management.  Management can now know what is happening inside the company as soon as it happens.  Secondly, it is getting the information to management in "real time"; that is, in time to do something about it.  For example, the production costs of a branch operation may be gradually increasing.  Without the assistance of the computer, these costs could get far out of line before coming to the attention of management.  With the computer, coupled with data communication facilities, however, any change in costs can be known at once and corrective action taken.

Management can now measure the immediate effect of management decisions. This is known as "information feedback." A familiar illustration of the principle of feedback is the interaction between the thermostat and the air conditioner, which constantly interact to keep the room at a predetermined temperature. In a similar manner, the feedback through the computer permits management to regulate and initiate changes in costs, prices, profit margin, inventories, production, and so forth, in line with a predetermined plan.

Telecommunication is also making it possible to centralize management. Top management in the central office can now have access to everything important that is happening at any corporate outpost as soon as it happens. An executive in the central office can have data on each branch at the same time that the branch manager can have the data. Decisions can be made and fed back to the branch as rapidly as they could be made at the branch. Centralized control of decentralized operations is now a reality.

**Time Sharing.** A fast-growing industry practice in the data processing field is time sharing, a process by which a computer system serves many independent users at the same time. An individual firm has an input-output device in his facility connected by communication lines to a distant central processor. The computer receives data arriving simultaneously from many users, and by giving each user a small piece of its time, processes the data almost immediately. The user has his own set of computer programs and also has access to public programs.

**Leasing.** Another industry practice is to lease, from an independent leasing agency, computer equipment to be installed on the lessee's premises. Under this arrangement, the leasing agent buys the data processing equipment specified by the user and then leases it to the user.

**Data Processing Service Centers.** Commercial data processing service centers provide computer service to small businesses and handle overflow loads for larger companies that have their own installations.

Considerable diversity exists among data processing services. Well-established centers may provide a complete data processing service: analyze customer requirements, offer consulting services, prepare computer programs, and implement the programs on their own equipment.

Most service centers offer *batch* processing (periodic processing of data that have accumulated over a period of time, such as a monthly accounts receivable or a weekly payroll). The work is done on a fixed schedule. Some centers use time-sharing equipment, and some even provide batch processing from remote facilities.

Many service centers have ready-made programs for such routine jobs as payroll, inventory, receivables, payables, labor distribution, and sales analysis. The centers will also prepare financial reports, complete marketing data, and do complicated scientific calculations.

*—Administrative Management Society*

**Information Retrieval and Exchange.** *Information service centers* have evolved to provide subscribers with business, scientific, and technical information by direct connection with computers over telecommunication facilities.

For example, a business can subscribe to a local credit rating service that in turn is affiliated with a regional or national credit service. One strategically located center can store the credit ratings of most businesses and millions of individuals in its area.

## Automation and the Secretary

Automated data processing, coupled with improved data communication, is producing significant changes in office work. A major shift in emphasis is evident in work done by office personnel. Office workers are freed of the drudgery of detailed computations and file maintenance, with many of such functions being taken over by machines. On the other hand, the demand for persons trained in automated data processing is rapidly increasing. And there is an ever-increasing demand for highly trained secretaries. Technology has not devised a way to replace the secretary; for, as someone said, "Machines will never charm the boss's guests nor cover up for him when he goofs, but they *will* free the secretary from petty jobs—make her a more important person.

Technology is changing the role of the secretary. As office work becomes more automated, the work of the secretary is becoming less routinized and clerical in composition and more supervisory and administrative in nature. Many of the routine duties involving copying, calculating, sorting, and recording that have consumed so much of the secretary's time can now be done by automated processes. The secretary has more time to devote to supervisory and administrative functions and to tasks requiring imagination and initiative. Thus her position becomes not only stimulating and challenging but more important as well.

The computer has, in part, changed the secretary's role of compiler of data to one of screener of data—a role that involves decision making on an administrative level. She may interpret, pull figures, and set up reports from computer output. She may set up material for input into the computer system.

The centralization of data—made possible through the computer with its interconnections with all the branches and divisions of a company—brings a flood of data into the executives' offices. These data pass over the top-level secretary's desk. The secretary must perform the decision-making function of deciding what data are to be fed to the executive. This screening function conserves the executive's time.

In a large company, the secretary inevitably becomes the liaison person between her executive and the data processing department or computer center. Consequently, she must understand both management and data processing in order to interpret what data her employer requires.

The introduction of automated equipment into the office demands that the office personnel adjust to new procedures—a problem complicated because of the natural tendency to resist change. New knowledges and skills must be developed. Old ways must be abandoned and new procedures accepted. Thus, the supervisory role of the secretary becomes increasingly important. The staff, under the supervision of the secretary, must be conditioned to accept the new procedure. Training must be provided and new work standards developed. Changes in personnel may also be required. All these factors add to the secretary's responsibilities, but they also add to the prestige of her position.

As the secretary becomes more involved in decision making and administrative and supervisory responsibilities—a trend that automation is accelerating—her preparation must be equal to the demands. A broad understanding of economics and business organization and management is essential.

## SUGGESTED READINGS

Awad, Elias M. *Business Data Processing*, 3d ed. Englewood Cliffs: Prentice-Hall, Inc., 1971.

Gentle, Edgar C., Jr. *Data Communication in Business, An Introduction.* New York: American Telephone and Telegraph Co., 1965.

Neuner, John J. W., B. Lewis Keeling, and Norman F. Kallaus. *Administrative Office Management*, 6th ed. Cincinnati: South-Western Publishing Co., 1972.

Wanous, S. J., E. E. Wanous, and Gerald E. Wagner. *Fundamentals of Data Processing.* Cincinnati: South-Western Publishing Co., 1971.

## QUESTIONS FOR DISCUSSION

1. What functions must the equipment at a computer installation perform?

2. Why is accuracy so important in feeding input data into a computer system?

3. Identify the three major classes of personnel required in computer installations.

4. The statement has been made that businesses could not return to manual processing of data even if they wanted to. Why would this be true?

5. It has been said that, although the computer has contributed a great deal to one segment of our society in making information accessible, it has created a social hazard to the individual desiring privacy and the restriction of personal information. What are some situations in which an individual might feel that his right to privacy has been violated?

6. Give examples of ways in which electronic data processing and developments in telecommunications are revolutionizing management processes in business.

7. It has been stated that in the future top management in business will be less concerned with personnel relationships and more involved in problem solving and abstract relationships. What is your reaction to this statement?

8. What is the relationship between data processing and data communication?

9. In what ways, if any, do you think improvements in telecommunications and electronic data processing will change the work of the secretary to a top executive in the future?

10. Decide whether you would use the words (italicized in the following sentences) dictated by your employer. Then use the Reference Guide to verify or correct your answers.

    (a) The *balance* of the order was shipped this afternoon.

    (b) Ten committee members were present, but the balance had asked to be excused.

    (c) Mr. Downs acted as chairman during the *remainder* of the meeting.

    (d) The *remainder* of the fund will be used for research.

■ **1.** Visit a computer installation in your community and prepare a report showing how the use of the equipment has reduced the amount of repetitive labor involved in the work of the office.

■ **2.** In the following bookkeeping applications, what are the step-by-step procedures in maintaining records, recording information, analyzing the data, and making decisions?

**Accounts Receivable**
**Accounts Payable**
**Payroll**

What types of input media for a computer installation would be appropriate?

# Chapter 19

## COLLECTING BUSINESS INFORMATION

Researching information for her employer is an office assignment that the administrative assistant or executive secretary, in her role as administrative assistant, finds exciting and rewarding. It is exciting because it challenges her initiative and resourcefulness. It is rewarding because she can provide her employer with needed information.

The executive secretary is expected to know how to locate resource materials. She may be able to anticipate her employer's informational needs, or he may delegate research assignments to her.

The following are illustrations of assignments that she might be expected to do:

**Check out a proposal by gathering the pertinent data the executive will need in his evaluation**
**Verify the accuracy of data submitted in support of a proposal**
**Gather the data the executive will need in preparing a proposal**
**Examine possible solutions to a problem, advantages and disadvantages, opinions of authorities, ways others solve the problem**
**Do the library research required by the executive in contributing to a project**
**Gather and organize information the executive will need in preparing a speech or an article for a professional magazine**

In such activities, the secretary has a look-it-up function and a presentation function. This chapter discusses the sources to which the secretary can turn to find the information. Chapters 20 and 21 discuss ways that the secretary may organize the data to make the most effective presentation.

## WHERE TO LOOK FOR INFORMATION

Needed information may be found in the *office of the executive or of the secretary*, in a *company library*, or in an *outside library*. An executive undoubtedly subscribes to publications devoted to his field; other materials are collected through his memberships in trade or professional organizations. What the employer reads is often his top aide's cue to what she should read. The executive often secures specialized reference

A telephone call to a specialized library may save a trip.

—*American Telephone and Telegraph Company*

books for his personal office library. The company also may provide materials for the reference shelf of the secretary or office supervisor—if she is enterprising enough to request the indispensable ones and to watch for pertinent new publications.

Many large corporations maintain a company library staffed with a technically trained librarian. In addition to a librarian, many companies have a research staff that locates information requested by each office. In this case the function of the secretary is to provide an accurate and exact request for information. In other situations the secretary must locate the information in the company library.

It may be necessary to go outside the organization for needed information. The first logical outside source is the public library. A number of cities have public libraries with specialized business departments and branches that provide invaluable assistance to the business interests in their area.

The *specialized* library is another source of information. *The Directory of Special Libraries and Information Centers*, published by Gale Research Company of Detroit, lists over 13,000 special libraries, their location, size, and specialty. A local Chamber of Commerce will frequently have a library on commercial and industrial subjects. Many business, technical, and professional societies or associations maintain excellent libraries whose use, generally, is limited to members. (Law libraries are often located in county and federal court buildings or at the local university or college of law.) Many cities provide municipal reference libraries for the public as well as for city employees. Hospitals and colleges of medicine maintain medical and surgical libraries. Art, history, and natural history museums have specialized libraries, as do colleges and universities. Some newspaper offices have large library collections that they may open to limited public use. The United States Department of Commerce maintains regional offices in the principal cities, making available the files of the publications of the Department.

The public or special library (through its reference department) may answer questions over the telephone. Naturally, only questions that can be easily answered are accepted. If the public library in the secretary's community renders telephone reference service and if the secretary has frequent need for such service, it is courteous for her to visit the library and introduce herself to the person in charge of the reference desk.

> "EVERY MAN has a right to his opinion, but no man has a right to be wrong in his facts."
>
> —*Bernard Baruch*

## USING THE LIBRARY

When a subject requires extensive searching or considerable listing and copying, the secretary usually goes to the library to do the work; but she needs considerable skill in finding the information about published materials from which she will make selections.

### Finding the Information

Her first task is to select research material from the various library indexes, guides, and catalogs.

**Books.** The index of books is the *card catalog*. This is a card file that shows the contents of the library just as a book index shows the contents of a book. In the catalog there are at least three index cards for each book; one card is filed by the author's name, one by title, and one or more by subject classification. Many of the cards contain "See also" notes, which indicate where similar or related information may be found. The cards are usually uniformly printed and available to libraries from the Library of Congress.

**Dewey Decimal System.** The Dewey decimal system, used in library classifications, is a type of subject filing. The subjects are divided into not more than ten general classifications numbered in hundreds from 000 to 900, inclusive. Each major class may be divided by units of ten, such as 100, 110, and 120. These classes may be further subdivided by units of one, such as 110, 111, and 112. Subdividing can be continued indefinitely by using the decimal point — for example, 126.1, 126.2, 126.21, 126.211, ad infinitum. Under this system, business information is found in the 650 groups.

**Library of Congress System.** In libraries using the Library of Congress designations (combination of letters and figures), business information is found under the major category *H* (social sciences).

**Published Indexes.** A publication, *Books in Print, U.S.A., An Index to the Publishers' Trade List Annual,* lists all books included in publishers' catalogs, by author, title, price, and publisher. This book is normally shelved in the reference section of the library.

The *Cumulative Book Index* (or the CBI as it is familiarly identified) is an index of most of the books printed in English all over the world and still available from publishers. The CBI lists each book in three ways — author, title, and subject. These king-sized volumes are normally shelved in the catalog department of the library.

**Pamphlets and Booklets.** Much valuable information is now published in pamphlet, booklet, or leaflet form. Such material is cataloged by subject and title in the *Vertical File Index* (a subject and title index

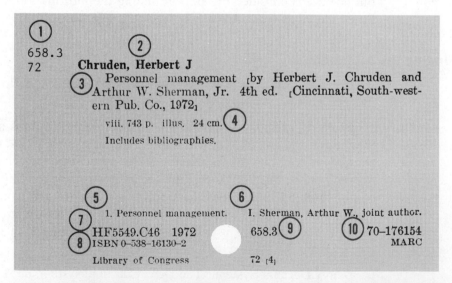

An author's card in a library catalog shows: (1) the classification and book number; (2) the author's name; (3) the title of the book, author or authors, edition, publisher, and date of publication; (4) text pages and the size of the book in centimeters; (5) the subject entry; (6) the joint-author entry; (7) the Library of Congress call number; (8) the International Standard Book Number; (9) the Dewey Decimal classification number; and (10) the serial number of the card.

to selected pamphlet material) that is published monthly.  The following
is a typical listing:

**Business Etiquette**
    **Your Best Business Behavior by Dorothy Diamond**
    **15 p il '71 Sportshelf Box 634 New Rochelle**
    **NY 10802 50¢**

This source of information can easily be missed during research on
a topic because the material may not be indexed in the library's catalog
nor shelved.  It is usually stored vertically in file drawers.

**News.** *Facts on File* is a weekly world news service published as a
one-volume, loose-leaf booklet with a cumulative subject index.

For newspaper references, the *New York Times Index* should be
consulted.  Supplements of this index are published monthly and
cumulative editions, annually.  Entries are arranged alphabetically
under name of subject. The *Wall Street Journal* publishes a similar index.

**Magazines.**  The best index on general magazines is the *Readers'
Guide to Periodical Literature*—a cumulative author and subject index
to articles appearing in periodicals that are on file in almost all main
public libraries.

Other indexes that will help the secretary to locate current informa-
tion in special fields are: *Biological and Agricultural Index, Art Index,
Applied Science and Technology Index, Bibliography Index, Business
Periodicals Index, Education Index,* and *Engineering Index.*

## Preparing Bibliography Cards

The first consideration in selecting material for examination is its
*date of publication*.  If current information is desired, an article on
missiles published ten years ago would be of little value; but twenty- or
thirty-year-old biographies of Benjamin Franklin would be worthwhile.

The second consideration is *content*.  Some listings describe the types
of information in the publications.  Such descriptions help in selecting
material to be researched.

For each reference selected for study, prepare a bibliography card.
On a 5- by 3-inch card record the library call number, the author's name,
the title of the publication (and article if it is in a periodical), the publisher, the date of publication, and the page reference.

Number the cards in the upper right corner in sequence, according
to each new source used.  The number that is thus assigned to a source
is used to identify all notes that are taken from it.  This method saves a
great deal of time in identifying the sources when the references are

The bibliography card (left, above) identifies the book as source No. 6. The card at the right conveniently shows pertinent material, organized and easy to reorganize before the actual writing of the paper.

copied or abstracted; besides, the cards serve as a permanent and detailed record of the sources used.

## Taking Notes

The secretary is now ready to study, evaluate, accept or reject material, and record the references on individual sheets or on cards 6 by 4 inches or larger. With cards or sheets of uniform size, instead of a shorthand notebook, the complete set of references can be sorted for use in drafting the outline and the report.

**Compiling Reference Cards.** Each reference card should give the following information in a standard form similar to that illustrated above:

Page number — written in the upper left corner (Do this first to avoid omitting it.)

Source — indicated by the number on its bibliography card

Topic — described in a conspicuous position, giving the nature of the reference

Information — written either as a direct quotation or as a summary statement (A direct quotation is written word for word and enclosed in quotation marks, and any omissions from the original are indicated by ellipses.)

**Abstracting.** A reference in abstract form should be identified as such, with the source and page number from which it was taken. A secretary who can prepare good abstracts can save her employer a great deal of reading time. She must develop the ability to pick out the salient points and to express them in summary form.

## COPYING MATERIAL

Fortunately, most libraries provide researchers with typewriters and copying machines. If possible, statistical tables should be copied by machine. If the secretary is taking verbatim notes on a single article, she should use her stenographic notebook and timesaving shorthand. The notes can be filed as a permanent record.

When library publications can be borrowed, the material can be taken to the office and typed or reproduced on a copying machine. The librarian will, in fact, often lend the secretary a noncirculating copy for a limited time, for libraries are eager to cooperate with business people and to have them make the fullest use of their collections.

## SOURCES OF GENERAL INFORMATION

Information sources are being updated and revised constantly, and new materials are being published regularly. It is necessary, therefore, to update any guide (including this chapter) with current sources.

### Atlases

An atlas is a collection of maps and statistical information regarding populations and geographic areas. *Rand McNally Commercial Atlas and Marketing Guide*, subscribed to by most libraries, contains not only geographic maps but also many economic maps. It really constitutes a map service; new and revised editions are furnished during the year. If the service is stopped, all material must be returned to the publisher.

### Dictionaries

One would naturally expect a dictionary to be a frequently used reference source of the secretary. Even though the office has a large unabridged dictionary, the efficient secretary will want an up-to-date desk-size dictionary within arm's reach. *Webster's New Collegiate Dictionary*, *The American College Dictionary*, and *Standard College Dictionary* are all acceptable in the latest editions.

There are also innumerable specialized dictionaries: bilingual ones for use in writing and translating foreign correspondence; and technical ones such as *A Dictionary for Accountants, Dictionary of Industrial Relations, Dictionary of Computers, A Dictionary of Occupational Titles, A Dictionary of Business and Scientific Terms, Hackh's Chemical Dictionary, A Dictionary of Statistical Terms, Encyclopedic Dictionary of Real Estate Practice, Thomson's Dictionary of Banking, Black's Law Dictionary, Encyclopedic Dictionary of Business and Finance, Modern Dictionary of Electronics, Hawley's Technical Speller, Dictionary of Physics and Electronics*, and the *Condensed Chemical Dictionary*.

New developments outdate technical dictionaries rapidly. Only the most recent editions can be considered dependably up to date.

## Directories (City)

A secretary to a lawyer or to an insurance man may be asked to locate or trace the address of an individual by a search through city directories when the name of the person is not listed in the telephone directory. Current and back issues of city directories are kept at libraries for the convenience of business users. The library collection of directories might contain the local city directory and also directories of all the cities in the state and of the major cities over the country.

City directories are not published by cities but by commercial enterprises for profit. Some of the very largest cities, such as New York City and Los Angeles, no longer have city directories. The North American Directory Publishers print a *City Directory Catalog*.

## Directories (Special)

There are also hundreds of classified directories serving many fields —so many, in fact, that a special guide to directories is published. The latest edition of *Guide to American Directories* lists more than 4,000 directories in over 300 major fields of public and private enterprise. Some of them are listed below.

1. Those that list individuals engaged in the same occupation—for example, the *American Medical Directory* which gives education and field of specialization of all physicians in the United States and Canada.

2. Those that provide biographical sketches of *selected* individuals. *Who's Who in America* is a biographical directory, reissued biennially, of notable living men and women. *Who's Who*, an international annual biographical dictionary published in London, contains mainly prominent English names. There are also many selective *Who's Who* references, such as *Who's Who in Labor, Who's Who in Commerce and Industry, Who's Who in the South* and *Southwest, Who's Who of American Women,* and *World's Who's Who in Finance and Industry.*

3. Those that list all the businesses or service institutions engaged in similar or related enterprises in the United States, such as *Thomas' Register of American Manufacturers,* and *American Bank Directory.*

4. Those that list businesses in foreign countries, such as *Jane's Major Companies of Europe, Standard Trade Index of Japan,* and *Fraser's Canadian Trade Directory.*

5. Those that serve as buyers' and consumers' guides. The best known is *MacRae's Blue Book,* a buying guide published annually. It also lists trade names and firms owning such names. Another typical buyers' guide is the *Hospital Purchasing File. Consumer Reports* published by Consumers Union and *Consumer Bulletin* published by Consumers Research Inc. are typical publications for consumers.

6. Those that provide such information as *Where to Find Statistical Information, Encyclopedia of Associations, A Businessman's Guide to Washington* (governmental agencies and their services), *A Businessman's Guide to Europe,* the *Encyclopedia of Sports,* and the *National ZIP Code Directory.*

## Encyclopedias

An excellent reference source is an encyclopedia. Only two are mentioned here. In addition to general information, the *Encyclopedia Americana* provides information on American cities and manufacturing and commerce. The *Encyclopaedia Britannica* is used to secure information on European countries and cities.

## Government Publications

Our government is a prolific publisher and a major source of information for the businessman. Some government publications may be subscribed to or purchased by the company. Others will be found on file in the reference department or business section of the public library, or in the municipal reference library of a city hall—all depending upon the subject matter. If the secretary works in a city that has a depository library (usually located in a larger library) designated by law to receive all or part of the material published by the government, she might turn to it for reference. Otherwise, she would go to one of the libraries or departments just described. If necessary, or if repeated use of a work seemed likely, the secretary would buy the publication.

In *The Monthly Catalog of U.S. Government Publications* the secretary will find a comprehensive list of all publications issued by the various departments and agencies of the United States Government, including those for sale by the Superintendent of Documents and those for official use only. A semimonthly list of *Selected United States Government Publications* is sent free to persons requesting the Superintendent of Documents to include their names on the mailing list.

Proceedings and debates of Congress are given in *The Congressional Record. The Congressional Directory* provides names and biographical facts of Senators and Representatives, composition of Congressional committees, information about special agencies and commissions of the government, and listings of our diplomatic representatives abroad and of foreign representatives here.

The *Official Register of the U.S. Government*, an annual, publishes names of those holding administrative or supervisory positions in the legislative, executive, and judicial branches of the federal government.

Publications of the U.S. Department of Commerce, Bureau of the Census, are based on data from censuses taken in various years including information on population, housing, business, manufacturing, and agriculture. Full census reports provide complete information. *The Statistical Abstract of the United States* (annual), however, presents summary statistics about area and population, vital statistics, education, climate, employment, military affairs, social security, income, prices, banking, transportation, agriculture, forests, fisheries, mining, manufactures, and related fields. Data on all cities over 25,000 in population are given in the *City Supplement* to the *Statistical Abstracts*.

The U.S. Department of Commerce, Bureau of Foreign and Domestic Commerce, publishes the annual *Foreign Commerce and Navigation of the United States* that gives detailed statistical records of the foreign commerce of the United States: articles exported and imported, rates of duty and duties collected, and a complete registry of vessels involved in foreign trade. *International Commerce Weekly* provides information for those engaged in trade with other countries. The *Survey of Current Business* (issued monthly) reports on the industrial and business activities of the United States.

Publications of the Department of Agriculture provide agricultural and marketing statistics and information for increasing production and agricultural efficiency. Department of Labor publications deal mostly with labor statistics, standards, and employment trends. Their official publication is the *Monthly Labor Review*.

Economic and agricultural data on many subjects may be acquired from various state governments. The secretary should address inquiries to the departments of health, geology or conservation, and highways; to the divisions of banks, insurance, and statistics; to industrial and public utilities commissions; or to the research bureaus of state universities. Pertinent information about executive, legislative, and judicial branches of state governments is given in the *Book of the States* which is published every two years by the Council of State Governments.

## Yearbooks

Yearbooks are annual reports of summaries of statistics and facts. *The World Almanac and Book of Facts*, which is the most popular book of this type, contains many pages of statistics and facts, preceded by an excellent index. One reference librarian has said, "Give me a good dictionary and *The World Almanac*, and I can answer 80 percent of all questions asked me." It covers such items as stock and bond markets; notable events; political and financial statistics of states and cities; statistics on population, farm crops, prices, trade and commerce; educational data; and information on the postal services. Because of its wide coverage and low price, the secretary might request the executive to purchase a copy of *The World Almanac* each year for office use. Another yearbook of this type is the *Information Please Almanac, Atlas, and Yearbook*, published by Simon and Schuster.

The *Statesman's Yearbook*, published in London, provides factual and statistical information on countries of the world. Data are provided on type of government, area and population, religion, education, justice, defense, commerce and industry, and finance. The *International Yearbook* and *Statesmen's Who's Who* analyze developments of international significance.

## SOURCES OF BUSINESS INFORMATION

Sources of business information, like general information, are constantly being revised and new materials published regularly. This listing of specific business sources, therefore, is to serve as a guide and should be supplemented with new sources as they appear.

### Abstracting Services

So vast is the volume of technical literature published in many areas that engineers, scientists, and business executives find it difficult to keep abreast of new developments. To help bridge this information gap, some large companies subscribe to an abstracting service that specializes in a specific field. An example is the American Petroleum Institute's Abstracting and Indexing Service. Highly trained specialists abstract thousands of journals, publications, and scientific papers from all parts of the world. The abstracts are distributed to subscribers.

Some of the abstracting services feed abstracts and selected references into a computer. The computer arranges the material alphabetically by subject. A computer-driven phototypesetter prints out indexes periodically and can provide an immediate printout of all abstracts on a specific subject. The recipient can determine from the abstract whether he wishes to read the original and complete document.

The National Federation of Science Abstracting and Indexing Services, Washington, D.C., publishes *A Guide to the World's Abstracting and Indexing Services in Science and Technology*.

### Subscription Information Services (General)

Management often subscribes to information services relating to business conditions in general. These services present information from more direct and limited sources than those found in the popular publications. A service may use loose-leaf form so that superseded pages can be destroyed and new and additional ones inserted easily. It may be the secretary's duty to see that the new material is filed in its proper place in the service, according to the instructions sent by the publisher. These services include those listed on the next page.

Babson's Reports Inc. Two bulletins are issued: *Investment & Barometer Letter* (weekly) and the *Washington Forecast Letter* (weekly).

The Bureau of National Affairs, Inc. This privately owned company reports government actions affecting management, labor, law, taxes, finance, federal contracts, antitrust and trade regulations, international trade, and patent law. It publishes a *Daily Report for Executives.*

*The Kiplinger Washington Letter.* This weekly confidential letter analyzes and condenses economic and political news for subscribers.

The Conference Board. Over 4,000 subscribers support research in the field of business economics, financial, personnel, and marketing administration, international operations and public affairs administration. Included in the service is a monthly magazine — *The Conference Board Record* and a desk sheet in Bulletin form — *Weekly Desk Sheet of Business Trends.*

*Research Institute Recommendations.* This weekly newsletter analyzes economic and legislative developments and makes tax recommendations.

## Subscription Information Services (Specialized)

The secretary should be acquainted with the subscription services for specialized fields described below:

Credit. Dun and Bradstreet Credit Service. This service collects, analyzes, and distributes credit information on retail, wholesale, and manufacturing companies.

Financial. (Most brokerage houses provide investment information to prospective and present customers.) Moody's Investors Service. This Service publishes *Moody's Stock Survey, Moody's Bond Survey, Moody's Dividend Record, Moody's Bond Record,* and *Moody's Handbook of Common Stocks.*

Standard and Poor's Services. Publications include *Corporation Records, Dividend Record, Listed Stock Reports, Over-the-Counter* and *Regional Exchanges Stock Reports, Stock Guide, Industry Surveys, International Stock Report, The Outlook, Transportation Service Stock Summary, Poor's Investment Advisory Survey, Called Bond Record, Status of Bonds, Convertible Bond Reports, Bond Guide, Municipal Bond Selector, Register of Corporation Directors and Executives.*

Law, Tax. Commerce Clearing House Services. These services are especially useful to lawyers and accountants. The CCH Topical Law Reports (over 100 loose-leaf publications) provide assistance on such problems as federal tax, labor, trade regulation, state tax, social security, securities, bankruptcy, trusts, insurance, and aviation.

Prentice-Hall Services. These loose-leaf current publications cover the latest laws, rules, and regulations with interpretations and comments. Most aspects of federal and state laws with respect to business and taxation are covered. In addition, *Accountant's Weekly Report, Insurance and Tax News (*a biweekly newsletter), *Lawyer's Weekly Report,* and *Executive's Tax Report* (weekly) keep subscribers up to date.

**Office Administration.** *The Word Processing Report.* Published twice monthly, these reports cover industry trends, word processing equipment and systems, and analyses of case studies.

**Real Estate.** Real Estate Analyst Reports. These monthly, loose-leaf reports include: *The Real Estate Analyst, Real Estate Trends,* and *The Digest Service.*

**Trade.** The Bureau of National Affairs, Inc. In addition to providing general business services, this organization publishes *Antitrust and Trade Regulation Report, Federal Contracts Report, International Trade Reporter, Export Shipping Manual, The United States Patents Quarterly,* and *Daily Labor Report.*

## Newspapers and Periodicals for Executives

Periodicals coming into the office can be divided into two types — general and specialized.

**General Periodicals.** The alert secretary scans general business magazines received at the office or at her employer's desk for material that may be of immediate or possible interest to the executive and also to her. Typical business magazines are:

*Barron's.* An investor's magazine published weekly by Dow Jones & Co., Inc.

*Business Week.* A periodical covering factors of national and international interest to the business executive. Statistics reflect current trends.

*Dun's (formerly Dun's Review).* This monthly magazine covers finance, credit, production, labor, sales and distribution.

*Forbes.* A semi-monthly magazine on corporate management for top executives in business and finance.

*Fortune.* This monthly magazine features articles on specific industries and business leaders. It also analyzes current business problems.

*National Observer.* Factual articles on world affairs and economic and political developments of special interest to the business executive are provided by this periodical published by Dow Jones & Co., Inc. in newspaper format.

*Nation's Business.* Published monthly by the Chamber of Commerce of the United States, this business magazine concerns political and general topics.

**School of Business Publications.** In addition, the executive may subscribe for the business magazines published by some of the larger university schools of business. Well-known magazines of this type are the *Harvard Business Review* (bimonthly) and the *Journal of Business* (quarterly), University of Chicago.

**Special Articles.** In the business sections of such weeklies as *Time* and *Newsweek* and the special articles in *The U.S. News and World Report,* the reader can learn a great deal about current business trends.

The researcher can find valuable information in specialized periodicals and digests.

—*American Telephone and Telegraph Company*

**Newspapers.** *The New York Times* is a daily newspaper covering world, domestic, and financial news. The *Wall Street Journal*, primarily an investor's newspaper, is published daily and covers current business news and lists daily stock reports.

**Specialized Periodicals.** It is common for a company to belong to several trade associations, each of which helps it with a different aspect of its business. In addition, the executive may belong to several professional associations. These associations issue regular magazines to their members, publishing articles and statistics of current interest. *The Standard Periodical Directory* lists over 50,000 United States and Canadian periodicals.

The *Business Periodicals Index* is the primary source of information on a wide range of articles appearing in business periodicals.

When seeking data on a specific magazine or newspaper, the secretary might consult *Ayer's Directory of Newspapers and Periodicals* (annual), or *Ulrich's International Periodicals Directory* providing such information as name of publication, editor, publisher, date established, technical data, and geographic area served. Another source of specialized magazines is the *Readers' Guide to Periodical Literature*. More than one hundred well-known magazines (such as the *Architectural Record, Changing Times, Consumer Reports, Foreign Affairs, Monthly Labor Review*, and *Time*) are indexed in each issue and their articles cataloged under appropriate headings.

## Handbooks

Handbooks have been published in many areas of business. They are highly factual and are written to give a general survey knowledge (with the minimum use of time and effort) about a field. A few of the many handbooks that have been published include: *Handbook of Business Administration, Business Executive's Handbook, Accountants' Handbook, Business Finance Handbook, Financial Handbook, Handbook of Successful Tax Procedures, Office Administration Handbook, Financial Executive's Handbook, AMA Management Handbook, Handbook of Employee Selection, The Sales Manager's Handbook, Production Handbook*, and *Handbook of Modern Marketing*.

Among a number of handbooks written for the secretary employed in a specialized office are handbooks for the legal secretary, medical secretary, school secretary, and others. (See page 196.)

## Secretary's Reference Shelf

In addition to the secretarial handbooks and reference materials needed for transcription (page 196), the secretary may collect other worthwhile reference books; or she may be asked by the executive to purchase them for the office. What is on the secretary's reference shelf should depend on the nature of her job and the background information she will need. A useful, inexpensive reference is *How to Use the Business Library*. This manual is revised periodically and would be a valuable adjunct to the office library or secretary's reference shelf. Among other source books of information are the following:

Abridged encyclopedias—such as *The Columbia Encyclopedia* (one volume), comprised of very brief articles. It is particularly strong on biography and geography; or the *Lincoln Library of Essential Information* (two volumes), that classifies information into twelve broad subject fields, rather than alphabetically.

An annual book of statistics—such as the *Statistical Abstract of the United States, The World Almanac* and *Book of Facts* or the *Commodity Year Book*.

An atlas or gazetteer — such as the *Rand McNally Standard World Atlas* or *Webster's Geographical Dictionary*.

A book of quotations — such as Bartlett's *Familiar Quotations* or *The Home Book of Humorous Quotations*.

The secretary's reference shelf should surely include a technical handbook that covers the area of work of the executive.

# SUGGESTED READINGS

Downs, Robert B. *How to Do Library Research.* Urbana: University of Illinois Press, 1966.

Gates, Jean K. *Guide to the Use of Books and Library*, 2d ed. New York: McGraw-Hill Book Company, 1969.

Johnson, H. Webster. *How to Use the Business Library with Sources of Business Information*, 4th ed. Cincinnati: South-Western Publishing Co., 1972.

Knight, Hattie M. *One Two Three Guide to Library.* Dubuque: William C. Brown, Publishers, 1970.

Morse, Grant W. *The Concise Guide to Library Research.* New York: Washington Square Press, Inc., 1966.

Wasserman, Paul. *Encyclopedia of Business Information Sources*, Vol. 1. Detroit: Gale Research Co., 1970.

## QUESTIONS FOR DISCUSSION

1. In your new position as secretary to the administrative manager of a business consulting firm, you have been given permission to purchase three desk reference books. Which books would you choose? By what criteria did you make these choices?

2. Does the reference department of your public library render telephone service? If so, what limitations are placed on it? Is there a special business department or branch?

3. If your employer is involved in scientific research and gives highly technical dictation, where would you turn for help in learning the vocabulary?

4. If your employer disagreed with the rules of good usage that you follow in your transcription, what would you do?

5. It is difficult to determine how long reference material should be retained in an office. In each of these cases, what factors would determine your decision?

   (a) Catalogs from suppliers
   (b) Back numbers of professional and technical magazines
   (c) Advertisements of competitive items
   (d) House organs of your company
   (e) Copies of *The Statesman's Yearbook*

6. In the following sentences insert the proper word for those enclosed in parentheses or rephrase the sentences so that there is no doubt as to the meaning. Then use the Reference Guide to verify or correct your answers.

   (a) New statistics are published (every two years).
   (b) Data are requested (twice a month).
   (c) Summaries are compiled (every two months).

7. Show how you could, in a piece of formal writing, avoid the use of *above* in the following sentences:

   (a) The interpretation of the above statistics is important to any conclusion we reach.
   (b) The above is subject to more than one interpretation.

■ **1.** Your employer has asked you to prepare an annotated bibliography on the landscape office design, using only sources published within the last five years. Type the bibliography.

■ **2.** Assume that you are secretary to the general counsel of one of the subsidiaries of a major manufacturing firm. Your employer has just been transferred to the home office and has just arrived in the office. He tells you that he has at least ten crates of books to be unpacked and arranged on his bookshelves. You are to supervise the arrangement of the books on the shelves. Also, he asks you to devise a system of control of these books, as he expects that many of the staff will want to use his material. What would be your plan of action for arranging the books on the shelves? What would be your system of control?

■ **3.** For Problem 3 in Chapter 20 you will be asked to prepare a business report on one of the following subjects. In preparation, you are now to do the necessary reading, prepare bibliography cards, and take the necessary notes.

(a) Turnover of office personnel
(b) A job evaluation program for office employees
(c) Professional organizations for business women
(d) For the woman—marriage and/or career
(e) A plan for the improvement of communication in the office
(f) Success in supervision of office employees
(g) Salaries of office workers
(h) The concept of word processing centers

(i) The use of employment tests in the selection of office workers
(j) The effects of automation on the secretarial profession
(k) Reduction in the 5-day work week
(l) In-service training for the office workers
(m) Types of fringe benefits in major organizations
(n) Improving the productivity of office workers

■ **4.** Examine a copy of the *World Almanac* or the *Information Please Almanac*. Write a description of the general classes of information. Include one or two examples of interesting facts you found it to contain.

■ **5.** Assume that in your work you are called upon to seek the following information. Prepare a list of the answers (identify by letter) and your source of information.

(a) Who is chairman of the board of American Telephone and Telegraph Company? Where would you find biographical data about him?
(b) What is the address of the national headquarters of Kiwanis International? What is the total membership?
(c) What was the population of New Orleans at the last official census?
(d) Who are members of the Interstate Commerce Commission?
(e) What is the total circulation and the advertising rate of *Fortune*?
(f) What is the annual crude petroleum production of Indonesia?
(g) What products are manufactured by Harold L. Palmer Company, Inc., Livonia, Michigan?
(h) What are the five principal business centers in the state of Arkansas?
(i) Who said "The man who makes no mistakes does not usually make anything"?

# Chapter 20

## PRESENTING STATISTICAL INFORMATION

The reliance upon quantitative data is the most significant change in business decision making in recent years. The computer can provide the business executive with data pertinent to each detail of business operations. The task remains, however, to convert the data into information that is meaningful and comprehensible to the reader. Tables, charts, and graphs are extensively used for interpretation. A well-constructed table or chart can convey a picture of business operations more quickly and more clearly than words or numbers. Thus, business management relies heavily upon visual media to convey information.

Chapter 19 pointed out that the executive secretary, in her role as administrative assistant, sometimes has the function of gathering data and also of organizing them for effective communication to others. For example, to support a proposal to establish a word processing center in the company, an executive needs facts about the experiences of other companies with word processing centers, on the various cost factors involved, on the attitudes of employees, and so forth. Gathering the needed data is but the first step. The second is organizing them. Tables and graphs are effective devices for communicating. The administrative assistant with the ability to take masses of figures and organize them into meaningful tables and graphs is exceptionally valuable to the executive.

Giving life to figures, which well-planned tables and graphs really do, calls for a thorough knowledge of the techniques of table and graph construction, good planning, and imagination. The several steps involved in this type of work—compiling, classifying, and presenting data in tables and graphs—are discussed in this chapter.

## COMPILING AND ORGANIZING DATA

The data with which the secretary works come from many sources. Some of them are compiled within the company. Other information, however, must be obtained from such secondary sources as magazines, yearbooks, and reports of outside agencies.

National Insurance Corp.
Life Policies and Amounts
December 31, --

| Districts | Agents | Policies | Amount (Thousands$) |
|---|---|---|---|
| *Atlanta* | | | |
| Florida | 14 | 1950 | 6240 |
| Georgia | 9 | 1089 | 3049 |
| North Carolina | 25 | 2046 | 10744 |
| South Carolina | 18 | 1926 | 3659 |
| Total | 66 | 7011 | 23692 |
| *Boston* | | | |
| Maine | 8 | 608 | 1276 |
| Massachusetts | 7 | 588 | 2387 |
| Vermont | 19 | 1957 | 6262 |
| Total | 34 | 3153 | 9925 |

From Annual Report of District Offices
Compiled by R. C. 1/21/-- Checked by L. H.

A data work sheet should indicate the source, the compiler, and the checker. The work sheet should be filed with the finished tabulation, with the adding-machine tape attached as proof of totals.

The data must be assembled onto a working form or forms so that totals can be obtained, averages and percentages calculated, and the information summarized. This process of transferring facts from the source documents to working forms is called *compiling* the data. The simplest compilation of data is a pencil-written tabulation similar to the one illustrated at the top of this page.

## Methods of Classifying Data

The objective in compiling data is to organize information into some type of meaningful classification. Data can be classified in any of five ways: (1) alphabetic sequence, (2) kind, (3) size, (4) location, or (5) time.

```
                    CONTINENTAL PRODUCTS

            NUMBER OF ACCOUNTS AND TOTAL SALES
                     OF WILLIAM MOYLE
            IN 5 LARGEST CITIES IN EASTERN IOWA

            FIRST AND SECOND QUARTERS OF 19--

                                              SALES
NAME OF CITY    NAME OF ACCOUNT      1/01/-- - 3/31/--     4/01/-- - 6/30/--

BURLINGTON      GRAYS DRUG COMPANY          349.16              1,214.62
                MILLERS VARIETY             430.11                237.46
                PURITY DRUGS              1,113.02                899.34
                A. J. WALKER                46.39
                RICHARD WESSELS           2,304.19              3,321.76
                                          4,242.87*             5,673.18*

DUBUQUE         CAMERON PHARMACY            88.62              1,114.05
                DRAGER BROTHERS             83.23                 34.77
                EVERYBODYS MARKET          442.89                233.84
                ZEISS BROTHERS             134.77
                                           749.51*             1,382.66*


                                        43,376.07**          47,418.38**
```

In many offices, machine tabulation has supplanted manual compilation of data. From punched cards or tape, the computer calculates and prints the data on perforated, accordion-folded sheets like that shown above.

1. An *alphabetic sequence* of data is often used when the data are compiled for reference. For instance, the data on the worksheet compilation might list the names of the district offices in alphabetic sequence and the names of the states in each district, also in alphabetic sequence.

2. A *kind grouping* of data is used when the items are kinds of objects, characteristics, products, and so on. An example of kind of grouping is a table entitled, "Retail Trade in U.S., 1973, by Kind of Business." The number of stores and the year's sales are broken down into several main groups, such as food stores and apparel stores. Under each of these are listed the data for each of the types of stores included in the group.

3. *Size variations* may be shown in two ways: (a) in an *array*—that is, with the items listed in ascending or descending order, such as a table of the fifty greatest ports in the world with the ports arranged in the order of net tonnage in descending order; (b) in a *frequency distribution*—that is, according to the number in each size class. A frequency distribution is used instead of an array when the size classes can be grouped advantageously. Tables of age distribution are usually shown in this way; for example, the number of persons between the ages of 10 to 14, 15 to 19, and on as far as needed, instead of the number of persons 10 years old, 11 years old, and so on.

4. A *location listing* is used to show the data by geographic units—such as cities, states, and countries. Real-estate data are often listed this way, as are commodity sales on a national scale.

5. *Time-of-occurrence or time-series listings* are very common. The listing may be made by days, weeks, months, years, decades, and so on.

**466**        *Part 7* • COLLECTING, PROCESSING, AND PRESENTING BUSINESS DATA

AVERAGE BUSINESS LETTER COSTS
FOR THE YEAR 1973[a]

| Cost Factor | Average Cost per letter | Percentage of Total Cost |
|---|---|---|
| Secretarial Time | $0.99 | 29.90[b] |
| Fixed Charges[c] | 0.86 | 26.00 |
| Dictator's Time | 0.72 | 21.75 |
| Nonproductive Labor[d] | 0.26 | 7.85 |
| Mailing Cost | 0.21 | 6.34 |
| Materials | 0.10 | 3.02 |
| Filing Cost | 0.17 | 5.14 |
| Totals | $3.31 | 100.00 |

[a]Based on data supplied by the Dartnell Corporation, Chicago.
[b]Expressed to the nearest 1/100 of 1%.
[c]Depreciation, overhead, rent, light, and similar items.
[d]Time lost due to waiting, illness, vacation, and other causes.

An array may list items in descending or ascending order. Vertical lines may be used to separate columns and the ends of the table may be left open. The footnotes are placed directly below the table and are identified by use of lowercase letters.

After data have been collected, they may be translated into either averages or percentages so that comparisons can be made. To say that sales in Peoria were 35 percent greater this month than last month is easier to interpret than to say that sales last month were $50,000 and this month, $67,500.

In some instances, it may be more helpful to know the average salary of clerks in the purchasing office than to know the highest and the lowest salary paid. The use to be made of the data determines which figures would be of most value.

**Averages.** One way to help the reader understand a set of figures is to compute averages of some type. (An average is a single value used to represent a group.) But which of the averages in common use should you choose? The one used most often is the *arithmetic average* or, more technically, *arithmetic mean*. It is determined by adding the values of the items and dividing that total by the number of items. If the weekly payroll for 120 employees is $24,000, for example, the average pay would be $200.

The *mode* is a second kind of average. It is the value that recurs the greatest number of times. The data are arranged in a frequently distribution to determine the mode. For example, the mode in the following distribution is the class interval $200.01 to $210.00, because the greatest number of earned amounts fall in that range.

| Weekly Earnings | No. of Employees |
|---|---|
| $190.01 – 200.00 | 2 |
| 200.01 – 210.00 | 26 |
| 210.01 – 220.00 | 19 |
| 220.01 – 230.00 | 9 |
| 230.01 – 240.00 | 5 |

The *median* is an average of position; it is the midpoint in an array. In order to determine it, the data must be arranged in an array; that is, in either ascending or descending order. Then it is necessary only to count the number of items and find the mid one, which is the median. For example, assume that five students have the following amounts in their checking accounts:

| | |
|---|---|
| Student A............. | $500 |
| Student B............. | 190 |
| Student C............. | 175←——MEDIAN |
| Student D............. | 160 |
| Student E............. | 5 |

The median is $175; on the other hand, the mean is $206. Obviously, the mean is affected by extreme cases (the student with an abnormally large checking account and the one who is almost "broke"). This kind of influence is why the median is usually selected as the average that comes nearest to indicating the true state of affairs when there are extreme cases in the data.

**Percentages.** Percentages help in making numbers understandable and the relation of various items to one another and to the total more easily grasped. In the table on page 467, the last column shows the percentage each cost factor represents of the total cost. The statement, "The secretarial cost in producing a business letter is $.99," has less meaning than "The stenographic cost in producing a business letter is $1 or 31.3 percent of the total cost of producing the letter."

*Percentage relatives* or *index numbers* are used to compare the extent or degree of changes. They are relative because they are based on a value at some specific time and that base must be clearly defined. For example, in 1929 there were approximately 20,000,000 telephones in the United States; in 1934, 17,000,000 telephones; in 1940, 22,000,000; in 1952, 45,000,000; in 1960, 66,500,000; in 1964, 84,167,000; and in 1971, 120,218,000. The percentage relatives, based on the 1929 figure as 100, are 85 for 1934, 110 for 1940, 225 for 1952, 332.5 for 1960, 420.8 for 1964, and 601.09 for the 1971 index.

# PRESENTING DATA EFFECTIVELY

A problem that confronts a secretary working with numeric data is determining on the most effective presentation. Tables are preferable for exact representations, whereas graphics are better when quick identification of relationships is important.

## Tables

Three types of tables are used for writing business reports: *general-purpose* tables—those to be used for reference; *special-purpose* tables—those that direct the eye and mind to specific relationships of significance; and *spot* tables—unnumbered tables which appear within paragraphs of the report. General-purpose tables are usually placed in the appendix. Most of the tables of statistical data included in business reports are special-purpose tables. The table on page 468 is an example of the spot table.

A table should be self-explanatory. It should be kept simple and designed for rapid reading. The incorporation of too many elements in one table detracts from its readability and effectiveness. When planning a table, keep one question in mind, "Precisely what is this table to show?" All data that do not apply should be excluded.

Another word of caution is that statistics should not distort the true situation. To avoid misrepresenting facts when you present statistics you may want to read *How to Lie with Statistics.*[1]

After the table has been developed, it may be well to dramatize the material presented in it by a chart or graph. In other words, the chart does not replace the table; it supplements it. Tables provide details; charts present relationships but not minutae and would not be satisfactory to the reader who seeks exact data.

## Planning the Table Layout

It is almost impossible to type a well-balanced table, allowing sufficient space for all items and margins, unless the work is carefully planned. The facts and the figures to be tabulated must be analyzed carefully before the various headings and column arrangements are determined. The best method of planning a table is to make a penciled rough draft.

After this plan is drawn, the secretary can save herself time (and often grief) by using the backspace-from-center method when tabulating.

---

[1]Darrell Huff, *How to Lie with Statistics* (New York: W. W. Norton & Company, Inc., 1954).

## Suggestions for Typing Tables

Additional suggestions will help you plan and type an effective table.

**Title.** The title should be complete and clearly worded. The title, subtitle, and column headings should make the table self-contained. If the data represent a period of time, either the title, the subtitle, the column headings, or the reference to the data source should indicate the period covered. Type the title in all capitals with no terminal period. Break a title too long for one line at the division of a thought.

| | |
|---|---|
| *POOR:* | ANNUAL SALES OF ELECTRONIC EQUIPMENT BY MAJOR MANUFACTURERS IN THE UNITED STATES TO LATIN AMERICAN COUNTRIES |
| *GOOD:* | ANNUAL SALES OF ELECTRONIC EQUIPMENT BY MAJOR MANUFACTURERS IN THE UNITED STATES TO LATIN AMERICAN COUNTRIES |

If there are several tables presented in a report, it is advisable to number the tables to facilitate reference.

**Abbreviations.** In order to save space, abbreviations may be used in column headings; but they should never be used in titles.

**Columns.** For easy reference, the column headings may be numbered consecutively from left to right. Columns of related data should be placed closer together than other columns. Major divisions of groups of columns can be indicated by wider spaces or by double vertical rules.

**Alignment.** In tabulated words and phrases, the left margin should be kept even. In tabulated figures, the right margin must usually be kept straight. When decimal fractions involving different numbers of places to the right of the decimal point are listed, the decimal point must be kept in vertical alignment.

| *Correct* | *Incorrect* | *Correct* | *Incorrect* |
|---|---|---|---|
| Adding machine | Adding machine | 1,476.0 | 1,476 |
| Calculator | Calculator | 32.7 | 32.7 |
| File cabinet | File cabinet | 11,148.0 | 11,148 |

**Amounts.** A comma should be used to separate every three digits in amounts, but it should not be used with the digits after a decimal point. For example: *1,125.50* and *21.16184*.

For sums of money the dollar sign should be used with the first amount in a column and with each total.

| *Correct:* | | *Incorrect:* | |
|---|---|---|---|
| | $1,456.26 | | $1,456.26 |
| | 362.35 | | $  362.35 |
| | 18.46 | | $   18.46 |
| | $1,837.07 | | $1,837.07 |

To rule lines on the typewriter, place the pencil or pen point at an angle in the cardholder notch. For horizontal lines, move the carriage from left to right. For vertical lines, release the variable line spacer and turn the platen forward or backward.

*—IBM Corporation*

**Readability.** *Leaders*, or lines of periods, aid the reader by carrying the eyes across a wide expanse of space from one column to another. Leaders are usually typed with a single space between periods. Periods on successive lines should be in vertical alignment. When long columns are single-spaced, skipping a line every three, four, or five rows improves readability.

**Rulings.** Rulings may improve the appearance of a table. They may be typed with the underline key or made with pencil or a ball-point pen.

A double ruling is used at the top of the table two lines below the title. Single rulings should divide the stub and box headings from the rest of the table. A single ruling should also end the table. Vertical rulings should separate the columns. Rulings may be omitted at the sides.

**Units.** The unit designation of the data must be given (inches, pounds, and so forth). Generally, this information is provided above the columns as a part of the heading or subheading.

Leave space above and below a column heading.

**Special Notes.** If the meaning of any item in the table is not clear or must be qualified, an explanation should be given in the form of a footnote. Footnotes are also used to indicate the source of secondary data.

To identify footnote reference in numeric data, use symbols (24,961*) or lowercase letters (24,961[a]). A number used to reference a footnote (24,961[1]) can be confused as being part of the numeric data.

NATIONAL INSURANCE CORPORATION
LIFE POLICIES IN FORCE
DECEMBER 31, 19—

Boxed Heading

| District | Number of | | Total Amounts (Thousands) |
|---|---|---|---|
| | Agents | Policies | |
| Atlanta. . . . . . . . . | 66* | 7,011 | $ 23,692 |
| Boston . . . . . . . . . | 34 | 3,153 | 9,925 |
| Chicago . . . . . . . . | 18 | 1,016 | 5,017 |
| Cleveland. . . . . . . | 9 | 2,114 | 10,170 |
| Dallas . . . . . . . . . | 21 | 4,118 | 12,375 |
| Dover . . . . . . . . . | 7 | 846 | 8,751 |
| Kansas City. . . . . . | 5 | 718 | 9,278 |
| Omaha . . . . . . . . . | 20 | 3,875 | 18,117 |
| Newark . . . . . . . | 16 | 2,110 | 13,476 |
| Totals | 196 | 24,961 | $110,801 |

*Includes South Carolina, added since last year.

This table was prepared from the work-sheet compilation on page 465. Leaders and skipped lines have been used to improve the readability of the table. To avoid confusion of reading large figures, the amounts are shown in thousands. Thus 23,692,000 is shown as 23,692.

**Reference.** The name of the person responsible for the preparation of the table should be indicated on the file copy at least. When the data come from a secondary source, such as a publication, the source should be indicated on the table.

**Variety and Emphasis.** Both variety and emphasis on relationships can be given to the typed copy by using italics, boldface, and type of different sizes and styles, or by varying the placement of the column totals. Two typewriters, one with pica type and the other with elite, can be used. Footnotes and column headings can be typed in elite type, and the body of the table typed in pica type. Changing the type elements on the IBM Selectric can provide even wider variations. Also, a wide-carriage typewriter and oversize paper can be used for a table that cannot be accommodated on standard equipment and paper.

## Checking the Typed Table

Every typewritten table must be checked for accuracy. Proofreading requires the help of another person, who should read the original draft while the secretary checks the typed copy. Reading figures for check purposes is an oral technique that has a fairly definite prescribed routine, indicated by the examples given below. The words in the examples that are connected by a hyphen should be read as a group; the commas indicate pauses:

    **718 seven-one-eight**
    **98,302 nine-eight, comma three-oh-two**
    **24.76 two-four, point, seven-six**
    **$313.00 three-one-three even (or no cents) dollars**
    **77,000 seventy-seven thousand even**

For copy in columnar form it is usually advisable to read down a column rather than across the page. This procedure provides a double check because, in most instances, the typing work has been done across the page. If the table includes totals, the amounts in each column should be added and checked against the total.

After the accuracy of the typed table has been verified and errors corrected, the original draft of the table should be filed in a personal folder kept by the secretary or attached to, and filed with, the typed file copy of the final draft. If anyone who reads the typed copy discovers an error, the filed copy of the original data will enable the secretary to determine whether the error occurred in the original material, which may have been supplied to the secretary, or whether the error was made in the process of typing the table.

## Graphic Presentation

A graph is a statistical picture. It presents numerical data in visual form, making them more easily analyzed and remembered. The average person can remember a graph, yet he is unable to remember the columns of figures upon which the graph is based. Taking the hard facts of business and organizing them in visual form to make comparisons easy, to emphasize contrasts, and to bring out the full force of the message that figures can tell is a challenging opportunity.

Construct graphs on your typewriter or with the help of commercially available aids. The most widely used commercial graphing material is found in the Chartpak kit, which contains self-adhering bar and line tapes in various designs and colors. With such a kit the amateur can make charts that are very effective—even dramatic. Then there are the professional chart makers. Believe it or not, the *Yellow Pages* in New York (Manhattan) alone contain over thirty listings under *Charts*.

Alphabet packs, such as Prestype, can also help the secretary produce an effective graphic presentation. The line graph on page 475 was prepared by a secretary untrained in art, using such materials. The secretary needs a basic knowledge of the various types of graphs. An "Idea" folder can be set up in which examples of each type (both typewritten and commercially prepared) can be placed, with notes concerning their suitability for certain data.

## Preparing Charts and Graphs

In making any chart or graph, no matter how simple, it is best to rough out a working copy first. When the final copy is prepared, the graph should be framed on the paper. The bottom margin should be slightly larger than the top margin. The margins on the sides should be equal unless the pages are to be bound at the left. If the necessary guide points are marked lightly in pencil, they can be erased with an art gum eraser after the inking in is completed.

The title of the chart or graph should indicate its nature concisely. It should be centered above or below the chart, and its lettering should be the largest or the most heavily emphasized on the chart. The use of lettering guides is recommended. The source of the data and the date of compilation can be placed in one of the bottom corners at either margin. Even when this information is omitted from the presentation copy, it must be recorded on the working copy.

**Line Graphs.** A commonly used type of graph is the *line graph*. It is most effective in showing fluctuations in a value or a quantity over a period of time, such as variations in production, sales, costs, or profits over a period of months or years. Thus, the line graph is an effective way to depict a comparison of trends over a period of time.

The line graph on page 475 emphasizes the positive relationship that existed between net profit and the amount spent for advertising over a particular five-year period.

Follow these suggestions for preparing line graphs:

1. Prepare a working copy on printed graph or coordinate paper and the final or presentation copy on plain paper.
2. Place periods of time on the horizontal scale at the bottom of the graph; record variations in quantities or numbers on the vertical scale.
3. Always show the *zero* point. To prevent the curve from occurring too high on the chart, show a "break" in the chart with two wavy horizontal lines to indicate the part that you have omitted. (See page 475.)
4. To avoid distortions, plan the size of your graph. It is good practice to make the width at least one and one-half and not more than one and three-fourths times the height. A rise can be made to appear very steep and thus sharp or quite gradual, depending upon the relation of height to width.
5. If possible, position all lettering horizontally on the chart.
6. Work with no more than four or five lines on a graph, giving each a legend or identification on the graph. Make each line distinctive in character by using different colors or by using these lines: heavy solid (—), light solid (—), dash (---), dots (...), or dot dash (.-.-.-.).

# COMPARISON OF NET PROFIT WITH ADVERTISING EXPENDITURES

In Thousands of Dollars

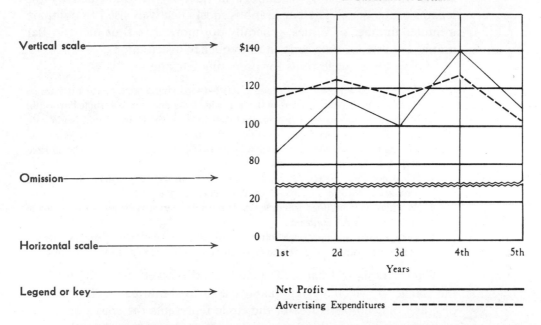

Vertical scale————————→

Omission————————→

Horizontal scale————————→

Legend or key————————→

This line graph shows the *zero* point, uses two wavy lines to indicate the omission that positions the significant data properly, and gives a key or legend identifying the two items being plotted. As many as four or five items can be plotted, provided the lines are not too close together.

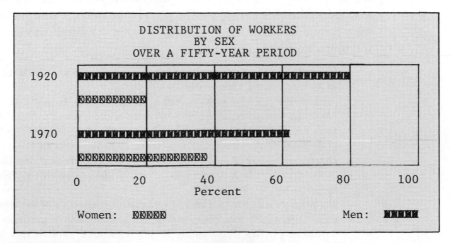

Source: Women Workers Today, U.S. Department of Labor, Employment Standards Administration, Women's Bureau, Washington, D.C., 1971, p. 1

For this typewritten horizontal bar graph, the heavy bar was typed by striking over upper-case *M, W, A,* and *V.* The light bar was typed by striking over uppercase *X* and *O.*

**Bar Graphs.** The bar graph presents quantities by means of horizontal or vertical bars. Variations in quantity are indicated by the lengths of the bars. The bar graph is most effectively used to compare a limited number of values, generally not more than four or five. Bar graphs are used in time series and frequency distributions.

Follow these suggestions for preparing bar graphs:

1. For best appearance, when space is left between single bars, space the bars so that there is a distance between them ranging from one half to a whole bar width.
2. Except for time series, the quantities indicated on the chart should begin with *zero* (0). In a chart where starting at 0 makes the chart too tall or too wide, omit that portion after 0 on which all bars would appear and indicate the omitted portion by a pair of break lines.
3. When possible, arrange bars in ascending or descending order. If they are arranged according to time, chart the earliest period first.
4. Bars may be in outline form or solid. If the bars represent different items, shade or color them for contrast.
5. To type a bar, use uppercase letters (X, W, N, $), a heavy strikeover (X over 0), or a combination of letters and characters (as in the lower graph on page 475).

**Circle Graphs or Charts.** The circle chart is an effective way to show the manner in which a given quantity is divided into parts. In this type of graph the complete area of the circle represents the whole quantity, while the divisions within the circle represent the parts. Thus, the illustration shows not only the relationship of each part to the whole, but also of each part to every other part.

The circle chart may be used to present such data as how the sales dollar is spent; how taxes paid by a firm are divided among local, state, and federal governments; or the percentage of store purchases made by men compared with that made by women. Follow these suggestions for preparing circle graphs:

1. Convert the data to be presented into percentage form. Let the circumference of the circle equal 100 percent.
2. Arrange the elements to be plotted according to size, largest first.
3. Mark the top center of the circumference of the circle, the "12 o'clock" position. From this point, moving in a clockwise direction, mark off that percentage of the total that each segment represents, beginning with the largest segment.
4. Determine the size of each segment. *If a protractor is used*, the circumference of the circle equals 360, or a total of 100%; thus a segment representing 10% would be 36°.
   *If a protractor is not available*, divide the circumference of the circle into four equal parts (each part representing 25%). Each fourth part may in turn be divided into halves (representing 12½% segments). Follow this division plan until the size of segment desired is obtained.
5. If space permits, identify each segment by a caption inside the segment. Shade or color the segments to provide contrast.
6. Type the titles of the sections horizontally.

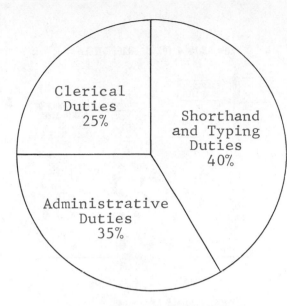

Clerical
Duties
25%

Shorthand
and Typing
Duties
40%

Administrative
Duties
35%

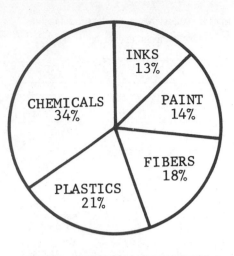

INKS
13%

PAINT
14%

CHEMICALS
34%

FIBERS
18%

PLASTICS
21%

## SALES VOLUME BREAKDOWN
## BY PRODUCT

This partially typewritten circle graph
shows the relationship of the sales of
each product to each other product
and to the total sales volume.

Note that the secretary has used the
black- and red-inked portions of her
typewriter ribbon for different effects.

## DAILY WORK DISTRIBUTION
## OF THE
## EXECUTIVE SECRETARY

This partially typewritten circle graph
shows the relationship of the duties of
the executive secretary by classification.

## THE EFFECT OF RECORDS LOSS BY FIRE

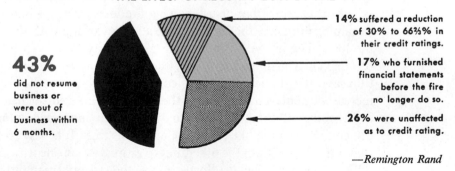

**43%**
did not resume
business or
were out of
business within
6 months.

**14%** suffered a reduction
of 30% to 66⅔% in
their credit ratings.

**17%** who furnished
financial statements
before the fire
no longer do so.

**26%** were unaffected
as to credit rating.

—*Remington Rand*

Notice how, in this commercially prepared circle or "pie" graph, the black section dramatizes the effect of records loss by fire and indirectly promotes the sale of fireproof files and
safes. To emphasize the point being made, the artist disregarded some of the usual points
of form for graphs.

MEDIAN WEEKLY WAGE FOR OFFICE WORKERS

EMPLOYED IN CLEVELAND, OHIO

January, 197-

| | Typist | Stenographer | Secretary A |
|---|---|---|---|
| 180 | | | $$$$$ |
| 160 | | | $$$$$$$$$$ $$$$$$$$$$ |
| 140 | | | $$$$$$$$$$ $$$$$$$$$$ |
| 120 | | $$$$$$$ $$$$$$$$$$ | $$$$$$$$$$ $$$$$$$$$$ |
| 100 | $$$$$$$$$$ $$$$$$$$$$ | $$ $$$$$$$$$$ | $$$$$$$$$$ $$$$$$$$$$ |
| 80 | $$$$$$$$$$ $$$$$$$$$$ | $$$$$$$$$$ $$$$$$$$$$ | $$$$$$$$$$ $$$$$$$$$$ |
| 60 | $$$$$$$$$$ $$$$$$$$$$ | $$$$$$$$$$ $$$$$$$$$$ | $$$$$$$$$$ $$$$$$$$$$ |
| 40 | $$$$$$$$$$ $$$$$$$$$$ | $$$$$$$$$$ $$$$$$$$$$ | $$$$$$$$$$ $$$$$$$$$$ |
| 20 | $$$$$$$$$$ $$$$$$$$$$ | $$$$$$$$$$ $$$$$$$$$$ | $$$$$$$$$$ $$$$$$$$$$ |

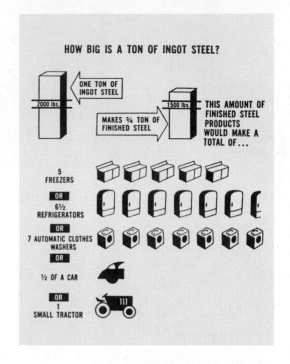

—*American Iron and Steel Institute*

In this pictorial graph the dollar-sign symbol ($) in each bar represents $1. With larger amounts, each $ can represent $100, $1,000, $10,000, or more.

While the secretary will not do the actual drawing of a pictorial chart, she may do much of the planning for the graph and be responsible for the preparation of the drawings by a commercial artist.

**Pictorial Charts.** One of the more interesting developments in graphic representation is the use of pictorial charts. They are generally an adaptation of one of the other types of graphs in which drawn symbols are used to represent the types of data being charted.

For example, a bar chart showing fire losses may be illustrated with streaming fire hose, the length of the stream varying with the amount of the loss. The growth of telephone service may be shown by drawings of telephones arranged in a line, each telephone representing so many thousand telephones. It is not considered good practice to represent increases by enlarging the size of the object symbolized, such as augmenting the size of the telephone to indicate an increased number; it is difficult to compare like objects of different sizes. It is easy to determine that one is larger than the other, but to estimate that one is twice or three times as large is difficult. Furthermore, the symbol frequently gives the impression that the item and not the quantity increased in size. Indicate size or growth by more symbols rather than larger symbols as shown at the left above.

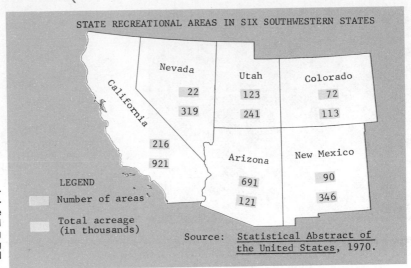

STATE RECREATIONAL AREAS IN SIX SOUTHWESTERN STATES

| | | |
|---|---|---|
| Nevada | Utah | Colorado |
| 22 | 123 | 72 |
| 319 | 241 | 113 |
| | Arizona | New Mexico |
| 216 | 691 | 90 |
| 921 | 121 | 346 |

California

LEGEND
Number of areas
Total acreage (in thousands)

Source: Statistical Abstract of the United States, 1970.

To illustrate her employer's report on recreational facilities, the secretary constructed this map chart, using color to give meaning to the figures presented on the chart.

**Map Charts.** Maps are often used to depict quantitative information particularly when comparison is made of geographic areas. After the selection of the proper map, follow these suggestions in preparing the map chart:

1. Outline the geographic areas, either by use of color, shading, or crosshatching.
2. Provide a legend to explain the meanings given to the colors, shadings, or crosshatchings.
3. If quantities are involved, figures can be placed inside the geographic area. Other symbols representing quantities, such as dots, may also be used.

### Limitations of Charts and Graphs

While charts or graphs are useful in presenting comparative data, they have certain limitations. The number of facts presented on any one graph is usually limited to four or five. It is best to use a table when six or more items are involved. A second limitation is that only approximate values can be shown on charts or graphs.

A third limitation is that it is possible for a graph to be drawn with mathematical accuracy and still give a distorted picture of the facts being presented. For example, the overall width of a line graph determines the angles of the plotted lines. A graph that is too narrow may indicate a much sharper rise and fall in the lines than the data indicate. In the same way, a graph that is too wide may tend to give the impression of a much more gradual fluctuation than may have actually occurred.

The London office of the American Express International Banking Corporation keeps its records constantly updated by means of this visual wall chart.

*—American Express*

## Process and Flow Charts

One of the most widely used tools in office management is the process or flow chart. It is used to determine the most effective, simplest, and least expensive means of accomplishing a task. The flow chart traces a unit of work as it flows through the office. Symbols with connecting lines are used to trace a step-by-step sequence of the work from point of origin to point of completion. The basic symbols are shown on page 481. A template can be purchased for drawing these symbols. While the meaning of each symbol has become fairly standardized, a key can be provided to prevent any misunderstanding.

Graphic data processing equipment now permits man and machine to exchange graphic information at electronic speed. Businessmen work directly with *graphics*, charts, curves, sketches, and drawings generated on a cathode-ray-display tube. The images can be recorded on film. (See Chapter 18.)

## Organization Chart

An organization chart is a graphic presentation of the organizational structure of a business. It points out responsibility relationships and answers two basic questions: (1) What are the lines of authority (who reports to whom)? (2) What are the functions of each unit (who is responsible for what)?

A business organization is seldom static. It is changed by new personnel, new divisions, new responsibilities, and realignment of old responsibilities. The organization chart, therefore, is frequently revised. The technique of preparing and updating an organization chart is part of the "know-how" that every secretary needs. On page 482 are suggestions for preparing an organization chart. (See also Chapter 2.)

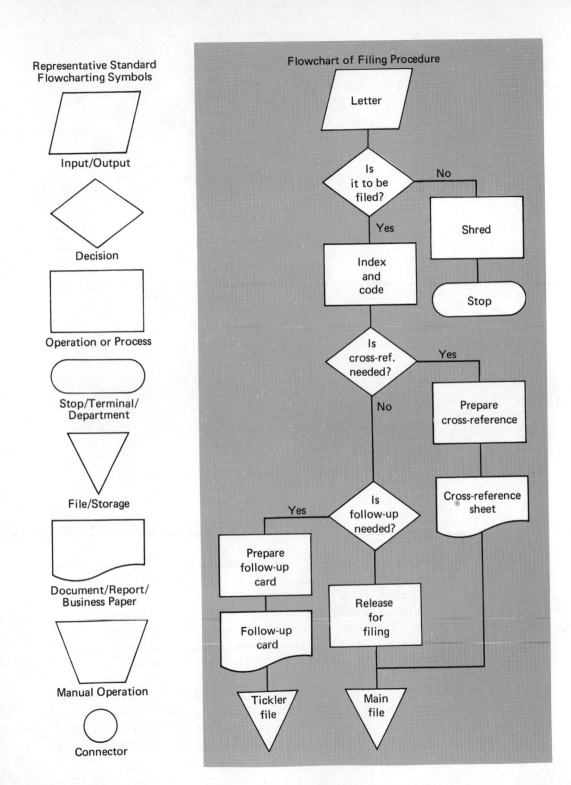

Representative Standard
Flowcharting Symbols

Input/Output

Decision

Operation or Process

Stop/Terminal/
Department

File/Storage

Document/Report/
Business Paper

Manual Operation

Connector

Flowchart of Filing Procedure

Letter

Is it to be filed?

No

Yes

Shred

Stop

Index and code

Is cross-ref. needed?

Yes

No

Prepare cross-reference

Cross-reference sheet

Is follow-up needed?

Yes

Prepare follow-up card

Release for filing

Follow-up card

Tickler file

Main file

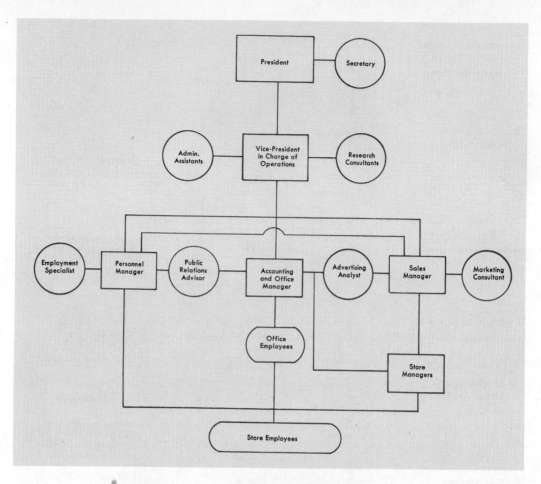

On this organization chart, the four levels of administrative authority are clearly identified. The administrative staff is differentiated from the support staff. Note that the secretary to the president is not under the supervision of the office manager.

1. **The chart should be simple.** A complex chart can confuse more than it can help.
2. **Responsibility should flow downward in the chart** with each level clearly identifiable. Lines of authority should be easily identified.
3. **When the intersecting of a line is unavoidable, the *pass symbol* (a half-circle "detour" in an otherwise straight line) is used.**
4. **Different symbols differentiate policy-making positions (line) from support positions (staff).**

The organization chart shown on this page shows a line-and-staff relationship. Such a chart would be supplemented with a functions chart on which the responsibilities of each position would be identified. To show on one chart both authority relationships and functional responsibilities detracts from its visual simplicity.

# SUGGESTED READINGS

Balsley, Irol Whitmore, and Jerry W. Robinson. *Integrated Secretarial Studies*, Jubilee ed. Cincinnati: South-Western Publishing Co., 1964.

Dawe, Jessamon, and William Jackson Lord, Jr. *Functional Business Communication*. Englewood Cliffs: Prentice-Hall, Inc., 1968, pp. 465–482.

Famularo, Joseph J. *Organization Planning Manual*. New York: American Management Association, 1971.

Lesikar, Raymond V. *Report Writing for Business*, 3d ed. Homewood, Illinois: Richard D. Irwin, Inc., 1969, pp. 299–323.

Rogers, Anna C. *Graphic Charts Handbook*. Washington: Public Affairs Press, 1961.

## QUESTIONS FOR DISCUSSION

1. What is meant by the statement, "Business decisions are not based on raw data, but on information derived from data"?

2. What kind of graphs should be prepared to present the following data?

   (a) The number of men employees as compared with the number of women employees of a company for each year of a five-year period

   (b) The amount paid in one year for taxes to the city and county governments compared with the amount paid to the state and federal governments

   (c) The average consumption of electricity over a 24-hour period in order to identify peak-load periods

   (d) Amounts two companies spent for research over four years.

3. Corporations usually use graphs extensively in their annual reports to stockholders. Financial tables and statements, however, are generally used in presenting data to boards of directors and to banks. Why are graphs used in the one case and tables in the other?

4. What type of graphic presentation would you recommend for the following data?

   (a) Total sales in the U.S. by districts for one year

   (b) Sales by product in six districts for one year

   (c) Total company sales over a twenty-year period

5. A consultant firm with a total of 35 employees reported in a community wage study that its average wage (arithmetic mean) was $13,000. An examination of the records revealed that the firm had ten high-paid executives, each receiving over $30,000 a year. What would be your criticism of the reported average wage figure?

6. What is the secretary's responsibility in a situation in which she is aware that her employer is issuing false statistical information? Would it make any difference whether the information was going to an outside agency or to another official in the firm? What should she do if the information is misleading but not illegal?

**7.** Tell how you would indicate the following kinds of omissions in quoted matter. Then use the Reference Guide to verify or correct your answers.

Research has barely begun, **(words omitted here)** and no fair estimate of additional time required can be given **(closing words of sentence omitted here)**. We hope three months will be sufficient but can make no promises. **(sentence omitted here)** Two of the technicians begin new assignments October 1.

**8.** Tell how you would punctuate the following kinds of changes in quoted matter. Then use the Reference Guide to verify or correct your answers.

**(a)** To show a correction:
This material is of excellent *actually inferior* quality.

**(b)** To show an uncorrected error:
The *author's* styles are similar.

**(c)** To show an interpolation:
Since publication *1960* the situation has changed.

## PROBLEMS

■ **1.** Your employer tells you that the company is considering the establishment of a new branch office. The proposed location has narrowed to:

Phoenix, Arizona
St. Petersburg, Florida
Grand Rapids, Michigan
Charlotte, North Carolina
Elyria, Ohio

He asks you to make a comparison of the 1960 and 1970 population reports for these five cities as one of the bases on which the Board of Directors will make its final decision.

**(a)** Prepare in pencil a tabulation of the data that you secure from a reference source. Compute the percentage of increase or decrease in population during the ten-year period, and arrange the table in descending order. In calculating your percentages, round your population figures to the nearest thousand.

**(b)** Type the table in good form, making one carbon copy. If necessary, prepare a pencil layout.

**(c)** Keep a record of the time you spend on this project and prepare an itemized report of the cost of pre-paring this table for your employer. Assume that your salary is $140 for a 40-hour week.

■ **2.** Preparatory to establishing a policy on sick leave, your employer asks you to make a study of the number of days of absence from work because of illness and other causes (excluding vacations) of the 70 employees in the Des Moines office. From the records, you obtained the total number of days each employee was absent. They are as follows:

| | | | | | | |
|---|---|---|---|---|---|---|
| 26 | 8 | 17 | 15 | 17 | 14 | 13 |
| 16 | 7 | 5 | 47 | 20 | 25 | 19 |
| 12 | 20 | 11 | 15 | 9 | 4 | 41 |
| 18 | 27 | 19 | 11 | 19 | 12 | 13 |
| 8 | 3 | 44 | 18 | 24 | 17 | 15 |
| 18 | 14 | 13 | 10 | 2 | 37 | 20 |
| 28 | 16 | 15 | 15 | 14 | 11 | 9 |
| 1 | 32 | 19 | 30 | 18 | 11 | 12 |
| 10 | 6 | 13 | 15 | 33 | 17 | 21 |
| 16 | 11 | 13 | 8 | 7 | 14 | 12 |

**(a)** Prepare a frequency distribution of the days absent. Use a class interval of five days (one work week), such as 11 to 15, 16 to 20. Include in the table the percentage of employees who were absent in each frequency class.

**(b)** Determine the modal class interval.

■ **3.** The following amounts are the June sales per day of a product.

| Amount | Amount |
|---|---|
| $118.23 | $  9.61 |
| 41.32 | 18.23 |
| 91.73 | 107.16 |
| 63.24 | 26.31 |
| 36.74 | 83.17 |
| 18.92 | 67.92 |
| 87.65 | 74.26 |
| 27.11 | 68.31 |
| 16.94 | 17.08 |
| 78.26 | 10.66 |
| 124.36 | 94.33 |
| 97.08 | 101.09 |
|  | 89.31 |

(a) Prepare in pencil a tabulation of the sales so that you can determine the median. What is the median sale for June?

(b) Calculate the arithmetic average or mean of the June sales.

■ **4.** The following figures represent the sales volume for National Industries for one year. Prepare a line graph of the data. What implications can you give about seasonal fluctuations and general performance for the two years?

| | First Year | Second Year |
|---|---|---|
| January . . . . . . . . | $86,857 | $114,273 |
| February . . . . . . . | 69,623 | 92,526 |
| March . . . . . . . . | 38,972 | 64,159 |
| April . . . . . . . . . | 34,284 | 60,844 |
| May . . . . . . . . . | 40,485 | 69,273 |
| June . . . . . . . . . | 37,737 | 76,294 |
| July . . . . . . . . . | 40,852 | 74,858 |
| August . . . . . . . . | 46,085 | 82,437 |
| September . . . . . . | 49,592 | 80,158 |
| October . . . . . . . | 55,846 | 83,628 |
| November . . . . . . . | 54,249 | 87,849 |
| December . . . . . . . | 61,292 | 94,958 |

# Chapter 21

## ASSISTANCE WITH REPORTS, PROCEDURES WRITING, AND PUBLICATIONS

One of the very important areas where the secretary may assist her employer is that of preparing business reports. Nowhere else is the employer-secretary teamwork better exemplified than in business writing. Each has a contribution to make. Whether your employer represents top management, middle management, or front-line supervision, he is actively involved in some kind of report writing, varying from the informal interoffice memorandum to the formal, bound report. He may even prepare manuscripts for publication or be responsible for procedures writing for the company. As a team member, you will be expected to be an expert in the language and display of material; and you may even be asked to be a critic of the report content. Further, you may be completely responsible for the preparation of routine business reports.

This chapter discusses reports, procedures writing, and manuscripts for printing. It gives specific instructions for the organization of reports, and illustrates techniques for making material attractive and interesting. This information will be useful to you in your role as administrative assistant.

## REPORT WRITING

The primary purpose of a business report is to transmit objective information that, in turn, stimulates management action. A report is used to plan, organize, and implement business operations; it contains factual information presented in clear, concise language.

Reports are used within the company or outside the company. For internal use, reports are *vertical* (up and down the company ranks) or *horizontal* (across management lines). They are *formal* (written) or *informal* (both written and oral). As business becomes more complex, so do management problems, and the weight of report writing and report increases. Every year, millions of business reports are written — and generally it is management personnel who must digest and react to the information.

## Report-Writing Routine

There is considerable difference in the routine for writing a report and the routine for writing a letter. The executive writes and rewrites a business report until he has presented the subject matter with precise clarity. His routine is something like this:

He collects the information.

He formulates a broad or detailed outline of the contents.

He checks the logic of his organization of content.

He drafts the report in longhand or dictates it. The secretary types it in rough-draft form.

He (and perhaps the secretary, too) rechecks the organization of the material for better structure and edits it sentence by sentence for clarity and correctness. The secretary types another draft.

He checks again the organization and editing. The secretary types it (or supervises its typing) in final form.

Executives vary in their skill and procedures in writing reports. Every executive, however, edits and polishes successive drafts until the final report is as clear, concise, and logical as he can make it.

## The Secretary's Responsibility

Although the employer seldom delegates to the secretary the responsibility of writing an important report, he may request that she research information or assemble data and statistics. Generally, he will rely on the secretary to edit the report for clear language, to eliminate repetitive words and phrases, to check spellings and meanings of words, and to double-check all figures. He may suggest that she assume the role of the reader in editing, to insure that the report as written will be understood.

In addition, the secretary is responsible for the typewritten presentation of the report in logical sequence and in attractive style. She may have a file of sample reports to guide her in this work.

In matters of editing and completing the final typewritten draft, the secretary is expected to be the expert. This is an established contribution in the employer-secretary teamwork of business writing.

## The Form of a Report

Some companies have developed style sheets for all or for special reports. If such is the case, the form indicated in the style sheets will be used as standard practice. In other cases, the writer follows his own preference, but *consistently*.

A short report may consist of only the body or informative text. A long, formal report may have, in addition to the body, various introductory parts and appendixes, the order for which is shown on page 488.

| Introductory Parts: | Cover or title page (or both) |
| --- | --- |
| | Preface or letter of transmittal, including acknowledgments |
| | Table of contents |
| | List of tables, charts, illustrations |
| | Summary |
| Body of the Report: | Introduction, including purpose of the report |
| | Main body of the report |
| | Conclusions and recommendations |
| Supplementary Parts: | Appendix or reference section |
| | Bibliography |
| | Index |

Notice that the summary *precedes* the main body of the report. This arrangement benefits the busy executive who may be interested in or have time to read only a synopsis of the report. Those who need or want complete information read the entire report.

Of the three main parts of a report (introductory, body, and supplementary), the body is usually developed first and typed in all but final form before the other parts are prepared. For this reason, the development of the body of a report is likewise discussed first here.

## DEVELOPING THE BODY OF THE REPORT

Even though the executive is responsible for the report, he will sensibly and logically work with the secretary as a team member.

### The Outline

A methodical executive first sets up a topic outline or framework of the report containing all the important points that he wishes to cover. He may make and use only a pencil draft, or he may submit it to a superior for final approval—in which case the secretary types the outline in proper form (on one page, if possible). This outline may later serve as the table of contents and the heading framework for the report.

No main heading or subheading in an outline ever stands alone. For every *I* there is at least a *II*, for every *A* a *B*. (When an outline contains a "single" heading, a thoughtful reading will usually reveal that the heading actually is part of another point, or misplaced, or irrelevant.) The main headings and subheadings should be phrased accurately and concisely *in parallel style*. They can be short constructions, long constructions that tell the story, or even complete sentences; but once the style is established, it must be consistent and parallel throughout.

In the following partial first-draft outline of an article on executive-secretary teams, notice the wordy and nonparallel phrasings of the main headings and subheadings and the concise, parallel form of the revision.

```
  I.   WORST TRAITS OF A TYPICAL SECRETARY

       A.  Search me--I don't own the place
       B.  Has to be told to do everything
       C.  Can't remember

 II.   WHAT SECRETARIES DISLIKE MOST ABOUT BOSSES

       A.  Treats me like a piece of office scenery
       B.  Too many five-minutes-to-five emergencies
       C.  Doesn't realize I have a good mind too
```

```
  I.   WORST TRAITS OF SECRETARIES

       A.  Gives impression of being uninterested
       B.  Shows very little initiative
       C.  Forgets details and instructions

 II.   WORST TRAITS OF EXECUTIVES

       A.  Treats secretary too impersonally
       B.  Has needless five-minutes-to-five emergen-
           cies
       C.  Ignores intellectual capacity of secretary
```

## The Rough Draft

A carefully written formal paper is typed one or more times in rough-draft form. A rough draft is generously spaced and accurately transcribed with little thought of final form or appearance. The purpose of the rough draft is to get the writer's thoughts on paper—to give him something tangible to edit and improve. Rather than a waste of time, this is a vital step. In typing rough drafts, follow these practices:

1. The paper used is less than letterhead quality but is sufficiently strong to withstand erasing during the editing process. Many offices use colored paper.
2. Carbon copies are not made unless they are expressly requested or unless an extra copy is needed to be cut into strips in reorganizing the material.
3. Plenty of room for write-ins and transfer indications is provided by use of triple spacing and wide margins on all four sides.
4. Each successive draft is given a number and dated. Each page is numbered in sequence and sometimes carries the draft number and date also.
5. Each successive draft is carefully checked and proofread so that subsequent drafts will contain valid material.
6. Typing errors are X'd or lined out rather than erased if time is short.
7. Quoted matter, if several lines in length, is single-spaced and indented in the same form as in the final copy because changes in quoted matter are unlikely.
8. Footnotes are typed at the bottom of the page, or on a separate sheet, or as shown on page 490.

A simple method of incorporating a footnote into a rough draft is
shown in this example[1]--that is, to type the footnote immediately

---

[1]J Marshall Hanna, Estelle L. Popham, and Rita Sloan Tilton,
Secretarial Procedures and Administration (6th ed.; Cincinnati:
South-Western Publishing Co., 1973), p. 513.

---

below the line in which the reference number appears, separated
from the textual matter above and below by lines across the page.

Save all rough drafts until the report is completed and presented,
even though they have been superseded, because the executive sometimes decides to use material from an earlier draft.

## TYPING THE BODY OF THE REPORT

The final version of the report measures the executive's skill in
concise, logical writing and the secretary's skill in sustained, attractive. meticulous typing. As the secretary begins the final typing, she
should vow to make haste slowly, taking time to design an attractive
page layout. Keeping a dictionary and a punctuation guide within arm's
reach is also a must.

Most reports require multiple copies. Prepare carbon copies as you
type the original, photocopy the original for distribution, or type the
copy on a master for reproduction.

### Page Layouts

There are two kinds of typed page layouts: the *traditional* which
looks much like a standard printed page of a textbook; and the *nontraditional* in which the units of typing are creatively arranged and
displayed. The successful secretary must be alert to ways of presenting
facts in nontraditional layouts as well as in traditional ones. By varying
margins, line spacing, indentions, capital and small letters, spacing between letters and words, underlining, placement of various parts, using
white space generously, and devising charts, drawings, and graphs, she
can achieve results that will greatly enhance the effectiveness of a report.

**Indentions.** Paragraphs may be typed flush with the left margin or
indented 5, 10, 15, or even 20 spaces. For single-spaced reports blocked
or with paragraph indentions, double-space between paragraphs. In
blocked double-spaced work, triple-space between paragraphs.

**Margins.** The suggestions that follow will help the secretary maintain uniform margins.[1] Simplify the typewriting job by placing a *special guide sheet* directly behind the page being typed. Use ordinary bond or other serviceable paper (or onionskin, if carbon copies are necessary). The guide sheet, illustrated here for a leftbound manuscript) should be ruled with India ink, other dark ink, or colored pencil that will be visible through the top sheet.

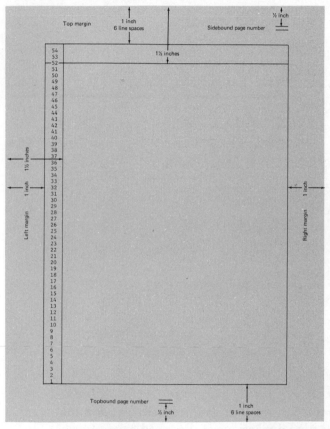

A Special Guide Sheet

1. In the *upper right corner* and *centered at the bottom* are short lines positioned so that a page number typed to rest on them will leave a ½-inch top and 1-inch side margin or a ½-inch bottom margin, as desired.

   Usually, only topbound manuscripts are numbered at the foot of the page; but if a first page of an unbound or leftbound manuscript is to be numbered, the number is centered at the foot of the page as for a topbound manuscript.

2. The vertical rule 1½ inches from the left indicates the left margin setting. The extra ½ inch is for binding.

3. The vertical rule 1 inch from the right indicates the right margin of the copy. Keep the right margin as even as possible. No more than two or three letters should extend beyond the vertical line. Use a word-division manual for speedy and correct decisions about end-of-line hyphenations. Avoid hyphenating words at the end of more than two consecutive lines, and and never end a page with a hyphenated word. Do not end or begin a line with a 1- or 2- letter syllable.

4. Two horizontal lines (1 inch and 2 inches from the top of the sheet) mark the top margins of the manuscript. The first page begins on Line 13, which leaves a 2-inch top margin. Subsequent pages start on Line 7, which leaves a 1-inch top margin. (Position the typewriter cylinder to type on the first line of writing *below* the rules shown.)

---

[1]Adapted from *A Manual of Style for the Preparation of Papers and Reports*, 2d ed., by Erwin M. Keithley and Philip J. Schreiner.

5. The horizontal line 1 inch from the bottom edge of the paper indicates the last line available for typing. Plan to carry at least 2 lines of a paragraph forward to a new page. Plan the last line of the body of the material to allow for any footnotes that go on the page.

6. The vertical center rule shows the horizontal centering point of the page, the point equidistant between the marginal rulings at left and right.

**Titles.** Notice the differences in impact weight of the titles shown below. Which do you like best? Why?

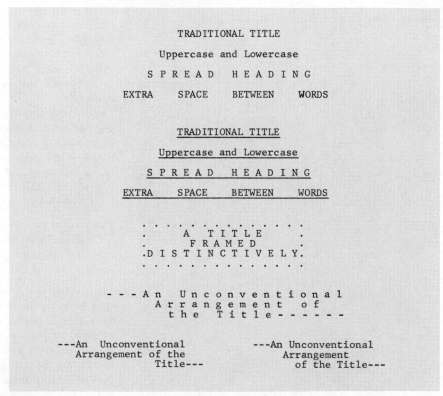

Every typewritten title is a part of a black-and-white picture. Therefore, select a style that is attractive in width and weight and that is in satisfying proportion to the dimensions of the typed page. It is hard to *visualize* which form of title is best. But you can try them out for size, weight, and appearance by typing several experimental arrangements of the title, cutting them out, and laying each one on a full page of similar typing. The best one will become evident.

**Headings and Subheadings.** Headings and subheadings are used to guide the reader through the report. The criterion for their wording is: Does the heading clarify the content and increase readability, and is the construction parallel to other headings?

In general, headings and subheadings parallel the outline. Note their arrangement in this book and their usefulness in preparing the reader and in showing the relative importance of subject matter.

Both headings and subheadings can be varied by placement, by use of capitals and small letters, and by indention, as shown in the illustrations at the right. The styles illustrated here are unusual and would be used only where there was a need for an eye-catching, dramatic effect.

Before the secretary types the report, she plans a guide to the form and position of each heading and subheading, of each margin and indention, and of all line spacing. This plan, typed in a form easily referred to, is called a style sheet.

```
                    TITLE  OF  REPORT


                        A MAIN HEADING

The text begins here without indention and is single-spaced.
Four line spaces have been left below the title and two line
spaces below the main heading.

A First Subheading


                  T I T L E   O F   R E P O R T

A MAIN HEADING      A main heading typed at the side must be broken
APPEARS HERE        into two or three short lines.  The text begins
                    five spaces to the right of the longest line in
the main heading, and the resulting line length used for one more
line than the heading contains.  Three line spaces have been left
below the title.

        Subsequent paragraphs have been indented 15 spaces
and one line space left between paragraphs.


    A FIRST SUBHEADING


            For attention value, this heading has been typed on
a separate line with four line spaces above and three below it.

        A Second Subheading.  This heading has been indented
to paragraph point, with the text following on the same line.  Two
line spaces have been left above it.

            Caution.  The adoption of an unusual style such as
this requires extra checking for consistency, or the effect will
be lost.
```

## Quoted Matter

Reports often quote material from other sources, either directly or indirectly, and must give credit to these sources. For indirect quotations or references, a footnote suffices. Direct quotations are handled in the following ways:

1. Quotations of *fewer than four lines* are typed in the body of the paragraph and enclosed in quotation marks.
2. Quotations of *four or more lines* are usually single-spaced and indented from the left margin or from both margins.
3. When a quotation of *several paragraphs* is not indented, quotation marks precede each paragraph and follow the final word in the last paragraph.
4. A *quotation within a quotation* is enclosed in single quotation marks.
5. *Italicized words* in the quotation are underscored.
6. *Omissions* are shown by ellipses—three spaced (or unspaced) periods within a sentence, four periods at the end of a sentence.

7. *Inserted words (interpolations)* are enclosed in typewritten brackets, using the underscore and diagonal: $\lfloor\ \ \rfloor$. Parentheses cannot be used, as they often occur naturally in the context and the reader could not identify matter enclosed in them as inserted matter.

8. A *footnote reference* showing the source should be made for the quotation unless the source is identified adequately in the text.

Permission to quote copyrighted material must be obtained from the copyright holder when reports are to be printed or duplicated and given public circulation, except for material published by a governmental agency. Full information should be sent with the request including the:

1. Text leading up to the quotation
2. Lines to be quoted, or page and line locations in the publication from which lengthy material is being quoted
3. Credit line or complete footnote reference
4. Title and publisher of the publication in which the quoted matter will appear

## Footnotes

Footnotes are numbered in sequence on each page, throughout each section, or throughout the entire report. There is an advantage in numbering footnotes anew with each page or section—if footnotes are inserted or deleted, only the numbers on the page or within the section need be changed. Styles of typing footnotes may be reviewed in the footnote and bibliography style guide in the Communications Guide in Part 10.

## Numbering Pages

Usually the typist saves time by waiting until the body is typed before typing page numbers. Anticipating changes, she numbers the top sheet of each carbon assembly in pencil as it is completed, thus keeping unpaged copy in order. After the supplementary sections and the preliminary pages have been typed, page numbers can be typed for the body of the report.

Arabic numerals without punctuation are placed at the upper right corner of the body and supplementary parts of the report. The preliminary pages preceding the body are numbered in small Roman numerals at the bottom center.

## PREPARING AND TYPING THE OTHER PARTS

The order in which the other parts of a report are prepared varies, but inserting page numbers on the table of contents must be one of the last steps. In the following discussion the concluding supplementary parts and then the introductory parts are considered.

## Appendix or Reference Section

In a formal report an *appendix* or *reference section* devoted to supplementary information, supporting tables and statistics, or reference material follows the body of the report.

## Bibliography

A report that is based upon a study of published materials frequently includes a bibliography, listing the source material. Such a bibliography is called a *selected bibliography*. Many business reports are based on factual information within the company, and there is no need to refer to outside source material.

Sometimes the secretary is requested to prepare a *comprehensive bibliography* listing all the material published on a subject for a selected period of time. An *annotated bibliography* contains an evaluation or a brief explanation of the content of each reference.

A bibliography reference is very similar in form to a footnote in that it cites the author's name, the title of the publication, the publisher, and the date. If there is an editor, a translator, or an illustrator, his name may be included. The price and complete details on the number of illustrations, plates, diagrams, and so on can be included if this information will be of value to the ones who will use the bibliography. Specific chapters or sections and their inclusive page numbers should be stated if the entry refers to only a certain part of the book or periodical.

## Indexing Procedure

An *index* is included only when it is felt that there will be occasion to use it. A detailed table of contents usually suffices. When an index is necessary, use a copy of the report and underline in colored pencil each item on each page that should be included in the index. Each underlined item and its page number are written on a separate slip. The completed slips are then sorted into alphabetic order, and a typed index is prepared from them.

*Transmittal,* ×*letter of, for a* ×*report*

*496*

The index slip for an item on the next page of this book is shown. The X's indicate that cross-reference slips were made and listed under *Letter of transmittal for a report* and *Report, letter of transmittal for.*

## Letter of Transmittal

Frequently a *letter of transmittal* is bound into the report and performs a function similar to the preface of a book. It gives authorization for the report, details of its preparation, the period covered, acknowledgement of persons who contributed materials and other such information to help the reader understand the depth and breadth of the report and arouse his interest in studying it. (See page 499.)

The letter of transmittal is typed on the regular business letterhead and is signed in ink. It is reproduced on the same kind of paper used for the other pages of a duplicated or printed report, and the signature is duplicated rather than handwritten.

## Summary

The summary is a concise review of the entire report and its findings. It includes a statement of the problem, its scope, the method of investigation, conclusions, and recommendations. It is objective in nature and is written to give the reader a clear understanding of the facts in the report. The length of the report determines the length of the summary; however, recommended style is to limit the summary to one page.

## Title Page

The *title page* may provide an opportunity for artistic typing. Even a report of five or ten pages is improved with a title page. One designed by the secretary should be simple if the report is typed in traditional form. If the report is typed in nontraditional form, the secretary should try for distinction and artistic display of the information.

The title page must contain the essential facts for identifying the report—the title, for whom it is prepared, by whom it is submitted, the date, the place of preparation. The essential facts vary with the contents and the readers of a report. An interoffice report may require only the title and the date. The executive should approve the title page; he may have definite opinions on the inclusion and arrangement of certain items.

## Table of Contents

After paging the report, the secretary prepares the table of contents that precedes the report. This table lists the main topics or chapter titles and page numbers, possibly conforming to the original outline. It may be useful to list subheadings and their page numbers as well. Rough out the table of contents to get an idea of its vertical length and the horizontal length of the items before deciding on the final style.

The next five pages present parts of a report typed in acceptable form.

A FEASIBILITY STUDY

OF THE REDUCTION

IN THE WORKDAY WEEK




Prepared for

Electro-Mag Company
1606 North McVickers Street
Chicago, Illinois




Submitted by

Northshore Research, Inc.
2500 Diversey Parkway, West
Chicago, Illinois

June 30, 197-

**Title Page for a Left-Bound Report**

TABLE OF CONTENTS

Page

Table of Contents Page for a Left-Bound Report

**NORTHSHORE RESEARCH, INC.**

*2500 Diversey Parkway, West*                                           *Chicago, Illinois  60647*
                                                                          *(312) 771-4890*


                                        June 30, 197-


Mr. August F. Snyder, President
Electro-Mag Company
1606 North McVickers Street
Chicago, IL  60639

Dear Mr. Snyder:

        The feasibility study, authorized by you on January 1
of this year, concerning a reduction in the workday week in
your organization is now complete.

        The conclusions were reached after thoroughly investi-
gating your organization's production schedule, quality standards, time and motion studies, and after conferences at random
with management personnel and employees in the plant.  A survey
of employee opinion was also made.

        It is recommended that the Electro-Mag Company under-
take a trial period of the four-day work week for at least six
months and, at its conclusion, evaluate the results of the trial.

        Working with you and your staff has been a pleasure.
Our gratitude is expressed to the many employees of the Electro-
Mag Company who cooperated with us in making this study.

                                        Respectfully yours,

                                        *Alfred J. Wainright*

                                        Alfred J. Wainright
                                        Director of Research


rt


**Letter of Transmittal for a Left-Bound Report**

SUMMARY

The feasibility study of a change in the workday week for the Electro-Mag Company reveals the adaptability of the company to such a reduction. The advantages would be the increased utilization of personnel and physical plant and the reduction in costs, while achieving the proposed production schedules. The change in workday week also eliminates the need for additional plant facilities to achieve the production level. In addition, employees of the company favor the change.

We recommend that:

1. The Electro-Mag Company make plans immediately to initiate a trial period of the four-day work week

2. The trial period be no less than six months

3. Work be scheduled from 7:30 a.m. to 11:30 a.m. and from 12 noon to 6 p.m., Mondays through Thursdays

4. An evaluation of the merits of the four-day work week be made at the end of the trial period

Depending upon the results of the evaluation, it may be desirable to consider a trial period of the three-day work week.

ii

Summary Page for a Left-Bound Report

A FEASIBILITY STUDY

OF THE REDUCTION

IN THE WORKDAY WEEK

INTRODUCTION

## The Problem

To better utilize the human and physical resources
of the Electro-Mag Company, the possibilities of a change in
the workday week have been explored. Alternatives to the
five-day work week are provided and evaluated.

## Purpose of the Report

Because of the increase in the demand for the products of the Electro-Mag Company and the lack of areas for
expansion of the physical plant of the company, this feasibility study has been undertaken to suggest alternative means
of increasing the present production capacity of the company
while utilizing only the available plant facilities. The
possibility of a reduction in the workday week and the further
utilization of three eight-hour shifts are considered.

## Definitions

The terms used frequently in this report are defined here.

Workday. The established workday at the Electro-Mag
Company consists of eight hours, beginning at 8:30 a.m. and
ending at 5 p.m. A one-half hour break for lunch is provided.

**First Page of a Left-Bound Report**

# PROOFREADING, FINAL CHECKING, ASSEMBLING, AND BINDING

After all the typing is finished, four important steps remain: proofreading, final checking of mechanics, assembling, and binding. (All figures and computations would, of course, have been checked *before* the final typing.)

## Proofreading

Each typed page of the final copy of the report is proofread word for word and figure for figure. A practical plan is to use the last carbon copy for checking, boldly marking all corrections on it, and filing it permanently. The careful worker goes through the material at least twice—the first time comparing the copy with the original for accuracy of typing and for omissions, and a second time for consistency of style and form. If possible, proofread the copy with someone as a team.

## Final Checking

Use a final-check sheet and go through the report once for each factor listed below. This final check has caught many an embarrassing error and is, in fact, a device that can well be used for all work involving detail and accuracy. Check the following items *on each set* of the report unless a copying machine has been used.

1. Indicated corrections made on every page
2. Correct references to page numbers, tables, or figures
3. Correct sequence of page numbers (necessary for each set even when a copying machine has been used)

## Assembling

The final report is submitted in complete sets, with the ribbon copy on top. The typed pages are assembled in reverse order—that is, the bottom page is laid out first, face up. In this way, you can see any blank or mutilated pages during assembly. When you have collated a complete set, joggle the pages horizontally and vertically until they are exactly aligned.

## Binding

Binding is the last step in preparing a report. The most popular form of binding is the staple. When only one staple is required, position it diagonally in the upper left corner (/not —). When a wider margin has been left for binding at the top or at the left, use two or three staples along the wide margin, parallel with the edge of the paper.

If a report that is to be stapled proves to be too thick, use double stapling, inserting the staples in proper position from the front and then inserting a second set in the same spots from the back.

Some offices prefer sturdier and more permanent types of binding. Some of these bindings require special supplies and equipment, such as metal eyelets, punches, wire spiral devices, or plastic combs. A convenient and attractive cover in transparent plastic with a snap-on spine is available.

## PREPARING COPY FOR THE PRINTER

When typewritten work is to be sent out of the office for printing or duplicating, the secretary types the copy in a complete, accurate, and easy-to-follow form. Since the copy is to be followed exactly, she does not rely on others for necessary punctuation, for correct spelling, or for the improvement of the copy in other ways. Of course she retains a file copy for ready reference.

If possible, however, she should discuss styling with the person who is to be responsible for the work. Together they should develop a style sheet showing the type to be used for main headings and subheadings, for footnotes, for bibliography, and for captions.

### Manuscript

Prepare a manuscript that is to be typeset according to the following guidelines:

1. Type all copy double-spaced on one side of 8½- by 11-inch sheets, with one or preferably two copies. Leave generous side margins. Quoted material or other text matter to be set apart should be single-spaced and indented on both sides.

2. Key all typewritten copy to its exact position on a page layout.

3. Number all sheets in the upper right corner. Two or more compositors may work on the same assignment, so correct numbering is imperative.

4. Type incidental changes, or write them clearly in ink, between the lines or in the margins.

5. Typewrite a long addition on a separate full-sized sheet and give it an inserted page number, as 16a; indicate on page 16 the point at which the insertion is to be made.

6. Draw a heavy line through words to be omitted.

7. Give explicit directions. With the help of a compositor, specify size and style of type faces and amount of leading (space between lines) desired.

8. Use a single underline to indicate *italics*, a double underline for SMALL CAPS, and a triple underline for REGULAR CAPS. To indicate bold face, use a wavy underline.

9. Number footnotes consecutively. They may be typed on the page to which they pertain; between full-width rules directly under the line in which the reference occurs; or at the bottom of the page but separated from the text by a short line; or all in sequence on a separate sheet.

10. Provide titles and number tables and illustrations consecutively with Arabic numerals. Send with the manuscript a full list of all tables and illustrations.

11. Include a title page showing the title, the author's name and address, and perhaps the date.

12. Send the original copy to the printer. Do not fasten the sheets together. Keep them flat by placing them between strong cardboards or in a strong box. Wrap the manuscript in strong paper.

13. Send the manuscript by first-class mail.

## Magazine Articles and Press Releases

At times the executive may be asked to submit an article for magazine publication. The secretary simplifies the editor's job of judging the space needed for the copy by typing a sample paragraph from a recent issue of the magazine line for line. She can then determine the average line length and the number of lines to an inch of printed material. She can then type the material to conform to this gauge. Headings for the copy should be consistent with those used in the magazine. A covering letter giving the approximate number of words in the article also aids the editor.

If the approximate length requirements of the article are known in advance, the secretary types a rough-draft version with double spacing in the average line length of the magazine copy. This copy is given to the executive with a close estimation of the amount of space presently accounted for. As he revises the copy, the executive can lengthen or shorten the article. Copies of the published material should be kept in a file so labeled.

Press releases should be addressed to the City Editor unless a definite person (such as the Financial Editor) is specified. Publicity and news releases are discussed on pages 213 and 214.

## Reading Proof

It is customary for the printer to submit proofs. The secretary usually does the checking for errors, but the executive should be given an opportunity to approve revisions.

The first proof is usually in galley form—long sheets containing one column of printed copy, the column width as on the final printed page. Each kind of error or change to be made is indicated by a proof-readers' mark (illustrated on page 505). The place of the correction is

# PROOFREADER'S MARKS

## INSERT MARKS FOR PUNCTUATION

ˇ Apostrophe

[/] Brackets ·

: ☉ Colon

˄ ⸜/ Comma

ˣˣˣ/ Ellipsis

!/ Exclamation point

-/ Hyphen

˄ ⌃ Inferior figure

···/ Leaders

(/) Parentheses

⊙ Period

?/ Question mark

˅ ⸝⸝ Quotation mark

; ⸜ Semicolon

˅ ˅ Superior figure

## OTHER MARKS

|| Align type; set flush

*bf* Boldface type

× ⓧ Broken letter

≡ Cap Capitalize

C+sc Capitals and small capitals

ℐ Delete

ℬ Delete and close up

˄ Insert (caret)

*ital* Italic, change to

*Bf ital* Italic boldface

*stet* Let type stand

*lc* Lower case type

⊔ Move down; lower

⊓ Move up; raise

⊏ Move to left

⊐ Move to right

¶ Paragraph

no¶ ⊏No new paragraph

out s.c. Out; omit; see copy

Ⓖ Reverse; upside down

rom Roman, change to

↶ Run in material

run in Run in material, on same line

# Space, add (horizontal)

> Space, add (vertical)

⌒ Space, close up (horizontal)

< Space, close up (vertical)

sp Spell out

tr ∽ Transpose

(?) (?) Verify or supply information

*wf* Wrong font

# / same / lc > All marks should be made in the margin on the line in which the error occurs; if more than one correction occurs in one line, they should appear in their order separated by a slanting line.

Errors should not be blotted out.

indicated in the text, and the kind of correction to be made is written in the margin on the same line. If there is more than one correction in a line, the proofreaders' marks in the margin are separated by conspicuous diagonal lines as shown in the illustration on page 505.

The printer submits the second proof in page form. This new proof must be again meticulously read and corrected. Page numbers and page headings are shown in this proof and are usually checked as separate individual operations. This is often the final opportunity for the author to catch errors and to make changes.

## PROCEDURES WRITING

Procedures writing has been called "verbal flow charting." It lists step by step the logical sequence of activities involved in a given task, so that an employee can perform an operation by following instructions. Procedures writing serves to control as well as to communicate. It controls how things are to be done as it instructs employees in the steps to follow in recurring operations.

Writing good procedures seems deceptively simple, but to eliminate extraneous material is extremely difficult. Effective procedures writing is one of the most valuable forms of business writing because it saves time and money.

Writing procedures is a sophisticated process — so much so, in fact, that some companies assign one person to write procedures, thus maintaining uniformity. It is important that procedures be written in a simple, direct style, using terms easily understood by all who will be expected to interpret and follow them in the intended manner.

Procedures for a department or for an operation are usually collected in a loose-leaf notebook that can be updated by adding and deleting pages as new procedures are issued. It is helpful to include an index in the manual for easy reference.

### A Sample Procedure

Assume that several mix-ups occurred because there was no standard procedure for reserving the board room for special meetings. Finally, your employer decides to put you, his administrative assistant or secretary, in charge of scheduling the room. He wants your help on writing a procedure to be sent to all office employees, outlining the steps to be taken in reserving and using the room.

There are at least four formats that can be used: *traditional, improved traditional, job breakdown,* and *playscript.*

Insert in Section IV, <u>Use of Special Rooms</u>,
following page 16 and label 16a, <u>Board Room</u>.

The person requesting use of the Board Room files
a written request with the administrator of office
services at least one week before the date of the
meeting, indicating the name of the group involved,
the exact time of the meeting, its expected duration, and the expected attendance.

The administrator of office services immediately
notifies the applicant in writing whether the room
is available and, if so, notifies the custodial
staff in writing of the necessary room setup and
the duration of the meeting, giving instructions
for any necessary special cleaning.

The person requesting the room checks the room one
hour before the meeting and provides any special
supplies needed, and checks lighting and temperature.

The traditional format above features prose-style writing and uses little spacing variation.

Insert in Section IV, Use of Special Rooms, 16a.

<u>Board Room</u>

<u>The person requesting use of the Board Room</u> files
a written request with the <u>administrator of office
services</u> at least one week before the proposed
meeting, indicating:

    1.   The name of the group involved
    2.   The exact time of the meeting
    3.   Its expected duration
    4.   The expected attendance

<u>The administrator of office services</u> immediately
notifies the applicant in writing whether the
room is available and, if so, notifies the <u>cus-
todial staff</u> in writing of:

    1.   The necessary room setup
    2.   The duration of the meeting
    3.   Instructions for any necessary special
       cleaning

<u>The person requesting the room</u> checks the room one
hour before the meeting and provides any special
supplies needed, and checks lighting and temperature.

Note that in the illustration of the *improved traditional* format above, variations in spacing,
use of the underline, and tabulations give emphasis to the appropriate points.

**Job Breakdown.** With the job breakdown the logical sequence of action is reflected in the *Steps*. The *Key Points* represent cautions to the worker at the points where he is likely to make mistakes. The *Steps* tell the worker what to do; the *Key Points* tell him how to do it.

Every *Step* does not have to have a *Key Point*, and there may be more than one *Key Point* for one operation.

Insert in Section IV, Use of Special Rooms, 16a.

B O A R D   R O O M

| Steps | Key Points |
|---|---|
| 1. File a written request with the administrator of office services. | 1a. Do this at least one week before the date of the proposed meeting. |
| | 1b. List name of group to use room, time of meeting, the expected duration, and the expected attendance. |
| | 1c. Make entry in tickler file for a date well in advance of the meeting to check on receipt of clearance. |
| 2. Receive clearance from the administrator of office services. | 2. Follow up tickler entry if clearance is not received promptly. |
| 3. On day of meeting, check the room one hour before the meeting. | 3. Be sure that room is clean, the temperature is comfortable, and a sufficient number of chairs are positioned for the participants. |
| 4. Distribute necessary supplies. | 4. Provide water and paper cups or glasses, ash trays, note pads, and sharpened pencils. Check the lighting and adjust the rheostats if necessary. |

**Playscript.** The playscript format[1] answers the question, "Who does what?" It utilizes the team approach in completing office tasks. The actor is easily identified, and what he does starts with an action verb in the present tense. According to the man who developed this technique, playscript is really a form of flow chart, and any step that backflows rather than proceeds by forward action can immediately be spotted, and gaps in the logical steps can also be quickly detected, just as backflow is revealed in a flow chart.

Insert in Section IV, Use of Special Rooms, p. 16a

Subject:   RESERVING BOARD ROOM FOR SPECIAL MEETINGS

| Responsibility | | Action |
|---|---|---|
| Requesting Employee | 1. | Prepares a written request at least one week before the date of the proposed meeting, including name of group, time of meeting, duration, and expected attendance. |
| | 2. | Sends request to administrator of office services |
| | 3. | Enters tickler to follow up approval |
| Administrator of Office Services | 4. | Notifies the applicant in writing whether the room is available |
| | 5. | Notifies custodial staff in writing of necessary room setup, duration of meeting, and need for any special cleaning |
| Requesting Employee | 6. | Checks the room one hour before the meeting for number of chairs and temperature level of room |
| | 7. | Distributes necessary supplies and checks lighting |

## Selecting the Format

A traditional person or a traditional company would probably adopt the improved arrangement of the traditional format. A more venturesome author in search of eyecatching appeal would probably choose the

[1]Leslie Matthies, *The Playscript Procedure* (New York: Office Publications Inc., 1961).

job breakdown or the playscript. In a procedure involving one operator, the job breakdown might be chosen, for it has the advantage of cautioning against wrong moves. It looks more complicated than the playscript, however. The playscript would probably be selected for writing procedures involving more than one worker.

## SUGGESTED READINGS

Archer, Robert M., and Ruth Pearson Ames. *Basic Business Communications.* Englewood Cliffs: Prentice-Hall, Inc., 1971.

Becker, Esther R., and Evelyn Anders. *The Successful Secretary's Handbook.* New York: Harper & Row, 1971, pp. 271–284.

Dawe, Jessamon, and William Jackson Lord, Jr. *Functional Business Communication.* Englewood Cliffs: Prentice-Hall, Inc., 1968, pp. 402–511.

Hay, Robert D. *Written Communications for Business Administrators.* New York: Holt, Rinehart, and Winston, Inc., 1965, pp. 253–406, 441–467.

Keithley, Erwin M., and Philip J. Schreiner. *A Manual of Style for the Preparation of Papers and Reports,* 2d ed. Cincinnati: South-Western Publishing Co., 1971.

Lazzaro, Victor. *Systems and Procedures, A Handbook for Business and Industry,* 2d ed. Englewood Cliffs: Prentice-Hall, Inc., 1968, pp. 253–261.

Matthies, Leslie. *The Playscript Procedure.* New York: Office Publications, Inc., 1961.

Robinson, David M. *Writing Reports for Management Decisions.* Columbus: Charles E. Merrill Publishing Co., 1969.

Shurter, Robert LeFevre. *Written Communication in Business,* 3d ed. New York: McGraw-Hill Book Company, 1971.

## QUESTIONS FOR DISCUSSION

1. Why might a written procedure be called a "verbal flow chart"? Why is it difficult to write procedures?

2. If you were responsible for getting a company brochure published, how would you prepare for a conference with the printer?

3. Suppose your employer is in conference with his superior, going over a report which you and he have prepared. He discovers an error in an amount and calls you in and says that you made the error. He petulantly asks if you failed to check the figures. You remember distinctly that the amount is one which he took from a statement prepared by someone else in your department. How would you answer?

4. If you had obtained all the data available on a certain subject and an executive had drafted a report based on this information, what would you do if in the morning's mail you received a business magazine containing an article which covers a new angle of the subject? Would you call the executive's attention to the new material, knowing that it would mean a rewrite job?

5. In what ways will a report differ if it is intended for individuals (a) who know little about the subject matter or (b) who are technicians of the

subject matter? Give examples of types of reports written for each category.

6. In the printed copy of the lecture "The Care and Feeding of the Mind" by Professor Jacques Barzun there appears the following paragraph. Punctuate it as you would if it were dictated to you. Then use the Reference Guide to check your answers.

> The lesson is don't be afraid to *lend* your mind. It is a perfectly safe loan you are sure to get it back possibly with interest and in any case the very act of wrapping it around an alien thought will keep it in stretching trim. Give heed to any idea that is proposed to you and see where it leads. Don't judge by first appearances and don't fear a permanent imprint on the pure white page of your mind. You can always wind up with Euclid's favorite conclusion you remember how he starts by saying Let ABC be larger than DEF. You let him foolish as his idea appears from the diagram and pretty soon he reassures you by exclaiming Which is absurd!

7. Type the information in the blanks in the following sentences. Then use the Reference Guide to verify or correct your answers.

   (a) The typewriter is _____ years old. (8)

   (b) We are asking _____ for the typewriter which is _____ years old. ($20, 14)

   (c) To be exact, the mimeograph is _____ years, _____ months, and _____ days old. (15, 8, 4)

## PROBLEMS

■ **1.** Type each of the following titles twice (eight different arrangements). Divide the titles into two or more lines if necessary, and center each line horizontally on the page. Allow six line spaces between titles. Indicate your preference of the resulting styles.

(a) Opportunities for Women in Business Management

(b) How Data Communication Creates Total Business Systems

(c) Women Who Work

(d) The Increasing Influence of Women in the Economy

■ **2.** As administrative assistant to the vice-president, operations, of a large manufacturing firm, you are assigned the supervision of two young assistants. You have given them the responsibility of opening and sorting the office mail. You decide to prepare a procedural statement in playscript style covering this activity. Before you begin writing, you analyze the cycle of the operation, determine the actors involved (the two assistants, mail messenger, and yourself), analyze each action in the operation, and identify any office forms used in the process. Write the statement of procedures. (You may wish to refer to Chapter 7).

■ **3.** From the bibliographical notes that you prepared for Problem 3 in Chapter 19, page 463, develop a business report on one of the ten topics given (or a topic of your own choice which your instructor has approved). Use graphs or tables if you think they will improve your presentation.

**4.** To provide some practice for yourself in using proofreaders' marks, indicate the method of marking (both in the text material and in the margins) changes listed below. Set up three columns headed *Change Desired in Text, Proofreaders' Mark in Text, and Proofreaders' Mark in Margin.*

(1) Insert the word *more*.
(2) Change the word *readnig* to *reading*.
(3) Delete the word *usually*.
(4) Show a space in *ofthis*.
(5) Even up the left margin where the letters have been set a space too far to the left in one line
(6) Write the word *think* in solid capitals.
(7) Show an apostrophe in the word *womens*.
(8) Capitalize the word *congressional*.
(9) Insert a hyphen in *selfemployed*.
(10) Indicate a new paragraph in the copy.
(11) Italicize the word *usually*.
(12) Use lowercase correctly for the words *History, Algebra, Social Studies*, and *English*.
(13) In marking the copy for the preceding question, you inadvertently indicated that the word *English* should be written in lower case too. Show that you want the original capitalization to stand.
(14) Transpose *two only* to *only two*.
(15) Use less space between words.
(16) Use small caps for the paragraph heading, *Characteristics of the New Process*.
(17) Use quotation marks around *shot in the arm*.
(18) Indicate no paragraph.
(19) Indicate that type does not match.
(20) Delete the hyphen in *readily-available service*.
(21) Insert a comma between *pens* and *and*.
(22) Center and type in solid caps the paragraph heading: *Introduction*.
(23) Change *thimk* to *think*.
(24) Indicate leaving more space after a colon.
(25) Increase the amount of space between lines.
(26) Move copy to the right to align.
(27) Indicate correct spelling of *state room*.
(28) Delete the apostrophe in *it's*.
(29) In the title *A Manual of Style for the Preparation of Papers and Reports*, the words *for the Preparation of Papers and Reports* have been crossed out. Indicate that these phrases should be retained.
(30) Delete the comma: *He finished the report, and got it on his superior's desk before leaving the office that afternoon.*

**5.** Using information in the Communications Guide, type correctly as a footnote and as bibliography item the following information:

(a) An unsigned article, "Making U.S. Technology More Competitive," on pp. 44–49 of *Business Week*, January 15, 1972.
(b) A book written by Ray A. Killian entitled *The Working Woman a Male Manager's View*, published by American Management Association in 1971. It contains 214 pages. The footnote refers to page 79.
(c) A chapter entitled "Training and Developing Office Workers" in *The Dartnell Office Administration Handbook*, published by the Dartnell Press, Chicago, Illinois, in 1967, J. C. Aspley, Editor. This chapter appears on pages 228–259.
(d) An article by David W. Barr, President, Moore Business Forms, Inc. called "Improving Office Productivity" in the January 1972 issue of *The Office*. The footnote refers to material on page 80.

# Part 7

# CASE PROBLEMS

William Mueller was purchasing agent for a large corporation. Although his primary responsibility was purchasing raw materials for the factory, he was also in charge of buying all office equipment. He was highly regarded inside the company because of his ability to "drive a hard bargain" and was credited with saving the company many thousands of dollars every year. He regarded price as a prime factor in purchasing equipment and sought no recommendations from company personnel as to typewriters, calculating machines, or duplicating equipment. He attended the business equipment shows regularly and was on good terms with business equipment salesmen.

Marilyn Towson, secretary to a vice-president, felt that she should be interested in developments that would increase her productivity and the quality of her work. She read secretarial and office management magazines regularly, visited showrooms of business equipment companies, and also attended business equipment shows.

At the annual business equipment show, she met Mr. Mueller. He was visibly annoyed at her presence and said jokingly, "Well, well, look who's here. What are you trying to do — train to take over as purchasing agent?"

After leaving Mr. Mueller, Marilyn tried out an automated typewriter that she felt would allow her to improve her preparation of the annual report for offset. The machine had an error-correction device and could justify margins automatically. The salesman offered to send the typewriter to her office for a trial. Marilyn wondered whether she should accept the offer and what strategy she could use to get approval for its purchase if the machine lived up to her expectations.

**Should she have ordered the machine on a trial basis?**

**Should she have presented her case to Mr. Mueller?**

**Should she have discussed her needs with her employer?**

**Should she have dropped the whole idea and continued to use what she regarded as inferior equipment?**

## 7-2  GETTING COOPERATION OF STAFF AND SUPERIORS

The office was relatively peaceful, and each worker was performing his regular duties with dispatch. Then the possibility of a merger loomed. Extensive reports would be needed immediately; and Henry Bronwell, the corporate treasurer, worked with his secretary, Ellen Burchard, through the whole weekend. They planned the work to be done before the crucial big meeting on Thursday. They roughed out the reports to be presented. Since some of the necessary information was not available in Mr. Bronwell's office, he told Ellen that she would have to get it from his colleagues.

Ellen's shorthand notes included the following work instructions:

"Because I'll be in meetings downtown all of Monday and Tuesday, you'll have to get the information necessary before you can complete the reports. Don't, though, intimate that there is any possibility of a merger. Pull Jerry and Rita off their regular jobs to get the report out."

Ellen reached home Sunday night exhausted, discouraged, and apprehensive. How, she wondered, could she enlist the cooperation of Jerry and Rita, especially since she was not free to tell the reason for their assignment to a special project? Mr. Bronwell had the authority to reassign them, but he did not realize that he had never officially given Ellen such authority, assuming that being his secretary carried the authority. Ellen, however, realized that Rita especially resented Ellen's giving her any work instructions.

She worried, too, about her relations with some of her superiors and wondered how to approach them to ask for data without appearing to be officious. On the other hand, she felt pleased and gratified by Mr. Bronwell's confidence in her ability to handle this difficult assignment and vowed to merit his trust.

**What approach could Ellen take to get the support of those whom she must supervise? How could she get the cooperation of her superiors?**

## 7-3  THE SECRETARY'S LOYALTIES

Ethel Kinney was secretary to Harold Roberts, sales manager of Brown-Haskins Manufacturing Company. During the five years since Mr. Roberts had joined the company, his career had been spectacular; and he had increased sales by 34 percent. He was out of the city about half the time and, because of his overly long hours, did not hesitate to take an occasional day off after a strenuous trip.

During the past two months, however, his unaccounted-for absences had reached alarming proportions. He had not come to the office at all the previous week although he was not on official vacation. He had telephoned from home every day and had dictated several letters and telegrams. On Monday he had asked Ellen to tell the president of the company that he, Mr. Roberts, was in San Francisco working on the Johnson order.

**What should Ethel say to her employer? Where do her loyalties lie — with her employer or with the corporation?**

# Financial and Legal Facets of Secretarial Work

*Part* **8**

A close relationship exists between the financial and the legal aspects of secretarial work. Both, therefore, are included in this section although the financial and legal responsibilities of the secretary-administrative assistant vary with the type of organization, the size and function of the office, and the extent of the executive's interests. Usually, the secretary is not primarily responsible for handling the executive's personal checking account, insurance and investment records, and tax data; but she assumes an "assist" role—a role that the executive both appreciates and rewards.

# Chapter 22

# BANKING SERVICES AND RESPONSIBILITIES

A secretary's responsibilities for banking and handling financial records will depend upon the size of the office in which she is employed. In a small office, the secretary may do all the office banking and keep most or all of the records of the business. In a large office, however, her financial duties may be confined to assisting her employer with his personal banking or to keeping a petty cash fund. Although the secretary may devote but a small amount of time each day to these duties, they represent exacting and confidential responsibilities. They are exacting because they involve handling money — other people's money. They are confidential because financial matters are always personal.

Whether a secretary's financial duties are extensive or limited, she may expect to perform some, if not all, of these functions: make bank deposits, write checks, cash checks, pay bills, reconcile bank statements, handle petty cash funds, and record incoming funds. Although specific practices and methods vary somewhat, the basic banking procedures of all banks are similar.

## THE CHECKING ACCOUNT

The new secretary with financial responsibilities must be identified at the bank as representing the executive or his business. If the executive wishes the secretary to sign checks for the withdrawal or payment of personal or company funds from his account, or to indorse and cash checks made out to him, he must authorize the bank to honor her signature. The bank may require the executive to sign a special authorization form, or to arrange for the secretary to add her signature to his signature card on file at the bank. Some banks require that the secretary be issued a power of attorney (page 592) to perform these functions.

### Accepting Checks

Accepting a check that is given in person or received through the mail requires precautions to assure that the check is valid — that it has been properly prepared. Examine these points: (a) date — to see that the check is not postdated (dated later than current date), (b) amount — to determine that the amount of payment is correct, (c) figures — to be sure that the amount written in figures agrees with the amount written in words, and (d) indorsement — to see that an indorsement, if required, has been properly made. To have a deposited check returned by the bank because it was improperly written is time consuming, inconvenient, and sometimes expensive.

Before depositing a check and while the details are still available, be sure to record the information needed for the accounting records on a receipt form or in a record book.

## Depositing Funds

To make a deposit, the secretary presents to the bank teller a deposit slip (see page 520) listing the amounts being deposited in duplicate (or a passbook), and the deposit itself, consisting of currency, coin, indorsed checks, and money orders.

**Preparing Coins and Bills for Deposit.** Banks prefer that coins and bills, if in sufficient quantity, be put in the money wrappers that the banks furnish. Coins are packed in paper rolls as follows:

| Denomination | Number of Coins to a Roll | Total Value of Coins in Roll |
|---|---|---|
| Pennies | 50 | $ .50 |
| Nickels | 40 | 2.00 |
| Dimes | 50 | 5.00 |
| Quarters | 40 | 10.00 |
| Halves | 20 | 10.00 |

Bills of each denomination are made into packages of $50, $100, and so forth. The packages are separated into all-of-a-kind groups with each bill laid right side up and top edge at the top. Torn bills are mended with tape. A paper bill wrapper—a narrow strip with the amount printed on it—is wrapped tightly around the bills and securely glued.

The depositor's name or account number should be stamped or written on each roll of coins and package of bills. Receiving tellers of banks do not stop to count packaged money when taking deposits, but someone counts it later in the day. If the depositor's name or account number appears on each roll or wrapper, mistakes can be easily traced.

Extra bills are counted and stacked, right side up, the largest denominations on the bottom and the smallest ones on top and fastened with a rubber band. Extra coins are counted, placed in an envelope, identified, and sealed.

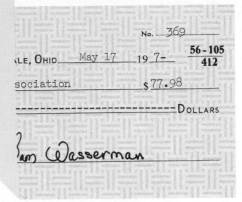

For deposit and
credit to the
account of
57  May 20, 197--
M and B Association

No. 369

ᴸᴱ, Oʜɪᴏ    May 17    19 7--    $\frac{56-105}{412}$

ociation    $ 77.98

- - - - - - - - - - - - - - - - - - - - - - - Dᴏʟʟᴀʀs

ᵃᵐ Wasserman

Indorsements are properly made across the back of the left end of checks and money orders, as is shown on the restrictive indorsement illustrated here.

**Preparing Checks for Deposit.** In order to deposit a check, the payee indorses it on the back; however, banks accept checks for deposit that are indorsed by a representative of the payee. The indorsement may be rubber-stamped or written in ink. In fact, a bank may accept an occasional check that lacks an indorsement. Some banks stamp the back of such a check with a statement such as, "Credited to account of payee named within—absence of indorsement guaranteed."

Notwithstanding the last sentence, it will be the secretary's responsibility to indorse every check for deposit. If the name of the payee is written differently on a check from the account name, indorse the check twice: first, as the name appears on the face of the check, and again, the exact way the account is carried. A rubber-stamp indorsement (showing the name of the bank, the name of the account, and the account number), obtained from the bank where the executive banks or from an office-supplies store, is the most time-saving method. Companies that receive a large number of checks can use a machine that will indorse checks at a high rate of speed. If a check is to be deposited, a pen signature need not be added to a rubber-stamp or machine indorsement.

There are several standard indorsements:

1. *A restrictive indorsement* (shown above) is one in which some condition attached to the indorsement restrains the negotiability of the check or renders the indorser liable only upon a specified condition or conditions, such as "For deposit," or "Upon delivery of contract." A restrictive indorsement is commonly used when checks are being deposited. Checks indorsed "For deposit" need not be signed personally by the depositor but can be indorsed or stamped by the secretary. The "For deposit" qualification automatically keeps the check from being used for any purpose other than for deposit to the account of the depositor whose name appears in the indorsement.

2. An *indorsement in full* or *special indorsement* (shown first below) gives the name of a specified payee, written before the indorser's signature. This indorsement identifies the person or firm to which the instrument is transferred. A check indorsed in this way cannot be cashed by anyone without the specified payee's signature.

The words "Pay to the order of First National Bank" in the illustration at the right identify the name of the bank to which the check is being transferred. For further transfer, the First National Bank must indorse the check again.

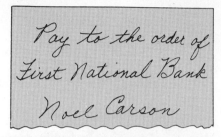

3. *A blank indorsement* consists simply of the signature of the payee, making the check payable to any holder. This indorsement, therefore, should never be used except at the bank immediately before the check is being deposited or cashed. A check should never be indorsed at the office or sent through the mail with a blank indorsement. If it is lost, the finder can turn it into cash.

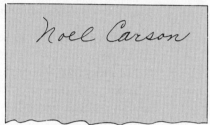

## Magnetic Ink Numbers

Data processing equipment now reduces the manual work involved in handling checking accounts. The American Bankers Association has adopted a uniform system of MICR (magnetic ink character recognition) that provides for preprinting the bank's transit number and the depositor's account number in magnetic ink characters in a uniform position at the bottom of the checks. When a check is received at the bank, the date, amount of the check, and other coded information also are recorded in magnetic ink characters at the bottom of the check. Optical character recognition (OCR) equipment sorts the checks according to issuing bank and account numbers, computes totals, and posts to the depositors' accounts. This sorting, totaling, and posting is done electronically and at speeds of several hundred checks a minute.

A preprinted deposit slip for a MICR system is illustrated on page 521, along with a check identified by magnetic-ink characters.

When an automated system is in use, the depositor can use only those deposit slips and checks that have been specifically printed to show his account number. If a depositor does not have his deposit slip or check at the time of a deposit or withdrawal at the bank, the bank clerk can handle the transaction.

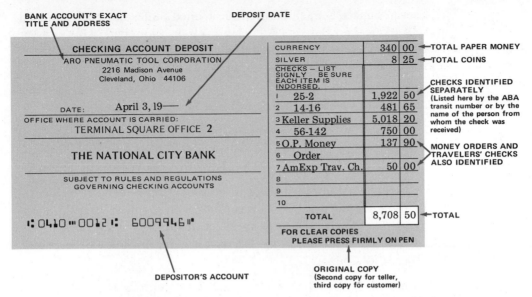

CHECKING ACCOUNT DEPOSIT

ARO PNEUMATIC TOOL CORPORATION
2216 Madison Avenue
Cleveland, Ohio 44106

DATE: April 3, 19—

OFFICE WHERE ACCOUNT IS CARRIED:
TERMINAL SQUARE OFFICE 2

THE NATIONAL CITY BANK

SUBJECT TO RULES AND REGULATIONS
GOVERNING CHECKING ACCOUNTS

⑆0410⑉0012⑆ 6009946⑉

| | | | |
|---|---|---|---|
| CURRENCY | | 340 | 00 |
| SILVER | | 8 | 25 |
| CHECKS — LIST SIGNLY BE SURE EACH ITEM IS INDORSED. | | | |
| 1 | 25-2 | 1,922 | 50 |
| 2 | 14-16 | 481 | 65 |
| 3 | Keller Supplies | 5,018 | 20 |
| 4 | 56-142 | 750 | 00 |
| 5 | O.P. Money | 137 | 90 |
| 6 | Order | | |
| 7 | AmExp Trav. Ch. | 50 | 00 |
| 8 | | | |
| 9 | | | |
| 10 | | | |
| | TOTAL | 8,708 | 50 |

FOR CLEAR COPIES
PLEASE PRESS FIRMLY ON PEN

← TOTAL PAPER MONEY
← TOTAL COINS

CHECKS IDENTIFIED SEPARATELY
(Listed here by the ABA transit number or by the name of the person from whom the check was received)

MONEY ORDERS AND TRAVELERS' CHECKS ALSO IDENTIFIED

← TOTAL

DEPOSITOR'S ACCOUNT

ORIGINAL COPY
(Second copy for teller, third copy for customer)

**Completing a Deposit Slip.** Many types of deposit slips are used. Most banks have deposit slips designed especially for use with automated equipment, usually in multiple sets with interleaved carbon or NCR coating. The deposit slip shown above is designed for automated processing.

**Account Numbers.** Each depositor has an account number with which the bank's automated equipment identifies the depositor's account; therefore, the account number must appear on the deposit slip. The bank provides the depositor with a supply of deposit slips either printed with his account number in magnetic ink characters or with space provided for the depositor to record his account number.

*Check-Stub Entries*     *Bank-Check Entries*

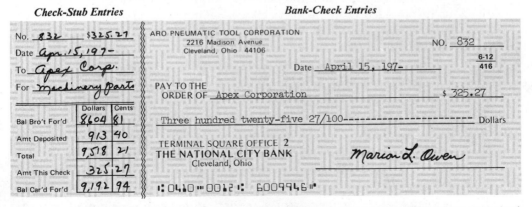

No. _832_ $325.27
Date _Apr. 15, 197–_
To _Apex Corp._
For _Machinery parts_

| | Dollars | Cents |
|---|---|---|
| Bal Bro't For'd | 8,604 | 81 |
| Amt Deposited | 913 | 40 |
| Total | 9,518 | 21 |
| Amt This Check | 325 | 27 |
| Bal Car'd For'd | 9,192 | 94 |

ARO PNEUMATIC TOOL CORPORATION
2216 Madison Avenue
Cleveland, Ohio 44106

NO. _832_

6-12
416

Date _April 15, 197–_

PAY TO THE
ORDER OF _Apex Corporation_                 $ _325.27_

_Three hundred twenty-five 27/100_----------------------- Dollars

TERMINAL SQUARE OFFICE 2
THE NATIONAL CITY BANK
Cleveland, Ohio

_Marion L. Owen_

⑆0410⑉0012⑆ 6009946⑉

Note that the series of magnetic-ink identification numbers at the bottom of this bank check are the same as those of the preprinted deposit slip at the top of this page.

**Check Numbers.** Each bank in the United States has been assigned an ABA (American Bankers Association) transit number. This number is usually printed in small type in the upper right portion of the check, to identify the bank for clearing-house functions. Illustrated, the numbers mean:

City or State     ⟶    25 - 2 ← Specific bank in the city or state

                      412 ← (4) Federal Reserve District
                            (1) Branch in the district
                            (2) Number of days required to clear the check

Some banks require each check listed on the deposit slip to be identified by using the two top ABA transit numbers, in this case 25-2, unless the check is drawn on the bank in which the deposit is made. In this case, the check is identified by the name of the maker of the check. (See illustration, page 521.)

**Listing Checks.** When a large number of checks is regularly deposited, common practice is to list the checks on an adding machine and to attach the tape to the deposit slip, listing only the total on the deposit slip. Some banks, however, who prefer that all checks be shown on the deposit slip, provide "long" deposit slips for such use.

**Listing Other Items.** Money orders, bank drafts, travelers' checks, and interest coupons are listed with the checks on the deposit slip. Certain government, municipal, and company bonds provide interest coupons attached to the bond. On the due date the coupon can be detached from the bond, placed with a deposit slip in an envelope provided by the bank, and deposited. A separate envelope must be used for each class of coupon.

Some banks require the depositor to fill out a certificate of ownership (provided by the bank) before accepting the coupons for deposit.

## Banking by Mail

*Depositing by mail* has become very popular because of the time it saves. The secretary in a small office may make most or all of the bank deposits by mail. Various kinds of mail-deposit slips and envelopes are provided by different banks. All checks must be indorsed "Pay to the order of (name of bank)" or "For Deposit Only," signed, and listed on the mail-deposit slip. The deposit slip and indorsed checks are placed in an envelope and mailed to the bank. Currency should never be deposited in this manner unless sent by registered mail. By return mail, the bank sends the depositor a receipt, along with a new mail-deposit slip and envelope.

## After-Hours Banking

At many banks, deposits may be made and cash withdrawn after banking hours.

**Night Depository.** Some businesses use the *night depository* for funds collected after banking hours. The bank provides the depositor with a bag in which to lock the deposit. The depositor then can drop the bag through a slot accessible from outside the bank at any time during the night. On the next banking day, a bank teller unlocks the bag and makes the deposit. The depositor later stops at the bank to pick up the empty bag and his deposit receipt. If the depositor prefers, however, the bank will leave the deposit bag locked until the depositor arrives to make the deposit personally. Branch banks and evening banking hours further add to the convenience of the depositor.

**Cash Withdrawals.** For the convenience of customers who need limited amounts of cash after banking hours, some banks have installed automated banking equipment outside the bank. This equipment dispenses cash at any hour to customers who have been issued a bank-sponsored credit card (Master Charge, BankAmericard) and who have been assigned a separate secret code number. To withdraw cash, the customer inserts his card into the cash dispenser, enters his code number on a keyboard, and presses a button that specifies the amount he wants to withdraw. Within seconds the cash and a charge slip emerge from a slot in the dispenser. The amount of the withdrawal is charged automatically to the customer's checking account — or to his credit card account for a withdrawal larger than his checking account balance.

Cleveland, O. ........ *January 4,* 19.—

To The Cleveland Trust Company:- You are hereby notified that

........ *Ann Kane, Secretary* ........

is authorized to draw all or any part of the balance now or at any future time standing to my credit in my ........ *checking* ........

Account No. *890-12314* with your company. This authority to remain in full force until you receive written notice from me of its revocation.

Signed ........ *Howard E. Durst*

An account holder can authorize a specified person to draw on his account by completing and signing an authorization that is stamped on the back of his signature card at his bank.

## Checking Account Withdrawals

Banks provide a variety of check forms and checkbooks: one check with attached stub to the page; three or more checks to the page; pads with interleaved copy sheets or with attached *vouchers* (a form used to record the purpose and other details of the payment). Many businesses use prenumbered checks imprinted with the name of the business. The secretary is responsible for ordering a new checkbook before the old one is completely used. Banks usually bind an order sheet into the checkbook toward the back. The secretary merely mails the page and receives a new checkbook shortly thereafter.

**Completing Check Stubs.** Complete the stub *before* you write the check. Failure to do so frequently results in the details of a check being forgotten. In addition to showing the number of the check, the date, the name of the payee, and the amount, the stub should provide other data for classifying or breaking down the disbursement in the accounting or tax records. For example, if the check is for a part payment, an installment payment or a final payment, that fact should be noted. If the amount covers several items, (such as payment for two or more invoices), each should be listed. If the check is in payment of an insurance premium, the name of the insured and the policy number should be listed.

| COMMERCIAL ACCT. NUMBER |
|---|
| *890–12314* |

The undersigned hereby assent(s) to and agree(s) to be bound by the present and all future Rules and Regulations of **THE CLEVELAND TRUST COMPANY** governing commercial accounts, and ACKNOWLEDGE(S) RECEIPT OF A COPY OF SUCH PRESENT RULES AND REGULATIONS.

| SIGNATURES | BIRTH DATE |
|---|---|
| 1. *Howard E. Durst* | *3/8/20* |
| | BIRTH DATE |
| 2. *Howard E. Durst* | *6/1/50* |
| *by Ann Kane, Secretary* | HOME PHONE NO. *671-2459* |

MAIL ADDRESS AND ZONE NO. *236 Euclid Road, Cleveland , Ohio*

OTHER ADDRESS *1283 State Bldg. Cleveland —*   MOTHER'S 1ST NAME 1. *Nina*

BUSINESS OR EMPLOYER *Attorney – Durst & Durst*   MOTHER'S 1ST NAME 2. *Maude*

INTRODUCED BY OR BANK REFERENCE   BUSINESS PHONE NO. *341-3478*

PLACE PAYING INSTRUCTION STAMP HERE

| THIS SPACE FOR BANK USE ONLY | DATE OPENED | 1ST DEPOSIT | OPENED BY | CLOSED |
|---|---|---|---|---|
| B-94 4-59 | | $ | | |

The form of the secretary's signature on line 2 of this signature card shows that she is merely signing for the account holder. To allow the bank to identify the two valid signers for this account, additional information is provided: the birthdates of each signer and the first name of the mother of each signer.

**Writing Checks.** A check is a negotiable instrument and imposes certain legal responsibilities on the maker. Therefore, it must be written with care to insure that no unintended liability is created. For example, an altered check is not cashable. If a bank cashes such a check, the bank must assume any resulting loss. However, if it can be shown that the maker failed to use reasonable precautions in writing the check, thus making alteration difficult to detect, the maker must assume any resulting loss. Consequently, always type checks or — if necessary — write them in ink (never pencil). Follow these steps:

1. Be sure that the *number* of the check corresponds with that on the stub. If the checks are not numbered in printing, number all checks and check stubs upon starting a new checkbook.

2. *Date* the check on the exact date that the check is being written. Occasionally checks are postdated—that is, dated ahead to a time when sufficient funds will be in the checking account. This is a questionable practice, however.

3. Write the name of the *payee* in full and correctly spelled. For correct spelling, refer to bills, letterheads, or the telephone directory. Omit titles such as *Mr., Mrs., Miss, and Dr.* On checks written to a married woman, use her given name: *Ruth Hill*, not *Mrs. John R. Hill.*

4. In writing the *amount*, use large, bold figures written close to the dollar sign and sufficiently close together to prevent the insertion of other figures. In spelling out the amount, start at the extreme left, capitalizing the first letter only, and express cents as fractions of 100:

Three hundred forty and no/100————————————————————**Dollars**

Two huhdred thousand eight hundred sixty-four and 65/100————————**Dollars**

Two thousand seven hundred and 35/100————————————————**Dollars**

To write a check for less than \$1, circle the amount written in figures and write "Only" before the spelled-out amount. Cross out "Dollars" at end of line.

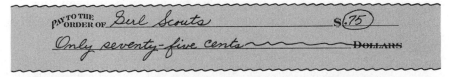

5. Fill any *blank space* before or after the amount with hyphens, periods, or a line.

6. The *purpose* of the check, such as "In Payment of Invoice 6824," may be written in a corner of the check, if space permits, or across the end of the check.

Never cross out, erase, or change any part of a check. If you make an error, write "VOID" conspicuously across the face of both the check and the stub. Save a voided check and file it in numerical order with the canceled checks returned from the bank. Since it is easy to alter the impressions made by a worn ribbon, type checks with a fresh ribbon. Keep the checkbook in a safe place, and guard its confidentiality.

COLUMBUS EMPLOYEES
FEDERAL CREDIT UNION
CHARTER No. 286

24614

COLUMBUS, OHIO _July 1_ 19 7- 25-1/412

PAY TO THE
ORDER OF Joseph L. Klingensmith                    $ 98.96

Ninety-eight 96/100                          VOID          DOLLARS

GRANDVIEW OFFICE                    COLUMBUS EMPLOYEES FEDERAL CREDIT UNION

THE OHIO NATIONAL BANK.
COLUMBUS, OHIO.                     _Stanley Eisenberg_
                                    ASSISTANT TREASURER

⑆0412⑆0001 811⑈8⑈06095⑈

COLUMBUS EMPLOYEES FEDERAL CREDIT UNION    COLUMBUS, OHIO          DETACH BEFORE DEPOSITING CHECK

| | DR. | CR. | POSTED | |
|---|---|---|---|---|
| SHARES | 4,225.27 | .00 | 4,225.27 | BOOK NO. |
| LOANS | .00 | | | COLUMBUS EMPLOYEES FEDERAL |
| DIVIDENDS | 98.96 | | 98.96 | CREDIT UNION |
| EXPENSE | .00 | | | 1800 KING AVENUE · COLUMBUS, OHIO 43216 |
| MISC. | | | | |
| CASH | 98.96 | .00 | 98.96 | |

A voucher check consists of the check and a detachable stub that shows the purpose of the check and various data necessary for record keeping.

**Writing Checks for Cash.** A check for funds for the personal use of the account holder can be written to *Cash* as the payee and signed by the account holder. A check so written is highly negotiable: Anyone in possession of it can turn it into money. The cautious person, therefore, will use this form only when writing the check on the bank premises. (The bank asks the person receiving the money to indorse the check, even though the payee is *Cash*.)

The executive may expect the secretary to keep him supplied with cash. On banking days, she simply asks, "Do you need money?" If he does, she can write the check and either present it for his signature or, if authorized, sign it herself. After cashing the check, the secretary should keep the currency separate from her own, placing the money in an envelope that she seals and puts in a safe compartment of her handbag.

## Procedure to Stop Payment on Checks

After a check has been issued, payment can be stopped unless the check has been cleared by the bank upon which it was drawn. This procedure may be necessary when a check has been lost, stolen, or incorrectly written. Most banks make a charge for this service.

To stop payment, telephone the stop-payment desk of the bank and give the name of the maker, the date, number and amount of the check, the name of the payee, and the reason that payment is to be stopped. The bank clerk will search the checks on hand to see if the item in question has cleared. If it has not, he will process the request for a stop-payment. Then you must dispatch either a letter of confirmation or a stop-payment form supplied by the bank. When you are sure that the stop-payment request is in effect, write a replacement, if necessary.

### Reconciling the Bank Balance

Each month the bank returns to the account holder the *canceled* checks (checks that have cleared during the month) along with a statement that lists each deposit and withdrawal and any other items, such as a service charge or stop-payment charge. The account holder then checks the accuracy of his checkbook records and files the canceled checks as proof of payment.

When the statement and canceled checks are received, the final balance on the statement and the bank balance in the checkbook are compared and the difference between the two records accounted for. This process is called *reconciling the bank balance.*

Many banks print, on the back of the bank statement, instructions and a form for reconciling the bank balance. This printed form may be used, or the reconcilement may be typed on a separate sheet and attached to the bank statement.

**Procedure.** The following is a systematic procedure for making the reconciliation:

1. **Compare the amount of each canceled check returned by the bank with the amounts listed on the bank statement. (The canceled checks are generally returned in the order in which they are listed.)**

2. **Arrange the canceled checks in numerical sequence.**

   (For customers with large check volumes, some banks sort the checks into numeric sequence by magnetic ink number and print the bank statement with all check numbers listed numerically and the uncashed checks identified by number, all electronically. While there is a small charge for this service, it greatly speeds the reconciliation of bank statements.)

3. **Compare the returned checks with the checkbook stubs. Make a distinctive check mark on the stubs of canceled checks. Compare also the amounts of deposits shown on the stubs with those shown on the bank statement. List and total any that were omitted.**

4. **List the outstanding checks, showing the check number, the payee, and the amount. Total the outstanding checks.**

5. **Add the total unlisted deposits to the bank balance; subtract the total amount of the outstanding checks. The remainder is the corrected bank balance.**

6. **The bank will list service charges (if they have made any) among the withdrawals on the bank statement. Subtract the amount of the service charges, and any**

other deductions made by the bank, from the balance shown on the last check-book stub for the period being reconciled. The resulting figure should be the same amount as the corrected bank balance. If so, you must deduct the amount of the service charges from the balance on the checkbook stub that is currently the last one used. The remainder will be the true *current* balance in the account.

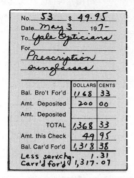

As shown in the illustration at the left, an entry must now be made on the *current balance* (not the last stub of the reconciliation period) for any service charge or other charge by the bank.

**Locating Errors.** If the two adjusted balances — statement and stub — do not agree, first check the computation on the reconciliation sheet to make sure there is no error. If there is none, make sure that:

*No check has been omitted in the reconciliation.* Go through the check stubs (one by one) and see that each one is included among the checks either cleared or outstanding. Also check that each check has a stub.

*No deposit has been omitted.* Cross check the deposits in the check stubs with those on the bank statement.

A deposit made by mail on the date that your bank statement is prepared will not appear on the statement. Add this deposit to the bank statement balance on the reconciliation sheet.

If there is still an error, either the bank has made an arithmetical error in the statement, or more likely there is an error in the stubs. First check the accuracy of the *amounts forwarded* on each check-stub page. If these are correct, the arithmetical computations for each stub should be examined. When the error is located, mark the stub where it occurs: "Error—should be $_____; corrected on Stub #_____." Then make the compensating adjustment on the last stub.

Enter the amount of the error on the reconciliation statement and show where the error occurs and where it is corrected in the check stubs. After the proper check stub (the last transaction covered by the bank statement), write "Agrees with bank statement, (*date*)." Then you can easily find the starting point for next month's reconciliation.

**Filing Canceled Checks.** File the bank reconciliation conveniently for the next reconciliation. You will need the records of checks now outstanding. Keep canceled checks inside the folded bank statements and file the statements chronologically, or file the bank statements chronologically and the checks numerically in a separate place. Save canceled checks, as they are evidences of payment; they constitute legal receipts. The retention period must be established by company policy.

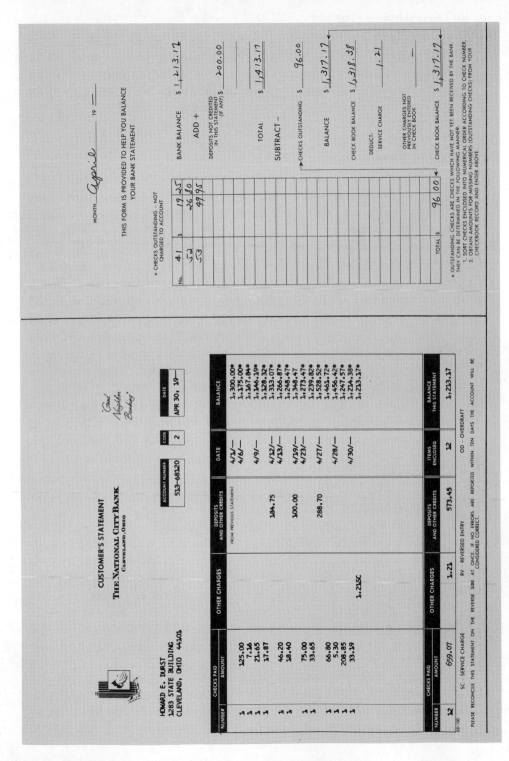

The monthly bank statement shows the checks paid, the deposits received, and any other deductions made from the account, such as the $1.21 service charge.

Printed on the back of many bank statements is a convenient form for reconciling the bank balance.

## Follow-up on Outstanding Checks

Investigate any check that has not cleared through the bank within a few weeks of its date of issue. The payee may not have received the check, or may have misplaced or lost it. A letter or telephone call to the payee will clarify the matter. If the check is apparently lost, cancel the old check in the checkbook, forward a stop-payment order to the bank, and issue a new check.

## Bank Safe-Deposit Boxes

Frequently the executive rents a *safe-deposit box* from his bank. This is a metal box locked by two keys into a small compartment in the bank's safe-deposit vault. The bank has very strict rules about access to safe-deposit boxes. The customer must register each time he goes to his box; a bank employee accompanies him to the box, opens one of the locks with his key, and opens the other lock with the customer's key. The box itself is then removed and taken by the customer to a private room. Ordinarily securities, wills, insurance policies, notes, gems, and other small valuable articles are protected by safe-deposit storage. Rent is usually billed annually and is deducted from the customer's checking account if he has one. (The rent is a deductible income tax item.)

The executive must sign a special banking form if he wishes his secretary to have access to his safe-deposit box. She may have two responsibilities relative to safe-deposit-box work: (1) to maintain a perpetual inventory of its contents in duplicate, one copy to be kept in the box, the other in her office; and (2) to guard the key carefully.

## Special Bank Services

Some banks provide a number of special services for their checking-account customers.

**One-Check Payroll Service.** If a number of employees maintain checking accounts at the same bank, a one-check payroll plan may be used. In place of writing a separate check for each employee, the employer sends the bank one check covering several employees. A list of the employees and the amount to be deposited to each account is attached to the check. The bank deposits the amount to the employee's account and withdraws the total amount from the employer's account.

**Dividend Deposit Plan.** Banks will collect dividend payments for customers. Under this plan, the stockholder requests the companies in which he holds stock to send all dividend payments directly to the bank for deposit in his checking account.

**Freight Payment Service.** Companies that have a large number of freight bills find it difficult to process the paper work and make payment within the time limit established by the Interstate Commerce Commission. Some banks provide a freight-payment service. The carrier sends the freight bill directly to the customer's bank. The bank deducts the amount of the bill from the customer's account and credits it to the carrier. Monthly, the bank sends to the customer a complete listing of all freight bills paid and charged to his account. Corrections for overcharges and unapproved bills are made at that time.

**Investment Services.** Most banks provide a number of investment services: investment advice, credit information, collection of matured bonds, shipment of securities for customers, and buying and selling of United States Treasury bonds, certificates, and bills.

**One-Check Service.** The check and the credit card have become standard for paying most bills, with a consequent increase in the number of checking accounts. This growth is reflected in the number of checks being written. In 1939, an estimated 3 billion checks were issued, while by 1972 the number had grown to over 24 billion checks a year — with a growth rate of 1 to 2 billion a year. Banks need ways to reduce the check volume and, at the same time, increase their services to checking-account customers. One promising development is the multipurpose-check service identified by titles like Super Check, Bill Payment Service, and One-Check Service.

In the One-Check Service plan, the bank issues to the depositor a special check listing on its face numerous local concerns (stores, utilities, finance companies, and the like). Beside the name of each appropriate

**SUPER CHECK**

THE FIRST NATIONAL BANK & TRUST COMPANY IN MACON
MACON, GEORGIA  *February 10,*  197—  No. 43

Please pay to: charge my Checking Account

| | $ | | $ | | $ |
|---|---|---|---|---|---|
| 1st Nat'l Bk. & Tr. | | Davisons | | Rich's | |
| Master Charge | | Fickling & Walker | | Sears | 27.31 |
| American Oil | | Flint Electric | | Shell Oil | |
| Atlanta Gas Light | | GMAC | | Southern Bell | |
| BP Oil | | Ga. Power | 31.48 | Standard Oil | |
| Bank Americard | | Goldmans | | Stephens | |
| Belk-Matthews | | Griffith Mortgage | | Tenneco Oil | 173.42 |
| Board of Water Comm. | | Gulf Oil | | Texaco | |
| Burden-Smith | | Home Federal | | R.S. Thorpe | |
| Cherokee Farms | | Humble Oil | | Union Oil | |
| Chi-Ches-Ters | | Macon Federal | | Zayre | |
| | | Macon Telegraph & News | | SUPERCHECK CHARGE | .60 |
| | | Macon TV Cable | | TOTAL | 232.81 |
| | | Murphy, Taylor & Ellis | | | |
| | | Jos. N. Neel | | | |
| | | Newberry's | | Signature | |
| | | J.C. Penney | | *Don Armstrong* | |
| | | Powell's Pharmacy | | | |

⑆061⑆2⑉00471⑆            61

creditor, the customer inserts the amount to be paid, totals the amounts for all payments, and dates and signs the check. He encloses the bill stubs with the check and sends them to the bank. The bank then credits the account of each payee indicated, and deducts the total from the maker's account, along with a fee of 50 to 75 cents for the multipurpose check. Some banks provide a choice between having the total amount deducted from the checking account or having it charged to a bank credit charge account.

The one-check service permits one check to replace a number of checks, thereby greatly reducing the paper work of the depositor, the bank, and the payees.

**Computerized Banking.** The ultimate goal of the banking industry is a cashless, checkless society in which a computer handles the complete exchange of funds between two parties. A few centers are trying such a system on an experimental basis. The system represents the merging of the depositor's checking account and the bank-issued credit card. Under the system, a computer terminal is installed in each store or business establishment, and the computer terminal is connected by regular telephone circuits with the bank's computerized accounting data center. For example, when a customer makes a purchase at a store, the sales clerk inserts the customer's bank-issued credit card into the store's terminal. Using a conventional telephone, the clerk dials the bank's computer storage facilities (thus connecting the store terminal to the bank's data center). On the store's terminal keyboard, the clerk enters the amount of the purchase. The computer responds by authorizing the purchase, deducting the amount from the customer's checking account, and adding it to the merchant's account — all without a single piece of paper changing hands. And the entire transaction takes only 15 seconds!

## PAYING BILLS

An executive seldom turns over his personal bill paying to a new secretary. It is one of the responsibilities that a secretary acquires or, frequently, assumes. First, the secretary may be asked to address the envelopes. Then when the executive is rushed, he may say, "Will you write these checks for me?" It is then that the secretary can show that she is capable of handling this responsibility. *Bill paying* consists of:

1. Verifying the items and checking the computations on each bill
2. Filling in the check stub (Be sure to itemize and identify the payment in order to use the stub in accounting processes or in preparing income tax returns.)

3. Making out the check
4. Writing on the face of the invoice or the statement the date, the number, and the amount of the check used in payment
5. Addressing the envelope
6. Tearing off the invoice or statement stub to be mailed with the check
7. Attaching the stub from the bill to the check and inserting both under the flap of an addressed envelope ready for presentation to the executive for signature

## Verifying Bills

When the executive gives the secretary bills to pay, she can assume that he approves their payment; but she should verify the prices, the terms, the extensions, and the additions.

*Invoices* (itemized listings of goods purchased) must be checked against the quoted prices and terms or with records of previous prices paid. Monthly *statements* (details of accounts showing the amount due at the beginning of the month, purchases and payments made during the month, and the unpaid balance at the end of the month) can be verified by comparison with invoices and sales slips, check stubs, and other records of payments made on the account.

*Bills for services* (utility companies, for example) are usually accepted as they are, although the toll statement with the telephone bill is checked very carefully. Before paying bills for professional services, the secretary should obtain the personal approval of the executive.

TELEPHONE
703-598-2738

# THE OLD DOMINION COMPANY

492 Broad Street     Richmond, Virginia 23219

| | MONTH | DAY | YEAR |
|---|---|---|---|
| | 1 | 11 | 7- |

SOLD TO   W. R. BROOKS
1970 CAREW TOWER
CINCINNATI, OHIO  45202

YOUR ORDER NO. B-479
SALESMAN   J. LONG
SHIP VIA    BEST WAY

| QUANT. | COMMODITY | CODE NO. | PACK | SIZE | NET PRICE | EXTENSION | |
|---|---|---|---|---|---|---|---|
| 2 | DESK MODULES, WALNUT | 472A | | 6'6" | 242.00 | 484 | 00 |
| 2 | DESK MODULES, WALNUT | 472B | | 5'4" | 179.00 | 358 | 00 |
| | SALES TAX | | | | | 42 | 10 |
| | | | | | | 884 | 10 |

Paid 2/8/7-
Check No. 43

This invoice is ready for filing. The check marks indicate that the extensions have been checked. The number and date of the check sent in payment has been noted.

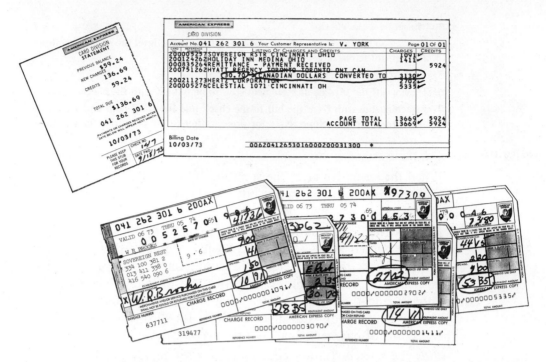

Note the items to be compared for accuracy in the credit card statement and enclosed receipts.

Arrangements can be made under which the utility company sends your utility bill directly to your bank. The bank pays the bill, deducts the amount from your account, and includes the paid bill with your bank statement at the end of the month.

## Credit Card Statements

To avoid carrying large amounts of cash or travelers' checks, many business and professional men use credit cards (American Express, Diners' Club, Carte Blanche, and the like) when traveling and when paying local entertainment expenses. Credit card statements also are helpful in preparing expense reports and in verifying travel and entertainment expenses for income tax reporting.

When making a purchase with a credit card, the purchaser signs a bill or receipt and receives a copy. Later he receives a monthly statement for all charges made to that card during the month, along with the signed receipts. The executive may delegate to the secretary the responsibility for checking his monthly credit card statement, which requires careful inspection of the signature on each receipt and a comparison of the amount on the enclosed receipt with that on the receipt given at the time of purchase.

## Filing Paid Bills

Some logical system should be set up for filing paid bills, for they provide the key to the canceled checks. If there are only ten to twenty bills each month, the secretary can place all of them in one file folder. If there are many, she may set up an alphabetic file for them; or she may use a subject file, keeping together all of the utility bills, the insurance bills, the bills for supplies, and so on. Whenever a question arises concerning the payment of a bill, the secretary should be able to locate the annotated bill giving the check number and then to get the canceled check from the files for evidence.

## Making Payments by Other Forms

Although most of the payments handled by the secretary will probably be made by ordinary check, she may on occasion use one of several special checks or money-order forms that can be obtained at the bank (usually at a nominal charge).

**Certified Check.** A regular depositor's check that is guaranteed by the bank on which it is drawn is called a *certified check*. To obtain such a check, the secretary takes the executive's personal check to the bank and asks that it be certified. After seeing that sufficient funds are in the account to cover the check, a bank official stamps on the face of the check "CERTIFIED," adds an official signature, and immediately charges the account with the amount of the check.

**Official Check.** A check written by the bank on its own funds is known as an *official check* (sometimes known as a cashier's or treasurer's check). Such a check can be issued to a bank customer who does not have a checking account. The amount of the check plus a service fee is paid to the bank clerk, who then writes the check to the specified payee. This form is most frequently used to transfer relatively large sums of money. (Banks use official checks to pay their own expenses.) The

Use certified checks when the payment of a sum of money is required to bind a contract, to guarantee fulfillment of a contract, or to make settlement between stock brokers, bond dealers, and others. (A stop-payment order cannot be issued against a certified check.)

**Official Check**

NEW YORK, N. Y. April 11, 19__    Nº 2492

## Union National Bank
1-30/210

PAY TO THE ORDER OF David A. Stewart                 $178.50

The sum of $178 and 50 cts _____ DOLLARS

OFFICIAL CHECK

Raymond P. Bateman
CASHIER

⑈0210⑈0030⑈ 323 940 8⑈

**Bank Draft**

No. 195    First National Bank    13-1/420
Camden, Ohio June 20, 19__

PAY TO THE ORDER OF Consolidated Lamp Co    $1247.55

The sum of $1247 and 55 cts _____ DOLLARS

TO
FIRST NATIONAL BANK
CINCINNATI, OHIO

Charles L. Grosvenor
CASHIER

⑈0420⑈000 1⑈ 103 404 7⑈

secretary requests that the official check be made payable to her employer, who must then indorse it in full to the ultimate payee. The check then stands as proof of payment.

**Bank Draft.** A *bank draft* is a check written by the bank on its account in another bank located in the same or in another city. A purchaser pays the bank the exact amount of the draft plus a small fee for issuing the draft. Properly indorsed, the bank draft can then be cashed at the bank on which it is drawn. It is used for the same purpose as an official check and differs only in that the bank draft is drawn by the bank on funds it has on deposit in another bank while an official check is drawn by the cashier on funds in his own bank.

When there is need to transfer funds quickly, the bank can telegraph (cable, if to a foreign country) its corresponding bank in another city directing it to transfer funds to a designated person or company.

**Bank Money Order.** A *bank money order* (*personal money order* or *registered check*) is similar to that issued by the post office but less expensive. It is sold primarily to persons without a checking account who wish to send money through the mail and can normally be cashed at any other bank — at home or abroad; it is negotiable and transferable

**Bank Money
Order**

by indorsement. The amount of a single bank money order generally is not more than $200, but there is no restriction on the number of bank money orders that may be issued to the same person to be sent to the same payee. The purchaser is given a receipt for his records.

The bank money order is more frequently used than an official check or a bank draft when the amount of money transferred is relatively small. It differs from an official check in that the names of both the purchaser and the payee appear on the money order.

In addition to the forms discussed here, payments may be made by other money orders (postal, telegraph, or express); or cash may be sent by registered mail under special circumstances. Refer to the index of this book for further explanation of these methods of payment.

## THE PETTY CASH FUND

Payments of small amounts for postage, bus and taxi fare, collect telegrams, donations, delivery charges, and incidental office supplies are frequently made from a *petty cash fund*. In many instances the fund is entrusted to the secretary.

The size of the fund will vary according to the demands made upon it. If the fund is large, it should be kept in a locked cash box and stored in the office safe or vault at night. If it is small, it can be kept in a small box or an envelope. In any event, the fund should be locked at night in a desk drawer, a file drawer, or the safe.

### Petty Cash Records

The petty cash fund is usually set up with a stipulated amount, such as a $20 fund. Each replenishment of the depleted fund brings it up to $20 again. For example, after the secretary has disbursed $18.50 from the fund, she has on hand $1.50. The reimbursement check to the petty cash fund is for $18.50. The executive may prefer to write a check for a full $20 each time, or he may give the secretary $10 one time and $15 another. A purely personal fund can be any size desired.

Each item listed in the Paid column of a petty cash record requires a receipt.

## Petty Cash Report

In replenishing the petty cash fund, the secretary should prepare a summary report of all payments made.

Each expenditure should have a receipt covering it for an accounting record. If receipts are used consistently, the total money in the cash box plus the total of the receipts should equal the amount of the fund.

Keep a record of the receipts and the disbursements. Balance the record whenever the funds get low — or periodically, if the executive prefers. Some of the expenses itemized in a petty cash record may be income tax deductible; file the records and examine them at tax-return time. Make petty cash entries at once, for they are difficult to recall later. A practical form of a petty cash record is shown below.

Stationery stores sell pads of petty cash vouchers (or receipt forms).

| PETTY CASH VOUCHER | | No. 56 |
| --- | --- | --- |
| $ *3.00* | | Date *January 4, 19--* |
| PAID TO | *Post Office* | |
| FOR: | *Stamps* | |
| | Received Payment | *R. L. Reed* |

# CREDIT AND COLLECTION INSTRUMENTS

The executive secretary's financial responsibilities may extend to such credit and collection instruments as notes, drafts, and certificates of deposit. Because these papers can be transferred or negotiated by the holder to someone else, they (together with checks and other substitutes for cash, such as bank drafts and money orders) are known as *negotiable instruments*.

## Notes

A *promissory note*, more commonly referred to as a note, is a promise by one person (known as the *maker*) to pay a certain sum of money on demand or at a fixed or determinable future date to another person or party (known as the *payee*). A promissory note is illustrated below.

$660.00        Phoenix, Arizona    August 7    19__
Four months                        AFTER DATE _I_ PROMISE TO PAY TO
THE ORDER OF _James Bailey_
Six hundred sixty 00/100                                —DOLLARS
PAYABLE AT _Second National Bank_
VALUE RECEIVED WITH INTEREST AT _6_ %
NO. _13_    DUE _December 7, 19__         _Robert Shaw_

Frequently, collateral is requested to pledge the payment of a note. In this case the instrument is called a *collateral note*. Collateral can be salable securities (stocks, bonds), a real estate mortgage, or anything that represents ownership and is exchangeable. When an obligation is fully paid, the collateral is returned to the borrower. If it is not paid, the creditor can convert the collateral into cash.

Some notes bear interest, paid at maturity when the *face* of the note is due. On a noninterest-bearing note, the loan-making agency deducts in advance the "interest" (known as the *discount*) from the face of the note. The remainder is called the *proceeds*. For instance, a borrower who gives a bank a 3-month, noninterest-bearing note for $1,000 would receive $985 if the discount were computed at the rate of 6 percent.

The amount and the date of a partial payment on a note are written on the back of the note. When the secretary makes a partial payment on a note for the executive, she should make certain the payment is recorded on the back of the note in her presence, for the note is held by the lender until it is paid in full. If she makes the payment in full, the indorsed note should be turned over to her, for then it is a legal record that the obligation has been discharged.

## Commercial Drafts

A draft is a written order by one person on another to pay a sum of money to a third person and is generally used as a collection device. In the commercial draft illustration on this page, Ankromm and Son owe $539.62 to King and Wilson, who give this draft to their bank in Topeka for collection. The bank forwards the draft to its correspondent bank in St. Louis, which presents it for payment to Ankromm and Son. When the draft is paid, the proceeds are sent to the Topeka bank and thence to King and Wilson.

This draft is a *sight draft* for it instructs that it is to be paid "at sight." A *time draft* is payable at some future time and reads "thirty days after date" or some other stipulated period of time.

Drafts are frequently used as a means of collecting before delivery for goods shipped by freight. The merchandise is shipped on an *order bill of lading*, which requires that the receiver present the original copy of the bill of lading to the railroad company before obtaining possession of the merchandise. The bill of lading with the draft attached is sent to the bank in the town of the buyer. When the merchandise arrives, the purchaser pays the draft at the bank, obtains the bill of lading, and claims possession of his goods at the freight office.

## Certificates of Deposit

A certificate of deposit is a promissory note issued by a bank to a depositor. It is negotiable (ownership may be transferred from one party to another by indorsement and delivery) as it contains the five basic elements of a negotiable instrument:

1. It must be in writing and be signed by the maker or drawer.
2. It must contain an unconditional promise or order to pay a definite sum.
3. It must be payable on demand or at a fixed or at a determinable future time.
4. It must be payable to order or to bearer.
5. It must identify the drawee with reasonable certainty.

## Discounting Notes and Drafts

Business firms accept notes, time drafts, and installment contracts from customers in payment for merchandise and may convert these instruments into cash before they are due for payment. This is done by "selling the paper" to a bank or finance company. The bank deducts interest (discounts the paper) and gives the seller the cash proceeds. The bank, in turn, holds the paper until maturity and collects from the customer. The ownership of notes and drafts is transferred by indorsement in the same manner as that used for checks.

## Foreign Remittances

When a payment or remittance is to be made to a person or business firm in a foreign country, the following forms of payment may be used.

**Currency.** United States currency, or foreign currency purchasable through your local bank, may be sent abroad. Most foreign countries regulate the amount of currency that may be so transferred. Your bank will advise you as to the legal restrictions. Currency payments, of course, would be sent by registered mail.

**Cable Money Order.** Either your bank or Western Union will cable money abroad for you. The cable money order is generally payable in the currency of the country to which it is being sent. Cable money orders are speedy but expensive.

**American Express Money Orders.** Money orders payable in a foreign currency may be purchased at any American Express Company office. Express money orders may be made payable to the purchaser or to another person or firm. American Express will arrange for the transfer of the money order to the person or firm in the foreign country to whom it is payable by cable, airmail, or mail; or the purchaser, if he elects, may receive the money order and transfer it by mail or some other means. Express money orders are payable in the foreign country at the office of the American Express Company or at the bank in the foreign country identified in the money order.

**International Money Order.** See page 297.

**Foreign Bank Draft.** A bank draft payable in a foreign currency can be purchased at your local bank. As with currency, most foreign countries limit the amount of money which may be transferred. The bank will arrange for the transfer of the draft; or the purchaser, if he elects, may transfer it by mail or by some other means. This method of payment or transfer of funds would be used when large amounts are involved.

## SUGGESTED READINGS

Becker, Caroline J. *Using Bank Services*. Washington: American Bankers Association, 1970.

Klein, A. E., Supervisory ed. *The New World Secretarial Handbook*. Cleveland: World Publishing Co., 1968, pp. 261–281.

*Office Work in the Field of Banking, Manpower White Glove Training Manual*. Milwaukee: Manpower, Inc., 1967.

## QUESTIONS FOR DISCUSSION

1. As Miss Hill, a secretary, was leaving for lunch, her employer, Mr. Roger, asked her to deposit his salary check in the bank. Mr. Roger indorsed the check by writing his name on the back of the check. Miss Hill placed the check in her purse. While at lunch and before the deposit was made, Miss Hill's purse was either lost or stolen.

   **(a) What poor business practices were evident in this situation?**
   **(b) Upon discovery of the loss, what should the secretary do?**

2. What precautions or safeguards should a secretary observe in writing checks? Explain why each precaution is important.

3. A secretary follows the practice of placing all personal bills (home expenses, charge accounts, and so forth) of her employer on his desk when received. She makes no follow-up on them on the basis that she has no responsibility for her employer's personal financial matters. Would you agree with the secretary's evaluation of her responsibility?

4. On a check stub certain items are added to the previous balance and other items are subtracted from the previous balance. Name as many plus items (additions) and as many minus items (subtractions) as you can.

5. Indicate the steps that should be followed in replenishing the petty cash fund. Include (a) method of proving the petty cash fund, (b) procedure for determining the amount required to replenish the fund, and (c) description of the check that would be written to replenish the fund.

6. Do you think that the secretary is ever justified in borrowing for her personal use from the petty cash fund?

7. When making a payment from the petty cash fund, one secretary always insists that the person to whom she is paying the money sign or initial the petty cash receipt. Considering that most petty cash payments are for very small amounts, is this precaution necessary?

8. When a bank draft is purchased, it may be drawn in favor of the person or business to whom payment is being made, or in favor of the person making the payment and indorsed by him to the creditor. Which do you think is the better method? Why?

9. A fruit grower located in Portland, Oregon, is shipping by railway a large quantity of fruit to a dealer in Chicago. He wishes to be certain of obtaining payment for the fruit before it is delivered to the dealer. The dealer, in turn, wants the fruit delivered in Chicago before he makes payment. Outline the procedure that would be followed by the shipper and by the buyer (dealer) in handling this transaction.

**10.** Your employer asks you to send $300 to his daughter at the University of Mexico, Mexico City. How do you send the money?

**11.** If necessary, correct the following. Then use the Reference Guide to check your answers.

(a) Deposits reached a new high during the month of May.

(b) Working together in such close proximity caused friction between the two tellers.

(c) The posting machines are both alike in appearance.

(d) The action of the court bars out the possibility of our obtaining an early settlement.

(e) Enclosed herewith is our certified check in payment of the account.

## PROBLEMS

■ **1.** A deposit includes the following checks, bills, and coins:

### Checks

| | |
|---|---|
| 27-10 | $124.80 |
| 45-12 | 16.25 |
| 27-10 | 115.25 |
| 14-8 | 76.10 |

### Bills

| | |
|---|---|
| 4 | $20 bills |
| 16 | $10 bills |
| 21 | $5 bills |
| 155 | $1 bills |

### Coins

| | |
|---|---|
| 19 | Halves |
| 62 | Quarters |
| 73 | Dimes |
| 45 | Nickels |
| 103 | Pennies |

(a) Indicate how the checks should be indorsed for deposit in the First National Bank by Ames, Inc.

(b) For each denomination of bills give (1) the number of bills that would be wrapped, (2) the value of the wrapped bills, (3) the number of unwrapped bills, (4) the value of the unwrapped bills, (5) the value of all bills of all denominations.

(c) Repeat the process for the coins.

(d) Determine the total amount of the deposit.

(e) Indicate specifically how the bills and coins in the deposit would be presented to the bank teller.

■ **2.** Prepare the reconciliation of the bank statement.

The bank statement showed a balance of $948.39 on March 31. Examination of the bank statement provided the following information: A deposit for $211.80 made by mail on March 31 was not shown on the statement. A service charge for $3.50 had been deducted by the bank. The bank had also deducted $12 rent for a safe deposit box and $6.50 for printing of checkbooks. All checks written were returned with the bank statement with the exception of checks No. 87 for $118.20, No. 96 for $178.48, and No. 97 for $1.92.

The check-stub balance on March 31 was $883.59.

■ **3.** Your office has a $30 petty cash fund that is stored in a small metal box and locked in a file cabinet at the end of the day. Entries are made in a petty cash book that contains the following columns: Cash Received, Cash Paid, Postage, Office Supplies, Donations, and Miscellaneous. The largest single expenditure permitted from the fund is $4. Prenumbered petty cash vouchers are used.

Since you are turning the responsibility for the fund over to an assistant, you prepare written directions, specifying details for:

(a) Safekeeping of the fund

(b) Making payments from the fund

(c) Replenishing the fund

Prepare the instructions.

# Chapter 23

## INVESTMENT AND INSURANCE RECORDS

An executive may have extensive investments in securities and real estate, and most executives carry insurance protection for their families and businesses. Many of these investment and insurance transactions come across the secretary's desk; in fact, much of the routine work may be her responsibility. Her thoroughness, or lack of it, can affect her employer's tax liability. For example, the buying and selling dates for securities determine a long-term or a short-term capital gain or loss. These dates come from the secretary's record of the transactions. The adequacy of a reimbursement for a fire or burglary loss may depend upon the quality of the property inventory that she maintained.

While a secretary need not share her employer's interest in stock market fluctuations and his enthusiasm for the financial section of the newspaper, the more she knows about buying and selling securities, keeping property and insurance records, and other financial matters, the more valuable she will be to him and the more satisfaction she will get from her work. And, after all, reading the *Wall Street Journal* can become a pleasant and rewarding habit.

## SECURITIES

A corporation can secure capital by issuing stock or by borrowing money through bonds. *Stocks* are evidence of ownership in the corporation; *bonds* are evidence of creditorship — that is, of a loan to the corporation.

### Stocks

Ownership in a corporation is divided into units known as *shares of stock*. A stockholder is an owner of one or more shares of stock, and his ownership is shown by a paper known as a *stock certificate*. The stockholder receives *dividends* in return for his investment in the corporation. Dividends are paid from the earnings of the company either in cash or in additional stock referred to as a *stock dividend*.

**Kinds of Stock.** Stocks fall into two general classes, *common* and *preferred*. Holders of common stock are usually the only ones who have the right to vote in the stockholders' meetings. The rate of dividends paid on common stock is not fixed.

Preferred stock usually has a fixed dividend rate and a preference over common stock in first payment of dividends and in the first distribution of assets if the company is liquidated. Preferred stock may be *cumulative* or *noncumulative*. With cumulative preferred stock, any unpaid preferred-stock dividends accumulate and must be paid before any distribution can be made to common stockholders. Noncumulative preferred stock does not contain a provision to pay dividends in arrears.

Preferred stock also may be *participating* or *nonparticipating*. It is participating only if the stockholder is entitled to share with the common stockholders in any additional dividend disbursement after an agreed rate is paid on the common stock.

Some preferred stock is *convertible*; that is, the owner has the privilege of converting it into a specified number of shares of common stock at any time he chooses. Most preferred stocks are *callable*; that is, they are redeemable at the option of the issuing corporation at the redemption price specified in the stock certificate.

Stock may be *par-value* or *no-par-value* stock. *Par value* refers to a value ($1, $5, $10, $100) printed on the stock certificate. This printed value has no significance in determining the market price of the stock, which is measured by the stock's earning power — past, present, and future. Many companies today, therefore, do not print any value on their common stock. It is then known as no-par-value stock.

**Stockholders' Meetings.** Stockholders' meetings are held annually. Members of the board of directors are elected at this meeting by the

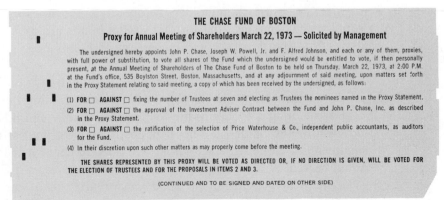

A proxy is sent to the stockholder for his optional use. The form usually indicates the names of those to whom the voting rights are being assigned and, in some cases, provides the stockholder with a place to indicate whether he wishes his stock to be voted for or against certain proposals to be decided at the stockholders' meeting.

stockholders present in person or by proxy. The board, in turn, elects the officers of the company at one of its regular meetings.

A notice of the stockholders' meeting, accompanied by a proxy form and a proxy statement, is sent to each stockholder entitled to vote. The notice gives a description of the business that is to be transacted. A *proxy* is a legal instrument assigning one's voting privilege to a specified person or persons. If directors of the corporation are to be elected, the proxy statement indicates the names of the persons nominated for whom the stockholder's proxy will be voted.

The stockholder may attend the meeting and vote in person; he may sign and send in the proxy and thus cast his vote; or he may simply choose to do neither and thus fail to vote his stock.

If the executive usually attends the stockholders' meeting, the secretary should see that the date of the meeting is recorded on his calendar. If the meeting is to be held out of town, she should discuss travel arrangements with him.

**Annual Reports.** Most companies send annual, and usually also quarterly, reports to stockholders. Such reports usually include a review of the company's activities and its financial statements.

Some executives study these reports carefully and then have them filed. If this is your employer's habit, file them with other such reports or in the separate folder for that stock.

## Bonds: Regular or Coupon

A *bond* is a certificate containing a written interest-bearing promise to pay a definite sum of money at a specified time and place. The interest due must be paid to bondholders before stockholders can share in the profits of the company, and for that reason bonds are considered safer investments than stocks. The ownership of bonds does not give the investor voting rights in the company.

There are two general classes of bonds—coupon bonds and registered bonds. *Coupon bonds* are payable to the person holding them. If the bond or the interest coupons are lost or stolen, they can be converted into cash by the holder. Coupon bonds, therefore, present a security responsibility to the secretary who is entrusted to care for them. Bonds should be kept in a safe-deposit box.

Coupons are cut from the bonds on or after their due date and presented at a local bank for collection. Some banks make a small charge for this collection service. Bond coupons can be listed on a bank-deposit slip.

*Registered* bonds are decidedly less worry to the secretary. Such bonds are registered by the issuing corporation, which mails the interest and principal payments to the registered holders. If the bond is lost, the owner still receives his payments; and the bond certificate can be replaced.

Corporate bonds are usually issued in $1,000 units. The selling price, however, is quoted as though they had a $100 denomination. Thus, if a corporate bond is said to sell at 97⅝, it actually sells at $976.25, a discount of $23.75 from its maturity value.

## Stock Market Trading

Most stocks and bonds are purchased and sold through a stock exchange, such as the New York Stock Exchange (known as the "Big Board"), the American Stock Exchange (Amex), the Midwest (Chicago) Stock Exchange, the Pacific Coast Stock Exchange, and the Toronto Stock Exchange. A number of smaller organized exchanges are found in different parts of the country in large cities. On the New York Stock Exchange only securities listed on the exchange are traded on its floor; the American Stock Exchange and other exchanges permit trading in unlisted securities.

Some stocks and bonds are purchased in the *over-the-counter* market, which is not a place but a method of doing business; that is, the transaction is handled privately through a bank, a broker, or a securities dealer and does not go through any of the stock exchanges. A buyer or seller of the security is located, and the sale price is arrived at by negotiation. Most over-the-counter transactions are limited to unlisted securities (stocks and bonds of relatively small local companies that are not listed on an exchange).

Buying and selling of stocks and bonds on the stock exchange is handled through a *broker*. Stock certificates sold through brokers are not passed from owner to owner; the seller turns in his certificates to the broker who sends them to the transfer agent for cancellation. The transfer agent employed by the corporation is usually a bank, which keeps a record of the specific owners of stock certificates by names and numbers. The agent fills in a new certificate with the name supplied to him, writes in the number of shares the certificate represents, has it signed and countersigned, and forwards it to the broker for delivery to the new owner or for deposit to the credit of the owner's account at the brokerage firm. As a service to investors, some brokerage firms will hold all stocks and bonds owned by an investor and send him a monthly statement or inventory of his holdings, listing the amounts received as dividends or interest that month.

The term *mutual funds* is used to identify investment companies (or investment trusts). These investment companies sell shares to individual investors and use capital raised in this manner to purchase additional securities. These stocks and bonds are known as the *portfolio* of the investment company. The individual with limited funds is offered a chance to own (indirectly) an interest in many companies and types of securities because these investments are diversified among bonds, preferred stocks, and common stocks, and also among many corporations.

Specialized mutual funds are available to investors wanting to purchase specialized securities—for instance, insurance, chemicals, or other stocks offering growth possibilities or high income.

**Stock Market Information.** The financial pages of leading newspapers report daily the stock transactions at major exchanges. The number of shares sold and the selling price for all stocks listed and traded in that day on each exchange are reported. Sales and prices of bonds are also reported in separate tables.

Stocks listed on the exchange on which there was no trading—that is, no sales were made of the stock on the day being reported—are printed under a special "Bid and Asked" section. This section gives the closing bid and asking price for the stock. For example, AmFinani bid 42½, asked 44½. This means no American Finance stock was transferred and that there was an offer to buy at 42½ and an offer to sell at 44½.

In addition to the daily stock market report and financial news that appear in the newspapers, information on security prices, trends, and business conditions may be obtained from such sources as *Wall Street Journal, Business Week, Barron's, Financial World, Forbes, Magazine of Wall Street and Business Analyst, The Exchange, American Investor, Moody's Stock Survey,* and *Commercial and Financial Chronicle.* Several large brokerage firms and some banks also publish special reports on securities.

There are a number of investment advisory services, such as Moody's Investors Service Inc., Babson's Reports Inc., United Business and Investment Service, and Financial World Research Bureau. Most of these organizations analyze the stock market and for a fee provide investors with detailed information on companies, lists of stocks to watch, stocks that represent "good buys," stocks to "sell." They also analyze the individual's stock holdings and provide other data that an investor may need. Such service is also available from the broker with whom an investor has an account.

**Market Averages.**  A number of stock averages are designed to serve as barometers of the stock market — that is, to indicate whether the market is rising or falling.  Probably the best known are the Standard and Poor's Index and the Dow-Jones Averages.  The Standard and Poor's Index is based on the price of 500 stocks and is computed hourly each trading day.  The Dow-Jones Averages include four separate averages — one for industrials (stocks of industrial corporations), one for rails, one for utilities, and a composite average of 65 stocks, intended to measure trends in all divisions of the market.  The market averages are published in leading newspapers and are reported on television and by radio.

**Market Terminology**.  Certain standard terminology is used in placing orders for the purchase or sale of stock.

**Market Order.**  A *market order* instructs the broker to buy or sell a security at once.  No price is indicated and the order is executed "at the market"; that is—at the best price obtainable.

**Limited Order.**  A limited order instructs the broker to buy or sell a security at a certain price only.  If the transaction cannot be consummated at the designated price, the order is not executed.

**Day Order.**  The day order is good only for the day on which it is given; *GTW Order* is "good for this week"; a *GTM Order* is "good this month"; and a *GTC Order* (open order) is "good till canceled."

**Stop Order.**  The investor using a stop order instructs the broker to buy or sell "at the market" whenever the security moves to a specified quotation.

**Short Sale.**  The investor sells short—that is, sells securities that he does not own in anticipation of buying them later at a lower price.  To negotiate the sale, he, or his broker, borrows the stocks temporarily.

**Bid and Offer.**  The price at which a prospective buyer will purchase and the price at which a prospective seller will sell is called *bid and offer*.  This quotation involves over-the-counter sales.

**Yield.**  The *yield* is the percentage of return (for one year) on one share of stock, computed at the current market price or at the price paid by an owner.

**Ex Dividend.**  A company declares a dividend to be paid to all stockholders as of a given future date.  Stock sold during the intervening period may be sold *ex dividend*; that is, the *seller* and not the *purchaser* of the stock will receive the unpaid declared dividend.

## NEW YORK STOCK EXCHANGE TRANSACTIONS

| 197–<br>High | Low | | Sales in<br>100s | Open | High | Low | Close | Net<br>Chg. |
|---|---|---|---|---|---|---|---|---|
| 85 3/4 | 54 | AbbtLb 1.10 | 205 | 58 1/8 | 59 3/8 | 58 | 58 1/8 | + 1/8 |
| 60 | 45 | ACF Ind 2.40 | 9 | 50 5/8 | 50 5/8 | 50 1/2 | 50 5/8 | |
| 17 1/2 | 10 1/2 | AcmeClev .80 | 14 | 12 5/8 | 13 | 12 5/8 | 13 | + 3/8 |
| 64 3/4 | 39 1/2 | Acme Mkt 2b | 41 | 44 5/8 | 44 3/4 | 44 1/2 | 44 3/4 | + 1/8 |
| 14 3/4 | 12 | AdmsEx 86g | 42 | 12 7/8 | 13 1/4 | 12 3/4 | 12 7/8 | |
| 54 1/2 | 39 1/2 | AetnaLf pf2 | 2 | 52 1/2 | 52 1/2 | 52 1/4 | 52 1/4 | – 1/2 |
| 46 3/4 | 32 1/4 | Akzona la | 94 | 32 3/4 | 33 | 32 1/4 | 32 1/2 | + 1/4 |
| 1 | | 2 | 3 | 4 | 5 | 6 | 7 | 8 |

### Key

1 The price range (high and low) of the stock in the year to date

2 The name of the company and a description of the stock. The rate of annual dividend paid per share based on the last quarterly or semiannual declaration is listed next. Special and extra dividends are not included unless noted by a legend letter following the dividend rate. Check the legend at the end of the stock listing for interpretation of the letters. The following legend explains the letters used in the illustration above:

   a — Also extra or extras    b — Annual rate plus stock dividend
   g — Declared or paid so far this year    pf — preferred stock

3 The number of shares of stock sold during the day (in hundreds)

4 The price of the first (*opening*) sale of the stock for the day

5 The *highest* price the stock reached during the day. Stock quotations are in eighths of a point (dollar). Thus 76⅛ means a price of $76.125 per share; 76¼ ($76.25); 76½ ($76.50); 76⅝ ($76.625).

6 The *lowest* price for which the stock sold during the day

7 The *last* (*closing*) price for the stock at the end of the day

8 The difference between today's last price and the last price of yesterday. The plus sign (+) indicates an increase in the last price today over yesterday's last price; the minus sign (−) indicates a decrease.

The stock-market-page illustration shown above provides the following information: To this date this year, Abbott Laboratories common stock has sold at a high of 85¾ ($85.75) and a low of 54 ($54). The stock paid $1.10 in dividends last year. During the day 20,500 shares were sold. The stock opened at 58⅛ ($58.125). It reached a high of 59⅜ ($59.375), and the lowest amount for which it sold was 58. The last sale for the day was at 58⅛. This was up ⅛ from yesterday's closing.

*Round and Odd Lots.* Most stocks listed on the stock exchanges are traded in 100-share units, called *round lots.* An order for anything less than 100 shares is known as an *odd lot.* A small additional commission charge is made for handling *odd-lot* transactions.

*Stock Split.* A company may split its stock to lower the market price. In a *stock split,* the company issues to each stockholder a specified number of additional shares for each share he now owns. For example, if it is a three-to-two split, the stockholder will receive three shares in exchange for each two shares he owns.

**Stock Rights.** When a corporation plans to sell additional stock, each existing stockholder may be given a stock warrant indicating the number of shares that he is entitled to purchase at a designated price, usually slightly below the market. If the stockholder chooses not to exercise his stock purchase rights, he has the option of selling his rights to another party.

**A Brokerage Transaction.** To understand the procedure of a brokerage transaction, let us follow through a hypothetical one in which the secretary shares responsibility.

1. **The purchaser, or his secretary, places an order with the broker to buy 25 shares of U.S. Steel common "at the market," (generally by a telephone call.)**

   (The secretary makes a full memorandum of the order; the date, the time, and the order placed. The broker *executes* the order on that date—the trade date.)

2. **When the broker has made the purchase through the stock exchange, he sends an invoice called a** *confirmation* **for the purchase of the stock to the buyer.**

   (The invoice or bill for the purchase or sale of securities is called a *confirmation* because the broker is acting as an agent, and he confirms by means of the invoice the instructions given to him. The confirmation lists the name of the stock and description, the number of shares purchased or sold, the price per share, extension, commission charge, tax, postage, and total.
   The *secretary* compares the confirmation with the memorandum of the order to make sure the order has been carried out correctly.)

3. **The purchaser, or his secretary, sends a check to the broker by the settlement date (which is five business days after the trade date).**

4. **The broker arranges for the transfer of the stock to the purchaser.**

   (If the executive has the brokerage company retain the stock, his account will be credited and the stock will be reported on the next monthly inventory statement. If he retains his own stock certificates, the certificate will be forwarded to him by registered mail. If delivery is made to the executive, the secretary, upon receipt of the stock, records the stock certificate number on the confirmation. She transfers all the information from the confirmation to the executive's permanent record.
   The secretary may attach the confirmation to the stock certificate, or she may file the confirmations chronologically under the broker's name so that they will be available when the stock is sold. The sales confirmation may be filed with the executive's copy of his income tax return.)

| JAN | FEB | MAR | APR | MAY | JUN | JUL | AUG | SEPT | OCT | NOV | DEC |
|-----|-----|-----|-----|-----|-----|-----|-----|------|-----|-----|-----|

(Dividend Date)

STOCK: Detroit Edison, common
BROKER: Merrill Lynch  DIVIDENDS: Mar., June,
FILED: Safe deposit box, City National  Sept., Dec.

| Date | Certificate Number | How Acquired | No. of Shares | Cost per Share | Total Cost* |
|------|--------------------|--------------|---------------|----------------|-------------|
| 1/18/-- | H21601 | Purchased | 100 | 41 1/2 | 4,189.75 |
| 5/20/-- | H29861 | New cert. for H21601 after sale 40 shares | 60 | | |
| 12/4/-- | H32504 | 5% stock dividend | 3 | | |
| | | | | | |
| | | | | | |

*Includes postage, insurance, and commission.

| RECORD OF SALES | | | | | | |
|-----------------|--|--|--|--|--|--|
| Trading Date | Shares Sold | Selling Price | Gross Amount | Int. or State Tax | Commission Paid | Net Amt. Received |
| 5/20/-- | 40 | 43 3/4 | 1,750.00 | 2.43 | 22.50 | 1,725.07 |
| | | | | | | |
| | | | | | | |

A separate record card or sheet for stock transactions should be kept for each lot of securities. Purchases and sales are recorded on the front of the card as illustrated. Dividends are recorded on the ruled form on the back of the card. A metal tab can be used to indicate the dates on which to expect dividends. The card should show where the securities are kept.

**Delivery of Securities.** When securities held personally by the executive are sold, they are ordinarily delivered to the broker's office by the secretary or by messenger, or are sent by registered mail and insured, accompanied by a covering letter describing the securities in full. Include the owner's name and such items as the company name, amount, and certificate number for each stock certificate or bond enclosed. Request a return receipt.

**Records of Securities.** One good rule for the secretary to follow in keeping financial records for securities is to use a separate page or card for each lot. The illustration given above shows a convenient form and indicates the information that would be recorded on each group of securities.

The "where kept" notation is important information that should be recorded about any valuable paper. Papers tucked away in unusual safekeeping spots known only to the owner often remain hidden when they are desperately needed in his absence.

| Date Purchased | Security | No. of Shares | Price per Share | Total Cost |
|---|---|---|---|---|
| 4/15/59 | Cleve. Elec. Illum. Co., common | 100 | 52 1/4 | $5,269 |
| 6/10/60 | Disney, common | 200 | 30 1/4 | 6,084 |
| 3/7/73 | Knight News | 100 | 52 1/8 | 5,278 |

The executive should have at hand a typed alphabetic list of his securities. The secretary may wish to prepare the list in triplicate: a copy for the executive's desk, one for the files, and one for her own records. She should list separately (for a given company) each purchase of stock made on different days or at different prices.

**Stock Certificate Numbers.** When all the stock covered by one certificate is sold, the certificate is surrendered to the broker as part of the sale. When only a portion of a block of stock covered by one certificate is sold, the certificate is also turned over to the broker; but the investor receives a new certificate for a total of the unsold shares. This procedure requires a change in the certificate number on the stock records. For example, in the stock record illustrated on page 552, the 40 shares that were sold were from the block of 100 shares covered by Certificate Number H21601. This fact was indicated. The new certificate number for the 60 unsold shares is also recorded.

# REAL ESTATE

A secretary may be commissioned to do any or all of the tasks incident to the executive's real estate activities—to care for the valuable papers necessary to real-estate transactions, to do the banking work, and to keep simple, complete records of income and expenses.

## Buying Property

When real property is purchased, the title of ownership is transferred by means of a properly executed written instrument known as a *deed*.

**Deeds.** There are two types of deeds—warranty deed and quitclaim deed. In a *warranty deed* the grantor or seller warrants that he is the true and lawful owner, that he has full power to convey the property, and that the title is clear, free, and unencumbered. In a *quitclaim deed* the grantor quits his claim to the property; that is, he relinquishes his claim but does not warrant or guarantee the title.

A deed must be signed, witnessed, and acknowledged before a notary public. It should be *recorded*—that is, entered on public record, at the courthouse in the county where the property is located. Deeds, mortgages, and leases are valuable legal documents and should be kept in a bank safe-deposit box or in a fireproof vault or safe.

**Legal Terms.** Other legal terms frequently used when the title to real estate is transferred are:

*Mortgages*—formal written contracts that transfer interests in property as security for the payment of the debt (Mortgages must be signed, witnessed, and recorded in the public records the same as a deed. The law considers the mortgagor [the borrower] as owner of the property during the period of the loan.)

*Junior (Second) Mortgage*—a mortgage that is subordinate to a prior mortgage

*Amortization*—mortgage or loan repayment plan that permits the borrower through regular payments at stated intervals to retire the principal of the loan

*Foreclosure Proceedings*—legal process used to satisfy the claim of the lender in case of default in payment of interest or principal on a mortgage

*Option*—an agreement under which an owner of property gives another person the right to buy the property at a fixed price within a specified time

*Appurtenances*—rights of way or other types of easements that are properly used with the land, the title to which passes with the land

*Easements*—privileges regarding some special use of another person's property, such as right of way to pass over the land, to use a driveway, or to fish in a stream

*Fixtures*—those articles that are permanently attached to real estate, such as buildings, fences, and electric wiring in a building

*Land Contract*—a method of payment for property whereby the buyer makes a small down payment and agrees to pay additional amounts at intervals (The buyer does not get a deed to the property until a substantial amount of the price of the property is paid.)

## Property Records

Permanent records of property owned are kept for several reasons, to determine the value of the property, to show the outstanding debt: to use in tax reporting, and to use as a basis for setting a satisfactory selling price.

A separate record should be kept for each piece of property owned and should include information similar to that shown on page 555.

**Investment Property.** Property held for rental income or to be sold at a hoped-for profit is *investment property*. The secretary's employer may own several such pieces, or he may be employed to manage such property for other owners, for which service he receives a fee. Managing property means negotiating with the tenants, keeping the building in repair, and handling certain of the finances—collecting rentals, paying expenses, and so on.

```
Type and Location          Commercial property
      of Property          127 North Webster Avenue
                           Tucson, Arizona  85715

Title in Name of:      Robert C. and Mary K. Folley

Date Acquired:         2/21/7-   Purchase Price:        $76,500

Mortgage(s):           Main Savings and Loan          $40,000
                       First Federal Bank               5,000

Assessed Evaluation
for Taxes:             $39,000

Remarks:  Deed is filed in home safe
```

| Income from Rentals | | | Mortgage Payments Int. and Princ. | | | Expenses | | |
|---|---|---|---|---|---|---|---|---|
| Date | Item | Amount | Date | Item | Amount | Date | Item | Amount |
| 2/10 | Rent | 510.00 | 2/28 | I.+P. | 310.00 | 3/10 | Taxes | 500.00 |
| 3/10 | Rent | 510.00 | 3/31 | I.+P. | 310.00 | 3/10 | Water | 48.20 |
| 4/10 | Rent | 510.00 | 4/30 | I.+P. | 310.00 | 4/16 | Plumb. | 46.85 |
|  |  |  |  |  |  |  |  |  |

Keep a property record similar to this form for each piece of property. At the end of each year all the income and expenses related to each piece of property can be conveniently organized for preparation of the income tax report.

Tenants may be required to sign *leases* prepared by the secretary. Printed lease forms (see Chapter 25, pages 599–600) are available in stationery or legal-supply stores. The pertinent facts must be filled in on the form and the signatures affixed. These forms should be checked with an attorney to be certain they set forth the exact conditions desired.

The secretary keeps detailed records of income and expenses on each piece of investment property because all income must be reported and all expenses are deductible on tax returns.

To keep accurate data on each unit, the secretary can follow the plan suggested here.

1. Set up an individual file folder for each rental unit, such as each suite of offices, each apartment in a building, or each house. As each unit would be identified on the file folder by the number or address, an alphabetic index of tenants' names giving their rental location would serve as a helpful cross reference.

   File in this folder everything pertaining to the unit of rental, such as correspondence, the lease, bills for repairs or improvements, lists of any special fixtures or furniture provided, rental amount.

2. Use a miscellaneous folder (or folders) for the building in general to take care of the items that cannot be charged to a specific rental unit, such as janitor service, repairs to the exterior of the building or corridors, taxes, and other such items.

The record of all receipts and expenses paid can be written right on each folder, or on a card or sheet filed inside each folder. Preferably, such records are kept on separate sheets in a loose-leaf book where the chance of their being lost is considerably reduced.

The banking of money collected from investment property and the payment of bills for such property should be handled carefully. It is extremely important that the deposit slips be completed so that every deposit can be identified and that every check stub be labeled to be charged against a specific rental unit or building.

**Personal-Property Records.** To provide necessary information in event of death or other contingency, the secretary is often asked to keep a file of the executive's personal property, such as an inventory of household goods, a description and the location of family jewels and heirlooms, insurance policies, and the names and addresses of certain key people involved in his personal affairs. Such information and materials should be placed in sealed envelopes, labeled, and kept in the safe-deposit box or fireproof office safe.

## Tickler Card File

There are many recurring expenses on property, such as mortgage payments (usually due monthly), tax payments (due annually or semi-annually), and insurance premiums (due quarterly). On income property, the rent is usually due on a certain day each month. To make sure that income is received when due and that recurring expenses are paid on time, a tickler card should be prepared for each item so that the card can be used continually—refiled under the next pertinent date after it comes to the front on the current reminder date.

In addition to interest and mortgage payments, use tickler cards for:

```
File date:  12th of each month

Mortgage payment due:  15th of each month
(Mail check no later than the 12th)

Duplex, 906 Seneca Street

Amount of check:  $225.00

Make check to:  Estate of Frank Foster
Send check to:  Willis and Thompson
                148 Baker Bldg.
                110 W. 7th Street
                Fort Worth, TX  76102

Final payment date:  April 15, 1979
```

The tickler card for a monthly mortgage payment identifies the property, shows the file date, due date, amount of payment, to whom payment is to be made, and where the check is to be sent.

*Taxes*—Indicate for each kind of tax payment: kind of tax, payment date, amount, to whom to make the check payable, where to send the check, and whether or not a return must accompany the payment.

*Insurance Premiums*—See page 559 for information to be shown.

*Rent Receipts*—For each rental unit show location, amount of rent, name and mailing address of tenant, and any special information regarding collection or interpretation of rent payment.

### Source Materials

If the secretary's employer has extensive real estate holdings or is engaged in the real estate business, he may subscribe to an information service, such as the *Prentice-Hall Real Estate Service.*

There are a number of periodicals that specialize in providing current information on real estate, a few of which are *Builders Journal, Real Estate Weekly, Builders and Realty Record, National Real Estate Investor, The Appraisal Journal, National Real Estate and Building Journal, Journal of Property Management,* and *Building Reporter and Realty News.*

The *Handbook of Real Estate Forms*[1] would be a valuable addition to the secretary's reference shelf.


## INSURANCE

Insurance can be grouped into three general classes—personal, property, and liability. *Personal insurance* includes the many kinds of life, accident, and health insurance. *Property insurance* covers loss from impairment or destruction of property, such as fire, earthquake, burglary, and automobile collision. *Liability insurance* protects the insured against losses resulting from injury to another, such as public liability, workmen's compensation, and employer's liability.

The individual or business purchasing the insurance is called the *policyholder.* The *policy* is the written contract that exists between the policyholder and the insurance company. The insurance company may be referred to as the insurer or the *underwriter.* The policyholder makes periodic payments to the insurance company for the policy. These payments are called the insurance *premium.*

The secretary has three responsibilities regarding the executive's insurance; namely, to see that the premiums are paid promptly so that there will be no lapse in protection, to keep summary records on each kind of insurance for the executive's information, and to store the policies and related correspondence in a safe place.


### Premium Payments and Renewals

Insurance premiums are payable in advance. Those on property insurance are usually paid annually or for a term of three or five years. Premiums on life insurance may be paid annually or in monthly, quarterly, or semiannual installments.

---

[1]E. J. Friedman, *Handbook of Real Estate Forms* (Englewood Cliffs: Prentice-Hall, Inc., 1957).

—*MacManus*

The secretary must follow up on payment of insurance premiums, as well as cancellations and indorsements (changes in the policy). In this illustration the secretary is updating the policy by attaching an indorsement received from the insurance company.

Many life insurance policies allow a 28- to 31-day grace period in making premium payments. If the premium is due and payable on August 16, payment of the premium may be made any time before September 16. If the premium notice does not specify the grace period, the secretary should inquire from the insurance company if a grace period is allowed.

Checks in payment of premiums must be drawn in sufficient time to have them signed and sent to the insurance company or agent before the expiration date. It is the secretary's responsibility to avoid any insurance policy lapse caused by failure to make premium payment.

In addition to seeing that premiums are paid, the secretary should also arrange for the cancellation of policies when the protection is no longer needed. A policy can be canceled by telling the insurance company or agent of the cancellation and returning the policy. The premium for the unexpired period of the policy is refundable. The secretary should place a follow-up in her tickler file to check on the receipt of the premium refund.

## Insurance Records

The beginning secretary will know nothing of her employer's personal insurance commitments, but she may be fortunate enough to inherit a summary record from her predecessor. More likely, however, she herself will set up this record from any policies on file in the office and from notices of premiums due as they arrive.

Methods of keeping insurance records vary, but in general the records consist of an insurance register and a premium payment reminder, usually in the form of a tickler card. The register would contain information similar to that shown in the illustration. Some secretaries record insurance policies on separate sheets

In correspondence, be sure to include the *policy number*. If the correspondence relates to a claim, include the *claim number* assigned by the insurance company.

in a small loose-leaf notebook. Thus, when a policy is no longer in force, she can remove its sheet. Others prefer to use a separate register for each type of insurance: life, property, and liability. Certainly the executive's personal insurance and that of the business or office should be kept in separate registers.

Use a separate tickler card for each policy, and file the cards according to premium-payment date. This helps to avoid the lapse of a policy or a penalty for late payment of a premium.

The insurance index card illustrated on page 560 provides all the information necessary. The data may be placed on separate cards, in an insurance register, or both.

| INSURANCE REGISTER | | | | | | |
|---|---|---|---|---|---|---|
| Company and Name of Agent | Policy No. | Type and Amount | Date Issued | Amt. of Premium | Date Due | Grace Period |
| N.Y. LIFE V. Getty | 29 22 84 | Ord. Life on Mr. B. $20,000 | 3/2/55 | $284 Semi-an | 2/2 8/2 | 30-day |
| N.Y. LIFE V. Getty | 37 86 21 37 86 21 | Term $10,000 on Mrs. B. | 1/9/68 | $175 Annual | 5/6 | 30-day |
| CONN. GEN. T. Ramsey | H261 162 | Fire on household goods $20,000 | 1/12/72 | $249 Annual | 12/12 | |

Columns to provide appropriate information can be added as needed. When a policy expires, draw a line through the description to indicate the policy is no longer in force.

## TYPES OF INSURANCE

*Personal Insurance* — Protects against the results of illness, accident, and loss of income because of illness, accident, or death.

Life: Endowment  
     Limited payment life  
     Ordinary life  
     Term

Health: Hospital care  
       Medical fees  
       Surgical fees  
       Loss of income

*Property Insurance* — Protects from financial loss resulting from damage to insured's property.

Automobile collision  
Burglary and employee theft  
Fire  
Fire — Extended coverage (windstorm, lightning, riot, strike violence, smoke damage, falling aircraft and vehicle damage, most explosions)  
Plate glass  
Standard boiler  
Valuable papers  
Vandalism

Marine: Barratry  
       Burning  
       Collision  
       Mutiny  
       Piracy  
       Sinking  
       Standing

*Liability Insurance (Casualty)* — Protects against claim of other people if insured person causes injury or property damage to others.

Automobile liability  
Bailee insurance  
Elevator insurance  
Libel and slander

Premise and operations liability  
Public liability  
Product insurance  
Workmen's compensation

*Credit, Fidelity, and Surety* — Protects against losses from:

Bad accounts (Credit)  
Title (Surety)

Employee embezzlement  
  (Fidelity)

---

File an index card for each insurance policy in a tickler file. This provides a convenient record of the insurance and serves as a reminder notice for renewals and premium payments.

```
File date:  December 26, 197-

Expiration date:  January 4 each year

Type:  Fire insurance on office furniture

Amount:  $5,000  With:  Mutual Insurance Co.
                         5352 First St., City

Policy No. X438832
Date of issue:  January 5 each year
Premium:  $48.20
Policy filed:  First National Bank
```

## Property Inventory

The importance of keeping an up-to-date property inventory can be fully appreciated only by someone who has experienced a fire or burglary loss. To present a claim for a loss, the insured must "furnish a complete inventory of the destroyed, lost, damaged, and undamaged property with cost and actual cash value." This is difficult to do after the loss has taken place. A property inventory also serves a second important purpose. It shows how much insurance should be carried. Property values change; and unless the inventory is updated periodically, property may be overinsured or underinsured.

On her own initiative, the secretary may wish to keep an inventory of the furniture and equipment in the office. She should encourage her employer to provide details for an inventory on the furniture and valuables in his home. She should periodically update the inventory with him.

## Storage of Policies and Inventory Records

Since insurance policies must be examined occasionally for data on coverage, beneficiaries, rates, cash value, indorsements, and the like, the policies should be readily available — but in a safe place.

If the policies are kept in a file, you may find it convenient to remove them from their protective envelopes and place each policy in a separate folder. Identify the front of the folder with the name, address, and telephone number of the agent, and the policy number. Such a plan makes it possible to file with each policy any important correspondence, itemized lists of property covered, indorsements, and other pertinent data that affect the conditions of the insurance contract.

When insurance policies are stored in the office, there is always the possibility of their loss by fire. As a precaution, type a list of the policy numbers, insuring company, coverage, and amount. Your employer should store this list in his home safe. Thus, if the office records are destroyed, they can be more readily reconstructed.

Since an insurance policy *is* a contract, you can discard it when it has expired and keep your file cleared. First, however, you should call or write the agent to make certain that no claim on the policy is pending and that it has no continuing value.

## Fidelity Bonds

A *fidelity bond* is insurance on an employee's honesty. Most employers carry such insurance on those employees who handle large sums of money. The bonding company investigates the employee's character and the supervisory and control methods in force in the employer's business. No bond is sold if the applicant's character is questionable or if office conditions would make it easy to embezzle company funds.

Blanket fidelity bonds covering the entire personnel are bought by banks and other financial institutions. They protect against losses by embezzlement, robbery, forgery, and so on.

To be asked to take out a fidelity bond is no reflection on your character. Actually it indicates that you are considered competent to be entrusted with company funds.

## Action in Emergency

When disaster strikes, the secretary has an opportunity to prove that she is the cool-headed, responsible type that can think and act quickly. Others may be so excited and involved in the emergency that they fail to think of procedures. Insurance companies make these suggestions:

> After a fire, as soon as the situation is under control, notify the insurance company immediately by phone and confirm the call by wire. The insurance company may be able to have an inspector on the scene to witness the damage and save a lot of paper work later on.
>
> Immediately report to the police any losses by theft.
>
> Keep accurate and separate records for cleanup, repairs, and charges made by outside contractors. The items are all part of the insurance claim.
>
> When an accident occurs, interview witnesses on the spot. Signed statements carry much weight and refresh memories in settling claims. If possible, take pictures at the scene.

## WHERE-KEPT FILE

In the event of the sudden death of an executive, his family will need immediately certain financial information. The secretary can be of great assistance in such an emergency if she maintains a folder containing up-to-date information that will be needed. The following information might be included:

> *Bank Accounts*—the name and address of each bank in which an account is kept, the type of account, the exact name of account, and the name of bank contact (if the executive has one)
>
> *Birth Certificate*—where it can be found
>
> *Business Interests*—list of the executive's business interests
>
> *Credit Cards*—record of names and account numbers
>
> *Income Tax Record*—where past returns are filed; the name and address of the tax consultant
>
> *Insurance Policies*—location of insurance records (If these records do not contain detailed information on life, health and accident, hospitalization, and medical

insurance policies, the information should be placed in the folder. The name and address of the insurance adviser should be filed also.)

*Real Estate Investments*—location of detailed property records

*Passport*—where it can be found

*Safe-Deposit Box*—the name of the bank, the box number, and location of key

*Social Security*—the social security number

*Stocks and Bonds*—location of detailed investment records

*Tax Accountant* — name of

*Will*—location of the original and copies of the will; date of the latest will; name of attorney who prepared the will; executor's name and address

## ADMINISTRATIVE FUNCTIONS

The administrative assistant to an executive may be expected to perform a number of administrative functions related to the property, investments, and insurance coverage of the company and of the executive for whom she works. The college-trained secretary brings to her position a background of courses in economics, accounting, business law, and, in some cases, real estate and insurance. All of these courses contribute to her competency.

As an administrative assistant she may be asked to:

1. **Prepare an investment prospectus** on stocks that are under consideration for investment. This activity would involve checking investment service reports for gathering data on products, past performance, background of company officials, forecasts for the area and for the company, comparison with competitors, and so forth. Such data are available in the business section of a public library and in special libraries.

2. **Update the investment portfolio** of the company or of the executive. The updating process would involve analyzing (1) the rate of yield on each investment, (2) profit trends, and (3) the outlook for the company. For some classes of stock, charts showing the fluctuations in the market may need to be prepared and updated at regular intervals.

3. **Supervise and follow through on repairs and improvements** made to investment property. Frequent visits to the location of the property and careful study of the repair or construction contract would be necessary.

4. **Handle the details related to processing the sale or purchase of real estate.** This activity involves such details as having the title searched for liens and mortgages, obtaining title insurance, and processing and recording the deed.

5. **Review at regular intervals the insurance policies** in force and arrange for revision in insurance coverage in keeping with changing values of the property. The responsibility includes cancelling unneeded policies and being alert to new insurance needs.

6. **Process an insurance claim.** This responsibility involves compiling the records necessary to support a claim—cost records, appraisal of loss, and proof of loss.

## SUGGESTED READINGS

Brandt, Catherine. *A Woman's Money — How to Protect and Increase It in the Stock Market*. West Nyack: Parker Publishing Co., 1970.

Doris, Lillian, *The Real Estate Office Secretary's Handbook*. Englewood Cliffs: Prentice-Hall, Inc., 1966.

Engel, Louis. *How to Buy Stocks*, 4th ed. Boston: Little, Brown & Co., 1967.

*How to Read a Financial Report*. New York: Merrill Lynch, Pierce, Fenner & Smith, Inc., 1971.

Klein, A. E., Supervisory ed. *The New World Secretarial Handbook*. Cleveland: World Publishing Co., 1968, pp. 282–299; 320–337.

Levy, Herla Hess. *What Every Woman Should Know About Investing Her Money*. Chicago: Dartnell Corp., 1968.

*Office Work in the Field of Insurance, a Manpower White Glove Training Manual*. Milwaukee: Manpower, Inc., 1965.

Stabler, Charles Norman. *How to Read the Financial News*, 10th ed. New York: Harper & Row, 1965.

## QUESTIONS FOR DISCUSSION

1. A secretary whose employer invests in securities must know a number of stock market terms. What does each of the following terms mean? (Refer to outside sources for the meanings of terms with which you are not familiar.)

| | |
|---|---|
| bear market | margin |
| "blue-chip" stocks | market value |
| book value | mutual fund |
| bull market | option |
| ex dividend | "over-the-counter" |
| float | rails |
| growth stocks | sleeper |
| industrials | stock dividend |
| investment companies | utilities |

2. In what way can a stockholder participate in determining the policies of a company in which he owns stock?

3. Your employer is considering an investment in United Airlines (Unit Air) stock. He asks you to compile a report for him on the stock. What type of information would you include in the report? What would your information sources be?

4. In addition to stock prices, what information does the financial section of the newspaper contain? Would you recommend that the secretary read this section regularly?

5. Assume that you keep the records of your employer's personal investments. If he died, should you turn these records over to his widow, or should you wait until the executor of the estate is appointed and turn the records over to him?

6. In the event of fire or theft, all financial records (including stock certificates, bonds, and insurance policies) may be lost. What precautions

should a secretary take and/or suggest to her employer that would minimize such losses?

7. An owner of a small grocery store with six employees wishes to protect himself against all possible insurable losses. What types of insurance would he obtain? (He owns the building in which the store is located.)

8. Your employer asks you to have a mortgage recorded. What does this mean, and how would you carry out his instructions?

9. Your employer owns several pieces of rental property. You are responsible for keeping the records. What records would you keep?

10. Write the following years in Roman numerals.

    **1900     1918     1945     1950     Current year**

Convert these Roman numerals to Arabic numbers:

    **D          M          MDCDXLVIII**

11. Type the information in the blanks in the following sentence.

    **One historian thinks it dates back to _____ and another to _____. (*anno Domini* 175, before Christ 200)**

Consult the Reference Guide to verify or correct your answers.

## PROBLEMS

■ **1.** Your employer owns the following securities:

200 shares...American Natural Gas, common, (ANatGas)

100 shares...Coca Cola, Common (CocaCol)

75 shares...Consolidated Edison, 5% preferred, (Con Edis pf 5)

5 bonds...New York Telephone, (NY Tel 4½s 91)

200 shares...Standard Oil of Indiana (StOilInd)

500 shares...United Gas of Canada (Un Gas Can)

(a) **Prepare a report showing the current market value of your employer's security holdings. (Use the closing price of the security on the date of the report.)**

(b) **Your employer purchased the shares of American Natural Gas stock at 25. He receives a quarterly dividend of 57½¢ per share. Determine the rate of yield that he receives on his investment and the rate of yield at the *current* market price.**

■ **2.** When you obtain employment as a secretary, you may be able to participate in some form of employee group insurance. So that you may know something about these arrangements and how they operate, investigate the employee insurance plan maintained by a local company and report to the class the details of the plan.

Include in your report the types of insurance available, how the premiums are paid, and the status of the insurance upon termination of employment with the company.

■ **3.** Your employer owns a professional building that cost him $120,000. The building houses 18 offices. Six offices rent for $350 per month, ten for $300, and the remaining two for $250 per month. All the offices were rented throughout the year except four of the $350 offices, which were vacant three months each while being redecorated. The following expenses were incurred during the year in operating the building: management fee, 5% of the rental income; janitorial and maintenance service, $800 per month; supplies, $1,150; utilities,

$2,900; taxes, $7,560; repairs, $9,835; redecorating $8,250; and miscellaneous expenses, $875. Prepare a report showing the income, expenses, and net income for the year and the annual percent of return on the investment in the building.

■ **4.** Your employer has investments in stocks; a piece of rental property; and insurance policies on himself, wife, son, home, and automobiles. You decide to set up a tickler file to assist you in keeping track of these personal financial transactions. Prepare a 5- by 3-inch card identifying the information that you would record on

(a) **each insurance policy**
(b) **the rental property**
(c) **each security**

# Chapter 24

## PAYROLL PROCEDURES AND TAX DUTIES

Federal and state laws require all employers to keep detailed payroll records. Time records must be maintained, employee earnings and deductions must be recorded, payroll checks must be prepared, and tax reports submitted. In a large business, much of this work is done in a special payroll division and, unless employed in that division, the secretary would have few if any of these duties to perform. In a small office, however, she may handle all of the payroll work. The secretary's payroll responsibilities, therefore, are usually determined by the size and function of the office in which she works.

Regardless of the nature of her payroll responsibilities, every secretary can assist in the preparation of her employer's annual income tax return. Throughout the year she can systematically collect pertinent income tax data so that, when income tax return time comes, the facts and figures are readily available. No employer expects his secretary to assume the role of a tax adviser, but the "assist" role that she can assume is one that he appreciates.

## PAYROLL PROCEDURES

Payroll work is detailed and demands mathematical accuracy. In addition, it requires an understanding of the forms and reports that are legislated by the Federal Insurance Contribution (Social Security) and Fair Labor Standards Acts, income tax laws, federal and state unemployment compensation acts, and any pertinent local legislation.

The payroll is also a security responsibility. Payroll information is confidential. The secretary, therefore, must guard all payroll facts. Not only must the actual payroll checks and records be secured, but all payroll computation sheets must be destroyed because they provide the inquisitive person with a source of information. When working on the payroll, the secretary should place all information in a desk drawer if an interruption requires her to leave her desk.

## Social Security

Under the Social Security system most business, farm, and household employees and self-employed persons are provided an income in old age and survivor benefits in event of death. Social Security also provides a nationwide system of unemployment insurance and hospital and medical insurance benefits (known as Medicare) for persons of age 65 or over.

To pay most of these social security benefits, both employees and employers contribute an equal amount. Medical insurance (for persons of age 65 or over) is optional and is financed jointly by contributions from the retired insured person and from the federal government.

**Social Security Numbers.** Each employer and employee must obtain a social security number to identify himself in the government records. For the employer the number is called an *identification number*, while the employee must obtain an *account number*.

To obtain an account number, file an application form (Form SS-5) with the nearest social security office or post office. You will receive a card stamped with your account number. If the card is lost, a duplicate can be obtained. If you change your name or need to make other changes, report them on Form OAAN-7003 to the Social Security Administration. The secretary may find it convenient to have the following social security forms on hand:

**SS-5 — Application for Social Security Number (or Replacement of Lost Card)**
**OAAN-7003 — Request for Change in Social Security Records**
**OAR-7004 — Request for Statement of Earnings**

The social security administration recommends that every three or four years each employee request a statement of his account (Use Form OAR-7004) to make sure that his earnings have been reported properly.

The social security card shows the account number like that assigned to each individual protected under the Social Security Act. Note that the card has two parts—the upper part to be carried by the employee in his billfold, and the lower part to be detached and filed with other valuable papers for reference. The individual retains the same account number throughout his life.

**F.I.C.A. Tax Deductions.** Under the Social Security Act both the employer and employee pay *F.I.C.A.* (Federal Insurance Contribution Act) *taxes* at the same rate. A summary of the present tax rates and those scheduled for the future (subject to change by Congress) is shown in the table at the right.

Each employee's tax is deducted from his wages each payday; the employer accumulates these amounts for each employee and forwards them (together with his own tax payment) to the Internal Revenue Service Center for his region.

PRESENT AND FUTURE F.I.C.A. TAX RATES
(In Percentages)

| Year | Employer | Employee | Self-Employed |
|------|----------|----------|---------------|
| 1973–77 | 5.85* | 5.85* | 8.0* |
| 1978–80 | 6.05 | 6.05 | 8.25 |
| 1981–85 | 6.15 | 6.15 | 8.35 |

*Levied on the first $10,800 of a person's earnings each year.*

To illustrate, assume an employee earns $100 a week and is paid at the end of each week. At the rate of 5.85 percent the employer deducts $5.85[1] for the employee's F.I.C.A. tax and contributes an equal amount for his share. At the end of the quarter (13 weeks), the employer remits to the government a total of $152.10.

Self-employed persons (such as farmers, architects, and contractors) are required to pay at a rate that is approximately three fourths of the total paid by the employer and the employee on the same income. A self-employed individual reports and pays his F.I.C.A. tax simultaneously with his income tax.

**Unemployment Compensation Tax Deductions.** Under the Social Security Act, employers of four or more workers must pay a federal tax levied to pay the administrative costs of the state unemployment laws.

Most employers are also subject to a state unemployment tax. This tax, in most states paid by only employers, provides funds from which unemployment compensation can be paid to unemployed workers. The tax rate in most states is 2.7 percent of earnings up to $3,000 yearly on each employee. The employer's contributions to state unemployment compensation funds are reported on special forms filed quarterly.

In some states the unemployment tax is levied on employees as well as employers. In these states, the tax is deducted by the employer from the employee's wage. The employer submits quarterly to the state amounts deducted along with his contribution.

---

[1]The amount is usually obtained from a table (Circular E, Internal Revenue Service).

## Withholding (Income Tax) Deductions

The federal government requires most employers to withhold a certain amount from each wage payment to an employee as an advance payment on his income tax. The amounts withheld are remitted to the regional Internal Revenue Service Center at the time the F.I.C.A. taxes are paid. The term *wages* used in this connection includes the total compensation paid for service such as wages, salaries, commissions, bonuses, and vacation allowances.

The amount of income tax withheld depends upon the amount of wages received and the number of personal exemptions to which the taxpayer is entitled. Each employee must file with his employer, immediately upon reporting to work, an Employee's Withholding Exemption Certificate (Form W-4) to indicate the number of personal exemptions to which he is entitled. These are:

**An exemption for himself**

**An exemption for his spouse (unless his spouse claims her own exemption)**

**An exemption for each dependent (unless his spouse claims them)**

**An additional exemption if the taxpayer or his spouse is 65 years of age or over or is blind**

The amount of tax withheld is then computed from a table (Circular E) provided by the Internal Revenue Service.

A number of cities and states tax personal income. The percentage of deduction and the form of payment vary; for example, one city may have the employer deduct 1 percent from every payroll check issued and remit the total deductions at the end of each quarter of a calendar year. Some states and cities require individuals to file annual income tax returns.

**The following forms are needed for payroll records:**

*W-2* . . . . . . . . . . . . . Wage and Tax Statement

*W-3* . . . . . . . . . . . . . Reconciliation of Income Tax Withheld and Transmittal of Wage and Tax Statements

*W-4* . . . . . . . . . . . . . Employee's Withholding Exemption Certificate

*501* . . . . . . . . . . . . . Federal Tax Deposit

*940* . . . . . . . . . . . . . Employer's Annual Federal Unemployment Tax Return

*941* . . . . . . . . . . . . . Employer's Quarterly Federal Tax Return

*State Unemployment Return; other state and city report forms as required*

# CALENDAR OF PAYROLL PROCEDURES

• *On Hiring a New Employee:*

Have the employee complete Form W-4 (Employee's Withholding Exemption Certificate). Record employee's social security number and number of exemptions. File the certificate for safe keeping.

• *On Each Payment of Wages to an Employee:*

Withhold the proper amount of income tax and F.I.C.A. tax (refer to the instructions and tables supplied by the Internal Revenue Service and also to city and state information, if necessary). Make all other deductions.

As part of the payroll check or as a separate statement, a detailed record of total wages, amount and kind of each deduction, and net amount should be furnished to the employee.

• *Within 15 Days after the Close of Each of the First Two Months of Any Calendar Quarter:*

If income and F.I.C.A. taxes withheld total $200 or more, but less than $2,000, by the last day of the first month and/or by the last day of the second month in a calendar quarter, the full amount must be deposited in a Federal Reserve Bank or authorized bank by the 15th of the next month. Use Form 501. (Federal Tax Deposit).

If the total amount of undeposited taxes is less than $200 by the last day of the second month of a calendar quarter, the full amount may be paid with the quarterly tax return (Form 941).

• *On or Before Each April 30, July 31, October 31, and January 31:*

File *Form 941 (Employer's Quarterly Federal Tax Return)* with the regional Internal Revenue Service Center. Remit with it the full amount due; that is, the total amount of income and F.I.C.A. taxes withheld during the quarter less total of Federal Tax Deposits Receipts (Form 501).

The *State Unemployment Return* is usually filed at this time.

• *On or Before January 31 and at the End of an Employee's Employment:*

Prepare *Form W-2 (Wage and Tax Statement)* showing the total wages, total wages subject to withholdings for income tax, the amount of tax withheld, the total wage subject to F.I.C.A. tax, and the amount of tax withheld.

> The government-prepared Form W-2 consists of four copies — two copies given to the employee (for his own record and for his annual income tax return); one copy for the Internal Revenue Service Center, one copy for the employer's record. To save paper work, many large firms print their own W-2 forms with five or six copies. The additional copies are given to the city and state (that is, for records of income tax withheld) if they require them.

• *On or Before January 31 of Each Year:*

File *Form 940 (Employer's Annual Federal Unemployment Tax Return)* to report payment of federal unemployment taxes under the Federal Unemployment Tax Act.

File *Form W-3 (Reconciliation of Income Tax Withheld from Wages)* to provide a summary statement that enables a comparison of the total income taxes withheld as reported on all Form W-2s and the total amount of income tax withheld as reported on the four quarterly Forms 941.

*Retain payroll records for a period of FOUR YEARS.*

## Other Payroll Deductions

In addition to the deductions required by federal and state legislation, other payroll deductions—such as hospital care insurance (hospitalization), group insurance premiums, stock and bond purchases—may be made. In most firms these deductions are voluntary, and usually the authorizations may be canceled by the employee at any time.

Most employers furnish with each wage payment an itemized listing of all deductions made for taxes or other purposes from the employee's wage. This information is usually provided on a form attached to the check, to be removed and retained by the employee when the check is cashed. At the end of each year, the employer is required to furnish each employee with a Withholding Tax Statement (Form W-2) that shows the total earnings and tax deductions. The employee attaches one copy of Form W-2 to the place indicated on the income tax return form.

## Fair Labor Standards Act

There are primarily two classes of remuneration—*wages* at a rate per hour and *salaries* at a rate per week or month. Persons receiving wages are usually paid only for the hours they work; persons receiving salaries are usually paid for the full pay period even though they may be absent from work for brief periods. To differentiate, employees are called "hourly" and "salary" employees respectively. Office employees are almost always paid salaries although record-keeping requirements at times may make practical the payment of office employees on an hourly basis.

Most hourly and salaried employees come under the provisions of the *Fair Labor Standards Act*, which sets a minimum hourly wage and requires that each employer keep a record of the hours worked by each employee and that each employee be paid at a rate at least fifty percent greater than his regular hourly rate for all time over forty hours during a work week. Professional workers and executives are excluded from the provisions of the act.

Some companies pay overtime for all work beyond a specific number of hours a day. In other companies no overtime is paid salaried workers, but compensatory time off is given instead.

The Fair Labor Standards Act does not require the filing of overtime reports to any governmental office, but records must be kept on file for four years in the employer's office on nonexempt employees for the perusal of a government examiner at any time he chooses to look them over. Detailed information about this legislation may be obtained from the nearest office of the Wage and Hour Division, Department of Labor.

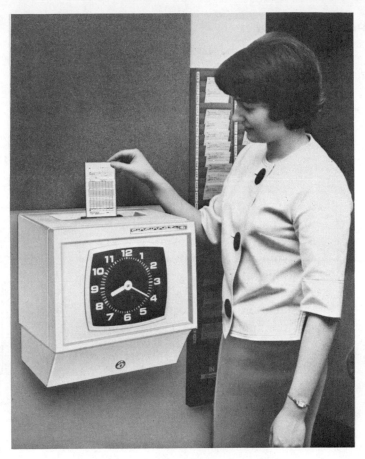

The employee takes her time card from a card rack and slips it into an electrically operated time-recording clock that stamps the exact time of entering or leaving on the card.

—*Cincinnati Time Recorder Co.*

## Time Records

Hourly workers, such as factory and department-store employees and some salaried workers, "punch in" and "punch out" each time they enter and leave their places of employment. The time is stamped on a time card. At the end of the payroll period the cards are collected and the pay is computed from the time stampings. A time card is illustrated on the opposite page.

Instead of using a time clock, salaried employees may sign in and out on a ruled sheet; or the secretary may be responsible for checking each person in and out daily on such a time sheet. Time records are not necessary in computing salaries, but it is advisable to keep them. The psychological effect in itself tends to cause employees to be more punctual. A second reason is that such records may be the basis of paying overtime earnings or balancing time off with overtime worked. Then too, there are various reports that require records of the overtime or time off of salaried employees.

## Payroll Records

Federal legislation requires employers to keep payroll records. These usually include a form similar to that on page 575, to be completed each pay period. In addition, an employee's earning record is usually kept for *each* employee. Data from payroll records are transferred periodically to the employee's earning record, preferably each pay period. The employee's earning record form illustrated on page 575 provides quarterly totals for the required quarterly tax reports, as well as the annual total. Even though the laws affecting payroll taxes are changed from time to time, a comprehensive record similar to that illustrated will provide the basic data from which to compile almost any type of payroll tax report.

SOC. SEC. NO. 696-44-2878

PAY PERIOD ENDING 4/30/--

CLOCK NO. 12

NAME Nancy Daniels

WITHHOLDING TAX EXEMPTIONS 1

| REG. HOURS | RATE | AMOUNT | F.I.C.A. TAX | TOTAL EARNINGS |
|---|---|---|---|---|
| 35½ | 2.10 | 74.55 | 5.10 | 87.15 |

| O.T. HOURS | RATE | AMOUNT | INC. TAX WITH. | TOTAL DEDUCTIONS |
|---|---|---|---|---|
| 4 | 3.15 | 12.60 | 10.20 | 19.15 |

| TOTAL HRS. | | AMOUNT | GROUP INS. | NET PAY |
|---|---|---|---|---|
| 39½ | | | .50 | 68.00 |
| | | | HOSP. | |
| | | | 3.35 | |
| | | | OTHER | |

TOTAL

| Days | | | | | | | Hours |
|---|---|---|---|---|---|---|---|
| 1 | Σ 8⁰⁴ | Σ 12⁰¹ | Σ 12⁴⁸ | Σ 4³² | | | 7¼ |
| 2 | P 7⁵⁴ | P 12⁰² | P 12⁵² | P 3⁵⁸ | | | 6¾ |
| 3 | ⅀ 7⁵⁸ | ⅀ 11³⁰ | ⅀ 12⁵⁴ | ⅀ 4³⁶ | | | 7 |
| 4 | ℉ 7⁵⁹ | ℉ 12⁰³ | ℉ 1²⁸ | ℉ 4³¹ | | | 7 |
| 5 | ℞ 7⁴⁶ | ℞ 12⁰² | ℞ 12⁴⁹ | ℞ 4³⁰ | ℞ 5⁰⁰ | ℞ 9⁰⁵ | 11½ |
| 6 | | | | | | | |
| 7 | | | | | | | |
| | IN OUT MORNING | | IN OUT AFTERNOON | | IN OUT OVERTIME | | 39½ |

## Requesting Salary Check

If a secretary is the lone employee in a firm, her payroll duties include reminding the executive that it is payday—a somewhat embarrassing necessity for the new or young secretary. A not-so-obvious way is to ask, "Shall I write out my salary check for your signature?" or "Do you want me to cash a check this noon for my salary?" Never wait until two minutes before leaving time and meekly and hesitatingly say, "This is payday." Remind him at a timely moment. The lawyer, doctor, or branch-office representative under whom the secretary is likely to be the only employee is a matter-of-fact businessman who wants to pay his secretary promptly but who frequently forgets that important day and may not wish to be delayed at the last minute.

## Administrative Responsibilities

In her supervisory and administrative role, the executive secretary may be involved in salary administration. For example, she may be

# PAYROLL RECORD

FOR PERIOD ENDING   March 15, 19--

| | EMPLOYEE | EXEMP-TIONS | EARNINGS | | | DEDUCTIONS | | | | | NET PAY | CHECK NO. |
|---|---|---|---|---|---|---|---|---|---|---|---|---|
| | | | REG. | OVER-TIME | TOTAL | FICA TAX | WITH. TAX | GROUP INS. | HOSP. | TOTAL | AMOUNT | |
| 1 | Allen, John | 1 | 400.00 | 15.00 | 415.00 | 24.28 | 68.60 | .50 | 3.35 | 96.73 | 318.27 | 123 |
| 2 | Bauer, Thomas | 2 | 420.00 | | 420.00 | 24.57 | 54.10 | .50 | 8.85 | 88.02 | 331.98 | 124 |
| 3 | Cowan, Robert | 1 | 360.00 | | 360.00 | 21.06 | 60.20 | .50 | | 81.76 | 278.24 | 125 |
| 19 | Scott, Martha | 2 | 400.00 | | 400.00 | 23.40 | 50.70 | .50 | 8.85 | 83.45 | 316.55 | 141 |
| 20 | Weyer, Louis | 1 | 320.00 | 10.00 | 330.00 | 19.31 | 51.80 | .50 | | 71.61 | 258.39 | 142 |
| | TOTALS | | 7,600.00 | 280.00 | 7,880.00 | 460.98 | 1,421.24 | 10.00 | 119.60 | 2,011.82 | 5,868.18 | |

Shown above is a partial page from a basic payroll record. According to the needs of her specific situation, the secretary may either purchase standard forms at a stationery store or design a form with the number of columns and lines that she requires and duplicate the form herself. If requirements are large enough to justify having the form specially printed, the company will likely have a payroll department.

# EMPLOYEE'S EARNINGS RECORD

| | 19-- PERIOD ENDING | EARNINGS | | | DEDUCTIONS | | | | | NET PAY |
|---|---|---|---|---|---|---|---|---|---|---|
| | | REG. | OVER-TIME | TOTAL | FICA TAX | WITH. TAX | GROUP INS. | HOSP. | TOTAL | AMOUNT |
| 1 | 1/15 | 400.00 | | 400.00 | 23.40 | 50.70 | .50 | 8.85 | 83.45 | 316.55 |
| 2 | 1/31 | 400.00 | | 400.00 | 23.40 | 50.70 | .50 | 8.85 | 83.45 | 316.55 |
| 3 | 2/15 | 400.00 | | 400.00 | 23.40 | 50.70 | .50 | 8.85 | 83.45 | 316.55 |
| 4 | 2/28 | 400.00 | 15.00 | 415.00 | 24.28 | 50.70 | .50 | 8.85 | 84.33 | 330.67 |
| 5 | 3/15 | 400.00 | | 400.00 | 23.40 | 50.70 | .50 | 8.85 | 83.45 | 316.55 |
| 6 | 3/31 | 400.00 | 20.00 | 420.00 | 24.57 | 54.10 | .50 | 8.85 | 88.02 | 331.98 |
| | QUARTER TOTALS | 2,400.00 | 35.00 | 2,435.00 | 142.45 | 307.60 | 3.00 | 53.10 | 506.15 | 1,928.85 |

| | YEARLY TOTALS | 9,600.00 | 180.00 | 9,780.00 | 572.13 | 1,240.40 | 12.00 | 212.40 | 2,036.93 | 7,743.07 |
|---|---|---|---|---|---|---|---|---|---|---|

| NAME | ADDRESS | SOC. SEC. NO. | KIND OF WORK | DEPT. |
|---|---|---|---|---|
| Scott, Martha | 261 Rose Avenue Atlanta, Georgia | 561-245-4800 | Secretary | Sales |
| NO. DED.  2 | | MARITAL STATUS  M | | |

In addition to the payroll record shown at the top of the page, the secretary must keep an individual record for each employee involved. Again, her specific requirements will determine the number of columns and the data to be recorded.

asked to perform such administrative functions as to recommend promotions and salary increases for members of the office staff, to assist in determining compensation for office personnel, to determine work standards, to examine and propose incentive plans for the office, to evaluate office employees, and to make recommendations for transfers and dismissals. The manner in which these functions are carried out plays an extremely important role in determining office morale.

An essential to a sound salary-administration plan is that each employee be paid a fair and reasonable compensation for work done. This requires some form of job analysis. Before making recommendations involving salary administration, the secretary needs to be thoroughly familiar with the competencies required for each position under her supervision and to have some measure of the quality and quantity of the work produced by each staff member. Job analysis and employee evaluation are two administrative areas in which the secretary may need to obtain background knowledge.

The executive secretary also may find an awareness of union and legislative regulations regarding labor to be helpful.

## THE EXECUTIVE'S INCOME TAX

The secretary can assist the executive in the preparation of his annual income tax return by:

**Being alert to items that he must report as income and items that he may take as deductions**

**Accumulating such items throughout the year with supporting papers and records for use at income tax time**

**Following up to see that returns are filed and payments are made**

The performance of these duties demands certain basic understandings as to what constitutes taxable income, what deductions are allowable, and how to organize the material to make it readily accessible.

### Income Tax Files

The *income tax files* generally consist of income and deduction records, supporting computations and memorandums, previous years' tax returns, and a current income tax file folder or portfolio. To avoid the possibility of filing current tax materials with those of previous years, large expansion portfolios may be used and all the income tax material related to a given year filed in that portfolio and labeled "Federal Income Tax, 19—." All supporting records of income tax returns should be retained indefinitely.

At the beginning of each year a portfolio should be set up for income tax materials for the year, and all such data (bills, canceled checks, reports, itemized listings, receipts) should go into this portfolio. Thus, when the executive is ready to prepare his tax report, all the essential records and reference materials will have been accumulated.

## Records of Taxable Income

A record of the executive's personal income may be maintained in a special record book where each item is individually recorded. In most instances, however, no separate record book will be kept. The tax information will consist mainly of deposit slips to which identifying notations have been attached, copies of receipts, statements of earnings and deductions from salary checks, dividend statements, notations of entries for interest in savings accounts, and other notations which the secretary files in the income tax portfolio. As personal income may be derived from many sources and be received at irregular intervals, the secretary must be able to identify taxable income and must be alert in seeing that a notation on each income item gets into the tax portfolio.

The following items are *taxable income*:

**Wages, Salaries, and Other Compensation.** The gross amount (amount before deductions for such items as income tax, old-age benefit contributions, employee pensions, hospitalization, and insurance) received from wages, salaries, commissions, fees, tips, and similar sources is taxable. In addition to these items, awards and prizes of money or merchandise, amounts received in reimbursement for expenses that are in excess of the actual business expenses incurred, and bonuses are also taxable income.

**Dividends.** Cash dividends on stock when paid in cash are generally taxable. Stock dividends, however, may or may not be taxable depending on whether the stockholder had the privilege of electing to take either stock or cash. Since some dividends may be wholly or partially exempt from taxation, a complete record of all dividends received should be maintained. Those dividends which are not taxable can be eliminated at the time the tax return is prepared.

At the beginning of the year, corporations usually send stockholders a form stating either the total dividend paid per share for the previous year or the total amount of dividends paid to the addressed stockholder. Watch for and file this information in the income tax portfolio.

**Interest.** With the exception of interest on state and municipal bonds and some U.S. Government bonds, all interest received is taxable. Thus, interest received from corporate bonds, mortgage bonds, notes, bank deposits, personal loans, accounts in savings and loan associations, and most U.S. Government bonds should be itemized and recorded.

**Gains on Sale or Exchange of Property.**  Profit from the sale of property is fully or partially taxable depending upon the length of time the property was owned and upon other circumstances.  In order that the exact profit may be determined, it is essential that detailed property records be kept on each property item.  Real estate, stocks, and other securities are property items.

**Proceeds from Annuities and Endowment Life Insurance.** A portion of income from annuities and endowment life insurance is taxable.

**Rents Received.**  Income received from rents is taxable.  The owner of property from which rents are received is entitled to deductions for depreciation, mortgage interest, taxes, repairs, insurance, agent's commission, and other ordinary and necessary expenses of operating the property. Property records should be kept on each rental unit owned. (See page 556.)

**Royalties.**  Royalties include income received from writings, works of art, musical compositions, and from inventions and patents.

All expenses incurred in producing property (such as patents and books) that provide a royalty income are deductible.

**Income from a Profession or a Personally Owned Business.**  All income from a profession or a personally owned business is taxable after deductions for all ordinary, necessary operating expenses have been made.

**Nontaxable Income.**  Even with nontaxable items, the secretary should strive to keep as complete a record of all income as her working situation permits.  The data will then be available when the tax return is being prepared.  Incomes which are not taxable or incomes from which deductions are allowable can be examined and properly excluded or recorded by the tax consultant at the time of preparation of the tax return.  On the basis of her limited knowledge of tax laws, the secretary should not assume the responsibility for excluding income items from the tax data she compiles.

## Records of Tax Deductions

A detailed record of each of the following allowable tax deductions should be kept in the tax portfolio for aid in the preparation of the income tax return.

**Alimony.** Periodic alimony or other payments in lieu of alimony under a decree of divorce or of separate maintenance are allowable as a personal deduction by the husband in the year of payment.

**Bad Debts.** Uncollectible and uncollected debts resulting from either business or personal relationship are deductible.

**Casualty and Theft Losses.** Losses resulting from fire, storm, flood, or theft are deductible if not reimbursed by insurance. Damage to the taxpayer's automobile resulting from an accident would be deductible to the extent not covered by insurance.

**Child Care.** Expenditures for child care up to a certain amount are deductible by widowers and employed women under certain special circumstances.

**Contributions.** Contributions to organizations or institutions devoted primarily to charitable, religious, educational, scientific, or literary purposes are deductible. Examples would be contributions to schools and colleges, churches, hospitals, American Cancer Foundation, Girl Scouts, Salvation Army, and United Appeal. Charitable gifts to individuals, political organizations, social clubs, or labor unions are not deductible.

Nonreimbursed expenses (use of automobile, postage, out-of-town telephone calls) incurred while serving in a campaign to collect funds for a charitable, religious, or educational organization are considered a contribution to the organization and are deductible as such.

**Education.** The cost of improving job-related competencies may or may not be deductible depending upon meeting criteria established by the Internal Revenue Service. This would include tuition, books, and professional journals.

**Interest.** All interest paid on personal debts may be deducted. This deduction includes interest paid on such items as bank loans, home and property mortgages, and installment loans on the family automobile.

**Medical and Dental Expenses.** Medical and dental expenses are not restricted to those of the taxpayer but may also include his family and dependents. Medical care insurance up to a certain amount and medical expenses over a certain amount are deductible. To claim this deduction, the taxpayer is required to furnish the name and address of each person to whom such expenses were paid, the amount, and the approximate date of payment.

```
                    TRAVEL EXPENSE REPORT

From/to    Houston to Chicago          Date(s) Feb. 5-7, 197-

Purpose    To attend convention of National Dental Trade Ass'n

                                                        Cost

Transportation  Air/economy                          $152.00

Hotel           Palmer House - 2 nights                56.00

Meals           2/5      $ 9.00
                2/6       12.50
                2/7        8.00                         29.50

Other           Tips              $ 8.00
                Taxi               12.50
                Convention reg.    10.00
                Airport parking     8.00                36.50

                                        Total       $274.00

Receipts attached

    Hotel
    Braniff
    Convention registration
```

Travel expenses may be forgotten if they are not recorded promptly. At the completion of each business trip, the secretary should obtain from the executive the data she needs to complete a report of travel expenses. Unless the expenses are reimbursed by the corporation, she should file the report with attached receipts in the income tax portfolio.

**Taxes.** Such personal taxes as the following are deductible: state or local income taxes, personal property taxes, real estate taxes, state or local sales taxes, and state and local gasoline taxes.

**The Executive's Business Expenses.** *Traveling expenses* incurred by the executive when he is away from home in connection with his business or profession and for which he is not reimbursed are deductible. These expenses include such items as airline tickets, excess-baggage charges, airport transportation services, car rentals, automobile expenses, bus and subway fares, taxi fares, meals (only if away overnight), hotel/motel expenses, tips, telephone/telegraph expenses, and laundry.

*Entertainment expenses* for business purposes (customers, agents, clients, professional advisers) are deductible. The wife of an out-of-town guest may also be included. Meals, including tips, theatre and other tickets are recognized entertainment costs. Even club dues are deductible provided the club is used primarily for entertaining business guests. Deductions for entertainment, however, are subject to detailed examination by the Internal Revenue Service. A detailed record similar to the one illustrated on page 581 should be prepared, identifying each guest and his business connection, and supported by receipts if the total cost is $25 or more.

*Gifts* up to $25 in value are deductible when given for a business purpose. Each gift deduction, however, must be supported by a record showing date, cost, reason for giving, and the name and business connection of the recipient.

Many executives use credit cards in paying for travel and entertainment expenses. The secretary should identify each travel and entertainment expenditure on the monthly credit card statement and file it, or a copy, in the income tax portfolio. She should keep this record current.

**Other Deductions.** Other allowable deductions that apply in specific cases are: safe-deposit-box rental when income-producing items are stored in the box, cost of uniforms and their upkeep when they are essential, moving expenses (within certain limitations), and repairs of business property. The secretary should add to her master list of deductible items those items that are pertinent to the executive's situation.

### Tax Guides and Forms

The secretary can be of more assistance to the executive in handling his income tax materials if she has studied an income tax guide. She should be familiar with the various tax forms and know how to choose the proper ones and where and how to file them. Such familiarity will help her to follow intelligently the instructions regarding completion of the forms.

GUEST LIST

(Business Entertainment)

Date    April 10, 197-

Guest(s)    George Snyder
            Frank Fletcher
            Rupert Ramsey
            John Malinowski
            (All of the V. M. Massey Co.)

Explanation    Lunch at the country club
               to discuss contract renewal

Total cost    $26.78 plus 15% tip, $30.78
              Receipt attached.

GRILL    36234

Maketewah Country Club

| | | |
|---|---|---|
| 2 | Onion soup | 1.20 |
| 3 | Shrimp cocktail | 4.50 |
| 2 | Special salad bowl | 5.00 |
| 2 | Filet sole | 6.00 |
| 1 | Small steak | 4.00 |
| 5 | Coffee | 2.00 |
| 3 | Pecan pie | 1.80 |
| 2 | Lemon sherbert | 1.00 |

| SUBTOTAL | 25.50 |
|---|---|
| SALES TAX | 1.28 |
| TIP | + 15% | 4.00 |
| TOTAL | 30.78 |

Signature    Walter Randall

A record must support each entertainment expense. If the total cost is $25 or more, a receipt must be attached. At the end of each day, the secretary should check her appointment book and flag any appointment that has involved deductible expenses. The next day she can obtain the needed information from the executive, prepare the report, and file it with attached receipts in the income tax portfolio.

## FORMS USED FOR FILING INDIVIDUAL INCOME TAX RETURNS

*File on or before April 15 Following the Close of the Calendar Year:*

*Form 1040 (U.S. Individual Income Tax Return)*—a two-page return (called the "long form") that may be used for *any* amount of income. All deductions can be listed in full, and all computations are made by the taxpayer.

*Form 1040-SE (Declaration of Estimated Tax for Individuals)*—filed by every citizen who can reasonably expect to receive more than $500 from sources other than wages subject to withholding; or can reasonably expect gross income to exceed—

(1) $20,000 for a single individual, a head of household, or a widow or widower entitled to the special tax rates;

(2) $20,000 for a married individual entitled to file a joint declaration with his spouse, but only if his spouse has not received wages for the taxable year;

(3) $10,000 for a married individual entitled to file a joint declaration with his spouse, but only if he and his spouse have received wages for the taxable year;

(4) $5,000 for a married individual not entitled to file a joint declaration with his spouse.

The estimated unpaid tax may be paid in full at the time of filing the declaration form; or it may be paid in four equal quarterly installments (payable on April 15, June 15, September 15, and January 15). The first installment payment must accompany the declaration.

**Tax Guides.** The following publications can be obtained from the office of the Internal Revenue Service, free or for a nominal charge: *Your Federal Income Tax*; *Tax Guide for Small Business*; *Employer's Tax Guide* (Circular E); *Farmers' Tax Guide*; *Tax Guide for U.S. Citizens Abroad*; and *Casualties, Thefts, Condemnations*. Inexpensive tax guides can also be obtained at book stores.

**Tax Forms.** One set of blank forms is mailed to each taxpayer; additional copies needed for drafting the return may be obtained from the local office of the Internal Revenue Service and usually from banks and post offices or reproduced on a copying machine. The forms used for filing individual income tax returns are discussed above. The Internal Revenue Service has ruled that reproduction of tax forms, schedules, and supporting data on office copying machines is acceptable. Forms may be prepared in pencil and reproduced on a copying machine, thus avoiding the necessity of recopying or typing the form.

Copies for the files should be made on a copying machine of all supplementary information and supporting data such as receipts, statements, expense reports, and other items that may be attached and mailed with the tax return.

# A CHECK LIST FOR COMPUTING INCOME TAX

As you keep a tax portfolio or prepare the income tax return, check this list of common items that are deductible or nondeductible from adjusted gross income.

| | Deductible | Nondeductible |
|---|:---:|:---:|
| Alimony and separate maintenance payments taxable to recipient............. | √ | |
| Automobile expenses (car used exclusively for pleasure) | | |
|     State gasoline taxes imposed on consumer.............................. | √ | |
|     Interest on finance loans............................................. | √ | |
|     License fees......................................................... | | √ |
|     Ordinary upkeep and operating expenses................................ | | √ |
| Burglary losses (if not covered by insurance)........................... | √ | |
| Casualty losses not covered by insurance (fire, flood, windstorm, lightning, earthquakes, etc.)................................................... | √ | |
| Charitable contributions to approved institutions........................ | √ | |
| Domestic servants (wages paid)......................................... | | √ |
| Dues, social clubs for personal use..................................... | | √ |
| Employment fees paid to agencies....................................... | √ | |
| Federal income taxes.................................................. | | √ |
| F.I.C.A. taxes withheld by employer..................................... | | √ |
| Fines for violation of laws and regulations.............................. | | √ |
| Funeral expenses...................................................... | | √ |
| Gambling losses (to extent of gains only)............................... | √ | |
| Gift taxes............................................................ | | √ |
| Gifts to relatives and other individuals................................. | | √ |
| Income tax imposed by city or state..................................... | √ | |
| Inheritance taxes..................................................... | | √ |
| Interest paid on personal loans......................................... | √ | |
| Life insurance premiums............................................... | | √ |
| Medical Care Insurance Premiums (including Blue Cross and Blue Shield). Limited to 50% of premium cost with a $150 maxmium................. | √ | |
| Medical expenses in excess of 3% of adjusted gross income (including the cost of artificial limbs, artificial teeth, eye glasses, hearing aids, dental fees, hospital expenses, premiums on hospital or medical insurance) to extent not covered by insurance........................................................ | √ | |
| Political campaign contribution up to $50 ($100 on a joint return).......... | √ | |
| Property taxes, real and personal....................................... | √ | |
| Residence for personal use | | |
|     Improvements and street assessments................................ | | √ |
|     Insurance.......................................................... | | √ |
|     Interest on mortgage loan........................................... | √ | |
|     Loss from sale of.................................................... | | √ |
|     Rent paid.......................................................... | | √ |
|     Repairs............................................................ | | √ |
|     Taxes............................................................. | √ | |
| Sales taxes, state and local............................................ | √ | |
| Traveling expenses attending professional meetings...................... | √ | |
| Traveling expenses to and from place of business or employment............ | | √ |
| Uniforms for personal use including cost and upkeep, if not adaptable for general use (nurses, policemen, jockeys, baseball players, firemen, trainmen, etc.) ... | √ | |
| Union dues........................................................... | √ | |
| Use taxes imposed on consumers under state law......................... | √ | |

## Typing and Mailing Tax Returns

The tax return contains confidential information. The secretary, therefore, will do the typing herself, even though she has an assistant for routine typing jobs. Before typing, each figure must be checked for accuracy; then the return must be typed and proofread carefully. Before mailing the form, the secretary should check to see that it has been properly signed and that materials to accompany the return have been securely attached to the finished form as directed.

At the foot of the first page of the federal tax forms, space is provided for "Signature of preparer other than taxpayer." This does not mean the signature of the secretary who has merely collected tax data or typed the form. The signature is to be that of a tax consultant or attorney who has prepared the return and who assumes responsibility for its validity.

As the mailing of all tax returns is a very important responsibility, the secretary should see to the mailing of them herself. Do not put them in the regular office mail, send them through the mailing department, or trust them to a clerk or anyone else to post. The secretary should note on the file copy the exact time and place where she personally mailed each return. A certificate of mailing may be obtained from the post office as legal proof that the return was mailed. If such a certificate is obtained, attach it to the file copy of the return.

If an Estimated Tax Declaration has been filed, the secretary must remind her employer when quarterly tax payments are due (June 15, September 15, and January 15). A good idea is to place cards in your tickler file at appropriate points.

## Late Filing

The taxpayer who is late in filing his return is assessed a penalty. Under certain circumstances, however, an individual may obtain permission to file his federal income tax return after the April 15 deadline by submitting Form 2688 (Application for Extension of Time to File Tax Return) or by writing a personal letter to the Internal Revenue Service. Extensions may be granted if the circumstances are beyond the control of the taxpayer—absence abroad, illness, loss of records, or inability (beyond the taxpayer's control) to assemble the required data.

## SUGGESTED READINGS

Bower, James B., and Harold Q. Langenderfer. *Income Tax Procedure.* Cincinnati: South-Western Publishing Co., 1972.

Keeling, B. Lewis, and John A. Pendery. *Payroll Records and Accounting.* Cincinnati: South-Western Publishing Co., 1972.

Klein, A. E., Supervisory ed. *The New World Secretarial Handbook.* Cleveland: World Publishing Co., 1968, pp. 300–319.

1. Some businesses observe the policy of making information on salaries paid available to all employees. Other businesses keep all salary information highly confidential. Which policy do you think would build the best employee morale?

2. You are responsible for preparing the payroll and distributing salary checks to members of the office staff. How would you answer questions directed to you regarding the salary of a fellow employee? regarding your own salary?

3. The payroll in large organizations is usually prepared by the payroll department. Most secretaries, therefore, do not have this responsibility. Why then should a secretary be familiar with payroll procedures and payroll taxes?

4. The Social Security Act requires that the self-employed person pay a F.I.C.A. tax approximately fifty percent higher than the employed person. Why?

5. One of your assistants, who is your senior in age and tenure in the company, has the habit of arriving at work a few minutes late each morning. As a corrective measure you design a register sheet and ask each member of your staff to sign in and out each day. There is considerable opposition to your regulation by the other members of your staff on the grounds that they are salaried, not hourly employees. What is the difference between a "Salaried" and an "Hourly" employee, and how would you respond to this objection?

6. Assume that an employee's salary is $1,350 a month.
   (a) **In what month will his last F.I.C.A. tax be deducted?**
   (b) **On how much of the employee's salary for that month will the F.I.C.A tax be calculated?**

7. Identical information is written on the statement that accompanies the employee's pay check, the payroll record, and the employee's earning record. Suggest a way of recording this information in one writing.

8. It is said that the secretary should play an "assist" role in the preparation of her employer's income tax return. What does this mean to you?

9. The Internal Revenue Service requires a taxpayer to document all traveling and entertainment expenses for which a tax deduction is claimed. What is the secretary's role in compiling this information?

10. What precautions should the secretary observe in typing and mailing her employer's income tax return?

11. Insert the information in the blanks in the following sentences. Then consult the Reference Guide to correct your answers and tell which reference entry you used in each case.

(a) They sell for _____ each. ($0.50)

(b) Your letter of _____ was delayed. (September 25)

(c) He mailed it on the _____ of September. (25)

(d) You have _____ _____ grace. (thirty-one days)

(e) Production has increased _____ _____. (thirty-three and one-third %)

(f) Production has increased _____ _____. (8%)

(g) Everything is at _____ and _____. (6's and 7's)

(h) There is a _____ _____ grace period. (25 day)

(i) There is a _____ _____ interim. (3 day)

(j) His _____ _____ vacation began Monday. (3 week or 3 weeks)

12. Tell what terminal punctuation mark is used after each item in an enumeration if the units are:

(a) Run-in words or phrases    (d) Run-in sentences

(b) Tabulated words or phrases    (e) Tabulated sentences

(c) Run-in clauses

Consult the Reference Guide to verify or correct your answers.

13. Tell when you use a comma to separate units in a series. Then consult the Reference Guide to verify or correct your answers.

## PROBLEMS

■ 1. Obtain one of the following payroll forms, study the instructions for completing it, and be prepared to present to the class a description of the form and the method of completing it.

SS-4 . . . . . Application for Employer Identification Number

SS-5 . . . . . Application for Employee Account Number

941 . . . . . . Employer's Quarterly Federal Tax Return

W-2 . . . . . . Wage and Tax Statement

W-4 . . . . . . Employee's Withholding Exemption Certificate

OAAN-7003 . . . Request for Change in Social Security Records

■ 2. To accumulate information for a tax file, a secretary must have some understanding of taxable income and allowable deductions. From the following list, select those income items that are taxable and those expense items that are deductible. Arrange the items alphabetically and type them in a form convenient for reference. You may need to check reference sources to identify the tax status of certain items.

*Income Items*

Payment for writing magazine article

Interest from municipal bonds

Bonus from employer

Prize — paid vacation to a resort as a prize for the "Best Idea" contest

Rent received on property inherited from a relative

Dividends on corporation stock

Interest on U.S. Government bonds

Merchandise received from employer

Interest on deposits in savings and loan association

Payments from accident insurance

Property inherited from a relative

Payment for a speech to a service club (not related to business or profession)

Royalties received from a patent

Profit from sale of building lot originally planned for home

### Expense Items

Contribution to an old friend
Tips paid for service while on business trip
Federal income tax paid during year
Interest on loan on family automobile
Contributions to Girl Scouts
Contributions to a political party
Interest on loan on home
Driver's license fee
State income tax
Property loss resulting from theft
Federal Social Security tax
Retail sales tax (state)
Employment fees paid to agency
Life insurance premiums
Traveling expenses to and from employment
Union dues
Repairs on home
Gift to a customer
Expenses incurred in acting as chairman of United Appeals fund drive

■ **3.** Jacob Wertman is paid $3.20 per hour and an overtime wage of one and one-half times his hourly rate. All hours over 36 are considered overtime. He works 39 hours during the last week in March.

(a) What are his gross earnings for the week?

(b) If the F.I.C.A. tax rate is 5.85% and there is a $24.80 federal income tax deduction, and a 2% state income tax deduction, what are his net earnings?

(c) To determine Mr. Wertman's total earnings for the first three months of the year, where would you look?

Chapter **25**

# LEGAL FACETS OF SECRETARIAL WORK

Secretarial work inevitably involves some contact with legal vocabulary, legal papers, legal correspondence, and legal procedures. The extent of involvement depends, of course, upon a number of factors. Certainly the secretary in a legal office spends much of her time working with legal terminology, documents, and formalities. On the other hand, the secretary in the corporate president's office may have only an occasional legally related function. But whether a secretary's legal work is frequent or only occasional, it is exacting and requires some basic understandings.

This chapter makes no effort to identify all the legal papers or procedures with which a secretary may work. It does, however, describe some of the more commonly used legal documents, discusses secretarial procedures related to preparing legal papers, and suggests reference sources to which the secretary may turn for assistance.

It may be that a secretary finds legal work attractive and that she decides to become a trainee in a law firm, in the legal department of a large corporation, or in the government. In that case she can build upon the content of this chapter with a specialized training program to become a certified legal secretary or legal assistant; both are attractive and challenging fields. She may even decide to study law and prepare for the bar—certainly a worthy and attainable goal.

## FREQUENTLY USED LEGAL DOCUMENTS

Business transactions such as sales, negotiable instruments, or the formation of agencies frequently involve parties from different jurisdictions. Naturally, complexities and problems arise in preparing the legal documents to cover conflicting laws of the federal government and the 50 states. To expedite legal procedures, a number of uniform statutes have been enacted, the most recent and most important one from the standpoint of the businessman being the Uniform Commercial Code. The legal documents described here conform to this code.

## Contracts

Many people in the business world are concerned with the legalities of buying and selling of goods, property, and services. Every buying and selling activity constitutes a contract between or among the persons concerned. Decisions made and actions taken with outside people by a secretary (in the name of the executive or his office) often are contractual agreements enforceable by law. A *contract* is an enforceable agreement, either oral or written, which involves legal rights and responsibilities. Some contracts, such as those for the purchase of real estate, must be in writing; but *all* important contracts should be written, even though this is not a legal requirement. A contract may be in the form of an oral agreement, a sales slip, a memorandum, a contract form, a promissory note, or a letter.

**Content.** In typing a contract, the secretary should check to see if the following essential information is included:

- Date and place of agreement
- Names of parties entering into the agreement
- Purpose of the contract
- Duties of each party
- Money, services, or goods in consideration of contract
- Time element or duration involved
- Signatures of the parties

Prepare enough copies of a contract so that each party will have one for his file. (If prepared in a law office, an additional copy is made for the law office files.) When the executive sells his services by contract (as do engineers, architects, builders, and real estate representatives), the secretary may have a standard form to use as a model; but usually there are items peculiar to each contract that make it necessary to vary the fill-ins each time. Printed forms are available for most common legal documents. Since some contracts must follow a statutory model or must contain specified provisions, it is recommended that the secretary use them or follow legal advice when preparing specified provisions.

**Care Before Signing.** All contracts should be carefully read by all parties before they are signed. Not only will mistakes, misunderstandings, and fraud be avoided, but also matters can be determined such as: (1) what responsibilities are assumed by each party, (2) exactly what is offered at what price, (3) how payment is to be made, (4) whether or not material can be returned, and (5) when and how the contract can be terminated.

**Contracts Made by the Secretary.** As has already been pointed out, the secretary often acts (in a legal sense) as the deputy of the executive; that is, she knowingly—and sometimes even unknowingly—executes contracts. This situation places responsibility on the secretary to exercise caution in making commitments, in requesting work to be done by outside agencies, in quoting prices or making offers to purchase, and in signing purchase or repair orders, sales orders, or agreements on her own initiative, for such commitments may be contractual.

The executive naturally relies on his secretary's recommendation on many orders or agreements (contracts) that he signs. The mere fact that the secretary presents the contract for machine repair service to him for signature implies her indorsement of its contents. For example, the secretary makes all the arrangements for redecorating the office or for the purchase of a new office machine. The executive signs the contract on the presumption that his secretary has checked all details and verified that the contract is correct and understood. A secretary may save her employer the time of reading "the fine print" if she annotates the important points of the contract and attaches this annotation to the contract when it is submitted to him for signature.

**Filing Contracts.** A contract copy should be filed carefully, for it is a legal instrument necessary to prosecuting any deviation from the contract. It is well to place the contract in a No. 10 envelope and mark plainly on the outside, "Signed contract between . . . ." This can be filed permanently in the company's or person's file or in a separate "Signed-Contracts" file; or if it is important enough, in a safe-deposit box. In some companies, such legal papers are kept in asbestos envelopes as a protection against fire.

## Wills and Codicils

The requirements regarding the drawing of wills and codicils are rather technical and vary among the states. Hence, they should not be drawn without proper legal supervision or direction.

**Wills.** A *will* is a legal instrument whereby a person provides for the disposition of his property after his death. A *testator* (man) or *testatrix* (woman) is the one who makes the will. One who dies without having made a will is said to die *intestate*. A *nuncupative* will is an oral one and is valid only as to personal property; land may not be devised by a nuncupative will. A will in the handwriting of the testator is called a *holographic* will.

A will may be *revoked* by mutilation, cancellation, destruction, or the execution of a new will. Every will should contain a provision stating that any and all previous wills are revoked even though the testator does not remember ever having made another will.

To *probate* a will is to prove its validity to the court for the purpose of carrying out its provisions. An *executor* (man) or *executrix* (woman) is the one named by the testator to carry out the provisions of a will.

**Codicil.** A *codicil* is a supplement that makes a change in the will, deletes or adds something to it, or explains it. It must be signed and witnessed with all the formalities of the original will.

A person asked to *attest* (witness) a will or codicil need not read the provisions and, of course, does not try. He is merely witnessing the signature of the testator and assuring the beneficiaries that the testator was in sound mind when he signed the will. A will presented for witnessing should have only the signature area visible, thus preventing any chance reading of the contents.

## Copyrights

Creative work reproduced for sale or public distribution may be *copyrighted*. Copyrighting applies not only to printed matter, such as books and periodicals, but also to photographs, pictorial illustrations, musical compositions, maps, paintings, and movies.

To copyright is to register a claim with the federal government to a piece of original literary or artistic work. A copyright grants the exclusive right to reproduce a creative work or to perform it publicly. Registering is done either by the originator of the work or the one reproducing and marketing copies. Copyrighting tends to prevent a dishonest or careless person from stealing another's creative work and marketing it as his own.

The increased use of photocopying equipment increases the necessity for the protection of a copyright. (Recent changes in the copyright laws have modified certain restrictions relative to reproducing materials to be used for educational purposes.) Copyrights run for 28 years and can be renewed once for 28 more years. A copyright can be obtained by filing the appropriate forms with the Register of Copyrights in Washington, D.C.

## Patents

A *patent* may be obtained by a person who has "invented or discovered a new and useful art, machine, manufacture, or composition of matter, or any new and useful improvement thereof—not known or used by others in this country before. . . ." Literature on the procedure for securing a patent can be obtained from the Superintendent of Documents, U.S. Government Printing Office, Washington, D.C. 20402.

Legal specialists usually are employed to prepare the patent application, the first step in negotiations between the Patent Office and the inventor.

A patent grant gives the exclusive right to make, use, and sell the patent. A patent must be applied for by the inventor. After the patent has been granted, it can be sold outright or leased, in which case the inventor is paid a royalty for its use. A patent expires at the end of seventeen years and can be renewed only by an act of Congress.

## Trademarks

The Patent Office also registers trademarks for goods moved in interstate commerce, giving evidence of the validity and ownership of the mark by the registrant and of his right to use the mark. The registration term covers 20 years. However, during the sixth year of registration, an affidavit must be filed with the Patent Office showing that the trademark is being used or that its nonuse does not signify intention to abandon the mark.

## Affidavit

An *affidavit* is a written declaration made under oath that the facts set forth are sworn to be true and correct. The word itself means "he has made oath." An affidavit, made by an *affiant*, must be sworn to before a public officer (such as a notary, judge, or a justice of the peace).

For example, evidence of citizenship is required before an applicant can obtain a United States passport. If the person seeking a passport has no birth certificate, he may use an affidavit from a relative declaring that the passport applicant was born in the United States.

## Proxy

A *proxy* is a written authorization (similar to that shown in Chapter 23 on page 545) empowering another to vote or act for the signer. Proxy forms are solicited from all stockholders prior to annual or special meetings of a corporation.

The secretary may be responsible for collecting proxies for the company in which she works, or she may call to her employer's attention a proxy form from a corporation in which he holds stock.

```
                        POWER OF ATTORNEY

            KNOW ALL MEN BY THESE PRESENTS, that I, CAROLINE B.
   HUGHES, of the City and County of San Diego, State of Cali-
   fornia, by these presents do make, constitute, and appoint
   GEORGE DAVIS, of the City of Jamul, County of San Diego, State
   of California, my true and lawful attorney, for me and in my
   name, place, and stead, to negotiate for the purchase of the
   structure and property situated at 111-113 West Third Street,
   City and County of San Diego, State of California, known as
   Hidalgo Towers; and I hereby ratify and confirm all that my
   said agent or attorney will lawfully do, or cause to be done,
   in connection with this purchase.
            IN WITNESS WHEREOF, I have hereunto set my hand and
   seal this____day of _____, 19--.


                                   _____L.S.
                                         Caroline B. Hughes
```

The legal form *Power of Attorney* would be notarized in a form similar to that shown on page 594.

## Power of Attorney

The executive may vest his secretary with a *power of attorney*—the power to act for him. The document itself sets forth the powers given. It may authorize the secretary to sign checks and other legal documents for the executive. It may be made for an indefinite period, for a specific period, or for a specific purpose only. Only a tried-and-true secretary whose business integrity is unquestioned earns this decidedly weighty responsibility of acting as her employer's agent.

Should the executive have power of attorney for someone else, the secretary sets up a special file and records all executions.

## POSSIBLE RESPONSIBILITIES FOR LEGAL PAPERS

The secretary may type legal papers completely, or she may fill in printed legal forms from dictation. She may also *witness* the signing of completed papers. She may extend her legal responsibility so that it is necessary for her to become a notary public. As a notary public she will acknowledge that a document was actually executed by the persons who sign it. Finally, she may be responsible for recording legal papers.

## Notary Public

Notarial commissions are issued by the secretary of state, the governor, or other designated official in the various state capitals. Application blanks will be furnished upon request by the appropriate official in the state in which the commission is sought, or they may be bought at a stationery store. (See pages 599–600.) There are usually a fee, an examination, and certain citizenship qualifications. Most states also require bond, which may be applied for on forms obtained along with the application. A notary public can purchase Error and Omission insurance to protect herself against liability for her acts.

The notary's appointment states the county or counties in which she is authorized to perform and the date of expiration of commission. It is necessary for her to buy a notary-public seal and a rubber stamp. The former is used to press into the document the seal showing her name, the county in which she is commissioned to act, and the seal of the state. The rubber stamp shows the date when the commission expires. Each notary receives local rules and instructions with which she must comply.

A notary does not scrutinize the document she is to certify. She gives the oath and verifies that the signature or signatures are genuine. If you should become a notary, remember not to be curious about what is in the paper you are certifying.

If the secretary is not a notary public, one of her responsibilities may be to arrange for the details related to having papers notarized. The names of two or three notaries public convenient to the office should be obtained. In some instances, it may be necessary to arrange a meeting time with the notary public and to notify all parties involved.

The notary public witnesses affidavits. She also signs *acknowledgments* and *verifications*, which are executed under oath. In an acknowledgment the person swears that his signature appearing on a document is genuine and was made of his own free will. A verification is a sworn statement of the truth and correctness of the content of a document to which the signer affixes his signature. All necessary signatures must be completed before the notary public signs the document.

```
STATE OF CALIFORNIA )
                    : ss.
County of San Diego )

        On (current date), before me, a Notary Public, in and
for said County and State, personally appeared MARSHA SCHOMBURG,
known to me to be the person whose name is subscribed to the
within instrument, and acknowledged that she executed the same.

        WITNESS my hand and official seal.


                        _____
                              Notary Public
```

## Preparation of Legal Papers

Legal papers can be divided into two classes:

1. *Court Documents.* **These vary considerably and must follow the specifications of the particular court in the city, county, state, and federal government. They include such documents as** *complaints, answers, demurrers, notices, motions, affidavits, summons, subpoenas.*

2. *Noncourt Legal Documents.* **These include such legal papers as contracts, wills, leases, powers of attorney, agreements, and many others. They give formal expression to legal acts and are legal evidence if court action or litigation becomes necessary.**

The form of legal papers is standardized in some respects; in others, it varies with the wishes of the court and with personal preference.

**Paper Size.** Traditionally, all legal documents were typed on 8½- by 13- or 14-inch hard-to-tear white paper called *legal cap.* Legal cap is printed with a red or blue vertical double rule 1⅜ inches from the left edge and a single rule ⅜ inch from the right edge. *Brief* paper, 8½ by 10½ inches, also with ruled margins, was used for legal briefs and memorandums; for some documents each line on a sheet was numbered. Although many courts still require legal cap for court documents, there is a trend toward using the standard 8½- by 11-inch sheet because this size can be microfilmed for storage in court files. Before typing a court document, the secretary should learn the requirements of the particular court.

**Copies.** Multiple copies of legal documents are usually required. For example, all parties to a contract receive a copy, file copies are necessary, and the attorney retains one or more copies for his office. Before the copying machine came into common office use, multiple copies were made with carbon paper. Sometimes two or more typings were necessary to provide a sufficient number of legible copies of a document. Now the copies can be made on the copying machine and, if so, the secretary types only the original and makes the copies from the original on the copier. In some offices the secretary types the original and, on color-coded tissue-weight paper, a file copy; she then makes all other copies from the original on the copier.

*Copies* can be used and referred to as *duplicate originals* if they are signed and made to *conform* in all respects to the original (to contain all the copy shown on the original).

After the paper has been *executed* (the original and duplicate originals made valid by necessary procedures, such as signing, witnessing, perhaps notarizing, and recording), all the distribution copies and the office file copy must be *conformed* by typing in the signatures, dates, and all other data that were added in executing the paper.

**Type.** For legal papers, pica type is preferred and may be required for court documents. In any case, do not use the "fancy" typefaces like *script*, *italic*, or *gothic*.

**Margins, Spacing, and Centered Titles.** On paper with printed marginal rules, type within the rules by one or two spaces. On unruled paper, use 1½- inch left and at least ½-inch right margins. Top margins are 2 inches on the first page and 1½ inches on subsequent pages. Bottom margins are 1 inch.

For most legal papers, use double spacing, with a triple space above side headings. Very long documents are sometimes single-spaced to avoid exceptional bulkiness.

Two inches from the top of the first page, type the title of the paper in all capitals, centered between the rules. Divide at a logical point and double-space a heading that is too long for one line. Leave 2 blank line spaces below the title.

**Hyphenation.** Learn the preference for your particular situation. Sometimes the last word on a page must not be hyphenated; sometimes a divided last word is recommended to make the unwarranted insertion of pages more difficult. Avoid dividing words at the end of other lines.

**Paragraphs.** Indent ten spaces for paragraphs. To make difficult any unwarranted insertion of pages, do not end a page with the last line of a paragraph. Carry over two or more lines to the next page.

**Quoted Matter and Land Descriptions.** Indent five to ten spaces from the left margin; retain the right margin if desired, or indent five spaces. Indent another five spaces for a new paragraph in the quoted material. Indented quotations may be single-spaced.

**Page Numbers.** Legal documents frequently go through a series of drafts before the final one. Number and date each draft: the first typing, "First draft," the second, "Second draft," and so on. Keep all drafts until the final document has been typed and processed.

Center page numbers ½ inch from the bottom edge.

**Dates.** Spell out single-digit ordinal dates and type the year to conform: *the first day of June, nineteen hundred and seventy-three* (but *the 15th day of June, 1973*). Date every legal paper. If the first or last paragraph does not include the date, type the date on the last line immediately preceding the signature lines.

```
SUPREME COURT OF THE STATE OF NEW YORK

COUNTY OF NEW YORK

-------------------------------------- X

MARY ALICE CONNOR,

                              Plaintiff,

              -against-

GERALD DAVID ROBERTS,

                          Defendant.

-------------------------------------- X

         Plaintiff, complaining of defendant, by Stephen H.

O'Reilly, her attorney, alleges:

         FIRST:  That heretofore and on or about the fourth

day of October, 197-, the defendant caused to be written in a

letter to the plaintiff the following statement:

         "If you do not appear in this office by October
         10 with the money and notes, my attorney will be
         instructed to go to the District Attorney's office
         to procure a warrant for your arrest and Dodson will
         be notified that this money and notes were given you
         upon false representation."

         SECOND:  That said statement was published, as here-

inafter alleged, of and concerning the plaintiff to whom said

letter was addressed and consequently mailed.

         THIRD:  That by said statement the defendant intended

to charge the plaintiff with the crime of larceny.

         FOURTH:  That on information and belief that the

defendant did publish such statement by causing it to be read

and transcribed by his stenographer.

         FIFTH:  That said stenographer knew that said state-

ment referred to plaintiff and knew it intended to charge

plaintiff with the crime of larceny.

         SIXTH:  That said statement was untrue and malicious.

         SEVENTH·  That by reason of the premises, plaintiff
```

The form of legal papers varies from state to state. The complaint (a paper to be used in a court case) shown above is typed in a form acceptable in the state of New York. For this reason, the secretary who frequently types legal papers needs to compile an appropriate forms file.

**Numbers.** Numbers with legal significance (amounts of money, periods of time) have traditionally been written in both words *and* figures. For example, *Five Thousand Dollars ($5,000)* or *Ten (10) barrels* *of oil* or *Sixty (60) days* (but a *six-month period*). (For general number usage, follow the style preferred by your employer.)

Use the dollar sign with a number in conformity with the spelled-out version: *Sixty Dollars ($60), but Sixty (60) Dollars*. Capitalize all words of an amount except *and*: *Three Hundred Seventy-Five and 45/100 Dollars ($375.45)*.

**Reference Notations.** On the first page of the file copy in the upper left corner, type the full names of the recipients of all copies of the document.

**Names and Signature Lines.** If you know the exact signature that is to be used, type it in the body of the document in exactly that way. If you do not know the form of the signature, use the legal name—the full two or three names of the person without abbreviations or initials. The legal signature of a married woman preferably combines her maiden name with her married name, such as Dorothy Keller Brown—not Dorothy Ann Brown. Personal titles (*Mr., Mrs., Miss*) are not used; ordinarily neither are professional titles. To permit easy reference and identification, it is common practice to type in all capitals the names of individuals, businesses, agencies, and institutions named in a legal document.

At the end of a legal paper, type three lines for required signatures. These signature lines cannot stand alone on a page; arrange the body of the instrument so that at least two lines will appear on the page with the signatures. The lines extend from slightly right of center to the right margin, with two or three blank line spaces between them. Signature lines for witnesses begin at the left margin and extend to the page center.

TIME-SAVER. After preparing multiple copies of a legal paper that requires many signatures, attach a colored file flag at the appropriate point for each signer, using a different color for each one.

Some secretaries lightly pencil in the respective initials at the beginnings of the lines on which each is to sign. Other secretaries use a small "X" to mark the spot. In some jurisdictions the names must be typed under the signature lines. Names are typed on file-copy signature lines after some indication for *signed*, such as *Sgd*.

**Seals.** The abbreviation *L.S.* (*locus sigilli*, meaning "place of the seal") frequently appears at the end of lines on which parties to a paper sign their names. These letters have the legal significance of a wax seal. State laws determine whether or not a legal paper requires a seal.

**Insertions.** At the time of signing a legal paper, an insertion may be requested. An insertion is valid if the signers indorse it by writing their initials in ink near it. At the time of typing, however, an omission may not be inserted between the lines to avoid retyping the page.

**Erasures and Corrections.** Each page should be typed accurately, for an erased and corrected error can cast doubt on the validity of an item if it occurs in a vital phrase. For example, "*four* thousand acres" erased and changed to "*forty* thousand acres" (or "June *6*" changed to "June *5*") might raise a question of validity. An error in a single word in the straight text can usually be erased and corrected without question, but avoid erasing figures, dates, names, and places. If they must be erased, have the correction initialed.

**Proofreading.** The secretary unfamiliar with legal work should be particularly careful in proofreading her work, questioning terms that she does not understand. Novices have typed "the plaintiff praise" for "the plaintiff prays" and referred to the "Court of Common Please" or the "Court of Common Police" rather than the "Court of Common Pleas." They have embarrassed themselves by referring to a "notary republic." If you are not sure of your ground, FIND OUT!

Property descriptions, quoted material, and all figures and dates that appear in legal documents should be proofread twice because a minor discrepancy can be the basis of a litigation. Read a second time aloud to another person. Identify all capital letters, punctuation marks, and abbreviations.

## Standard Legal Forms

Undoubtedly your employer will engage legal counsel when preparing important legal papers. If, however, certain types of papers are often used, such as leases or deeds, the forms given in legal reference books can be used as guides. Avoid indiscriminate copying of such forms because the laws vary from state to state, and laws also change.

**Legal Forms.** Stationery stores that supply legal offices carry printed legal forms that concur with local laws. These are called *legal* forms or law blanks. Look in the *Yellow Pages* under the heading *legal forms* for sources of supply for printed blanks of such common documents as affidavits, agreements, deeds, leases, powers of attorney, and wills.

Many printed legal forms consist of four pages, printed on both sides of one sheet of 8½- by 28-inch paper and folded once to make four pages of 8½ by 14 inches. The form for the indorsement is printed on the fourth page. With this arrangement, binding of the pages at the top is unnecessary, and a cover is not used. When the front page (page 1) is turned, pages 2 and 3 will read as one continuous page down the full inside length of the document.

**Fill-Ins on Legal Blanks.** Fill-ins may range from a single letter or figure to words, phrases, or long lines of text. Printed lines are usually not provided in the blank spaces; the typist, therefore, must align the typing line with the printing line. Use the printed margins for typing full lines. As a precaution, rule a *Z* in ink to fill deep unused space.

**Carbon Copies of Legal Blanks.** To align typed information on carbon copies of printed forms, check the forms to be sure that all copies were printed at the same time. The legend 60M 7/6/7– indicates that 60,000 copies were printed on July 6, 197–. Roll the matched set carefully into the typewriter and then insert the carbons (as shown on page 89). Because aligning is difficult, you may prefer to type each blank individually, checking each one against the source document. If you do this, type *COPY* on all but the one to be used as the original.

**Riders.** When the space allotted for filling in conditional clauses or other provisions in a legal blank is not large enough for the typewritten material, leave sufficient space after the last line to permit a slip of paper containing the rest of the typewritten material (called a *rider*) to be pasted to the document. Use legal cap for the rider, and cut off any unused part of the sheet. Fasten the rider securely to the document and fold the rider to fit neatly within the backing sheet.

**Forms File.** Many legal documents that the secretary types are adaptations of previous ones. A forms file of commonly typed legal documents, therefore, can be an important time saver. Accumulate this file by making an extra carbon or copying-machine copy of representative legal documents at the time of the first typing. In the margin, add helpful notes such as the number of copies to be prepared, the distribution of the copies, and other pertinent data. In time, the file will contain most, if not all, of the legal documents produced in the office. You can then consult the file to determine the exact procedure for any document contained therein. Legal secretaries consider their forms file to be their most valuable reference source.

> TIME-SAVER. To insure that no line of the original copy of a legal document has been omitted in retyping, hold line-for-line typed copy beside the original — or align the copy over the original and hold them up to a bright light.

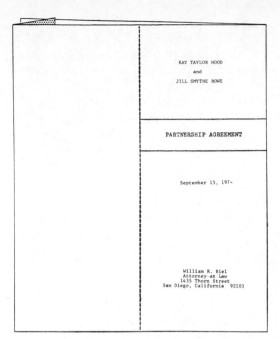

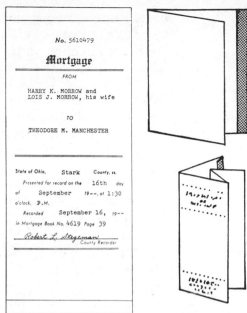

The *indorsement* (a description of the legal paper within) is typed on the outside of a cover as illustrated at the left above, or on a printed legal back as shown in the center. The correct folding of a legal back is shown at the right. Some offices file the folded documents in tall, narrow files with the indorsements in view; others use file drawers 16 inches wide and file unfolded legal papers with the first page to the front and the indorsements not visible.

To protect a legal document, use a single backing sheet ("legal back" or "cover") with dimensions that are about 1 inch wider and 1½ inch longer than the instrument. This sheet is usually blue and of tough, heavy-quality paper. After the back has been properly folded and reopened, the indorsement is typed. The typed pages are then inserted under the inch fold at the top of the backing sheet, and an eyelet or staple is placed at each side (about 1 inch from the top and the sides). Backing sheets may be color coded to differentiate types of documents.

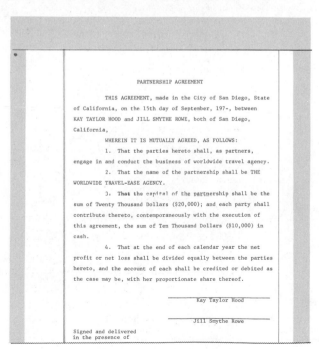

# This Lease Witnesseth:

**THAT** David R. Frey and Sophia G. Frey, husband and wife,
**HEREBY LEASE TO** Samuel B. Thompson
*the premises situate in the* City *of* Tampa *in the County of*
Hillsborough *and State of* Florida, *described as follows:*

Building to be used as a hardware store located at 865 Forest
Drive, Tampa, Florida,

*with the appurtenances thereto, for the term of* ten (10) years *commencing*
May 1, *19* --, *at a rental of* five hundred (500)
*dollars per* month , *payable* monthly.

SAID LESSEE AGREES *to pay said rent, unless said premises shall be destroyed or rendered untenantable by fire or other unavoidable accident; to not commit or suffer waste; to not use said premises for any unlawful purpose; to not assign this lease, or underlet said premises, or any part thereof, or permit the sale of* his *interest herein by legal process, without the written consent of said lessors; to not use said premises or any part thereof in violation of any law relating to intoxicating liquors; and at the expiration of this lease, to surrender said premises in as good condition as they now are, or may be put by said lessors, reasonable wear and unavoidable casualties, condemnation or appropriation excepted. Upon nonpayment of any of said rent for* ten *days, after it shall become due, and without demand made therefor; or if said lessee or any assignee of this lease shall make an assignment for the benefit of his creditors; or if proceedings in bankruptcy shall be instituted by or against lessee or any assignee; or if a receiver or trustee be appointed for the property of the lessee or any assignee; or if this lease by operation of law pass to any person or persons; or if said lessee or any assignee shall fail to keep any of the other covenants of this lease, it shall be lawful for said lessors,* their *heirs or assigns, into said premises to re-enter, and the same to have again, re-possess and enjoy, as in* their *first and former estate; and thereupon this lease and everything herein contained on the said lessor* s *behalf to be done and performed, shall cease, determine, and be utterly void.*

SAID LESSORS AGREE *(said lessee having performed* his *obligations under this lease) that said lessee shall quietly hold and occupy said premises during said term without any hindrance or molestation by said lessors,* their *heir or any person lawfully claiming under them.*

*Signed this* tenth *day of* April *A. D. 19* -- .

IN THE PRESENCE OF:

_____      _____

_____      _____

_____

(Over)

---

Insertions on this lease are typed on a printed legal form. Align typed copy with printed matter and use the same margins for insertions of typed lines. Do not use *$* sign if *dollars* is printed at the end of the space for inserting a sum of money. Proofread carefully to see that all insertions have been made.

This secretary is consulting the file of legal forms that she has compiled. On each form she has noted all the facts pertinent to completing and filing it.

## SOURCES OF INFORMATION FOR THE LEGAL SECRETARY

The legal secretary may obtain helpful information from the legal secretarial handbooks listed on page 604 and from the following publications. Most of these publications are available in local libraries.

*Martindale-Hubbel Law Directory* — a four-volume reference published annually listing lawyers and their addresses, as well as a digest of the laws of the 50 states and patent, copyright, and trademark laws

*Glossary of Legal Terms for Secretaries* — published by the United States Government Printing Office

*The Lawyer's Handbook, Black's Law Dictionary, Legal Writing Style* — published by West Publishing Company, St. Paul, Minnesota

*Legal Secretary's Encyclopedic Dictionary, Sletwold's Manual of Documents and Forms for the Legal Secretary* — published by Prentice-Hall, Inc., Englewood Cliffs, New Jersey

*NALS Docket* — a bimonthly magazine published for members of the National Association of Legal Secretaries, Suite 1003–04, Barrister Hall, 29 South LaSalle Street, Chicago, 60603

*Local Law Bulletin* — (daily or weekly) — a record of court calls and current news about meetings of interest to the legal profession

Catalogs of printing companies that provide legal forms

The National Association of Legal Secretaries provides a contact with other legal secretaries and promotes interest in professional development. Those who qualify for and pass its six-part examination become Certified Professional Legal Secretaries. (See page 658.)

## SUGGESTED READINGS

Blackburn, Norma D. *Legal Secretaryship*. Englewood Cliffs: Prentice-Hall Inc., 1971.

Leslie, Louis A., and Kenneth B. Coffin. *Handbook for the Legal Secretary*. New York: McGraw-Hill Book Co., Inc., 1969.

Miller, Besse May. *Legal Secretary's Complete Handbook*, 2d ed. Englewood Cliffs: Prentice-Hall, Inc., 1971.

National Association of Legal Secretaries. *Manual for the Legal Secretarial Profession*. St. Paul: West Publishing Co., 1965.

Sletwold, Evangeline F. *Sletwold's Manual of Documents and Forms for the Legal Secretary*. Englewood Cliffs: Prentice-Hall, Inc., 1965.

## QUESTIONS FOR DISCUSSION

1. A lease is a contract, and standard lease forms are available at legal supply companies. These forms provide blank spaces for the insertion of variable data. Usually more space is provided than is needed for the fill-in.

   (a) How can you be sure that all copies of a purchased lease form are identical?

   (b) What variable data might be typed on the lease form?

   (c) What may be done to prevent additional insertions after the lease has been signed?

   (d) How many copies of the lease should be made?

2. What is the difference between the secretary's action in signing an acknowledgment in her capacity as notary public and in signing a service contract for office machines? in witnessing a will and in signing a lease for an apartment?

3. The suggestion has been made that in typing a will, each page prior to the final page be terminated with a hyphenated word. This is contrary to recommended manuscript- or letter-typewriting procedure. Why would this exception be appropriate for this legal instrument?

4. The secretary in an adjacent office asks you to witness the signatures on a contract. When you reach her office, you find that the signatures have already been affixed; and you are asked to sign as a witness. What would you do?

5. What is the procedure for becoming a notary public in your state?

6. Your employer asks you to rush out a legal paper that must be signed by persons waiting in his office. You type it quickly, check it even more quickly, and hand it in. After the signers leave, you notice you have made a serious error in a date. What would you do?

7. Through the influence of the Roman Empire, Latin became the early language of government and law. Many Latin words and phrases continue to be used in legal documents. What is the English translation of each of the following Latin terms?

| | |
|---|---|
| ex delicto | nunc pro tunc |
| in personam | pro tem |
| pendente lite | et ux |
| per stirpes | stare decisis |
| bona fide | causa |
| | scilicet (ss) |

Where would you look to obtain the correct shorthand outline for these terms?

8. What precautions are required with signatures to legal documents?

9. If an executive gives a power of attorney to his secretary, can she bind him on all contracts that she signs?

10. Select the words in these sentences that have been converted to unconventional parts of speech. Then consult the Reference Guide to check your answers.

(a) Take care of that rush first.

(b) She has a secretary look about her.

(c) The company inspector comes next week.

(d) He powers the invention with gasoline.

## PROBLEMS

■ 1. It has been recommended that a secretary should accumulate a file of legal forms for reference purposes. Prepare a typing instruction sheet that could be inserted in the front of such a file. Include typing instructions for:

(a) Margins
(b) Spacing
(c) Paragraph indention
(d) Writing dates
(e) Paging
(f) Writing figures
(g) Typing names
(h) Typing quoted matter
(i) Preparing forms for signatures
(j) Fill-ins in legal blanks
(k) Correction of errors

■ 2. Type the following affidavit; make one carbon copy.

State of Ohio, County of Franklin. Richard L. Cummings, being duly sworn, deposes and says that he has been employed by and has worked for the Majestic Furniture Company, 5813 North High Street, City of Columbus, County of Franklin, State of Ohio, continuously for the past fifteen years.

Sworn to before me this
(*use current date*)

_____
Notary Public
My commission expires (*Date*)

■ 3. Use a manual listed on page 604 or another source as a guide in typing a power of attorney. Prepare one and two (original and two carbons), using the information given below and the current date. Below the signature line, type an acknowledgement to be signed by a notary public in San Diego. Prepare legal backs for the first two copies.

Mr. Frank R. Wright, of San Diego, California (San Diego County), wants to make his brother, George L. Wright, of the same city, his attorney for the purchase of the residence and land at 2342 Camino Del Rio in San Diego.

■ 4. Type the following agency contract; make one and two and use the current date.

### AGENCY CONTRACT

(¶) This agreement, made and entered into on this, the _____ day of _____, 19--, by and between the GENTRY PRODUCTS CORPORATION, a corporation of Butte, Montana, the party of the first part, and PETER S. ELLIOT, of Boise, Idaho, the party of the second part, (¶) WITNESSETH: That, whereas, the party of the first part is about to open a branch office, to be located in Boise, Idaho, for the sale of its products, the said party of the first part hereby engages the services of PETER S. ELLIOT, the party of the second part, as manager of that office. (¶) The party of the first part hereby agrees to pay to the party of the second part a monthly salary of Twelve Hundred Dollars ($1,200), payable on the last day of every month, for a period of one year from the date of this contract. (¶) The party of the first part hereby agrees to pay all reasonable office expenses, including rent and salaries of such help as shall be agreed upon from time to time between the parties hereto. (¶) The party of the second part agrees to give his undivided time and attention to the business of the party of the first part and not to engage in any other business or occupation while in the employ of the party of the first part. (¶) The party of the second part also agrees that he will be governed at all times by the instructions of the party of the first part with regard to all contracts entered into with third persons for the party of the first part, that he will render a report of each and every sale at the time of such sale, giving a detailed account of the products sold, the prices, and the terms of the sale; and that he will submit each month to the party of the first part an itemized list of office expenses. The party of the second part agrees also to make all collections for products sold by his office and to make remittances of funds on hand as directed by the party of the first part from time to time.

(¶) IN WITNESS WHEREOF, the parties have hereunto affixed their hands and seals on the day and in the year first above written.

### GENTRY PRODUCTS CORPORATION

_____ (SEAL)
Paul K. Singleton, President

_____ (SEAL)
Peter S. Elliot

Witnesses:

_____

_____

# Part 8

# CASE PROBLEMS

Norma Wilson was secretary to the dean of the School of Business at XYZ University.  The Dean was to present a paper on Friday in a distant city, and the 30-page paper was then to be submitted for publication in the proceedings of the symposium.

On Thursday Nancy planned to type the final draft of the paper, for which she had done much of the research herself.  As she settled down to the typing, the Registrar called to remind her that all teaching schedules for the following semester were due in his office by five o'clock that day.  On Monday she had sent a rough copy of proposed schedules to all members of the division with a request from the Dean that each member initial his schedule if he approved it or submit by Wednesday evening a request for revision and his reason for asking for the change.  In checking the returned schedules, she found that Professor Lawler, a usually dissident faculty member, had not been heard from.  She called his secretary, who said, "Professor Lawler is never in on Thursday.  That's the day he works at the Research Council.  It's on his class schedule filed in your office."

Norma then telephoned the Registrar that the Dean's material would be delayed until Monday at 10:30 because he had not heard from all of his faculty members.  Just as she was starting on the report, the Dean called an emergency meeting involving a disciplinary matter; and, as was customary, he asked Norma to take notes.  Since both the meeting and the report were short, Norma transcribed her notes as soon as she returned to her desk.

At 11:30 Norma started on the research paper again.  She discovered that she had omitted two page references on footnotes when researching the information.  Instead of taking her lunch hour, she made a quick trip to the library to secure the missing information.  Before resuming her typing, she telephoned to ask Professor Lawler's secretary to bring the missing schedule to her office just as soon as the professor came in on Friday.  Then she placed a note on the Dean's desk that the schedules would be delayed until Monday and asked if he wanted to approve them before she typed them.  (He attended the Council for Deans at ten o'clock every Monday.)

A constant stream of faculty and student visitors delayed the report even more.  At three o'clock the Dean rushed out of his office saying, "May I have the manuscript so that I can familiarize myself with it this afternoon?  I want to read it smoothly tomorrow, and that requires practice."

Norma had to admit, "It's not ready yet, Dean. There's just too much work in this office for one person. I can give you a rough draft in about twenty minutes, and I can mail the final corrected manuscript tomorrow afternoon if you give me the name and address of the editor of the proceedings."

The Dean, visibly annoyed, retreated to his office, muttering, "I gave it to you on Wednesday morning. You knew I had to have it today. Maybe you should try to plan your work better."

**What errors in work organization did Norma commit?**

## 8-2 THE SECRETARY AS CONFIDANTE

During the coffee break, Edna Miller found Connie James, a word processor in tears in the lounge. She put her arms around Connie and said, "Connie, what on earth is the matter with you?" Connie dried her tears and poured out a month of resentment against Miss Wiley, the coordinator of the Center. "She's always getting on my back because I can't punctuate my letters the way she wants them. I learned in school to put a comma where there is a pause. Now she expects me to know all about complex and compound sentences, appositives, direct address, and all the rest of it. I guess she wants me to be a grammar book, for goodness sakes. You should have heard her the other day when Mr. Jackson sent back two letters because one of them had a proofreading error and the other one had *supersede* spelled with a *c*. Anyway, she is supposed to proofread our letters a second time, so why didn't she find those errors? She's not perfect either. She said that I had taken the training program and should be able to handle the job now. She even said that she expects all of us girls to be language specialists! Me a language specialist? When I worked for Mr. Allen, he liked the way I punctuated all right."

Edna comforted the girl and told her that they didn't have time to talk any more now but could meet for lunch the next day. Because she believed in her company's policy of trying to salvage an unsatisfactory worker, she even sent a grammar book on which she had leaned for years down to the Center for Connie.

All the rest of the day Edna pondered her role.

**Should she have listened to Connie's complaints about a colleague — someone promoted to the job of coordinator from a secretarial job exactly like her own?**

**Should she have taken a "hands-off" attitude?**

**Should she regard herself as the ears of her employer and report to him the problems that are arising during the period of transition to the word processing center type of organization?**

**What should she say to Connie at lunch?**

# Your Professional Future

*Part* **9**

This section looks to your future. The college-trained secretary faces almost endless opportunities for employment. Obtaining the right position, one that offers both job satisfaction and advancement, however, is a result of careful planning. Management-level positions await those who continue to grow professionally and who assume and execute tasks of responsibility. The proven secretary is a likely candidate to fill an administrative post.

# Chapter 26

## SELECTING THE RIGHT POSITION

This chapter focuses on *you*, the young college student and the mature, college-trained woman, as you begin to seek full-time employment in the business office. Although secretarial positions have certain common elements, wide differences do exist. In evaluating each job prospect, you will be considering such factors as the location and size of the office, the difference in personnel policies, and the specialties of the job. Because your success on the job will depend, in large measure, on the satisfaction that you derive from the position, it is extremely important that your selection be consistent with your goals, your interests, and your abilities.

## TYPES OF OFFICES

One of the many advantages of secretarial work is that employment opportunities exist in communities of almost every size. Although most secretaries work in the downtown area of cities, many attractive positions are open in the suburbs, in industrial complexes adjoining cities, and in small, outlying towns. From a secretary's viewpoint, each type of location offers certain benefits. The "best" location is a matter of choice.

### Downtown Locations

In addition to the many large offices in a downtown area, there are also innumerable small offices — some located in high-rise office towers, others in small storefront buildings. As a secretary working downtown, you will have lunchtime opportunities to browse and shop. And you will see and be tempted to buy more of everything — clothes, accessories, and gadgets.

Though travel time and parking rates for private automobiles present problems, public transportation is more likely to be conveniently available. Another consideration is the wide choice of eating facilities and afterwork entertainment.

Suburban office facilities take advantage of the open areas to lend a parklike atmosphere to their grounds. Note the natural wooded area, the attractive landscaping, and the sunny patio with umbrella-shaded tables in this picture.

—*Volkswagen of America*

### Suburban Locations

In the industrial suburbs, large manufacturing concerns are located along public transportation routes. Also found in each suburban community are a real estate office or two, an insurance agency, offices of several doctors and dentists, a school board, small stores, a city hall, and similar small offices.

The suburban position may be very close and convenient to your apartment or home, or it may be located miles across town. There will be far fewer choices of restaurants than in the downtown area, but lunch costs will probably be lower. Your company may operate a restaurant serving food at cost. It may even be the practice to take your lunch and eat in the lounge.

### Outlying Locations

Many large industrial plants are located on main highways on the edges of cities but in rural-like open spaces. To get to them, employees must drive or ride in a car pool, which can be expensive. Employee restaurants are often operated at or below cost. Sometimes attractive recreation facilities are provided for the employees.

## Small Communities

Secretarial positions in small communities offer many advantages including lower living cost, and little or no transportation cost. However, salaries in such communities tend to be lower than those paid in the urban centers.

## Small Offices

Many secretaries choose to work in a one-girl office or where there are only a few persons—such as offices maintained by attorneys, architects, engineers, accountants, doctors, dentists, insurance agencies, real estate agencies, suburban banks, employment agencies, churches, schools, and company branches. They prefer the relaxed family atmosphere and casual dress of the small office. More important to the secretary, perhaps, is the wide variety of duties available to her. There is no one else to do the filing, handle the cash, make long distance calls, duplicate materials, sort and send out mail, and purchase supplies. In this position she is the master of all trades.

**Personnel Policies.** One of the advantages of working in a small office is the freedom offered. The hours of work are usually established, but the secretary knows the volume of work and when time permits may take longer lunch hours, leave early, or take a day off.

Small offices usually have general personnel policies rather than clearly defined ones. This may or may not be to the advantage of the secretary. There may be no limit to sick leaves and emergency absences, or there may be no provision at all for them.

There are a few definite disadvantages to working in a small office. Generally, there is a limit to the amount of salary a small office can pay. The ceiling may be set by circumstances of the business and not by the competence of the secretary. Instead of giving specified salary increases at definite intervals, the employer is likely to consider each salary increase individually when he gets around to it. Another disadvantage is the absence of social opportunities in the work situation. The secretary, particularly in the one-girl office, may find herself isolated.

**Administrative Opportunities.** In some small offices, the secretary must assume a great deal of administrative responsibility, but rarely is she given an administrative title or status. The employer, depending upon the nature of his work, may be out of the office much of the time and the responsibility for running the office falls on the secretary. In such situations, the secretary is pretty much her own boss.

—I. Magnin

—European Health Spa

The secretary in a small urban office may find more variety in noontime activities outside the office than she would in a large, self-contained building in a suburban area. From a downtown office she can quickly reach numerous shops and recreational facilities.

Three- and four-girl offices frequently provide excellent opportunities to gain supervisory experience. In such situations, the senior secretary may supervise the work of the office staff along with her other duties.

## Large Offices

The work of the secretary in the large office tends to differ in many respects from that of the secretary in the small office. In the large office many of the business routines are performed by special departments. Telephone duties are handled by switchboard operators; postal and shipping chores, by the mailing and shipping department; the purchasing department orders supplies—to mention a few. (See Chapter 2.) On the other hand, in addition to her communication responsibilities the secretary in the large office may handle travel details, research business information for the executive, draft reports, sit in on conferences and write the proceedings, and perform many other services.

In some offices, her work may involve administrative and supervisory responsibilities only, with the dictation and transcription duties being handled in the word processing center. In all large offices, though, the impact of automation is evident. Automation is adding to the decision-making responsibilities of the secretary and relieving her of many clerical routine duties. (See Chapter 18.)

**Personnel Policies.** Personnel policies must be clearly defined and followed in large offices. Singling out an individual employee for special privileges can be damaging to office morale. The personnel policies of a large company usually cover such matters as:

**Hours of work, lunch hour, rest periods**
**Overtime pay or compensatory time off**
**Eligibility for vacation; length of vacation**
**Number of days allowed annually for emergency sick leave**
**Days considered as holidays (days off with pay)**
**Salary range for each job; frequency and extent of salary increases**
**Fringe benefits**

There is opportunity for advancement in a large organization. There are many steps up the secretarial ladder. In addition, there are supervisory and administrative positions to which the secretary can advance. Secretaries to top management are frequently administrative assistants both in duties and title.

**Fringe Benefits.** Many businesses and government agencies offer fringe benefits to their employees. They are called "fringe" because they are outside the realm of salary, and sometimes outside the realm of taxable income. In some instances, the fringe benefits cost the organization an additional 25 to 30 percent of the wages paid to the secretary.

*Group Life Insurance.* An insurance policy may be taken out on the employee. The employer may pay all or part of the premium. Usually, every employee is eligible, and rates are lower than for individual insurance of comparable coverage. The policy usually terminates when the employee leaves the company, but some policies have conversion features.

*Hospitalization Insurance.* Insurance for hospital and medical costs is offered to employees covering the employee and the members of his family. The company may pay the premium or may deduct the premium periodically from the employee's salary and pay it to the insurance company for him.

*Credit Union.* A credit union is a kind of employee-operated bank in which the employees can make savings deposits and from which they can obtain loans. A user must be a member since a borrower must purchase at least one share of stock. An employee can arrange to have an amount withheld from his regular pay check and deposited with the credit union.

*Stock-Purchase Plan.* A stock-purchase plan provides an opportunity to buy company stock from one's earnings. The employee may choose to have a set amount deducted from his salary toward the purchase of company stock. Many companies, within set limits, match the contributions of employees.

*Pension Plan.* In recent years, company pension plans have become more and more sophisticated. Sometimes a company purchases an annuity for an employee or sets aside funds from which to make pension payments to him when he retires. Often both the employer and employee contribute.

Pension plans can provide a major part of an individual's retirement funds. It is wise, therefore, to weigh the probability that you will want to remain with a company that you are considering. (See page 624.)

*Bonuses.* Some companies give employees bonuses at the end of profitable years, often substantial amounts. This is sometimes a better management policy than to increase and decrease wages to correspond with fluctuating profits. These bonuses may be in the form of cash or of company stock.

*Educational Opportunities.* Some organizations provide in-service educational opportunities at little or no cost to employees. For example, programs in management and secretarial training are common. In addition, employees are often reimbursed for educational expenses incurred in acquiring additional job-related training, making this fringe benefit especially attractive to an employee seeking promotion.

*Miscellaneous Benefits.* Companies dealing in a product or service, such as retailers and commercial airlines, offer employees attractive purchase discounts or travel plans. Some organizations provide numerous outside recreational facilities for employees and their dependents— golf courses, resorts, and the like. Generous vacation and sick leave periods are becoming more and more common. For the female worker, liberal maternity benefits have been written into many company policies.

## THE SECRETARY'S OPPORTUNITIES FOR SPECIALIZATION

Opportunities for employment are unlimited for the qualified secretary in almost every type of business and in every geographic area—and the opportunities for specialization are so excitingly varied that this book can discuss only a few.

—*E. I Du Pont de Nemours & Co., Inc.*

A doctor's secretary must be familiar with medical terminology. The American Association of Medical Assistants sponsors training programs for the medical secretary in which specialized duties and vocabularies are stressed.

## The Medical Secretary

A long-established and rapidly growing area of secretarial specialization is that of the medical secretary. She may work in a doctor's or dentist's office, for a clinic, a hospital, a pharmaceutical company, a public health facility, or even an insurance company.

While desirable, special training is not essential; learning on the job is always possible. A knowledge of Latin, however, is a distinct help in understanding the terminology. Courses in German, likewise, will prove helpful. Business schools, community colleges, the technical institutes, and some four-year colleges and universities offer programs for training the medical secretary. Besides training in the office skills and medical dictation, curriculums include a number of science courses, the study of medical terminology, and the accounting procedures common to medical offices. A rich variety of handbooks are available to the medical secretary and to the secretary who is contemplating this specialization.

In the one-doctor office, the secretary may serve as receptionist, bookkeeper, transcriber of case histories, secretary, and office manager. She may do routine technical duties like sterilizing instruments or taking temperatures. And, of course, she strictly adheres to the principles of medical ethics in keeping patients' medical records confidential. If she is the only employee in the office, the whole show is hers. So, too, is the responsibility for a smoothly run office.

In larger offices and in hospitals, her work will consist of transcribing patients' records, either from shorthand or machine dictation, and of the myriad details involved in smoothly, pleasantly, and comfortingly handling the patients in today's busy medical office. But regardless of the size of the office or organization, the secretary must be familiar with medical terms—both the meaning and the spelling—and with professional office procedures. And she must understand and keep up to date on medical and hospital insurance forms.

Medical secretaries can take the one-day examination administered by the American Association of Medical Assistants, Inc., for certification as Certified Medical Assistants, Administrative. Eligibility requirements are:

**A high school diploma or equivalent and three years' experience**

*or*

**One academic year in a college-level medical-assistant program and two years' experience**

*or*

**An associate degree or a two-year certificate program in medical assisting and one year's experience**

The examination consists of two divisions:

*Division I (General)*—covers medical terminology, basic anatomy and physiology, psychology, and medical law and ethics

*Division II (Administrative)*—covers oral and written communications, bookkeeping and insurance, and administrative procedures

## The Legal Secretary

Legal secretaries are among the highest paid in the profession, and rightly so. The work of the law office is exacting; an inaccurate record can be extremely expensive. The secretary must have a command of the English language and high typewriting and shorthand proficiencies. Working long hours—most of them under pressure—she must have a thorough knowledge of legal procedures and a real interest in the law.

The title *legal secretary* comes only after considerable experience in the field, many times after training from the senior secretaries in the law office. To give professional status to the legal secretary, the National Association of Legal Secretaries (International) sponsors, through its chapters, free training programs, an employment service, and a Professional Legal Secretary examination and certification program.

The examination has six parts: written communication skill and knowledge; human relations; secretarial procedures and office management; secretarial accounting; legal terminology, techniques, and procedures; and legal and secretarial skills. To be eligible for the examination, an applicant must be a member of NALS, must have had at least five years' experience as a legal secretary, and must present letters from five reputable persons, one of whom must be a member of the American Bar Association and another, the applicant's present employer.

Many of the peculiarities of the work of the legal secretary were described in Chapter 25. Actually, the legal secretary's work is highly varied and involves extensive contacts with people—the clients of her employer.

Occasionally, a secretary has become so fascinated with the profession that she has studied law at evening classes, passed the bar examination, and proudly changed the desk plate from "Secretary" to "Attorney."

## The Educational Secretary

Every community offers employment opportunities for educational secretaries in work that varies widely among positions. The secretary to the top school officials of a large city system will have duties similar to those of the secretary in business and industry. On the other hand, the secretary in the office of the small local school will perform vastly different duties. For example, she will probably have less dictation but may keep many more records, order materials and supplies, supervise duplicating, schedule facilities, work on master schedules, and plan group meetings. She will also meet school visitors and have close contacts with students, teachers, and parents.

The National Association of Educational Secretaries, a department of the National Education Association with offices in Washington, D.C., is constantly working for the improvement of salaries, retirement benefits, and tenure coverage for educational secretaries. The organization upgrades the profession by sponsoring a continuing academic program, conducting conferences, and distributing publications (*The National Educational Secretary*) and pertinent information. The NAES also sponsors a Professional Standards Program that issues five kinds of certificates (basic, associate professional, advanced professional, and master) based on education, experience, and professional activity. A college degree is required for the Professional Certificate. To be eligible for the examination, an applicant must be a member of NAES.

The technical secretary or administrative assistant needs a technical understanding as well as secretarial background to take part in the engrossing procedures of the scientific or engineering office. The demand for technical secretaries far exceeds the supply.

—*E. I. Du Pont de Nemours & Co., Inc.*

## The Technical Secretary

The technical secretary serves the engineer and the scientist—men who are at home in the laboratory but not in the office. To conserve the time of the highly paid scientific and engineering personnel, many companies provide each top-level scientist and engineer with assistants to perform routine functions and to free him for creative work. The secretary is a member of this "assist" team. Her function is to assume the office burden and to minimize the distractions and interruptions necessitated by office detail.

The "tech-sec" is probably as much an administrative assistant as she is a secretary. Her work includes not only the usual secretarial duties but such additional responsibilities as handling all or most of the correspondence from composition to mailing, maintaining the office technical library, at times gathering materials from other library resources, and proofreading and frequently editing scientific papers, as well as handling all details incident to their publication. She prepares engineering reports, checks materials against specifications and standards, and orders materials in compliance with specifications. The work is demanding and exacting, but the pay is exceedingly rewarding.

A strong background in mathematics and science is an asset to the "tech-sec," and to grow with the position requires continued study.

When you work as a technical secretary, you may expect to undergo security clearance if you are to be employed in a company having contracts with the Department of Defense of the United States Government. The maintenance of strict security control is becoming important to other companies as well, because of the possibility of the pirating of formulas, research findings, advanced designs, and so forth. The secretary must know how security is maintained for each classification from restricted data to top secret.

## The Public Stenographer

The secretary aspiring to be her own boss may find her niche in public stenography. A word of caution, however: the public stenographer must be a "jack of all secretarial trades." Only a secretary with a broad education, a wealth of office experience, and the highest level of skills should attempt to enter the field.

As the title implies, the public stenographer works for the public— that is, for anyone who comes along with secretarial work to be done. For this reason, her office is usually located in a hotel or off the main foyer of a large office building. She charges by the hour or job and may work for as many as half a dozen persons each day. The work ranges from taking highly technical dictation to recording speeches and testimony of witnesses, to typing legal documents, to purchasing a gift for the wife of a busy executive before he catches the four o'clock plane for home. A public stenographer is usually a notary public.

In the right location, the income is high; but much of the work is under time pressure. Being a public stenographer is not for the ulcer prone.

## The Temporary Service Secretary

One of the fastest-growing and unique services today is that of providing part-time office help. Kelly Services, Inc.; Western Girl, Inc.; and Manpower, Inc. are but a few of the organizations specializing in this service. Others are listed in the *Yellow Pages Directory* and are widely advertised in general publications. These organizations offer a corps of temporary workers to be deployed wherever required. They help the office that experiences intermittent periods of heavy workload, they fill in for employees who are on vacation or ill, and they provide the one-half secretary for the one-and-a-half-secretary office.

In addition to providing a service to business, these organizations provide a means of organized part-time employment to a large number of women who are unable, because of family obligations or other duties, to devote themselves to year-round, full-time jobs or who return to work after rearing a family.

The work of the "temporary" is as varied as is business. Calls for assistance come from all types of offices. The agency attempts to match the requirements of the job with the competencies of the temporary worker. Many a secretarial trainee in college has found that being a Kelly Girl for the summer has been profitable both financially and experience-wise. This is one way to cram a wide variety of experience into a short summer period.

## The Civil Service Secretary

More secretaries work for the government than for any other type of business or organization. Government positions offer certain advantages, such as assured annual increments, job security, a sound retirement system, and the opportunity for advancement based on merit. Working for the government, however, can lack the excitement and stimulation that is associated with a business involved in a competitive market. The work is frequently highly routinized, and imagination and initiative are not always appreciated and rewarded; however, a college-trained secretary who has initiative and ambition and who is highly selective when entering government service can advance to a position of great responsibility. The increasingly large number of women in high-level government executive positions attests to the opportunities there.

Being a Government Girl does not necessarily mean working in Washington, D.C., or for the federal government. In fact, only 11 percent of the federal employees work in the District of Columbia. Wherever there is a military installation, veteran's hospital, weather station, or federal bureau office, there are federal employees, including secretaries. State and local governments (combined) employ far more office workers than does the federal government. Thus, government jobs are found in towns and cities in America and in foreign countries.

The federal government, all states, and many municipal governments have a civil (meaning civilian) service merit system, which means that jobs are classified and appointments made on examination results. Stenographic posts are classified in the Federal government as GS3 (General Schedule 3) through GS6, and it is possible for a secretary to advance to GS7 and 8. There is a standard base salary, with annual increments, for each GS rating.

The United States is divided into ten regions with a U.S. Civil Service Office in each. To obtain information about a position, write to the regional office in which you wish to obtain employment. If you are interested in working in Washington, D.C., write the U.S. Civil Service Commission, Washington, D.C. You can also obtain information about Federal Civil Service examinations from your local post office.

## The Foreign Service Secretary

Does the prospect of serving as a secretary in the American Legation in Istanbul, Tokyo, Paris, Rio de Janeiro, or Copenhagen excite you? If so, you should examine the employment opportunities in the Foreign Service of the Department of State, United States Information Service (USIS), Agency for International Development (AID), and the Departments of Army, Navy and Air Force.

Working in a foreign country can be thrilling, but also exacting, and calls for a special kind of person—one who is willing to live in an exemplary fashion, for our foreign service personnel are on display 24 hours a day. Each staff member represents the United States and contributes to the success of our program. The Department of State, USIS, and AID, therefore, carefully screen all foreign-service personnel; and requirements are high. The basic requirements for a secretarial position in the Foreign Service of the Department of State are as follows:

- **21 years of age**

- **Single without dependents**

- **High score on a qualifying examination covering clerical aptitude, verbal ability, spelling, typing, shorthand**

- **Four years' office experience or the equivalent**
  **(A year in college is usually considered to equal a year of work experience; however, a minimum of one year of full-time secretarial experience is always required.)**

Competency in a foreign language is not required. If, however, you should have ambitions to advance to the position of a Foreign Service Staff Officer in the Department of State (there are many women in these posts), ability to speak and write a foreign language is required. Extensive study of a foreign language in college would be a strong plus factor when your application is evaluated.

The pay is comparatively good, with additional allowances for housing, cost of living, and special compensation for hardship posts.

A booklet entitled *Foreign Service Secretaries Assignment: Worldwide with the U.S. Department of State* can be obtained by writing the Employment Division, Department of State, Washington, D.C. 20402.[1]

---

[1]Information about foreign employment in the U.S. Information Service and AID can be obtained by writing to these agencies in Washington, D.C.

The office of Mrs. Ellen Brooks Cramp-
ton, staff editor with George Rainbird,
Ltd., of London, overlooks busy Marble
Arch and Hyde Park. Mrs. Crampton is a
graduate of Wittenberg University,
Springfield, Ohio.

### Work-Travel Plans

For several years secretaries from Europe, primarily England, have
invaded the United States secretarial market, giving the office an international image. Conversely, an increasing number of secretaries from
the United States are seeing Europe via a work-travel plan. International
units of temporary office-help services and employment agencies are
recruiting secretaries for work in England and on the Continent on a
working-vacation plan. One plan proposes an eight-week assignment
in London working for leading British firms or for British subsidiaries
of American corporations.

## SURVEYING EMPLOYMENT OPPORTUNITIES

A review of the help-wanted advertisements in most newspapers will
show that the highly qualified, college-trained secretary is in a position
to pick and choose. The problem, then, is one of job selection. There
are many dimensions to the selection process, as these questions reveal:

**Do you want to work in your local community, or do you hope to find employment
in a new location—a large city, a different part of the country, or abroad?**

**Are you the one-girl office type, or will you be happy only in an office crowd?**

**How well does the business relate to your special interests in art, music, sports,
medicine, accounting, social work, research, writing, politics?**

**Are you likely to be satisfied in the position a year from now? five years from now?**

Psychologists say that the key items in job satisfaction are a sense
of responsibility, satisfaction of achievement, opportunity for growth,
recognition from employer, and a feeling of being needed. The right
choice is not the result of luck but of careful analysis and action.

## Evaluating a Company

How do you judge a company as a potential employer? There is no sure test, but answers to the following five questions may help.

*What is the reputation of the company in the community?* **The community image of a company is the sum of many things—employee relationships, reputation for progressive management, sponsorship of community projects, and general leadership in civic and business activities.**

*How satisfactory are the employer-employee relationships* (company morale)? **Do the employees seem to be one big family with a common bond of enthusiasm, or are there undercurrents of distrust and backbiting?**

*Is the business financially stable?* **A business that is not economically sound cannot give its employees a feeling of financial security. Its wage policies and employee benefits will always depend on the profit picture.**

*Is the company expanding?* **A growing organization usually offers opportunities for advancement. Women stand a good chance for management positions in the new, expanding industries.**

*What opportunities for training and advancement are provided?* **Companies that provide special training programs or pay tuition in local universities and colleges merit special consideration.**

Don't overlook the opportunities in the small office—you may be happier there—and in the new company that is just getting under way. Being on the beginning team can be exciting and rewarding.

## Developing a Job Prospect List

No good sales campaign is ready for action without a *prospect list*. Your job prospect list should include potential employers who could offer the kind of employment opportunity you are seeking—location, size, interest appeal, permanence, and job satisfaction.

**School Placement Office.** The placement office of the school you have attended for your secretarial training can give you expert help in developing your prospect list and can assist you in making job contacts. Complete all forms necessary for registration promptly. Get acquainted with the placement office personnel. Discuss your employment needs with them freely and often. If they arrange a job interview for you, always report back after the interview. Solicit their advice and let them know you appreciate their assistance.

**Free Employment Agencies.** Employment agencies are a good source of prospective positions. Any person seeking employment may register without charge with one of the Employment Service offices of his state. Registration includes a comprehensive interview and a skills test so that you can be properly classified according to your abilities, personality traits, training, and experience. In order to keep on its active list, you must communicate with that office regularly.

Other free employment services are maintained by certain civic and religious organizations. In some cities the Chamber of Commerce gives help in securing employment.

**Private Employment Agencies.** Private employment agencies are in business to find people for jobs and jobs for people and, therefore, charge a fee for this service. In some states, regulatory bodies set maximum-fee limits on charges by agencies. Applicants registering with an agency sign a contract in which the fee terms are stated. A major advantage of a good agency is that it carries out a complete job hunt for the applicant, thus relieving her of much of the repetitive detail work involved in job hunting. Although in the past, job applicants paid the entire fee for the placement service, today the employer usually pays part or all of the fee charge in the higher-paid positions.

Private employment agencies perform a valuable service for the employer as well. The staff of the agency can expertly screen, test, and interview each applicant. The company then interviews only those who meet the company's specified qualifications.

Because many businesses use private agencies exclusively, keep in mind that many desirable positions are available only through an agency.

A private employment agency should be selected carefully. For a directory of reputable agencies, write to the National Employment Association, 2000 K Street, N. W., Washington, D.C. 20006. Agencies listed in the directory subscribe to a code of ethical practices. The directory will be especially helpful in locating an agency in a distant city where you would like to obtain employment.

**Newspaper Advertisements.** The classified section of the newspaper is an excellent source of information for the job seeker. Besides depicting the employment picture of the community, skill requirements and the "going" pay rates for secretarial positions are often stated. If a particular advertisement appeals to you, follow to the letter the directions given for making an application.

---

EXECUTIVE SECRETARY

If you are seeking a position which offers:

- Responsibility for your judgment
- Challenge for your ambition
- Superior starting salary for your economic desires
- A chance to exercise your creativity
- An opportunity to use your personality to meet and work with people

With a company that offers:

- An outstanding growth record
- Excellent benefit programs
- Newly decorated offices
- Highly qualified professional staff

And you offer the following qualifications:

- Excellent typing and shorthand skills
- Superior level of maturity
- Preferably at least 1 yr. secretarial experience and a 2-yr. secretarial course

Then please send brief résumé in confidence to Personnel Dept., P.O. Box 10313, Dayton, Ohio 45401

Firms that advertise for help in the classified columns sometimes use a *blind* advertisement like the one on page 626. A blind advertisement is one in which a key or box number is used for your reply and the firm name is not mentioned. A legitimate blind advertisement is usually inserted that way because the firm does not want to be bothered with interviewing large numbers of applicants. On the other hand, blind advertisements are sometimes used just to get names of sales prospects by someone who has something to sell.

**Friends, Relatives, and Associates.** You may wish to enlist the assistance of your friends, friends of your family, the businessmen with whom you have had some kind of contact, firms for which you have worked temporarily, people you have met through group contacts, and your teachers. Inform all of them that you are in the market for a position and that you would appreciate their help. Naturally, you should never make a nuisance of yourself. A report to the person who referred you to an opening, no matter what the outcome, is a matter of courtesy.

**Other Sources.** The *Yellow Pages* of the telephone directory provide a classified list of the local businesses to which you might apply. For instance, if you are interested in a position in an insurance company, you would find listed under *Insurance* all of the local companies.

Become an avid reader of the daily newspaper and watch all news items that would give you a clue to a possible job contact. New businesses are constantly opening, and items relating to jobs, changes, or expansions in business frequently appear in the newspaper.

**Job Prospects in Other Locations.** There are a number of information sources you may use to obtain job prospects in a distant city or area. The names of reputable private employment agencies in the city or area can be obtained from the directory of the National Employment Association. (See page 626.) Copies of the leading newspapers in the city or area can be examined at your local library. Names of companies can be obtained from the Yellow Pages of the telephone directory. Telephone directories for all major cities are kept in many public libraries. The Chamber of Commerce employment service can be contacted.

## Learning about a Company

You should exhaust all means of getting information on each of the firms on your prospect list. Telephone to find out the employment manager's name. Inquire of your friends, acquaintances, and instructors about the firm. Examine the company's advertisements that appear in papers and magazines. Study the annual report of the firm. A copy can usually be obtained by sending a request to the company.

Many large companies publish brochures describing job opportunities and employment policies of the company. Your college placement office may have them on file. If not, send a request to the company. If it is a small firm, you may inquire of its reputation from the Chamber of Commerce and the Better Business Bureau. Use separate file folders to accumulate pertinent material on each company.

Many firms will be eliminated as you proceed in this information-gathering campaign. When your prospect list is as complete as you can make it, check it and group your prospects by jobs you are best fitted to fill. Select the prospects with which you think you have the best chances for employment and which provide an interesting future.

## MAKING AN APPLICATION

A fundamental step in preparing to make an application for a position is to take an inventory of your knowledges, skills, strengths, and weaknesses in terms of the requirements of that particular position. What skills, understandings, and special qualities will the employer be seeking? What type of experience background will he expect? Do you have unique qualities that would be an asset in the position? What weaknesses in your preparation or background might the employer note? What plan do you have to correct these weaknesses?

The preparation of your personal data sheet will assist you in making this analysis.

### Your Personal Data Sheet

Sometimes called a *résumé*, *personal history*, or *dossier*, a personal data sheet is a concise, positive presentation of your background and abilities. Because your purpose is to gain a personal interview with the employer, your data sheet must arouse interest in your unique qualifications — must be an "appetizer." It must be short, preferably one page; if too long, it dulls the appetite.

There are two types of personal data sheets: a *general* one that is a record of your work history (illustrated on the next page) and a *qualifications* data sheet written with a specific position in mind. In the latter, experience related to the job in question is fully described and unrelated experience is omitted.

You will use your data sheet in a number of ways. It will accompany your letter of application in answer to classified ads and in pursuing job

## Letter of Application

689 Carroll Avenue
DeKalb, Illinois 60115
April 10, 1973

Mr. Howell Edmunds, Vice-President
Harmon Advertising Company
104 North Michigan Avenue
Chicago, Illinois 60202

Dear Mr. Edmunds:

The Placement Office at Northern Illinois University has told me of the opening in your office for a college graduate with some stenographic experience who can handle a large volume of dictation, relieve you of routine details, and meet the public well. Believing that I meet these qualifications, I should like to apply for the position.

You will see from the enclosed résumé that I have developed to a superior level the stenographic skills involved in secretarial work and have the ability to operate a number of office machines. You will also note that I have supplemented my course work here at the university with on-the-job experience during the summers.

As graduation nears, I am eager to begin a full-time position in the secretarial field. When you have analyzed my qualifications in terms of your needs and have checked my references, I should like very much to come to your office to talk with you about the position. I shall telephone you on Wednesday morning to ask for an appointment.

Sincerely yours,

Joanne Webster

Miss Joanne Webster

Enclosure

---

## Personal Data Sheet

Miss Joanne Webster                     Age:        21 years    Height:  5' 3"
689 Carroll Avenue                      Marital Status:  Single  Weight:  112 pounds
DeKalb, Illinois 60115
Permanent Residence: 127 Far Hills Road, Peoria, Illinois 61611

Objective:  A secretarial position requiring a volume
            of dictation and transcription and an
            opportunity for meeting the public

EDUCATION

Northern Illinois University               Major:   Secretarial Studies
College of Business Education              Minor:   English
Bachelor of Science Degree, June, 1973

Peoria High School
Peoria, Illinois
Diploma (5th in class of 174), June, 1969

Major Courses:
    Accounting                   Business statistics      Marketing
    Business communications      Data processing          Office machines
    Business law                 Economics                Office management

Secretarial Skills:  Shorthand dictation rate, 120 words a minute
                     Shorthand transcription rate, 35 words a minute
                     Typewriting straight-copy rate, 75 words a minute

Office Machines:  Mimeograph, direct-process, and offset duplicators; key-
                  driven, rotary, and electronic calculators; and adding
                  machines

EXPERIENCE

Summers
1970-71-72        John Hancock Mutual Insurance Co.     Stenographer (typing,
                                                         shorthand, filing)

9/71-6/72         Office of Dean of Women               Clerk (typing, filing,
                  Northern Illinois University           receptionist duties)

9/72-6/73         Business Manager, Kappa Delta

EXTRACURRICULAR ACTIVITIES

President         Secretarial Studies Club
Member            Alpha Pi Epsilon, Honorary Secretarial Fraternity
President         Future Business Leaders of America
Member            Kappa Delta Sorority, Chairman of Social Committee
                  and Business Manager (Senior Year)

REFERENCES (By Permission)

Dr. Lyle Maxwell, Northern Illinois University, DeKalb, Illinois 60115
Mr. Louis Ahearn, General Agent, John Hancock Mutual Insurance Company,
    3613 Devon Avenue, Chicago, Illinois 60645
Dr. Robert Kester (my minister), 1804 Woodstock Avenue, Peoria, Illinois 61611

openings. Give copies to friends, relatives, and business acquaintances to pass on to a prospective employer. Your college placement office will need one or more copies. Always take a copy to an interview. It enables you to list accomplishments and some of the extras that wouldn't be included in an application form.

Type each personal data sheet individually (do not duplicate), and include these fundamentals (the order of which can vary):

**Personal Data.** Every employer wants to know certain personal items about an applicant. He will likely want to know your:

| | | |
|---|---|---|
| **Full name** | **Age** | **Height and weight** |
| **Address** | **Telephone number** | **Marital status** |

A recent photograph attached to the data sheet is recommended. It is important, however, that the photograph be appropriate and not a casual snapshot.

**Objective.** A statement indicating the position that you seek projects your positive view of your qualifications and also provides the reader with an instant knowledge of the sort of job that you seek.

**Education.** Include complete pertinent information about your educational background.

*Schools Attended.* List all the colleges and universities that you have attended and the high school from which you were graduated. List the most recent schools first and give dates of graduation, diplomas received, degrees conferred, awards, and scholarships.

*Major Subjects.* The business courses that you completed should be listed. Include also courses related specifically to the position for which you are applying. For example, in applying for a secretarial position in an advertising office, you would list the English, art, and psychology courses taken.

*Secretarial Skills and Abilities.* Give your speed in shorthand dictation and transcription. List separately the business machines that you can operate, stating your operating ability. Say, for example, that you have operating knowledge on a machine, or expert ability if you have had considerable experience and can operate a certain machine well. Overrating your ability, however, may give your application a tone of superiority which may impress your potential employer unfavorably.

**Work Experience.** List your work experience in the order of recency or in the order of its importance to the position in question. For example, in applying for a secretarial position, list office experience (full and part time) first, giving inclusive dates of employment, the name and address of the employer, the title of the position held, and a brief description of it. If your work involved the supervision of others, be sure to include the fact. And don't forget to mention promotions.

You will need to exercise selectivity in preparing your list. If you have had extensive full-time office experience, it is not necessary to list all the part-time positions you may have held. If, however, as with most students, your work experience has been largely limited to summer and part-time employment while in school, you may wish to list all such work whether or not it was office work.

**Special Interests, Abilities, and Accomplishments.** Your extracurricular activities, special interests, and achievements may give the prospective employer an indication of what kind of person you are and how you would fit into his office; therefore, you should list:

1. *The extracurricular activities in which you have participated and the offices you have held.* Holding responsible offices in one or more activities or groups may be more impressive than parading evidence of membership in virtually every organization on the campus.

2. *Special honors received.* Recognition by awards and scholarships is evidence of your ability and perseverance.

3. *Special achievements if they have implications for the position you are seeking.* Your ability to read or speak a foreign language, awards for English composition or original writing, or special training in some field of science may be the specific point that influences the employer in your favor.

**References.** Three or four reliable references are adequate—business people, if possible. The longer and better they have known you, the more valid will be their evaluation of your abilities.

If you have had no experience, list teachers or administrators, preferably teachers of business subjects, who know you well. Always secure permission to use anyone's name as a reference before you list it.

The full name and full address (business address preferred) of each reference should be given with business title, if any, and the telephone number, if he can be reached by telephone. An indication of the circumstances under which each person has known you adds to the value of references.

**A Few Don'ts.** It is recommended that you do not mention your religion or race in your personal data sheet, and a simple indication of your marital status is sufficient. Details can be given in the interview, if they are important. Also save for the interview salary talk, as well as your reasons for leaving previous employment.

## Your Application Letter

An application letter, too, is a means to an end—that of obtaining a personal interview. It is an original letter written with the requirements of a specific job in mind. It should *summarize* on one page your qualifications and relate your experience to the available job. Finally, the letter requests a personal interview and tells the reader how to reach you. Bear in mind that your letter is but one of many that the employer receives. It is, therefore, extremely important that your letter stand out in the crowd. Make it win for you that personal interview!

**Solicited and Unsolicited Application Letters.** An application letter is *solicited* if you are responding to a help-wanted advertisement or are writing upon request of an employer (frequently a part of the screening process). Send a personal data sheet with a solicited letter of application.

*Unsolicited* application letters can be written as "feelers" to discover a vacancy or to follow up a reported vacancy. The same unsolicited-letter form can be used repeatedly with carefully made adaptations for each regarding any special requirements about which you know. It is a matter of opinion whether the personal data sheet should accompany an unsolicited application letter. Waiting to present it at a personal interview gives you the advantage of being able to tailor the data sheet to the available position.

**Basic Parts of an Application Letter.** Whether solicited or unsolicited, your letter should include the following four basic parts:

1. **An interesting and appropriate first paragraph**

> The position of secretary described in your advertisement in today's issue of the <u>Charlotte Observer</u> is a challenging opportunity. May I be considered for the position?
>
> Mr. Grant Lehman of your Sales Department suggested that I write to inquire whether you have . . . .
>
> Have you a place in your office for a college graduate who possesses good stenographic skills, who majored in English, and who participated in . . . .
>
> Dr. Martha Hall, Head of the Secretarial Science Department at Eastern State University, tells me that you have a secretarial position open for a college graduate with stenographic and word processing training. Will you please consider me an applicant.

2. **An appraisal of your qualifications as related to the needs of the position—not complete but just enough to convince your reader that he should see you**

> My interest in working in a publications office began in high school where I edited the school newspaper and yearbook. In college I completed a minor in English and journalism along with my secretarial studies. Work on the <u>Review</u>, the college . . . paper, contributed further practical experience.

**3. A statement of sources of additional information on your qualifications**

```
        Additional information on my qualifications can be obtained
by examining my credentials that are on file at the University
Placement Office, 473E Millett, . . . .

        The persons listed as references on the enclosed data sheet
can provide you with additional information on my qualifications.

        A call to Miss Marjorie Church, secretary at the University
Placement Office (277-3480), will provide any further details of
my qualifications that you may desire.
```

**4. A closing ("selling") paragraph suggesting an appointment and definite action**

```
        Because I cannot be called by telephone during business hours,
I shall telephone your office on Friday morning to ask for an
appointment for an interview.

        I should like very much to come to your office to talk with
you about the position.  When I telephone you on Wednesday morn-
ing, will you please let me know a time that would be convenient
for you to see me?
```

**Guides for Writing Application Letters.** There is no one formula for writing an effective application letter, but observance of these eight guides will be of great aid. The "few don'ts" given for preparing data sheets also apply to application letters.

*1. Address Letter to an Individual.* A letter directed "To Whom It May Concern" may never concern anyone. Find out the name and title of the person in charge of employment and use them. This information may be obtained from the switchboard operator of the company. The use of the name (correctly spelled) and title personalizes the letter and makes a favorable first impression.

```
Box H-816
Charlotte Observer
Charlotte, NC   28202

Gentlemen:
```

Obviously you cannot address your letter to an individual when you are replying to a blind advertisement. The correct address form and salutation for such a letter is shown at the left.

*2. Use "You" Approach.* One employment director says that nine tenths of the letters he reads begin with "I want . . ." or "I am interested in . . ." The potential employer feels like saying, "So what?" He wants to know whether you have a service for sale that fits *his* requirements. Your first objective, then, in both the letter and the interview is to show him that you understand the requirements of the position and to demonstrate to him how your qualifications meet his needs. If you adopt this attitude, your problem of enumerating a long list of "I did this" and "I did that" will be solved.

**3. Be Honest and Confident.** Your application letter can show a proper but not overemphasized appreciation of your ability. Above all, be *honest*. Your letter should be neither boastful nor begging. Employers are experts in detecting insincerity. Be specific about the position you want and the things you can do, but do not exaggerate. You may be called upon to prove your claims.

Do not be apologetic. If your experience is limited, you need not call attention to the fact. Concentrate on your positive qualities.

**4. Write an Original Letter.** Study as many effective application letters as possible to get ideas and suggestions, but write your own letter —in your own words and in your natural way of saying things. NEVER copy a letter of application and present it as your own.

**5. Be Brief.** A lot of thinking—but comparatively little writing— should go into an application letter. Remember that a famous letter writer once said, "I wrote a long letter because I didn't have time to write a short one."

If you enclose your personal data sheet, omit in your letter a detailed treatment of your education and experience. Your letter then must be an invitation to read the data sheet. The statement, "I am enclosing information about my training and experience," does little to persuade the reader to continue to your data sheet. Stimulate interest by such statements as, "An examination of my personal data sheet will show that I am well prepared by training and experience for secretarial work," or "My extracurricular activities, described in the enclosed personal data sheet, have prepared me to work with other people."

**6. Make Action Easy.** You are more likely to win an interview by saying, "I shall call you on Friday morning to see if you wish to arrange a personal interview," instead of saying "May I hear from you?" The purpose of the application letter is to get an interview. If you obtain one, your letter has done as much as you can expect it to do.

**7. Give the Letter Eye Appeal.** Make your letter attractive and absolutely faultless in conformity with the best rules of business-letter writing. Anything you say will be worthless if your message contains a typographical error. There must be no flaws in spelling, grammar, punctuation, typing, arrangement, spacing, placement, or wording. You should use a good quality of white bond paper of standard letter size. Your envelope should match the paper in quality. Letterhead paper should not be used, but your complete address (but not name) should be typed in the heading.

**8. Use the Correct Signature.** Four or five lines below the complimentary close, type your name. If you include *Miss*, *Mrs.*, *or Ms.* on the typed line, omit the title when you sign. If you type only your name, write (in parentheses) *Miss, Mrs., or Ms.* at the left of your signature. Use black or blue-black ink.

**9. File a copy of each application letter that you write.**

If you were a personnel officer, would you seriously consider interviewing the writer of the letter at the left?

## THE INTERVIEW

In preparation for the interview, you should go back to the front of this book and reread the discussion of traits requisite for success in secretarial work. The interviewer wants to know whether you have the traits discussed there. Put yourself in his place. What would *you* want to know about the applicant?

Though the time you spend with the interviewer may be short, you will be giving him a volume of information about yourself. He will form opinions based on your general appearance, your voice, diction, posture, attitude, and personality. Your conduct and manner during the interview and the written materials you present to him in your personal data sheet and application blank also tell him a great deal about you.

### Guides to a Successful Interview

Tend toward the conservative side in dress and appearance. Secretaries who hold the top jobs are natural looking, well groomed, and smartly but simply dressed. They shun extremes in hair style, makeup, and dress. Nails should be clean and well manicured. It is a good idea for you to hold a dress rehearsal before going for the interview. Make sure that you are satisfied with your appearance before you leave for the interview.

## A PREINTERVIEW CHECKLIST

Are you properly dressed and groomed for an interview?.............. ☐

Have you gathered all the information you need about the company—its products, its policies, its status in the community?................... ☐

Do you know the interviewer's name? If not, obtain it from the receptionist before the interview.............................................. ☐

Have you mentally formulated answers to the usual factual questions and also to possible unusual questions that the interviewer may ask?..... ☐

Are you prepared for an interview? Be sure to take—

- Your personal data sheet......................................... ☐
- Your Social Security card......................................... ☐
- A complete school record showing "To" and "From" dates........ ☐
- A tabulated summary of your college courses..................... ☐
- A record of your business skills and personal accomplishments (unless included on personal data sheet)....................... ☐
- Letters of reference (Some personnel experts question the value of open letters of recommendation. You may decide to omit them.).. ☐
- List of personal references (unless included on personal data sheet) ☐
- Your employment record, including dates, names, addresses of employers, duties performed, and name of immediate supervisor.... ☐
- List of questions you wish to ask the interviewer.................. ☐
- Your residence addresses for the past several years.............. ☐
- A pen and well-sharpened pencils................................ ☐
- A small notebook for dictation.................................... ☐
- A good pocket-size dictionary.................................... ☐
- An eraser and erasure shield..................................... ☐

Anticipate the questions the interviewer may ask. If you have thought through the possible questions, you will be less likely to be caught off your guard during the interview. So plan your answers to talk not too much nor too little; strive for the happy medium.

A card, a letter, or a note of introduction to someone in the organization is usually helpful. It may be a referral card from your placement office or a note on the back of a personal card, but it puts you in contact with the one you want to see.

Before leaving for the interview, use the preinterview check list at the top of the page to be sure you are well prepared.

**The Application Blank.** You may be asked to complete an application blank before you are interviewed. The application blank is as vital a part of your application as the interview. Many applicants are eliminated entirely on the basis of the way they fill out the application. Therefore, never treat it casually. Read it through carefully before you begin to fill it out.

Application blanks are usually planned with care. Every question on the blank serves a purpose for the interviewer. Although you may be unaware of the motive behind certain questions, answer every question exactly as you are directed and omit nothing. Draw a wavy line, write the word "none," or make some comment in blanks for which you have no answer. Think before writing any answer. Be certain that you write only in the space designed for each answer. Be careful that you follow instructions. For instance, print your name when the instructions tell you to print; put your last name first if you are so requested. The way you fill out the blank reveals far more about you than you realize.

The general neatness of the blank is important. Good handwriting is desirable because there is always need for longhand writing in office work, and no one in any office wants to decipher a scrawly, illegible hand. An application blank to be typed may be a disguised part of the typing test, so it should represent your best work.

**The Interviewer's Method.** The employment director of a company or a member of his staff conducts the preliminary interview. If he is favorably impressed, he sends the applicant to the immediate supervisor of the available position. In talking with applicants, the initial interviewer follows a set pattern:

> He — establishes rapport with the applicant.
>   — indicates who will make the final selection.
>   — reviews the applicant's work-experience record.
>   — asks questions related to the available job.
>   — leads into the closing of the interview.

## INTERVIEW REMINDERS

- Refrain from smoking during an interview.
- Keep your voice well modulated.
- Look directly at the interviewer when speaking or listening.
- Control your nervous actions and maintain good posture.
- Refrain from overtalking or undertalking.
- Be pleasant to everyone you meet in the office.
- At the end of the interview, thank the interviewer for his time and consideration and leave at once. Thank the receptionist also when you leave.

For a successful interview, keep in mind the interview pointers listed on the preceding page.

The interviewer will question you to encourage you to talk. Many of the questions will be routine and, although answered on your personal data sheet, may be asked again merely to put you at ease and to give you an opportunity to express yourself.

Some of the usual questions are:

**What is your education?**

**What is your special training for this work?**

**Do you live at home?  Do you have any dependents?**

**What business experience have you had?  By what firms have you been employed?  Why did you leave them—particularly the last one?**

**Why do you want to work for this company?  (What an opportunity to show that you know something about it!)**

**What salary do you expect?  What do you consider to be your strong points?  weak points?**

**Are you free to travel?**

**How long do you intend to work?**

In addition to these typical questions, the interviewer may include a few that are designed to throw an applicant off his guard and obtain a true picture of his personality.  Some of these questions may seem to be unusual and perhaps personally presumptuous, but they are all part of the interview technique and have a purpose.  Some questions of this nature are listed below.

## HOW WOULD YOU ANSWER THESE QUESTIONS?

1. If you were starting college over again, what courses would you take?
2. Are you engaged?  Do you expect to make a career of business?
3. Do you feel that your extracurricular activities repaid the time devoted to them?
4. How did your previous employer treat you?
5. What have you learned from some of the positions you have held?
6. Did you change your major field of study while in college?  Why?
7. Do you feel you have done the best scholastic work of which you are capable?
8. What special interests do you have?
9. Which of your college years was the most difficult?
10. What types of people seem to "rub you the wrong way"?
11. Do you think that grades should be considered by employers?
12. To what campus organizations do you belong?
13. Do you favor students having a greater voice in administering the colleges and universities?

If you have had business experience, it is quite logical that your previous employment will be a point of discussion in the interview.

You will probably be asked why you left your last position. Be prepared to answer this question and, whatever your reason for leaving, be sure to emphasize positive—not negative factors. Be truthful but brief. It is tactless and unethical for you to say anything detrimental about any former employer or firm for which you have worked, regardless of any personal feelings you may have. Always speak well of former employers. Nothing is gained by doing otherwise.

**The Salary Question.** Salary is always important, but don't pass up an interesting position for one that pays a few dollars a week more. If your work is challenging and interesting, your performance will soon merit a salary increase.

Your college placement office can obtain information about salaries. The Administrative Management Society publishes an annual survey of office salaries, fringe benefits, and working hours. The United States Department of Labor makes an annual occupational wage survey in the larger cities. The survey reports may be obtained from your Regional Office, Bureau of Labor Statistics.

Most large businesses have a salary schedule about which you can become informed before applying for a position. When the salary question comes up in the interview—and it usually does — the best response is "I am willing to start at your scheduled salary for a person with my background."

If, before leaving the interview, you are not told what the salary would be, it would be appropriate to inquire "What would be the starting salary for this position?" If the application blank asks "Salary Desired" and you do not wish to state a salary figure, write "Open" or "Your Schedule" in the space.

**Asking Questions.** An interview is a two-way street, and you will be expected to ask questions. In fact, your failure to do so may be interpreted as indicating a lack of genuine interest on your part. What will be the scope of your work? With whom would you be working? What opportunities will the position provide for advancement? Does the company promote from within? Is there a company training program for self-improvement? These are all thoughtful, intelligent questions that concern you. Questions about working hours, vacation schedules, coffee breaks, and so forth, are appropriate *if* you take care to give the impression that you are more interested in giving than in what you will get. If you are not shown, feel free to ask to see the prospective work station.

**Concluding the Interview.** You will probably know quite definitely when the interview is coming to an end. If the interviewer has shown interest and in any way has encouraged you but has not committed himself definitely about a position, it is permissible to ask directly, "When will your decision be made?" If this does not seem to be a fitting question, you might ask, "May I call back on Friday at two?"

The interviewer may rise, and that will indicate that the interview is at an end. You should rise too and thank the interviewer for his time. Do not offer to shake hands and do not delay when the time has come to depart. Make no attempt to prolong the interview. Leave at once, gracefully, pleasantly, and with dignity. Remember to thank the receptionist as you leave.

## Tests for Selecting Employees

If you have gained favorable consideration, you may be asked to take some form of test. It may be merely a letter or two to ascertain your ability in shorthand and typewriting. It may be a more general test or one designed to detect a wide variety of abilities. The main thing to remember is that you know how to do what is asked and to do it quietly, confidently, and efficiently.

## Evaluation of the Interview

A good practice after the interview is to evaluate your performance.

**Were your answers logical?**
**Did your conversation ramble?**
**Were you completely honest with the interviewer?**
**Were you convincing in your sales approach?**
**Did you keep your eyes directed to the interviewer?**
**Were you always courteous in your replies?**

Each interview can be a valuable learning experience. If you feel you did not make a favorable impression, consider why and begin now on a program of improvement.

Besides evaluating your own behavior, it is important that you decide whether this is the "ideal" job for you. Refer to the section *Evaluating a Company* on page 625 to assist you in your decision.

## Follow-Up of the Interview

If you decide you are interested in the position, a good follow-up letter, arriving within two or three days after the interview, may put your application on top. Include in the follow-up letter additional

Employers have learned that the mature woman, having successfully reared a family and managed a household, possesses the qualities of dependability, perseverance, and a sincere interest in her job.

selling points: qualifications not completely covered in the interview or additional emphasis of your strong points related to the position.

For some reason you may decide not to accept a position that has been offered. Certainly this situation demands a prompt, courteous, and straightforward letter of explanation and appreciation. The day may come when you need the goodwill of that company or person.

## POSTSCRIPT: A WORD TO THE MATURE WOMAN

There is an ever-increasing interest in you, the mature woman who wishes to return to the business office. Where once many employment offices were closed to older women, today employers are expressing favorable attitudes toward hiring them. Employers find that the mature woman is reliable, is less likely to leave their employ, has strong and permanent motives for working, and is able to work efficiently despite many distractions. In fact, many business firms are beginning to court the mature worker. One company in Cleveland, for example, is actually moving from its downtown location to the suburbs just to get nearer the market of suburban housewives.

The mature woman, like her younger counterpart, must formulate a plan of action. For all returning female workers, there are at least two stages in the plan—and for some women there are three. Stage One is the time of preparation, rebuilding confidence and competencies. Stage Two involves a survey of the job opportunities in the community for the mature worker. Stage three, the final one, is that of action, writing the personal data sheet and application letters and appearing for interviews. After completing Stage One, many women bypass Stage Two by going directly to an employment agency or a temporary service agency. In any event, all returning workers will be concerned with Stages One and Three.

## Stage One: The Preparation

The returning office worker uses this period to prepare her mind as well as her skills. She builds confidence in her ability as she rebuilds her office skills. She comes to grips with her reason for returning to work. If married, she wins the consent and support of her husband and the cooperation of any children still living at home. She takes an inventory of her strengths and weaknesses and decides, to some extent, on the type of office work that will suit her interests and abilities.

In the area of office skills, the mature woman invariably considers herself "rusty." She may also be aware that she is uninformed regarding the changes in business technology. Therefore, several months before seeking employment, she initiates a program of rebuilding her skills, either "on her own" or in a skill-refresher course. To update herself in the field of business, she may interview a secretary on the job, consult the various professional business and office magazines, or discuss the subject with a business educator.

## Stage Two: The Survey

Before beginning her search for employment, the mature woman needs to know the hiring practices of the large companies in her community. Is there an age barrier in initial employment? What types of offices hire returning workers? In most communities it is the small office—real estate, law, professional—or a branch office of a large company that employs mature female workers.

The survey of employment opportunities may very well include the temporary service agencies and others who require part-time workers. These avenues may lead to eventual full-time employment, while providing the means for rebuilding office knowledges and skills.

| Personal Data Sheet and Application Letter | Application Blank | Interview |
|---|---|---|
| Omit mention of age. There is no reason to mention it at this point.<br><br>List all your work experience, both paid and volunteer.<br><br>List your main interests. | If the blank provides for inserting your age, use your correct age, without embarrassment.<br><br>Complete the application blank with care. | Be completely honest about your reasons for wanting to return to work. Women have many valid reasons. Be prepared to answer this question.<br><br>Be prepared also to answer the typical questions asked in an interview. (See page 638.) |

In the mature woman's action plan, Stage Three itself has three steps. They are shown in the tables above.

### Stage Three: Action

At this stage comes the preparation of a personal data sheet and letters of application. If the suggestions offered earlier on these topics are observed, it is quite likely that appointments for interviews will follow. The mature woman may also want to observe the points made in the tables above.

Finally, don't be in a hurry to accept your first job offer. Evaluate each company and position in terms of your own goals and interests. Accepting an interim job may prevent your later accepting the very job that you were seeking.

The next interview just might be that *right* position for you.

AN OLDER woman didn't get a job because she gave her correct age on an application blank. The next time she was confronted with the question, she wrote: "I refuse to answer on the grounds that it might eliminate me."

## SUGGESTED READINGS

Albee, Lou. *Over 40—Out of Work?* Englewood Cliffs: Prentice-Hall, Inc., 1970.

Becker, Esther R., and Peggy Norton Rollason. *The High-Paid Secretary*. Englewood Cliffs: Prentice-Hall, Inc., 1967.

Butler, E. A. *Move In and Move Up*. New York: Macmillan Co., 1970, pp. 15–30 (personal data sheets).

King, Alice Gore. *Help Wanted: Female, The Young Woman's Guide to Job Hunting*. New York: Charles Scribner's Sons, 1968.

Pogrebin, Letty Cottin. *How to Make It in a Man's World*. New York: Doubleday & Co., 1970.

Winter, Elmer L. *Women at Work, Every Woman's Guide to Successful Employment*. New York: Simon and Schuster, 1967.

1. In some instances, large offices pay a beginning salary lower than that of smaller offices. In such cases, the fringe benefits offered employees in the large company are emphasized. What fringe benefits are offered that would be of value to the secretary with the following plans?

   **(a) To work only a few years until marriage**
   **(b) To work only to obtain money to continue her education**
   **(c) To make a career in business**

2. After carefully considering your training, interests, and special aptitudes, would you choose a specialization in the secretarial field (for example, legal, medical, technical, or educational)? If so, give the reasons for your choice.

3. In seeking your first position, what factors would be important to you in evaluating a company? How would you get the necessary information?

4. What circumstances would make it desirable for a secretarial applicant to register with a private employment agency?

5. Assume that you are considering a foreign-service assignment with the Department of State. Evaluate your interests, training, and experience for such an assignment.

6. After sending out a number of unsolicited letters of application, you are called for an interview. At that time you will be given shorthand, typing, and spelling tests. How would you prepare for this testing situation?

7. Some authorities say that references should not be listed on the personal data sheet, but a statement such as "References available upon request" should be included. What reasons, if any, are there for not including the references? Do you favor taking letters of reference to an interview?

8. The following introductory paragraph was used in a letter of application. What is your criticism of the paragraph? How would you suggest it be restated?

   "I have been looking for some time for a secretarial position similar to the one described in your advertisement in the paper, and I believe that I may have found just the opening that I have been searching for. You may consider this letter an application for the position."

9. Some applicants resent certain questions asked in interviews. They consider the questions to be prying into their personal affairs and to be irrelevant to their application. What would be your answers to such questions as:

   "Are you engaged?" "Do you have any debts?" "How do you usually spend Sundays?" "Do you use liquor or drugs?" "How do you feel about your family?" "Have you taken part in campus demonstrations?"

10. A highly qualified job counselor recommends that if, at the time of the interview, you are offered the position, you should ask for time to think it over—even though you definitely plan to accept. The delay is suggested so that the company will not think you make hasty decisions. Do you agree? Why?

**11.** Is it ethical to accept, without advising your potential employer, a position which he considers to be permanent but which you consider to be temporary, such as a position for the summer only, a position you intend to keep only until another position comes along, or a position to gain experience to qualify for a position in another company?

**12.** A compound word may be written as a solid word, joined with a hyphen, or written as individual words. Explain why the following groups of words are written as shown. Then consult the Reference Guide to verify or correct your answers.

    **(a)** shell-like, heel-less, re-employ, pre-establish
    **(b)** twenty-five, eighty-four, one-fourth, fifty-five
    **(c)** re-collect, re-form, fruit-less diet, re-count
    **(d)** S-curve, X-ray, U-turn, T-square, H-bomb
    **(e)** a make-believe plan, a two-hour session, a well-known enemy
    **(f)** ex-President, pre-Easter, semi-Dutch, anti-Freudian

**13.** Show which words you would capitalize in the following sentences. Then use the Reference Guide to verify or correct your answers.

    **(a)** I am sorry that I have not studied biology, chemistry, or physics; perhaps I can take a night course in one of them.
    **(b)** I received straight A's in secretarial practice and also in human relations in business.
    **(c)** I majored in languages: french, german, russian, and spanish.

## PROBLEMS

■ **1.** Assume that you are seeking a position as a secretary and you decide to reply to the following newspaper advertisement:

### WANTED: SECRETARY

For prestige company. Must type 60 WAM, take shorthand 100 WAM. Good telephone personality, ability to meet people. Send personal data sheet to Box 1853, *Times*.

Prepare a data sheet for your qualifications and a covering application letter.

■ **2.** Suggest situations in which each of the following experiences would be an asset in getting a position as secretary:

**(a)** Treasurer of student government
**(b)** Camp counselor in summers
**(c)** Beauty queen in college
**(d)** Salutatorian of high school class
**(e)** Checker at chain grocery
**(f)** Sunday School teacher
**(g)** Reared on a farm
**(h)** President of college club of secretarial students
**(i)** Summer in Europe
**(j)** Waitress in summer resort
**(k)** Editor of high school annual
**(l)** Major in chemistry
**(m)** Phi Beta Kappa
**(n)** Part-time worker in registrar's office
**(o)** Member of social sorority
**(p)** Voted "most original" by senior class
**(q)** Advertising manager of college newspaper
**(r)** Sales clerk in department store
**(s)** Member of glee club
**(t)** Member of production staff of Little Theater
**(u)** College champion in women's tennis singles

*due Fri.*

■ 3. Assume that you are applying for a specific position and are asked the following questions. Type your replies on a sheet of paper. In preparing your answers, try to analyze the motive behind the question.

(a) Why do you want to work for this company?
(b) What skills do you have?
(c) What salary do you expect?
(d) Do you intend to stay in the position permanently?
(e) Are you engaged?
(f) What hobbies interest you?
(g) What books have you read in the past three months that interested you?

(h) How much will your living expenses be?
(i) What experience have you had?
(j) What kind of grades did you make in college?

■ 4. Just before completing your secretarial training, you decide to survey the secretarial openings in your community by sending out a number of unsolicited letters of application. Using your own data and the names of local companies, prepare the letter, making sure that it is appropriate for each of the companies.

# Chapter 27

## PLANNING FOR A PROFESSIONAL FUTURE

Today, the woman office worker has more opportunity for professional advancement than ever before. The old myths and folklore regarding women in management positions are slowly being dispelled. Further, federal legislation barring discrimination by sex in employment assures women of acceptance in the man's business world. Although a recent New York survey shows that relatively few women hold top-level management jobs (of 100 major corporations 3.8 percent of management posts and 4.7 percent of professional jobs are held by women), some corporate giants, such as General Electric, Polaroid, and IBM, are undertaking specific measures to insure the professional advancement of women.

Statistics tell us that the average American woman will be active in the labor market for at least 25 years. Obviously, then, as you begin your career as a college-trained secretary, you should be concerned about your ability to go forward. You will want to move up in the business world; to do so, you must excel in every aspect of your job. Beginning with your first position, develop and follow a *Success Formula*.

## THE SUCCESS FORMULA

Prescriptions for success in business are as varied and legion as are the types of successful executives. If you are to succeed, you will have to develop your own formula. There are, however, certain basic rules that may help you to succeed in each position you hold and to gain professional status in business. These rules do not differ greatly from those that applied to your college program. Briefly stated they are:

1. **Get off to a good start.**
2. **Learn all you can about the company, the people with whom you work, and the requirements of your position.**
3. **Plan and systematize your work.**
4. **Display initiative.**
5. **Accept responsibility willingly.**
6. **Maintain a wholesome, positive attitude.**
7. **Continue to grow professionally.**

## Making a Good Start

Some companies have a well-planned program for inducting new employees into their positions. If you obtain a position in such a firm, someone will be assigned to welcome you, introduce you to your colleagues, show you your work area, perhaps take you to lunch, tell you something of the history of the organization, possibly show you a movie about your new company, and provide you with booklets describing company policies and benefits.

Many companies, however, have no organized induction program. If you are fortunate, the secretary whose place you are taking will remain on the job for a few days to train you. In many cases, though, you will report to an executive whose secretary has already left, and you sink or swim alone.

**First Impressions.** Everyone in the office will form first impressions of you, just as you will of them. The very same things you considered important when you made your application for the position will continue to be important as you try to succeed on the job. Because you were hired, you can assume that you made a satisfactory first impression on your employer. Now you must make a satisfactory first impression on those with whom you work — and strive to make this impression a permanent one.

You will be under critical and detailed inspection that first day. Your dress, your grooming, and everything you do and say will be observed. At this point, exercise good judgment by first being an attentive *listener*. It is a human trait to be defensive toward an outsider or a newcomer until that person wins one's goodwill and approval. Don't be disconcerted by this; if you understand it, you will be encouraged to make your associates like and accept you. Remember that their approval is most important to your future welfare and your happiness.

Begin your first day on time, allowing plenty of time for the things that Fate seems to have in store for that first trip to a new job! Being even a few minutes late will require an explanation to your employer, a situation that you will find uncomfortable.

**Learning Names.** Certainly one way to create a good first impression is to learn promptly and pronounce correctly the names of those with whom you work. Associate the name with a mental picture of the person, as you are introduced or as soon as possible. An effective plan is to write the name and practice pronouncing it. Then address the person by name at every appropriate occasion. Drawing a floor plan showing the location of the desks and the names of their occupants will help you through that first week.

**Observing Ground Rules.** New employees are expected to learn quickly the company's regulations relative to rest periods, lunch hours, personal telephone calls, coffee breaks, smoking, and other similar activities. Some of these rules may be in writing; others will have been established by custom but are nonetheless binding. One of the surest ways to get off to a poor start is to be a rule breaker. Ignorance is a poor excuse. The only safe policy is to find out the rules and customs of the office and observe them.

**Office Friends.** Every office with several employees (some say more than *two*!) has its cliques. You will want to move slowly in identifying yourself with one particular group. And you will want to be especially wary of office gossips. The secretary who has friends throughout the company and who varies lunch dates to include people from all departments and from other companies is not only popular but is also better able to serve her employer.

Friendliness should extend to all employment levels — the goodwill of the office messenger, the custodian, and the duplicating machine operator is important to your success.

## Learning About the Company

From the first moment, your overall program will be to learn as much as you can, about everything you can, as soon as you can.

In some companies a job analysis, job description, or job specifications for your new position will be available in a company manual and will give you an idea of the scope of your duties. To serve your employer effectively, you need to learn about the organization quickly so that you can interpret his wishes and carry out his directions without distracting him with requests for elementary information.

Learn as quickly as possible the names of customers, the names of your employer's close associates, his most frequently used telephone numbers, his most frequently used phrases in dictation, and the technical language of the company. The more you know and the more ready you are with the information, the quicker you will become valuable to your employer and the organization.

## Company Manuals

Most organizations have one or more company manuals or instruction sheets for office routine. A general office manual will usually explain the organization of the company, the relationships of the various offices and departments, the general rules and regulations, and information that affects all employees — the date and method of distributing paychecks, descriptions of company benefits, and a list of the holidays observed by the company. Some manuals give directions for the work of all departments (or merely one department); others are procedural manuals for initiating and completing specific activities of the company.

Operating manuals are often available for the various machines and equipment in the office, and most large companies have style manuals or other forms of direction for setting up correspondence and company forms. If your office has such a manual, spend many of your spare moments studying and thoroughly digesting everything that has a bearing on your work — almost to the point of memorization.

**The Office Files.** The office files offer a wealth of information to the new secretary. Previous correspondence, incoming and outgoing, will indicate the type of correspondence you can expect and will also be an excellent source of terminology and technical language. As you look through the files, list the terms with which you are unfamiliar. Note your employer's letter-writing style, his proper title, and where and how to file letters and records. Become familiar with the various forms and types of stationery of the company.

**Other Sources of Information.** Special types of records are often available to the secretary: scrapbooks or collections of clippings about the executive, the company, or its products are sources of background information. Many organizations publish a periodical (known as a *house organ*) written by and about its employees. Back issues of these will tell you a great deal, as will journals of the particular industry.

One way to determine the actual scope of your position is to acquaint yourself with the duties of other company employees. Seeing how your job relates to theirs will help you understand not only your own job but also the total functions of the office.

**Questions.** Of course you must ask questions; but make them few and make them count. There are two kinds of questions: *Learning* questions help you find out things you need to know; they are excellent questions. *Leaning* questions are those about something you really should know or could research for yourself; they are the kind that you should avoid.

There is a time and place for questioning. During the first few days of your work, whenever possible, accumulate your problems and questions by making notes, and ask them all at a logical time in one session with the executive or with your temporary mentor. As you compile your list, however, be sure that it does not include a problem that you could have solved for yourself.

The other employees will usually be helpful in answering questions, but you must remember that they have full-time work to do themselves. Sometime later you will probably have an opportunity to repay those who have helped you by returning the favor when they need extra help.

## Planning Your Work

Useful tools in organizing and scheduling your work are the tickler and pending files, desk reference manuals or files, and the chronological file. (See Chapter 2.) Learn the office time schedule concerning mail deliveries, regular meetings attended by your employer, and peak work-load periods. Establish a calendar of known future appointments, meetings, events, and deadlines. Before you can determine an efficient routine for performing your job, you must distinguish between priority and routine tasks.

You will not learn all you need to know the first day on the job; but as you become familiar with your duties, you will be able to schedule and systematize your work effectively.

**The Secretary's Desk Manual.** Every secretary needs her own secretarial desk manual — a loose-leaf notebook in which she has compiled company information and detailed instructions on the correct procedure for handling the duties peculiar to her desk. Not only is such a manual a real time-saver, but it is a real help to the executive in training a new or a temporary secretary — for in it can be found the answers to most of the questions that he would ordinarily be asked.

```
                    DATES TO REMEMBER

    Mr. Roskamp's Family

        Birthdays

            Mr. Roskamp - August 14, 1934
            Mrs. Roskamp - September 20, 1938
            Peter, Jr. - April 9, 1964
            Beverly - April 11, 1967
            Gordon - March 30, 1969
            Mr. Roskamp's mother - June 25, 1914

        Wedding Anniversaries

            Mr. and Mrs. Roskamp - June 17, 1962
            Mr. Roskamp's parents - June 25, 1932
            Mrs. Roskamp's parents - September 29, 1930

    Mr. Roskamp's starting date with company - August 1,
    1957

    My starting date with company - June 20, 1970

    Mr. Roskamp's annual reunion with college friends -
    third weekend in May
```

A page of a typical secretarial desk manual is shown here. It contains dates significant to the executive and the secretary.

Build your desk manual as you acquire the necessary information. You can start some sections, such as correct letter form and mailing procedures, immediately. Accumulating others will require time and experience. You may want to prepare a breakdown of your duties by time periods: daily, weekly, monthly, and annually. If you are always busy during the day, take the time to do the bulk of the preparation after office hours. The first draft will be the most time consuming: once written and thoughtfully indexed, the manual can be updated quickly and easily.

*Company Information.* Undoubtedly one of the first sections of the manual will consist of pertinent company information. If your employer is a supervisor or an executive of a large company, include an organizational chart showing the lines of authority and the person in each executive and supervisory position. In addition, the following information should be helpful to the secretary new on the job:

Addresses and telephone numbers of branch offices and subsidiaries

Names and titles of supervisory personnel at branch offices and subsidiaries

Company rules and regulations—hours of work, lunch hour, coffee breaks, and the like

Company policies (vacations, sick leave, insurance, and other fringe benefits) in summary form

Telephone numbers of specific office services

*Who's Who Directory.* Another section of the manual will likely be a directory of the persons with whom the executive has frequent contacts. Individual circumstances will determine whether to subdivide into *in-company* and *outside* listings. At any rate, the list should include:

1. Those with whom he frequently corresponds
2. Those with whom he frequently talks on the telephone
3. Frequent office visitors
4. His professional or service people (his attorney, doctor, broker, automobile serviceman, etc.)

To build up the set of names for the directory, jot down each one as it comes to your attention. Then prepare a card for each name, listing the following information:

1. The correct name of the person
2. The name and address of his company or organization
3. The telephone number (area code, extension number)
4. The salutation and complimentary close for correspondence, if not standard
5. The way the executive signs his name, if other than the usual way
6. The identity of the person in relationship to the executive (such as relative, school friend, attorney)

There are always a few favored correspondents with whom the executive uses more friendly and intimate forms of salutations and closings. To know who is so treated and what forms to use is of real help to anyone unfamiliar with handling the executive's dictation. A person customarily addressed "Dear Charles" or "Dear C. J." does not relish receiving the formal salutation, "Dear Mr. Giles."

To be of the most use, the manual should include generous cross references of affiliations and identifications. For example, if you have Mr. Ericson's name as sales manager of Acme Metal Company and

Mr. Curry's name as advertising manager of the same company, make up a cross-reference slip for Acme Metal Company and list on it the address of the company, and the names of Mr. Ericson, Mr. Curry, and any others in that company with whom the executive has contacts.

Likewise, if Mr. Robert Nolan is the executive's attorney, make out a slip for "Mr. Robert Nolan, Attorney," and a cross-reference slip headed "Attorney, Mr. Robert Nolan."

When all the name and cross-reference cards have been made out, sort them alphabetically. Type the names and cross-references on the loose-leaf pages. For any letters that frequently begin names, leave a full page. Insert the pages, with an appropriately tabbed divider page, into the manual. Later, type and paste or staple any change of address over the permanent entry until time permits retyping the page. (Some secretaries prefer a card file or small Rol-Dex file.)

*Clients and Projects Directory.* When the executive is a professional man with a succession of important clients, customers, projects, or jobs, a special section in the manual is necessary. Provide a page for each person or project, listing such information as the title of the job, the work to be performed, pertinent data, terms, and special procedures that the secretary must follow. A list of all persons importantly connected with the job is also helpful. Here too, cross-referencing should be freely used.

*Procedures Sections.* Provide topical sections in the manual explaining how to handle various secretarial duties. The outline on pages 654 and 655 covers some of the routine duties common to secretarial positions. Add sections as they become necessary.

*Personal Data Section.* In addition to the major items that comprise the basic desk manual, many secretaries add a personal section. This section contains the unusual reminders — dates and events of special significance to her executive and any personal information known by the secretary, such as:

**Biography of employer or a complete listing of educational achievements, employment records, awards, and community services**

**Birthdays and anniversaries of certain people in the company and in the employer's family**

**Important numbers—Social Security, passport, and credit cards**

**Insurance policies—numbers, amounts, and payment dates (unless already in an insurance register)**

**Memberships in professional and civic organizations—offices held, meeting dates, dues, committee assignments, and so on**

TOPIC OUTLINE FOR A DESK MANUAL

I. CORRESPONDENCE

    A. Procedure for handling:
       1. Incoming mail
          a. Model interoffice memorandum form
          b. Number and distribution of copies
       2. Outgoing mail
          a. Model letter form(s)
          b. Number and distribution of copies
          c. Postage (procedure for obtaining)
    B. Mail schedules

II. DIRECTORY (For information, refer to pages 652-653 of this book.)

III. FILING

    A. Centralized filing system
       1. Materials that go to centralized file
       2. Procedure for release of materials for filing
       3. Procedure for obtaining materials from filing
    B. Secretary's file (full explanation of filing system)
    C. Transfer and storage policies

IV. FINANCIAL DUTIES

    A. Bank account
       1. Procedure for making deposits
       2. Procedure for reconciling the bank statement
       3. Disposition of canceled checks and bank statements
       4. Location of bankbook and checkbook
    B. Payments of recurring expenses like membership dues and miscellaneous fees
       1. Dates of payments
       2. Procedures for payments
    C. Petty cash
       1. Location of fund
       2. Regulations covering expenditures from fund
       3. Filing of receipts
       4. Procedure for replenishing fund

V. LEGAL FORMS

    A. Models of all forms regularly used
    B. Instructions for completing
    C. Number and distribution of copies
    D. Name and address of notary public to be used

VI.   OFFICE MACHINES

    A.   Inventory (serial numbers and purchase date of all
        machines
    B.   Repair services (service contracts, name and telephone
        number of each serviceman)

VII.  SUPPLIES

    A.   List of supplies to be stocked
       1.   Quantities of each to be ordered
       2.   Names and addresses (or telephone numbers) of
          suppliers
    B.   Procedure for obtaining supplies
    C.   Procedure for controlling supplies

VIII. SUBSCRIPTIONS TO PUBLICATIONS

    A.   Names, number of copies, renewal dates
    B.   Procedure for renewal
    C.   Routing of publications in office

IX.   PUBLIC RELATIONS

    A.   News releases
    B.   Announcements
    C.   Personal data sheet for executive

X.    TELEPHONE PROCEDURES

    A.   Placing a toll call
    B.   Recording toll charges
    C.   Accepting collect calls
    D.   WATS lines
    E.   Leased lines
    F.   Conference calls

XI.   TELEGRAMS

    A.   Model telegram
    B.   Number and distribution of copies
    C.   Procedure for sending
    D.   Procedure for recording charges

XII.  TRAVEL

    A.   Notes on employer's travel and hotel preferences
    B.   Names and telephone numbers of persons in travel agency
        or airlines office
    C.   Location of timetables
    D.   Model itinerary
    E.   Method of ticket pickup
    F.   Expense report form
       1.   Number and distribution of copies
       2.   Receipts required

Bob Stagg, Augusta plant engineer, was recently named "Executive of the Year" by the North Augusta, (South Carolina) Chapter of the National Secretaries Association.

Bob was chosen from 52 other executives who were recommended for the honor by their secretaries.

Secretary Bev Jones Cummings nominated her boss for numerous reasons, including his ability to develop the potential of those on his team and his efforts to encourage his subordinates to make decisions and accept responsibility.

A major point in her recommendation was Bob's positive attitude towards change. "Unlike some," said Bev, "he doesn't shrink from change. Unlike others, he doesn't sit there and let it creep up on him. Instead, he takes the initiative and . . . looks for a better way of doing things."

In the photo on the left, Bob is shown accepting his "Executive of the Year" trophy from Bev.

— Moonbeams, *published by the Procter & Gamble Company, September, 1972.*

## Displaying Initiative

A sure clue to a superior secretary is the initiative that she displays in her job. In the beginning you are, of course, expected to adapt to the established procedures; however, as you become more familiar with the office operations and your employer's work, you can begin to make more independent decisions.

From the first day on the job, react to everything around you. Listen and make mental notes of information that you may need later. Learn to anticipate your employer's requirements. Perceive what needs to be done, and do it without being told. Soon experience will enable you to devise more efficient methods for certain tasks, to make decisions on your own, and to be more creative on the job. A display of initiative on the job is an excellent recommendation for a promotion.

## Accepting Responsibility

A myth about female office workers is that they do not want additional responsibility. In some cases, of course, this may be true of men *or* women. Many women, however, recognize that accepting responsibility and doing so willingly is a prerequisite for getting ahead.

As you refine your performance on the job and thus increase your work output, your employer naturally will turn to you for additional help. It may be work of a personal nature that you feel is not a part of your job. This, however, is far from the truth. By taking care of his personal files and correspondence and by assisting him with his outside activities, you leave his time available for vital company business.

If your employer asks you to do a project that you consider to be beyond your ability, regard it as a sign of his confidence in you. An executive is not likely to give a secretary a project that he knows she cannot handle. Therefore, accept the assignment graciously, think it through, and then begin to work on it.

Accept graciously, also, a request that you work overtime to complete an important matter. This something "extra" is appreciated and generally remembered. Another secretary in the office may ask your help with some assigned work. If you have the time, work with her. Besides building a spirit of cooperation, you may learn something useful.

For the secretary who desires to succeed, it is important that she work willingly with her employer and strive to relieve him of as many business details as possible.

## Maintaining a Positive Attitude

On occasion, a secretary may become disgruntled, unhappy, or discouraged with her job. Although a natural tendency is to display such feelings, it is extremely important to maintain a wholesome, positive attitude toward your employer, your company, your fellow employees, and yourself.

An example of such a situation might have to do with the prospect of change. Human nature seems to resist change, and the secretary faces changes in her job more today than ever before. Changes involving personnel, machines, company policy, and procedures are commonplace; thus, you must remain flexible in your thinking and adapt to the changes being made. Let your acceptance serve as an example to your colleagues and subordinates. A secretary who is positive in her thinking is a trusted member of the boss-secretary team.

## Growing Professionally

The business world makes heavy demands on those who would get ahead. Only those who believe, with sustained dedication, in what they are doing can meet the demands. Your attitude toward your work and your point of view come from within yourself, but you will have a difficult time keeping others from discovering them and mentally labeling you accordingly.

The certified professional secretary represents the highest standards of her field.

— *National Secretaries Association*

Your activities while you are in your initial position will determine your development toward professional status. You will need to learn all that you can while you are in the office, but you can also make your out-of-office activities contribute to your growth.

Certification programs for areas of secretarial specialization — medicine, law, and education — are offered through the professional organizations in these fields. The certification programs of the American Association of Medical Assistants, Inc., the National Association of Legal Secretaries (International), and the National Association of Educational Secretaries were described in Chapter 26. Secretaries who do not choose to specialize, however, can work toward becoming a *Certified Professional Secretary*.

In addition, management training programs are becoming available to the secretary. A secretary who advances to a management position may wish to take the examination for the Certified Administrative Manager certificate. (See page 660.)

**Certified Professional Secretary.** A certified professional secretary (CPS) is one who has successfully passed an examination administered by the Institute for Certifying Secretaries of the National Secretaries Association (International). She holds a Certified Professional Secretary Certificate indicating her accomplishment.

The certificate is the sign of achievement of the profession. It indicates that the secretary has a wide background in the field of business that may qualify her for promotion to management. Many employers (among them Philco-Ford, Montgomery Ward, Union Carbide, and branches of the federal government) provide programs geared toward CPS certification.

The CPS examination is divided into six sections: Environmental Relationships, Business and Public Policy, Economics of Management, Financial Analysis and the Mathematics of Business, Communications and Decision Making, and Office Procedures. The two-day examination is given only once each year in May in the over one hundred testing centers in the United States, Canada, and Puerto Rico.

The examination is open to both men and women, and membership in NSA is not required. There are certain educational and experience requirements, but it is possible to take the examination before meeting the secretarial experience requirements. (A student planning to graduate by August 31 of a given calendar year can take the CPS examination in May of that year. Those who graduate after August 31 must wait until the following year; however, to meet eligibility requirements, they must take the exam within 12 months of receipt of the diploma or degree.)

*Candidates with Previous Work Experience.* Secretaries with work experience must meet *one* of the following sets of requirements:

1. High school graduation or equivalent, plus a minium of three years' secretarial experience (one of which must have been a continuous 12-month period with one employer and within the past five years). All experience must have been within the past 25 years. For each year of high school not completed, two additional years of secretarial experience can be substituted.
2. Two years of post-high-school formal education, plus a minimum of two years of verified secretarial experience (one of which must have been a continuous 12-month period with one employer and within the past five years). All experience must have been within the past 25 years.
3. College degree plus 12 months' cumulative secretarial experience within the past five years.

Candidates meeting one set of these requirements and passing all six parts of the examination are issued the CPS certificate.

*Candidates Without Previous Work Experience.* Candidates who take and pass the examination before acquiring work experience must meet *one* of the following sets of requirements:

1. Two-year certificate, diploma, or an associate degree from an accredited school of business, two-year college, technical institute, or four-year college; then two complete years of secretarial experience.
2. Baccalaureate or advanced degree; then one complete year of secretarial experience.

Candidates who have met one set of these requirements and have passed the six parts of the examination are issued the CPS certificate. To prepare for the examination, obtain a study outline and bibliography, at no cost, by writing the Institute for Certifying Secretaries at 616 East 63d Street, Kansas City, Missouri 64110. You should plan now to include the coveted CPS rating in your professional development program.

**Associations.** You are urged to join professional organizations such as the National Secretaries Association (International), The Business and Professional Women's Clubs, and, if you are eligible, the American Association of University Women. Depending upon the nature of your employment, you may wish to affiliate with one of the following organizations:

**American Association of Medical Assistants, Inc.**
**Association of Desk and Derrick Clubs of North America (Oil)**
**National Association of Bank-Women Inc.**
**National Association of Educational Secretaries**
**National Association of Legal Secretaries**

As you advance up the business ladder, you may become eligible to join the Administrative Management Society, the Altrusa International, Soroptimist Club, or Zonta International.

If you are not a joiner, you can, of course, derive many of the same benefits from self-directed reading and study.

**Seminars for Secretaries.** Several professional organizations offer seminars for women in business. The local chapters of the National Secretaries Association (International) conduct workshops and seminars for secretaries. The Dartnell Institute of Management sponsors a series of secretarial training seminars in major U.S. cities. The Administrative Management Society and the American Management Association also offer seminars for women. Many companies have sent secretaries to these workshop seminars. Generally, however, the individual secretary must request from her employer the financial support to attend these programs.

**Management Training Programs.** Large businesses offer management training programs, and women are invited to participate in such programs more often than in the past. Many women executives have taken this route to the executive suite. At Montgomery Ward, for example, qualified women are eligible for all management training programs.

To be considered, the college-trained secretary must prove herself in each and every secretarial position, and must make known her commitment to the job, which means her job comes first — before social life, vacations, and just about everything.

**Certified Administrative Manager.** The secretary who advances to a management position can apply for a Certified Administrative Manager (CAM) certificate. The Administrative Management Society, an international organization, sponsors the CAM program. Candidates must pass a five-part examination on personnel management; financial management, control and economics; administrative services; systems and information management; and an in-depth case-study analysis. The examination is given twice each year.

Complete information about eligibility can be obtained from the Administrative Management Society, Director of Professionalization, Administrative Management Society Headquarters, Willow Grove, Pennsylvania 19090.


## AN ADDENDUM

All aspects of being a professional secretary do not necessarily come within the purview of the Success Formula. The secretary will want to utilize additional avenues on her way to the top. At all times, she must *work* to get ahead. She must acknowledge that she is no more important than her employer. Knowing this, she must promote him and identify herself with management and management concepts. The line between what is personal and what is business related may be difficult to distinguish. The secretary must not lose sight of this nor — in her desire for recognition — forsake her loyalty to her boss and her company.

### Work to Get Ahead

As stated earlier, the secretarial profession is exactly what you make it. If you stay in your own little niche, doing only the work that has been assigned to you, you are likely to remain in the same position and at about the same salary indefinitely. Advancement is very much up to you. Each time you find a way to free your employer of some task, you will become more valuable. Each time you assume a new responsibility and prove yourself equal to the task, you will be better qualified for that coveted advancement.

This statement does not mean that you barge in before you are sure or that you muscle in or infringe on the work of your co-workers—a sure way to insure your being thoroughly disliked—but it does mean that if you expect to get ahead, you must be a "self-starter," alert to opportunities to prove your value by assuming more responsibility.

In your rush to get ahead, don't overlook the fact that there are no substitutes for competence and confidence. Competence comes at a high price—a price paid in hard work, study, and dedication. A capacity for growth must be coupled with the self-discipline necessary to carry out a sustained effort toward growing with a job. Confidence is not only what you believe you can do, but also what others believe. If those up the ladder get the impression that you are striving for their jobs or standing on their shoulders in your climb, you will have destroyed the first rung on the ladder of advancement.

Build an impressive record of service to your employer and to others. Continue to promote your own individuality by maintaining a wholesome balance between business and social life, by developing interests and hobbies, and by cultivating friendships. Be well informed on the topics that interest you. Most of all, be *yourself* during each work day. A highly respected woman bank president who started as a secretary has this advice: "You reach the executive suite by the road called Hard Work, a trail often littered with carbon paper and typewriter ribbons. Prove your worth, and someone in the organization will discover you."

## Promote Your Boss

The more important your employer appears in the eyes of others — his boss, his customers or clients, his friends — the more important you appear too. Here are some suggestions to follow.

1. **Keep your executive's personal data sheet up to date. Many executives have a prepared data sheet which they may submit when applying for membership in a professional organization or when supplying a biographical sketch prior to a speech or publication. This sheet needs to be updated regularly.**

2. **Watch the newspaper and magazines for press notices that mention your executive. See that they are clipped, identified, and filed. They can be rubbercemented into a scrapbook. Many men are too modest to handle or supervise such a task, so the secretary should take the initiative. If the executive is very much in the public eye, he may subscribe to a clipping service. Incidentally, posting clippings about your executive on the bulletin board is one way of letting everyone in the office know that your boss, too, is important.**

3. **Keep his committee folders in good order and up to date. When he rushes off to a meeting, he will present a good image in the eyes of the other committee members.**

4. **Watch the news for items concerning your executive's business associates and friends. When they are honored or promoted, draft a letter of congratulations for your executive's signature and give it to him with the clipping.**

5. **Look for news reports about new firms or plants that might be potential customers. Your executive will be watching for these items also, but it does no harm for you to say "Did you happen to see this in yesterday's paper?"**

As a secretary, however, do not forget that there is no better way to promote the image of your employer than to see that all work going out of his office is flawless and is turned out with dispatch. Mistakes, delays, and sloppiness can type a man as well as his secretary.

The secretary who relieves her executive of routine tasks and who is alert to opportunities to prove her value as an assistant qualifies as a logical choice for an administrative opening.

## Identify Yourself with Management

The position of secretary to a major official of the business is not one that you step into or inherit because you have completed a college program or degree. These positions must be earned and are usually filled from the inside. Therefore, you will probably start on a lower level, but your goal is eventually to associate yourself with top management.

To work effectively on this level, the secretary must develop the ability to look at problems from the management point of view. This trait requires an orientation into management thinking through reading the same magazines that management reads, such as *Fortune*, *Nation's Business*, *Business Week*, *Wall Street Journal*, *Forbes*, *The Office*, *Administrative Management*, and others; through becoming concerned with management problems; and through studying management books and taking management courses, if available.

The emphasis of much of your secretarial training has been on following instructions, observing directives, carrying through on decisions that have been made, and assuming the initiative in a relatively narrow range of operation only. The management point of view, however, involves determining courses of action, making decisions, giving directions, and delegating authority and responsibility. To shift to the management outlook, the secretary must view problems basically from the "other side of the desk." This transition requires a carefully planned program of self-education, orientation, and discipline.

You will need to grow every day of your working life. If the time comes when you cannot keep up with your employer, he will probably begin to look for a secretary who can. If you continue to grow with the executive for whom you work, you will have a position as long as you want it; and the possibilities for advancement become limitless.

As you grow into your management role, you will gradually be performing more supervisory functions. The higher up the management ladder you climb, the greater your supervisory responsibilities will be. Chapter 28, the final chapter in this text, will discuss management and supervisory problems.

## SUGGESTED READINGS

Anastasi, Thomas E., Jr. *A Secretary Is a Manager*. Burlington, Mass.: Management Center of Cambridge, 1970.

Aspley, J. C. *The Dartnell Office Administration Handbook*. Chicago: Dartnell Corp., 1967, pp. 505–506 (information needed by the beginning worker).

Becker, Esther R., and Evelyn Anders. *The Successful Secretary's Handbook*. New York: Harper & Row, 1971, pp. 50–53 (secretarial manuals).

Lauria, Marie. *How to Be a Good Secretary*. New York: Frederick Fell, Inc., 1969.

Parr, May. *Poise for the Successful Business Girl*. Chicago: Dartnell Corp., 1970.

## QUESTIONS FOR DISCUSSION

1. Many secretaries have been successful in being promoted to management positions. Given the opportunity to interview one of these women, what questions would you ask?

2. Getting off to a good start with co-workers is important to success. What would you include in a list of "do's and don'ts" for new employees?

3. Assume that you are employed to replace the secretary to an executive of a large company and that the secretary has already left when you report. List sources that you could use for information about:

    (a) The organization of the company
    (b) The name of the customers
    (c) The technical language of the firm
    (d) Your employer's letter-writing style
    (e) The company mailing routine
    (f) The procedure for requisitioning supplies
    (g) The names of other office employees
    (h) The lines of authority of the office
    (i) The form for preparing business reports
    (j) The products manufactured by the company
    (k) The form and style for an itinerary

4. As a secretary, you have always willingly given a helping hand to your colleagues when they needed it. You find that they are relying so heavily on your help that you cannot complete your own work. How can you help your co-workers to organize their time and work?

5. Secretaries are warned not to be "too ambitious." What are some of the ways that a secretary might appear overambitious and thus create an unfavorable impression in the office?

6. Do you think that an executive should load his secretary with work that is entirely of a personal nature and unrelated to the company? Is he justified if doing it means that some company work is left undone?

7. Personnel changes in company organization have resulted in your being assigned a second employer. In your own mind you question whether you can handle the work of another person. What attitude should you take with your present employer and the new one?

8. You unavoidably overhear several secretaries discussing your employer unfavorably and unjustly. What is your responsibility in this case?

9. It has been said that a secretary to top management in business must think like top management. What does this mean to you?

10. Explain the difference in meaning between the two words in each set, and illustrate the correct meaning of each word in a sentence. Then consult the Reference Guide to verify or correct your answers.

advice; advise                     descendant; descendent
allude; elude                       disillusion; dissolution
amount; number                   disinterested; uninterested
appraise; apprise                  illusion; allusion
comedian; comedienne          ingenious; ingenuous
complement; compliment        practical; practicable
confidant; confidante           predominant; predominate

11. Use the proper form of *alumnus* in each of the following sentences. Then consult the Reference Guide to verify or correct your answers.

(a) The _____ of the University of Wisconsin presented a scholarship. (men and women graduates)

(b) The Princeton _____ of this region will hold their annual picnic. (men graduates)

(c) The Vassar _____ of each city meet regularly. (women graduates)

(d) She is an _____ of Swarthmore.

(e) He is an _____ of Dartmouth.

## PROBLEMS

■ 1. Select the professional association with which you would most like to affiliate as a secretary. Write a report, giving a description of the organization, its objectives, activities, membership requirements, and services to members.

■ 2. Prepare a report on the CPS examination. Your report should include how the examination is administered, areas covered, eligibility for admission, location of test centers, and advantages of securing the CPS designation.

# Chapter 28

## FULFILLING YOUR ADMINISTRATIVE ROLE

This decade has accelerated the consideration of more and more secretaries for promotion to middle management positions—secretaries who have shown an interest in the company, who have proven themselves in their positions, and who have cooperated with the management team and with colleagues. Most likely these women have participated in management seminars and management training programs.

Among the reasons for this change in attitude toward women in management is the recognition by executives of the management potential of the proven secretary. Nationwide, business and industry are acknowledging the rising aspirations of women and are implementing plans to better utilize women employees. In fact, many personnel officers are reserving for the next few years specified numbers of promotions for women employees. Recent legislation barring discrimination in employment by sex has had an important influence on the increasing equality of opportunities and pay for women.

Thus, the secretary may well have to ask herself: Do I want additional responsibility? Do I want to devote more of my time and thoughts to my work than I do at present? Do I want to be available for travel? Do I want to supervise others? Naturally, the answers to these questions rest with the individual. For some women, family responsibilities may make it impossible to devote more time than the regular working hours. Other women may not wish to take work home with them, often a requirement in higher-level positions. Then, there are those secretaries who are both qualified and willing to assume the responsibilities of management positions.

If the administrative position appeals to you, answer these questions:

**What will be your strategy?**

**How will you fulfill this role?**

**What will be your management style?**

**Will you emulate a man whom you admire in a similar job?**

**Will you follow the team-effort approach, or will you be autocratic and perhaps detached from employees and their problems?**

No doubt you will experiment and discover for yourself the method that works best for you; you will eventually develop your own style of leadership.

In this, the final chapter of this book, are suggestions to help you prepare for your administrative role.

Four areas of responsibility are discussed: how to develop the potential of your employees, how to facilitate smooth human interactions, how to improve work operations, and how to continue your own development so that you become increasingly capable of managing and supervising.

# MAKING THE RICHEST USE OF HUMAN POTENTIAL

As a supervisor or administrator, you will need to work *through other people* to accomplish your goals. That is why some people who are excellent practitioners themselves are not good supervisors or administrators—although a person who is not a natural leader may, through effort and education, develop competencies for these responsibilities. The importance of learning how to work through people accounts for the increasing emphasis on the behavioral sciences in college curriculums in business administration, in business books and magazines, and in management seminars.

In the first place, it is necessary to recruit the best possible people for the jobs to be filled. After that, ways must be found for developing those selected so that they can realize their greatest potential.

## Recruiting the Best Possible People

The actual recruitment is usually the responsibility of the staff of the personnel department. Before they begin any recruiting, however, they study the complete job description and the educational, work-experience, and skill requirements for the position. Later, potential employees who have met screening standards are sent to the immediate supervisor for final approval or rejection. (Note the word *rejection*; the supervisor, being close to the job, may recognize valid reasons why the proposed candidate would not be effective in the work situation. It is best to say *No* now and avoid later trouble.)

An objective of every company is promotion from within; as an effective supervisor or administrator, you should include as one of your objectives the development of replacements and personnel for new jobs. You should also learn to anticipate personnel requirements. It has been said, and wisely, that every executive, administrator, and supervisor should have an understudy or intern. No division, department, or section of an organization should be left to press the panic button upon the promotion, retirement, or demise of its director.

The problem of applying a functional system of promotion from within is closely allied to the following discussion of growth of employees' potential. When office workers at a day-long seminar on work performance were asked to list their expectations from the job, high on the list was "the feeling that I have some place to go—that I'm not in a dead-end job."

## Developing the Employee's Potential

If the employees under your supervision achieve optimum performance, they will thereby multiply tremendously the human resources in your segment of the organization. All of your supervisees' capabilities, not just yours alone, will be at work for you. And your success depends on their growth as well as your own.

The way in which you supervise these employees and how they perceive their jobs will affect their job performance. It is important to generate in every employee the feeling: I MATTER. Further, every employee wants and needs to know how he[1] stands. As his supervisor, you must evaluate him and assist him in reaching his full potential.

**Effective Supervision.** Supervision is the most demanding responsibility of a secretary or an administrator. As a supervisor, she must *think*, and in addition be a master of human relations. Then, after evaluating a situation, she can make decisions based on logical thought processes. These decisions must be justifiable because, on occasion, it may be necessary to initiate policies unpopular with her supervisees. In such cases, the secretary must have the fortitude to defend her actions.

As a secretary-supervisor, you direct the work of your subordinates and are accountable for the work that they produce. You must:

—Assign, schedule, coordinate, and approve the work of the office force.
—See that each individual receives any necessary on-the-job training.
—Provide the employee with objectives and a sense of direction.
—Set and maintain high standards for all office workers, including yourself.
—Establish an office climate of cooperation and confidence.
—Relate well to employees under your direction.

As an example of a supervisory situation, place yourself in this position and consider how you would react: You are secretary to an executive and you supervise two employees: Susan, who is married and the mother of two children; and Robin, who is single. It is late Friday afternoon. For the past week Susan and Robin have been typing an extremely confidential report with a deadline of 5 p.m. Friday.

---

[1]In this discussion of the secretary as an administrator, the authors have elected to use the indiscriminate third-person pronouns, *he* and *his* in referring to office employees.

Although the typing will be completed by the deadline, the proofreading of the 200 pages is sure to run into overtime hours; therefore, your employer has agreed to an extension of time. You, of course, plan to serve as one of the proofreaders. Unfortunately, however, Robin's vacation begins at five o'clock and Susan, with her family responsibilities, does not like overtime work. As the office supervisor, you can arbitrarily assign the work to Robin or Susan; or you can talk over the situation with the two women in the hope that one will volunteer her services. Naturally, the best course to follow is the latter. Since Susan and Robin have been given a part in the decision (an axiom in successful supervision), it is likely that one or both women will cooperate.

In the example cited, however, a truly effective supervisor would have realized earlier that the work would require overtime for completion and would have arranged the overtime work for another evening, thus avoiding the Friday crisis.

## IS MY WORK FULFILLING?

Almost 50% of the working population reports dissatisfaction with the kind of work they are doing. A great many of these would choose another line of work if they had it to do over. You can check your current satisfaction by answering TRUE or FALSE to each.

1. By my own choice, I spend a good deal of extra time on my work (either at home or on the job). _____
2. What I earn or can earn is clearly the main thing that motivates me. _____
3. My family seems to be basically proud of my work. _____
4. I have not acquired any worthwhile friendships where I work. _____
5. My line of work provides a basic service that helps the country or people in some important way. _____
6. My work uses hardly any of my aptitudes or talents. _____
7. I know that I have contributed significant things to my company. _____
8. Hard work and personal commitment do not pay off at my company. _____
9. My work has provided financial stability for me and my family. _____
10. I am in a line of work or a company that is out of step with the times. _____

*For a perfect score you should have answered all odd-numbered items TRUE, and all even-numbered items FALSE. If you got 8 or more right, your job must be meeting many important needs. However, if you missed 5 or more items, your current work situation probably falls short in social and psychological fulfillment (although it may be O.K. in meeting your financial requirements).*
*— EGO-QUIZ, by Dr. Harry J. Cargas and Dr. Richard C. Nickeson*

Rose H. Scott, office administrator in the department of scientific development at A. H. Robins Company, suggests six principles for the successful delegation of work.[2]

1. **Select the jobs to be delegated and get them organized for turnover. Try routine jobs first. Break down the job into logical steps and sequences and define the procedure in writing, if possible.**

2. **Pick the proper person, a person who will be able to understand the work and be capable of doing it along with the present workload.**

3. **Prepare and motivate the delegatee. Make the employee want to cooperate by building her confidence.**

4. **Turn over the work and make sure it is fully understood. Explain the job yourself, using every written and graphic aid at your disposal.**

5. **Encourage independence. Give the delegatee a chance to learn.**

6. **Maintain control. Don't abdicate responsibility for the job.**

**Job Motivation.** Recently it was estimated that the level of human productivity in this country is at only 50 percent of its potential. If the statement is indeed true, workers are producing only one half as much on the job as they are capable of doing. What makes people work to their fullest potential? Experts suggest that the key to maximum production is motivation, and the generator of this motivation is the immediate supervisor.

Perhaps the fact that a worker is not motivated in his job is obvious: increased tardiness, absenteeism, and poor performance indicate his discontent. The problem for the supervisor, then, is to determine the cause and then, as much as possible, attempt to remedy the situation.

Your responsibility is to inspire your subordinates to work to their full capacity. Recognize and reward the employee who works to his fullest potential. How you motivate subordinates will determine whether they achieve the goals you have set for the office.

For an employee to work at his highest level, he must be made to feel that what he is doing is important and that he is a part of the company team. He must feel that his supervisor has confidence in his ability. He seeks and must receive recognition as an individual through assignments of responsibility. He is encouraged to do what he is capable of doing. This is how people work, and this is how they are motivated.

**Job Satisfaction.** Closely allied to job motivation is the need for job satisfaction. Each individual has a set of needs applying to his job situation that he must satisfy. Certainly, he wants to be happy in his work; probably he wants company recognition of his ability, to do a

---

[2]Rose H. Scott, "My Six Rules for Effective Delegation," *Administrative Management* (June, 1971), p. 72.

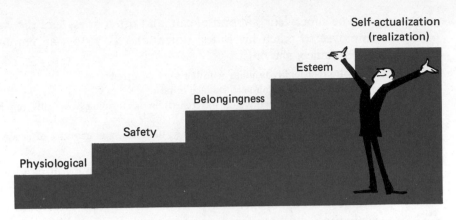

This chart, based on A. H. Maslow's research, shows not only the importance of self-actualization but the fact that it must follow the achievement of more basic needs in a well-defined hierarchy.

better job, to have a decision in the activities of his job, to have the opportunity to get ahead, and to have some measure of security. Therefore, you must determine the personal needs of your subordinates and provide a working situation that fulfills these needs. To be cooperative, your subordinates must be personally satisfied in their jobs.

For instance, the secretary-supervisor can assist her subordinates in achieving job satisfaction by:

**Giving each employee complete responsibility for the preparation of one section of a report or one unit of work**

**Granting increased authority in the accomplishment of office tasks**

**Allowing employees to participate in making decisions that affect their work (as pointed out in the example given earlier)**

Research studies by behavioral scientists such as Abraham Maslow have helped management personnel to determine the needs of employees. Maslow[3] identified a *hierarchy* of human needs: psychological, safety, belongingness, esteem, and self-actualization. He indicated that once a lower need is fairly well satisfied, a worker can be motivated only by a desire to satisfy the next-higher need. His work suggests that managers must help employees to realize their upper-level needs before complete job satisfaction—and thus higher productivity—can be obtained.

**Evaluation of Supervisees.** Every employee wants to know how he is doing in his job; as his supervisor, you are responsible for informing him. Your evaluation can be either formal or informal. (See Chapter 2.)

[3]A. H. Maslow, adapted in *Personnel Management*, 4th ed., by Herbert J. Chruden and Arthur W. Sherman, Jr. Cincinnati: South-Western Publishing Co., 1972, p. 296.

The supervisor's appraisal can, and often does, lead the way for the employee to reach his fullest potential. To assess an employee's job performance, she must:

—Be thoroughly familiar with the work involved
—Have a set of job-performance criteria
—Be aware of individual differences in performing the skills required by the position
—Consider such factors as accuracy, neatness, and quantity of production
—Be able to *communicate* her evaluation

The importance to an employee of an evaluation cannot be over-stated. Assume that you are responsible for the yearly evaluation of Robin and Susan, mentioned earlier. It is time for Robin's first-year evaluation, and you feel that, in general, she has done a good job. In the past few weeks, however, you have noticed a change in her performance and in her attitude. She is cooperative but sullen; her work is not up to former standards. Reluctant to make negative statements in her record, you decide to disregard the last few weeks' performance and complete the form on the basis of her previous record, feeling sure that something personal is bothering her and that it will work out in time. Also, you decide not to mention these points in your conference with her.

> ### 14 IMPORTANT WORDS AND 1 UNIMPORTANT WORD
>
> The 5 most important words: *That was a good job.*
>
> The 4 most important words: *What is your opinion?*
>
> The 3 most important words: *Will you please?*
>
> The 2 most important words: *Thank you.*
>
> The 1 least important word: *"I"*
>
> —Author Unknown

Is this the best course of action? Surprisingly, many supervisors in this situation would react in exactly the same way, tending to avoid possible unpleasant incidents and, in general, not wanting to become involved in the personal problems of their employees. Yet it is the supervisor's responsibility to maintain the work level in her department or group and to assist the employee in every way to be a happy and effective worker. An unpleasant situation should be faced and an attempt made to resolve any problems as soon as possible.

## FACILITATING SMOOTH HUMAN INTERACTION

An essential part of your supervisory role is the facilitation of smooth human relationships, and in this role you may be called upon to get the facts in cases where personalities clash, to evaluate those facts, and to make recommendations for restoring harmony.

## Communicating Effectively

At all times it is important for the supervisor to keep open the lines of communication with employees and thus be able to maintain established policies.

In one management study, supervisors and managers at all levels were asked to appraise communication within their organizations. Overwhelmingly, they reported that communication from above was appallingly ineffective but that their own communication downward was excellent. The importance of effective two-way communication is conveyed in the slogan used in one company: *You're down on what you're not up on.* Only if people understand what is happening will they support it. Middle managers have a dual responsibility: to keep the people upstairs informed of their performance and to keep their supervisees apprised of what management is doing and wants done.

*Horizontal* communication (between managers on the same level) is also essential; but communication on this level is more difficult because the communicators are less adept than they are in vertical channels.

Whether with personnel above, on, or below your level of authority, your *ability to communicate* can facilitate the human interaction that results in increased productivity. In fact, costly management programs have as a major objective the teaching of the ability to communicate.

**Work Instructions.** Work instructions can be given orally or in writing. Oral instructions have certain advantages over written ones, in that a sensitive supervisor knows immediately whether a subordinate understands the instruction, using facial expression and the employee's questions as clues. It is recommended, however, that complicated instructions be given both orally and in writing.

Often supervisors need to write job instructions or work procedures, perhaps to update a company or procedural manual or to see that instructions are available, understood, and followed. Here the important points are:

How to perform a certain procedure
Why that specific type of performance is desirable and important

**Personnel Policies.** A supervisor is responsible for interpreting management policy to workers in such a way that whatever conformity is needed is secured. Usually this means explaining the reasons behind such policy and the benefits that will accrue from its enactment. A problem arises if the supervisor is not in sympathy with the policy, but it must be stated unequivocally that there is an unavoidable obligation to support all company policies. Conversely, there is an equal obligation to communicate to management suggestions for change—either your own or those of your supervisees.

```
                            March 14, 197-

Mr. B.

Ken Jenkins of G & P called and asked if their order
No. B7248, which now calls for 1,500,000 Told cartons,
regular size, could be increased to 2,000,000 with
the same delivery schedule.

I called Sales Service at the plant, and they are check-
ing on the availability of paperboard and openings in
their production schedule.  Art Showalter is to call
me this afternoon.  If there is any problem involved,
I'll let you know.  Otherwise, I'll call Mr. Jenkins
and give him the information.  O.K.?


                            Evelyn
```

This secretary has assumed responsibility in her employer's absence for a routine but important matter. She has also *communicated* to her employer the action she has taken and how she plans to follow through on the action.

**The Administrative Assistant's Communications.** Much of the administrative assistant's work involves effective communication. You may need to collect and to supply information verbally; to write letters for your employer's signature; and to compose reports and memorandums for transmittal vertically throughout the organization. The administrative assistant frequently represents the company to outsiders and is often responsible for the company image.

## Succeeding in a Dual Role

The dual role of secretary-supervisor is complicated by several factors, for she must plan all her supervisory duties around her executive's schedule. His work and demands must have first priority, and all other duties may be immediately interrupted at his beck and call. Therefore, she is not free to plan or supervise in the same way that a full-time office supervisor can.

Part of her time she operates on the same level as those she supervises. She performs the same kinds of tasks. Thus, her subordinates tend to think of her as one who is on their own work level and not as an administrator, so they may not readily accept her authority.

While these factors tend to make the secretary-supervisor's life rather hectic at times, they can be surmounted, as proven by the many highly successful executive secretaries and administrative assistants who are cast in this dual role. Your ability to cope with such situations may well determine how far up the executive ladder you may expect to aspire.

Secretaries who have succeeded in filling a dual role in a business organization make these suggestions:

1. Work with the other administrative personnel in the office in establishing clearly defined lines of authority and operate within this framework.

2. Know thoroughly what you want done. Make definite assignments. Be specific in your instructions and take the time *to explain why.*

3. Organize the work to be done. This means planning ahead and avoiding—insofar as possible—emergency deadlines and "pressure" situations.

4. Understand and develop fair standards of performance. If your standards are fair, your subordinates will accept them and expect you to enforce them.

5. Be a ready and good listener. Many a problem has been solved by simply letting the person describe it.

6. Solicit ideas and suggestions. After all, there may be a better way. Give full credit to staff members when passing ideas up the administrative channel. Never, never claim their ideas as your own.

7. Openly praise good work but criticize in private.

8. Delegate responsibility. To assume all the responsibility yourself may be a good trait in a secretary but a bad one in a supervisor.

9. Remember that everyone has basically the same needs and drives as you— namely, the satisfaction of *achievement,* the need for *recognition,* the opportunity to *create,* the challenge of *growth,* a sense of *belonging,* and a feeling of *security.*

## FACILITATING WORK FLOW TO ACHIEVE PRODUCTION GOALS

In addition to human relationships, other factors are involved in achieving work goals: sound business decisions; provision of the best possible physical environment through scientific utilization of space, selection and maintenance of appropriate equipment, choice and control of supplies best suited to the job; control of the quality and quantity of work; and systems and procedures analysis.

Anyone aspiring to a managerial position must understand business and office organization, labor-management relations, and business law and ethics. Formal business administration courses in these areas, plus special management seminars, would be helpful. Your study will now become *functional* rather than *theoretical*. Note how your viewpoints can change:

**What are the provisions of *my* company's union contract?**

**What is the legal implication of *this* decision? in *my* company's area?**

**How can I apply the principles of business ethics and psychology to *this* situation?**

**Do *my* attitudes contribute to good relations among my fellow workers?**

## Observing Lines of Authority

People are jealous of position and are often insecure in their jobs. The surest way to arouse the animosity and suspicion of colleagues— but one frequently used by the novice—is to ignore lines of authority and bypass someone when working out a problem. Strict adherence to office protocol and to lines of authority is essential to business harmony. Even if you think you know "who knows what," and it is not the person designated on the organization chart with that responsibility, don't make the serious error of ignoring the existing line of authority. Many a bright young potential manager has cut his career short by violating this imperative dictum.

## Making Sound Business Decisions

Sound decisions are usually based on facts, and facts are secured from reading about research conducted by others or through conducting your own. After a certain procedure has been followed in a project, the outcomes should be evaluated. Objective analysis of results is essential to sound business decisions—application of research techniques to business problems, in other words. Using research as a basis for sound business decisions, though, requires the ability to read, develop, and interpret *raw* data as well as classified or statistical data such as that found in charts and graphs.

Computers are helping in the collection of business data upon which to base management decisions. The latest applications lie in the field of business simulation: If we take this action, what will be the result? By feeding into the computer various proposed courses of action, management can secure a quantitative estimation of results.

**Recommendations to Superiors.** One of the first evidences of management potential is your reluctance to dump your problems in the lap of your superior for solution. On the Army staff, all problem interviews are handled on a "staff-work-accomplished" basis. The person with the problem is required to present all data along with a recommendation of at least one solution, but preferably several alternate ones—not a bad technique for business to follow too. After a problem is once identified, the person closest to it should be in the best position to work out a solution and to recommend a course of action.

**The Decision Formula.** Decision making is a part of everyone's job. Routine decisions can be made quickly and with relatively little mental exercise; but important decisions take considerable time, thought, and effort. Making the *important* decisions is the responsibility of management personnel. In arriving at the proper course of action, successful decision makers:

—**Determine exactly what the problem is and write it down.**
—**Develop a list of alternative solutions to the problem.**
—**Examine the advantages and disadvantages of each possible solution.**
—**Select the best solution and review all the ramifications of this choice.**
—**Implement (and later evaluate) the chosen course of action.**

You can train yourself to be a successful decision maker (and problem solver) by following these steps in even the routine decisions you face in the office.

**Your Own Decisions.** You will have to learn what decisions to make on your own initiative and which ones you should refer to your superior along with all pertinent supporting data that will help him to make a wise choice. Experience will guide you, for employers vary. Some like to delegate as much work as possible and will give a free hand once you have proved your capability. Others just naturally cling to authority and their prerogatives in decision-making. Learn to adjust to the type of employer with whom you find yourself working.

In general, though, you should make routine decisions, keeping the employer informed of them but releasing him for more important jobs. Your freedom to make decisions will probably increase when he develops confidence in your decision-making ability.

## Physical Environment

If you have the opportunity to improve the physical environment of your office, review the wealth of articles in business periodicals and the discussions of office supplies and equipment in Chapters 4 and 6. Solicit the help of equipment salesmen and management groups. Develop a sound trade-in rotation plan so that you can stay within your budget and still keep equipment up to date. Investigate rental and leasing plans, as well as purchase. Study office layout and design in current magazines and books.

You have already developed a fund of information about office supplies (See Chapter 4). You will probably be responsible for ordering them. Get competitive prices, and save money for your company by choosing wisely. Plan far enough ahead for delays in deliveries without inconveniencing your staff. You will also control the supplies procured. As you know, pilferage is a serious factor that can be curbed only by careful surveillance. Supplies should be issued only on requisition, and it is your responsibility to review the requisitions periodically to see whether any employees are filing requests out of proportion to their reasonable needs.

## Applying Measurement Methods

Output in highly repetitive clerical operations has been successfully measured, and realistic quantitative standards have been established. In the management literature you can find standards for such processes as straight-copy and letter typing, addressing envelopes, filling in form letters, or cutting stencils. Your own systems and procedures staff will help you in setting standards. Qualitative standards are not as easy; just remember that the quality of all the work from your department is your responsibility. Until an employee demonstrates that her work is consistently usable, proofread EVERYTHING from her typewriter.

## Using Systems and Procedures Analysis

Management of office work is becoming scientific, with the greatest advances being made through the systems approach, an analysis of the flow of work with the objective of cost reduction. In many companies a systems and procedures staff is available for the scientific study of problems in individual offices. Although these specialists may be called upon for studies of a particular problem, the office administrator will want to become familiar with recent developments in this field and learn to make applications of recent developments.

The use of the computer has forced the development of systems and procedures techniques. The computer cannot function without systematically presented data. It is necessary, therefore, to analyze the flow-of-work processes into orderly sequences before programming the computer. Now such analysis is carried into noncomputer activities.

## Understanding Computer Applications

Anyone concerned with office operations today MUST consider computer applications and understand how the resulting flow of business information thereby facilitates the solution of more and more business problems. New opportunities to harness the capabilities of the computer must be sought continually.

The secretary is the liaison between the executive and both in-company and out-side administrators.

## CARRYING YOUR OWN WEIGHT

As you achieve administrative status, you will be expected more and more to carry your own weight—to be able to act "on your own." But you can ruin your whole future unless you demonstrate that you are primarily concerned with implementing your supervisor's goals and developing his objectives, not your own. In a way, your role resembles that of the understudy; do not upstage the star. This final section will discuss ways in which you can become more helpful to him.

### Developing Your Ideas

Try to develop your own creativity. Look at a problem from as many angles as you can find and search out all possible sources of information about it through readings, company files, college and intra-company courses, visits or telephone calls to related organizations, and active participation in professional organizations.

If you do have an idea, share it with your employer. A written memorandum is usually the best medium, for writing the idea forces

```
        TO:      JWV
      FROM:      Eileen Ayers
      DATE:      April 17, 197-
   SUBJECT:      Suggested solution for delivery problems

 McAdam and Graham's chief complaint is the lack of follow-through on day-to-day
 changes in their releases on blanket orders.  Following are two steps that
 should be taken immediately and a third step that entails a choice of alternatives.

      1.  As branch manager, you should have a personal talk with the sales backup
          men at the plant to explain the technical problems and problems that
          result from their "forgetting" to follow up on "unimportant details."

      2.  You should establish and get official approval of a bypass of line-of-
          authority in emergency situations.

      3.  This office should immediately initiate feasibility studies on at least
          three long-term communications improvements:
          a.  Investigation of possible telecommunications service (Data-Phone, etc.)
          b.  Rental of computer time in which our customer could input their re-
              quirements and data be transmitted to our plant and this office
          c.  Information on the latest means of graphic presentation of production
              schedules with devices for instantly recording changes.
```

A thoughtful secretary may be able to see a problem more objectively than her employer can. She may also have more time to think through and research the answer to a situation that is "bugging" her busy executive.

you to clarify it and to express it succinctly. Also, the written memorandum can be used for later referral.

Do not be jealous of the idea. Sometimes if you make a suggestion, it may be modified greatly before it is finally adopted. Your adaptability may result in the decision of a group or a person to do what you basically want done even though compromise is necessary. And, finally, you may not be given credit for your ideas. The question becomes: Which is better, to have your idea adopted—or to get credit for it even though it is not accepted? Usually, you prefer having your idea accepted.

## Improving Communication Skills

You will try to improve your communication skills, for even presidents of companies and countries continue to search for clearer and more persuasive ways of telling their story.

You will find yourself on committees where you will want to influence the actions of others. Remember the "staff-work-accomplished" approach (page 676); and make sure that when you speak, you are making a constructive suggestion.

Plan what you are to say: Your well-presented communication will reduce your superior's reading time. Write and rewrite to reduce verbiage. Abstract material and present it graphically. Arrange material to highlight all the salient points. Become a master at presenting the heart of the matter in one succinct paragraph.

Consider the possibility of expressing your ideas in articles and talks. Too many people are afraid to attempt public speaking or writing for publication. Yet these are tremendous aids to personal development and creativity; they make you clarify and organize your thoughts effectively. Public speaking teaches you to "think on your feet." You can learn to judge the reactions of your listeners and emphasize or rephrase a point according to your interpretation of your listeners' reactions.

## Developing Personal Specialties

Work to develop one or more specialties for which you are known throughout the organization. For instance, maybe you have talent in chart-making and have a collection of materials for dressing up graphic presentations. Maybe you are the departmental authority on records management and have recently visited a demonstration in retrieval of computerized business data. Maybe you are studying for an advanced degree in labor relations. Your specialty can be used not only to the department's advantage but also to your own.

## Summarizing Your Dual Role

This entire chapter has been devoted to ways of assisting your employer. These final suggestions summarize what has been said. They are designed to speed you toward supervisory or administrative success.

Your superior is probably primarily concerned with establishing policy. But companies do not just run themselves once the policy is established. Your most important function may be to implement the policy established and follow through to see that it functions. This means systematic reporting to your employer so that he knows what is going on. He must be apprised of results so that he can make modifications that seem desirable or are essential.

You will also relieve your employer of as much administrative detail as possible, representing him at certain meetings, seeing callers, answering letters, preparing memorandums and reports, making arrangements for travel and meetings, ghostwriting, and doing endless preliminary steps for his decision or approval.

At the heart of your success, though, lies your answer and his to the questions: Are you carrying out instructions? Are you representing him? If he frequently says, "Never mind; I'll handle it myself," you can be sure that you are not carrying your own weight. If he says to others about you, "I don't know what I would do without her; she practically runs the office for me," you can be sure that you are indeed fulfilling your administrative role.

## SUGGESTED READINGS

Anastasi, Thomas E., Jr. *A Secretary Is a Manager*. Burlington, Mass.: Management Center of Cambridge, 1970.

Aspley, J. C. *The Dartnell Office Administration Handbook*. Chicago: Dartnell Corp., 1967, pp. 228–259 (training office workers), pp. 271–280 (overcoming barriers to communication), pp. 519–551 (measuring employee performance).

Becker, Esther R., and Peggy Norton Rollason. *The High-Paid Secretary*. Englewood Cliffs: Prentice-Hall, Inc., 1967, pp. 27–34 (understanding your co-workers), pp. 35–44 (supervising others).

*Behavioral Science Concepts and Management Application*. New York: The Conference Board, 1971.

Ingoldsby, Patricia, and Joseph Focarino. *The Executive Secretary: Handbook to Success*. New York: Doubleday & Co., Inc., 1969, pp. 214–226 (delegating work).

Jennings, Eugene E. *Routes to the Executive Suite*. New York: McGraw-Hill Book Co., Inc., 1971.

*Job Design for Motivating*. New York: The Conference Board, 1971.

Kaiser, Julius B. *Managing the Paperwork Jungle*. Chicago: Dartnell Corp., 1971.

Morgan, John S. *Improving Your Creativity on the Job*. New York: American Management Association, Inc., 1968.

Place, Irene, Charles B. Hicks, and Robin L. Wilkinson. *Office Management*, 3d ed. Boston: Allyn and Bacon, Inc., 1971, pp. 205–221 (systems analysis), pp. 284–295 (work measurement).

*Time Magazine*, Special Issue: The American Woman. (March 20, 1972).

## QUESTIONS FOR DISCUSSION

1. What problem is presented when the executive hands his secretary a letter and says, "Tell Tom Becker's secretary to get an answer from Becker and then have her draft a reply for my signature?"

2. Male skepticism about women in administrative positions is evidenced by such statements as:

   Women try to promote two careers simultaneously—business woman and homemaker. Their interest and time are divided.

   The absenteeism rate of women in business is triple that of men.

   Women approach problems emotionally rather than intellectually. They are too sensitive to criticism and are too gossipy. They crack under strain.

   Women bosses are overcritical slave drivers. They have clawed their way up the success ladder and tend to be overbearing to their subordinates.

   Women dislike working for women. They much prefer to work for a man.

   How accurate are these criticisms? Recognizing that these attitudes do exist, what can the secretary do to overcome them?

3. Outline your personal plan for achieving an administrative title.

4. Your company usually follows the policy of promoting from within. As the office supervisor, you find it necessary on one occasion to recruit a replacement from outside the company. What is your responsibility to the employees in your office?

5. Your employer has given you a tedious, complicated, and confidential assignment of a clerical nature. You have two assistants who could do the work. Should you do the work yourself or delegate it? Why?

6. One of your assistants is especially capable in performing the various tasks of her position. How can you assist her in reaching her full potential on the job?

7. If the secretary has developed a new procedure for reporting credit information to the sales department, would it be better to present the idea to her employer, the vice-president in charge of sales, or to the head of the credit department?

8. What would you consider to be the most important factors to job satisfaction?

9. Give an example from your experience of a routine decision that the secretary herself should make. Give another example of a decision that should have been referred to the employer — along with all available data for reaching the decision.

10. What is the relationship of a systems and procedures staff to an operational unit?

11. What specialty do you have that might be developed into a plus factor in your job?

12. How can you be sure that you are representing your employer as he wishes when you carry out your administrative duties?

13. A middle management position in your firm is open, and you understand that your employer is considering you for that position. In your own mind you feel you are not yet prepared for such a post. You know you need additional academic training. If you are offered the position, should you accept?

## PROBLEMS

■ 1. In developing a feasibility study for a word processing center, your employer requests that you compare letter costs in your office with those reported in the national study shown in the table on page 467. He asks that you collect and report the data.

To obtain data, you keep a production record for one week for Miss Wright who devotes full time to taking dictation and transcribing. She recorded and transcribed 120 letters during the week.

The cost division of the Accounting Department provides you with the following cost information:

**Miss Wright's salary**.....$120 a week
**Dictator's time**...........14 hours at a cost of $6.50 an hour

Fixed charges (depreciation, supervision, rent, light, interest, taxes, insurance, pension, and similar overhead)..............40% of labor cost

Labor cost: Miss Wright's salary plus cost of dictator's time

Nonproductive cost (time lost by Miss Wright and dictator due to waiting, illness, vacation, and other causes)................15% of labor cost

Materials (amount used during week)...............$12.60

Mailing cost for 120 letters (postage and labor).........$18.40

Filing cost for 120 letters (labor and materials).......$12.60

Prepare a memo containing the total cost of producing the 120 letters and the cost per letter with a breakdown showing the amount and percentage of the cost that each factor represents. Include in your memo a discussion of the experiences of other companies that have word processing centers.

■ **2.** Your employer is concerned about the loss caused the company by employee absenteeism. He gives you the following chart and asks you to compute cost figures. Further, he requests that you include in your report (for his investigation) general categories for possible causes of excessive absenteeism (such as inadequate recruitment procedures).

Total sick days paid
   previous 12 months    _____
Average daily pay
   multiplied by
   total sick days        _____
Annual cost              _____
Total accrued 5-yr.
   expense               _____

You learn from the Accounting Department that in the last year 2,450 sick days have been paid and that the average daily pay is $30.

■ **3.** One of your assistants has resigned and you must find a replacement. In your review of applications, what type of information will be important to you? How will you conduct the interviews? Will the age of the applicant make a difference? How will you determine human relations skills of the applicant? Prepare a check sheet by which to evaluate each applicant. Assign relative importance to items with a total of 100 points.

# Part 9

# CASE PROBLEMS

Upon graduation from college, Edith Harvey was employed by the Beckwith Chemical Corporation. At the time of the employment interview, the personnel manager asked her if she intended to stay with the firm for a period of time, as induction of new employees is very expensive and the company wants to employ only permanent staff. She said *Yes*.

She was assigned as secretary to William Brower, one of four district sales managers, and felt that the position offered unusual opportunities for promotion.

After she had been on the job for three months, she overheard the following conversation: "Did you know that Jim Lucas is going to be appointed all-company sales manager? I guess that Bill Brower will be pretty disappointed." "Why should he be? Everybody knows that he isn't going anywhere in this company."

Even though Edith was happy working with Mr. Brower and liked both the company and the chemical world, she resigned at once to look for another job.

During the customary exit interview, she evaded the question of the reason for her leaving because she felt that she should be loyal to Mr. Brower. She replied that a personal problem had arisen that made it necessary for her to work nearer home.

**Did Edith have a responsibility to the company to remain? Is she right in resigning to find a job in which she can go along with her employer on the promotion road?**

Martha Vernon was selected as secretary to Mr. Hylton, president of Jones-Harum Office Equipment Company. She had expected that her apartment mate and co-worker, Sophia Downing, would get the promotion because of her excellent performance ratings. Sophia had also been a secretary with the company three years longer than had Martha.

The choice came as a complete surprise to Martha. The only explanation that she could think of was that she had been on special assignment to Mr. Hylton for three months while her own employer was in Europe.

Martha decided that the best way to forestall hard feelings on Sophia's part was to have a frank discussion of the situation with her immediately, before Sophia had had time to brood and build up resentment. Martha felt that if she could win her best friend's cooperation, the two of them would present a united front in the office that would win Martha the support of the staff, who might otherwise resent Martha's rapid rise in the company.

**Did Sophia have a valid complaint against the company? against Martha?**

**Was Martha's decision to bring the problem out into the open a wise one?**

**What approach could she have made in so awkward a situation?**

**Can you plan the conversation?**

## 9-3  SECRETARIAL ETHICS

Elise Larson was secretary to Mark Hopper, sales manager of the Jacobs Office Furniture Company. The company rented a list of sales prospects from Orville Evers, owner of a direct mail company, and used the list in a nationwide promotion.

In an independent personal effort, Mr. Hopper secured a patent for an electric wastepaper basket and started its manufacture in a small factory of his own.

Since distribution was his major problem, he used the sales prospect list rented by the Jacobs Office Furniture Company. He sent the advertising material out from his office, using the Addressograph plates that had been prepared for the Jacobs company. Elise, of course, knew of this mailing.

While Mr. Hopper was out of town, Orville Evers, owner of the direct mail company, stormed into the office with the advertising for the electric wastebasket and the envelope in which it had been mailed. He indignantly explained to Elise that one address on his rented lists was fictitious and contained a key word used to detect just such unauthorized uses.

Mr. Evers demanded the return of the list on the spot. He also insisted that Elise give him the Addressograph plates to take with him when he left the office.

**What should Elise do?**

**What is her responsibility to Mr. Hopper? to the Jacobs company?**

# Part 10

# Reference Guide

### How to Use the Guide

This Reference Guide is divided into nine main divisions. The headings for these divisions are boxed in heavy rules at the right. In direct alignment behind each heading is the visible rule on the page that starts the material of the heading. These pages will start *main divisions*. The main divisions are arranged alphabetically, as are the items within them. (The Communications and Postal Guides, however, are presented last—out of alphabetical order.)

In the items in this Guide, the styles of type have special meanings. Headings of the main divisions always appear in red in all capital letters. Headings for the next order are in **boldface letters.** Items under these secondary headings are in ***boldface italics***.

*Example*: You want to know whether or not to set off by commas the word *too*.

Step 1. Turn to PUNCTUATION (using the visible rule aligned with the boxed heading for PUNCTUATION at the right).

Step 2. Find the subdivision **Comma**, listed alphabetically under PUNCTUATION.

Step 3. Under **Comma**, find *too*, listed alphabetically under **Comma**.

Cross-references within the Guide will use the type styles as shown above. For instance, in the main division ABBREVIATIONS, you will find the listing shown below.

**Degrees**—See CAPITALIZATION; **Degrees.**

Because CAPITALIZATION appears in all capitals, you know it is one of the main divisions. Because **Degrees** appears in boldface type, you know that you will find the item listed alphabetically under CAPITALIZATION.

# INTRODUCTION

The English language in all its forms (usage, vocabulary, punctuation) is ever changing. Its study is fascinating and challenging. No part of this book will be of more value to a secretary than the English-usage section of this Reference Guide will be.

Handbooks and dictionaries *report* usage at different levels but are not arbitrary authorities. Nor does this Guide presume to be authoritative. It, too, *reports* current acceptable business usages.

When more than one usage is reported in this Guide, it is because there is *divided* usage — dictionaries and handbooks do not agree. A secretary, therefore, cannot assume that her reference books stand alone as supreme authorities on usage. But once she has selected one of a choice of forms, she should use that form consistently.

Formal English usage is followed in reports, dignified letters, papers for publication, and the like.

Colloquial English usage often occurs in friendly business letters. A word marked *colloquial* in the dictionary means that it occurs in spoken English, in conversation at an educated level. Because most spoken English is informal, colloquial usage suggests the informal level. In this guide, colloquial expressions are labeled *informal*.

Standard business English may be used in business correspondence because the nature of business writing is distinctly different from that of other writing. Standard business English is direct and to the point; its economy of words saves time for the writer and for the reader. Frequently, the purpose of a business letter is to obtain a favorable result or to create a friendly reaction. These purposes can often be realized by a conversational, spoken-English tone. Thus colloquial English can be appropriate to and desirable in business writing.

Business English often gives a new meaning to an old word — or uses it as an unusual part of speech, such as *to power your engine*. Businessmen often coin needed words (like *finalize* and *know-how*, both of which have been accepted into the language — by business writers and by the publishers of *Webster's Third New International Dictionary*). When confronted with a coined word or expression, the secretary must decide whether she will call attention to it by quoting or underlining it. If a word as used appears in her dictionary, she needs neither quotation marks nor italics.

Punctuation practices are always changing. The trend is toward less punctuation at the informal level although full, correct punctuation is still required at the formal level. Keep in mind that the purpose of punctuation is to help make your meaning clear to your reader. Use the punctuation that will fulfill this purpose.

**GENERAL RULE:** In formal typewritten text, spell out all words that would be conspicuous if abbreviated. Use abbreviations in informal writing and in tables, footnotes, records, billing, and technical writing. In formal writing, use periods after any abbreviations although periods are often omitted in informal writing.

## Ampersand

Use *and* unless you know that the company in question prefers the ampersand.

> Building and Loan Association
> American Telephone and Telegraph Company
> Norfolk & Western Railway

## At the beginning of a sentence

Even in informal writing, spell out or move from the beginning of the sentence.

> Procter & Gamble officials announced today that . . .
> The announcement by P & G officials that . . .

## Capitalization of

Follow the style of the unabbreviated form of the word.

> versus, vs.          Fahrenheit, F.
> ante meridiem, a.m.  Associated Press, AP

## Coined verb froms

Add an apostrophe and *s*, *d*, or *ing*.

> She c.o.d.'s everything.
> We are o.k.'ing the payment.
> The committee n.g.'d the proposal.

**Degrees**—See CAPITALIZATION; **Degrees.**

## Dimensions and weights

a. Spell out in formal writing; use abbreviated designations in informal; use symbols in technical writing and business forms only.

> Formal: An area six miles by two miles . . .
> Informal: Please refer to item No. 3 . . .
> Technical: Test #27 showed 12° less variation . . .
> Business forms:
> 62 #474, 8' x 12"     8 cu.ft.     1 qt.     6 qts.

b. In the metric system, do not use periods at the end of abbreviations. Singular and plural forms are alike.

> 1 m          1 meter
> 10 m²        10 square meters
> 5 m³         5 cubic meters

## Esq.

This title of courtesy, always in abbreviated form, follows a man's name. No other title or college degree is used with it.

> Alan R. Lane, Esq.
>   *not:*
> Mr. Alan R. Lane, Esq.
> Alan R. Lane, Esq., Ph.D.

## Geographic names

In formal text, do not abbreviate County, Fort, Mount, Point, and Port.

> He was born in Mount Pleasant, Michigan.
>   *but:*
> Mr. Herbert Hazelton
> 622 Grand Avenue
> Mt. Pleasant, MI  48858

## Government agencies and labor organizations

Government agencies, international organizations, and labor groups are often abbreviated with neither spaces nor periods.

> WHO        World Health Organization
> ICC        Interstate Commerce Commission
> AFL-CIO    American Federation of Labor-
>            Congress of Industrial Organizations

## Honorable

Do not abbreviate when preceded by *the*. See USAGE; **Honorable.**

> the Honorable A. R. Lane

## Jr., Sr.

These designations may be used with titles and academic degrees with or without comma.

> Mr. Alan R. Lane, Sr., President
> Prof. Alan R. Lane, Jr.
> Alan R. Lane Jr., M.D.

See PUNCTUATION; **Comma**; *Jr., Sr.* and USAGE; **Jr., Sr.**

## Months

Do not abbreviate names of months or days of the week except in tabulations, citations, references, and the like.

## Names of companies

Follow the style of the company in the use of abbreviations and symbols.

    Wm Taylor & Sons        Saks Fifth Avenue

## Names of persons (initials, contractions)

a. Follow the style in which the person signs his name.  Space after initials.

    Jay R. Penske      R. Floyd King      E. A. Fox

b. With more than two initials, internal spacing may be omitted.

    A.R.J. Simms    *or:*    A. R. J. Simms

c. When a letter is not actually an initial, follow the style used by the person.

    J Marshall Hanna      Harry R Turner

**d.** Do not use a period with contractions of names.  (Use contractions only when necessary to meet space requirements in tabulations, forms, etc.)

    Rob't Riemenschneider    Dan'l Falkenhausen

## Organizations

Names of well-known associations, societies, and companies are often abbreviated, sometimes with periods but without internal spaces.

    AMA      American Management Association
    Y.W.C.A.  Young Women's Christian Association
    IBM      International Business Machines
                  *but:*
    AFL-CIO, EST, PTA, ABC (or A.B.C.),
    CBS (or C.B.S.), NBC (or N.B.C.), A.S.P.C.A.

## Periods with abbreviations

Follow with a period each part of an abbreviation that represents a word unless common usage is without periods.

    c.o.d.            *not:*        cod
    i.e.                           ie
    a.m.                         am
                  *but:*
    AFL-CIO, cc, FM, IOU, PBX, UFO, VHF, UHF

See ABBREVIATIONS ; **Time (b).**

## Period with other punctuation

a. A period ending an abbreviation precedes other punctuation.

    If you call at 10:15 a.m., we . . . .

b. Use only one period when an abbreviation ends a sentence unless the abbreviation is enclosed in parentheses.

    Please call at 10:15 a.m.
    The price is $18 for the lot (not per sq. ft.).

## Plurals of abbreviations

a. For most, add *s.*

    gals., yds., Drs., bbls.

b. For abbreviations in all caps, add *s.*

    C.P.S.s        CPSs        R.N.s        RNs

c. For abbreviations consisting of single lower-case letters, add *'s.*

    c.o.d.'s        cc's        btu's

## Possessives of abbreviations

To form singular possessive, add *'s*; to form plural possessive, add *s'*.

    CPS's salary        CPSs' salaries

## Publications, parts of

Spell out in typewritten text.  Abbreviate in references and footnotes.  Follow the capitalization of the spelled-out form or the one used by the organization.

    Vol. II; Vols. II and V        p. 17; pp. 17-26
    Ch. 3; Chs. 3 to 6          Art. VII; Arts. I–VI

## Reverend

Do not abbreviate when preceded by *the*.

    Rev. A. B. Lane        the Reverend Mr. Lane

## II, 2d, or 2nd

When known, the form that the person uses should be followed.

    Mr. A. B. Lane, II        Mr. A. B. Lane II
    Prof. B. F. Lane, II      Prof. B. F. Lane II

See PUNCTUATION ; **Comma**; *Jr., Sr., II, III* and

## Spacing within abbreviations.

See ABBREVIATIONS ; **Organizations.**

## States and territories

a. Do not abbreviate in typewritten text.

b. Abbreviate in tabulations, footnotes, business forms, and the like.

c. In letter addresses, abbreviate only to achieve balanced line lengths. Use the special 2-letter abbreviations with the ZIP code number *only*. See POSTAL GUIDE; ZIP code.

## Street addresses

a. Do not abbreviate *Street*, *Building*, *Road*, *etc.* in typewritten text. Abbreviate in inside and envelope addresses only to achieve balanced line lengths.

b. Do not abbreviate one-word compass designations that apply to the street name.

210 North State Street     210 Plaza North
*but:*
210 First Street, N.W.

## Time

a. Abbreviate *a.m.* and *p.m.* in expressions of time, preferably in lowercase letters.

b. Abbreviate standard time zones in all caps without periods or spaces.

EST, EDST, CST, MST, PDST, GMT

c. A.D. precedes the year; B.C. follows the year.

A.D. 1973                79 B.C.

See NUMBERS; Time of day.

## Titles

a. Abbreviate courtesy titles.

Mr., Mrs., Ms., M., MM., Mme., Mmes., Mlle., Messrs.

b. In textual matter or addresses, do not abbreviate business titles (*president*, *general manager*, *etc.*) if a courtesy title is also used. Trend is to omit title if it creates an address of more than four lines.

Mr. Howard Hansen, President
Uniflex Corporation
788 East 17th South
Salt Lake City, UT  84104

c. Designating titles in addresses may be abbreviated.

Prof. A. B. Lane          Dr. M. P. Wolf

GENERAL RULE: When you can find no rule or example to guide you, do not capitalize.

## Ages (eras)

Dark Ages, Middle Ages, space age, stone age, Renaissance period, Victorian era

## Astronomical bodies

Except *earth*, *moon*, and *sun*, capitalize the specific names of astronomical bodies.

Mars, the North Star, the Southern Cross, the Big Dipper, Sirius, Canis Majoris

## Bible

Capitalize the word *bible* and its derivatives when they refer to the Scriptures but not when they refer to a handbook.

a Biblical reference, the Bible
That dictionary is my bible.

## Buildings

a. Capitalize names of office buildings.

the Stowe Building, Carew Tower

b. Capitalize names of public buildings only when used as a proper name.

Go to the Kent County Courthouse.
I'll be at the courthouse until two o'clock.

## Business names

Follow the style used by the business.

South-Eastern Tool Co.; tish evans, decorator

## Compound words

See WORDS; COMPOUND

## Congress

Capitalize when the word or its derivatives are used as proper names.

the Congress of the United States, the Senate, the House, the Eighty-Ninth Congress, the second session of Congress
*but:*
The delegates met in congress to decide what action the association would take.

## Countries, regions, and compass points

a. Capitalize names of countries, continents, and their derivatives.

the United Kingdom, the Continent, the continent of North America, European travel, French cuisine

b. Capitalize regions used as proper nouns or adjectives.

He lives in the West on the north bank of a river.
He flew to the Coast on business.
the people of the Far East (the Near East)

c. Do not capitalize points of the compass when they merely indicate direction.

They live east of Grand Rapids in the city of East Grand Rapids.

## Courses of study

Capitalize a specific course name but not the names of fields of knowledge unless they are proper nouns.

He passed Algebra III.
A secretary must excel in spelling.
He has a good background in mathematics.
She majored in French.

## Degrees

a. Capitalize abbreviations of degrees. Capitalize a spelled-out degree that immediately follows a name; otherwise, capitalize or not, as you prefer.

Professor J. W. Knapp, Ph.D., will . . . .
Dean John W. Knapp, Doctor of Philosophy, . . . .
The degree of Doctor of Education (or doctor of education) is . . . .

b. Type abbreviations of degrees with periods and without internal spaces. Set off with commas.

Alan J. Lane, B.S., will . . . .
Frank Santos, B.A. in Ed., will . . . .

c. Bachelor, master, and doctor degrees are *earned*, and in that order. Honorary degrees are *conferred* for some special reason.

d. In biographical references, list all degrees in chronological order — or give all earned degrees chronologically, then honorary degrees chronologically.

e. In letter addresses, the only degrees commonly used are M.D. and D.D.S., and then only if *Dr.* is omitted.

Michael Gavlak, M.D.
Dr. Michael Gavlack
Dr. Ray Stevens
*not:*
Dr. Michael Gavlak, M.D.
Dr. Ray Stevens, D.D.S.

f. In textual matter, for a degree that follows a name, use only the highest degree in each field. With it, before the name, you may use any title except *Mr.* (and *Dr.*, if one of the degrees is a doctorate).

Professor Grace Weber, Ph.D., is . . . .
Dean Russell Olderman, M.B.A., is . . . .
Mrs. Margaret Linderman, B.S. '73, is . . . .
*not:*
Mr. A. J. Black, Ph.D., is . . . .

## Epithets

Capitalize when used with a proper name or as a proper name.

They called him Golden Rule Smith.
He gave all the difficult jobs to Mr. Nice.
Cincinnati's Big Red Machine lost the World Series in 1972.
You can have high standards of behavior without being a Goody Two Shoes.

## Federal, government, national, state, etc.

Capitalize these words when they are part of a proper name. Otherwise, follow your own preference. The style trend is toward non-capitalization.

the Federal Reserve Bank, a federal tax, a Federal tax, the state capital, the State Capitol

## First words

a. Of direct quotations, capitalize as follows:

He said, "That's fine."
"That's fine," he said, "for you."
"That's true," he said. "You're right."
He explained: There is a reason . . . .

b. Of clause-type questions, do not capitalize first words and leave only one typewriter space.

What will happen if you are not ready? if you miss the plane?

c. Of phrase-type questions, use same style as for clause-type.

> How is the sailing? the swimming? the fishing?

d. Of internal independent clauses or phrases, capitalize as follows:

> The problem is, How can we do it?
> The fact is — Too little, too late!

e. Of lines of poetry, capitalize first word of each line.

> I ask of thee, beloved Night —
> Swift to thine approaching flight,
> Come soon, soon!
> — Shelley

f. Of sentences, always capitalize.

g. Of thoughts, capitalize as follows:

> I thought:   He knows now.

## Freshman, sophomore, junior, senior

Capitalize only when used as a proper name.

> As a senior you will . . . . The Junior Class plans . . .

## Government

See CAPITALIZATION, **Federal.**

## Governmental agencies

a. Capitalize names of specific bureaus, departments, commissions, etc., and the shortened form of a specific name.

> the Civil Service Commission   the Commission
> the Internal Revenue Service   the Service

b. Do not capitalize when used generally.

> He asked me which bureau handled such matters, and I replied that the Bureau of Labor and Statistics would help him.

## Holidays, holy days, days of special observance

Capitalize all holidays and holy days.

> Christmas, Easter, New Year's Day, Mother's Day, Passover, Yom Kippur, Fourth of July, Labor Day, Valentine's Day

## Hyphenated words

a. Capitalize any part that is a proper noun or adjective.

> the North-South game, mid-August, pro-American

b. Handbooks do not agree on the capitalization of hyphenated words in headings.  Use one style consistently.

> The Internal-Combustion Engine
> *or:*
> The Internal-combustion Engine

## Locations with identifying numbers

Capitalize unless the designation *No.* is used.

> Room 10, Column 3, Figure 72, Table 4

*Exceptions:*   Do not capitalize *page, verse,* or *line.*

> See page 18,  verse 6,  line 3.

See NUMBERS; **Room numbers, Serial and policy numbers.**

## Measurements

Do not capitalize units of measurement.

> 6 ft.      3 qts.      4 lbs.      5 tons

## Military units

Capitalize, as *Twenty-first Division.*

## Months, names of

Always capitalize.

## Nation

Capitalize *nation* only when used as a synonym for the United States (or a specific country).

> This great Nation will long endure.

## National

See CAPITALIZATION; **Federal.**

## Organizations and clubs, names of

a. Capitalize the proper name of an association, club, order, etc.

> the National Association of . . .
> the University Club of Akron
> the Urban League

b. Capitalize words like *club, organization,* etc., only when used as a proper name.

> Mr. Vincent will meet you at the Club for lunch.
> Children enjoy forming clubs and holding meetings.
> They belong to a bowling league.

## Personifications

Always capitalize.

> We watched Dusk, in her blue velvet gown, settle herself in the valley.

## Persons, names of

Follow the style, if known, used by the person.

> Anne Obrien,  Mr. de Rossett,  Mr. DeGraff

## Political groups

Capitalize as follows:

> the Democratic Party, a Democrat, the Republican Party, a Republican, the Communist Party, a Communist, the Labor Party, a Laborite
>
> *but:*
>
> a republican form of government, a democracy, a communistic government

## Races and peoples

Always capitalize.

> Caucasian(s), Negro(es), Polynesian, Micronesian, Asian

## Relatives

Capitalize when used as a designation with a name or alone as a proper noun.

> Have you seen Uncle John, Mother?
> My father enjoys playing golf, but my uncle does not.
> Thank you, Dad, for the delicious candy.

## Religious faiths and denominations, sacred books, hallowed beings

a. Capitalize all such words and their derivatives.

> Roman Catholic(s), Jewish, Protestantism, the Bible, the Scriptures, Allah, the Old Testament, the Koran, the Blessed Virgin, Buddhism, Methodists

b. Handbooks vary on capitalizing pronouns referring to the Deity. Usually they are not capitalized when the noun form precedes them in a sentence.

> God commanded his people.
> We know He loves His children.

## River, lake, ocean, mountain

Capitalize when part of a proper name (but not when used with more than one name).

> the Atlantic Ocean, Lake Cumberland, the Smoky Mountains, the Missouri River
>
> *but:*
>
> the Atlantic and Pacific oceans; the Ohio, Mississippi, and Missouri rivers; Spring, Torch, Houghton, and Higgins lakes
> The Great Lakes are sometimes called "inland seas."

## Roads, routes, streets, and thoroughfares

Capitalize when part of a proper name.

> State Route 17, Lincoln Tunnel, the Ohio Turnpike, Interstate 75, the Oakland Ferry, Madison Road, Fifth Avenue, Brockdorf Drive, Brooklyn Bridge
>
> *but:*
>
> The streets and highways were clogged with holiday traffic.

## Schools

Capitalize *school, high school, college,* or *university* only when part of a proper name.

> Mrs. Isabelle Knapp, who taught at South High School, was an excellent English teacher.
> From among many fine universities, he chose to attend the University of North Carolina.

## Seasons, names of

Do not capitalize unless personified.

> We had a rainy spring but a dry summer.
> Old Man Winter is due to arrive soon.

## Ships, names of

Capitalize and underline or merely capitalize.

> Wayne and Edith sailed on the France.
> We cruised the Caribbean on the Mermoz.

## Shortened names

Capitalize well-known shortened forms of proper names.

> the Street [Wall], the Continent [of Europe], the District [of Columbia], the Gulf [of Mexico], the Coast [Pacific]

## State, county, city, district, ward, etc.

a. Capitalize when part of a proper name unless they *precede* the proper name.

> New York State, the state of New York, the Second Ward, the County Clerk of Courts, Boone County, Fountain Square

b. Capitalize or not when they stand alone or are used as adjectives.

> File your state (State) tax return.
> There was a county (County) election.

### *The* as part of a title

a. In textual matter, capitalize *the* if it is actually the first word of the title but not if it occurs internally in the title.

> A statement in The New York Times ....
> We read An Economic History of the United States.

b. The trend in informal writing is to lowercase an initial *the* of titles.

### Titles of books, magazines, newspapers

See PUNCTUATION; **Special Element, Titles of Published Matter,** page 713.

### Titles of persons

a. When used alone, capitalize *president* and *vice-president* in referring to the heads of a sovereign nation.

> the President's speech, the Vice-President's speech, the President of Mexico

b. Capitalize titles that are used as designations preceding a name. (Some handbooks also capitalize any title used instead of the person's name.)

> Please read President Lane's letter.
> A letter from Mr. A. B. Lane, president of ....
> A directive from the president (President) states ....

c. Although most authorities hyphenate *vice-president*, common usage tends to omit the hyphen in a title designation before a proper name.

> Vice President Albert Andrews reports that ....

d. Do not capitalize the following titles when they are used alone in a general way.

> priest, rabbi, pastor, cantor, superintendent, minister, rector, judge, consul, professor

### Titles of plays, songs, articles, speeches, laws, acts, etc.

See PUNCTUATION; **Special Element, Titles of Published Matter,** page 713.

### Trademarked names

Capitalize unless the trademark uses lowercase letters as a distinctive style or the word has become a generic term.

> Vaseline, Coca-Cola, Dacron, Thermo-Fax, Scotch tape, Pyrex, Xerox, Crisco, mimeograph, cellophane, nylon

### Weeks of special observance

Always capitalize.

> There was widespread observance of Holy Week.
> Many banquets are held during National Secretaries Week.

### Whereas; Resolved

Capitalize and punctuate in one of these ways:

> WHEREAS, The ....          Resolved, That ....
> WHEREAS the ....           RESOLVED, That ....
> WHEREAS, THE ....          Resolved, That ....

---

## NUMBERS—Page 695

GENERAL RULE: In typewritten text, spell out all numbers under a certain specified one; usage, however, varies as to what this number should be. Follow the rule of your office or select one of those below. Make it your General Rule to be followed consistently.

---

SPELL OUT:
- Numbers under 10 (all agree on this)
- Numbers under 11 or 13
- Numbers under 100 that do not require hyphens
- Numbers under 101
- All numbers under 100 plus those over 100 that can be written in three words or less (as *one hundred nine, twelve hundred eighteen*)

---

### Addresses

a. House numbers: Always spell out the number *1*. (Some handbooks spell out numbers *1* through *10*.) Otherwise use figures.

> One Fifth Avenue
> Ten Park Terrace *or* 10 Park Terrace
> 182 Dearborn Street

b. Street numbers: Follow your general rule in spelling out small-numbered streets. There is no consensus on the use of ordinals with street numbers and on the style of separating house and street numbers. In forming ordinals, *2d* and *3d* are favored in current usage over *2nd* and *3rd*; or the cardinal number may be used. To separate the house and street number, use a compass indication, if possible, or one of the styles shown below.

> *Preferred:*
> 22 North 72d Street  (72nd Street)

> *Without compass indication:*
> 22 Seventy-second Street (Seventy-Second Street)
> 22 – 72d Street        22 – 72 Street
> 22, 72d Street        22, 72 Street

## Ages (in years)

a. Spell out approximate ages.

> Sally is nearly twenty-one.
> Her brother is about twenty-five.

b. Use figures for exact ages (without commas).

> He is 19 today.
> I am 22 years 3 months 11 days old.

c. When an age precedes a noun, follow the General Rule.

> A two-year-old child is full of energy.
> The 20-year-old house was in good condition.

## Approximations

a. Usually, approximate numbers are written out when they can be expressed in one or two words.

> Approximately eighty people attended.

b. If other numbers will occur in the same paragraph that will be written in figures, be consistent and use figures for all.

> Between 90 and 125 people attended.

## At the beginning of a sentence

Spell out, even when other numbers will be written in figures.

> Sixty-three students passed the test.
> Fifty years ago, only 575 people lived in that village.

## Centuries

Spell out, according to most handbooks.

> The twentieth century has been a dramatic one.

## Chapters, sections, pages, paragraphs, verses, lines, etc.

Use Arabic or Roman numerals according to the way the unit is numbered. (Note the style of capitalization.)

> Chapter IX          Paragraph 2
> Chapter 6           lines 3–11 (3 to 11)
> Volume II           page iv, page 1002
> Volume 3            verse 18
> Part 7              Section 4(b)

## Commas with figures

a. The comma may be omitted in four-digit numbers in typewritten text.

> We sent 1475 units by motor express.

b. Use a comma between two adjacent numbers.

> Regarding yesterday's test, out of 22, 18 passed.
> In 1973, 493 students took that course.

See NUMBERS; **Consistency within a sentence (b).**

## Compound numeric adjectives

a. Hyphenate a number-noun combination preceding a noun. Follow the General Rule for expressing numbers.

> a 768-page book, a 54-inch map, 40- and 50-yard bolts
> *or* forty- and fifty-yard bolts

b. Dimensions written before a noun are hyphened, using the singular form, but dimensions written after the noun are not hyphened and use the plural form.

> a 40-foot line, a line 40 feet long
> 5- by 3-inch cards, cards 3 by 5 inches

## Congress, sessions of

Spell out and capitalize as follows:

> Ninety-first Congress, first session
> *or:*
> Ninety-First Congress, first session

## Consistency within a sentence

a. Treat alike all numbers in a group unless one begins a sentence.

> Your three orders of 8, 25, and 110 dozen . . . .
> Eight, 25, and 110 dozen were . . . .

b. Spell out only one of two consecutive small numbers (usually spelling out the shorter word).

> We need two 8-foot boards.
> We need 8 two-foot boards.

c. Spell out a small number that is different in context from a large number.

We sold 625 units in nine months.

## Dates

a. Express and punctuate dates as shown in the examples. (A comma in parentheses shows that its use is optional.)

On May 22, 1973, we . . . .
On May 22 (,) we . . . .
On May twenty-second (,) we . . . .
On the 22d we . . . .
On the twenty-second we . . . .
On the 22d of May (,) we . . . .
On the 22d of May, 1973, we . . . .

b. Express two or more consecutive dates as follows:

On May 22, 23, or 26 we . . . .
In May, June, and July 1973 we . . . .
In May, June, and July of 1973 we . . . .
From May 4 to May 11 the . . . .
In our letters of May 4 and 7, we . . . .

c. In legal documents dates are often spelled out as follows:

On this tenth day of May in the year of our Lord one
    thousand nine hundred and seventy-three . . .
. . . this tenth day of May, A.D. 1973 . . . .

See NUMBERS; **Years.**

## Decades

Express in numbers or spell out as follows:

the 1970s, the 1970's, the seventies, the mid-seventies,
    the '70s, the 70's

## Decimals

a. Express in figures. With numbers less than *1*, use a cipher before the period except when the decimal begins with a cipher. In columns of numbers that include decimals, align the numbers at the decimal point.

22.33
0.56
.045

b. Do not use commas after a decimal point.

1,072.604361

## Degrees of temperature or angles

Express in figures.

8 degrees below zero, 4° above zero, a 45-degree
    angle, an angle of 45 degrees

## Distances

Express in figures except for fractions.

an 825-mile flight
a distance of 825 miles
about a mile and one half away
a three-quarter-mile stretch of highway

## Dividing numbers at end of line

*Figures* should never be divided at the end of a line. Avoid dividing spelled-out numbers except for hyphened numbers, which may be divided at the hyphen.

## Enumerations

See PUNCTUATION; **Special Element, Enumerations,** page 711.

## Fractions

a. As a noun or adjective, a fraction takes the singular or plural form according to the noun or pronoun that follows it.

Half the work is checked.
Half the tests are checked.
Half of it is checked *or* half of them are checked.

*Exception:* In a mixed fraction of one, the *noun* following is plural and the *verb* is singular.

Probably one and one half tons is enough.

b. Spell out fractions of less than one, but hyphenate only when used as an adjective; do not hyphenate if either element is already hyphenated.

a one-third share
one third of the shares
a seven twenty-fifths share

c. In typing fractions in multiple-copy work, *make* the fractions for greater legibility 1/2 (not ½). Key fractions may be illegible on the carbon copies. (In a writing, use all made or all key fractions.)

1/2 and 3/4 (not ½ and 3/4)

**d.** In typing fractions in figures, do not use commas in four-digit numbers.

    1/1000      1279/10000

**e.** In typing mixed fractions, space before a made fraction but not before a key fraction.

    46 1/4,  46¼

### Hyphenated numbers

Hyphenate all spelled-out compound numbers between twenty-one and ninety-nine.

### Market quotations

Express in figures.

    He bought 4s at 102 3/8.

### Measurements

Express in figures except for fractions under *1* and sometimes small whole numbers that would usually be spelled out. Note that an exact measurement, like an exact age, is written without commas.

    8 ft. 10 in. by 12 ft. 6 in.
    36 miles on two gallons of gas
    8½″ by 11″ paper *or* 8½- by 11-inch paper
    three-fourths bushel of tomatoes

### Millions and billions

*Million* and *billion*, spelled out, may take the place of the ciphers in a number.

    7.9 million, $25 million, 6 billion

### Money

**a.** For amounts in *even dollars*, express in figures and omit ciphers for cents. Spell out a small amount if preferred — or if it ends a sentence.

    a cost of $600, a saving of $125
    It cost two dollars. It cost $22.

**b.** For amounts in *dollars and cents*, always express in figures.

    Our quotation is $1.13 each.

**c.** For amounts in *cents*, spell out *cent* or *cents*. Use figures or spell out the number.

    a 2-cent tax, 6 cents, six cents, 88 cents,
    a one-half-cent increase, a ½-cent increase, an increase of one-half cent

**d.** Amounts in *legal documents* are usually spelled out and followed with the amount in figures in parentheses. Words are usually capitalized.

    price of Two Hundred Dollars ($200)
    price of Two Hundred (200) Dollars
    price of two hundred dollars ($200)

### Percent

Dictionaries vary on the usage of figures, the % symbol, and the spelling of *percent*.

    6 percent, six percent, 6 per cent, six per cent, 6%

### Periods of time

**a.** Express exact periods of time (those that include year, month, and days) in figures without commas.

    They paid interest for 1 year 6 months and 12 days.

**b.** In informal writing, periods of time may be expressed in possessive form. In formal writing, reword to avoid the possessive form.

    After six weeks' intensive research, we found . . . .
    After intensive study for a period of six weeks, we found the solution.

### Plurals of numbers

**a.** Form plurals of numbers by adding either *s* or *'s*.

    1900s *or* 1900's
    20s and 30s *or* 20's and 30's

**b.** Form plurals of spelled out numbers in the usual manner, as *tens*.

### Political subdivisions

Spell out and capitalize, as *the Fourth Ward*.

### Possessives of numbers

Form singular possessive by adding *'s*; form plural possessive by adding apostrophe to plural form. Except for informal writing, reword to avoid the possessive form for inanimate objects.

    a 60-day option *or* 60 days' option
    $25's worth, ten cents' worth

### Roman numerals

**a.** Roman numerals are numbers expressed in letters, usually uppercase. (Lowercase is used for preliminary page numbers of books or reports and in the *Page* column of the table of contents for preliminary pages.)

b. Arabic numbers and their equivalents in Roman numerals are shown below. Note that the Roman numerals are aligned at the right.

| 1 | I | 4 | IV | 10 | X | 500 | D |
| 2 | II | 5 | V | 50 | L | 1,000 | M |
| 3 | III | | | 100 | C | | |

c. Repeating a letter repeats its value. (This is done up to three times.) Placing a letter of lesser value before another subtracts its value; this is done rather than repeating a letter four times.

20 = XX, 30 = XXX, 40 = XL, CM = 900

d. Placing a letter of lesser value after one of greater value adds the value of the letter.

13 = XIII, 14 = XIV, 16 = XVI

e. A dash over a number multiplies it by 1,000.

$5{,}000 = \overline{V}$, $1{,}000{,}000 = \overline{M}$

## Room numbers

a. Always express in figures. Do not use commas in room numbers of 1000 and over.

The class met in Room 8.

b. The designations *room* and *suite* are omitted when the name of the building follows.

1948 Carew Tower, 2006 John Hancock Building

See CAPITALIZATION; **Locations.**

## Round numbers

In typing large round numbers, use figures, spell out in the fewest possible words, or combine words and figures.

1,500 *or* 1500       62,000 *or* sixty-two thousand
520,000,000 *or* five-hundred-twenty million *or* 520 million

## Serial and policy numbers

Express in figures. Copy internal spacing if known. Do not use commas, but you may use internal spacing to aid the reader.

No. 3718960, Policy 3 718 960, #3 71 89 60

See CAPITALIZATION; **Locations.**

## Sequential numbers

The hyphen may be used to indicate the omission of the word *through* between two numbers.

on pages 37-65       during August 21-26

## Time of day

a. Express *even* hours as follows:

11 a.m., 11 o'clock, eleven o'clock
12 noon, 12 midnight (*to avoid confusion*)

b. Express other times as follows:

a quarter to ten, (*of* ten), 1:20 p.m.

c. Write 24-hour-clock time as follows:

0045 (12:45 a.m.), 0715 (7:15 a.m.), 1530 (3:30 p.m.)

## Weights

See NUMBERS; **Measurements**

## Years

Express as follows:

A.D. 1973, 400 B.C., class of '75, mid-1974

See NUMBERS; **Periods of time** and **Sequential numbers.**

PLURALS—Page 699
POSSESSIVES—Page 700

## PLURALS

GENERAL RULE: Dictionaries give irregularly formed plurals of words. Given a choice between a foreign and an English plural, use the English.

*Exception:* Use the plural that is most familiar for the subject matter.* For instance, people in the advertising field use *media* in referring to modes of advertising. In the following list, the *preferred* usages (according to *Webster's Third New International Dictionary*) are shown in italics.

| English Plural | Foreign Plural |
| --- | --- |
| *appendixes* | appendices |
| criterions | criteria |
| *curriculums | curricula |
| *focuses* | foci |
| *gymnasiums* | gymnasia |
| *indexes* | indices |
| maximums | *maxima* |
| *mediums* | *media |
| *memorandums* | memoranda |
| minimums | *minima* |
| radiuses | *radii* |
| *referendums* | referenda |
| spectrums | *spectra* |
| tempos | *tempi* |
| *ultimatums* | ultimata |

## Abbreviations, plurals of

See also ABBREVIATIONS; **Plurals and Compound words and phrases.**

a. Pluralize the main word.

attorneys general, major generals, judge advocates, notaries public, trade unions, assistant postmasters general

b. Pluralize the main word in a compound that ends in a prepositional phrase.

chambers of commerce, commanders in chief, attorneys at law, powers of attorney, points of view, bills of lading

c. When a preposition is hyphened to a noun, pluralize the noun.

lookers-on, passers-by, hangers-on, runners-up, listeners-in, goings-on

d. When *neither word is a noun*, pluralize the last word.

also-rans, come-ons, follow-ups, go-betweens, higher-ups, trade-ins

## Cupful, handful, etc.

Add *s*, as *cupfuls*.

## Letters used alone

a. With capital letters, add '*s* or *s*.

B's *or* Bs

b. With lowercase letters, add '*s*.

a's, b's, c's

## Numbers, plurals of

See NUMBERS; **Compound numeric adjectives (b)** and **Fractions (b)**, and **Plurals of numbers.**

## Proper names

a. Add *es* to names ending in sibilants.

the Jameses, the Morrises, the Foxes, the Perezes, the Lorches, the Marshes

b. To other proper names (even those ending in *y* or in a vowel), add *s*.

the Americas, Eskimos, the Alvarados, the Johnsons, the Bachs, the Lillys, the Montessoris, the Murrays, the Randolphs

## Word used as a word

Add '*s* or form plural regularly.

10 yes's and 3 no's *or:* 10 Yeses and 3 Noes

## POSSESSIVES

GENERAL RULE: If a possessive form looks or sounds displeasing, reword the sentence to avoid it. For instance, *the climate of Kansas City, Kansas* is more pleasing than is *Kansas City, Kansas' climate*.

Ordinarily, possession is not shown for inanimate things. Avoid: *a contract's terms, a pen's top*. Acceptable in business writing: *the company's policy, the corporation's brochure*.

## Abbreviations

See ABBREVIATIONS; **Possessives.**

## Alternative possession

Each noun should be possessive.

Is it a man's or a woman's handwriting?
Did he go to the mayor's or the commissioner's office?

See POSSESSIVES; **Joint possession.**

## Appositives

To indicate possession when an appositive is used, add the possessive ending to the appositive or reword the sentence.

Pay Dave the Printer's bill.
It is Mr. Lane, our manager's, idea.
It is our manager, Mr. Lane's, idea.
It is the idea of Mr. Lane, our manager.

## Compound words

Add the possessive ending (usually '*s* for both singular and plural) to the last word.

He read his son-in-law's letter.
His sons-in-law's gifts arrived today.
A passer-by's hat blew into the street.
Three passers-by's heads turned in unison when the cars collided.

## *Else* phrases

Add '*s*.

I saw no one else's grade.
Matthew took someone else's coat inadvertently.

## Gerunds

Gerunds take the possessive form.

Allen's thinking was confused.
The girls' singing was well received.

See USAGE; **Gerund (b).**

### Joint possession

To indicate joint possession, add the possessive ending to the last of two or more nouns (unless a lack of clarity would result).

> Bob and Rita's dinner party was a success.
> Drs. Hanna, Popham, and Tilton's book was printed last week.
> *but:*
> They saw Jim's and Patty's daughter at the pool *not:*
> They saw Jim and Patty's daughter at the pool.

### Money's worth

Use possessive form with this idiom, as *five dollars' worth, $20's worth.*

### Multiple and compound proper names

a. In proper names of several words, add the possessive ending to the last word according to POSSESSIVES; **Sibilant sounds,** or reword to avoid the possessive form.

> Haskins & Sells's report *or* the report from Haskins & Sells
> the Scott Company's letter
> John, Jr.'s graduation
> the Senator from Michigan's speech

b. In proper names some words are considered *descriptive* rather than possessive. Follow official style, if known.

> Artists Supplies, Inc.
> Citizens National Bank

### Numbers, possessive forms for

Form the singular possessive by adding *'s.* Form the plural possessive by adding the apostrophe to the plural form or by rewording to avoid the possessive form.

> $12's worth, four days' work, 30 days' option, a 30-day option

See NUMBERS; **Possessives of numbers.**

### Plurals of possessives

Form the plural of a word first, then add the possessive ending.

> The workmen's tools were lost.
> The women's decision was announced.

### Separate possession

See POSSESSIVES; **Alternative (separate) possession.**

### Sibilant sounds

a. For one-syllable words and those whose last syllable is accented, add *'s.*

> Mr. Jones's car, Mrs. Mendez's report

b. For two-syllable words (singular or plural) whose last syllable is not accented, add only the apostrophe.

> Mr. Roberts' office, the Joneses' house

c. For words not ending in sibilant sounds, add *'s.*

> the senator's vote, the people's choice

### Time phrases

Form possessives regularly or convert to adjective phrases.

> They returned from a three weeks' trip.
> They returned from a three-week trip.

See NUMBERS; **Time of day** and **Years.**

## •Apostrophe

a. Use an apostrophe to indicate possession. See PLURALS AND POSSESSIVES (POSSESSIVES) and ABBREVIATIONS; **Plurals.**

b. Use an apostrophe to form the plural of abbreviations, letters, and figures. See PLURALS AND POSSESSIVES (PLURALS) and ABBREVIATIONS; **Plurals** and NUMBERS; **Plurals.**

c. Use an apostrophe to indicate omitted letters. Do not use a period after a contraction.

> ne'er    Rob't *not:* Rob't. (with a period)

d. Do not use an apostrophe with a shortened or clipped word such as *phone, photo, plane.*

## •Brackets

Type brackets using the diagonal and underline key /thus/.

### Inner parentheses

Use brackets for a set of inner parentheses.

> It is in her textbook (Secretarial Reports /2d edition only/, page 7).

### Quoted matter

a. *Copied errors (sic):* Use brackets to enclose the Latin word *sic,* meaning *thus,* to indicate that an error has been copied exactly.

> "The Rosevelts /sic/ came to America . . . ."

b. *Corrections:* Use brackets to enclose a correction in quoted matter.

> "Mr. Willson /Wilson/ stated that . . . ."

c. *Interpolations:* Use brackets to enclose an interpolation (matter inserted to clarify or question) in quoted matter.

> "They /his brothers/ claim the property."
> "Testimonial letters /solicited?/ are on file," according to the *New York Times.*

## •Colon

Use a colon to indicate that some closely related matter follows.

### After a clause

a. A colon after a clause indicates that a restatement or amplification follows:

> My intuition said: Stop now.
> This much is certain: We must act within a week.

b. A complete sentence following a colon may or may not begin with a capital letter, depending on the emphasis that is desired.

> To succeed is not easy: it takes constant effort.

c. A quoted sentence after a colon always begins with a capital letter.

> Constance Armstrong once stated: "Slow learners require explicit directions, clearly worded."

### Before an enumeration

a. Use a colon before a run-in enumeration when the introductory words are an independent clause.

> They will use three criteria: (1) the importance of the topic, (2) the purpose of . . . .
> *but:*
> The three criteria are (1) the importance of the topic, (2) the purpose of . . . .

b. Use a colon before tabulated enumerations.

> The three criteria are:
> 1. The importance of the topic
> 2. The purpose of the study
> 3. The scope of the findings

c. With *namely, i.e., for instance,* and the like, substitute a semicolon. If the items are tabulated, use no introductory word.

> . . . a number of aptitudes; namely, loyalty, honesty, and vitality.
> Without *namely:*
> . . . a number of items were missing:
> 1. An antique jug
> 2. A complete set of Shakespeare
> 3. A small cherry cabinet

### Before a quotation

Use a colon before a quotation of a sentence or more.

See PUNCTUATION; **Special Element, Quoted Matter;** *Poetry,* and *Several paragraphs* and *Several sentences (a),* page 712.

### Before a series or list

Introduce a series or list with a colon, a comma, or a dash.

See PUNCTUATION; **Special Element, Series (f),** page 712.

### With other punctuation

The colon follows a closing quotation mark.

## •Comma

Because the use of the comma is often necessary to clarify an intended meaning, the rules for comma usage cannot be stated to cover all situations.

Custom and accepted style, however, do dictate certain usages for formal writing. Therefore, in formal writing, observe all the comma rules.

In each piece of business writing, use the comma with consistent style — either following all the rules in every sentence or limiting its use to those necessary for clarity.

### Appositives

An appositive adds information about the word that precedes it.

a. Set off nonrestrictive appositives with commas.

> Janice, the star of the play, became ill.

b. Do not set off one-word appositives.

> My partner Clark is out of town.

c. Do not set off an appositive that is quoted, underlined, or typed in all capitals.

> The phrase "by your leave" is . . . .
> The warning mail early appeared in . . . .
> The book TIME WILL TELL reveals that . . . .

d. Set off an emphatic appositive with a dash. See PUNCTUATION; **Dash**; *Appositives*.

### Breaks in continuity

Use the comma to set off words that break the continuity of a sentence.

> It is the most unusual, if not the most difficult, problem that we face.
> It is best, we believe, to approach the . . . .

### But

a. Use a comma before *but* when it joins two independent clauses that do not have internal commas.

> They planned to go skiing this weekend, but they changed their plans when the snow melted.

b. Use a comma before *but* when it joins short independent clauses only if they are contrasted in meaning.

> The idea is good, but it is costly.
> It was raining but we didn't stop playing.

c. Use a comma with *but* only when it is a conjunction.

> The idea is good but costly.
> The idea is not only good but also practical.
> Everyone but Jane voted against the motion.

d. When *but* begins a sentence, no comma is used unless a parenthetical phrase follows it.

> This was true in the past. But in view of . . . .
> But, as you know, we agreed . . . .

### Cities and states

In textual matter, set off the state name as you would an appositive.

> He was born in Salisbury, North Carolina, in 1956.

### Clauses, independent

A compound sentence consists of two or more independent clauses that may or may not be joined by a conjunction. If one of the independent clauses contains a comma, use a semicolon between independent clauses.

> Your order for chairs, tables, and lamps was received July 12; the items were shipped on the 15th.
> If the weather is fair, we will meet in the courtyard; but if it is rainy, we will meet in Room 103.

### Clauses, dependent (subordinate)

a. When a subordinate clause precedes an independent clause, set it off with a comma. Subordinate clauses begin with such words as *although, when, if, unless, because, who, that*, etc.

> If you have not heard by the 12th, please wire.

b. Set off *nonrestrictive* clauses with commas. Whether a clause is restrictive or nonrestrictive depends on *what you mean*.

In the nonrestrictive clause below, the writer is considering only one book; and the book happens to be lying on the desk.

> She needed the book, which was lying on the desk.

The same sentence written *without* a comma indicates that among two or more books, the one on the desk was the one needed. Thus the clause is *restrictive*.

> She needed the book which was lying on the desk.

### Clarity, commas for

Use a comma to avoid misreading or ambiguity.

After all, the effort is secondary.
Please call in, in a few days.
Inside, the office was full of activity.
In that office, organization is stressed.

### Commands within a sentence

Set off with commas a mild command within a sentence.

In this case, remember, it is important to . . . .

### Consecutive adjectives

See PUNCTUATION ; **Commas;** *Two consecutive adjectives.*

### Contrast or emphasis

a. Use commas to set off elements that are in emphatic contrast to the rest of the sentence. They usually begin with *not* or *but not.*

It is to be used, not abused.
It may be certified, but not insured.

b. Commas set off single emphatic words.

Again, let me say that I agree in principle.
Many insist, rightfully, upon being heard.

### Dates

See NUMBERS ; **Dates.**

### Degrees, academic

See CAPITALIZATION ; **Degrees.**

### Dimensions, weights, etc.

Do not separate the parts with commas.

10 feet 2 inches by 12 feet 6 inches

### Direct address

Commas set off words in direct address.

Thank you, Miss Canter, for helping.

### Etc., et cetera

Commas set off *etc., and so forth, and so on,* or *and the like* in a sentence. (Abbreviate *et cetera* only in technical or informal writing.)

Art, drama, music, and the like, are well supported.

### Exclamations, mild

A mild exclamation within a sentence is set off with commas.

The plane, thank goodness, arrived on time.

### Gerunds

A gerund is a verb form used as a noun. Unless its noun usage requires a comma, do not set off a gerund. Do not confuse gerunds with participles (verbal phrases used as adjectives).

*Gerund:* Observing their reactions was amusing.
*Participle:* Observing their reactions, we were amused.
*Gerund as an appositive:* His hobby, collecting stamps, is a rewarding one.

### Identical consecutive words

See PUNCTUATION ; **Comma;** *Clarity, commas for.*

### Inc., Ltd.

Set off with commas *Inc.* and *Ltd.*

Perhaps Tressel, Inc., stocks it.
George Rainbird, Ltd., published his book.

### Infinitives

An infinitive is a verbal phrase that can be used as a noun or an adjective. Do not set off unless its noun usage requires commas.

To act on your proposal, we must first . . . .
To act on your proposal requires that we . . . .
We intend to act on your proposal.
Our next step, to act on your proposal, requires . . . .
Our next step is to act on your proposal.

### Introductory phrases

Long prepositional phrases or verbal phrases that begin a sentence are set off with commas.

At the earliest possible date, will you please . . . .
Beginning with Question 4, will you write . . . .
            *but:*
At the moment we do not anticipate . . . .
Write out your answers beginning with Question 4.

See PUNCTUATION ; **Commas;** *Participial phrases.*

### Jr., Sr., II, III

a. Use a comma *before* any of these seniority designations if the person uses a comma in his signature. In a sentence, use a comma after the designation if it is preceded by one.

Write Robert Lane, II, about it.
Notify Ralph Miller Jr. to come to the meeting.

b. Do not follow the possessive with a comma.

Call Richard Adams, Jr.'s home.

See ABBREVIATIONS ; **Jr., Sr.**

## Like

When *like* introduces a nonrestrictive phrase, set off the phrase with commas.

> The future, like the weather, is unpredictable.
> A spectator sport like football can be enjoyed either at the stadium or on television.

## Myself, himself, yourself, etc.

Do not set off intensive pronouns with commas.

> Mr. Lane himself approved it.

## Numbers, commas with

See NUMBERS; **Commas, Decimals, Measurements, Periods of time, Round numbers, Serial and policy numbers.**

## Of (before locations or affiliations)

A comma may precede *of*.

> Mr. Robert Krause, of Haines & Hamby, wrote . . . .
> Mayor Albert Flick, of East Burlap, announced . . . .
> The mayor of the city announced that . . . .

## Omitted words

A comma can replace omitted words that are clearly understood.

> Mr. Lane left on Sunday; Mr. Baker, on Tuesday

## Opinions, introductory expressions of

A comma follows introductory words like *fortunately*, *naturally*, *obviously*, etc. A semicolon precedes them if they join two clauses.

> It was raining; fortunately, I had my umbrella.

## Parenthetical expressions

If a pause is required, set off with commas such parenthetical expressions as *however*, *therefore*, *nevertheless*, *accordingly*, *consequently*, *moreover*, etc. When these expressions join two clauses, a semicolon precedes them, as shown above under

## Opinions, introductory expressions of.

> The trend, however, is to use fewer commas.
> We should, nevertheless, know the rules.

See PUNCTUATION; **Semicolon;** *Clauses (f).*

## Participial phrases

Use a comma after an introductory participial phrase.

> After studying your proposal, we feel . . . .

## Questions within sentences

See PUNCTUATION; **Question Mark;** *Question within sentence (a), (c).*

## Restrictive and nonrestrictive elements

a. A *restrictive* element defines, limits, or identifies the noun that it modifies. It indicates that the noun is one specific, individual thing. Do not set off with commas.

> The person *who composed that letter* needs to develop tact.

b. A *nonrestrictive* element describes or amplifies the noun that it modifies. It can be dropped without changing the *basic* meaning of the sentence. Set it off with commas.

> The writer of that letter, *which is a prize example of how to lose customers*, needs to develop tact.

## Series, lists, commas in

See PUNCTUATION; **Special Element, Series,** page 712.

## Such as

When *such as* introduces nonrestrictive elements, set off the element with commas. Do not use commas with restrictive elements.

> We order office supplies, such as paper, pencils, and typewriter ribbons, from them.
> An excuse such as this cannot be accepted.

## Too

When *too*, meaning *also*, occurs within a sentence, set it off with commas. Informal writing omits the comma when *too* ends a sentence.

> We believe, too, that the plan is good.
> We believe that the plan is good, too.
> We believe that the plan is good too.

## Transitional expressions

See PUNCTUATION; **Comma;** *Opinions* and *Parenthetical expressions* and **Semicolon;** *Clauses (c).*

## Transposed elements

Set off with commas sentence elements that are out of their natural order.

> That he talks convincingly, we agree.

### Two consecutive adjectives

Set off with commas two consecutive adjectives if the words can be reversed or if *and* can be inserted with no change in meaning.

> Red is a brilliant, intense color.
> It was a long, difficult journey.
> We have a new alkyd paint.
> That is a good secretarial procedure.

### Verbal phrases, introductory

See PUNCTUATION; **Commas;** *Gerunds* and *Infinitives* and *Participial phrases.*

### With other punctuation

Place the comma inside closing quotation marks but outside a closing parenthesis. Do not use a comma before an opening parenthesis.

> "Getting that order," he told me, "will assure your getting a bonus."
> The order was the largest this year (as far as I know), and it will need a good follow-up.

### Words that answer

Set off with commas such words as *yes*, *no*, *certainly*, *well*, etc. as follows:

> Certainly, we plan to send a delegate.
> Yes, we received your letter.
> Well, we have finally finished that project.
> > *but:*
> We certainly are looking forward to seeing you.
> We asked them and they said Yes.

### Yet (conjunction)

Use a comma or a semicolon before *yet* when it joins two clauses. (*Yet* can be an adverb.)

> We approve it, yet we wish it were better designed.
> We approve it; yet we wish it were better designed.
> We have not approved it yet.

---

### •Dash

### Appositives

Set off with dashes an emphatic appositive or one with internal punctuation.

> Speed — the desire of all typists — comes with practice.
> Even though the facts — the local labor market, the new tax law, and our long-range plan — seem valid, we cannot take action until . . . .

See PUNCTUATION; **Comma;** *Appositives.*

### Change in thought or structure

Set off with dashes an abrupt change in thought or sentence structure. The dash goes after internal punctuation.

> The typist turned in thirty perfect letters — Isn't that amazing? — on her first day.

### Credit lines, reference sources

See PUNCTUATION; **Special Element, Quoted Matter;** *Credit lines and reference sources,* page 712.

### Emphasis

For special emphasis, set off a word or phrase with dashes.

> These are the newest — and the best — available.

### Incomplete sentence

Use a dash to indicate that an unfinished sentence trails off into nothingness or that the omitted part is obvious.

> Your kindness so overwhelms me that —
> Telephone Mr. Lane today or — !

See PUNCTUATION; **Special Element, Ellipses,** page 711.

### Placement at end of line

In typewritten text, type the dash at the end of a line of typing rather than at the beginning of the next line.

> Although the main problem — the local labor market — remains unsolved, we . . . .

### Repetition of a word or phrase

Use a dash before an emphasized repetition.

> We are introducing a new plan — a plan that . . . .

### Series, lists

See PUNCTUATION; **Special Element, Series,** page 712.

### Summation

A dash precedes the summation of a series.

> Her hard work, her friendliness, her attitude — all tend to inspire us.

---

## •Exclamation Point

### Exclamatory elements

a. Use an exclamation point after a forceful remark or command.

> Ouch! your logic hurts.
> Mail it today!  You'll be glad.

b. Use a comma after expression of mild force or surprise.

> Good work, but we expected it from you.
> Truly, it is not to be taken so lightly.

### Extreme emphasis

Indicate the extreme in emphasis with an exclamation point.  Note the decreasing emphasis in these examples:

> This means a 200% profit!
> This means a 200% profit.
> This means a 200% profit.

### Irony

Use an exclamation point enclosed in parentheses to indicate that a word or expression is used ironically.

> Your conscientious (!) follow-up caused us to lose the order.

### O, Oh

a. With *Oh* use an exclamation point or a comma, depending on the degree of forcefulness you intend.

> Oh! what a surprise your letter was.
> Oh, that reminds me.  You are to be here . . . .

b. *O* is always coupled with a name in direct address (in solemn or poetic writing).

> O Hamlet, what a tragic day . . . .

### Rhetorical questions

Use an exclamation point for emphasis.

> How can we ever convince him!

### With other punctuation

Place the exclamation point inside or outside closing punctuation marks, depending upon the relation of the enclosed matter to the sentence.

> "Don't be a litterbug!" is a worthy slogan.
> What a clever "riposte"!

## •Hyphen

### Capitalized compound words

a. If the base word is capitalized, hyphenate to form a compound.

> pre-Christmas, anti-American, pro-French, un-American, ex-Republican party leader

b. In titles and headings, capitalize words that you would capitalize without the hyphens.

> An Off-the-Record Report
> A Middle-of-the-Road Leader

See CAPITALIZATION; **Hyphenated words** and **Titles of persons.**

### Clarity

Use the hyphen to clarify your meaning.

> A *little-used car* is not the same as *a little used car.*

### Compound words as adjectives

a. Hyphenate two or more words used as a single modifier when they *precede* the noun.  In most instances no hyphen is needed when the modifier follows the noun.

> He received on-the-job training.
> That company provides training on the job.
> We asked for an up-to-date report.
> The report is up to date.

b. In modern usage the hyphen is omitted in frequently used, one-thought modifiers that are instantly clear to the reader without the hyphen.

> the civil rights movement, a long distance call, the data processing equipment, the post office workers

c. Do not hyphenate:

1. An adverb-adjective combination

> a highly technical report, an unusually warm day, a barely legible copy, a frequently used word

Note, however, that some adjectives end in *ly* and therefore would not come under the rule.

> a surly-looking person, the friendly-appearing clerk

2. An adjective-possessive combination

> a six months' vacation

3. A two-word proper adjective used before the noun.

> of Scotch Irish descent, the Mason Dixon line

4. A modifier that is a foreign phrase

our per diem rate

5. A modifier enclosed in quotation marks

That is a "brain trust" idea.

6. Comparative modifiers — unless required for clarity

He is the highest ranking officer present.
Of the three, this is the shortest appearing one.

*but:*

I have never seen a slower-moving van.
I have never seen a slower moving van.

See NUMBERS; **Compound numeric adjectives.**

## *Identical words with different meanings*

Use a hyphen to prevent misreading a compound.

We plan to re-cover the furniture.
Will we recover damages for that?
Because the bank returned their check, we must re-collect the amount due.
Do you recollect when that happened?

## *Letter prefixes*

Hyphenate a compound with a letter prefix.

L-shaped, U-turn

## *Numbers*

Hyphenate spelled-out compound numbers, as *thirty-second, twenty-two, ninety-nine.*

See NUMBERS; **Ages, Consistency within a sentence, Fractions, Sequential numbers.**

## *Prefixes, hyphenated*

The following prefixes are almost always hyphenated.

| self | self-sufficient |
| ex | ex-champion |
| vice | vice-consul |

## *Prefixes, joined*

Compounds with the following prefixes are usually written as one word.

| anti | antifreeze |
| bi | bimonthly |
| book | bookmark |
| circum | circumnavigate |
| co | coplanner |
| dis | disaffect |
| extra | extracurricular |

| fore | foreknown |
| hydro | hydrochloride |
| hyper | hypertension |
| in, un | incapable |
| inter | international |
| mis | mistold |
| non | nonconductor |
| out | outdistance |
| over | overanxious |
| pre | premeeting |
| pro | proexercise |
| post | postdate |
| re | restyle |
| trans | transcontinental |
| tri | tricity |
| un | unsuitable |
| where | whereas |
| semi | semicircular |
| | *but* semi-independent |
| under | underestimate |
| up | update |

See PUNCTUATION; **Hyphens;** *Compound words as adjectives (b)* and *Identical words with different meanings.*

## *Prefixes with mixed usage*

Some prefixes are either hyphenated or joined to a base word according to the part-of-speech usage.

air     half     high     ill

a. Noun compounds are usually written as two words.

an air mass, a half frown, a high spot

b. Most adjective compounds are hyphenated.

an air-mixed liquid, a half-sincere offer
a high-flown phrase, an ill-conceived plan

c. Most verb compounds are hyphenated.

to air-mix, to half-approve, to high-hat

## *Series of hyphenated words*

In a series of repeated compounds, the hyphen is repeated but the base word is used only in the last compound. This is sometimes called suspended hyphenation.

There were two-, three-, and four-time winners.

## *Suffixes*

The following suffixes are usually joined to the base word unless the resulting word is long.

| like | a childlike look, a gasoline-like odor |
| hood | childhood, widowhood |
| free | carefree, frostfree, complication-free |
| proof | fireproof, burglar-proof |
| wide | nationwide, statewide, worldwide |

## •Parentheses

### Capitalization within

Within parentheses, capitalize only proper names. A complete sentence is not initially capped if it is within another sentence.

> He subscribes to the Columbus (Georgia) Blade.
> We played bridge (do you play it?) all evening.

### Function of parentheses

Enclose in parentheses any words, phrases, clauses, or sentences that explain, verify, illustrate, define, identify, and so on.

See PUNCTUATION; **Special Element, Enumerations;** *Parentheses with,* page 711.

### Inner parentheses

Enclose in inner parentheses or brackets any parenthetical matter *within* parenthetical matter. See PUNCTUATION; **Brackets;** *Inner parentheses.*

### With other punctuation

a. No punctuation is used before an *opening* parenthesis.

b. Appropriate punctuation precedes and follows a *closing* parenthesis.

> At the meeting (April 2) we . . . .
> At the last regular meeting (April 2), we . . . .
> At the next meeting (May 5?), we . . . .
> Were you at the last meeting (April 2)?
> The meeting will start at the regular time (10 a.m.).

---

## •Period

Use the period after declarative and imperative sentences, commands phrased as questions, abbreviations, initials, and numbers or letters in enumerations. Refer to:

ABBREVIATIONS
CAPITALIZATION; **Degrees**
NUMBERS; **Decimals, Money, Time of day, Years**
PUNCTUATION; **Quotation marks;** *With other punctuation* and **Special Element, Ellipses,** page 711 and **Special Element, Enumerations,** page 711.

---

## •Question Mark

### Direct and indirect quotations

Use a question mark at the end of a direct question, a period at the end of an indirect question.

> *Direct:* When did you order it?
> *Indirect:* He asked when you ordered it.

### Doubt or conjecture

Use a question mark in parentheses to question the accuracy of a statement or to indicate that it is but a conjecture.

> He worked there for five (?) years.

### Question within a sentence

a. Use a question mark at the end of a sentence that contains a clause questioning the whole sentence. Set the clause off with commas.

> He promised, didn't he, to call?

b. If a clause questions only the part preceding it, use the question mark after the clause and set the clause off with dashes.

> As a graduate of Yale — or is it Harvard? — he has. . . .

c. Use a question mark immediately after a quoted question or one in apposition to the word *question.*

> One question "Can you finish it in time?" must be asked.
> The question, Can you finish it in time?, must be asked.

### Requests phrased as questions

Use a period after a polite request in question form to which no direct answer is expected.

> *Direct question:* Can you come on the 29th?
> *Polite request:* Will you please send me your latest catalog.

### Series of questions with a sentence

See CAPITALIZATION; **First words (b), (c).**

### With other punctuation

Refer to the specific mark (listed alphabetically in this division, PUNCTUATION).

---

## •Quotation Mark

### Conversation

a. In literary writing, narration is often interspersed with a person's spoken words.

> "Right you are, Buck. I'll watch my step." Tod nodded slowly, his gray eyes thoughtful. "It's No. 2 they are after, isn't it? More money there."

**b.** Dialogue or direct conversation is punctuated as follows:

> He said, "That's fine."
> "That's fine," he said, "for you."
> "That's true," he said. "You're right."
> "When can you come?" he asked.
> "Oh, come now!" he answered.

**c.** A word-for-word personal or telephone conversation is typed in any quickly typed, easily read style. All speakers must be fully identified at the start.

> Telephone call — 6/10/73 — 2:50 p.m. Mr. Alan King called Mr. Willis Burt
> K  Hello, Willis, how are you?
> B  Fine, Alan. What can I do for you?
> K  I need some steel rods fast!
> B  I'll try my best. What sizes?

### Familiar sayings

Quoting or underlining a familiar saying (although unnecessary) can enliven a typed text. If the saying is used as an adjective, however, hyphens are sufficient.

> If "good things come by threes," I am especially blessed, for I have four to report.
> This is a good-things-come-by-threes report.

### Quoted matter

See PUNCTUATION; **Special Element, Quoted Matter,** page 712.

### Titles of published matter

See PUNCTUATION; **Special Element, Titles of Published Matter,** page 713.

### With other punctuation

**a.** Place closing quotation marks: after a comma or period; before a semicolon or colon; before or after other marks according to usage.

**b.** Other than the quotation mark, use only one punctuation mark at the end of a sentence even though the sentence structure suggests two.

> I read that article "Why Punctuate?"

**c.** With a double question, use only one question mark — either inside or outside the quotation mark.

> Have you read "Why Punctuate?"
> Have you read "Why Punctuate"?

### Words different in tone

**a.** Enclose in quotation marks (do not underline) words of a different tone, like popular terms, terms, unusual meanings, and slang expressions.

> A "man of distinction" like you . . . .
> Your "invitation" arrived and . . . .

**b.** Omit the quotation marks if *so-called* is used.

> Your so-called invitation arrived and . . . .

See PUNCTUATION; **Question mark,** *Doubt or conjecture.*

### Words used as words

Enclose in quotation marks or underline words that are defined or pointed out.

> The term coffee break means . . . .
> His pet word is "dynamic."
> She spelled "practice" with an "s."

---

## •Semicolon

### Clauses in compound sentences.

**a.** If a main clause contains commas, use a semicolon between clauses.

> A good dictionary, they say, is a secretary's best friend; and a good grammar is her loyal pal.

**b.** When two long main clauses are not joined by a conjunction, use a semicolon between them.

> I wrote him about the Baker order last Monday; his reply didn't get here until this morning.

**c.** If a transitional word or phrase joins main clauses, use a semicolon before and a comma after it. Some transitional words are:

| | | |
|---|---|---|
| also | namely | nevertheless |
| hence | for example | therefore |
| then | consequently | whereas |
| thus | furthermore | that is |
| yet | moreover | for instance |

> The need is pressing; therefore, we must . . . .
> Several of our policies need study; for example, . . . .
> They have not replied to our letter; moreover, they . . . .

**d.** When a very short transitional word joins two main clauses, the comma may be omitted.

> The need is pressing; thus we must have . . . .
> The contract has been signed; hence we no longer . . . .

**e.** With transitional words or phrases, the comma can replace understood words.

> We have an important matter to discuss; namely, a pension plan.

### Run-in enumerations

With a series of enumerated clauses, use a colon before the first figure and a semicolon before the following figures.

> The agenda for the meeting includes these items: (1) We will choose a replacement for Bob Jones; (2) we will vote on two tabled motions; and (3) we will set the date for the sales meeting.

See PUNCTUATION; **Special Element, Enumerations;** *Capitalization of units,* at the right.

### With other punctuation

A semicolon arbitrarily follows a closing quotation mark.

> He said, "There will be no increase"; however, we hope he is wrong.

---

## Special Elements of Punctuation

### •Ellipses

*Ellipses* (omission marks) consist of three spaced or unspaced periods within a sentence. If the omission is at the end of a sentence, the period ending the sentence makes a fourth period in the ellipsis.

Ellipses are used:

a. To indicate an omission of a phrase, a sentence, or more from quoted matter

> ". . . because it is so well written . . . and so timely . . . we should like to reprint . . . ."

b. To show that a series continues (in place of *et cetera*)

> Answer every third question (3, 6, 9 . . .).

c. To show passage of time in narrative

> He rose slowly . . . tried to steady himself . . . fell forward.

d. To show that a statement is unfinished or dies away

> Your reason makes us wonder . . . .

See PUNCTUATION; **Dash;** *Incomplete sentence.*

### •Enumerations

#### Capitalization of units

a. *Run-in enumerations of complete sentences:* If a main clause introduces a series of complete sentences, capitalize and punctuate in one of the following ways.

> We cited three objections: (1) Time is limited. (2) The cost is excessive. (3) We lack the trained personnel.
>
> *or:*
>
> We cited three objections: (1) Time is limited; (2) the cost is excessive; and (3) we lack the personnel.

b. *Run-in enumerations of words and phrases:*
1. With introductory main clause

> We cited three objections: (1) limited time, (2) excessive cost, and (3) lack of trained personnel.

2. With introductory sentence fragment:

> Our three objections are (1) limited time, (2) excessive cost, and (3) lack of trained personnel.

c. *Tabulated enumerations:*
1. With complete sentences, use conventional capitalization.

2. Common usage is to capitalize the first word (and any proper words) with words and phrases.

> The colors are:
> 1. Light beige
> 2. Pale yellow
> 3. Charcoal gray

#### Introductory colon

A *run-in* enumeration introduced by a complete sentence takes a colon; a *tabulated* enumeration always requires a colon, as shown in the example immediately above.

#### Parentheses

Use parentheses around figures in *run-in* enumerations as shown in the preceding examples.

#### Punctuation after items

*Run-in independent clauses (sentences):* Use semicolons or periods and a terminal period.

*Run in words or phrases:* Use commas and a terminal period.

*Tabulated sentences:* Use terminal periods.

*Tabulated words or phrases:* Omit terminal punctuation.

## •Quoted Matter

To identify the exact words of a speaker or a writer as such, enclose them in quotation marks, set them off by indention, or both.

### Copied errors (sic)

To identify errors copied per se from quoted matter, use typewritten brackets.
See PUNCTUATION; **Brackets;** *Quoted matter (a).*

### Corrections

To indicate corrected matter in quotations, use typewritten brackets.
See PUNCTUATION; **Brackets,** *Quoted matter (b).*

### Credit lines and reference sources

The source of quoted matter is given (1) in the text, (2) in a footnote, or (3) in a credit line following the indented quotation.

> The article "Facsimile Equipment" in the July, 1972, The Office says:
>
> "In the coming year, our economy will continue to grow stronger,"[1] states a leading . . . .
>
> Four be the things I am wiser to know:
> Idleness, sorrow, a friend, a foe.
>         — Dorothy Parker

See COMMUNICATIONS GUIDE; **Footnote construction,** page 739.

### Inserted words (interpolations)

Enclose in brackets any words inserted into quoted matter.
See PUNCTUATION; **Brackets;** *Quoted matter (c).*

### Omissions

Use ellipses to show omission of words or sentences in quoted matter.
See PUNCTUATION; **Special Element, Ellipses, (a),** page 711.

### Poetry

Introduce quoted poetry with a colon. Separate it from the text by line spaces and centering. Copy line lengths, indentions, and capitalization.

### Quotation within a quotation

Enclose the inner quotation in single quotes.

> "He needs more 'get up and go' if he is to succeed," the manager commented.

### Quoted sentence fragments

Enclose them in quotation marks.

> The letter said that she is "pleasant and conscientious" but that she "lacks initiative."

### Several paragraphs

Indent quoted matter of several paragraphs and introduce with a colon; identify the source. Usually, omit quotation marks with indented matter.

### Several sentences

a. Use a colon to introduce several quoted sentences.

b. Indent from both margins four or more quoted lines, usually without quotation marks.

c. Type quotations of less than four lines in run-in style with quotation marks.

### Single sentences

Enclose a single quoted sentence in quotation marks. Introduce with a colon. See PUNCTUATION; **Quotation marks;** *Conversation (b).*

### Single words

> He said, "Think!"

### Words in italics

When typing copy from printed form, underline any words that are printed in italics.

> Current usage of the word hardware is . . . .

---

## •Series

a. Use commas between units in a series if none contain internal commas.

b. Use semicolons between units if one or more contain internal commas or if the commas would confuse the meaning.

> Please send copies to James Martin, president, Anco; Inc.; Peter Andrews, treasurer, Peerless Foundry; and Bruce Parish, treasurer, Mills and Johnson.

c. Some writers omit the comma before the final connective in a series.

> a choice of tan, ivory, and gray.
> a choice of tan, ivory and gray.

d. Omit punctuation if all units are joined with connectives.

> It comes in tan or ivory or gray.

e. Set off with commas the expressions *and the like*, *and so forth*, and *etc.*

> He is reading books, articles, reports, and the like, for information.

f. To introduce a series or list, use either introductory words properly punctuated or punctuation alone, as follows:

> many colors; for example, beige, ivory, and cream.
> many colors — for example, beige, ivory, and cream.
> many colors, such as beige, ivory, and cream.
> good colors, for example, are beige, ivory, and cream.
> many colors: beige, ivory, and cream.
> many colors — beige, ivory, and cream.

PUNCTUATION; **Dash;** *Summation.*

### •Titles of Published Matter

#### Books, magazines, newspapers

Type in all capitals, or capitalize the important words and underline the entire title. Even when *the* is a formal part of the title, it is often disregarded.

> in yesterday's NEW YORK TIMES
> in the New York Times of
> in The New York Times of

*Exception:* Do not type in all capitals nor underline the word *Bible* (Scriptures).

#### Parts of published works

Enclose in quotation marks the title of any subdivision or unit of a published work (chapters, articles, features, columns, etc.)

> In the "Reference Guide" of SECRETARIAL PROCEDURES AND ADMINISTRATION . . . .
> Refer to "Motivation and Job Satisfaction" in Personnel Management, fourth edition.
> According to "Review and Outlook" in the Wall Street Journal . . . .

*Exception:* Do not enclose in quotation marks the titles of books of the Bible.

#### Movies, songs, lectures, plays, sermons

Capitalize important words and enclose title in quotation marks.

#### Titles with hyphenated compounds

See CAPITALIZATION; **Hyphenated words** and PUNCTUATION; **Hyphen;** *Capitalized compound words (b).*

### •Underlining

Underline two or more words as follows:

a. With closely related words (a title, phrase, or clause) use a solid underline.

> Send the items by parcel post if they will arrive by May 7; if not, use airmail.

b. With a series of distinct items, underline each word but not punctuation or spaces.

> We desperately need your cooperation, loyalty, and friendship if we are to complete this project.

#### Emphasis

Underline any words to be emphasized.

#### Foreign words or phrases

To indicate that a word or phrase is from a foreign language, underline it.

> His manner has a certain je ne sais quoi.

See WORDS: FOREIGN.

#### Italics

In preparing copy for the printer, underline all words that are to be printed in italics.

#### Titles of published matter

See PUNCTUATION; **Special Element, Titles of Published Matter,** this page.

#### Words used as words

See PUNCTUATION; **Quotation marks;** *Words used as words.*

| USAGE—WORDS AND PHRASES | —Page 713 |

The entries in the this division of the Reference Guide consist of common *acceptable* usages for words or phrases that are often misused and about which information is not commonly available in standard dictionaries.

GENERAL RULE: Devote some time to becoming familiar with the items in this division. After that—*when in doubt; look it up.*

### *A* or *an* before the letter *h*

Common usage is as follows:

> a historic (or historical) event, an honor, a hotel, a habitual trait, a humble (if you pronounce the *h*), an humble (if you do not)

## Ability to
Ability *to*, plus verb (ability to influence), not *of* (ability of influencing)

## About, at about
Use one or the other — not both.
> Leave at noon. Leave about noon.

## Above
a. In all levels of writing, this word is used as a preposition and an adverb.
> Her office is two floors above mine.
> It is as blue as the sky above.

b. In business writing it is sometimes used as a pronoun or adjective.
> Consider the above carefully.
> The above price is f.o.b. our factory.

## Absolve
To *free from*, as to *absolve from blame.*

## Accede
To *assent to*, as to *accede to your request.*

## Accept, except
a. *Accept* means to agree or to receive; it is always a verb.
> I accept your offer. She accepted the gift.

b. *Except* as a preposition means but.
> Everyone replied except Mr. Slade.

c. *Except* as a verb means to exclude.
> Once that clause was excepted, the motion passed.

## Accompany
To be accompanied *by* someone or in association *with* something.
> Mr. Slade was accompanied by Mr. Howard.
> The report was accompanied with a letter.

## Acquiesce in
To acquiesce *in*, not *to.*
> He acquiesced in the matter of the bonus.

## Acronyms
Acronyms are words from the initial letters or syllable of two or more words. They are not enclosed in quotes nor underlined. Plurals, possessives, and tenses are formed regularly. (WAC, snafu, HUD)

## A.D.
See NUMBERS; **Years**

## Adapt, adopt, adept
To adapt (change or make suitable), to adopt (to accept or put into practice), to be adept (expert)
> They adapted the device to their needs.
> They formally adopted the proposal.
> He is adept in (*not* at) training beginners.

## Adhere, adherent
To adhere (hold fast) *to*, as *adhere to our policy;* an adherent *of*, as *an adherent of that policy*

## Advice, advise
*Advice* is a noun meaning a recommendation; *advise* is a verb meaning to counsel.
> I can advise you, but will you follow my advice?

## Adverse, averse
*Adverse* means antagonistic; *averse* means disinclined and is milder.
> The proposal met adverse reactions.
> Joseph is averse to manual labor.

## Affect, effect
a. *Affect* is a verb meaning to influence.
> The weather affected our sales.

b. *Effect* as a noun means result.
> The weather had an adverse effect on our sales.

c. *Effect* as a verb means to accomplish or produce.
> The delegates effected a compromise.

## A la or à la
Except in formal or in specialized writing, the accent is dropped in typewritten text.

## All, all of
Use *all* with nouns, *all of* with pronouns.
> Check all the reports; check all of them.

## All, any, none, some, more, most
These words may be either singular or plural, depending on the intended meaning.
> None of the money has been collected; none of the bills have been paid.

## All right

This is the only correct spelling. *Alright* is incorrect.

## All together, altogether

*All together* means in the same place; *altogether* means entirely.

> The correspondence is all together in one folder.
> He is altogether too casual in his manner.

## Allude, elude

*Allude* (to refer indirectly); *elude* (to avoid)

> They alluded to a possible wage increase, but eluded making a positive statement.

## Allusion

See USAGE; **Illusion, allusion.**

## Already, all ready

*Already* is an adverb meaning previously, *all ready* is an adverb-adjective compound meaning completely ready.

> Are you all ready to go? Mr. Adams has already left.

## Altar, alter

*Altar* is a noun referring to worship; *alter* is a verb meaning to change.

> They decorated the altar.
> The tailor altered Mr. Davis' suit.

## Alternative

In strict usage an *alternative* is one of *two* possibilities. It is defined and commonly used as one of *several*.

## Alumna, alumnae, alumnus, alumni

An *alumna* is a woman graduate or former student (plural, *alumnae*).

An *alumnus* is a man graduate or former student (plural, *alumni*).

*Graduate* or *graduates* is a good substitute word.

## Among, between

Generally, *between* implies *two; among, more than two.* In choices, comparison, distinctions, and interrelationships, however, *between* is used with more than two.

> Games between the six schools have been scheduled.
> Differentiate between *to, too,* and *two.*

## Amount, number

*Amount* is commonly used of money and of that which cannot be counted; *number*, of things that can be counted.

> The unusually large number of speculators accounted for the large amount of speculation.

See USAGE; **Number, numeral, figure.**

## Amounts, quantities

An amount or quantity takes plural forms unless it refers to one unit.

> *A unit:* Ten yards makes one slipcover.
> *but:*
> Ten teams are participating.

## *And* in compound subjects

Compound subjects of two or more words joined by *and* take plural verbs and pronouns unless the words together comprise one thing.

> Our sales manager and our advertising director have sent in their reports.
> Our sales manager and advertising director has sent in his report.
> A pen and a pencil were found after the meeting.
> A matching pen and pencil makes a welcome gift.

## And/or

This informal phrase indicates a three-way choice. *Come Monday and/or Tuesday* means to come Monday or Tuesday or both days. In formal writing, say: *Come both Monday and Tuesday or both days.*

## Angry

One is angry *at* or *about* things, *with* or *at* people.

> He is sure to be angry with (*or* at) Mr. Lane about the oversight.
> He is sure to be angry at having to wait.

## Any

Use singular or plural verbs and pronouns according to intended meaning.

> Was any of the dessert left?
> Are any of the students eligible for the prize?

See USAGE; **All, any, none, some, more, most.**

## Anyone, any one

a. *Anyone* (with accent on the first syllable) is written as one word. *Any one* (with accent on the *one*) is written as two words and is usually modified by a prepositional phrase.

> Anyone is welcome to register. (*Anyone*)
> Any one of your men can do the job. (*Any one*)

b. This hint also applies to *anyway, any way; everyone, every one;* and *someone, some one.*

## Anxious, eager

Both *anxious* and *eager* mean earnest desire, but *anxious* denotes worry.

> We look forward eagerly to your visit.
> We are anxious to meet your requirements (but worried that we may fail).

## Appraise, apprise

*Appraise* means to set a value on; *apprise* means to inform.

> The adjuster will appraise the damage and will apprise you of his estimate.

## Appropriate

To appropriate (take) *something;* to appropriate (set aside) *for;* to be appropriate (suitable) *to* or *for.*

> The city appropriated the land.
> They appropriated money for the land.
> The cover is appropriate to the book.
> A suit is appropriate for office wear.

## Apropos

To be apropos *to* or *of* (pertinent to)

> His remark was not apropos to the occasion.

## Apt, likely, liable

a. Do not use *apt* for *likely* or *liable; apt* means suitable or qualified (*apt phrasing*).

b. *Likely* means probably (*likely to refuse*).

c. *Liable* means susceptible to something unpleasant (*liable to break*) or responsible (*liable for damages*).

## As, usage of

> *Adverb:* Write as often as possible.
> *Preposition:* He said it as an afterthought.
> *Conjunction:* The students took notes as I read to them.

Do not use *as* for *because* or *since.*

> Because (*not* as) you were late, we missed the plane.

## As — as, not so — as

In regular comparisons use as . . . as; in negative comparisons in formal writing use not so . . . as.

> This design is as attractive as that one.
> This design is not so attractive as that one.
> This design is not nearly so attractive as that one.

## As to

Usually a single preposition like *in, for, of, on, about, whether* etc. is preferable.

> He commented on (as to) your idea.
> Let me know whether you can come.
> *not:*
> Let me know *as to* whether you can come.

## As well as, together with

Because the noun or pronoun *preceding* either of these phrases is the subject of the sentence, subsequent nouns or pronouns do not affect the verb.

> The report, as well as the schedules, is finished.
> The schedules, together with the report, are finished.

## B.C.

See NUMBERS; **Years.**

## Bad, badly

Use *bad* with a linking verb because it is an adjective. *Badly* is an adverb and is used with regular transitive and intransitive verbs.

Linking verbs and predicate adjectives:

> He feels bad about losing. She looks bad.
> The news tonight sounds bad. The weather is too bad for a picnic.
> *but:*
> He played badly in the tournament. He was injured badly in the accident. The home team played the game badly and lost, which made them feel bad.

## Bail, bale

*Bail* means something pledged for security or to dip a liquid from a vessel. *Bale* is a bundle or a package.

> The prisoner was released on bail.
> They bailed the water from the leaky boat.
> Pick up 15 bales of paper from the dock.

## Balance, remainder

Balance means the amount of money in an account (the bank account or credit account with a firm). To use *balance* for *remainder* is colloquial. See USAGE ; **Colloquial.**

> Send the remainder (*or* rest) of the order.
> Colloquial: Send the balance of the order.

## Bases, basis

*Bases* is the plural of *base* and *basis*.

## Because of

See USAGE ; **Due to.**

## Between

See USAGE ; **Among, between.**

## Biannual, biennial, semiannual

*Biannual* means twice a year; *biennial*, once in two years; *semiannual*, every half year.

## Bimonthly, semimonthly

*Bimonthly*, every two months; *Semimonthly*, twice a month.

## Blond, blonde, brunet, brunette

*Blond* and *brunet* are masculine; *blonde* and *brunette* are feminine.

## But that, but what

*But that* is formal; *but what*, colloquial.

> We never dreamed but that they would accept our offer.
> We didn't know but what they might refuse.

## Can, could, would

*Could* is the past tense of *can*. *Can* and *could* imply ability. Use *would* with *could* in a related clause.

> If you would meet with us, we could select the items.

See USAGE ; **May, might.**

## Can, may

In formal writing, use *can* for ability; *may*, for permission, doubt, or possibility.

> This model can be used for . . . .
> This model may be discontinued.
> You may find that . . . .
> Tell him that he may leave when he is finished.
> He can finish by noon if he hurries.
> The job may take longer than we can foresee.

## Cannot, can not

*Cannot* is more generally used. Some writers feel that *can not* is more emphatic.

> I can *not* believe it!

## Cannot help but

This phrase is unacceptable. Use instead:

> We can but advise you (*or* we cannot but) . . . .
> We can only advise you . . . .

## Cannot (can't) seem to

This phrase is informal. Use *seem unable* to in formal writing.

> They seem unable to decide.
> They can't seem to decide.

## Canvas, canvass

*Canvas* is a noun (a cloth). *Canvass* is a verb meaning to survey or solicit.

> The cartons were covered with canvas.
> Mr. Lindsay will canvass the employees for the United Appeal drive.

## Capacity

*Capacity* is a noun meaning ability or measure of content.

> A capacity to listen will help you make friends.
> He has a capacity for making friends.
> The tank has a capacity of five hundred gallons.

## Capital, capitol

Use *capital* unless you are talking about the building that houses a government. Capitalize *capitol* only when it is part of a proper name.

> We visited the State Capitol in Lansing, Michigan.

## Cite, sight, site

*Cite* means to quote; *sight* means vision, *site* means location.

> He cited some good examples in his lecture.
> They sighted another ship on the horizon.
> We chose the site for our new branch plant.

## Claim

As a verb, *claim* has an antagonistic overtone. *Say* and *feel* are more tactful.

See USAGE ; **Euphemisms.**

## Coincidence, coincident, coincidental

*Coincidence* is a noun meaning a series of apparently unrelated events. *Coincident* is an adjective meaning "in the same space or time" or "of a similar nature." *Coincidental* means "as a result of a coincidence."

Our meeting on Main Street was a coincidence.
Our meeting was coincidental.
His appointment is to be coincident with the reorganization of the company.

## Colloquial

A word or meaning marked *colloquial* in a dictionary is used in the conversation of educated people. Colloquialisms are acceptable in informal writing and friendly business letters.

## Comedian, comedienne

*Comedian* is masculine; *comedienne*, feminine.

## Complected, complexioned

Always use *complexioned*, as *light complexioned*.

## Complement, compliment

*Complement* means to complete, fill, or make perfect; *compliment* means to praise.

He complimented Miss Shelley on her good work.
Her attention to detail complements his energetic salesmanship.

## Confidant, confidante

*Confidant* is masculine; *confidante*, feminine.

## Congress, sessions of

See CAPITALIZATION; **Congress** and NUMBERS; **Congress, sessions of.**

## Connected with, in connection with

These wordy phrases usually can be shortened to *with* or *in* — or omitted entirely.

We received your bill for services in (*not* in connection with) the study of our plan.

## Consensus of opinion

Purists object to this phrase as redundant, but Webster says it ". . . is now generally accepted as in good use."

See USAGE; **Redundancy.**

## Considerable

As a noun, *considerable* is colloquial. Use the word as an adjective.

There was a considerable amount of waste.
*Colloquial:* We had considerable to discuss.

## Consist of, consist in

To *consist of* means composed of; to *consist in* means to be comprised of.

The mixture consists of four herbs.
Experience consists not only in doing things repeatedly but also in learning from them.

## Consonant

To be *consonant in* or *with* means to be in agreement in or with.

## Consul, council, counsel

*Consul* means a representative; *council* means an assembly; *counsel* means advice or to advise.

The French consul addressed the town council.
He counseled the members to check their passports.

## Consult

To consult *about* something or merely to consult (Usually *with* is redundant.)

The heirs consulted the lawyer about the will.

## Contact

Dictionaries label the use of *contact* as a verb colloquial; handbooks, a business usage.

*Noun:* We wish to establish a business contact in Brazil.
*Verb:* Please contact our Denver office soon.

## Contingency, contingent

*Contingency* is a noun meaning a fact that depends on the existence of another fact or event. *Contingent* is the adjective form.

There is one contingency: The strike may delay our plans.
Our plans are contingent upon (*or* on) settlement of the strike.

## Continual, continuous

*Continual* means constantly repeated with only small breaks between; *continuous* means constantly without break.

There were continual interruptions.
The machine has been in continuous use since May.

**Contractions**

See PUNCTUATION; **Apostrophe (c).**

**Conversation**

See PUNCTUATION; **Quotation marks;** *Conversation.*

**Conversions of word usages**

See WORDS: COINED; **Conversions.**

**Correlate**

To correlate (connect systematically) *one thing and another thing;* to correlate *with.*

> This course correlates study and on-the-job training; it correlates learning with doing.

**Could**

See USAGE; **Can, could, would.**

**Credible, creditable, credulous**

*Credible* means believable; *creditable,* praiseworthy; *credulous,* ready to believe on weak evidence.

> We find his story credible, but his suggestion is not creditable.
> He is not so credulous as to accept your explanation.

**Data**

*Data* is the plural form of the Latin *datum.* Business usage gives *data* plural forms when the thought is plural, singular forms when reference is to a unit.

> Data are processed electronically at incredible speeds.
> The data supporting our conclusion is enclosed.

**Date (chronological)**

> It dates from (*not* back to) 1970.

See NUMBERS; **Dates and Years.**

**Date (appointment or engagement)**

This usage is variously termed *informal, slang, familiar, colloquial* in the meaning of a social engagement with a member of the opposite sex.

**Degrees, academic**

See CAPITALIZATION; **Degrees.**

**Descendant, descendent**

Avoid possible misspelling by using *descendant,* which can be either a noun or an adjective. (*Descendent* is only an adjective.)

> Descendent from the ceiling was a crystal chandelier.

**Differ**

One thing differs *from* another; Persons differ *with* each other.

> One author's style differs from that of another in many ways.
> He differs with us on that point.

**Different from**

Different *from* is always correct. Different *than* is sometimes used when followed by a clause.

> This shipment is different from the last one.
> The circumstances were different than (*or* different from) those he recalled.

**Dimensions**

See ABBREVIATIONS; **Dimensions and weights.**

**Discriminate**

To discriminate *against* or *between*

> They were unjust to discriminate against the worker for those reasons.
> We must be careful to discriminate between the new dress codes for business and actual poor taste.

**Disillusion, dissolution**

*Disillusion* means destroying an illusion; *dissolution* means dissolving.

> We were disillusioned to learn his true character.
> The dissolution of the company forced cancellation of many contracts.

**Disinterested, uninterested**

*Disinterested* implies an unbiased, unprejudiced interest; *uninterested* implies the absence of any interest.

> Ethics requires a CPA to be disinterested in the success of his clients.
> He is uninterested in books of fiction.

**Distinguish**

To *distinguish* between (even if more than two); to distinguish one from another; to be distinguished *for*

> It is difficult to distinguish between the three sizes of type.
> This form can be distinguished from that one by noting its form number.
> He is distinguished for his speaking ability.

## Doubt

a. To express doubt, use *if* or *whether*.

I doubt if there is time.
He doubts whether she will attend.

b. To express the lack of doubt, use a negative and *that*.

I do not doubt that there is time.
I have no doubt that there is time.

See PUNCTUATION; **Question mark;** *Doubt.*

## Due to

a. The use of this phrase as a preposition is controversial. Purists strenuously object to it. Use *owing to* or *because of*.

Owing to (*or* because of) faulty brakes, we drove slowly.
*not:*
Due to faulty brakes, we drove slowly.

b. In the usage below, *due* is correct as a predicate adjective followed by the infinitive phrase *to arrive*.

Flight 72 was due to arrive at 9:05 p.m.

## Each

As a pronoun, *each* is singular; as an adjective, it does not affect the verb.

*Pronoun:* Each of the plans has its advantages.
*Adjective:* They each have their good points.

## Eager

See USAGE; **Anxious, eager.**

## Effect

See USAGE; **Affect, effect.**

## Either, neither

These words as adjectives or pronouns take singular forms.

*Adjective:* Either day is convenient.
*Pronoun:* Neither has replied to my letter.
Neither of them has replied.

## Either — or, neither — nor

a. When these connectives join subject words, the *word that is nearer the verb* determines the use of singular or plural verbs and, in some cases, the person of the verb. Usually, place the plural word nearer to the verb.

Either Mr. Lance or his associates are going.
Neither the reports nor the book is here.

b. Reword to avoid an awkward construction.

Either he is coming or I am.
*not:*
Either he or I am coming.

## Else's

See POSSESSIVES; *Else* phrases.

## Eminent, imminent

*Eminent* means high, lofty, distinguished; *imminent* means impending or threatening.

Our speaker is an eminent scientist.
The clouds indicate that a storm is imminent.

## Enthuse

This verb, a back-formation from the noun *enthusiasm*, is labeled informal by most dictionaries. Do not use *enthuse* in formal writing.

He enthused at great length about the plan.
He was enthusiastic about the plan.

## Enumerations

See PUNCTUATION; **Special Element, Enumerations,** page 711.

## Equivalent

As an adjective, *to* or *in;* as a noun, *of*

His position is equivalent to that of director.
The value of these items is equivalent to that of the items you ordered.
The two machines are equivalent in quality.
The contents are the equivalent of three pounds.

## Errors in quoted matter

See PUNCTUATION; **Brackets;** *Quoted matter (a).*

## Etc., and so forth, et cetera

If *et cetera* is dictated, the secretary usually transcribes it as *and so forth* or *etc.* To avoid them, substitute *and the like.*

We must have all sales reports, expense reports, budgets, and the like, by the tenth of each month.

See PUNCTUATION; **Special Element, Series (e),** page 712.

## Ethics

This word takes singular verbs and pronouns when it means a set of practices; plural forms when it means individual ones.

> Professional ethics prohibits our advertising.
> In some instances his ethics have been questionable.

## Euphemisms

*Euphemisms* are softened, tactful phrases for blunt or harsh facts. Some common ones are:

> For *buried:* laid to rest
> For *discharged:* left our employ
> For *the rich:* the leisure class
> For *died:* passed away
> For *claim:* say *or* feel
> For *is:* seems
> For *poor:* underprivileged, modest

## Euphony

Euphony (pleasing speech sounds) can be achieved by:

— Avoiding the harsh or ugly sounds (*f's, b's, ch's, t's, ug's, og's*)
— Repeating pleasant sounds
— Using rhythmically accented syllables

> *Choppy:* We are glad indeed to be able to advise you . . . .
> The account balances do not differ from the beginning balance sheet.
> *Euphonious:* We are pleased that we can tell you . . . .
> The record of all receipts and expenses . . . .

## Everybody, everyone

a. These take singular verbs and pronouns.

> Everyone is asked to wire his opinion.

b. For the distinction between *everyone* and *every one*, see USAGE; **Anyone, any one.**

## Except

See USAGE; **Accept, except.**

## Exclusive

To be exclusive *of* or *with*

> The price mentioned is exclusive of tax.
> His line of apparel is exclusive with our shop.

## Excuse

See USAGE; **Pardon, excuse.**

## Explicit, implicit

To be *explicit in* or *on* means to explain or to "spell out"; to be *implicit in* or *on* means to imply but not actually state something that can be understood or inferred.

> Catalogs are explicit in describing items.
> The letter was quite explicit on that issue.
> The president's approval of that point was implicit in his approval of the full report.

## Farther, further

In formal English, *farther* is used for distances (far way); *further*, for advancement or degree, often with *into*. At the informal level, however, *further* is used for all.

> The airport is a mile farther on this road.
> We can go into the matter further tomorrow.
> Is Chicago farther from here than New York is?

## Federal

See CAPITALIZATION; **Federal.**

## Female

*Female* is used in records and statistics but is not acceptable as a synonym for *woman*, *lady*, or *feminine*.

## Few

As a subject, *few* is a collective pronoun that takes a plural verb and a singular modifier.

> A few are ready now. Only a few plan to come.

## Fewer, less

In strict usage, *fewer* refers to things that can be counted; *less*, to things that must be measured.

> Fewer persons attended the conference this year.
> Less time and effort are required to do the work with this appliance than with that one.

## Fiancé, fiancée

*Fiancé* is masculine and *fiancée* feminine for a betrothed couple.

## Flaunt, flout

*Flaunt* means to wave; to display boastfully. *Flout* means to treat with contempt or insult.

> She constantly flaunts her wealth.
> To flout rules and regulations is ill advised.

## Follow-up, follow up

Follow-up is a noun or adjective; follow up is a verb.

A follow-up will be necessary on this order.
Write a follow-up letter on May 2.
Be sure to follow up on this tomorrow.

## Fractions

See NUMBERS; **Fractions.**

## Further

See USAGE; **Farther, further.**

## Gerund

a. A gerund is a verbal (ending in *ing*) used as a noun. Gerunds can be used in all noun usages.

Subject: You learn that editing takes time.
Object: She learned editing from the senior editor.
Predicate noun: Rewriting is not editing.

b. In formal writing a possessive is used with a gerund (with the exception shown below).

His editing included Chapter 10.
The team's winning made the crowd happy.
George's finding the error was most helpful.

*Exception:* The possessive form is not necessary with a compound or inanimate modifier.

The No. 2 mill breaking down caused a delay.
The mill (*or* mill's) breaking down caused a delay.

## Good, well

To *feel good* and to *feel well* are not synonymous. Both *good* and *well* are adjectives and *feel* (in this usage) is a linking verb. Use *well* to mean *in fine health;* use *good* to mean pleasant or attractive.

Usually, when you feel well, you look good.
I feel well and energetic.
He feels good about his promotion.

See USAGE; **Linking verbs.**

## Got, gotten

Both words are the past participle of *to get.*

## Government

This word takes singular verbs and pronouns.

The government is setting up its budget.

See CAPITALIZATION; **Federal.**

## Graduated

Use either *graduated from* or *was graduated from.* In letters of application, use the latter form — in case your reader is a word purist.

Formal: He was graduated from Indiana University.
Informal: He graduated from Indiana University.

## Honorable

Use this title of respect during term of office. In an address the first name or initials and surname follow *Honorable* or *Hon.* In writing about the person, use the styles below.

Address: Hon. Alan Lane, Honorable A. R. Lane
In text: the Honorable Alan Lane, the Honorable Mr. Lane *not:* the Honorable Lane

See ABBREVIATIONS; **Honorable.**

## *Hope* phrases

Do not use *in hopes of* and *no hopes of.* Use the singular form.

We sent the letter to Fairbanks, Alaska, in the hope of reaching Dr. Hanna.
We have no hope of meeting that delivery date.

## However

Avoid starting a sentence with *however* as a transitional word. Used as an adverb, *however* can start a sentence.

Transitional: We waited for hours; however, he . . . .
As adverb: However you advised him, he did not . . . .

## Identified with

This term, when it means *associated with,* is colloquial according to some dictionaries.

## Idioms

a. An *idiom* is an expression or phrase that is somehow peculiar — an arbitrary grouping of words that is often illogical in construction or meaning but is acceptable in usage. Some common American idioms are *to make ends meet, to take pains, laid up with a virus, by and large,* and *to catch a cold* or *bug.*

b. A prepositional idiom is one in which the combination of words has a special meaning. Some common ones are *to live up to, to live down* something, *to put up with* something, *to set up, to set about* something, *to hand over,* to *bring up* a point.

**If clauses**
See USAGE; **Subjunctive mood**

**Illusion, allusion**
*Illusion* means a deceptive appearance; *allusion*, something referred to.
> He alluded to the illusion of added space that the new wall mirror provided.

**Imply, infer**
To *imply* means to give a certain impression; to *infer* means to receive a certain impression.
> Your question implies that you don't understand.
> I infer from your question that you don't understand.

**In, into, in to**
*In* implies a set location; *into*, movement to a location; *in to*, the adverb *in* and the preposition *to* (usually with a verb).
> He is in his office; he went into his office; he went in to answer the telephone.

**In connection with**
Use *connected with*.

**In person**
See USAGE; **Personally, in person.**

**Inc.**
See PUNCTUATION; **Comma;** *Inc., Ltd.*

**Incidence, incident, incidental**
*Incidence* means the occurrence of; *incident*, pertaining to (as an adjective); *incidental*, occurring by chance or unrelatedly.
> The incidence of hepatitis is higher in that area.
> The satisfactions incident to teaching outweigh the dissatisfactions.
> There are intangible advantages incidental to his job.

**Inconsistent**
To be inconsistent *in* or *with*
> He is inconsistent in his arguments.
> His statements were inconsistent with his record.

**Increase**
For business usage, see USAGE; **Raise, increase, increment.**

**Incredible, incredulous**
*Incredible* means unbelievable; *incredulous*, unbelieving.
> Frankly, I'm incredulous; his story is incredible.

**Infinitives**
a. An infinitive is the simple, basic form of a verb, such as *to go, to see, to do.* The *to* is dropped (and understood) after some verbs: *make it (to) work, help them (to) get,* etc.
> Make him (to) rest, if you can.
> We helped him get started on his project.
> They need not come until four.

b. Use an infinitive phrase as follows:
> *Noun, as subject:* *To go* will be a privilege.
> *Noun, as object:* He wants *to talk* with you.
> *Adjective:* The place *to go* is Spain.
> *Adverb:* He saved his graduation checks *to go* to Italy.
> *Absolute:* *To exaggerate* a bit, the trip was great!

c. A split infinitive occurs when a word or phrase separates *to* and the verb. Use a split infinitive only when necessary for clarity or emphasis. Notice in the examples below how the emphasis of meaning changes slightly with a shift of the infinitive.
> We want to understand it fully before signing.
> We want to *fully understand* it before signing.
> Later on, they began to actually enjoy jogging.
> Later on, they actually began to enjoy jogging.

**Ingenious, ingenuous**
*Ingenious* means inventive; *ingenuous* means candid or artless.
> Despite her ingenuous manner, she devised an ingenious solution to the problem.

**Inside of a, within**
In statements referring to time, the phrase *inside of a* is colloquial for *within.*

**Intransitive verbs**
See USAGE; **Transitive verbs.**

**Irregardless**
*Irregardless* is a nonstandard word; use *regardless.*

**Irony**
See PUNCTUATION; **Exclamation point** and **Quotation marks,** *Words different in tone.*

**Its, it's**
Use *its* as a possessive; *it's*, for *it is.*
> Its concept is new. It's a new concept.

## Job, position

Both words mean a post of employment but with this distinction: A laborer who uses physical effort has a *job* and is paid *wages* at an hourly rate. A worker with special training or ability has a *position* and is paid a weekly or monthly *salary*. In personnel terminology, *job* is used for both because it is short; for example, *a clerical job*. (*Job* is also used for a unit of work.)

## Junior, Senior, Jr., Sr.

*Junior* is usually dropped after the death of the father of the same name. *Senior* or *Sr.* is unnecessary and is almost never used unless the two identical names are closely associated (such as business partners) or unless each is so well known that a distinction is needed.

See ABBREVIATIONS; **Jr., Sr.** and PUNCTUATION; **Comma;** *Jr., Sr., II, III.*

## Kind, kinds

Use singular verbs and pronouns with *kind*, plural with *kinds*. This guide applies also to *type, types; class, classes*, etc.

> That type of machine performs well.
> The two types of machines used were . . . .
> *Avoid:* That kind of *a* machine performs well.

## Later, latter

*Later* means after a time; *latter* means the second of two things.

> I shall reply later.          I prefer the latter.

## Latest, last

a. While these words can be synonymous, a common distinction is to use *last* to mean at the end in time or place; *latest*, to mean following all others in time only, but not necessarily being the end.

> This is the latest edition of the book. It is not the last edition because we have started to work on the next edition.

b. *Last* can also mean the next before the present.

> Our latest model is gray; our last model was white.

## Lay, lie

a. The transitive verb *to lay* means to put in place. Its principal parts are *lay, laid, laid*.

> Lay the mail down.
> He laid the mail down.
> He has laid the mail down.

b. The intransitive verb *to lie* means to recline or rest on. Its principal parts are *lie, lay, lain*.

> The mail lies on the table.
> It lay there yesterday.
> It has lain there all week.

See USAGE; **Transitive verbs.**

## Lead, led

The past tense of *lead* is *led*.

> He led the opposition.

## Leave, let

*Leave* means to depart; *let*, to permit or allow.

> Leave the sample with us.
> Let our sample speak for itself.

## Lend

See USAGE; **Loan, lend.**

## Less, lesser

*Less* implies that which is smaller in extent but not countable: *less haste, less noise*. *Lesser* implies a difference in extent between two: *the lesser evil, a lesser work*.

## Like

a. All reference books agree on these usages:

> *Adjective:* . . . in a like situation.
> *Pronoun:* . . . letters, reports, and the like.
> *Preposition:* . . . type like a professional.

b. Usage of *like* for *as* or *as if* is not accepted in formal writing.

> *Informal:* The report reads like he took pains with it.
> *Formal:* The report reads as if he polished it.

See USAGE; **As, usage of.**

## Linking verbs

These verbs *connect* a subject with a predicate noun or adjective. Some examples are:

> to be (am, is, was, has been, etc.), act, appear, become, feel, get, grow, look, seem, sound, taste, turn

See USAGE; **Good, well.**

## Loan, lend

Although some writers use *loan* as a noun only, dictionaries show both *loan* and *lend* as verbs. The principal parts are *loan, loaned, loaned,* and *lend, lent, lent.*

## Look

When *look* means *appear* (a linking verb), use adjectives with it; when it means to see with the eyes, use adverbs.

   *Adjective:* Mr. Snyder looked very weary.
   *Adverb:* He looked wearily at the stack of papers.

## Loose, lose

*Loose* means not tight; *lose,* to suffer a loss.

   It is easy to lose a loose button.

## Lot of, lots of

Avoid these phrases in business writing. Use instead: *many, much, a great many, a considerable number,* and the like.

## Ltd.

See PUNCTUATION; **Comma;** *Inc., Ltd.*

## Mathematics

Use singular forms when you mean the *science* of mathematics.

## May, might

*Might* is the past tense of *may.* Both imply permission, possibility, or opportunity; *can* implies ability.

   The letter says that Mrs. Lee may sell the house.
   She might have sold it, but she reconsidered.
   The realtor says that he can sell it.

See USAGE; **Can, could, would.**

## Million

See NUMBERS; **Millions.**

## More nearly, most nearly

These phrases are used in formal writing to express comparative and superlative degrees for adjectives that cannot be compared, as *a more nearly perfect circle, the more nearly square design.*

## More than one

Although this phrase is plural in meaning, the subject that follows it takes a singular verb.

   More than one rule was ignored.

## National

See CAPITALIZATION; **Federal.**

## Necessary

This word is an adjective. It can be used in business writing to soften a phrase like *you must.* The noun form is *necessity* or *need.*

   It is necessary that you (*or:* You must) . . . .

## Necessity, need

Use *necessity of* or *for* or simply *need.*

   There is no necessity for this step.
         *or:*
   There is no need for this step.

## Neither

See USAGE; **Either, neither.**

## Neither — nor

See USAGE; **Either — or, neither — nor**

## News

This word takes singular verbs and pronouns.

   The latest news is that . . . .

## No

See USAGE; **Yes, no.**

## Nobody

This word takes singular verbs and pronouns.

## None, no one, not one

*None* can be either singular or plural; *no one* and *not one* take singular forms.

   None of the students were bored.
   None of the money was spent on improvements.
   Not one of us was able to be there.

See USAGE; **All, any, none, some, more, most.**

## Not, and not

When either of these two introduces a phrase in contrast to the subject, the subject determines whether the verb is singular or plural.

   Results, not wishful thinking, count.
   Your record, and not your promises, counts.

## Nothing but, nothing else but

Use *nothing but*.

> We can add nothing but our thanks.

## Not only, but also

a. In this construction the noun closer to the verb determines whether the forms used are singular or plural.

> Not only the orders but also his report was late.
> Not only the report but also the orders were late.

b. When this construction is used with main clauses, use the comma between them.

> Not only was it their first visit here, but it was also their first trip by air.

See PUNCTUATION; **Comma;** *But* and USAGE; **Parallel construction.**

## Notorious

This word means *well known for unfavorable reasons*. Used *noted, famed, celebrated*, etc. to imply favorable reasons.

## Not so — as

See USAGE; **As — as, not so — as.**

## Number

See USAGE; **Amount, number.**

## Number, numeral, figure

Use *number* to express the idea of a quantity or sum of something. Numbers can be spelled out or expressed in *numerals* or *figures*.

> We spell out small numbers like *two, five, ten*.
> We use figures for large numbers: 1,243, etc.
> There were 15 apples in the basket; *15* is the *number* of apples expressed by the *figures 1* and *5*.

## Number of

The meaning intended determines whether this phrase takes singular or plural forms.

> The number of replies that we received is gratifying.
> A number of the replies were critical of our policy.

## O, Oh

See PUNCTUATION; **Exclamation point;** *O, Oh*.

## Of

See PUNCTUATION; **Comma;** *Of*.

## Off, off of

Use *off* alone.

> The part fell off the machine.
> The boy jumped off the wall.

## OK, O.K., okay

Use *okay* in formal writing, *OK* or *O.K.* in informal.

## Older, oldest

Use *older* in comparing two things, *oldest* in comparing more than two. This guide applies to *elder* and *eldest* also.

> He was the elder of two sons.
> Which of the two books is the older edition?
> They presented an orchid to the oldest mother present.
> but:
> My older brother is a doctor; my younger brother, a student at Stanford.

## One

See USAGE; **We, they, one, you.**

## One's, ones

> Saving one's money is a good habit.
> Those forms are not the right ones.

## One of the

In formal writing, constructions like *one of the people who* and *one of the things that* take plural forms. In spoken English, the singular forms are often used.

> *Formal:* He is one of the directors who agree that . . . .
> *Informal:* He is one of the people who thinks that . . . .

## Oneself

*Oneself* is preferred to *one's self*.

> Taking oneself too seriously is a foolish practice.

## Only

a. Take care to place *only* where it limits according to the meaning of the sentence.

> Only the typists type form letters (not the secretaries).
> The only typist who types form letters is Alice.
> She only types; she does not take dictation.
> She types only form letters requested by the sales department.
> Alice types form letters only when she has spare time.

**b.** Do not use *only* as a preposition for *except* or *but*.

> *Incorrect:* No one is interested only Mr. Lane.

## On, onto, on to

See USAGE; **In, into, in to.**

## Or

When *or* joins two subject words, the verb agrees with the nearer word.

> Only one or two are needed.
> No pencils or paper was furnished.

## Oral, verbal

According to the dictionaries, *oral* means spoken; *verbal* refers to words, spoken or written. Although both are commonly used for *spoken*, use the dictionary meaning in formal writing.

> She presented the material verbally and supported it graphically with maps and charts.
> His oral agreement is tantamount to a written contract.
> *Informal:* His verbal contract is . . . .

## Out of date, up to date, etc.

Hyphenate these expressions only when used *before* the noun.

> His report is up to date.
> Her up-to-date records saved the day.

See PUNCTUATION; **Hyphen;** *Compound words as adjectives.*

## Owing to

See USAGE; **Due to.**

## Pair, pairs

The plural of *pair* is either *pair* or *pairs*.

> They sent only ten pair(s) of gloves.

See USAGE; **Two-part objects.**

## Parallel construction

If two or more sentence parts are joined by one or more conjunctions, the parts should be of like kinds; that is, all single words of the same part of speech, all phrases, or all clauses.

> The shipment was returned not only because it was late but also because two items were incorrect. (*connecting two clauses*)
> *not:*
> The shipment was returned not only for being late but also because two items were incorrect. (*connecting a phrase and a clause*)
>
> A good secretary not only is prompt but also shows initiative. (*connecting two verb phrases*)
> *not:*
> A good secretary is both prompt and shows initiative. (*connecting an adjective and a verb phrase*)
>
> Our plan is to decide on the type of building, to choose an architect, and to let the contracts. (*connecting infinitives*)
> *not:*
> Our plan is to decide on the type of building, choosing an architect, and letting the contracts. (*connecting an infinitive and participles*)

## Pardon, excuse

*Pardon* is used for things of considerable importance; *excuse* for less important ones.

> The company was pardoned for its apparent negligence when the facts were revealed.
> Please excuse the slight delay in answering.

## Participles, dangling

A participial construction should modify a related, logical word except when the construction is absolute (modifying nothing).

> *Dangling:* Leaving the office, the letter was dropped.
> *Logical:* Leaving the office, I dropped the letter.
> *Absolute:* The situation having developed, let's accept the changes it necessitates.

## Passed, past, pastime

*Passed* is the past tense and past participle of the verb *to pass*. *Past* is a noun or an adjective meaning previously, a preposition, or an adverb. *Pastime* (often misspelled *passtime* or *pasttime*) is a diversion.

> They passed the time by reading.
> Go two blocks past Elm Street.
> This bill is past due.
> In the past my favorite pastime was reading.

## Peeve

The noun *peeve* is not given in all dictionaries. The verb *peeve* is labeled *colloquial*.

## People

This word takes plural verbs and pronouns.

> Many people express their wishes in a national election.

## Percent, per cent; percentage

While both styles are in common use, the trend is toward *percent*. *Percentage* is always one word and never used with a number. *Proportion* is often better in formal writing.

See NUMBERS; **Percent.**

## Person, individual, personage, party, people

A *person* is a human being; an *individual* is one apart from a group; a *personage* is a person of importance; a *party* is a legal term for person (other usage is slang). Use *persons* for small numbers, *people* for large masses.

> The will of the people prevailed.
> The rule affected only thirty persons.

## Personal, personnel

*Personal* means private; *personnel* means a body of persons.

> The letter was personal.
> He drove his personal car, not the company car.
> The office personnel were dismissed at 2:30.

## Personally, in person

These terms intensify meaning. Avoid using them in formal writing.

> I personally guarantee each one.
> Mr. Lane made the award in person.

## *Place* compounds

In formal writing, use *anywhere, everywhere, somewhere, nowhere,* and the like. Although some dictionaries recognize *anyplace, everyplace,* and *someplace,* they label them *informal or standard.*

See USAGE; *Where* **compounds**

## Politics

This word is commonly used with singular verbs.

## Position

See USAGE; **Job, position**

## Practical, practicable

*Practical* means sensible, efficient, or useful. *Practicable* implies something that can be put into practice.

> My practical secretary has suggested a practicable method for handling follow-ups.

## Precedence, precedents, precedent

*Precedence* means priority or preference; *precedents* is the plural of the noun *precedent* and means an earlier occurrence; *precedent* (preSEEdent) is an adjective and means earlier in order.

> The guests were seated according to the precedence of their diplomatic positions.
> There are several precedents for that decision.
> The precedent decisions that apply to this case must be considered.

## Predominate, predominant

*Predominate* is a verb meaning to control or surpass; *predominant* is the adjectival form.

> The good features of the plan predominate over its bad ones.
> The predominant features of the plan are good.

## Prefixes

See PUNCTUATION; **Hyphen;** *Prefixes, hyphenated* and *joined.*

## Prepositions

Prepositions should end a construction only to avoid awkward phrasing or when used in a prepositional idiom.

> A collective noun takes a singular verb when the *group* is thought of.
> He left his car to be worked on.
> The widow felt that she had nothing to live for.

For prepositional idioms, see USAGE; **Idioms (b).**

## Presume to, presume upon

These are prepositional idioms, each with its own meaning.

> He presumed to offer advice to the company president.
> He presumed upon our generosity.

## Prerequisite

As a noun, a *prerequisite for;* as an adjective, to be *prerequisite to.*

## Principal, principle

a. *Principal* as an adjective means main; as a noun, it means the main person or a capital sum.

> The principal actor was outstanding in his part.
> The principals in the legal case are present.
> Mrs. Palmer invested the principal of the trust fund and spent the interest therefrom.

b. *Principle* is a noun meaning a rule, guide, truth, etc. It never refers to a person.

> He follows the principle of "least said, soonest mended."

## Privileged to, privileged from

These are prepositional idioms.

> They were privileged to hear a great symphony.
> They were privileged from taking the examination.

## Proved, proven

Although either word may be used as the past participle of *prove, proved* is preferred.

> You have proved (proven) your point.

## Proposition

Correctly used as a noun, *proposition* means an assertion or dignified proposal. Do not use this word as a verb.

## Public

As a noun this word is commonly used with singular verbs and pronouns but can take the plural at times.

> The public quickly tires of its favorites.

## Quantities

See USAGE; **Amounts, quantities.**

## Raise, increase, increment

Business uses all three words for a higher wage or salary. *Raise* is the common word (in Britain, *rise*); *increase* is the more dignified word; *increment* is a personnel word.

## Real, really

Use *real* only as an adjective, *really* is an adverb.

> What really worries us is that the real facts are so obscure.

## Reason is

*The reason is* takes a predicate-noun (or noun-clause) construction. *Because* is a conjunction for adverbial clauses; do not use it here.

> The reason we failed is that (*not* because) we were not prepared.

## Recipe, receipt

*Recipe* means a method of procedure (commonly referring to preparing food); common usage for *receipt* is a written statement that something has been received.

> Mrs. Edwards would like to have your recipe for beef Wellington.
> We are enclosing a receipt for your payment.

## Redundancy

Redundancy is the needless use of words. The phrases below are redundant. In each one, the italicized word is sufficient for clarity.

| both *alike* | *depreciate* in value |
| close *proximity* | month of *April* |
| *continue* on | *repeat* again |
| customary *practice* | two *twin sisters* |

See USAGE; **Consensus of opinion.**

## Remainder

See USAGE; **Balance, remainder.**

## Requisite

See USAGE; **Prerequisite.**

## Resolve

To *resolve* (settle) *something;* to *resolve* (determine) *that;* to *resolve* (separate) *into.*

> We resolved the problem before the deadline.
> We resolve that it won't recur.
> The problem resolved itself into three issues.

## Resolved

See CAPITALIZATION; **Whereas, resolved.**

## Restrictive clause

See USAGE; **That, which, who** and PUNCTUATION; **Comma;** *Restrictive and nonrestrictive elements.*

**Reverend**

Use a first name, initials, or title between *Reverend* and the surname.

> Rev. Maxfield Dowell, the Reverend M. A. Dowell, the Reverend Dr. Dowell (in a reference to him)

See ABBREVIATIONS; **Reverend.**

**Salary, wages**

*Salary* usually refers to a fixed amount paid for a given period; *wages* usually refers to a fixed amount paid for each hour worked.
See USAGE; **Job, position.**

**II, 2d, 2nd**

See ABBREVIATIONS; **II, 2d, 2nd** and PUNCTUATION; **Comma;** *Jr., Sr., II, III.*

**Self (intensive) pronouns**

See PUNCTUATION; **Comma;** *Myself, himself, yourself, etc.*

**Series, lists**

See PUNCTUATION; **Special Element, Series,** page 712.

**Set**

See USAGE; **Sit, set.**

**Shall, will**

*Will* is commonly used for first, second, and third person, future tense. In formal writing, however, express first person, future, with *shall*, second and third persons, future, with *will*. To express the emphatic future, reverse the usages of *shall* and *will*.

> We shall be happy to accept your offer.
> Nevertheless, I *will* take a stand on this matter.

**Should, would**

*Should* is used in uncertainty; *would* is used mainly as a conditional auxiliary verb.

> He should be ready to go soon.
> Do you think we should sign the contract?
> I would have gone except for a previous appointment.
> They would like Italy, I'm sure, once they were there.

**Sic**

See PUNCTUATION; **Brackets;** *Quoted matter (a).*

**Sit, set**

a. *Sit* is intransitive; a person or object sits. The principal parts are *sit, sat, sat.*

> We sat in the lounge and chatted.

b. *Set* is transitive (except when it means to jell or coagulate); a thing is *set* or *placed.* The principal parts are *set, set, set.*

> You *set* something down, and it *sits* there.
> Yesterday you *set* something down, and it *sat* there.

See USAGE; **Transitive verbs.**

**Slow, slowly**

Both words can be adverbs. Both *drive slow* and *drive slowly* are correct.

**So-called**

See PUNCTUATION; **Quotation marks;** *Words different in tone (b).*

**Species**

This word is both singular and plural.

> That species is extinct.
> These species were grouped for study.

**Split infinitives**

See USAGE; **Infinitives (c).**

**Sr., senior**

See ABBREVIATIONS; **II, 2d, 2nd** and PUNCTUATION; **Comma;** *Jr., Sr., II, III.*

**State**

See CAPITALIZATION; **Federal.**

**Stationary, stationery**

*Stationary* means stable or fixed; *stationery* is writing paper.

**Statistics**

Use plural forms except when you mean the science of statistics.

**Street addresses**

See ABBREVIATIONS; **Street addresses.**

## Subjunctive mood

In formal writing, the subjunctive mood is commonly used in contrary-to-fact clauses, clauses expressing doubt, clauses expressing wishes, regrets, demands, recommendations, etc.

> *Subjunctive mood:*
> If he were here, he would agree with me.
> If time were available, I would come.
> If that be true, we must act now.
> I wish I were confident of the outcome.
> We recommend that it be tried.

> *Conventional (indicative) usage:*
> I know he was here because he left a note.
> If he was (*not* were) here earlier, he didn't leave a note.
> If she was planning to go, she didn't tell me.

Professor Porter G. Perrin in his book *Writer's Guide and Index to English* says that, actually, subjunctives are a trait of style rather than a matter of grammar.

## Such as

See PUNCTUATION; **Comma;** *Such as*

## Suffixes

See PUNCTUATION; **Hyphen;** *Suffixes* and WORDS: COINED; **Suffixes**

## Superior

As an adjective, to be superior *to* a person *in* rank; as a noun, to be the superior *of*.

## Sympathetic

To be sympathetic (favorable) *to* or *toward* is colloquial. It is often used in business writing, as *we are sympathetic to the idea*.

## Tactics

Use plural verbs and pronouns except when you mean a military science.

## Tantamount

To be tantamount (equivalent) *to*.

## That, which, who

a. *That* and *which* are not always interchangeable. *That* is preferred for introducing a restrictive clause.

> The phrasing that you suggest is good.
> The book that you recommended is excellent.

b. *Which* is preferred for introducing a nonrestrictive clause.

> The new phrasing, which seems clearer, is better.
> Your help, which we need badly, will save the day.

c. *Who* refers to persons, personified objects, and sometimes to animals. *Who* can introduce either restrictive or nonrestrictive clauses.

> The members who favored the amendment voted *Yes.*
> Mr. Jones, who was out of town, voted by proxy.
> Native Dancer, who won many important races, was a famous racehorse.
> Lady Luck, who had apparently deserted us, returned; and the rain stopped.

d. In formal writing, do not omit *that* as a conjunction.

> *Formal:* We feel that this proposal is fair.
> *Informal:* We feel this idea is a good one.

## They

See USAGE; **We, they, one, you.**

## Till, until

*Until* is preferred at the beginning of a sentence.

## Titles of books, articles, etc.

a. A title used as a noun takes singular forms.

> *Executives Report* says in its latest issue . . . .

b. For form and style for typewritten titles, see PUNCTUATION; **Special Element, Titles of Published Matter,** p. 713.

## Titles of persons

See ABBREVIATIONS; **Titles** and CAPITALIZATION; **Degrees** and **Titles of persons.**

## Together with
See USAGE; **As well as, together with.**

## Trademarks
See CAPITALIZATION; **Trademarked names.**

## Transitive verbs
Dictionaries label verbs *transitive* or *intransitive*. Transitive verbs take objects. Intransitive verbs do not.

> *Transitive:* Send the letter today.
> *Intransitive:* She arrived this morning.

b. Some verbs are transitive *and* intransitive.

> *Transitive:* I wrote a full report.
> She left her luggage at the hotel.
> *Intransitive:* I wrote yesterday.
> She left yesterday.

## Two-part objects (scissors, gloves, etc.)
Words like scissors, while singular in meaning, take plural verbs and pronouns. Preceded by *pair of*, they take singular forms.

> The scissors are sharp.
> The gloves are new.
> This pair of gloves is new.
> Two pair (*or* pairs) of gloves were lost.

## Type of
*Type* is a noun or verb; do not use it as an adjective.

> This type of process is new.
> *not:*
> This type process is new.

## Uninterested
See USAGE; **Disinterested, uninterested**

## United States
Use *the* before *United States* in formal writing, rephrasing if necessary to avoid an awkward construction. (If necessary, substitute *American*.)

> According to laws of the United States . . . .
> *not:*
> According to United States laws . . . .

## Until
See USAGE; **Till, until.**

## Verbal
See USAGE; **Oral, verbal.**

## Verbal phrases
See USAGE; **Infinitives** and **Participles, dangling.**

## Vest
To vest *with* authority; to vest authority *in* a person or agency.

> The courts vest a guardian with power to administer an inheritance.
> Administration of the estate was vested in the trust department of the bank.

## Vice-president
See CAPITALIZATION; **Titles of persons.**

## View
As a verb, *to view with;* as a noun, *in view of* or *with a view to.*

> We view it with indifference.
> In view of the time, we will adjourn.
> With a view to prompt action, we . . . .

## Void
This word is a noun, a verb, or an adjective.

> His resignation left a void in our company.
> Please void check No. 435.
> She was void of any spark of enthusiasm.

## Vulnerable
To be vulnerable (assailable) *to* something *in* some way or place.

> He was vulnerable to criticism in his business practices.

## Wages, salary
See USAGE; **Salary, wages.**

## Weights
See ABBREVIATIONS; **Dimensions and weights** and NUMBERS; **Weights.**

## Well
See USAGE; **Good, well.**

## We, they, one, you
In business writing, these pronouns are used as indefinite pronouns to refer to the group that the

writer represents.  Use them consistently within a sentence or a paragraph.

> We wired our reply.
> If one considers it, he (*or* one) sees that . . . .
> If they reject it, we must then . . . .

### Whereas

See CAPITALIZATION ; **Whereas, resolved.**

### *Where* compounds

*Anywhere, everywhere, nowhere,* and *somewhere* are adverbs and are written as one word. See USAGE ; *Place* **compounds.**

### Whether, whether — or, whether or not

a. In indirect questions, *whether* is preferred to *if*.

> They asked whether he had come.
>> *not:*
> They asked if he had come.

b. For alternatives, use *whether — or* or *whether or not*.  Avoid awkward constructions.

> State whether you will go or stay.
> State whether or not you will go.
>> *not:*
> State whether you will go or not.

### Which, who

See USAGE ; **That, which, who** and **whose.**

### While, awhile

a. Use *while* as a connective for time or as a noun.  *Awhile*, an adverb, is written as one word.

> While Mr. Lambert was out, his caller arrived.
> Once in a while, we find that . . . .
> He left awhile ago.

b. *While* can be used for *although*, but it should not be used for *and*.

> While we see your point, we do not agree.
>> *not:*
> We order nails from the H & P Company, while we order hammers from Black and Burns.

### Who, whom

Use *who* as the subject of a verb, *whom* as the object of a verb or a preposition, or as the subject of an infinitive.

> Send it only to those who asked for it.
> Who do you think will be made chairman?
> Everyone upon whom I called accepted.
> Whom shall I ask first?
> Whom did they ask to be chairman?

### Whose

Use *whose* as a possessive conjunction if *of which* would be awkward.

> The manual for systems and procedures, whose author is unknown, is excellent.
>> *but:*
> A large box, the contents of which were unknown, stood on the loading dock.

### Will

See USAGE ; **Shall, will.**

### Within

See USAGE ; **Inside of a, within.**

### Yes, no

Type these words in any of these ways (but consistently in a writing).

> He will probably say "Yes."    He will probably say Yes.
> He will probably say "yes."    He will probably say yes.
> He will probably say Yes.

See PUNCTUATION ; **Comma;** *Words that answer.*

### Yet

See PUNCTUATION ; **Comma;** *Yet.*

### WORDS: COINED

Coined and picturesque words do not need quotation marks or underlining if they are

WORDS:COINED; COMPOUND; DIVISION; FOREIGN—Page 733

hyphenated or if they are appropriate to the context; set them off only to avoid misinterpretation or to label them as clever usage.

> Her shrug-of-the-shoulders attitude . . . .
> The regulations were written in officialese style.

### Conversions

A *conversion* is the unconventional use of a word. Enclose the word in quotation marks only if the reader may think it a grammatical error or if you want to label it as clever usage. (See next page.)

a. A noun or noun phrase converted to an adjective:

> She wore her *mistress-of-the-manor* expression.
> He is a *meat-and-potatoes* man.
> He was in his *comedian* mood.

b. An adjective or adverb converted to a verb:

> We *nonstopped* to Dallas.
> He *low-keyed* his way into making the sale.
> They *perhapsed* so often that we knew they were uninterested.

c. A noun converted to a verb:

> The boy *dogged* his father's footsteps.
> She *apple-pied* us until we could scarcely move.
> They *museumed* their way across Europe.

### Hyphens

Use a hyphen to connect compound coinages. See WORDS: COINED; **Conversions** and **Prefixes** and **Suffixes.**

### Prefixes

Handle words coined with prefixes according to the following:

ABBREVIATIONS; **Coined verb forms** and PUNCTUATION; **Hyphen;** *Letter prefixes* and *Prefixes, hyphenated.*

### Suffixes

a. If a word coined with a suffix would be hard to read, use a hyphen.

> He is an uh-er and ah-er (*not* uher and aher).

b. *-able and -ible.* In coinages, use the suffix -*able*, not -*ible*.

| | | |
|---|---|---|
| electable | put-downable | yesable |
| convinceable | bypassable | |

c. *-er and -ee.* Join -*er* to indicate the person acting, -*ee* to indicate the person acted upon. If the verb ends in *e*, drop one *e*.

> maintainer, maintainee    berater, beratee
> telephoner, telephonee    persuader, persuadee

d. *-ish.* Join to the word unless a hyphen is needed for clarity.

| | | |
|---|---|---|
| hindsightish | sixty-ish | tycoonish |

e. *-ize.* Join to a noun or adjective to form a verb, as *winterize*. If the word ends in a vowel, hyphenate, as *Sohio-ize, bureau-ize*.

f. *-like.* Join the suffix -*like* to the word unless the word ends in *l* or an awkward word would result. See USAGE; **Suffixes.**

g. *-proof.* To imply imperviousness, add -*proof* to the base word. Use a hyphen only if the word ends in *p* or *if* an awkward word would result. See USAGE; **Suffixes.**

h. *Other suffixes.* To coin a word with any other suffix, look up the suffix in the dictionary and follow the form of the examples given.

---

## WORDS: COMPOUND

*Compounds* are written solid, hyphenated, or open (as separate words). First consult a dictionary for the proper form of a compound. If the word is not given, consult this Reference Guide under one of the following headings:

CAPITALIZATION; **Hyphenated words** and **Titles of persons**

NUMBERS; **Compound numeric adjectives** and **Fractions** and **Hyphenated numbers**

POSSESSIVES; **Compound words**

PUNCTUATION; **Hyphen; Capitalized compound words, Compound words as adjectives, Letter prefixes, Prefixes (hyphenated and with mixed usage), Suffixes**

USAGE; *Place* compounds, *Where* compounds

WORDS: COINED

---

## WORD DIVISION

Typewriters without proportional spacing cannot and need not maintain the even right margins of typeset material. But because the reader will be distracted both by an unduly ragged margin and by excessive end-of-line word divisions the best course is to follow (judiciously) these rules:

a. DO NOT DIVIDE:

1. One-syllable words

| | | | |
|---|---|---|---|
| freight | through | straight | brought |

2. Words of five or fewer letters (preferably *six* or fewer)

| into | after | until | proper | notice |

3. Abbreviations, numbers, dates, names of persons (Avoid separating titles, initials, and professional and scholastic degrees from a name. If necessary to divide, do so at a logical point: May 14,/1974 or Mr. James A./ Hanover.)

4. Two-letter first or last syllables

5. Contractions

| couldn't | you'll | doesn't |

6. The last word in over two successive lines of typing

7. The last word in a paragraph or on a page

b. Divide hyphenated words only at the hyphen.

| self-criticism | profit-sharing |

c. Divide words:

1. After an internal one-letter syllable

| criti-cism | tele-vision | sepa-rate |

*Except:* Do not divide *able, ible, icle, ical, cial,* or *sion.*

| biolog-ical | change-able | deduct-ible | spe-cial |

2. Between two vowels separately pronounced

| radi-ator | sci-ence | cli-ents | situ-ation |

3. Preferably at a prefix or suffix

| mis-spelled | driv-ing | depart-ment | exten-sion |

4. Between double consonants unless the base word ends in the double consonant

| neces-sary | capil-lary | car-rier | excel-lent |
| will-ing | tell-ing | careless-ness | staff-ing |

*but:*

| discus-sion | impres-sive | impres-sion |

5. To improve readability by putting as much of a word on a line as is practical, even though the word has several acceptable points of division

considera-tion (*not* consid-eration)
documenta-tion (*not* docu-mentation)
inadequa-cies (*not* inade-quacies)

WORDS: FOREIGN

The English language has evolved from the combination of and additions from various languages, mostly Germanic. The practice of borrowing and adding foreign words is a continuing one; therefore, the secretary often needs to present foreign words in typewritten form.

a. Many "foreign" words have been so accepted into the language that they are considered *Anglicized*. Do not underline Anglicized words. Some common Anglicized words are:

| chauffeur | faux pas |
| chic | fete |
| cliche | hors d' oeuvre |
| coiffure | laissez faire |
| coup d' etat | Liebfraumilch |
| creche | maitre d' hotel (maitre d') |
| du jour | naive |
| eclair | Noel |
| entree | passe |
| ersatz | precis |
| facade | soupcon |

b. Typeset material often uses diacritical marks even with Anglicized words. Some common diacritical marks are:

| ´ | Acute accent (French, Spanish) |
| ` | Grave accent (French, Italian, English) |
| ^ | Circumflex (French) |
| ¨ | Dieresis (French, English), crema (Spanish), Umlaut (German) |
| ~ | Tilde (Spanish) |
| ¸ | Cedilla (French) |

If you find it necessary to use diacritical marks, insert them in ink as shown below.

mañana                tête-à-tête

c. Some foreign terms that are commonly underlined in typewritten material are shown below.

COMMUNICATIONS GUIDE —Page 736

| anschluss | mañana |
| cognoscente | noblesse oblige |
| de trop | nouveau riche |
| entre nous | rapprochement |
| et al. | vis-à-vis |
| joie de vivre | zeitgeist |

**THE C. J. KREHBIEL COMPANY**
PRINTERS AND BOOK MANUFACTURERS
ESTABLISHED 1871

3962 VIRGINIA AVE. (FAIRFAX)    CINCINNATI, OHIO 45227    AREA CODE 513
271-6035

December 10, 19--

Mr. Edward Caldwell
Akron Chamber of Commerce
74 South Main Street
Akron, Ohio 44308

Dear Mr. Caldwell

This letter is typed in block style with open punctuation.
Every line begins at the left margin. Only essential punctuation marks are used in the opening and closing lines.

The distinctive feature of this letter style is that the
date, the inside address, the salutation, the attention line
(when used), all lines in the body, the complimentary close,
and all signature lines begin at the left margin. No tabulator stops are necessary.

Typing time is accordingly reduced. First, time required
to set tabulator stops and to use the tabulator is saved.
Second, by omitting all except the essential punctuation
marks, the number of typing strokes is decreased.

The use of "open" punctuation is appropriate with this letter
style.

Cordially yours

*James Harvey*

James Harvey, Consultant

ao

---

AMERICAN TELEPHONE AND TELEGRAPH COMPANY
195 BROADWAY, NEW YORK, N. Y.  10007
AREA CODE 212    393-9800

December 10, 19--

Mr. Thomas James
Caswell-Higgins Associates
Suite 385, Maumee Tower
Toledo, Ohio 43604

Dear Mr. James

    SUBJECT:  The Modified Block Letter Style

This letter is typed in modified block style with blocked
paragraphs.  Open punctuation is used in the opening and
closing lines.

Contrast this style with the block style, and you will notice that the date line has been moved to begin at horizontal
center (although it would be appropriate also to end at the
right margin) and that the closing lines have been blocked
at the horizontal center of the letterhead.  All other lines
begin at the left margin.  These modifications of the block
style give the style its name--modified block.

When an attention line is used in this style of letter, it
is begun at the left margin.  If a subject line is used, it
is begun at the left margin or centered over the body of
the letter a double space below the salutation.

Although open punctuation is used in this letter, it is
equally appropriate to use mixed punctuation.

                    Sincerely yours

                    *David M. Balz*

                    David M. Balz, Director

mac

---

**Packaging** CORPORATION OF AMERICA

2029-30 CAREW TOWER • CINCINNATI, OHIO 45202 • AREA 513 621-9248
A Major Component of Tenneco Inc.

December 10, 19--

Mr. William Summers
The Electromagnetic Corp.
One Erieview Plaza
Cleveland, Ohio 44114

Dear Mr. Summers:

    This letter is typed in modified block style with in-
dented paragraphs.  Mixed punctuation is used in the opening
and closing lines.  This punctuation style calls for a colon
after the salutation and a comma after the complimentary
close.  All other end-of-line punctuation is omitted in the
opening and closing lines, unless a line ends in an abbreviation that requires the usual abbreviation period.

    Note that the date line is centered (although it could
have been typed to begin at center or to end at the right
margin); the subject line is centered; the first line of
each paragraph is indented 5 spaces (although 10- or 15-space
indentions are also commonly used); the closing lines are
blocked at the horizontal center of the letterhead.  All
other lines begin at the left margin.

    Although mixed punctuation is used in this letter, it
would be equally acceptable to use open punctuation.

                    Sincerely yours,

                    *George R. Sanders*

                    George R. Sanders

ok

---

 **ADMINISTRATIVE MANAGEMENT SOCIETY**
*Cincinnati Chapter*
AMS Formerly NOMA

Dated Today

Ms. Office Secretary
Better Business Letters, Inc.
1 Main Street
Busytown, U. S. A.

SIMPLIFIED LETTER

There's a new movement under way to take some of the monotony out of
letters given you to type, Ms. Secretary.  The movement is symbolized
by the Simplified Letter being sponsored by AMS.

What is it?  You're reading a sample.

Notice the left block format and the general positioning of the letter.
We didn't write "Dear Miss -----," nor will we write "Yours truly" or
"Sincerely yours."  Are they really important?  We feel just as friendly
toward you without them.

Notice the following points:

1. Date location
2. The address
3. The subject
4. The name of the writer

Now take a look at the Suggestions prepared for you.  Talk them over
with your boss.  But don't form a final opinion until you've really
tried out The Letter.  That's what our secretary did.  As a matter of
fact, she finally wrote most of the Suggestions herself.

She says she's sold--and hopes you'll have good luck with better (Simplified) letters.

*Arthur E. Every*

ARTHUR E. EVERY - STAFF DIRECTOR, TECHNICAL DIVISION
cc:  R. P. Brecht, W. H. Evans, H. F. Grebe

---

**Four Basic Letter Styles.** (1) Block style, open punctuation, (2) Modified block style with blocked
paragraphs, open punctuation, (3) Modified block style with indented paragraphs, mixed punctuation,
(4) AMS Simplified style

*William Allen*

Charlton Apartments
Charlton Bay, Massachusetts 01507

December 10, 19--

Dear Henry,

The inside address typed at the end of a letter removes the business touch and tone from the letter and makes it more personal.

This letter form is used also for very formal letters, such as letters to public officials and honored persons. In addition, letters of appreciation or sympathy or congratulations are typed in this form.

The reference initials are omitted. If the person receiving the letter knows the writer well, it is not necessary that his name be typed as part of the signature.

Cordially,

*Bill*

Mr. Henry D. Ransom
302 Peachtree Street
Atlanta, Georgia  30308

---

**Packaging** CORPORATION OF AMERICA  Form 11-0001-1

## INTEROFFICE MEMORANDUM

TO : New Members of the
      Stenographic Pool

FROM: Judith L. Rees
      Correspondence Supervisor

DATE : December 10, 19--

SUBJECT: Interoffice Correspondence

The interoffice or interdepartment letterhead is used, as the name implies, for correspondence between offices or departments within the company. One advantage of this form is that it can be set up quickly. For instance, this letter requires settings for only the margins and one tabulator stop. Titles (Mr., Mrs., Dr., etc.), the salutation, the complimentary close, and the formal signature are usually omitted.

Triple-space between the last line of the heading and the first line of the message. Short messages of no more than five lines may be double-spaced; longer messages should be single-spaced.

Reference initials should be included. When enclosures are sent, the enclosure notation should appear below the reference initials.

sva

**Interoffice Memorandum**

**Personal and Formal
Style Typed on
Personal Letterhead**

---

## FORM AND PLACEMENT OF ENVELOPE ADDRESS PARTS FOR OPTICAL CHARACTER READERS

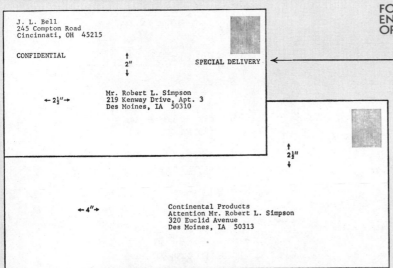

### Notations to Post Office
Begin at least three line spaces above the address, below the stamp. Type in all capital letters. Underline if desired. Such notations include:

AIRMAIL
SPECIAL DELIVERY
REGISTERED
HAND STAMP

See also page 239.

### On-Receipt   Notations
Type (in all capitals) a triple space below the return address and 3 spaces from the left edge of the envelope. Such notations include:
HOLD FOR ARRIVAL
PLEASE FORWARD
CONFIDENTIAL
Type an *attention line* immediately below the company name.

### Requirements for Optical Character Readers
Post office optical character readers are programmed to scan a specific area on all envelopes; so the address must be completely within this read-zone, *blocked in style, single-spaced.* The state abbreviations shown on page 751 (typed in uppercase) must be used. An apartment or room number should follow the street address *on the same line.* Acceptable placements for a No. 10 and a No. 6¾ envelope are specified in the illustration above.

# PROOFREADER'S MARKS

## INSERT MARKS FOR PUNCTUATION

| | |
|---|---|
| ᵛ | Apostrophe |
| [/] | Brackets · |
| : ⊙ | Colon |
| ⌃ ᵔ/ | Comma |
| ×××/ | Ellipsis |
| !/ | Exclamation point |
| -/ | Hyphen |
| ⌃ ⌃ | Inferior figure |
| · · ·/ | Leaders |
| (/) | Parentheses |
| ⊙ | Period |
| ?/ | Question mark |
| ᵛᵛ ᵛᵛ | Quotation mark |
| ; ⊙ | Semicolon |
| ᵛ ᵛ | Superior figure |

## OTHER MARKS

| | |
|---|---|
| ‖ | Align type; set flush |
| bf | Boldface type |
| × ⓧ | Broken letter |
| ≡ Cap | Capitalize |
| C+sc | Capitals and small capitals |
| ℰ | Delete |
| ℬ | Delete and close up |
| ∧ | Insert (caret) |
| ital | Italic, change to |
| Bf ital | Italic boldface |
| stet | Let type stand |
| lc | Lower case type |

| | |
|---|---|
| ⊔ | Move down; lower |
| ⊓ | Move up; raise |
| ⊏ | Move to left |
| ⊐ | Move to right |
| ¶ | Paragraph |
| no ¶ ⊏ | No new paragraph |
| out s.c. | Out; omit; see copy |
| �6 | Reverse; upside down |
| rom | Roman, change to |
| ⟵ | Run in material |
| run in | Run in material on same line |
| # | Space, add (horizontal) |
| > | Space, add (vertical) |
| ⌒ | Space, close up (horizontal) |
| < | Space, close up (vertical) |
| ⓢⓟ | Spell out |
| tr ∩ | Transpose |
| (?) ⑦ | Verify or supply information |
| wf | Wrong font |

All marks should be made in the margin on the line in which the error occurs; if more than one correction occurs in one line, they should appear in their order separated by a slanting line.

Errors should not be blotted out.

738          *Communications Guide* • PROOFREADER'S MARKS

One author → [1]W. K. Kuhn, The Evolution of Economic Thought (2d ed; Cincinnati: South-Western Publishing Co., 1970), p. 207.

Two authors (and editor) → [2]E. Jerome McCarthy and J. A. McCarthy, Integrated Data Processing Systems, ed. Durward Humes (New York: John Wiley & Sons, Inc., 1966), p. 74.

Ibid. → [3]Ibid., pp. 111-113.

Three authors → [4]A. B. Carson, Arthur E. Carlson, and Clem Boling, Secretarial Accounting (9th ed.; Cincinnati: South-Western Publishing Co., 1972), p. 59.

Four or more authors → [5]M. E. Jansson et al., Handbook of Applied Mathematics (4th ed.; New York: D. Van Nostrand Co., Inc., 1967), p. 42.

Unpublished material → [6]Morris R. Ingraham, Updating Secretarial Training Procedures, a mimeographed report by the Cogshall School of Business, 1973.

Op. cit. → [7]Carson, op. cit., p. 63.

Government agency → [8]U.S. Treasury Department, Internal Revenue Service, Your Federal Income Tax, Publication No. 17 (Washington: U.S. Government Printing Office, 1972), p. 87.

Magazine article → [9]"The Wacky World of the Eurodollar," Newsweek (March 19, 1973), p. 73.

Article from a bound volume → [10]John T. Dunlop, "New Forces in the Economy," Harvard Business Review (Boston: Graduate School of Business Administration, Harvard University, 1968), Vol. 46, No. 2 (March-April, 1968), p. 121.

Newspaper article → [11]Albert R. Hunt, "Tax Reform: Still over the Horizon," Wall Street Journal (March 5, 1973), p. 12, col. 4.

Loc. cit. → [12]Dunlop, loc. cit.

**FOOTNOTE CONSTRUCTION:** Indent to paragraph point; single-space; double-space between items. Use quotation marks with titles of publication *parts*; underline titles of *complete* publications. *Ibid.* refers to the immediately preceding source; *loc. cit.* refers to the same location of a previous citation with intervening footnotes; *op. cit.*, to a different page of a previous citation.

Three authors → Carson, A. B., Arthur E. Carlson, and Clem Boling. Secretarial Accounting, 9th ed. Cincinnati: South-Western Publishing Co., 1972.

Article from a bound volume → Dunlop, John T. "New Forces in the Economy," Harvard Business Review. (Boston: Graduate School of Business Administration, Harvard University, 1968), Vol. 46, No. 2 (March-April, 1968), p. 121.

Newspaper article → Hunt, Albert R. "Tax Reform: Still over the Horizon," Wall Street Journal. (March 5, 1973), p. 12, col. 4.

Unpublished material → Ingraham, Morris R. Updating Secretarial Training Procedures, a mimeographed report by the Cogshall School of Business, 1973.

Four or more authors → Jansson, M. E. et al. Handbook of Applied Mathematics, 4th ed. New York: D. Van Nostrand Co., Inc., 1967.

One author → Kuhn, W. E. The Evolution of Economic Thought, 2d ed. Cincinnati: South-Western Publishing Co., 1970.

Two authors (and editor) → McCarthy, E. Jerome, and J. A. McCarthy. Integrated Data Processing Systems, edited by Durward Humes. New York: John Wiley & Sons, Inc., 1966.

Government agency → U.S. Treasury Department, Internal Revenue Service. Your Federal Income Tax, Publication No. 17. Washington: U.S. Government Printing Office, 1972.

Magazine article → "The Wacky World of the Eurodollar," Newsweek. (March 19, 1973), p. 73.

**BIBLIOGRAPHY CONSTRUCTION:** Present the items alphabetically by the first word of an item that is not an article. Start each item at the left margin; indent subsequent lines 5 spaces. Invert the order of only the first author's name. Give page references only for citations of *parts* of publications. Omit parentheses around publication facts except for periodicals.

# FORM AND ARRANGEMENT OF BUSINESS LETTER PARTS

| Letter Part | Line Position | Horizontal Placement | Points to Be Observed | Acceptable Forms |
|---|---|---|---|---|
| DATE | If a floating date line is used, the date is typed from 12 to 20 lines from the top of the letterhead or plain sheet, depending upon letter length. A fixed date line is usually typed a double space below the last line of the letterhead. | *Block, AMS Simplified Styles:* Even with left margin. *Modified Block Style:* Begun at center of the sheet; to end flush with right margin; or according to the letterhead. | 1. Do not abbreviate names of months. 2. Unusual 2- and 3-line arrangements are not commonly used. 3. Do not use *d, nd, rd, st,* or *th* following the day of the month. | December 14, 19-- <br><br> 2 May 19-- <br><br> (Used primarily in government and military correspondence.) |
| ADDRESS | *With Floating Date Line:* Typed on 4th line below the date. *With Fixed Date Line:* Typed from 3 to 9 lines below the date, depending on letter length. *Government Letter:* Typed on the 14th line. *Personal Style:* Placed at the left margin 5 or 6 lines below the last closing line. | Single-spaced with all lines even at left margin. Use at least three lines for address. Place business title at end of first line or beginning of second line, whichever gives better balance. For a long company name indent the second line 2 or 3 spaces. | 1. Follow addressee's letter-head style. 2. Do not abbreviate *Street* or *Avenue* unless it improves appearance. 3. For the name of a town or city, do not use *City.* 4. Use postal zip codes in addresses. 5. Do not use % for *In Care Of.* (This follows the name line.) | Miss Rose Bannaian Manager, Rupp Steel Co. 2913 Drexmore Avenue Dallas, TX 75206 <br><br> Mr. Russell H. Rupp 68 Devoe Avenue Dallas, Texas 75206 <br><br> (Refer to the Reference Guide for specific comments.) |
| ATTENTION LINE | *Preferred:* Typed a double space below address and a double space above salutation. | Typed even with left margin or begun at the paragraph point. | 1. Do not abbreviate *Attention.* 2. Unnecessary to use *of* as in *Attention of Mr. R. H. Rupp.* | Attention Mr. R. H. Rupp Attention Purchasing Agent Attention Mr. L. Cox, Agent |
| SALUTATION | Typed a double space below last line of address or a double space below attention line. (Note: Omitted in the AMS Simplified style and in interoffice correspondence.) | Typed even with left margin. | 1. Use *Gentlemen* for a company, a committee, a numbered post-office box, a collective organization made up entirely of men (or of men and women). 2. In addressing women, substitute *Ladies* or *Mesdames* for *Gentlemen; Madam* for *Sir; Miss* or *Mrs.* for *Mr.;* use *Ms.* when the marital status of a woman is unknown. | Dear Mr. Rupp Gentlemen Dear Sir: Dear Russell: Dear Ms. Willis My dear Mrs. Cox |

| Part | Placement | Style | Guidelines | Examples |
|---|---|---|---|---|
| **SUBJECT (or REFERENCE) LINE** | Typed a double space below salutation. Some printed letterheads indicate position for subject or file number (usually at the top of the letterhead). | Typed even with left margin in the block and AMS styles. (In the AMS style, the word "Subject" is omitted and the line is typed in all capitals a triple space below last line of address.) *Modified Block Style:* Typed even with left margin, at paragraph point, or centered. | 1. *Subject* may be typed in all capitals or with only first letter capitalized. *Subject* may be omitted; if it is used, it should be followed by a colon. 2. Do not abbreviate *Subject*; capitalize important words in the subject line. | Subject: Pension Plan<br>SUBJECT: Pension Plan<br>Pension Plan<br>PENSION PLAN<br>Your File 987<br>Reference: File #586<br>Re: File 586 |
| **BODY** | Typed a double space below salutation or subject (reference) line. *AMS Simplified Style:* Typed a triple space below subject line. | *Block Style:* First line of each paragraph typed even with left margin. *Modified Block Style: First* line of each paragraph typed even with left margin or indented 5 or 10 spaces. | 1. Keep right margin as even as possible, avoiding hyphens at ends of lines where possible. 2. For enumerated material, indent 5 spaces from both margins and double-space after each item. (In the AMS style, indent listed items 5 spaces except when numbered.) | Single-space lines of paragraphs; double-space between paragraphs. A short one-paragraph letter may be double-spaced with indented paragraphs. |
| **SECOND-PAGE HEADING and BODY** | *Heading:* Begin approximately 1" (6 blank lines) below the top edge of the sheet. *Body:* Begin on the 3d line from the heading, using the same margins as for the preceding page. Do not begin with the last part of a divided word. Include at least two lines of a paragraph. | Mr. Jerry W. Robinson<br>Page 2<br>(Current Date)<br><br>Mr. Jerry W. Robinson   2   (Current Date) | Type the second and succeeding pages on plain paper. The heading is typed even with the left margin in block form or in a one-line arrangement (illustrated below). Use the one-line arrangement if a page might be crowded. | |
| **COMPLIMENTARY CLOSE** | Typed a double space below the last line of letter body. Omitted in the AMS Simplified letter style and in interoffice correspondence. | Begin at the center except in block style where the complimentary close is typed even with the left margin. | 1. Do not extend the longest of closing lines noticeably beyond right margin. 2. Capitalize first word only. 3. Avoid contractions. | Very truly yours,*<br>Sincerely yours,*<br>Cordially, or Cordially yours,*<br>Respectfully yours,<br>*Also written with *Yours* as the first word |
| **COMPANY NAME** | If used, typed a double space below the complimentary close. | Typed even with the beginning of the complimentary close. | 1. Capitalize all letters. 2. Type name exactly as it appears on letterhead. | TRIMOUNT CLOTHING COMPANY<br>JOHNSON & RAND SHOE CO. |

| Letter Part | Line Position | Horizontal Placement | Points to Be Observed | Acceptable Forms |
|---|---|---|---|---|
| SIGNATURE (Name and Title of Signer) | Typed 3 blank lines below complimentary close (or company name, if used). *AMS Style:* All capital letters at least 4 lines below last line of body. NOTE: If both the name and title are used, they may be typed on the same line or the title may be typed on the next line below the typed name. The style giving the best balance should be used. | Typed even with first letter of complimentary close (or company name, if used). *AMS Style:* Even with left margin. | 1. Capitalize important words in title. 2. When dictator's name appears in letterhead, use the title only. 3. Do not use *Mr.* in typing a man's name. (See pages 197–198 for secretarial signatures.) | Harold A. Wenchstern / Director of Personnel / Bruce Ryan, Manager / Purchasing Department / *AMS Style:* / LOUIS K. COX - AGENT |
| IDENTIFICA-TION NOTATION | Typed a double space below or on the same line with the last of closing lines. | Typed even with the left margin. (For a complete discussion on the use of reference initials, see page 193.) | Omit dictator's initials when his name is typed as part of closing lines. | jc    JWR/jc / jwr/jc JWR:jc / JWRobinson/jc |
| ENCLOSURE | Typed a double space below the identification notation. | Typed even with the left margin. | While *Enc.* and *Encl.* are not preferred forms, they are in common use because they save time. | Enclosure   Enc.   Encl. / Enclosures 3    Enclosures / Encs. 2      Catalog #23 / Enclosures: Check    Price List #8 / Contract |
| POSTSCRIPT | Typed a double space below the identification notation or the last typed line. | Indent or block the postscript according to the style used in other paragraphs of the letter. | Initials of the writer may be typed below the postscript in place of a second signature. | P.S. / Or omit the P.S. and write in the same form as a paragraph in the letter. |
| CARBON-COPY NOTATION | Typed a double space below the identification notation or the last typed line. (If notation not to appear on original, type at top of carbon copies.) | Typed even with the left margin. (When typed at the top of carbon copies, may be centered or placed at the left margin.) | 1. *cc* or *Copy to* are generally used to indicate "Carbon Copy to." 2. Use *BC* for "blind copy," if notation is typed on carbon copies only. | cc: / BC / cc: Mr. H. R. King / Miss K. Neilen / Copy to Mr. H. R. King, Cashier / BC to HRKing |
| MAILING NOTATION | Typed midway between date and first line of address; may be typed two lines below the last typed line. | Typed even with the left margin. | 1. Typed in all capital letters. 2. May be typed on carbon copies only. | AIRMAIL / SPECIAL DELIVERY / REGISTERED MAIL / CERTIFIED MAIL |
| SEPARATE-COVER NOTATION | Typed a double space below last typed line. | Typed even with the left margin. | Indicates method of transportation and number of envelopes or packages. | Separate Cover - Express / Separate Cover - Mail 2 |

## CORRECT FORMS OF ADDRESS AND REFERENCE

| Person and Address (Envelope and Letter) | Salutation | Complimentary Close | In Referring to the Person; Informal Introduction | In Speaking to the Person |
|---|---|---|---|---|
| **U. S. PRESIDENT**<br>The President<br>The White House<br>Washington, D. C. 20500 | Sir<br>Mr. President<br>Dear Mr. President<br>My dear Mr. President | Respectfully yours<br>Very truly yours | The President<br>Mr. (Name) | Mr. President<br>Sir (in prolonged conversation) |
| **WIFE, U. S. PRESIDENT**<br>Mrs. (Last Name Only)<br>The White House<br>Washington, D. C. 20500 | Dear Mrs. (Last Name Only)<br>My dear Mrs. (Last Name Only) | Respectfully yours<br>Sincerely yours | Mrs. (Last Name Only) | Mrs. (Last Name Only) |
| **U. S. VICE PRESIDENT**<br>The Vice President<br>United States Senate<br>Washington, D. C. 20510 | Sir<br>My dear Mr. Vice President<br>Mr. Vice President | Respectfully yours<br>Very truly yours<br>Sincerely yours | The Vice President<br>Mr. (Name) | Mr. Vice President<br>Mr. (Name) |
| **U. S. CHIEF JUSTICE**<br>The Chief Justice<br>The Supreme Court<br>Washington, D. C. 20543 | Sir<br>Mr. Chief Justice<br>Dear Mr. Chief Justice | Respectfully yours<br>Very truly yours<br>Sincerely yours | The Chief Justice | Mr. Chief Justice |
| **U. S. ASSOCIATE JUSTICE**<br>Mr. Justice (Name)<br>The Supreme Court<br>Washington, D. C. 20543 | Sir<br>Mr. Justice<br>My dear Mr. Justice<br>Dear Justice (Name) | Very truly yours<br>Sincerely yours | Mr. Justice (Name) | Mr. Justice<br>Mr. Justice (Name) |
| **CABINET OFFICER**<br>The Honorable (Name)<br>Secretary of (Office)<br>Washington, D. C. 20520<br><br>The Secretary of (Office)<br>Washington, D. C. 20520 | Sir<br>My dear Mr. Secretary<br>Dear Mr. Secretary<br><br>Madam<br>My dear Madam Secretary<br>Dear Madam Secretary | Very truly yours<br>Sincerely yours | The Secretary of....,<br>  Mr. (Name)<br>The Secretary of....<br>  Mr. (Name)<br>The Secretary of....; (Name)<br>  Mrs. or Miss (Name)<br>The Secretary<br>  Mrs. or Miss (Name) | Mr. Secretary<br>Mr. (Name)<br><br>Madam Secretary<br>Mrs. or Miss (Name) |
| **SPEAKER OF THE HOUSE OF REPRESENTATIVES**<br>The Honorable (Name)<br>Speaker of the House of Representatives<br>Washington, D. C. 20515 | Sir<br>Dear Mr. (Name)<br>My dear Mr. Speaker<br>Mr. Speaker | Very truly yours<br>Sincerely yours | The Speaker, Mr. (Name)<br>Mr. (Name)<br>The Speaker | Mr. Speaker<br>Mr. (Name) |

## CORRECT FORMS OF ADDRESS AND REFERENCE (Continued)

| Person and Address (Envelope and Letter) | Salutation | Complimentary Close | In Referring to the Person; Informal Introduction | In Speaking to the Person |
|---|---|---|---|---|
| **U. S. SENATOR, SENATOR-ELECT**<br>The Honorable (Name)<br>The United States Senate<br>Washington, D. C. 20510<br>or<br>The Honorable (Name),<br>Senator-Elect | Sir<br>Dear Senator (Name)<br>My dear Senator (Name)<br><br>Madam<br>My dear Senator (Name)<br>My dear Mrs. or Miss (Name) | Very truly yours<br>Sincerely yours | Senator (Name) | Senator (Name)<br>Mr. (Name)<br>Senator (Name)<br>Mrs. or Miss (Name) |
| **U. S. REPRESENTATIVE**<br>The Honorable (Name)<br>The House of Representatives<br>Washington, D. C. 20515<br><br>Representative (Name)<br>The House of Representatives<br>Washington, D. C. 20515 | Sir<br>My dear Representative (Name)<br>My dear Sir<br><br>Madam<br>Dear Representative (Name)<br>My dear Mrs. or Miss (Name) | Very truly yours<br>Sincerely yours | Representative (Name)<br>Mr. (Name)<br>Representative (Name)<br>Mrs. or Miss (Name) | Mr. (Name)<br>Mrs. or Miss (Name) |
| **U. S. GOVERNMENT OFFICIAL**<br>The Honorable (Name)<br>Director of Bureau of the Budget<br>Washington, D. C. 20503<br>Librarian of Congress<br>Washington, D. C. 20540 | Sir<br>Dear Mr. (Name)<br>My dear Mr. (Name)<br><br>Madam<br>Dear Mrs. or Miss (Name)<br>My dear Mrs. or Miss (Name) | Very truly yours<br>Sincerely yours | Mr. (Name)<br>Mrs. or Miss (Name) | Mr. (Name)<br>Mrs. or Miss (Name) |
| **AMERICAN AMBASSADOR**<br>The Honorable (Name)<br>American Ambassador<br>Paris, France | Sir<br>My dear Mr. Ambassador<br><br>Madam<br>My dear Madam Ambassador | Very truly yours<br>Sincerely yours | The American Ambassador[1]<br>The Ambassador<br>Mr. (Name)<br>Madam Ambassador<br>Mrs. or Miss (Name) | Mr. Ambassador<br>Mr. (Name)<br>Madam Ambassador<br>Mrs. or Miss (Name) |
| **AMERICAN MINISTER**<br>The Honorable (Name)<br>American Minister<br>Ottawa, Canada | Sir<br>My dear Mr. Minister<br><br>Madam<br>My dear Mrs. or Miss (Name)<br>My dear Madam Minister | Very truly yours<br>Sincerely yours | The American Minister,<br>Mr. (Name)[1]<br>The Minister; Mr. (Name)<br>The American Minister,<br>Mrs. or Miss (Name)<br>The Minister<br>Mrs. or Miss (Name) | Mr. Minister<br>Mr. (Name)<br>Madam Minister<br>Mrs. or Miss (Name) |

[1]In presenting or referring to American Ambassadors and Ministers in any Latin-American country, say "Ambassador of the United States" or "Minister of the United States."

# CORRECT FORMS OF ADDRESS AND REFERENCE (Continued)

| Person and Address (Envelope and Letter) | Salutation | Complimentary Close | In Referring to the Person; Informal Introduction | In Speaking to the Person |
|---|---|---|---|---|
| **U.S. REPRESENTATIVE TO THE UNITED NATIONS**<br>The Honorable (Name)<br>The United States Representative to the United Nations<br>New York, New York 10017 | Sir<br>Dear Mr. (Name)<br>My dear Mr. (Name)<br>*With Ambassadorial Rank:*<br>My dear Ambassador (Name) | Very truly yours<br>Sincerely yours | Mr. (Name)<br><br><br>Mr. Ambassador | Mr. (Name)<br><br><br>Mr. Ambassador |
| **FOREIGN AMBASSADOR IN U.S.**<br>His Excellency (Name)<br>The Ambassador of France<br>Washington, D. C. | Sir<br>Excellency<br>My dear Mr. Ambassador | Respectfully yours<br>Sincerely yours<br>Very truly yours | The Ambassador of.....,<br>Mr. (Name)<br>The Ambassador<br>Mr. (Name) | Mr. Ambassador<br>Mr. (Name) |
| **FOREIGN MINISTER IN U.S.**<br>The Honorable (Name)<br>Minister of Italy<br>Washington, D. C. | Sir<br>My dear Mr. Minister | Respectfully yours<br>Sincerely yours<br>Very truly yours | The Minister of.....,<br>Mr. (Name)<br>The Minister<br>Mr. (Name) | Mr. Minister<br>Mr. (Name) |
| **AMERICAN CONSUL**<br>(Name), Esq.<br>The American Consul<br>United States Embassy<br>(Foreign City, Country) | Sir<br>Dear Mr. (Name)<br>My dear Mr. (Name) | Very truly yours<br>Sincerely yours | Mr. (Name) | Mr. (Name) |
| **FOREIGN CONSUL**<br>(Name), Esq.<br>The French Consul<br>(American City, State) | Sir<br>Dear Mr. (Name)<br>My dear Mr. (Name) | Very truly yours<br>Sincerely yours | Mr. (Name) | Mr. (Name) |
| **GOVERNOR OF A STATE**<br>His Excellency the Governor of (State) or<br>The Honorable (Name)<br>Governor of (State)<br>(Capital City, State) | Sir<br>Dear Governor<br>My dear Governor (Name) | Respectfully yours<br>Very truly yours<br>Sincerely yours | Governor (Name)<br>The Governor<br>The Governor of (State) | Governor (Name)<br>Governor |
| **MEMBER, STATE LEGISLATURE**<br>The Honorable (Name)<br>The State Senate or<br>The House of Representatives<br>(Capital City, State) | Sir<br>Dear Senator or Representative (Name)<br>My dear Mr. (Name) | Very truly yours<br>Sincerely yours | Mr. (Name)<br>Senator (Name)<br>Representative (Name) | Mr. (Name)<br>Senator (Name)<br>Representative (Name) |
| **MAYOR OF A CITY**<br>The Honorable (Name)<br>Mayor of the City of.....<br>(City, State) | Sir<br>Dear Mayor (Name)<br>My dear Mayor (Name) | Very truly yours<br>Sincerely yours | Mayor (Blank)<br>The Mayor | Mayor (Name)<br>Mr. Mayor |

## CORRECT FORMS OF ADDRESS AND REFERENCE (Continued)

| Person and Address (Envelope and Letter) | Salutation | Complimentary Close | In Referring to the Person; Informal Introduction | In Speaking to the Person |
|---|---|---|---|---|
| **JUDGE OF A COURT**<br>The Honorable (Name)<br>Judge of the ...Court<br>(Local Address) | Sir<br>Dear Judge (Name)<br>My dear Judge (Name) | Very truly yours<br>Sincerely yours | Judge (Name) | Judge (Name) |
| **MILITARY PERSONNEL**<br>(Rank) (Name)<br>Post or Name of Ship<br>City, State | Sir<br>Dear (Rank) (Name)<br>My dear (Rank) (Name) | Very truly yours<br>Sincerely yours | (Rank) (Name) | (Rank) (Name) |
| **CLERGYMEN (PROTESTANT)**<br>The Reverend (Name), D.D. <u>or</u><br>The Reverend (Name)<br>Parsonage Address<br>City, State | Reverend Sir<br>Dear Dr. (Name)<br>My dear Sir<br>My dear Mr. (Name) | Respectfully yours<br>Sincerely yours<br>Yours faithfully | The Reverend Doctor (Name)<br>Doctor (Name)<br>The Reverend (Name)<br>Mr. (Name) | Dr. (Name)<br>Sir<br>Mr. (Name) |
| **RABBI (JEWISH FAITH)**<br>The Rabbi of<br>Congregation (Name)<br>Local Address | Sir<br>My dear Rabbi (Name)<br>My dear Rabbi | Respectfully yours<br>Sincerely yours<br>Yours faithfully | Dr. (Name)<br>Rabbi (Name) | Dr. (Name)<br>Rabbi (Name) |
| **PRIEST (ROMAN CATHOLIC)**<br>The Reverend (Name), (Degree)<br>Local Address | Reverend Father<br>Dear Father (Name)<br>Reverend and dear Sir | Sincerely yours<br>Respectfully yours<br>Yours faithfully | Dr. (Name)<br>Father (Name) | Dr. (Name)<br>Father (Name) |
| **SISTER (ROMAN CATHOLIC)**<br>Sister (Name)<br>Local Address | Dear Sister<br>Dear Sister (Name) | Sincerely yours<br>Respectfully yours<br>Yours faithfully | Sister (Name)<br>Sister | Sister (Name)<br>Sister |
| **PRESIDENT (COLLEGE OR UNIVERSITY)**<br>Dr. (Name) <u>or</u><br>President (Name), (Degree)<br>Name of University<br>City, State | Dear Sir<br>Dear President (Name)<br>Dear Dr. (Name) | Very truly yours<br>Sincerely yours | Dr. (Name) | Dr. (Name) |

## POSTAL RATES, FEES, AND INFORMATION

(As of May, 1973—Consult Postmaster or *Postal Manual* for current information)

### FIRST-CLASS MAIL[1]

| Kind of Material | Descriptive Information | Postage Rate |
|---|---|---|
| All first-class mail, except postal and postcards weighing 13 ounces or less<br><br>(Over 13 ounces air parcel postal rates apply.) | Includes:<br>1. Matter wholly or partially in writing or typewriting, except authorized additions to second-, third-, and fourth-class mail<br>2. Matter closed against postal inspection<br>3. Bills and statements of account | 8¢ per ounce or fraction of an ounce (A rate per ounce means 8¢ an ounce or fraction thereof—a fraction of a unit being treated as a whole unit in the computation of charges.)<br><br>This rate applies to the U.S., Canada, and Mexico. |
| Single postal cards and postcards | Single postal cards—government cards with imprinted stamps.<br>Postcards—private mailing cards; stamps must be affixed. | 6¢ each |
| Double postal cards and postcards | Reply portion of a double postcard does not have to bear postage when originally mailed. | 12¢ (6¢ each portion) |
| Business reply cards | The senders return these free. | 8¢ each |
| Mail enclosed in business-reply envelopes | Weight not over 2 ounces<br>Weight over 12 ounces<br>A business must first obtain a permit to distribute business reply envelopes from the post office where they are to be returned. The senders return these free. | 8¢ per ounce or fraction plus 2¢ per piece<br>Air parcel post plus 5¢ per piece |
| Airmail<br>  Postal or postcards | Use airmail cards, or write *AIRMAIL* conspicuously above the address. | 9¢ each |
| Letters and packages | 9 ounces or less—Over 9 oz. Air Parcel Post rates apply. | 11¢ an ounce |
| Business reply cards | | 11¢ each |
| Airmail other than cards | Weight not over 2 ounces<br>Weight over 9 ounces | 11¢ an ounce plus 2¢ a piece<br>Air parcel post rate plus 5¢ a piece |
| | EXCEPTIONS (Nonmailable)<br>a. Letters, cards, and self-mailers less than 3 inches in width or 4¼ inches in length<br>b. Pieces having shapes other than rectangular<br>c. Cards having a thickness of less than 0.006 of an inch | |

[1]First-class mail is discussed on page 225. Weight limit, 70 pounds. Size limit, 100 inches in length and girth.

747

## SECOND-CLASS MAIL[2]

| Kind of Material | Descriptive Information | Postage Rate |
|---|---|---|
| Newspapers and periodicals | Must have second-class mail privileges | Single-Piece Rate: 5¢ for first 2 ounces, 1¢ each additional ounce or fraction, or fourth-class rate, whichever is lower |
| | Special rates for bulk mailing by authorized nonprofit organizations | Bulk Rate: If there are as many as 6 pieces bundled for delivery to one five-digit ZIP Code. See postmaster for rate. |

## THIRD-CLASS MAIL[3]

| Kind of Material | Descriptive Information | Postage Rate |
|---|---|---|
| Circulars, books, catalogs of 24 pages or more and other printed matter, merchandise, seeds, cuttings, bulbs, and plants | Weight less than 16 ounces | Single Rate: 8¢ for first 2 ounces, 4¢ each additional ounce or fraction |
| | Special rates for bulk mailing by authorized nonprofit organizations | Bulk Rate: quantities not less than 50 pounds or of not less than 200 pieces. |
| Keys and identification devices (cards, tags, etc.) | | 14¢ for first 2 ounces 8¢ for each additional 2 ounces |

## FOURTH-CLASS MAIL[4]

| Kind of Material | Descriptive Information | Postage Rate |
|---|---|---|
| Special fourth-class rate for certain books, films, museum materials, playscripts, and manuscripts, etc. | Package must be marked *Special Fourth-Class Rate* and title of contents shown. See local postmaster. | 14¢ for first pound or fraction of a pound. 7¢ for each additional pound or fraction |
| Library books and educational materials sent between educational, religious, and philanthropic institutions | Package must be marked *Library Rate*. See local postmaster. | 6¢ for first pound or fraction of a pound |
| | Postage is not differentiated by zone. | 2¢ for each additional pound or fraction |

[2]Second-class mail is discussed on page 225–226.
[3]Third-class mail is discussed on page 226.
[4]Special fourth-class mail is discussed on page 227.

# APO, MPO MAIL

Letter............................11¢
Air parcel post. Applicable airmail zone rate, maximum of 70 pounds

## FOREIGN AIRMAIL (Up to ½ oz.)

Aerogramme.......................................15¢
Canada and Mexico—Domestic Rates Apply.
Asian and African Countries......25¢
European Countries...............20¢
South American and Caribbean Countries.....15¢

## SPECIAL HANDLING

### Third- and Fourth-Class Only
SPECIAL HANDLING FEES (Fees in addition to postage)

| Weight | Fee |
|---|---|
| Not more than 2 pounds | 25¢ |
| More than 2 pounds but not more than 10 pounds | 35¢ |
| More than 10 pounds | 50¢ |

## SPECIAL DELIVERY FEES
(Fees in addition to postage)

| Class of Mail | Weight — Not more than 2 pounds | More than 2 pounds but not more than 10 pounds | More than 10 pounds |
|---|---|---|---|
| First class and airmail (including air parcel post) | 60¢ | 75¢ | 90¢ |
| All otherclasses | 80¢ | 90¢ | 1.05 |

## MONEY ORDER FEES

| Amount of Money Order | Amount of Fee Domestic |
|---|---|
| $0.01 to $10 | $0.25 |
| $10.01 to $50 | .35 |
| $50.01 to $100 | .40 |

## INSURANCE

FEES (IN ADDITION TO POSTAGE)

| LIABILITY | FEE |
|---|---|
| $0.01 to $15 | $0.20 |
| $15.01 to $50 | .30 |
| $50.01 to $100 | .40 |
| $100.01 to $150 | .50 |
| $150.01 to $200 | .60 |

Liability for insured mail is limited to $200.
Restricted delivery. (Not available for mail insured for $15 or less).....50¢
Return receipts. (Not available for mail insured for $15 or less):

## COD MAIL

Consult Postmaster for fees and conditions of mailing.

## CERTIFIED MAIL

Fee (in addition to postage)........30¢
Restricted delivery.................50¢

## REGISTRY

REGISTRY FEES (IN ADDITION TO POSTAGE)

| Declared actual value (No limit) | Fees — If mailer does not have commercial or other insurance | Postal Liability |
|---|---|---|
| $0.00 to $100 | $0.80 | Without commercial or other insurance—declared value. |
| $100.01 to $200 | 1.05 | |
| $200.01 to $400 | 1.30 | With commercial or other insurance—declared value or prorated |
| $400.01 to $600 | 1.55 | |
| $600.01 to $800 | 1.80 | |
| $800.01 to $1,000 | 2.05 | |
| HIGHER VALUES | Consult Postmaster for fees. | |

Maximum postal insurance for shipments NOT commercially insured.....$10,000
Maximum postal insurance for shipments commercially insured.....$1,000
Restricted delivery (additional fee)...........50¢

## RETURN RECEIPTS

Certified Mail—Numbered Insured—Registered
Requested at time of mailing:
Showing to whom and when delivered.....15¢
Showing to whom, when, and address where delivered.....35¢
Requested after mailing:
Showing to whom and when delivered.....25¢

## STAMPS, ENVELOPES, AND POSTAL CARDS

### ENVELOPES AVAILABLE

| Kind | Denomination — Cents | Less than 500 — Cents (each) |
|---|---|---|
| Regular | 8 | 10 |
| Airmail | 11 | 13 |

### POSTAL CARDS AVAILABLE

| Kind | Selling price each |
|---|---|
| Single | 6¢ |
| Airmail single (use for airmail only) | 11¢ |
| Reply (6¢ each half) | 12¢ |

### ADHESIVE STAMPS AVAILABLE

| Purpose | Form | Denomination and Prices |
|---|---|---|
| Ordinary postage | Single or sheet | 1, 2, 3, 4, 5, 6, 8, 10, 11, 12, 13, 15, 20, 25, 30, 40, and 50 cents; $1 and $5. |
| | Book | 24 8-cent: $1.92. |
| | Coil of 100* | 6, 8, 11, and 25 cents. |
| | Coils of 500 & 3,000 | 1, 2, 5, 6, and 8 cents. |
| | Coils of 3,000 | 25 cents. |
| Airmail postage (for use on airmail only) | Single or sheet | 8, 10, 11, 15, 20, and 25 cents, $1 airlift. |
| | Book | 8 11-cent. |
| | Coils of 100,* 500 & 3,000 | 11 cents. |

*Dispenser to hold coils of 100 stamps may be purchased for 5¢ additional.

## AIR PARCEL POST ZONE RATES[5]

| Weight over 7 ounces and not exceeding: (Lbs.) | Local Zones 1, 2, and 3 | Zone 4 | Zone 5 | Zone 6 | Zone 7 | Zone 8 |
|---|---|---|---|---|---|---|
| | | | RATE | | | |
| 1 | $1.00 | $1.00 | $1.00 | $1.00 | $1.00 | $1.00 |
| 1½ | 1.20 | 1.22 | 1.25 | 1.30 | 1.40 | 1.50 |
| 2 | 1.40 | 1.43 | 1.51 | 1.60 | 1.68 | 1.77 |
| 2½ | 1.60 | 1.65 | 1.76 | 1.90 | 2.02 | 2.16 |
| 3 | 1.80 | 1.86 | 2.01 | 2.20 | 2.36 | 2.54 |
| 3½ | 2.00 | 2.08 | 2.26 | 2.49 | 2.69 | 2.93 |
| 4 | 2.20 | 2.30 | 2.52 | 2.79 | 3.03 | 3.31 |
| 4½ | 2.40 | 2.51 | 2.77 | 3.09 | 3.37 | 3.70 |
| 5 | 2.60 | 2.73 | 3.02 | 3.39 | 3.71 | 4.08 |
| 6 | 3.08 | 3.23 | 3.58 | 4.03 | 4.43 | 4.88 |
| 7 | 3.56 | 3.73 | 4.14 | 4.67 | 5.15 | 5.68 |
| 8 | 4.04 | 4.23 | 4.70 | 5.31 | 5.87 | 6.48 |
| 9 | 4.52 | 4.73 | 5.26 | 5.95 | 6.59 | 7.28 |
| 10 | 5.00 | 5.23 | 5.82 | 6.59 | 7.31 | 8.08 |

## FOURTH-CLASS (PARCEL POST) ZONE RATES[5]

| Pounds | Local | 1 and 2 Up to 150 miles | 3 150 to 300 miles | 4 300 to 600 miles | 5 600 to 1,000 miles | 6 1,000 to 1,400 miles | 7 1,400 to 1,800 miles | 8 Over 1,800 miles |
|---|---|---|---|---|---|---|---|---|
| | | | | Zones | | | | |
| 2 | $0.60 | $0.65 | $0.70 | $0.75 | $0.80 | $0.90 | $1.00 | $1.05 |
| 3 | .60 | .75 | .80 | .85 | .95 | 1.10 | 1.20 | 1.35 |
| 4 | .65 | .80 | .85 | .95 | 1.10 | 1.30 | 1.40 | 1.60 |
| 5 | .70 | .85 | .90 | 1.05 | 1.20 | 1.45 | 1.65 | 1.90 |
| 6 | .70 | .95 | 1.00 | 1.15 | 1.35 | 1.60 | 1.85 | 2.10 |
| 7 | .75 | 1.05 | 1.10 | 1.25 | 1.50 | 1.75 | 2.10 | 2.35 |
| 8 | .75 | 1.10 | 1.15 | 1.35 | 1.60 | 1.90 | 2.30 | 2.60 |
| 9 | .80 | 1.15 | 1.20 | 1.45 | 1.75 | 2.05 | 2.45 | 2.85 |
| 10 | .80 | 1.20 | 1.30 | 1.55 | 1.90 | 2.20 | 2.65 | 3.10 |

[5]Parcel post is discussed on pages 226-227. Space permits publication of rates up to 10 pounds only although weights up to 70 pounds may be sent by either surface or air parcel post. Charts are available from the local post office. The charts above will enable the reader to compare costs of sending parcel post by surface and by air.

# TWO-LETTER STATE ABBREVIATIONS*
## Approved for Use with ZIP Code *Only*

| | | | |
|---|---|---|---|
| Alaska.................. | AK | Montana................. | MT |
| Alabama................ | AL | Nebraska................ | NE |
| Arizona................ | AZ | Nevada................. | NV |
| | | | |
| Arkansas............... | AR | New Hampshire........... | NH |
| California.............. | CA | New Jersey.............. | NJ |
| Canal Zone............. | CZ | New Mexico............. | NM |
| | | | |
| Colorado............... | CO | New York............... | NY |
| Connecticut............. | CT | North Carolina........... | NC |
| Delaware............... | DE | North Dakota........... | ND |
| | | | |
| District of Columbia....... | DC | Ohio................... | OH |
| Florida................ | FL | Oklahoma............... | OK |
| Georgia................ | GA | Oregon................. | OR |
| | | | |
| Hawaii................. | HI | Pennsylvania............ | PA |
| Idaho.................. | ID | Puerto Rico............ | PR |
| Illinois................ | IL | Rhode Island............ | RI |
| | | | |
| Indiana................ | IN | South Carolina........... | SC |
| Iowa.................. | IA | South Dakota............ | SD |
| Kansas................ | KS | Tennessee............... | TN |
| | | | |
| Kentucky............... | KY | Texas.................. | TX |
| Louisiana............... | LA | Utah.................. | UT |
| Maine................. | ME | Vermont............... | VT |
| | | | |
| Maryland............... | MD | Virginia................ | VA |
| Massachusetts........... | MA | Virgin Islands........... | VI |
| Michigan............... | MI | Washington............. | WA |
| | | | |
| Minnesota.............. | MN | West Virginia............ | WV |
| Mississippi............. | MS | Wisconsin............... | WI |
| Missouri............... | MO | Wyoming............... | WY |

*Canal Zone, District of Columbia, Puerto Rico, and Virgin Islands also included.

# Index

Rating scale for use by supervisors, 33
*Read in, read out* in data processing, 438
Real estate, deed, 553; investment property, 554; lease forms, 555; legal terms for, 554; personal-property records, 556; property record form, 555; property records, 554; repairs and improvements, 563; source material, 557; tickler file, 556
Recalling mail, 238
Reconciling checking account balance, 527
Records, payroll, 574; of taxable income, 577; time, for payroll, 573
Records forms for payroll, 570
Records management practices, 331
Recruitment, personnel, 667
Reference books, 180
Reference cards for reports, 452
Reference file, desk, 31
Reference Guide, 687; abbreviations, 689–691; capitalization, 691–695; introduction, 688; numbers, 695; plurals, 699; possessives, 700; punctuation, 701–713; usage, words and phrases, 713–733; words: coined; compound; division; foreign, 733–736
Reference materials, 188
Reference shelf, secretary's, 461
Refusal, letters of, 208
Register, mail, 148
Register of visitors, 44
Registered mail, 230
Regrets, formal, 211
Release, news, 213–214
Remailing mail, 237
Reminder letters, 207
Rent-a-car travel, 369
Report, letter of transmittal for, 496
Reports of conferences, 413
Reports, compiling, *see also* Reports, presenting data in and Reports, writing; abstracting, 452, abstracting services, 457; atlases, 453; bibliography cards, 451; card catalog, 449; city directories, 454; copying material, 452; Dewey Decimal System, 449; dictionaries, 453; encyclopedia, 455; handbooks, 461; journals of schools of business, 419; library catalog cards, illustration, 450; Library of Congress System, 450; newspapers and periodicals, 459–460; New York Times Index, 451; published indexes, 450; Readers Guide to Periodical Literature, 451; reference cards, 452; researching information, 447–449; secretary's reference shelf, 461; sources of information, 447–461; specialized libraries, 448; subscription information services, 457–458; taking notes, 452; U.S. Government publications, 455; use of library, 449; Wall Street Journal Index, 451; yearbooks, 456
Reports, presenting data in, array, 467; averages, 467; for graphs, 476; circle graphs, 476; classifying data, 465; flow chart symbols, 481; graphs, 473–478; limitations of graphs, 479; line graphs, 474; map charts, 479; organization charts, 480, 482; percentages, 468; pictorial charts, 478; process and flow charts, 480; tables, 469–472
Reports, writing, *see also* Reports, compiling and Reports, presenting data in; appendix, 495; assembling, 502; bibliography, 495; binding, 502; body of report, 488–494; final check, 502; footnotes, 494; form for, 487; guide sheet for, 491; headings and subheadings for, 492; horizontal, vertical, 486; illustrations of parts, 497–501; indentions, 490; letter of transmittal, 496; margins, 491; numbering pages, 494; objective, 486; outline for, 488; page layouts, 490; preparing for printer, 503; proofreading, 502; quoted matter, 493; rough draft for, 489; routine for, 487; secretary's responsibilities, 487; summary, 496; table of contents, 496; title page, 496; titles, 492; typing the body, 490–494
Reports of meetings, 404
Requesting material from files, 326
Requests, writing, 207

Requisition forms, purchase of, 82
Research and development division of a company, 23
Researching information, *see* Reports, compiling
Reservations, flight, 365; hotel, 379
Resolutions of meetings, 404
Responsibility, accepting, by secretary, 656
Résumé, 628–631; executive's, 662
Retention schedule, 331
Retrieval of data, 443
Returning mail, 236
Reverse-charge telephone service, 263
Ribbon mechanisms for typewriters, 69
Riders for legal documents, 600
Right margins, even, 100
Roll-out files, 306, 316
Rotary files, 318
Round and odd lots of stocks, 551
Routine duties, 26

# S

Salaries, secretarial, 6, 8
Sales department functions, 22
Scale, rating, for use by supervisors, 33
Schedule, daily work, 29
Scheduling appointments, 48
Second-class mail, 225; rates, 748
Second sheets of stationery, 72
Secretarial manuals, 196
Secretary, "A" and "B", 5; as administrative secretary with word processing center, 6; as hostess, 37; areas of work, 4; Certified Professional, 658–659; as correspondence secretary or word processor, 6; defined, 2; duties of, 3; established role, 3; limitations to career, 9; opportunities for advancement, 8; personal qualities, 10–14; salary, 6, 8; self-check for personality, 14; in word processing center, 6; *see also* Supervisory role of secretary
Secretary's desk manual, 651
Secretary (officer) of a company, 20
Securities, alphabetical list of, 553; bonds, regular or coupon, 546; broker, 547; brokerage transaction, 551; certificate numbers, 553; confirmation of sale, 551; deliveries of, 552; investment prospectus, 563; market averages, 549; portfolio, 563; proxy, 545; records of, 552; stock, kinds of, 544–545; stockholders' meeting, 545; stock market information, 548; stock market listing, 550; stock market terms, 549–551; stock market trading, 547; stock rights, 551
Selectric typewriters, 66
Sentences, clarity of, 202; conciseness of, 202; first, 203; forcefulness in, 202; one-thought, 202
Semicolon, 710
Seminars for secretaries, 660
Separate-mail items, 189
Series, 712
Shipping, *see also* Mail; air express, 247; air freight, 247, 249; bills of lading, 250; bus express, 248; chart of air cargo usage, 247; export broker, 250; express services, 246; guides for air shipping, 247; international, 250; international air cargo, 251; motor freight, 249; procedures for, 246; railway express, 246; water freight, 249
Short sale of stocks, 549
Signature card for bank, 523
Signatures, secretarial, on transcription, 191
Snap-out business forms, 78
Social Security forms, 568
Social Security for payrolls, 568
Software in data processing, 438
Sorting incoming mail, 144
Speakerphone, 293, 295
Special-character typewriter keys, 69
Special-delivery mail, 233
Special fourth-class mail, 233, 748
Special-handling mail, 233, 749
Specialization opportunities, 616
Specialities, developing personal, 681

Special typed characters, 97–98
Spelling aids, 177
Staff-work-accomplished, 676
Stamps, postage, 234, 749
Statements, credit card, 534; monthly, of checking account (illustration), 529
State-name abbreviations for ZIP Code use, 751
Stationery, 71–77; bond paper, 71; carbon paper, 73; erasability, 72; letterheads, 73; office forms, 77; requisitions and invoices, 82; second sheets, 72; specifications for, 74; specifications for letterheads, envelopes, and carbon paper, 74–75; storage of, 83; substance, 72; use of in transcription, 185; watermarks, 71
Stationery supplies, 71–77; information files of, 81; overbuying of, 82; quality of, 80; salesmen of, 81; sources of, 80
Station-to-station telephone calls, 267
*Statistical Abstract of the U.S.*, 455–456
Statistical data, *see* Reports, presenting data in
Stencil, cleaning the, 130; corrections on, 128; electronic, 123; filing the, 130; guide copy for, 126; guide points on, 130; handwork on, 130; kinds of, 125; placement of copy on, 126; proofreading the, 129; running off, 130; stocking and storing, 126; typing the, 127
Stencil (mimeographed) duplication, 115
Stencils and masters, preparation of, 122
Steps to secretarial success, 647
Stockbroker, 547
Stockholders' meeting, 545
Stock market listing, 550; publications, 548; trading, 547
Stocks and bonds, *see* Securities
Stock split, 551
Stop order for stocks, 549
Stop-payment on checks, 526
Storage or memory file for data processing, 435
Storage of stationery and supplies, 83
Strikeovers, 97
Style for bibliography and footnotes, 739
Styles for business letters, 736–737
Styles for reports, *see* Report, writing a
Subject filing, 310–311
Subheadings, report, 492
Subscription information services, 457–458
Success formula, *see* Techniques, successful secretarial
Summary of a report, 496
Supervisors, evaluation by, 671–672
Supervision, effective, 668; by secretary, 32
Supervisor's prayer, 33
Supervisory role of secretary, applying measurement methods, 678; decision formula, 677; developing personal specialties, 681; developing your ideas, 679; effective communication, 673; effective supervision, 668; evaluation of supervisees, 671–672; improving communication skills, 680; job motivation, 670; job satisfaction, 670; list of duties, 675; observing lines of authority, 676; personnel policies, 673; principles of work delegation, 670; recommendations to superiors, 676; recruiting personnel, 667; understanding computer applications, 678; using systems and procedures analysis, 678; work instructions, 073
Supplies, storage of, 83
Surety insurance, 560
Sympathy, letter of, 210
Systems and procedures analysis, 678

# T

Table of contents for a report, 496
Tables, layout for, 469–471; proofreading, for reports, 469–472
Tabulator key, decimal, for typewriter, 69
Tape, punched, for data processing, 425
Taped announcements by telephone, 263
Tapes, filing of, 319
Tasks, assigned, original, routine, 26–27
Tax, records of taxable income, 577; income, check list for computing, 583; deductions, 579–581; for executive, 576–